Third Edition

AN INTRODUCTION

TO

PERSONALITY

DONN BYRNE

KATHRYN KELLEY
State University of New York at Albany

Prentice-Hall, Inc., Englewood Cliffs, New Jersey 07632

Library of Congress Cataloging in Publication Data

Byrne, Donn Erwin.
  Introduction to personality.

  Bibliography.
  Includes indexes.
  1. Personality.   I. Kelley, Kathryn, joint
author.   II. Title.
BF698.B9 1980   155.2   80-22782
ISBN 0-13-491605-0

BF
698
.B9
1981

Printed in the United States of America

10 9 8 7 6 5 4 3 2 1

Editorial/production supervision and interior design: Jeanne Hoeting
Cover design: Wanda Lubelska Design
Cover photograph: Robin Lynn Byrne
Manufacturing Buyer: Edmund W. Leone

PRENTICE-HALL INTERNATIONAL, INC., *London*
PRENTICE-HALL OF AUSTRALIA PTY. LIMITED, *Sydney*
PRENTICE-HALL OF CANADA, LTD., *Toronto*
PRENTICE-HALL OF INDIA PRIVATE LIMITED, *New Delhi*
PRENTICE-HALL OF JAPAN, INC., *Tokyo*
PRENTICE-HALL OF SOUTHEAST ASIA PTE. LTD. *Singapore*
WHITEHALL BOOKS LIMITED, *Wellington, New Zealand*

This book is dedicated to:

MILES FRANCIS BYRNE

An Irish love of storytelling was one of his gifts. A grandfather and grandson read together and took turns at creating our own adventures. Stories of a monkey, an elephant, and a small boy were part of my reality. I wish that Nano were here to see that Jocko, Tusker, and Donn are still at it.

JEROME AUGUST KELLEY

He recounted to his grandchildren tales of his pioneer adventures in the Old West, from equal parts of experience and imagination.

CONTENTS

Three
THEORIES OF PERSONALITY: PSYCHOLOGISTS AND RESEARCH 79

Six
INTELLIGENCE: THE BASIC ABILITY   197

Seven
MANIFEST ANXIETY: THE EFFECTS OF EMOTIONALITY   242

Eight
NEED FOR ACHIEVEMENT: STRIVING FOR SUCCESS   279

PART THREE: BEHAVIOR AS A FUNCTION OF THE SITUATION

Nine
ATTRACTION: LIKING AND LOVING   327

Ten
AGGRESSION: HATING AND HURTING   369

Eleven
SEXUALITY: PLEASURE AND PROCREATION 412

PREFACE

The subject matter of personality psychology is guaranteed to be of potential interest to most of us, because we *are* the subject matter. One's response to political issues, school performance, fears and worries, orientation to success and failure, loves and hates, sexual concerns, and altruism are all grist for the mill of the field of personality. This branch of psychology, in other words, is about what we do and think and feel and imagine as we go about our everyday lives. As you read this book, keep that focus in mind. It's about you, those you know, and how all of us manage to interact in both pleasant and unpleasant ways.

To accomplish the task of explaining and describing personality, we have centered our attention on five matters. Four of these are represented in the four sections of this text, and the fifth will be found throughout the book. It should be noted that the material covered ranges from classic theory and research in the field to the most recent and up-to-date work being reported in psychological journals.

First, by way of background, you will be introduced to personality as it fits within the general scheme of scientific endeavor, the major theories of personality from Freud to social learning, and some of the basic concepts and issues involved in personality research.

Second, research on four major personality dimensions or traits will be presented in some depth. These topics were chosen because they consist of four different aspects of human concern (authoritarian beliefs and values, intellectual ability, anxiety and its effect on behavior, and motivational differences involving achievement) and because each has been the object of considerable research interest over the past several decades. These examples provide an illustration of personality research from the viewpoint of individual differences.

Third, there is a shift from such fairly consistent behavioral traits to four types of behavior that are found to be strongly influenced by situational variables. Again, the chosen topics cover a wide span of human activity (attraction and love, aggression, sexuality, and morality), and again they each represent a large body of research findings. They provide an illustration of personality research from the viewpoint of stimulus determinants.

Fourth, we turn our attention to the individual and try to draw together much of what has been discussed in the book. That is, on the basis of existing theory and research, there is an attempt to show how personality develops and functions in the complex interplay of external stimulation, distinct internal processes, and the lasting consequences of rewards and punishments.

Fifth, in each section of the book, we have labored to make this introduction to personality as interesting, as relatively painless, and as educationally valuable as possible. Each chapter is introduced by a brief story; some may be amusing, a couple are horrifying, and you may groan at the corniness of others. Their aim, altogether, is to get you intrigued by at least some aspects of the chapter to come. They serve, in fact, to illustrate important points just as do the photographs to be found throughout the text. Within each chapter, major terms are printed in **boldface** when they first appear, and these terms are given again in a glossary at the end of the book. A summary of the major points covered appears at the end of each chapter. Some students find it useful to read these summaries first, by the way, to gain an overview of what is most important. As you go through the chapters, you will also find three types of special inserts in tinted areas. These have three functions. Research Close-Up provides a somewhat detailed look at a study or a series of studies that are especially interesting, unusual, or important. What Do You Think? deals with matters that are open to discussion; you may find it worthwhile to compare your reactions with those of your fellow class members. Try It Yourself represents an opportunity to become involved in relatively simple research projects with yourself and others as the subjects. The relevance to everyday life of each topic covered in the text is stressed, including applications ranging from psychotherapy to restructuring portions of the environment.

One final note involves our thanks to those who contributed in a variety of ways to this project. At Prentice-Hall, special thanks must go to John Isley who was not only unbelievably patient over the past several painful years but who also made many positive suggestions that helped shape the book in its present form. We are also very grateful for the contributions of Jeanne Hoeting who supervised the book's production with a diligence and patience equal to John's. In addition, we greatly appreciate the work of Carolyn Smith, copyeditor and Anita Duncan, photo researcher. Among our colleagues we very much appreciate the comments and suggestions of Elizabeth Rice Allgeier, Gerald Clore, Kay Deaux, William Fisher, Carol Miller, and David Przybyla. Also, for their constructive reviews of our manuscript, we wish to thank John Davis, Southwest Texas State University; Stuart Fischoff, California State, Los Angeles; Margaret Fitch, Hendrix College; Alan Glaros, Wayne State University; Sanford Golin, University of Pittsburgh; Vernon Joy, Western Illinois University; John A. Popplestone, The University of Akron; Steven Reiss, University of Illinois, Chicago Circle; Joseph C. Speisman, Boston University; James S. Uleman, New York University, and Daniel S. Weiss, University of California, San Francisco. We also thank Robin Byrne who not only worked on the reference section but who took the photograph used on the cover.

Now that all of these preliminaries are done, the next part is up to you—read, think, learn, apply, and enjoy.

D. B.   K.K.

Part One

STUDYING THE BEHAVIOR
OF INDIVIDUALS

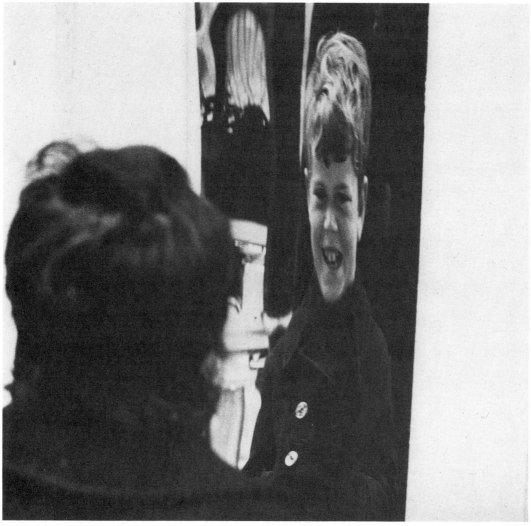

Mary M. Thacker, Photo Researchers

Chapter One

PERSONALITY PSYCHOLOGY: UNDERSTANDING HUMAN BEHAVIOR

In this chapter you will read about the following topics:

Special Inserts

Two primitive human beings squatted at the cave entrance, discussing a matter of some importance. Their language was a simple one and consisted in part of gestures and guttural sounds, yet they were able to communicate fairly well. Their conversation will, of course, be freely translated here. Toward the back of the cave a group of children of various ages huddled about the cooking fire. It was the time of year to harvest the crops that had been tended for many months, but the yield was clearly going to be a meager one. Long, hungry days and nights stretched before them. The woman was frightened. The man was too, but outwardly he expressed only anger.

Gulb pointed a hairy hand across the stream that marked off their territory. "Just look over there! Falmo's crops are twice the height of ours. His are green and ours are spotted with brown. His fruits and vegetables are plump and firm while ours are stunted and misshapen." He spat on the ground to express his contempt.

His companion, Brit, looked at him shrewdly from beneath her bushy eyebrows. "Why are his crops different from ours?"

Gulb grunted in pleasure at knowing the answer. "Because Falmo is in league with the evil spirits. He agreed to sell his soul in return for this bounty. Invisible devils make his crop lush while putting a hex on ours. I say we should kill Falmo tonight—as soon as it is fully dark. With my club I can crack his head open like a ripe cantaloupe."

"You are a superstitious fool, my mate." Gulb raised a clenched fist, but Brit motioned him away. "Wait, angry one, let me tell you what I know. I have watched Falmo and his woman since the beginning of the growing season. They did just as we did. They placed seeds and tubers in the ground. They carried water in gourds to moisten the earth when the rains were slow in coming. They pulled out the weeds to keep them from crowding out the young plants."

Gulb snorted. "We did all that, dumb woman, so our crops should be the same."

"But," Brit persisted, "Falmo also did something different. Just before planting time, he went fishing and brought back great baskets of small fish. Then, when the seeds were planted, the fish were planted at the same time in the same place."

Gulb laughed until the tears came to his eyes. "Planted fish! When you see trout growing on the bushes, let me know. In the meantime I will find much pleasure in smashing Falmo's fat skull."

"First let's find out if their strange custom explains their success with the crops. I have a plan. We'll plant fish with our seeds next year and see if our harvest improves."

"Maybe it will chance to be a good year, and we won't know whether the fish caused the change in our fields."

"You have a point. All right, then we'll just plant fish with half of our crop and see which half is better. That way we will be able to control for any accidental effects and still be able to determine whether the fish act as a causal factor."

Gulb looked thoughtful. "How will we decide if the experimental crop with the fish is really superior to the control crop that is planted in the usual way? Perhaps we will deceive ourselves and think we see differences where none exist."

"I have considered that problem," Brit replied. "We will measure the height of the plants in each crop as well as the weight of the fruits and vegetables we harvest from

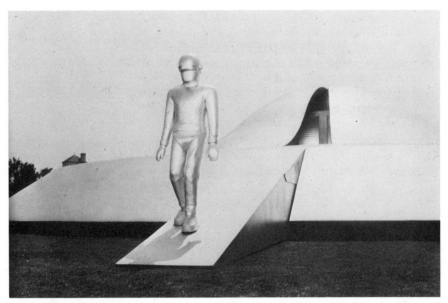

Figure 1-1. How would an alien being explain our behavior to the folks back home? (Springer/Bettman Film Archive)

each one. Then we will test the mean differences on each of these two dependent variables with a statistical technique that I worked out last night." She lovingly patted the calculator beads hanging from her bear-tooth necklace.

"Sounds good to me," said Gulb. "I wonder if the results could be published. For now, though, let's go back into the cave and have a bowl of monkey stew."

NO ONE KNOWS exactly how science began, and it is very possible that the story of Gulb and Brit is not accurate. The general idea, however, *is* accurate. At some point in the distant past, a few human beings began to devise a special way to answer their questions about the world around them: the **scientific method.** That method was first used to attempt to answer questions about agriculture and astronomy. Over time, other aspects of the physical world were subjected to scientific inquiry, and after many centuries the human body and its diseases became acceptable objects of study. During the past century science was extended once more, to include the study of behavior, and psychology came into being in the laboratories of Germany.

What is science? How can it be applied to human behavior? Can its methods really tell us anything about ourselves—why we love and hate, why we differ in intellectual ability and political ideology, why we have certain sexual needs, why we sometimes help a stranger in distress and sometimes do not? In this chapter some of the general features of science, especially a science of behavior, will be described. The following chapters describe a portion of what has been discovered about the most interesting phenomenon in the universe—us. An article in *Time* magazine a few years ago stated that "nothing raises eyebrows faster than the idea that science can find 'laws' of human behavior. Human differences are too vast for generalizations that apply with any exactitude to individuals." You may agree with that statement, but much of the rest of this book describes a surprising array of research suggesting that even *Time* (Feb. 14, 1964, p. 43) can be mistaken. First let's set the stage by getting an overall view of the scientific method and what it involves.

WHAT ARE THE GOALS OF A SCIENCE OF PERSONALITY?

Research and Theory: Trying to Make Sense of the World

We are animals who are bright enough to recognize that we are confronted by a threatening and confusing environment. We perceive ourselves to be the victims of discomfort, disease, natural disasters, and the sometimes unpleasant behavior of other human beings. Anything that might make order out of chaos by helping us understand and predict external events would clearly be to our benefit. Such an activity would be rewarding in that it would reduce fear and anxiety. If it also led to some degree of control over our surroundings, the rewards would be even greater. Such activities would be adaptive in an evolutionary sense, because the ability to predict and control any portion of the threatening environment increases the odds that a given individual will survive at least long enough to have offspring. Concepts that lead, for example, to the accurate prediction of seasonal changes, the securing of food, a way to protect oneself from predators, or some means to prevent disease would help preserve life and provide opportunities to mate.

Some of these new ideas must have been very daring and inventive. Imagine the first time someone tried to fertilize a crop (the American Indians really did plant fish with their corn), predict when the rainy season would begin, or open an oyster to eat it. The survival of a group would also be enhanced by passing on such knowledge to one's companions and to offspring. Specific concepts such as the regularity of the phases of the moon, the usefulness of a club as a weapon, the power of fire, the advantages of a wheel, the way to make gunpowder, or the relation between energy and matter need only occur once to one person. It can then become common knowledge.

The role of science in the learning process is sometimes confusing to college students (as well as their parents and other taxpayers); they sometimes find that their instructors are engaged in research rather than simply teaching. Though many people feel that they would rather pay for their own education than for someone's research, it is important to consider where knowledge comes from. "The lifeblood of a university is searching for new knowledge. If our only goal were to impart old knowledge, we'd be back in the days of the Medieval university" (Heller, 1977, p. 1). Research and teaching should be viewed not as incompatible but as mutually beneficial. Norman Cousins has also noted the importance of research to a university:

The governor of a great western state recently demonstrated his lack of education about education when he made some offhand and slurring reference to professors and teachers who loll around doing research when they ought to be carrying a full teaching load . . . What makes his attitude deplorable and dangerous is that the greatest investment any state can make in its future is through a great university. And the way to make a university great is not by teaching students to pass examinations but by creating an atmosphere congenial to the pursuit of knowledge. Such pursuit needs ample room for research (1978, p. 56).

All of humanity's intellectual products may be seen as attempts to make sense of the world, to gain predictive knowledge, and to achieve the means for controlling the world. At first, the concepts produced must have been fairly simple, such as the relation between fire and the feeling of warmth. In time, ideas were developed in more elaborate forms—pagan beliefs, myths, political ideologies, folk sayings, and science. There are many similarities among these seemingly different systems of ideas. Each involves the creation of abstractions, a narrow focus on a few crucial elements, and a simplification of that which is complex. Strangely enough, this process of abstraction, narrowing, and simplification leads to greater generality and, hence, broader understanding. Russel Lynes makes a similar point in a discussion of cartoonists: "This is not to say that the best cartoons are the most elaborate drawings of place and people. On the contrary it is the simplification of the complex by the deftest shorthand that evokes (as in the drawings of Steinberg) the most comprehensive view of the world" (1968, p. 23).

Figure 1-2 is a very general depiction of conceptual activity as a means of making sense of the world. The left- and right-hand portions of the figure represent, respectively, the problems and the goals of all conceptual systems. The center portion could be taken as a description of theology, communism, astrology, or physics. Such activities differ mainly in their procedures and in the kind of evidence they are willing to accept. The procedures and standards of science will be the focus of our attention with respect to the field of personality. There is, by the way, no need to compare different systems in an attempt to show that one is somehow better than another. There are no logical grounds on which to assert that science is better than, say, black magic. They are two different intellectual games with different rules. Science can be defended on practical grounds with respect

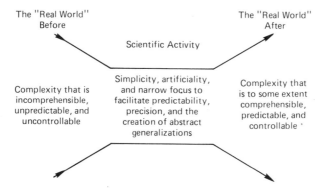

Figure 1-2. Many kinds of conceptual activity, including science, may be viewed as ways to focus attention on a narrow aspect of the complex world in order to understand, predict, and control it. Thorough knowledge of this aspect makes it possible to return to the world outside the laboratory with an improved ability to understand, predict, and control a portion of it.

to its past successes. Scientific conceptions have led to repeated instances of accurate prediction and to numerous techniques for controlling some portion of our surroundings. We may not be happy with all of the results of science, but one cannot argue that science is ineffective. Rain dances, human sacrifice, Grandmother's proverbs, astrology, voodoo, and palm reading have not done as well in providing either accurate predictions or useful technology (Henry, 1978).

On the basis of past success and future hope, science would seem to be one of humanity's more useful products. In what ways does scientific activity lead us to understanding, prediction, and control?

Understanding: Why? How?

What's in a Name?   Each of us wants to know why things happen in the world around us and we want to know how. When something is explained we feel better; understanding has been achieved. It is sometimes said that understanding is the basic goal of science. In one sense, however, an illusion of understanding is the easiest thing in the world to attain.

Simply naming an event or process often is sufficient to provide "understanding." Children gain some degree of mastery over the world by learning to name parts of it. A frightening noise becomes "thunder," and a strange creature that licks your face becomes a "puppy." Such names indicate that adults are familiar with the phenomena and are not afraid of them. The next time the event occurs, it is no longer mysterious; it has a label. The label provides a feeling of mastery. Once, when changing planes in the Dallas–Fort Worth airport, one of the authors offered to help a young mother who was traveling with two children. He took the somewhat frightened 3-year-old by the hand, and took the tram to another terminal.

When the boy was told that they were on a train ride just like the ones in Disneyland, his fear turned into joy and he repeated the words over and over as the car sped along the tracks. Once he had a name for his novel experience, it was no longer a source of fear. Such labels and categories *are* useful. They make it possible for us to code and process the information we receive from the world around us.

As we grow older, the same kind of word magic is still effective in reducing uncertainty and providing what seems to be understanding. We hear or devise explanations all the time. A murderer was motivated by watching violence on TV. A mathematician inherited his intelligence from one of his great-grandfathers, who was a "whiz at numbers." A permissive philosophy of child rearing brought about crime in the streets and topless bathing suits. A nurse explains her headaches by saying that they are psychosomatic. A student asked his instructor, "Why did the Eskimos develop the custom of abandoning their old people in the snow to die?" Attempting a joke, the instructor replied, "Because they subsist on a diet of whale blubber." Satisfied by this "explanation," thirty-five students carefully wrote the answer in their notes. Perhaps they expected to use it on the final.

After-the-Fact Explanations.   It is difficult to judge the kind of explanations we have been discussing if the event has already taken place. We are all creative enough so that almost any notion can be used as the basis of a convincing after-the-fact understanding of any event. This holds true whether the concepts are provided by well-developed scientific theory or by the delusions of a mental patient. Any ideas that depend entirely on their ability to offer "understanding" of what has already occurred are not likely to be destroyed by evidence to the contrary. A psychiatric patient complained to a visitor that the doctors were poisoning his soup. The visitor took a sip and said that it tasted all right to him. The patient nodded and said, "You see how clever they are?" Most evidence can be explained away just as easily after the fact.

"Why" questions are essential in building scientific theories, and understanding is clearly an important goal. What is needed is some way to determine when understanding has been achieved. In other words, how do you know when you understand something? Is there any way to distinguish among differing explanations? Is there any basis on which to judge some as more reasonable than others?

WHAT DO YOU THINK?

Explaining Animal Behavior: What Would a Venusian Say?

The task of the personality psychologist is a difficult one because the object of study is the end product of a great many processes that were neither observed nor controlled by the researcher. That is, most of our research focuses on relatively mature persons who have inherited certain attributes and have spent many years learning specific behavioral reactions (Dworkin, Burke, Maher, & Gottesman, 1976). At that point the psychologist steps in and tries to explain the differences among them and to predict their responses. That task is so difficult that the really amazing thing is that the science of personality is actually succeeding and that its explanations and predictions are steadily improving.

To get some idea of what this task is like, we'll consider some behavioral differences whose origins are actually known. You will be in the position of a personality psychologist faced with the problem of trying to make sense of some puzzling observations.

Your first project gets under way when you come across two different animals. One (known as a rabbit on this planet) is standing beside a musical instrument (called a piano), pawing at the keyboard. Another animal (known as an Irish Setter) is standing beside a window pointing its right elbow at a squirrel that is sitting on the lawn outside. Your task is to record what you observe, devise hypotheses as to the origins of these behaviors, and think of possible ways to test your hypotheses. After you have suggested as many possibilities as you can from the point of view of a Venusian, you might want to turn this page upside down to learn the right answers. Do you think the scientist from Venus might eventually arrive at the correct explanations?

Key

A rabbit has been taught to "play the piano" by means of the **operant conditioning** techniques developed by B. F. Skinner. Such complex behaviors are taught gradually through a **shaping** process in which rewards are given for behavior that constitutes a step toward the desired end product (such as piano playing). Eventually, in successive stages, an animal can learn to engage in very complex behaviors that would almost certainly never occur in the absence of deliberate teaching.

An Irish setter is enacting an inherited behavior pattern when he responds to the sight of a small animal such as a squirrel with a rigid posture, straight tail, total silence, concentration, and the pointing of one of his front legs. No one had to teach him this, and he has never even observed another dog engaging in pointing behavior. Yet, he began behaving in this way at a very early age, and his stance resembles that of other, genetically similar, Irish setters. This unlearned behavior has been adapted to his location indoors in that he has learned through trial and error that when he is inside a house he must stand up on his back legs in order to see a squirrel through the window.

Prediction: When? What?

If We Can Predict, We "Understand." The indication of understanding adopted by scientists is *prediction*. This particular criterion is perhaps the major distinction between science and most other conceptual

Figure 1-3. You are a behavioral scientist from Venus and have been assigned to study various species on the third planet from the sun. Since you and the Earthlings are not yet able to communicate very well you must go about the task without the benefit of any information they might have. (Photo courtesy of Roger Mellgren)

systems. Thus, we say that any attempt to increase understanding (naming or building complex verbal explanations) is of value only if the result is (1) a more accurate prediction of the original phenomena or (2) accurate prediction of other phenomena. For example, on what basis are friendships formed? Are we attracted to those who are very much like ourselves or to those who are different? Our culture provides little help—we are told that "birds of a feather flock together" *and* that "opposites attract." You can make a logical argument for either statement and can probably find examples among your friends to fit each. As we will see in Chapter 9, there is abundant evidence that similarity is a more powerful factor in attraction than complementarity. In countless situations it has been predicted—and confirmed—that similarity will lead to liking. Only under very rare and unusual conditions do people find themselves attracted to someone who is unlike themselves in certain ways. By comparing the predictive ability of two explanations of attraction, we have a firm basis on which to select the more accurate.

The term *prediction* is used here in a very general sense to mean any situation in which we make the statement, "If X is true, then we should be able to observe Y." It may be that Y actually occurred sometime in the past, so we are really "postdicting." For example, archaeological predictions may be tested by observing the remains of a culture that disappeared centuries ago. Likewise, various geological explanations of the composition of the moon were confirmed (or disconfirmed) by observations of lunar rocks that were older than humanity. Whether the predicted phenomenon is in the past, present, or future, scientific statements are expected to refer to observable effects. If someone tells you that the ancient Babylonians had transistor radios or that the moon is made of Kraft cheese or that people who masturbate develop hairy palms, that person should be able to make a predictive statement about what would constitute proper evidence. If this cannot be done, no matter how interesting the idea, science cannot deal with it. It can be seen that insistence on prediction provides scientists with a built-in system for correcting and improving their explanations.

Feeling It Versus Predicting It.   In our everyday lives, when we say that we *really* understand something, we often mean that there is a gut-level feeling of illumination. Holt (1962) pointed out that this intuitive feeling of knowing something is different from a predictive statement. As an example, he noted that social scientists feel that they understand juvenile delinquency if they can take variables such as economic status, the social disorganization of a neighborhood, and family structure and use them to predict the delinquency rate. That kind of formulation is not what most people are likely to think of as understanding. Instead, they feel that understanding might come from firsthand contact with a delinquent and his family, reading an exciting crime novel, or seeing a powerful movie that vividly portrays a delinquent. In that sense an artist is better able to provide "understanding" than a scientist. An artist can make you feel it. A scientist, on the other hand, can give you tools with which to predict it.

The two types of understanding are quite different, and each is important. Trouble sometimes arises when people fail to make this distinction and are disappointed to find that a scientific theory fails to stir the emotions or that a great artistic achievement fails to provide predictive accuracy. Science strives for intellectual insight while art strives for emotional insight. Ideally, both types of understanding can occur together. We once knew a graduate student who had spent several years conducting research on interpersonal attraction and was able to use a theory to devise experiments in which her predictions were usually confirmed. One day, in a seminar, she became engaged in a heated argument in which some class members expressed opposing views on some topic while others supported her. In the middle of this interchange she announced that to her amazement she suddenly realized what attitude similarity and dissimilarity truly involved. She meant that she now felt emotionally what she before had known intellectually.

Does an Accurate Prediction Indicate That Your Explanation Is Correct?   When a prediction or a series of predictions fails, the ideas that led to that prediction must be altered. What about the reverse situation? It may seem odd, but a successful prediction is no guarantee of the correctness of a theory.

For example, even when the earth was thought to be the center of the universe astronomers were able to make fairly accurate predictions of the movements of the moon, sun, and planets. The planets offered the greatest difficulty, but the astronomers solved this problem by proposing complex loop-the-loops as the orbits of the planets "around the earth." The only thing wrong with this theory was that it was not consistent with later data. When the sun was thought of as being located at the center of the planetary system, the new theory depicted each planet as traveling in a smooth orbit around this body. The new theory yielded the same accurate predictions provided by the old one, and in addition it enabled astronomers to account for observations that had been inconsistent with the earlier theory. It should be noted that all theories are tentative: They are accepted to the extent that they are consistent with existing data and are subject to change whenever new, inconsistent data become available.

Another example is provided by various ideas concerning the causes of yellow fever. At one time night air was believed to bring on the disease because when windows were kept closed at night there was some decrease in the likelihood of getting sick. The reason this idea led to accurate predictions concerning the prevention of yellow fever was that closed windows prevented mosquitoes from getting in. Once the idea that mosquitoes were the causal agent was proposed, a predictive test involved having volunteers expose themselves to mosquito bites. The test indicated that yellow fever developed after such exposure; therefore, night air had nothing to do with yellow fever. At another level the mosquito has nothing to do with it either, unless it is carrying the yellow fever virus.

In everyday life we may do the same kind of theorizing and predicting. A young girl told us about an idea she had when she was quite small. She believed that the world had once been black and white and had only later been changed to color. Her data were consistent with this belief. Old TV shows were black and white and new ones were in color. The same was true of movies that she had seen. Even in family photograph albums the switch from black and white to an all-color world could be observed. Thus, she had a powerful theory supported by convincing evidence. What evidence could you provide to disconfirm her theory?

Does an Inaccurate Prediction Indicate That Your Explanation Is Incorrect?   It is also true that a hypothesis can be *falsely rejected* when it fails to predict accurately. In science ideas must be rejected tentatively as well as accepted tentatively. A classic problem in comparative psychology is that of whether other animal species can be taught to use human language (Hahn, 1978). The idea of being able to talk to the animals is appealing to many of

us, not just to Dr. Doolittle. Because chimpanzees are highly intelligent, they have frequently been chosen as subjects in experiments designed to explore this possibility. The proposal that chimpanzees could be taught to communicate was tested by various investigators, who raised chimps from infancy so that their experience would be like that of a human baby. In the 1930s Winthrop and Luella Kellogg raised a chimp named Gua with their infant son; Gua could understand at least 100 words when they were spo ken to her, but she never tried to talk. In the 1940s Keith and Catherine Hayes spent many years in such an effort with a chimpanzee named Viki, yet they were able to teach her to make only three sounds (mamma, papa, and cup) that approximated English words (Hayes & Hayes, 1951). It was concluded, then, that even a very bright animal given intensive training could not be taught to use language.

Somewhat later Gardner and Gardner (1969) decided to start over again with the same hypothesis and a different method—one that was suggested by Samuel Pepys in 1651. They reasoned that chimpanzees are not naturally vocal but that they use their hands a great deal to gesture and to manipulate objects. A chimp named Washoe was selected for study, and the researchers undertook to teach her the sign language of the deaf. With a gestural language rather than speech, Washoe was able to learn thirty signs in twenty-two months and continued to add to her vocabulary each week. Even more surprising, she learned to combine signs into sentences such as "Give me a tickle," "Open the refrigerator for food and drink," "You, me go ride car, quick," and "Listen to the dog." Another chimp, Lucy, was trained in the same way and was even given a pet to care for, "Lucy's Cat." Lucy tried in vain to teach her pet to use sign language and to use the toilet; she seemed as frustrated by her failure as the psychologists who had tried to teach chimpanzees to speak (Bartlett, 1975). When the cat died, Lucy did not use the cat's name again until three months later, when she was looking through a copy of *Psychology Today*. She saw a photograph of herself and the cat, and began to make the sign for "Lucy's cat" over and over (Temerlin, 1975).

A male chimp has been observed to tell apparent lies; he pre- tends to have to go to the bathroom when he is bored with his lessons, and he sometimes blames his misdeeds on someone else (Kunen, 1977). Other chimpanzees have been taught sign language by researchers who were fluent in it because of deafness in themselves or their families; in such an environment learning was even more rapid and took place at an earlier age than with the original chimps (Gardner & Gardner, 1975). Going beyond sign language, other psychologists have taught their primate subjects to use a sort of typewriter. They press buttons to give orders to a computer and are rewarded with food, a tickle, and the like (Rumbaugh, 1976). More recently, similar research at Stanford with a female gorilla named Koko suggests that this species may be even better at sign language than chimps. All of these findings seem to indicate that the original hypothesis was correct but the method of testing it was wrong.

The difficulties involved in reaching a "final" conclusion about anything are demonstrated still further by more recent research on chimpanzees. An extensive investigation by Terrace, Petitto, Sanders, and Bever (1979) led to the conclusion that apes are only using the gestures as a way of obtaining a reward, much as a dog can learn to "shake hands" if that behavior is reinforced. These investigators found no evidence that their chimp (Nim) ever created genuine sentences by combining signs. When there was prompting by a human trainer, the ape's responses could easily be mistaken for sentences. Such considerations have led some to conclude once again that only human beings possess the ability to use language (Limber, 1977). Terrace (1979) suggests that future projects *could* find that chimps use language, but the chance for subtle and complex imitation has to be ruled out.

The fact that an idea may be accepted at one point and later rejected (or vice versa) may be a bit upsetting, but that kind of uncertainty is part and parcel of the way science proceeds. There is no way to find out anything about the "real world" except by noting the outcomes of predictions about it. Therefore, accurate predictions should be taken to mean that one's present theory is tentatively "correct" but that at some point it may be supplanted by a better one. Inaccurate predictions mean that one's present theory is tentatively "incorrect," but new ways of testing it may bring it back to life.

RESEARCH CLOSE-UP

Answers Can Be Elusive: Men, Women, and Sexuality

It is usually very frustrating for nonscientists to discover that every answer to every question in every scientific field must be a qualified one. There are no certainties and no absolute proofs. That is, any scientific pronouncement is introduced by the implicit statement, "To the best of our current knowledge, utilizing the methods now available to us, the data are consistent with the following conclusions." Such an implied statement is necessary whether one is studying a black hole in space, the structure of the double helix, the effects of supersonic airplanes on the ozone layer, or the effects of cigarette smoking on lung cancer. There is no final knowledge in science, no ultimate solution that is accepted beyond question and for all time. Whenever new methods and new data become available, it is always possible that old answers will have to be discarded in favor of new ones. This openness to new information and to change is an integral part of what makes the scientific method and the scientific approach to obtaining knowledge a powerful system—there is a built-in mechanism to prevent anyone from becoming forever stuck in the errors or half-truths of the past.

To illustrate the way in which answers can change, let's consider a specific behavioral question: Do males and females differ in sexual needs and sexual behavior? Many people feel that they already know the answer. Syndicated columnist George Crane (M.D., Ph.D.) points out frequently that men require more "erotic calories" than women and that a clever wife must pretend interest in sex even though she does not feel it, thus keeping her husband happily supplied with "boudoir cheesecake." In our culture we are all familiar with the stereotype of the female who uses her sexuality to trap a mate and then quickly switches to "Not tonight, dear; I have a headache."

Systematic data on sexual behavior and responsiveness were not available to anyone until the present century, when a few pioneers (e.g., Davis, 1929; Hamilton, 1929) began conducting surveys on the subject. The results of this type of research were not widely circulated, however, until the publication of the first two "Kinsey Reports" in 1948 and 1953 (Kinsey, Pomeroy, & Martin, 1948; Kinsey, Pomeroy, Martin, & Gebhard, 1953). Their findings with respect to male–female differences were very consistent and very clear, and the data fit in well with commonly accepted opinions. Men were much more sexually responsive and active than women, as indicated by the fact that they reported a greater tendency to masturbate, engage in premarital and extramarital inter-course, seek out erotic materials, and become aroused by reading or viewing pornography. Such data led to much theorizing as to why the two sexes have different sexual needs. For example, it was suggested that in prehistoric times it was adaptive for females to be sexually unresponsive because they had to concentrate on maternal duties while the males were out hunting, raping, fight-ing, and engaging in other manly pursuits; for that reason evolution tended to favor passive, nonsexual females and active, virile males. Marriage manuals used the survey findings as a basis for recommending that husbands guide their wives slowly and gently to sexual awareness because of the natural differences between the sexes. As an Irish housewife observed, "Men can wait a long time before wanting it, but we can wait a lot longer" (Messenger, 1977, pp. 73–74).

There was no reason for anyone to question the data or the theories and recommendations based on them until the late 1960s and early 1970s. Then three new types of data became available.

First, Masters and Johnson (1966) conducted a series of experiments in which male and female volunteers reported to a medical research laboratory in St. Louis to engage in masturbation and intercourse while being physiologically monitored. Such research had never before been attempted, and there were many findings that did not fit the picture of the unresponsive female. Both sexes were easily aroused by genital stimulation, and both showed similar patterns of excitement mounting to a peak at orgasm. At that point the sexes were found to diverge a bit in that males go through a refractory period during which they are not aroused by further stimulation; females, in contrast, continue to be responsive to stimulation and can go on to have a series of orgasms. To the amazement of some people, women were being described as sexually superior to men!

Second, a number of researchers in various parts of Western Europe and North America began conducting studies in which male and female volunteers were exposed to erotic stories, pictures, and movies in a laboratory setting. This kind of research had not been carried out before, and once again the data were surprising. Males and females were found to be equally aroused by erotic stimuli as measured by self-ratings and physiological indications of excitement (Byrne & Lamberth, 1971; Fisher & Byrne, 1978; Griffitt, 1973; Schmidt, 1975; Schmidt, Sigusch, & Schäfer, 1973). It seems that the earlier studies found differences only because it was not socially acceptable for females to seek out erotic stimuli. Females reported disinterest in and nonarousal by pornography *because they were unfamiliar with such material* (Gebhard, 1973). Though female experience with erotica has increased greatly in recent years (Bell & Lobsenz, 1977), *surveys* still show a sex difference in reported arousal while *experiments* indicate no such differences.

Third, questionnaire studies of sexual practices have continued to be conducted over the years. New data collected in this way reveal that our society has been experiencing a genuine change in behavior. In successive generations male–female differences in masturbation, premarital intercourse, extramarital intercourse, and so forth have steadily disappeared (Hunt, 1974). On college campuses today, for example, the sexual practices of male and female students are almost identical (Curran, 1977; DeLamater & MacCorquodale, 1979). All such findings suggest that past differences in attitudes and behavior were based on learning. There was cultural pressure to suppress female sexuality and encourage male sexuality.

What conclusions can scientific research provide with respect to male–female differences in sexual needs or expression? The answer, as with all questions, depends entirely on the data currently available. The answer in the 1950s would stress differences, while the answer today would stress similarities—even though both conclusions were based on solid research evidence. It should also be kept in mind that 30 years from now the answer may or may not be totally different.

Control: What Are the Practical Implications? Of What Use Is It?

In the laboratory the ability to **control** events means that the scientist can manipulate certain variables and predict accurately their effects on other variables. Such a reliable cause-and-effect relationship also means that it may be possible to control some aspect of the world outside the laboratory. What issues are involved in the application of scientific knowledge?

Knowledge for Its Own Sake Versus Solving Practical Problems. There is an old and honored tradition that places a high value on the principle that knowledge should be sought not for practical reasons but for its intrinsic worth. This tradition has been described by Walter Lippmann as follows:

If we say that the vocation of the scholar is to seek the truth, it follows, I submit, that he must seek the truth for the single simple purpose of knowing the truth. The search for truth proceeds best if it is inspired by wonder and curiosity, if, that is to say, it is disinterested—if the scholar disregards all secondary considerations of how his knowledge may be applied, how it can be sold, whether it is useful, whether it will make men happier or unhappier, whether it is agreeable or disagreeable, whether it is likely to win him a promotion or a prize or a decoration, whether it will get a good vote in the Gallup poll. Genius is most likely to expand the limits of our knowledge, on which all the applied sciences depend, when it works in a condition of total unconcern with the consequences of its findings. [1966, p. 19]

Despite this tradition, a certain amount of conflict tends to exist between those who are actively engaged in basic research and those who feel that the ultimate outcome of such work should be useful to society (Asimov, 1979). The general culture, as represented in funds available for research grants and popular articles describing scientific findings, is clearly oriented toward applying those findings for the benefit of humanity. Basic research seems less important and is sometimes viewed as a waste of time—or, according to one member of the U.S. Senate, a "golden fleece" of taxpayers (Shaffer, 1977). The single most notable area of agreement between the political left and the right is a negative attitude toward basic research (Kornberg, 1977). "If research isn't relevant, it must not be worthwhile." For some, *relevant* means "of immediate benefit in improving the quality of life," while to others it means "of practical utility in increasing industrial or military efficiency." It is no accident that research on both ancient and modern projects such as the telescope and jet propulsion was first supported because of the perceived utility in warfare.

The emphasis on useful applications isn't confined to nonscientists; a psychologist recently said, "I feel it is a waste of time and money to be doing research on far-fetched ideas of little or no practical use to mankind" (Crane, 1977, p. 30). Support for basic research can generally be obtained, however, by pointing out that such work has often led to findings of practical value. For example, prior to the early 1940s the work of atomic physicists was seemingly far removed from any "practical use to mankind." Today the applied aspects of this field range from death-dealing explosives to nuclear power plants. In addition, the history of science suggests strongly that working on applied problems has not always been the most effective way to solve such problems. One need only think of ancient alchemists attempting in vain to change lead into gold. It is also true, of course, that at times solutions come first; basic research may be conducted afterwards to discover how or why something works. For example, aspirin has long been used as a means of reducing pain, but the reasons for its effectiveness are still being sought.

The fact that there is not always a direct relationship between laboratory research and useful applications apparently is not generally understood. If we can agree that certain problems are critical, why don't scientists concentrate all of their efforts on solving those problems? In a field as highly developed as physics, it is frequently possible to set a goal (the atom bomb or a manned rocket to the moon) and, with enough money and engineering effort, achieve it. In less developed fields such as biomedicine and psychology, the creation of a multimillion-dollar Manhattan Project does not appear to be a useful way to proceed. A crash program to cure cancer or prevent crime is probably doomed to fail. It is not because we don't desire to solve such problems; rather it is because young sciences must proceed in a different way. Instead of identifying a problem and then seeking the solution, it is necessary to gain reliable knowledge and then seek a problem to which it can be applied (Azrin, 1977).

There are many instances in which experimental methods or findings are developed in basic research and later are found to be useful in solving some applied problem (Varela, 1977). Such research fallout may be accidental in that the concerns of those who conducted the original research were far removed from the use to which it is later put. For example, the accidental discovery of X radiation was of great importance in theoretical physics; at the same time, the use of X-rays in medical diagnosis was an application of that discovery to a quite different field. Townes (1968) has documented the basic research that led to the development of the laser beam, which then became a tool solving many applied problems. He notes that if the researchers had sought to build a more accurate clock, a better drill, a more sensitive tool for eye surgery, three-dimensional photography, and so forth, they would almost certainly not have started by studying the interaction between microwaves and molecules. Such work, however, *was* conducted simply to seek new knowledge and understanding. The applied payoff could not have been guaranteed, and the details of that payoff could not even have been guessed. The difficulty of making such guesses is illustrated by an editorial in the *New York Times* in 1903. It was predicted that very hard work might lead to the development of a flying machine in "from one to ten million years."

Two questions illustrate the different emphases that may be placed on the same finding: Is it relevant to the theory? Could it serve a useful purpose? Perhaps the ideal approach is one in which both questions are asked and the ideal finding is one that provides a "yes" to each (McElroy, 1977). Weinberg (quoted in Greenberg, 1966) proposed that science is like a basketball game in which a team keeps the ball moving; every now and then there is a chance to make a good shot. Basic research keeps knowledge moving; every now and then there is a chance to exploit it for some practical use. A similar idea was expressed by Charles Kettering, who said, "Keep on going and the chances are you will stumble on something, perhaps when you are least expecting it. I have never heard of anyone stumbling on something sitting down" (Austin, 1974).

Control Outside of the Laboratory: Value Judgments.   When scientific knowledge is applied, value judgments must be made. Should thousands of innocent civilians be killed to hasten the end of a war? Is it right to fluoridate a town's water supply over the protests of a frightened minority to aid in the prevention of dental cavities? Is it right to pass a sterilization law to decrease the incidence of mental retardation? Is it right to design advertising that will motivate people to drink a certain brand of beer? Is it right to maintain a sperm bank to which only highly intelligent, creative males are allowed to contribute? Is it right to design neighborhoods in such a way that personal isolation is decreased? These decisions are different from those usually required of scientists; there are no generally accepted standards for moral concepts such as "right."

Even if there were general agreement that a given application is right and proper, there is growing awareness that technology may have unforeseen and unwelcome results (LaPorte & Metlay, 1975). For example, the automobile was a tremendous improvement over the horse as a means of transportation, but it brought with it highway deaths, pollution, and the use of scarce energy resources. Birth control pills are the most effective way to prevent an unwanted pregnancy, but they also pose a variety of health hazards as side effects. Behavior modification is the most efficient therapy to bring about rapid changes in behavior, but this technique can also be used to "brainwash" people who oppose those in positions of power.

Any instance of control could be dangerous. It is difficult to know which is the more frightening image—the mad scientist, the unthinking bureaucrat, or the evil dictator. No one wants to be manipulated by forces beyond his or her control. As Farber (1964) has pointed out, however, there is no way to escape control. We are all controlled by our physical and social surroundings, and we all spend our lives being influenced by parents, teachers, advertisers, political leaders, columnists, and so forth. Thus, the choice is never really between control and freedom; rather, it is between accidental and purposeful control and between beneficial and harmful control. Clearly, the application of scientific knowledge *should* be carried out on purpose and for the benefit of humanity. Living up to that standard must be a primary concern of scientists and nonscientists alike.

So far we have discussed *why* individuals engage in scientific activity and *what* the goals of that activity might be. Now we will consider some of the details of *how* science operates.

In a book written many years ago to give the general public some understanding of what science is all about, James B. Conant (1947) stated that he hoped to dodge the problem of defining science, feeling that science could best be understood by reading about how various scientists have gone about their work.

Science is not defined by its tools or by the facts it has gathered. Scientific apparatus often seems forbidding at first, but almost anyone can learn how to use it. And the facts are available in written form for anyone who wishes to seek them out. Science, in fact, is a dynamic, often exciting, often frustrating process in which there is a continual interaction between observing and thinking. The process is not really mysterious, and the basic elements are fairly clear.

Observation: A Starting Point

A science of behavior has many possible starting points, but most include observations of behavior. The observation may be of oneself, others in one's everyday environment, animals, patients in therapy, or people serving as subjects in experiments.

What are the characteristics of **unsystematic observation?** At this stage there is no concern for experimental rigor. One of the most exciting and important aspects of science can be seen in the attempt of an acute observer to make sense of some aspect of the world. For example, a therapist notes that a patient can move her paralyzed hand after expressing hostility toward her father for the first time. A child psychologist hears a small girl attribute the blame for an accident to an object. A professor observes that his students seem to joke and laugh loudly just before an exam. If a person observes such events, wonders about them, and tries to make sense of them, he or she has engaged in the initial activity of a science of behavior. The aim is to arrive at fruitful concepts, which will then lead to more refined observations.

For example, you may have observed that when a large group of people are together at a restaurant or bar there is often much confusion when the bill arrives. Each person contributes what he or she feels is the right amount; someone adds up the cash; and the total includes little or no tip. Four psychologists who observed this phenomenon several times decided that one effect of such interactions would be a proportionally smaller tip for the waiter the larger the group served (Freeman, Walker, Borden, & Latané, 1975). To test this proposal they carried out a **systematic observation** by conducting a **field study** of tipping. They chose a restaurant in Columbus, Ohio, and asked eleven waiters to record the number of customers at each table, the size of the bill, and the size of the tip over a two-week period. The waiters were not told what the study was about until afterward. As may be seen in Figure 1-4, the hypothesis was confirmed. The greater the number of patrons at the table, the smaller the percentage of the tip. Such a study can also be described as **correlational research** because there was no manipulation of variables but, rather, observation of the correlation or connection between two variables.

Generalization: Going Beyond the Specific Observation

As soon as observations are expressed in ways that go beyond what was originally observed, **generalization** to a *class* of events is taking place. This process constitutes the first step or the most primitive level of theory building. We each gather a series of concepts, often unverbalized and often incorrect, that influence our views of behavior (Goodman, 1978). Novelists have been aware of these concepts for many centuries. Quite often a fictional character expresses a generalization or series of generalizations

Figure 1-4.   Results of a field study of tipping behavior in a restaurant. It was found that the waiter's tip was proportionally smaller as the number of customers at the table increased.

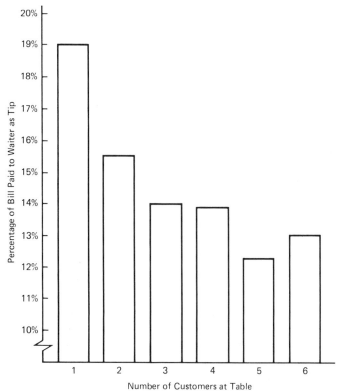

Number of Customers at Table

(Based on data from Freeman, Walker, Borden, & Latané, 1975)

about behavior. Thus, fiction has always contained a great deal of *potential* psychological wisdom.

Not only novelists but waiters, teachers, bus drivers, and sales-people observe human behavior and all develop general notions about it. "Fat people are jolly." "Mexican kids can't be trusted." "It's human nature to have wars and revolutions." "Any guy who walks like that must be queer." "Spare the rod and spoil the child." "Everybody's out to make a fast buck." "Blonds have more fun." Most people, of course, do not go beyond their original generalizations, and it is easy to fool oneself into believing that a relationship exists when it actually does not (Hamilton & Gifford, 1976). This is because most people do not have adequate means to check their ideas in order to discard the incorrect ones and expand on those that are valid. To move beyond the generalizations of everyday life and the pages of novels, one must specify **operational definitions** and engage in **empirical research** to test the validity of the generalizations. By operational definitions we simply mean the observable variables and procedures to which a generalization refers. In the field study of tipping, the size of the group was defined as the number of customers seated at each table, the size of the tip was defined as the percentage of the total bill that was given to the waiter, and the procedure involved the recording of this information by specific waiters in a specific restaurant over a specific time period. Empirical research is research that involves such observable elements.

The jump from an observation to a useful generalization is by no means automatic. Hilding (1975) wrote of his experience as an under-graduate in a bacteriology course in 1914. One day he noticed that the bacteria he was growing had a number of black spots surrounded by clear circles. He asked his instructor about it and was told that he must have been careless in cleaning the plate, thereby allowing it to be contaminated by mold. Hundreds of bacteriologists and their students must have observed the same thing in laboratories around the world. Only one person, Alexan-der Fleming, went from that observation to what now seems an obvious generalization: "If something diffuses out from a colony of molds which will prevent bacterial growth in culture, might this also prevent infection in man?" (Hilding, 1975, p. 703). The result of that generalization was penicil-lin. Such experiences make one wonder what important discoveries each of us must be missing as we go about our lives. In the words of scientist Szent-Györgyi, ". . . see what everybody else has seen, and think what nobody else has thought."

Verification: Testing the Accuracy of Generalizations

Outside of science, most people seem to rely mainly on **congruent valida-tion** to "test" their generalizations. That is, any new observations that are congruent with the generalizations are accepted as evidence that the ideas are correct. Contrary observations are ignored or forgotten. For example, the belief that members of some minority group are dirty may be confirmed by observing a few members of that group who are in need of a bath. But as a Jewish saying puts it, "*For instance* is not proof." The fact that some members of all ethnic groups (including one's own) may also be unclean, or that most members of the minority group in question are *not* dirty, can easily be overlooked.

In science, on the other hand, an effort is made to verify generalizations by seeking new data as objectively as possible. Pure objectivity probably can never be obtained, be it in science, everyday life, or newspaper reporting. We can try, though, to avoid the kind of blatant subjectivity suggested by the Irish tale of a Dubliner who took his family to England for a brief vacation. At the London zoo his youngest son ventured too close to the gorilla cage, where he was grabbed and pressed against the bars. The father rushed up to save his son by hitting the animal on the head so hard that he killed it. A British reporter was on the scene and said that he would write the story under the heading, "English Hero Saves Child from Monster's Attack." The father corrected him and pointed out that he was Irish. When the story appeared, the headline read, "Irish Thug Kills Child's Pet." In science such biases are likely to be much more subtle, but at any given time certain kinds of concepts, methods, and evidence are more appealing than others and hence are more likely to be accepted (Holton, 1973; Merton, 1975). The primary concern is to proceed in verifying generalizations in such a way that one is not deceived into accepting that which is not so or rejecting that which is. Even simple questionnaires can bias results by the way in which the questions are asked. In a letter to the *Houston Post* (March 25, 1979, P. 3B), Billy James Hargis reported the results of a mail survey he conducted. A sample of his questions is the following—"Are you willing to pull U.S. troops out of Korea and risk surrendering the country to the Communists after our boys bled and died on the Korean battlefield?" Phrased in that way, the item indicated that 503 respondents were in favor of removing the troops while 16,497 were opposed. Do you believe that different wording of the question might yield a different proportion of "yes" and "no" responses?

Whenever possible, scientists turn to **experimental research** to verify generalizations. Experiments are preferred to correlational studies because they can show that changes in one variable (the **independent variable**) result in or determine changes in another (the **dependent variable**). Ideally, any irrelevant variables are brought under **control** so that only the independent variable is operating; thus, any changes in the dependent variable are attributed to the effects of the independent variable. Besides the kind of systematic observation shown in the tipping study described earlier, it is also possible to conduct a **field experiment** in which something is *made* to happen in a natural setting. For example, Fisher, Fisher, and

Byrne (1977) conducted such an experiment in a drugstore in West Lafayette, Indiana. It was believed that the emotional responses of males who purchased condoms would be affected by the age and sex of the person from whom the purchase was made and that those responses would affect their opinions of the product. The subjects were male college students who entered a drugstore to buy a package of condoms. The researchers arranged for four types of pharmacist to be present behind the counter at different times—a male or a female who was either middle-aged or the same age as the subjects. Rating scales were filled out after the purchase. The subjects' most negative reactions were to the older female and to the male of the same age. It seemed reasonable that the older female would be a source of anxiety (some subjects felt as if they were buying a condom from their mother), but the negative reaction to the same-age male was unexpected. Such surprises set the stage for further speculation, which, in turn, leads to new and different kinds of verification.

Beyond such field studies, scientists usually prefer to conduct a **laboratory experiment** to determine the relation between an independent variable and a dependent one. In general, a laboratory setting provides the greatest precision in manipulating and measuring the variables under study, and the greatest control over irrelevant variables. The only negative feature is the artificial setting. This creates the danger that the findings may be **artifacts,** that is, something created by the experimenter and not what would happen naturally. Under the best of conditions, verification of a given relation would be obtained in all of the ways described here (a correlational field study, a field experiment, *and* a laboratory experiment), and there would thus be considerable confidence in the accuracy of the results.

TRY IT
YOURSELF

Barriers at the Drinking Fountain

A great deal of research in recent years has dealt with the concept of **personal space.** It is as if each of us carries around an invisible "bubble" into which very few people are allowed to enter. We tend to feel uncomfortable and move away if a stranger or even an acquaintance approaches us too closely. In our culture at least, a very close interpersonal distance is appropriate only for lovers or certain relatives. Most of us recognize this aspect of our world and try to avoid either being invaded or invading the space of others. For example, research has shown that people working at a library table (Fisher & Byrne, 1975), using a public rest room (Middlemist, Knowles, & Matter, 1976), or passing strangers on a sidewalk (Konečni, Libuser, Morton, & Ebbesen, 1975) tend to react negatively when others invade their personal space, and to avoid intruding on the personal space of others.

You can observe for yourself the way personal space operates by setting up a field experiment following a procedure devised by Barefoot, Hoople, and McGlay (1972). The hypothesis is that a personal space barrier induces strangers to avoid using a drinking fountain. Select a fountain along a hallway as the site of your experiment. You want to use personal space as an independent variable and to determine its effect on the dependent variable—taking a drink of water. To manipulate spatial factors, you want to create different conditions in which confederates are stationed at least two different distances from the drinking fountain. In one condition, the confederate can sit in a chair placed one foot from the fountain. In the other, the chair can be 10 feet away. For each condition, simply count the number of passers-by who stop and get a drink during the 30-minute test period. You would predict that more people will drink when the confederate is seated 10 feet away than when the chair is only one foot from the fountain.

Is that all there is to setting up an experiment? Not quite. There are some other details to consider, details that involve an attempt to control for other factors that may influence drinking behavior. Your goal is to hold everything else constant so that only personal space will be varying. If you read a professional article, it sometimes sounds as though various control procedures were inscribed somewhere on a sacred rock or the researcher had been provided with a secret book of rules. Actually, devising experimental controls is largely a matter of logic, reasoning, and common sense, and even the most experienced investigator may accidentally overlook something that proves to be crucial. *Before* you read the rest of this box, you might think a bit about the drinking fountain experiment and see if you can think of other factors that should be controlled. *After* you have read the next few paragraphs, you might try to think of possible additions to the list.

For one thing, what does the confederate do during the experiment? It is important that this person's behavior be the same in the one-foot and ten-foot conditions; for example, you would want to avoid smiling versus frowning or making eye contact versus looking away. Such things can even occur unconsciously when a confederate knows the hypothesis and is hoping that it can be confirmed. Findings obtained under such conditions can result from **experimenter effects** and thus be artifacts rather than genuine findings. One useful device would be to have the confederate read a book, try to maintain a constant expression, and avoid looking up at anyone approaching the drinking fountain. Going a step further, it is ideal if the confederate knows nothing about the research or what you expect to find; when the person who interacts with subjects is **blind** to the purpose of the experiment, as the waiters in the tipping study were, there is much less likelihood of their unwittingly affecting the results. Also, the confederates must be seated in such a way that their presence seems natural. If it is obvious that they are just sitting there as part of an experiment, **demand characteristics** are created. That is, subjects are provided with hints or clues as to what the experimenter is doing and what findings are expected. When that occurs subjects often either try to help the experimenter or try to sabotage the research. Obviously, it is essential to avoid such reactions.

Then one might consider the sex of the confederate. Since some research on personal space has shown that males and females react differently (especially when the opposite sex is involved), it would be wise to use *both* a male and a female confederate at each distance. If the male sat only at one distance (say, close) and the female only at the other (far), two variables would be **confounded.** In that situation any effects observed could be attributed to distance *or* sex *or* a combination of the two, and there would be no way to determine which variable was actually at work. To avoid any special effects that could be attributed to a particular individual's acting as a confederate, it would be best to have a fairly large number of different males and females as confederates. Another solution would be to have just one male and one female, trying very hard to make them as similar as possible with respect to obvious factors such as race, attractiveness, and style of clothing.

Then consider when you might conduct your experiment. Perhaps drinking behavior is affected by the time of day or the day of the week. So each condition should be run at the same time of day on the same day of the week at the same drinking fountain.

Finally, how do you record your data? Either the confederate or a hidden observer should keep a record of how many people of each sex stop to have a drink in each condition. If the number of possible drinkers tends to vary, it would be best to record the total number of people who pass by the fountain and calculate the *percentage* who stop to drink. After you have actually carried out the experiment, your instructor can show you how your data may be analyzed to determine whether the confederate's distance from the water fountain influences drinking behavior and whether the confederate's sex has any influence on the behavior of males versus females.

Perhaps conducting and helping to design this field experiment can serve to make research seem somewhat less formal and less mysterious as a way to answer questions about behavior.

Building Theories: The Value of More General Explanations

Theories are generalizations that go beyond the events involved in a specific observation. When someone proposes an explanation in the form of a theory, it becomes possible to deduce **hypotheses.** Further research can then be devised to test the accuracy of each hypothesis. If the hypotheses are confirmed, such data are said to be consistent with the theory and, hence, to provide support for it. If the hypotheses are *not* confirmed, the data are inconsistent with the theory; this suggests that the theory should be discarded or altered, *or* (as we saw with respect to the studies of chimpanzees) that the wrong method was used to test the hypothesis.

Sometimes people speak as if theories were of little value compared to solid facts—"It's just a theory." Actually, scientific activity moves forward *because* there are theories. The reciprocal importance of theories *and* facts has been suggested by former Treasury Secretary George Shultz who sang the following song at a VIP dinner in Manhattan:

A fact without a theory
Is like a ship without a sail,
Is like a boat without a rudder,
Is like a kite without a tail.
A fact without a theory
Is a tragic final act,
But one thing worse
In this universe
Is a theory without a fact.
        (*Time,* Feb. 26, 1973, p. 80.)

Without strongly held theories to guide what is sought in research and what is believed, science would not progress beyond simple descriptions and random findings (Holton, 1975). Even incorrect theories—such as that of Lovell, who believed that Mars was a dying civilization crisscrossed by canals—lead to the focusing of research interest and eventually to more accurate theories. Perhaps the ideal theorist is one who proposes an exciting explanation, clings to this explanation with an almost religious zeal as relevant data are obtained, and then is willing to abandon or alter it if a better theory comes along. As you might guess, the first two traits are encountered more frequently than the third one. It has even been argued by Paul K. Feyerabend, a philosopher of science, that scientific progress depends as much on rhetoric and propaganda as on rational argument (Broad, 1979). He indicates that since no theory (including Einstein's theory of general relativity) fits *all* of the facts perfectly, decisions about what is correct must rest in part on emotional considerations, including the power and prestige of the theorist.

The theories that psychologists have constructed to explain behavior are of several kinds. In the following two chapters several personality theories will be outlined. The earliest of these consist of very broad generalizations that were designed to explain all of human functioning. Because such theories relied more on observation and generalization than on verification, they do not meet our expectations of what fully developed scientific theory should be.

What *should* a theory be like? While some psychologists would disagree, many (e.g., Spence, 1960) take the physical sciences as a model. They believe that we first need a body of empirical laws that indicate in mathematical terms the relationship between variables. Next, highly generalized laws are created to bring together the lower-level laws. Finally, a complete theory is built. Such creations are elegant statements that explain a wide variety of phenomena, state a multitude of specific relations, and provide precise and accurate predictions.

In psychology, especially the field of personality, we have only begun to build that type of theory. We are beginning to devise behavioral laws analogous to those of the pendulum; we can dimly see laws analogous to the effect of gravity on momentum; and we can at least imagine a complete theory of behavior. To return to our examples, in the studies of tipping and condom purchasing it may have seemed that the investigators were simply looking at interesting and perhaps obvious aspects of their everyday world. In fact, each of those studies was related to the building of general laws that can be expressed in mathematical form. Only students with an algebra background will find these equations easy to comprehend, but the general idea should be clear. The tipping study stemmed from Latané's (1973) **social impact theory,** which indicates that the psychological impact of a group will be a power function, N^t, of the number of people actually present in the group (N = the number of people and the exponent t = the impact of additional group members and is less than 1). In the situation shown in Figure 1-4, the mathematical function is

$$\text{Tip} = \frac{.184}{N^{.22}}$$

The application of this idea to such phenomena as bystander intervention in an emergency and the tendency to report a theft will be described in Chapter 12.

The drugstore study was also part of a more general theory, the **reinforcement–affect model** of evaluative responses. Clore and Byrne (1974) proposed that the evaluation of any stimulus is a positive linear function of the weighted proportion of positive reinforcements associated with that stimulus. Thus,

$$\text{Evaluation} = m \left[\frac{\Sigma \text{PR} \cdot \text{W}}{(\Sigma \text{PR} \cdot \text{W} + \Sigma \text{NR} \cdot \text{W})} \right] + k$$

(Σ = the sum of, PR = positive reinforcements, NR = negative reinforcements, W = a weighting coefficient, and m and k are empirically derived constants.) In Chapter 9 this formulation will be applied to a variety of evaluative judgments ranging from interpersonal likes and dislikes to judicial decisions.

In general, then, it is suggested that a fruitful approach to building a theory of personality is to establish firm behavioral laws and construct small theories dealing with specific and limited events. Such mini-theories of personality would not be very broad in scope, but they would be powerful predictors. More general theories will eventually tie these mini-theories into a unified whole. In Chapter 13 the initial outlines of such a broad theory are presented.

PERSONALITY AS A FIELD OF PSYCHOLOGY

Knowledge About Human Behavior: An Urgent Need

From the viewpoint of the physical and biomedical sciences, the history of human development is one of constant and ever more amazing progress. At least in highly developed industrial nations, an astounding proportion of the general population is living in a manner that was not available to even the most wealthy and powerful citizens as recently as the early 1900s. Rosten (1974) pointed out that the richest leaders in history would marvel at the wonders that many of us take for granted, including the stereo phonograph, the instant camera, the ball point pen, the food on supermarket shelves—not to mention the metallic zipper. We enjoy an amazing degree of physical comfort, with central heating and air conditioning, king-size beds, automatic washers and dryers, vacuum cleaners, and refrigerator–freezers with automatic ice makers (regular or crushed). With a few exceptions, most major infectious diseases can be prevented or cured. With automobiles and airplanes, our mobility is miraculous. A manned satellite can cross the country in the time it took George Washington to travel from Mount Vernon to Washington, D.C. An inexpensive pocket calculator can provide instant answers to our math problems. We can sit in the comfort of our homes and view color photographs of the Martian landscape on our television sets. Almost continuous entertainment in the form of movies, television, radio, and recordings is available with the flick of a switch. It could be said that things are getting better and better, and we should all be filled with optimism.

People today, however, are less and less inclined to believe that science and technology are leading us to Utopia (Trippett, 1977). More depressing than any technological failure, though, is the way human beings behave. As Pogo once noted, "We have met the enemy and he is us." When we examine the behavior of our species during the twentieth century, change and improvement clearly are not the outstanding features. Just consider a few examples. The technical skills and organizational ability of a cultured and advanced European nation were directed toward the identification, arrest, transport, and efficient slaughter of several million "undesirable" men, women, and children. The distribution of wealth is so unequal that at the same moment in time one woman can pay $1 million for a piece of jewelry while another stays awake in a tenement room to keep the rats from eating the flesh of her sick baby. A student and former Boy Scout rode an elevator to the top of a university tower and shot over forty people at random before he himself was shot to death. A Latin American dictator employed a midget whose fearsome specialty was biting off the genitals of male political prisoners. Russian intellectuals who criticize their government are arrested, placed in mental hospitals, and tormented with advanced medical techniques. More children in the United States die annually as a result of physical abuse by their parents than from leukemia, cystic fibrosis, and muscular dystrophy combined. Uncontrolled population growth and exploitation of natural resources have resulted in overcrowded cities whose residents breathe filthy air and drink water that contains chemical and organic waste. Anyone who walks alone on the streets of a big city at night is risking his or her life. In the United States one marriage in three ends in divorce, and an unknown number of the rest bind bored, unhappy mates in loveless unions. The picture of human progress is badly marred when we focus on ourselves.

Chad Oliver once wrote a science fiction novel about a planet whose behavioral and physical sciences developed in reverse order to ours. The behavioral theories and technology of that planet were far superior to the ones on earth, while the physical sciences were still at a primitive level. In view of how things have worked out on our planet, Oliver's reversed world sounds appealing.

One possible solution to all of our people-centered problems would be the rapid development of behavioral science. This is not to suggest that psychologists or anyone else have all the answers. Rather, the hope would be that there is time for psychology and other fields to be as successful in pursuing the science of behavior as physicists have been in making sense of our physical surroundings. Some observers (e.g., Hampshire, 1977) feel that there is little hope for a science of behavior, but in a very real sense it may be the only hope we have.

Personality in Relation to Other Fields of Psychology

There are many areas of research within psychology. No psychologist studies all types of behavior. Thus, some of us deal only with animal learning; some are interested only in leadership behavior in small groups; and others concentrate on the development of mathematical models that describe behavioral laws. Where does the field of **personality** fall within psychology?

Whereas the background of experimental psychology lies in the laboratory approach to science, in which independent variables are manipulated to determine their effect on dependent variables, the historical background of personality psychology is much closer to everyday experience. For thousands of years before there were psychologists, there was general awareness of and interest in individual differences. People tend to describe others in terms of where they stand along a number of *dimensions*. Whether we are describing a political candidate, a blind date, a character in a novel, or a neighbor, the same sorts of dimensions are utilized in each instance. For example, people are described as relatively intelligent or stupid, kind or cruel, dominant or submissive, liberal or conservative, anxious or calm, contented or unhappy, ambitious or lazy, crazy or sane, devious or straightforward, creative or commonplace, social or unsocial, crude or refined, impulsive or cautious, interesting or dull, outgoing or withdrawn, and so on and so on. In fact, if one were to take any description of a person and list that person's position on all such dimensions, the end product is what we mean by the term *personality*.

With the birth of personality psychology, this interest in the dimensions of individual differences has grown in sophistication, and current work includes attempts to measure attributes of personality with some precision, to determine the extent to which relationships exist between and among personality dimensions, and to provide both qualitative and quantitative descriptions of people.

In this book *personality* will be defined as the sum total of all of the relatively enduring dimensions of individual differences. The *field of personality* is defined as that branch of psychology which deals with dimensions of individual differences and with situational determinants of behavior. Thus, behavior is viewed as determined by a combination of personality traits and situational factors.

In many respects personality is the broadest and least specific field of psychology. It has been described by Gardner Lindzey as the last refuge for general psychologists and also as psychology's garbage bin, in that any research that doesn't fit other existing categories can be labeled "personality." For this reason the work described in a book like this one touches on fields as diverse as social psychology, clinical psychology, learning, developmental psychology, physiological psychology, and others.

Psychologists are often roughly divided into *experimental* and *clinical* on the basis of broad areas of interest. The identity of the former group rests on the origins of psychology as a laboratory science, and the label "experimentalist" most often refers to someone who engages in research in the areas of learning, perception, or psychophysiology. Clinical psychology is largely a post-World War II phenomenon. While research methodology has long been included in the graduate training of clinicians, their specialty is the application of diagnostic and therapeutic skills to the identification and alleviation of the emotional problems of maladjusted individuals.

Psychologists in the personality–social area are somewhat different from both experimentalists and clinicians. They share a research orientation and methodology with experimentalists, but their research involves relatively complex human behavior. Like clinicians, personality psychologists are interested in the variables that determine human behavior, but they are much more inclined to focus on normal rather than abnormal functioning.

Division 8 of the American Psychological Association (APA) is de-

Table 1-1. A survey of personality and social psychologists indicates that they are employed in a variety of settings and engaged in a variety of different activities. The vast majority, however, engage in teaching and/or research at a college or university.

Employment Setting	Percentage	Activity	Percentage
College or University	72.7	Teaching	45.8
Federal government	5.1	Basic research	23.6
Nonprofit organization	4.9	Management	9.6
State government	3.4	Applied research	7.5
Private industry	2.4	Management, other than research/development	6.3
Medical school	2.2	Clinical research/investigation	2.2
Military, USPHS	1.8	Clinical practice	1.0
Nonprofit hospital/clinic	1.8	Report or technical writing/editing	0.9
Junior college	1.2	Development	0.8
Self-employed	1.0	Counseling practice	0.4
Secondary school system	0.9	Administration, psychological tests	0.2
Private hospital/clinic	0.7	Consulting	0.1
Other government	0.6	Design	0.1
Research center	0.5	Other	1.13
Other	0.6		

(Data from Cates, 1970)

voted to personality and social psychology, which in recent years has been one of the fastest-growing areas in the field. Between 1948 and 1960, the membership of Division 8 increased 297 percent; by comparison, that of Division 3 (experimental psychology) increased 40 percent and that of Division 12 (clinical and abnormal psychology) increased 189 percent (Tryon, 1963). Since about 1960, personality has emerged as a major field of specialization among doctoral candidates (Vance & MacPhail, 1964).

As of the late 1970s, Division 8 was found to have the largest membership of the various APA divisions with 4,372 members (McKinney, 1976.) It was also found to have a very young membership, a sign that this field has become more popular among graduate students and new Ph.D.'s. In terms of both number of members and publication of research, the personality–social area has grown faster than psychology as a whole (McGuire, 1968). Table 1-1 shows the employment settings and principal activities of personality and social psychologists who responded to the 1968 National Register of Scientific and Technical Personnel (Cates, 1970). It may be seen that most of these psychologists are employed in a college or university setting and are engaged in teaching and/or basic research.

AN OUTLINE OF THIS BOOK

This book is divided into four sections. The first section contains four introductory chapters. This chapter has attempted to introduce the notion that personality psychology is an area of scientific research, to point out the general goals toward which scientific activity is directed, and to give a brief overview of personality in relation to the rest of psychology. The following two chapters will summarize major personality theories that constitute both the classical theories proposed by analysts and the more modern contributions of psychologists. The fourth chapter returns to the topic of personality research and describes the intellectual turmoil within the field resulting from the conflict between the trait approach and the situational approach.

The second section of the book concentrates on individual differences. There are four chapters describing in some detail what is known about a representative sample of personality dimensions: authoritarianism, intelligence, manifest anxiety, and need for achievement. These traits were selected as examples because (1) there has been a considerable amount of research on each of them and (2) they represent quite varied kinds of personality dimensions. The four variables provide a sampling of research on differences in ideology, ability, emotion, and motivation.

The third section shifts to a discussion of the situational factors in behavior. There are four chapters describing what is known about the determinants of attraction, aggression, sexual behavior, and morality. Again, these topics were selected because each has been the subject of a great deal of research and because they represent a broad range of extremely important aspects of human behavior.

Thus, the study of personality will be approached in a relatively broad way to provide a picture of the variety of methods and approaches used in this field, as well as in a relatively narrow way to provide a close-up of a limited number of personality dimensions and important areas of human behavior. The emphasis throughout the book will be on research aimed at gaining knowledge about people and not on attempts to describe and characterize the actions of particular individuals. The final chapter of the book will show that it is possible to take variables that are usually studied one or two at a time and "put them together again" to describe any given person. The "molecular" way in which science must proceed does not eliminate the possibility of learning something about the "molar" functioning of a whole person—actually, it makes such learning possible. In this final chapter a unified picture of personality will be presented; personality development, personality structure, and personality functioning will be treated within a single theoretical framework.

SUMMARY

The scientific method was first developed to answer questions about astronomy and agriculture. This approach to knowledge was gradually extended to all aspects of the physical world and to all living organisms, including the human body and human behavior.

One of the many ways in which people have attempted to make

their lives more orderly and predictable is through science. The goals of science are understanding, prediction, and control. Without a clear criterion, understanding is not a satisfactory goal in that it is easy to achieve an illusion of understanding through simple naming as well as by devising after-the-fact explanations. Prediction may be defined as the primary goal of science and as a way of indicating when understanding has been achieved. An accurate prediction is no guarantee of the correctness of an explanation, however, and an inaccurate prediction does not always mean that the theory is incorrect. All theories are only tentatively right or wrong; it is always possible for new findings or methods to cause us to alter our ideas. When research has made it possible to predict accurately the effect of one variable on another, such knowledge may be used to control some aspect of the world outside the laboratory. There is an ancient academic tradition, unpopular on both the political left and the political right, that knowledge should be sought for its own sake rather than for practical reasons. A useful strategy in any science is to encourage basic research and at the same time seek to apply the knowledge thus obtained to the solution of practical problems. One difficulty in applying scientific findings is that value judgments must be made, and these judgments must be based on criteria that are external to science.

Science is a dynamic process involving both observation and generalization. Scientific activity begins with observation, often in informal, uncontrolled situations. When the observations are expressed in ways that go beyond that which has been observed, there is generalization to a broader class of events. Generalization is the first step or the most primitive level of theory building. Though people everywhere observe and generalize about behavior, the process of verification is unique to science. A primary concern of scientists is to carry out the verification process in such a way that one is not deceived into accepting that which is not so or rejecting that which is. The next step, theory building, involves the formulation of ever-broader generalizations that encompass basic laws. Theories make it possible to deduce hypotheses that lead to new attempts at verification. A comprehensive theory permits the unification of formerly unrelated empirical events within a single framework. One approach to theory building in psychology is to seek empirical laws, which become part of highly generalized laws, which in turn become the building blocks of a comprehensive theory.

The rapid progress of the physical and biomedical sciences is sometimes thought of as meaning that human development is a process of constant and almost miraculous improvement. A view of human behavior, however, presents a panorama of war, crime, and assorted cruelties for which behavioral science may be the only real solution. The background of experimental psychology lies in the traditional laboratory approach to science, in which independent variables are manipulated and their effects on dependent variables determined. The historical background of personality psychology is in the centuries-old habit of describing other people in terms of their positions on an almost infinite number of dimensions. Such descriptions eventually led to attempts to measure personality dimensions and study their determinants and correlates. The most distinctive feature of the field of personality at present is the tendency to combine experimental psychology with an interest in individual differences. An individual's personality is defined as the sum total of all of the relatively enduring dimensions of individual differences. The field of personality is defined as that branch of psychology which deals with dimensions of individual differences and with situational factors affecting behavior. The field of personality or personality–social psychology is a rapidly growing one that shares its research orientation with experimental psychology and its interest in complex human behavior with clinical psychology. The Division of Personality and Social Psychology is the largest division of the American Psychological Association, and this field has become very popular among graduate students and new Ph.D.'s during recent years. Most personality–social psychologists are employed in a college or university setting and are engaged in teaching and/or research.

SUGGESTED READINGS

BYRNE, D.   Paradigm research in personality and social psychology. In D. Byrne, *The attraction paradigm*. New York: Academic Press, 1971. Pp. 3–22. A description and explanation of the way basic and applied research may be conceptualized in these fields of psychology.

FROMKIN, H., & STREUFERT, S.   Laboratory experimentation. In M. D. Dunnette (ed.), *Handbook of industrial and organizational psychology*. Chicago: Rand McNally, 1976. Pp. 415–65. A detailed and useful description of the advantages of laboratory research, the pitfalls to be avoided in such research, and the relation between experimentation and application.

KUHN, T. S.   *The structure of scientific revolutions*. Chicago: University of Chicago Press, 1970. A very important and readable analysis of the way science normally progresses and, at times, undergoes dramatic change.

McCAIN, G., & SEGAL, E. M.   *The game of science*. Monterey, Calif.: Brooks/Cole, 1977. An entertaining and painless introduction to the scientific method and its place in society.

SKINNER, B. F.   The steep and thorny way to a science of behavior. *American Psychologist*, 1975, *30*, 42–49. An interesting and challenging description by the world's foremost behavioral scientist of the way science is applied to human behavior.

Chapter Two

THEORIES OF PERSONALITY: THE ANALYSTS

In this chapter you will read about the following topics:

The space probe had traveled thousands of light-years through the galaxy in a search for species that bore some resemblance to the life forms of the home planet. To the Mrdlngs, this meant finding creatures made of metal who ingested liquid nutrient, were able to move about, and could respond to external stimulation. Though most of the stars they visited were surrounded by one or more planets, the mission had not yet discovered any living organisms. Just when many members of the expedition had given up hope for success, they were pleasantly surprised when they scanned the third planet from a medium-sized star near the edge of the galaxy. After several weeks of observation, the commander transmitted the following initial summary prepared by his scientific officers:

The basic species here is a being resembling our own Glflns, though at a more primitive stage of development. As usual, our field work is being conducted primarily at their medical facilities where a steady flow of subjects is available. We do not comprehend much of their language as yet, but the hospitals seem to be called "garages."

The typical individual on the planet is metallic and moves about on four round wheel-like appendages. It seems that these creatures have built, or directed their small, soft-shelled slaves to build, a network of pathways that spreads in various directions across the continents. They seem to subsist on a liquid diet obtained from storage tanks located at convenient feeding centers. The liquid passes through a tube into a small mouth located in the rear section of the creatures' bodies. Most curious is the fact that their waste products are excreted in the form of a vaporous gas emitted from a tubular rear appendage.

Our studies of the garages make it clear that these "Glflns" are very fragile and sickly beings. At frequent intervals, they must be treated for such ailments as flat appendages, the sudden onset of internal noise, a tendency to belch black smoke, and/or the total inability to move. In many instances they must be pulled along to the medical centers by specialized rescue workers.

Much of their behavior is quite odd, and we have been attempting to build a workable theory to explain their actions. For example, they often must undergo treatment for the very severe injuries that occur when they dash headlong into one another or into some solid object beside their pathways. Death (known here as being "totaled") is not uncommon. Dr. Pqr has concluded that this is an inherently hostile species. For example, when there are many creatures on a pathway at once, they tend to move quite slowly while vocalizing in angry, unpleasant voices. This aggressiveness is frequently turned inward, however, and transformed into self-destructive acts. The clearest example is that, despite the obvious risk of injury, mutilation, and death, they travel at very high speeds whenever possible, especially between their cities. It should be noted that while Dr. Mg agrees as to the presence of aggressive and self-destructive tendencies, he feels that such behavior is the result of early experiences rather than inherited drives. He argues that the many scratches and dents on the patients provide evidence of abusive treatment during the developmental period which could be responsible for the violence displayed in adulthood.

In fairness, it must be added that young Dr. Mln rejects both theories. It is his belief that the creatures behave as they do in response to external conditions. They may be seen to bellow angrily when anything blocks their forward progress, when the colored lights at intersections do not alternate quickly enough, and in response to the noises made by their fellow creatures. Thus, if it were possible to alter their surroundings, their aggression should quickly decrease.

In a future report, we will describe the behavior of several much larger species that are probably related to the primary inhabitants. Despite their physical superiority, these lumbering creatures seem to play a servile role in this society; they have been trained to deliver goods from place to place. Such social class distinctions are thought to be based on genetic differences in ability.

How would you go about making sense of the behavior of automobiles if you had never seen them before? How would you explain gas stations, traffic jams, horn honking, speeding, and so forth? When behavioral science came into being at the beginning of the last century, equally difficult problems were undertaken as theorists attempted to figure out the behavior of their fellow human beings. Why do members of our species sometimes hate and kill, sometimes behave tenderly, and sometimes become emotionally disturbed? How can we explain dreams, creativity, falling in love? What motivates us—lust, power, ambition, reverence for a supreme being, the need for self-acceptance, the search for pleasure, or the fear of pain? The first attempts to bring some kind of order to this array of phenomena were made by psychotherapists dealing with disturbed and unhappy patients. The task they set for themselves was not only to try to help the individuals who had sought treatment but also to use the information obtained in this setting as a basis for understanding all human behavior. Thus at the beginning of this century **personality theory** was born. Such a theory is developed with the aim of describing and explaining the behavior of individuals. The insights of these pioneering theorists were sometimes wrong and sometimes not even verifiable but many of their ideas have had a continuing impact on the field of personality, on many other areas of behavioral science, and on our culture in general.

EXPLAINING BEHAVIOR: WHAT IS "HUMAN NATURE"?

Though the creation of a personality theory is a fairly recent undertaking, people have tried to explain their own actions and those of others throughout history. Many of these early explanations—and the assumptions on which they are based—continue to influence theory and research on personality. For that reason it will be useful to take a brief look at some of them.

All human beings are raised within a given culture, learn the language of that culture, and are molded by what happens to them throughout their lives to such a degree that there is no way to determine what **human nature** would be like without such influences. The desire to identify basic human characteristics may be one reason for the prevalence of legends about children being abandoned in the woods and raised by animals—from Romulus and Remus to Mowgli in *The Jungle Book* and even Tarzan (Miller, 1976; Shattuck, 1980). Even though there is no such thing as a "pure" human being who is free from cultural influences, this has not kept people from speculating about what factors might underlie human nature. Several themes have been stressed from the earliest philosophical writings to the most recent research on personality. Three of these will serve as illustrations. Most ideas about personality can be placed somewhere among the following three dichotomies. Basically, assumptions are made as to where human beings stand along the axes good-bad, rational-irrational, and internal-external control.

The Beast Within Versus the Noble Savage

One common assumption is that human beings are barely tamed beasts who are by nature aggressive, cruel, and warlike. It is believed that the only thing that keeps any of us from a life of killing, looting, and random sexuality is the restraining force of cilvilization, which molds us and controls us by means of religion, interpersonal pressure, and the forces of law and order. Those who make this assumption about humanity suggest that when such constraints are absent or weakened, the result is anarchy. Daily examples of warfare, crime, and the like throughout the world are seen as evidence supporting this view of humanity.

In contrast, human beings can be regarded as basically good and gentle, as peaceful as a band of timid deer munching on leaves in the forest. Those who view humanity in this way suggest that an uncivilized human being would be a "noble savage," honest, kind, and wise in the manner of the native Americans in *The Last of the Mohicans.* From this perspective trouble is caused by corrupt cities, cruel parents, unjust laws, poverty, and

TARZAN DID NOT ATTEMPT TO ESCAPE. IN FACT HE WELCOMED THE OPPORTUNITY TO TEST HIS NEW SKILL. QUICKLY HE UN-SLUNG HIS BOW AND FITTED A WELL-DAUBED ARROW.

Figure 2-1. One view of human nature considers us as Noble Savages who are basically good and honest. The infant Tarzan was raised by beasts in the jungle, and developed into just such a being. (New York Public Library)

other negative forces that create angry, twisted human beings. If these corrupting factors could be altered or destroyed, all people would be able to develop as unspoiled, happy creatures living in harmony with nature.

The Logical Computer Versus the Emotional Reactor

A second viewpoint also involves some basic assumptions about the manner in which we function. On the one hand, it is possible to emphasize our intelligence and ability to reason. Perhaps the best-known example of such an idealized version of rational behavior is Mr. Spock of *Star Trek*. Like a living computer, he responds to incoming information, uses any relevant facts he has acquired earlier, and then reaches the most logical conclusion possible. Have you ever read tips on how to choose a career, a car, or a mate? You are advised to add up the costs and the benefits with respect to each choice and then to make whichever decision would maximize benefits and minimize costs. Presumably, we could each function as rationally as Mr. Spock if only we would use our intellectual capacities. Apparently the creators of *Star Trek* did not view earthlings as behaving in this manner: Mr. Spock's intellectual approach is attributed to his Vulcan father.

The other extreme on this continuum is also depicted on *Star Trek*—it is the emotional, impulsive Dr. McCoy. Perhaps human beings respond not so much to logic as to their feelings. Like any other animal, we seek to obtain pleasure and avoid pain whenever possible. In addition, strong emotional states such as sympathy, love, and anger can propel us into doing things that we might avoid if we paused long enough to be logical. Further, it is suggested that we are not always *aware* of our reasons for acting. Thus, we can be viewed as unconsciously motivated and not always rational in what we do.

Internal Propulsion Versus Kites in the Wind

The third type of assumption about human nature involves the way our behavior is determined. Are we propelled by internal forces or by external ones? Much of personality theory has emphasized internal factors that are based either on inherited, genetically determined traits ("Blood will tell") or on that which is learned at an early age ("As the twig is bent, so grows the tree") (Wilson, 1978). Thus, individual traits are "set" either at conception or during childhood. From then on, one's personality is expressed in a consistent manner.

An opposite view is that most of our behavior is influenced by the situation in which we find ourselves. Thus, anyone can be shy or outgoing, brave or cowardly, kind or cruel, depending on the circumstances. This "situational" view of human behavior will be described in greater detail in the following chapter. A focus on the individual and his or her internal traits leads toward a concern with altering the person so that he or she is better able to adapt to the demands of external reality. The world is the way it is, and psychology's task is to find out how to mold people to fit that world. On the other hand, a focus on situational factors tends toward a concern with altering the situation so that it does not have a harmful effect on human beings. The world has many negative aspects, and it is psychology's task to find out how to make our surroundings better. These are two quite different positions, and they lead to quite different kinds of research, theory, and application.

A further aspect of this dimension has been suggested by attribution theorists (Nisbett, Caputo, Legant, & Marcek, 1973). We tend to view our own behavior as influenced by external factors but attribute what other people do to internal causes. "I cheated on the exam because the prof makes up unfair questions. *He* cheated because he's dishonest."

As you read about the personality theories described in the rest of this chapter, try to place each one with respect to these three dimensions. We'll return to this issue at the end of the chapter.

WHAT DO YOU THINK

Human Behavior Developing in Isolation

It should be clear that we can never reach a final answer to the question of what human beings are "really" like. We can only indicate what they are like under given circumstances. But the assumptions we make influence not only personality theory but also the way each of us feels about the chances for a lasting world peace, the causes of crime and the way to prevent it, the reasons for poverty and financial success, how best to raise children, and much else besides. Have you ever thought about your own position on such questions and how your beliefs and opinions reflect your basic assumptions?

As an exercise in thinking about these issues, imagine the following situation and then finish the story. A large group of preschool children is being flown by jumbo jet to a newly built amusement park on the coast of Australia. The event is both a promotional stunt and a special treat. The boys and girls were selected from all parts of the United States in an effort to achieve a representative mixture of ethnic groups, socioeconomic classes, and religious backgrounds. The youngest child is 2 and the oldest 6.

A sudden storm causes the pilot to change course. Then, as the plane is flying over an unpopulated tropical island in the South Pacific, a mysterious explosion forces the pilot to make an emergency landing. The plane spins roughly to a halt on a rocky beach, instantly killing the entire crew. Only the children survive. They are shaken up and frightened, but none of them is seriously injured.

After jumping from the plane through a crack in the fuselage, they soon find that the island is well supplied with fruits and berries and that there is a stream of pure water running down from a hill in the central portion of their new land. There are a few animals in the jungle, but none of them is dangerous. There are fish in the lagoon, and the weather is always warm.

When the plane disappeared, attempts were made to locate it and rescue any survivors. Because the flight had been off course, the search proved fruitless and the entire group of youngsters was assumed to have been lost at sea along with the pilot and crew. Now, 20 years later, a group of travelers is sailing on a small schooner that happens to stop at the island where the plane landed. To their surprise, there are several people on the beach of this supposedly uninhabited spot. The boat anchors in the lagoon, and several of the travelers go ashore. What do they find? What kind of society has developed here? Is it run democratically or is there a dictatorial leader? Is there one group or are there several competing ones? Are the survivors friendly or warlike? Do they work hard or are they lazy? Do they have rules and laws or does everyone do as he or she wishes? What kind of sexual customs have they developed? What is their language like? Does religion play a role in their lives? Do they pay any attention to racial differences? Have they created families? Do they behave as they probably would have if they had grown up in the United States or are they completely different? Do they tend to act like Mr. Spock or like Dr. McCoy?

When you complete this story you might want to read what others have written. Other members of your class might make very different assumptions about how human behavior would develop in this situation. In *The Lord of the Flies*, author William Golding supplies a chilling version of the society that such children would create.

PERSONALITY THEORIES AS APPROACHES TO UNDERSTANDING BEHAVIOR

For many psychologists, a theory of behavior is no different from a theory of any other natural phenomenon. We have taken the approach of the "hard" sciences as a model because the historical roots of psychological research are found in nineteenth-century biology and physics. For many of those who are interested in personality and clinical psychology, however, the historical roots of the field lie elsewhere—in the consulting rooms of nineteenth-century physicians who sought to understand behavior by building psychological models of human functioning (Rychlak, 1976). As a result, the formulations that we call personality theories have been somewhat more similar to the formulations of philosophers than to those of physical scientists. What are the implications of such differences?

In Chapter 1 scientific activity was described as moving from observation to generalization to verification to theory building. The crucial difference between the original personality theories and other theories of science has to do with verification. Such matters as operational definitions, controlled observations, and quantification are essential to scientific verification. Beginning with Sigmund Freud, personality theorists attempted to utilize a different kind of verification technique consisting simply of additional uncontrolled observations. We will examine some of the strengths and weaknesses of that approach in the following pages.

When someone with the brilliance and creativity of Freud engaged in theory building of this kind, the outcome was not a set of empirical laws or even an acceptable theory, but it was much more than a literary exercise. Many of his ideas have had an influence on research, and they have also influenced our artistic creations and even our general concept of human nature. The basic weakness of this approach should be noted at the outset. The proof of any scientific pudding is prediction and control, and the traditional personality theories do not always allow us to predict behavior or provide rules for controlling behavior. Even so, the early personality theories were interesting attempts to bypass the empirical procedures of science. They offer provoking insights into human behavior, and they have profoundly influenced human thought. For these reasons personality theories, however imperfect, are likely to continue to influence the kinds of variables we study and the kinds of explanations we consider reasonable.

THE PSYCHOANALYTIC THEORY OF SIGMUND FREUD

A Medical Researcher in Vienna

In Freud's (1935) own words, "I was born on May 6th, 1856, at Freiberg in Moravia, a small town in what is now Czechoslovakia. My parents were Jews, and I have remained a Jew myself." His family moved to Vienna when he was four. He completed medical school at the University of Vienna with the intention of becoming a research scientist. He was not greatly interested in learning about medical practice and spent much of his time in laboratory research. Shortly after receiving the M.D. degree in 1881, he joined the Institute for Cerebral Anatomy to conduct research. His salary was low, advancement in an academic research setting was hampered by a prevailing atmosphere of anti-Semitism. He therefore decided to seek the financial rewards of private practice. Even so, he remained interested in searching for answers to the problems confronting him; he thought of himself not as a physician but as a biologically oriented scientific scholar (Sulloway, 1980).

Freud was intrigued by a number of somewhat unorthodox approaches to the treatment of emotional problems. These included hypnosis as practiced by Jean Charcot, a French psychiatrist, and an unusual procedure devised by Joseph Breuer, a Viennese physician, that involved directing the patient to simply *talk* about his or her symptoms and problems. Freud did not find hypnosis very useful, but he was impressed by the "talking-out" technique. After a disagreement with Breuer concerning the role of sexual conflicts in hysterical symptoms, Freud went his own way in developing both **psychoanalytic theory** and the therapeutic techniques that constitute **psychoanalysis.** He himself felt that a major turning point in his thinking had come in July 1895, when he had his first insight into the nature of dreams. In the fall of that year he began what he called the Project for a Scientific Psychology (Gass, 1975). Freud worked during the period when the first psychology laboratories were being established in Germany. While these early psychologists were studying conscious processes, perception, and simple motor responses, Freud was trying to understand unconscious thought processes and complex human behavior.

Freud's life was devoted to the practice of psychoanalysis and to writing and developing his theory of personality in a steady outpouring of articles and books. His work attracted numerous disciples and led to the establishment of the International Psychoanalytic Association in 1910. In addition to his lasting effect on the practice of psychiatry, he had an important influence on psychology as well. While many members of the medical profession still considered Freud little more than a scandalous quack, G. Stanley Hall, an American psychologist, invited him to give an address at meetings commemorating the founding of Clark University. Late in Freud's life the Nazis overran Austria, and he managed to escape to England after ransom money had been collected by his friends and admirers. He died in London in 1939.

In discussing Freud's theories it is helpful to keep in mind the nature of his theory-building procedures. In therapy, his observations consisted mostly of what his patients said. Because the technique was new and unusual, Freud was in the unique position of hearing, in great detail, private thoughts, early memories, sexual secrets, dreams, wishes, and other details about the lives of numerous people. Even more than a priest in a confessional, Freud was exposed to aspects of human behavior that are not usually on public display. Because talking seemed to reduce the severity of symptoms and increase the patient's feeling of well-being, Freud could have been content to develop and practice an important new therapeutic technique. But he did much more than that. He tried to make sense of his observations, to explain what he heard, and to build his generalizations into a theoretical framework with the potential to explain all of human behavior. A number of writers have compared his methods to those of Sherlock Holmes. Why should talking about a long-forgotten childhood incident lead to a dramatic improvement in a physical condition? Why should a man report dreams in which he had intercourse with his mother? Why should a person be unable to think of what to say when confronted with hostile and aggressive words? Novelist Nicholas Meyer (1974) utilized the similarity between Holmes and Freud in *The Seven-Per-Cent Solution,* in which he has the fictional detective tell Dr. Freud:

This is most remarkable . . . Do you know what you have done? You have succeeded in taking my methods—observation and inference—and applied them to the inside of a subject's head. . . . You know, Doctor, I shouldn't be surprised if your application of my methods proves in the long run far more important than the mechanical uses I make of them. [p. 129]

Freud was a devoted exponent of the assumption that behavior is lawful and that it should be possible to identify the meaning of a person's dreams, slips of the tongue, lapses of memory, neurotic symptoms, or anything else. As his theory grew, he was constantly changing it on the basis of new observations, deductions, and efforts to overcome logical difficulties. It is interesting to note that Freud's concerns would have been severely restricted if he had bound himself to the methods and procedures of the experimental psychologists of his day. By going his own way he was able to deal with problems and generate ideas that were far beyond those considered by behavioral scientists. Even if the final outcome of Freud's endeavors turned out to be as literary as it was scientific (Schafer, 1976), what an impressive achievement it was!

Mapping the Structure of the Mind

Among Freud's earliest ideas was the concept of the human mind as an active region in which internal factors operate to influence external behavior. He stressed the importance of thoughts and motives of which the person is not even aware, and he viewed our interior landscape as a battleground on which there are tense struggles among competing forces. Thus, the three *states of consciousness* and the three *systems of personality* came to play a central role in Freud's theory.

States of Consciousness.   Freud divided mental functioning into three levels or states: conscious, preconscious, and unconscious. Whatever you are perceiving or thinking about at this moment is defined as your **conscious** functioning. This frequently means whatever a person can express in words. For example, if a woman feels a certain visceral sensation and says to herself, "I am hungry," that is a conscious experience. Included here are perceptions of internal and external events and the wishes and plans that occur in our thoughts and discussions.

The **preconscious** includes those memories from the past which are more or less available to consciousness when needed. If someone asks you your telephone number or your mother's maiden name or the capital of Illinois, you will probably be able to bring the material into consciousness, sometimes after a mental effort or struggle. The relation between conscious and preconscious material is seen in the tip-of-the-tongue phenomenon, in which the name of a song or a movie actor or whatever is almost, but not quite, recalled. Sometimes it is hours or days later that the forgotten material is suddenly and clearly remembered. Once we were at a student party, playing "TV Trivia." Someone asked who played the four leading characters on "Leave It to Beaver." Various people found it easy to remember that Jerry Mathers played the Beaver and Barbara Billingsley his mother. The father was more difficult, but after a while someone shouted out, "Hugh Beaumont." But no one could recall the name of the actor who played Beaver's brother, Wally. The game went on, the guests eventually went home, and still the question of Wally's real name went unanswered. About 4:00 the next morning one of us (DB) woke up with the sudden insight that the right answer was Tony Dow. Freud would have been pleased to note both that the correct name of the actor had been present in the preconscious all along and that the active process of trying to retrieve the name had continued despite being asleep. It has been suggested that the preconscious is like a darkened room in which consciousness is represented by a small speck of light that flits from point to point, much as Tinkerbell does in *Peter Pan.* In this instance, during sleep the actor's name was suddenly illuminated, and the problem was solved.

Freud described the **unconscious** as a storehouse of unacceptable images, including past events, current impulses, and desires of which one is not aware. Here we have a much larger and much darker room that the speck of light is unable to penetrate. In this vast area, thought processes can run free without constraint by rules of grammar or logic, realism, or moral issues. The unconscious material is threatening and must be held back so that it does not overwhelm the person with anxiety. Unconscious material can sometimes reach the surface, usually in disguised form; examples include dreams and hallucinations. The material can be deciphered or interpreted by someone who has been trained in the ways of the unconscious. In the words of Disney's Cinderella, "A dream is a wish your heart makes when you are fast asleep," but Freud would add, "Sometimes it's a very disguised wish." When unconscious thoughts burst through without distortions, they are likely to be disowned: "How could I dream such nonsense? I've never thought of things like that! Did I really say all of that when I was stoned?" Dreams can also involve creative functioning in which problems are solved and new ideas developed; people whose dreams are of this sort are found to be more creative then those whose dreams are less novel (Domino, 1976a).

The Three Systems of Personality. Observing the things that his patients felt and wanted, the things that they did and failed to do, and the things that they felt were right and wrong, Freud organized these behaviors into a conceptual scheme by suggesting that the personality is composed of three interacting systems: the id, the ego, and the superego. That is, he proposed that each thing we do is the end result of whatever compromises we work out among our primitive desires, the constraints of reality, and our acquired moral code.

In the beginning there is only the **id**, and it is totally unconscious.

Infants respond solely to desire—hunger, thirst, pain reduction. They want their needs fulfilled right now. Like the Cookie Monster on "Sesame Street," ME WANT COOKIE! Robert Louis Stevenson had a dream about the amoral creature in each of us and turned the dream into his story, "Dr. Jekyll and Mr. Hyde." This demand for immediate satisfaction of our bodily needs was labeled the **pleasure principle.** If satisfaction were always supplied instantly, our thought processes would remain as simple as those of infants. Hunger would lead to food, thirst to drink, and lust to sex, without delay, complications, or consequences.

We do not remain infants, so it is apparent that some other kind of functioning (i.e., **ego**) must develop. Freud proposed that, to survive, the person must begin to come to terms with the objective world. One must learn the difference between milk and the idea of milk, between the memory of mother's voice and her presence in the room, between what one wants and what is actually obtained. From this ability to distinguish reality from fantasy, there gradually develop behaviors that allow one to manipulate the real world. Included here is the tendency to plan ahead and then test the usefulness of the plan by trying it out. In contrast to the pleasure principle of the id, the workings of the ego are described as the **reality principle.** In Chapter 1 the development of science was described as a means of gaining the ability to predict and control the environment. Freud would describe those activities as ego functioning in the service of the reality principle.

The aim of the id is to obtain pleasure and avoid pain. The ego acts to gain the same ends within the constraints of reality. At this point, a third system develops. When parents are able to teach their child the traditional values of their society and when this moral code becomes internalized so that the child truly believes and genuinely feels the rightness of these values, the **superego** comes into being. The goal here is not pleasure but doing the right thing, being good, achieving perfection as defined by a given moral code. A more familiar term than *superego* is *conscience,* which refers to a kind of built-in reinforcement process that makes a person feel satisfied when doing right and guilty when doing wrong. At times the pleasure-oriented aims of the id are in direct conflict with the morality-directed aims of the superego. Most often, personality is seen as functioning fairly well, with the ego coordinating the demands of the id, the superego, and the objective world. Thus, the id tells us what we *want* to do, the superego tells us what we *should* do, and the ego decides what we *can* do.

Dynamics and Development

In addition to describing how mental processes function, Freud attempted to explain the motivational factors driving the total system and to account for individual differences in personality. We'll take a brief look, then, at his concepts of *personality dynamics* and *personality development.*

Energy and Instincts. Freud viewed each human being as a machine that consumes food, water, and oxygen and converts these into energy, which is then expended in both physical and mental work. Freud was strongly influenced by the thinking of physicists, and he assumed that the conservation of energy was as true in biology as in physics. Thus, energy could be stored, transformed from one state to another, or expended, but it could not be destroyed or lost from the system. Freud proposed that the source of psychic energy for personality functioning was instinctive physiological needs based within the id.

The resulting motivational theory is a familiar one in psychology. Bodily needs lead to conscious desires and to the behavior necessary to satisfy the need. When the need is satisfied, the organism comes to rest until another need arises. There are individual differences in the means adopted to satisfy each need and in the specific goal objects. For example, we can learn to eat very different kinds of food (ranging from a Big Mac to curdled mare's milk mixed with warm blood) and reduce our hunger pangs equally well. Freud classified instincts as those involving life—such as hunger and sex—and those involving death. **Libido** was the name he gave to the energy underlying the life instincts, but he had no equivalent name for the energy of the death instincts; the term **thanatos** is sometimes used. The life instincts ensure the survival of the individual and of the species, and Freud's interest was mainly with the sex instinct. For this reason, libido is often interpreted as sexual energy. The goal of the death instinct is to return the organism to the inorganic matter from which it came. The death wish is frequently frustrated by the life instincts; hence, other goals must be substituted for self-destruction. The frustration is resolved by turning the death wish on others in the form of the aggressive drive. The notion of a death instinct was prompted by observations of the widespread savagery unleashed in World War I. Had Freud lived beyond 1939, he might have become even more convinced that much of human behavior is impelled by the death instinct.

Anxiety and Defenses Against Anxiety. Freud (1926) stressed the role of **anxiety** as an unpleasant feeling that people try hard to avoid or reduce. Unlike fear, anxiety has no specific focus. It involves a general sense of helplessness like that of an infant who has been forced out of a safe, comfortable womb by the traumatic event of birth. Presumably, whenever that helpless feeling involving loss of security occurs in later life, we know again the terror we went through when we were born. Fanciful as they may seem, Freud believed that a series of events can evoke just such feelings—loss of one's mother, the threat of castration, rejection by a lover, and failure to measure up to the standards of one's own superego. One of the goals of therapy is to make the patient aware of the cause of his or her anxious feelings and insightful as to their current inappropriateness. For example, the end of a love affair can seem like the end of the world, but it helps to consider the possibility that one's emotional state may just be a reenactment of the **birth trauma.** With such ideas now conscious instead of unconscious, the person becomes free to deal with the situation in a realistic way. The loss is not that bad. There *are* other lovers to be found.

Anxiety is a signal that a threatening thought is about to enter consciousness. The ego reacts to such a threat by defending itself. The principal **defense mechanisms,** as outlined by Anna Freud, are repression, projection, reaction formation, and regression. They operate unconsciously, and they involve some distortion of reality. It's as if the ego fools itself. *Repression* is the major way by which the ego defends itself against the panic that would be caused by unleashing the unconscious. This mechanism includes forgetting, denial, and misperception. A boy feels sexually attracted to his sister, and that is threatening and evokes anxiety. The anxiety can be reduced if he is literally not aware of his sexual desires. *Projection* involves assigning the cause of the anxiety to an external source that is easier to deal with than one's own impulses. Unacceptable sexual desires can be denied as relevant to oneself; instead, they are attributed to someone else. Thus, the boy may be worried about black men, who, he decides, must be eager to rape young white women. With *reaction formation,* there is a reversal of impulse so that the original anxiety-evoking impulse is denied by the presence of its opposite. Thus, the boy could not be sexually attracted to his sister if he disliked her. If a given source of anxiety arises at a later stage, one way of solving the problem is to return to an earlier stage (*regression*). If the boy can remain a child in his thoughts and wishes and behavior, the sexual threat goes away.

Stages of Development.   During the first six years of life, according to Freud, each person passes through a series of stages. Freud was convinced that these initial years were crucial in forming the adult personality.

The first contact with the external world is through the mouth. The **oral stage** centers on the pleasures received from eating, sucking, and (later) biting. Freud reasoned that fixation at the early oral stage would lead to an **oral personality.** Dependency needs are tied to the early oral stage, in which a person passively receives help from others. In the movies, Lou Costello depicted a happy dependent oral character who was easily led astray by Bud Abbott. Research shows that people with oral traits actually do tend to conform to the wishes of an authority figure (Tribich & Messer, 1974). Fixation at the later oral stage would lead to an oral–aggressive personality with a need to abuse others verbally. Such phrases as "He nearly bit my head off" or "She has a sharp tongue" come to mind. Don

Rickles enacts the role of such a person very well as he insults the "hockey pucks" in his audience.

The next interaction between the child and the external world usually occurs by the time he or she is a year old. This involves the bowel functions and is known as the **anal stage.** The child takes pleasure in defecation but, when toilet training begins, is forced to regulate this behavior according to an external set of more or less arbitrary demands. Once again, a person's character is determined by the events that occur during this stage. Controlling one's bowel functions is a way of conforming to society's demands, pleasing parents, and delivering a product at the right time and in the right place. One type of **anal personality** is the *retentive* person who is characterized by conformity, stinginess, and excessive concern with neatness and order. Anal *expulsiveness* is seen as related to messiness and explosive displays of temper. Power in the adult world can be attained through either conformity or rebellion. In *The Odd Couple* Felix Unger and Oscar Madison reveal the problems that arise when these two types of anal personality try to live together.

The next arena of interaction between the individual and the external world has to do with the genital organs and occurs at about age four. In the **phallic stage** masturbation is discovered to be pleasant and enjoyable sexual fantasies are associated with touching one's penis or clitoris. Freud believed that males and females have different experiences at this stage. The boy's sexual fantasies involve his mother. This reminded Freud of the ancient Greek play in which Oedipus kills his father and marries his mother. With such incestuous desires, a little boy becomes afraid that his jealous father will castrate him as punishment. This situation of lust for the mother and fear of the father was labeled the **Oedipal complex.** Fear usually wins out in that **castration anxiety** causes the boy to give up his sexual longing for his mother and try to be as much like his father as possible. Ideally, this resolution of the conflict results in strong, nonsexual affection for one's mother ("How I love ya, how I love ya, my dear old Mammy") and identification with the powerful father ("My dad's tougher than your dad"). Both aspects of this resolution are summed up in the song "I Want a Girl Just Like the Girl Who Married Dear Old Dad." Another feature of this resolution is the development of a strong superego. When the Oedipal conflict is not resolved, Freud believed that a male is likely to become either a homosexual or a heterosexual who does not really love women but only uses them as sexual objects. Such behavior constitutes the **phallic personality.**

The experiences of the female during the phallic stage were always something of a puzzle to Freud, and his analysis of the situation has been the object of many justified attacks by women. He believed that the little girl, too, is sexually attracted to her mother. The problem here is not fear of the father but, rather, the discovery that the clitoris is "inferior" to the penis possessed by males. The result of this discovery, according to Freud, is **penis envy** and a feeling of hostility toward the mother for creating this anatomical defect. These problems (sometimes called the **Electra complex**) are more or less resolved when the girl rejects her mother as a sexual object and feels love and admiration for her father (as in "You're Daddy's little girl" and "My heart belongs to Daddy"). She decides that she can be like her mother and will produce a baby that will serve as a penis substitute. Freud also believed that since females do not face castration anxiety, they never develop strong superegos. The idea that females are not as morally strong as males is, of course, totally incorrect. Freud suggested that an unresolved Oedipal phase for females could result in a woman who flirts and teases men (the Southern belle), a coldly castrating career woman (Faye Dunaway in *Network*), or a lesbian.

In Freud's view, the events occurring during these three psychosexual stages establish the person's basic personality characteristics by the time he or she is six years of age. Between that age and puberty there is a **latency period** in which children repress their Oedipal concerns, lose interest in anything sexual, and segregate themselves into all-male and all-female play groups. It has been suggested that such behavior is culturally determined. In contrast, Harlow (1975) explains the latency period on the basis of his extensive observations of young monkeys. Males spontaneously play in a much more aggressive way than females. They form separate friendship groups before puberty because the females find the males too rough and the males find the females too passive and quiet. With puberty, however, each sex becomes motivated by other concerns, and the mature person (or monkey) moves on to the **genital stage,** in which adults react to a person of the opposite sex with sexual desire and affection. This permits the development of genuine friendships, love, and other nonselfish social attachments. Many people never entirely resolve the Oedipal conflict and hence never reach the genital stage. The final outcome of these various stages is the adult personality, which is shaped by what has happened during each developmental period.

RESEARCH CLOSE-UP

Showing the Effects of Unconscious Motives

Modern personality psychologists often criticize psychoanalytic theory because of the absence of a solid research base that would allow us to confirm or refute each of Freud's basic propositions. In recent years, however, several investigators have been able to devise ways of testing many Freudian hypotheses (Silverman, 1976). Here we will look at one program of research that shows how psychoanalytic theory can sometimes be tied to empirical evidence.

A central idea in this theory of personality is that thoughts and desires of which a person is unaware—material that is unconscious—can influence his or her feelings, create anxiety, and actually cause physical symptoms to develop. Freud had observed the expression of emotions and physical complaints and deduced the presence of unconscious motives as the cause. Scientists would be much more able to accept such ideas if the unconscious mechanisms could be manipulated in experiments. In this way the behavioral effects described by Freud could be predicted on the basis of a controlled manipulation of the proposed causes of that behavior. Such evidence would constitute impressive support of one aspect of the theory, but how could that sort of test be carried out?

One solution to this question has been provided by a series of experiments at Michigan State University (Karnilow, 1973; Perkins & Reyher, 1971; Sommerschield & Reyher, 1973). These experiments used hypnosis to create a situation involving sexual wishes, which were then "repressed" at the direction of the hypnotist. The crucial test of Freudian theory came when subjects were exposed to cues that were relevant to the repressed material—would the effects be like those described by Freud?

One of the procedures used involved the creation of a sexual scene with overtones of the Oedipal situation. The subjects, male college students, were told the following story while under hypnosis and then instructed not to remember it.

One evening while you were out for a leisurely walk, your attention was drawn to an attractive older women who seemed quite upset. She had lost her purse and did not have money for her bus fare. Wishing to help the woman, you took out your wallet, but discovered that you only had a $10 bill. Still wanting to help, you offered to accompany her to the bus stop and pay her fare. She, however, insisted that you accompany her to her apartment in order that she might repay you. You agreed, although somewhat reluctantly. Once within her apartment, she suggested that you might find some money. There were pieces of brass, gold, lead, steel, tin, platinum, bronze, iron, copper, silver, chromium, and other kinds of metal. . . . You also remember seeing some coins. There was a penny, a dollar, a nickel, a peso, a pound, one cent, a mill, a quarter, a dime, a shilling, a farthing, a franc, assorted coins, cash, and other kinds of money . . . she seemed very friendly and was reluctant to have you leave. After talking about the collection, she offered you a drink and snack. She then turned on the record player and invited you to dance. Gradually you became aware of some stimulating, but disquieting, thoughts and feelings. She was very good looking, and it seemed like such a pity to have all her beautiful softness and curves go to waste. She seemed to be silently inviting you by her physical closeness, glances, and words. Her heavy breathing indicated that she was becoming extremely aroused sexually. You were just starting to make love to her when it occurred to you that she was older, respectable, perhaps married, and undoubtedly very experienced. You wondered if you would be able to satisfy her, and thought of how traumatic it would be if she laughed at your advances. In spite of these thoughts, you found yourself becoming increasingly excited and aroused. You wanted to make love to her right there, but the telephone rang. While you waited, you became so aroused and excited that you could hardly speak.

You made a hurried excuse for leaving, promised to call her back and left the apartment. Later you learned that the only way you could attain peace of mind was to completely push the whole experience into the back of your mind.

Then the subjects were given a posthypnotic suggestion:

Now listen carefully. The woman I have told you about actually works in this laboratory. In fact, you will meet her briefly later on. After you are awakened, you will not be able to remember anything about this session. However, sexual feelings will well up inside of you whenever words associated with money or metal are mentioned. You will realize that the sexual feelings are directed toward the woman you will see shortly and you will want to tell me how you would like to express these feelings toward her. [Silverman, 1976, p. 631]

At this point the subject was awakened and shown a series of printed words, some of which were associated with the "repressed memory," such as *gold*, *steel*, *dollar*, and *peso*. After each word the subject was asked, "how are you doing?" Most of the subjects responded to these critical words (but not to control words) with such physical symptoms as headaches, nausea, sweating, or muscle tremors, as well as with feelings of guilt, shame, or disgust. They didn't remember the story, and they didn't know why they were responding as they did—that is, they were much like Freud's patients, who sought psychotherapy because of their unpleasant symptoms. In this instance, however, the reasons are clear, and "therapy" could be quickly applied so that the symptoms did not continue outside the laboratory. It should be noted that control subjects who simply *heard* the story without being hypnotized did not react to the critical words with such symptoms.

Research of this sort allows us to identify those aspects of Freud's theory which can be verified and to discard those which turn out to be incorrect (Fisher & Greenberg, 1977).

THE ANALYTICAL THEORY OF CARL JUNG

The Play of Opposites

Carl Jung was born in Switzerland in 1875, the son of a pastor. Though he had planned to go into philosophy or archaeology, he was impelled toward the natural sciences and medicine by a dream. He obtained an M.D. degree from the University of Basel. His main interest was psychiatry, and he worked in a mental hospital in Zurich. Like Freud, he studied for a time in Paris. Jung later taught at the University of Zurich, but eventually he quit in order to spend all of his time in private practice and in developing his theory.

A momentous event in Jung's life was his reading of Freud's first book, *The Interpretation of Dreams* (1900). He was immensely impressed by it and began gathering data that seemed to confirm Freud's ideas. Though Jung carried out several research studies, he later expressed strong doubts about the value of laboratory experiments and the collection of empirical data. Jung and Freud began corresponding in 1906, and when the International Psychoanalytic Association was founded, Jung was elected its first president. Freud and Jung had close ties, both professional and personal. Jung was seen as Freud's heir apparent in psychoanalysis, but their association came to an abrupt end in 1914, in part because of Freud's emphasis on sexuality. Jung then withdrew from Freud's group of psychoanalysts and began working on his own personality theory, which he labeled **analytical theory.**

During his years as a practitioner and theorist, Jung educated a great many therapists who traveled to Switzerland to undergo analytic training. He died in 1961 at the age of 85.

Analytical psychology never became as popular as psychoanalysis, and Jung has had less influence on the field of personality than Freud did. His two major contributions to personality research were the concept of introversion–extraversion and the word association technique. Jung's work is an interesting example of how the early therapists arrived at considerably different end products even though theorists like Freud and Jung began at the same point and used the same general techniques.

Jung himself has supplied a general overall description of his mode of theorizing: "I see in all that happens the play of opposites" (1961, p. 337). He traced his thinking to the influence of Goethe:

In my youth [around 1890] I was unconsciously caught up by this spirit of the age, and had no methods at hand for extricating myself from it. *Faust* struck a chord in me and pierced me through in a way that I could not but regard as personal. Most of all, it awakened in me the problem of opposites, of good and evil, of mind and matter, of light and darkness. Faust, the inept, purblind philosopher, encounters the dark side of his being, his sinster shadow, Mephistopheles, who in spite of his negating disposition represents the true spirit of life as against the arid scholar who hovers on the brink of suicide. [1963, p. 235]

The Unconscious as a Storehouse of Racial Memories

The Personal Unconscious.   Any experiences that have been unnoticed, forgotten, or repressed are contained in the **personal unconscious.** Such unconscious material tends to be organized into complexes; a **complex** consists of a collection of related concepts and images. Jung was interested in the word association test as a research tool, and the way people responded to this test suggested that there were clusters of related material that had a special meaning for each person. For example, if someone were to respond to a number of different stimulus words with references to controlling, dominating, and manipulating other people, that person could be described as having a power complex. Other groups of responses could lead to such diagnoses as mother complex, homosexual complex, or inferiority complex.

The Collective Unconscious.   One of Jung's primary concepts was quite far removed from other psychological and psychoanalytic theories. In the **collective unconscious** are the influences we inherit from our own ancestors, from the entire human race, and even from our animal forebears. Jung describes the general idea as follows:

> This psychic life is the mind of our ancestors, the way in which they thought and felt, the way in which they conceived of life and the world, of gods and human beings. The existence of these historical layers is presumably the source of the belief in reincarnation and in memories of past lives. As the body is a sort of museum of its phylogenetic history, so is the mind. There is no reason for believing that the psyche, with its peculiar structure, is the only thing in the world that has no history beyond its individual manifestation. Even the conscious mind cannot be denied a history extending over at lesast five thousand years. It is only individual ego-consciousness that has forever a new beginning and an early end. But the unconscious psyche is not only immensely old, it is also able to grow increasingly into an equally remote future. It forms, and is part of, the human species just as much as the body, which is also individually ephemeral, yet collectively of immeasurable duration. [1939, pp. 24*ff*]

The evolution of our anatomy is repeated from conception to birth as we develop from a one-celled organism into a complex human being. We resemble other species along the way and even, for a time, develop such specialized features as gill slits. But each of us ends up as a distinctly human organism. In a similar way, the evolution of experience is supposedly retained as an unconscious memory in the collective unconscious. Because we all have a common evolutionary history, we all share the same collective unconscious. These memories are not directly available to conscious thought, but they reveal themselves by predisposing us to respond to given stimuli in a given way. Thus there are a number of characteristics that are shared across otherwise quite different cultures, such as the tendency to believe in a supreme being, fear snakes, and love one's mother. Jung's explanation of these shared tendencies is that we share primitive ancestors who repeatedly had certain experiences. The predisposition affects behavior only if an appropriate stimulus is encountered. If one never saw a snake, for example, the primitive fear of snakes would never be aroused. We are predisposed to such a reaction, however, and our first contact with a snake should automatically arouse fear.

One of Jung's beliefs was that human beings can benefit by becoming aware of the wisdom stored in their collective unconscious. Many problems arise when a person ignores or behaves in opposition to the urgings of the collective unconscious. Much of Jung's therapeutic effort was directed at making patients more aware of these urgings.

Archetypes.   The **archetypes** are universal symbols in the collective unconscious. For example, there is a mother archetype, and this blends with our own experiences with our actual mother, who is frequently seen as

Figure 2-2.   The archetypes of the young hero (Harrison Ford's Hans Solo) and of the wise old man (Alec Guiness' Ben Kenobi) in *Star Wars* provides a guarantee that good will prevail. With the help of Luke Skywalker (Mark Hamill) and Chewbacca, they go forth to battle the evil forces on the Death Star. (Springer/Bettmann Film Archive)

an ideal figure because of archetypal influences. This archetype not only determines attitudes toward one's own mother but is reflected in art, literature, religion, and mythology—the Virgin Mary, the Earth Mother, Mary Worth, Whistler's Mother, the Fairy Godmother, and such customs as Mother's Day. There is also a very different mother archetype. Thousands of primitive experiences with angry and even cruel mothers lead to such figures as the Wicked Witch of the West, the she-devil, the whore, and the evil stepmother. Presumably, because an achetype is involved, children should be more frightened by the witch in *Snow White* than by any monster in a horror movie. Other archetypes include rebirth or resurrection, the young hero who can solve all of our problems, God, and the wise old man. When a movie such as *Star Wars* contains several archetypes, it is a box office hit.

One way in which archetypes are discovered is through observation of repeated themes in myth or art. Why do we find story after story of a divine being who comes to earth and mingles with its citizens? Why is a circular arrangement repeated in primitive drawings, early architecture, sculpture, Renaissance art, and the scribblings you made as a child? Jung's answer was that they are based on shared racial memories. Why does a certain theme in literature or drama have a universal appeal that goes beyond the artistic merit of the material itself? Why are people caught up by the primitive symbols of Moby Dick, Oedipus the King, and Prince Charming? The Indians of Mexico viewed Cortés as a god, and the Hawaiians had the same reaction to Captain Cook—in each instance the white explorer fit an ancient myth in the culture. The power of these symbols was taken by Jung as evidence that they evoked inherited memories from the collective unconscious.

Some Characteristics of the Personality

The Persona.   Many theorists have described behavior in terms of social roles in which we play a particular part in a given situation. In Jungian theory this idea is carried even further in that the **persona** represents the mask that each of us puts on. It reflects the role we are assigned to play in our interactions with others. If you are not aware of the difference between this public version of yourself and your true inner self, you become shallow and cut off from honest feelings and emotions. The search for inner truth in the form of encounter groups, mysticism, or drugs may be seen as a way of trying to get behind one's mask to discover who is really there.

The Anima and the Animus.   Jung observed that elements of both sexes are present in each of us. Each man's collective unconscious contains an achetype of femininity, the **anima.** Likewise, each woman's unconscious includes an archetype of masculinity, the **animus.** Failure to recognize these archetypes leads to emotional problems, as when a macho male fails to perceive his own gentleness and tenderness or a submissive female ignores her own ambition and drive. Unisex fashions and the women's movement may be seen as attempts to express recognition of the anima and the animus. In current psychological research there is much interest in identifying people who are able to express both masculine and feminine traits; they are said to be *androgynous* (Bem, 1975).

The Shadow.   The unconscious opposite of overt behavioral traits is the **shadow.** It is of great importance for a person to become aware of these unconscious trends. Whatever is emphasized consciously, the opposite is emphasized unconsciously. The shadow is the dark reflection of the selves of which we are aware. Jung believed that dreams reflected these unconscious aspects of our personality; for example, an extraverted person should have introverted dreams. Research suggests that he was wrong in that the expression of personality traits in dream content is actually similar to the conscious expression of these traits (Domino, 1976b).

Extraversion and Introversion.   Jung defined a basic individual difference as the direction taken by a person's motivational system in relation to the outside world. These inborn differences lead either to subjective functioning, in which the self is uppermost (**introversion**), or to objective functioning, in which the outside world is uppermost in importance (**ex-traversion**). Jung describes these attitudes as follows:

> [Introversion] is revealed by a hesitating, reflective, reticent disposition, that does not easily give itself away, that shrinks from objects, always assuming the defensive, and preferring to make its cautious observations as from a hiding place. [Extraversion] is characterized by an accommodating, and apparently open and ready disposition, at ease in any given situation. This type forms attachments quickly, and ventures, unconcerned and confident, into unknown situations, rejecting thoughts of possible contingencies [1928, p. 41]

This distinction was adopted by many theorists and has led to much research. Jung's assumptions about introversion–extraversion include the belief that these tendencies are inherited, that there is an unconscious development of the opposite trait, and that overdevelopment of either trait can lead to neurosis or psychosis.

Thinking, Feeling, Sensing, and Intuiting. Jung classified psychological functions into four categories. The two modes of judgment are the creation of ideas (**thinking**) and the evaluation of internal and external events (**feeling**). The two modes of apprehension are the objective perception of events (**sensing**) and the subjective perception of events (**intuiting**). These four functions commonly develop to different degrees, and the stronger member of each pair is emphasized while the weaker one is repressed. It is important to strive for equal functioning. When the introversion–extraversion dimension is considered together with the four functions, the result is a series of basic personality types, as shown in Figure 2–3. Research on these types using the Myers-Briggs Type Indicator (Myers, 1962) reveals several behavioral differences among members of the different categories. For example, one experiment compared introverted–thinking types with extraverted–feeling types on their ability to remember different kinds of material. As expected, the former group did better with familiar, impersonal tasks (remembering a series of numbers), while the latter group did better on a novel, personal task (remembering a series of faces) (Carlson & Levy, 1973).

The four functions are also relevant to a discussion of the meaning of **symbols.** Jung distinguished signs (sheriff's badge, American flag, H_2O) from symbols. The latter are words, ideas, or images that convey a relatively unknown thing that cannot be represented more clearly in any other way. The thinking and sensing functions are involved in responding to symbols, but intuition and feeling are much more important. A true symbol evokes feelings, fears, and wishes that are deeper than logical, rational thought processes. Examples are the cross for early Christians, the swastika for the Nazi party, and the number 13.

Stages of Development. Like Freud, Jung described a series of developmental stages. Unlike Freud, he described the changes that occur

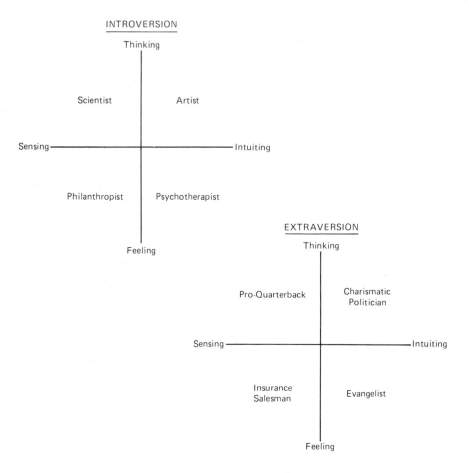

Figure 2-3. In Jung's theory there are two basic attitudinal dimensions (introversion and extraversion), two modes of judgment (thinking and feeling), and two modes of apprehension (sensing and intuiting). A person's position along these various dimensions indicates his or her basic personality type.

after childhood. Also, it seemed to Jung that it was misleading to suggest that all bodily satisfactions must involve sexuality.

The child faces the problems of nutrition and growth mainly in the first four years of life. Jung saw this as a presexual period during which one is learning to speak and to think, gradually becoming interested in the world beyond oneself and one's parents. Sexual functioning can begin when the person reaches puberty, but true sexual maturity does not always follow then—or ever. The parents are seen first as protectors and suppliers of nutrition and later as objects of sexual longing. Jung thus agreed with Freud about the incestuous desires of the Oedipal period.

Jung focused a good deal of attention on the changes of the middle years and old age. In middle age one's interests move away from the body and toward artistic, philosophical, and intellectual concerns. Religion becomes important as one tries to define one's relation to the external world. If a person fails to develop these interests and remains locked in the earlier stage of physical pleasure or work, development ceases.

Jung also described development in a more general way, in terms of the development of the human race. Thus, there is progress toward greater self-realization from one generation to another. He believed that evolution was as striking in personality as in biological structures and functions. Jung's description of our past development and future potential is a hopeful and optimistic one.

THE INTERPERSONAL THEORY OF HARRY STACK SULLIVAN

An American with a Social-Psychological Theory

Harry Stack Sullivan was an American psychiatrist. His approach to theory building was much like that of Freud and Jung, but once again the final product was quite different. Freudian theory is concerned with the personal unconscious and its control by the ego, the superego, and the demands of reality. Jung's theory may be seen as focusing on the collective unconscious, humanity's racial wisdom, and human evolutionary potential. In Sullivan's **interpersonal theory** the emphasis is on interpersonal relationships. Sullivan's position is compatible with the work of current psychologists in that he stressed observable interactions among people rather than the hypothesized inner workings of the psyche. In fact, he identified psychiatry with social psychology and pointed out that personality is an abstract construct drawn from social observations (Sullivan, 1950).

Sullivan was born on a farm in New York State in 1892. He had a lonely, unhappy childhood; when he was eight years old he became involved in a homosexual relationship—interestingly enough, both boys later became psychiatrists (Chapman, 1976). He received his M.D. degree in 1917 from the Chicago College of Medicine and Surgery, which he described as a "diploma mill." After serving in World War I he held medical posts with two government agencies before he entered the field that was to be his life's work. During a year at Saint Elizabeth's Hospital in Washington, D.C., he began his association with William Alanson White, a neuropsychiatrist. From the early 1920s until the early 1930s, he worked at Saint Elizabeth's Hospital, at the University of Maryland Medical School, and at the Enoch Pratt Hospital, concentrating largely on the problem of schizophenia. At that time psychoanalysts felt that schizophrenics could not be helped by psychotherapy, but Sullivan disagreed and was able to bring about improvement in many such patients. His next step was to set up a private practice in New York City. From an initial orientation that was somewhat Freudian, he moved toward developing his own theoretical position. During the late 1930s he became director of the Washington School of Psychiatry, which was funded by the William Alanson White Foundation. He also edited the foundation's journal, *Psychiatry*. He died suddenly in 1949 in Paris.

Sullivan was described as a shy and socially awkward man who nevertheless engaged in diverse successful roles—practitioner, teacher, editor, and administrator. Also, he remained a homosexual throughout his life. Unlike Freud and Jung, he did not produce a series of books. He published only one volume (Sullivan, 1947) during his lifetime. His other five books were assembled and edited after his death and are based on his lecture notes and recordings of his lectures.

The Self: A Defense Against Anxiety

Viewing personality as a verbal abstraction rather than a concrete entity, Sullivan found no reason to build a theory describing the elaborate details of "the personality." Rather, he noted that people interact with other people (present or absent, alive or dead, real or fictitious), and it is these interpersonal interactions that characterize human behavior. Our habits, our dreams, our hopes and fears, and everything else that distinguishes us from other animals all are made up of interpersonal concerns. Sullivan also recognized the power of social forces such as poverty and bigotry in shaping the ways in which human beings react.

Sullivan did find it useful to identify a few fairly stable aspects of personality. One of these is the **dynamism.** A dynamism is a recurring behavior pattern or habit. For Sullivan, the important human dynamisms are those involving other people. Many of the personality variables discussed later in this text, such as authoritarianism, anxiety, and achievement need, would be labeled dynamisms. Sullivan's main focus, however, was on the dynamism of **self.**

Sullivan described the self as a protective device that develops in interactions between an infant and its parents. Being completely dependent on the parents for physical well-being, the child becomes sensitive to parental approval and censure. From positive and negative parent–child interactions, the child learns that certain behaviors are approved, and these aspects of the self are perceived as good-me. Other acts are disapproved, and they are perceived as bad-me. The self system consists of the judgments made by parents and others, and it functions to protect the person from anxiety. The emphasis is on maintaining a consistent and positive self-picture, or good-me. Maintaining this self-image often requires misperceptions, forgetting, and other defensive maneuvers. Sullivan viewed inadequate or defensive self-functioning not as a product of internal malfunctions but as a product of an irrational society. If it were not for the unreasonable demands of parents and other members of society, the self system would not have to develop crippling defenses against anxiety. Thus, the task of the therapist was to establish a secure relationship and to support the patient's self-esteem.

Another interpersonal construct discussed by Sullivan was **personification,** or the concept one has of oneself or any other person. If another person is associated with positive experiences, one's personification of that person is favorable. If that person is associated with anxiety and pain, the personification is negative. Once such concepts are formed, there is a tendency to perceive the other person in a consistent way. This, of course, can interfere with accurate perception of his or her behavior. Widely shared personifications take the form of stereotypes and prejudice. If both positive and negative interactions have occurred, quite different personifications may be established side by side (e.g., good-me *and* bad-me, good-mother *and* bad-mother).

Modes of Experience and Stages of Development

Modes of Experience.   The most distinct of Sullivan's concepts was his notion of three modes of experience: prototaxic, parataxic, and syntaxic. **Prototaxic** functioning is the earliest and most primitive form of experience. For example, the infant is bombarded by sensations that it is unable to perceive as coherent or meaningful events. There is no relation between events, no sense of time, no distinction between self and the outside world.

As we begin to perceive meaning and relations and to distinguish self from the external world, our thought processes shift to the **parataxic mode.** The experiences and images may be erroneous or unrealistic, but the meaning is very real to the individual. To get a personal feel of the parataxic mode, readers who have access to their own preschool picture books might try leafing through and noting the special memories and meanings evoked by the pictures. A few years ago one of the authors came across a battered copy of a *Mother Goose* book that had been a favorite at about the age of three. The full-page picture of Jack Sprat and his wife brought a rush of memories—ancient fears and puzzling sensations linked with their ugly, angry faces. For a moment there was a glimpse of parataxic functioning several decades in the past. Similarly, returning to a town, a house, or a vacation spot that one has not visited since early childhood can evoke parataxic experiences. As adults, we may sometimes slip back to parataxic thinking and revive our childhood confusions. We know a woman who was never able to eat spaghetti because in early childhood she believed the noodles were actually dead worms. False perceptions and other defensive reactions to anxiety are labeled "parataxic distortions" in that a purely personal meaning interferes with realistic perceptions. Many of the

Figure 2-4. In Sullivan's theory, our interpersonal experiences provide us with positive *and* negative images of ourselves and of those around us. For example, we develop concepts of a "good mother" who is represented in stories about Fairy Godmothers who grant our wishes and of a "bad mother" who appears in stories in such forms as wicked stepmothers and evil witches. In Oz, Dorothy found both with Glenda the Good and the villainous Wicked Witch of the West. (Bettmann Archive)

thought processes of psychotics, such as delusions and hallucinations, represent parataxic functioning.

When one learns to perceive as others do and to share their language, beliefs, and explanations, one's thinking has entered the **syntaxic mode.** In this mode functioning depends on validation and agreement. Interpersonal communication is possible only for those who function syntaxically. It might be noted that the agreement may be quite arbitrary (e.g., the meaning of words and numbers) or inaccurate (e.g., the earth is flat); all that is necessary is that these symbols and meanings be shared. Sullivan suggested that most of us respond both syntaxically and parataxically in our everyday functioning. We communicate as if our language were entirely syntaxic, but we are also responding to parataxic meanings. Such dual functioning causes confusion and failures of communication. For example, if in a political discussion someone labels himself "radical," the subsequent conversation is going to be colored not by a dictionary definition of *radical* but by all the meanings, feelings, and positive and negative experiences each person associates with that word. One person may think of a radical as a political realist who sees that Democrats and Republicans are really quite similar. Another has in mind a bomb-throwing anarchist who wants to blow up bridges and government buildings. Still another has in mind social change and ideas about how to make the world a better place. Still another has an image of communist spies who want to undermine the nation. When these people discuss "radicals" it is easy to imagine the communication problems that can arise.

Stages of Development.   Sullivan's description of seven developmental stages was tied to interpersonal experiences rather than to internal
events or biological processes. Sullivan also recognized that the pattern of
development would vary from one culture to another and that his description was based on observations of European and American societies.

The first stage in Sullivan's sequence is *infancy,* the period from
birth to the development of speech. Oral activity is dominant in this stage
because oral behavior is the primary means of interaction between the child
and other people. The child's first concepts involve the nipple (either on
mother's breast or attached to a bottle), which can be associated with pleasure and satisfaction (good-nipple) or with anxiety and frustration (bad-
nipple). During this stage there is also a progression from prototaxic to
parataxic thinking.

The second stage is *childhood,* in which language develops and syntaxic thinking becomes possible. Interpersonal behavior at this stage involves playing with peers and being taught many skills by one's parents. In
addition, the child's self-image becomes clearer and the child begins to
learn the various roles he or she is to play—boy, girl, clown, mother's
helper, bully, or whatever. The child discovers that there are others who
dislike him or her and who may even be dangerous. Within the family, the
child may easily come to believe that everyone reacts with love and good
wishes; negative interactions outside the family can come as a great surprise.

The third stage, the *juvenile era,* coincides in our society with the
first years of elementary school. The child begins a life away from the
family in an expanded social sphere. Interpersonal interactions become
more complex, and the child must learn a variety of roles and interpersonal
strategies. The child develops a *reputation* and tends to see the world in the
stereotyped terms of his or her culture. Behavior also begins to be guided
by self-criticism and self-approval. For a great many people, the juvenile
stage is the final one.

The fourth stage, *preadolescence,* is characterized by the move from
completely egocentric concerns to the formation of an intimate relationship
with a friend of the same sex. This is the person's first genuine human
relationship—complete with affection, shared secrets, and mutual trust.
This is the first expression of love, which is the feeling that the satisfactions
and the security of another person are as important as one's own. When
this kind of relationship is not formed, the result is unhappiness, loneliness,
and impairment of future interpersonal functioning.

The fifth stage is *early adolescence.* During this period sexual relations are of central importance. There are, of course, physiological changes
that intensify sexual desire, but for Sullivan the most important aspect of this
period is the interpersonal expression of that desire. Adolescence is a confusing time in which sexual desire centers on members of the opposite
sex, sexual satisfaction is most likely to be achieved by oneself, and intimate

friendships usually exist with members of one's own sex. Maturity involves the fusion of desire, satisfaction, and intimacy with a member of the opposite sex. You might note that Sullivan's own sexual orientation did not fit his definition of maturity. Given the difficulty of working out such interpersonal relations in the context of taboos and learned guilt, it is hardly surprising that sexual behavior is frequently a source of severe conflicts or that the outcome of this stage often is not entirely satisfactory. Sullivan did not view sexuality in children or adolescents as a special problem except that society responds with anxiety and hence gives negative meaning to this kind of behavior. When people remain psychologically in the juvenile era, their heterosexual activity is limited to what Sullivan labeled "instrumental masturbation." The other person involved in the sexual act is not part of an intimate relationship but is merely an animate object providing physical pleasure.

The sixth stage, *late adolescence,* begins with the choice of one's preferred form of genital activity and moves toward the acquisition of a mature repertory of interpersonal relations.

If these stages are completed successfully, the person moves into *adulthood* and mature relations with other people. Sullivan believed that personality continues to grow throughout life and that the formation of close relationships, even in adulthood, can overcome problems created in earlier stages. Thus, his theory was an optimistic one. He felt that there is a natural tendency toward psychological health that is thwarted by unfortu-

Table 2-1.   Sullivan's Developmental Stages. Harry Stack Sullivan described the developmental stages in terms of the kinds of interpersonal relations in which an individual is engaged.

Stage	Time Period	Characteristics
1. Infancy	From birth until beginning of speech.	Oral activity. Progression from prototaxic to parataxic thinking.
2. Childhood	From beginning of speech until school entry.	Language develops and syntaxic thinking begins. Interaction with peers.
3. Juvenile era	First years of elementary school.	Complex interpersonal interactions.
4. Preadolescence	Last years of elementary school, overlapping with beginning of junior high school years.	Formation of intimate relationship with same-sex friend.
5. Adolescence	Last years of junior high school and beginning of high school years.	Sexual relations are of paramount importance.
6. Late adolescence	Last years of high school and beginning of college years.	Choice of preferred genital activity. Mature interpersonal relations.
7. Adulthood	Remainder of life.	If the previous six stages are completed successfully, the person becomes a truly human being.

nate interactions and/or by destructive forces in society. Sullivan's seven developmental stages are summarized in Table 2-1.

SOME ADDITIONAL THEORIES: ERIKSON, SHELDON, AND OTHERS

In addition to the pioneering contributions of Sigmund Freud, numerous analysts and psychiatrists created theories of personality during the first half of the twentieth century. We have just examined two of them—Jung with his emphasis on inherited predispositions and the play of opposites, Sullivan with his emphasis on the crucial role of interpersonal relations. We will now briefly examine some additional approaches.

Erikson: Developmental Stages

Erik Erikson studied psychoanalysis with Freud's daughter, Anna. Afterward, he moved to the United States and began work on a developmental theory of personality. Other personality theories indicate the importance of the developmental process, but with most of the stress on the early years. Erikson, in contrast, considered the entire life-span as the scene of development and change.

His initial interest was in the crises we each must meet and resolve as we pass through eight **stages of life** (Erikson, 1963). At each stage, as shown in Table 2-2, there is a characteristic crisis to be resolved, and there is a "good" (psychologically well adjusted) and "bad" (maladjusted) possibility at each stage. In contemporary Western cultures, at least, young infants and children face such problems as learning to trust others, fulfilling their basic needs, and feeling self-confident in the task of dealing with the world around them.

Children can learn either to take the initiative and gain a sense of competence or to be burdened by guilt and a sense of inferiority. In adolescence, it is necessary to establish one's own identity and role in life. There is an **identity crisis** because there are many possible alternatives, and we each must decide "who we are."

The problems of intimacy must be met in late adolescence and young adulthood. The choice is between genuine, warm interpersonal relationships and isolation and loneliness. In maturity the choice is between productivity in one's work and personal life versus stagnation and lack of change. Depending on how well each of us has been able to resolve each of life's crises, it is possible to meet the ultimate crisis of one's own death with a calm acceptance of the inevitable and a feeling that life was worthwhile. The opposite response is to view one's life as a total waste and to view death as the final unlucky break.

A successful resolution of the crisis at each stage makes it easier to progress to the next stage. Even if a crisis is incompletely or unsatisfactorily

Table 2-2. Erik Erikson's theory of personality describes the life-span as involving various stages stretching from birth to death. There are eight stages of life involving crises to be met and resolved either successfully or unsuccessfully. At the same time the person must progress through six stages of ritualization which involve his or her fantasies, play activities, and social roles.

Stages of Life: Crises to Be Met and Resolved	Stages of Ritualization: Fantasy, Play, and Social Roles
1. Sensory Stage - During an infant's first months, it learns to trust or mistrust other people.	I. Numinous Stage - Mother is a "hallowed presence."
2. Muscular Development Stage - During toilet training, the child learns to be confident and independent or to feel shame and self-doubt.	II. Judicious Stage - Judgments of right and wrong are applied to the behavior of self and others.
3. Locomotor Stage - As the child learns to crawl and then walk, he or she learns to take the initiative and express Oedipal desires or to feel guilty and repressed.	III. Dramatic Stage - The child acts out fantasies and tries out a variety of roles.
4. Latency Stage - During the early school years the child learns to feel confident of his or her abilities or to feel inadequate.	IV. Formal Stage - Established rules begin to govern both work and play.
5. Puberty Stage - As sexual maturation begins, the adolescent develops and accepts a personal identity or remains confused about character and role.	V. Ideal Stage - Beliefs about how things *should be* become all-Important.
6. Young Adulthood Stage - When an intimate relationship is sought, the person learns to establish true contact with another human being or retreats into lonely isolation.	VI. Generational Stage - Individual performs all of the adult rituals involved in marriage, parenthood, assuming occupational roles, grandparenthood, retirement, and death.
7. Adulthood Stage - In the middle years of life, each person becomes a productive and creative human being or one who complacently settles into an unchanging rut.	
8. Maturity - If the crises of the previous seven stages have been successfully met, the person must face the challenge of death as the ultimate fate—"was my life worthwhile?" The choice is between accepting death with a sense of integrity and self-worth or dreading death with a sense of despair and worthlessness.	

resolved, however, the person may return to it at a later time for additional work. Some have pointed to the *mid-life crisis* experienced by many adults as indicating that such problems as intimacy, identity, and productivity may return to haunt the middle-aged adult who reflects on the past. Especially among men, the solution frequently is a change in marriage partners, a new job, or a radical change in life style. In Erikson's terms, such individuals are still trying to resolve earlier crises from their past. Since the mid-life crises of women do not fit this pattern very well, some personality psychologists (Algin, 1979) have suggested that female development is incomplete or arrested at the stage of intimacy. It might be more accurate to suggest that Erikson's theory is better suited to explaining the behavior of men than

Figure 2-5. Erikson's developmental theory emphasizes the importance of a series of crises. In adolescence, each of us must face questions of identity—"Who am I?" Once this is resolved, individuals must try to learn to establish genuine contact with at least one other human being. (UPI)

of women. There may well be basic sex differences which determine the nature of generational crises.

Interestingly, Erikson (1977) has continued to build his theory in recent years by turning his attention to another aspect of the developmental process. In addition to the crises that one encounters, each person also goes through six **stages of ritualization.** This is a dimension of behavior that includes our innermost fantasies, the play acting involved in elaborate childhood games, and the "games" that adults play as they engage in the rituals of courtship, taking on occupational roles, becoming parents, and so forth. This culturally defined framework serves to make our acts seem meaningful and to unify our inner selves. Such rituals also serve to make the behavior of others in one's culture more or less predictable.

Despite the intuitive appeal of these various ideas and their scope, there has been relatively little research based directly on Erikson's theory (DiCaprio, 1974).

Sheldon: A Twentieth Century Typology

In a variety of ways, typological theories are quite different from the psychodynamic theories presented in this chapter and from the research-oriented psychological theories presented in the following chapter. Thus, they tend not to fit well in any grouping of theories. In addition, their emphasis on hereditary factors rather than learning is not accepted by most psychologists. Despite being both unusual and unpopular, they have played an interesting historical role in personality psychology.

The earliest recorded attempt to make sense of personality was put forth by the physician Hippocrates who lived in Greece before the time of Christ. He suggested a **typology**—a limited number of categories into which all people could be classified. Individuals were said to have one of four possible **temperaments.** Thus, each person was characteristically either cheerful, angry, depressed, or apathetic. As is true of most other typologies that have been created since, Hippocrates assumed that these behavioral characteristics were reflected in some physical attribute of the individual (bodily fluids in this instance) and that individual differences were based on heredity (Buss, Plomin, & Willerman, 1973).

One of the best known modern typologies was created by an American physician and psychologist, William Sheldon. He concluded that bodily characteristics fall along three dimensions and that there are three basic temperaments that correspond to these physical dimensions. As shown in Figure 2-6, the physical **somatotypes** consist of one's score (ranging from 1 to 7) along the dimensions of **endomorphy** (soft, round, overweight), **mesomorphy** (muscular, broad shouldered, athletic), and **ectomorphy** (thin, frail, angular). The corresponding temperaments are **viscerotonia** (sociable, tolerant, comfort-loving), **somatotonia** (energetic adventurous, bold, aggressive), and **cerebrotonia** (restrained, intellectual,

Figure 2-6.   In Sheldon's type theory of personality, people are said to vary along three dimensions in terms of their physical structure or somatotype. Based on bodily measurements, each dimension receives a score ranging from 1 to 7. These physical dimensions were hypothesized to be associated with three corresponding temperament dimensions (viscerotonia, somatotonia, and cerebrotonia). Shown here are the three extreme types (endomorph, mesomorph, and ectomorph) as well as an average body build (one who scores in the middle of each dimension).

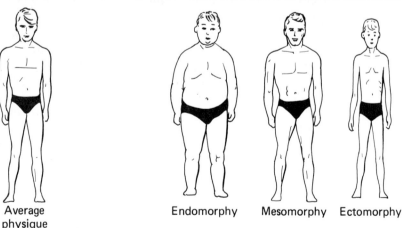

Average physique   Endomorphy   Mesomorphy   Ectomorphy

private). The average person is supposed to fall in the middle of each dimension (4–4–4) while the three most extreme types are those who score 7–1–1, 1–7–1, and 1–1–7.

Some research indicates that bodily characteristics correspond to temperament in the way Sheldon hypothesized (Walker, 1962), although the association is not nearly as strong as the theory suggests. In addition, some research shows that particular somatotypes are associated with distinct types of mental illness (Sheldon, Lewis, & Tenney, 1969). For example, endomorphs are most likely to develop emotional disorders such as depression, mesomorphs are likely to develop paranoid delusions about the motives of others, and ectomorphs are overrepresented among withdrawn, schizophrenic patients. Psychologists who are reluctant to accept biological explanations of psychological differences attribute the real but weak empirical support for Sheldon's theory to cultural stereotypes and to our reactions to those whose appearance fits these stereotypes. Thus, some people behave in ways specified by somatotype theory because others *expect* them to do so and treat them accordingly.

Other Analytic Theories

In addition to the theorists whose work has been described in this chapter, numerous other psychotherapists have followed in Freud's footsteps. Some proposed minor variations of emphasis with respect to existing theories while others created totally new and different formulations.

Among these theorists was an associate of Freud's in Vienna, Alfred Adler. His greatest disagreement with Freud was about the importance of the **need for power** as opposed to sexual need. Like Sullivan, Adler held that social interactions were all-important, but to him the critical matters were the will to power, dominance, and interpersonal superiority. As with Jung and Freud, Adler's theoretical differences with Freud led to personal and professional arguments and eventually to the end of their relationship. Adler became the founder of what is known as *individual psychology*.

Erich Fromm, another theorist who stressed interpersonal behavior, was interested in political matters. He attempted to make psychological sense of the appeal of such systems as Nazism and Communism to millions of people. Why would anyone deliberately choose a totalitarian society over a democratic one? Fromm's answer was a widespread **fear of freedom.** That is, freedom and democracy are potentially frightening because they involve making choices and the possibility of making the wrong choice. Freedom of opportunity also includes the possibility of failure. One answer to such threats is the security of an authoritarian society in which the decisions are left to others. Fromm felt that it was crucial for people to learn to face the risks of freedom in order to be able to enjoy its benefits. Ideally, a free society makes it possible for people to express love and tenderness and to value truth and justice.

In addition to Freud's daughter, Anna, there were several female analysts who made major contributions to the early personality theories. Karen Horney was a physician who argued for several modifications in psychoanalytic theory. For example, she suggested that penis envy may occur because of the different values placed on males and females in our society rather than because of innate reactions to the penis as superior to the clitoris. She also classified human needs as falling into three basic categories—tendencies to move *toward, away from,* or *against* other people. The approach needs include love, the avoidance needs include the search for independence, and the aggressive needs include the striving for power.

THE INITIAL PERSONALITY THEORIES: WERE THEY SUCCESSFUL?

Sigmund Freud, Carl Jung, Harry Stack Sullivan and the other early theorists constitute an important part of the history of personality psychology—physicians who attempted to build theories of human behavior in the absence of relevant research on human behavior. Such theories were dominant during the first half of this century. Before we turn to the contemporary psychological theorists, it might be useful to evaluate this early work with respect to the scientific goals of understanding, prediction, and control.

The theorists themselves sought mainly to understand human behavior. Baffling or mysterious behavior was easier to comprehend when constructs like the id, ego defenses, collective unconscious, and parataxic distortion were devised. They could be used to explain dreams and slips of the tongue, suicide and rape, psychosis and war, and many other puzzling things that people do. The problem, of course, is, "How do we know our explanation is correct?" How do we know that we understand these phenomena? If a student tells me, "I'd like you to meet my girl, Mom—I mean Pam," I can explain his mistake on the basis of an unresolved Oedipal conflict and propose that he was attracted to a partner who serves his unconscious incestuous needs. If he agrees, my explanation is confirmed. If he disagrees, I can point out his strong resistence to admitting repressed wishes into consciousness, thus again confirming my explanation. If he hits me in the mouth, he provides even stronger evidence of the anxiety aroused by my accurate interpretation of his verbal slip; further, he probably identified me as a threatening authority figure and reacted with the same primitive rage felt toward his father. If he gradually comes to accept what was said, he is showing insight and a widening of his consciousness. It should be clear that if someone really plays this kind of game the personality theorist couldn't lose. The explanation is "correct" no matter what. Personality theories that rely on subjective understanding provide no way to separate correct assertions from incorrect ones. The theoretical system is accepted or rejected on faith.

When we turn to the goal of prediction, it becomes very difficult to evaluate personality theories with total fairness. That is, the theories were not built with prediction in mind, and many are not expressed in predictive terms. What does it mean, predictively, to say that human beings first pass through an oral stage? We know that everyone begins life by sucking milk from a nipple, but nothing is added to our predictive ability by this knowledge. What can one predict from the notion that each man possesses an anima and each woman an animus? Of what use is it to say that the cognitive functioning of young infants is prototaxic when there is no way to verify such a statement and it leads to no predictions about the infant's behavior? One could take many of the constructs and propositions of existing personality theories and show them to be useless in scientific terms. The unfairness of this approach should also be obvious. It entails viewing a theoretical product with a very different pair of glasses than was used by the creators of the product. As we saw earlier in the chapter, it is possible to take *some* aspects of such theories and subject them to an empirical test. Thus, research can provide a very useful bridge between traditional personality theories and current psychological knowledge.

Finally, what have these theories accomplished in the way of application? It is possible to say that the obvious application has been psychotherapy, beginning with psychoanalysis. This is not entirely true. The development of therapeutic techniques may be seen as parallel to development of personality theory. If anything, the theories tended to grow out of observations made by those who were engaged in psychotherapy. It is true, however, that some specific aspects of therapy were influenced by theories of personality. For example, one therapist might stress sexual conflicts, another the patient's creative potential, and a third the anxiety aroused in interpersonal interactions.

It may be concluded, then, that personality theories have not achieved the goals of science. This conclusion does not in any way detract from the brilliance of those theories. It also does not suggest that it should have been obvious at the outset that scientific goals would not be met. Nor does it mean that personality theories have nothing to offer. Scientific success is not the be-all and end-all of human existence. For some time to come, novelists and personality theorists may have more to offer in helping us make sense of human existence than can be offered by psychologists engaged in laboratory research.

Early in this chapter it was pointed out that personality theorists differ in their basic assumptions about human nature. In Figure 2-7 the position of three theorists with respect to the three dimensions is indicated.

Despite the historic role of these personality theories, most current research in this field concentrates on formulations created by psychologists. We will examine some of these theories in the following chapter.

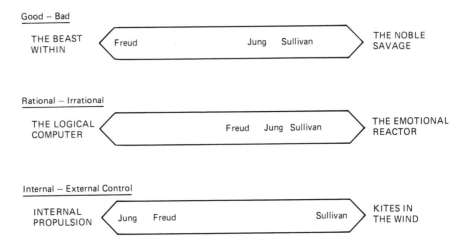

Figure 2-7. The three major personality theorists discussed in this chapter are shown with respect to their suggested positions on three dimensions involving assumptions about human nature. Would you suggest different placements? Where do you think the other theorists fall? Where would you place your own beliefs about human nature on each dimension?

SUMMARY

Several personality theories were developed in the first half of this century by practicing analysts. These theories attempted to describe and explain the behavior of individuals.

Though it is not possible to determine what is basic "human nature" that is not affected by culture, we nevertheless tend to make assumptions about what people are "really like." Three dimensions on which such assumptions differ are those that describe human beings as barely tamed beasts versus noble savages, logical computers versus emotional reactors, and the objects of internal versus external forces.

The earliest personality theories are different from most scientific theories because the analytic theorists tended not to use the empirical methods of science to verify their hypotheses.

Sigmund Freud (1859-1939) developed the therapeutic procedures of psychoanalysis. He also constructed the first major theory of personality. Convinced of the lawfulness of behavior, he tried to describe the human psyche using deductive methods like those of Sherlock Holmes. Mental functioning was classified as conscious, preconscious, and unconscious. Freud suggested that the personality is composed of three interacting systems: the *id* (concerned with immediate gratification of needs), the *ego* (concerned with the demands of reality), and the *superego* (concerned with matters of right and wrong). Freud viewed a human being as a machine that consumes nutrients, converts them into energy, and expends that energy in physical and mental work. The life instincts (*libido*) ensure the survival of the individual and the species; the death instinct (*thanatos*) strives to return the organism to inorganic matter and can be turned outward in aggressive behavior. *Anxiety* was defined as an unpleasant feeling involving a sense of helplessness. Anxiety is evoked by situations involving loss, beginning with the trauma of birth; defense mechanisms are used to reduce anxiety. Each person passes through a series of stages; the events that occur in each stage are crucial determinants of later personality traits—oral, anal, phallic (during which the Oedipus complex arises), and genital.

Carl Jung (1875–1961) was a Swiss psychiatrist who was an early colleague of Freud. He eventually broke away from Freud in terms of both personal friendship and professional association. He then developed his own personality theory, which is known as analytical psychology. Jung's concept of the personal unconscious was similar to Freud's, but he added the unique idea of a collective unconscious that contains influences inherited from one's own ancestors, the entire human race, and even our animal forebears. These inborn factors are not conscious, and they operate by predisposing us to respond to specific stimuli in given ways. Within the collective unconscious are images or ideas called *archetypes*. The *persona* is the mask we wear in social interactions. The *anima* and *animus* are the unconscious elements of the opposite sex that are present in men and women. The *shadow* is the unconscious opposite of our overt behavioral tendencies. People tend to expend their energies in either an introverted or an extraverted fashion. Jung also classified the psychological functions into two modes of judgment (thinking vs. feeling) and two modes of apprehension (sensing vs. intuiting). *Symbols* are words, ideas, or images that constitute the best possible way of expressing something that is relatively unknown. Unlike Freud, Jung did not conceive of development as being tied to sexual pleasure, and he focused on the developmental changes of later life, when the person is free to turn to artistic, philosophical, and intellectual activities.

Harry Stack Sullivan (1892–1949) was an American psychiatrist who also worked as an educator, editor, and administrator. Sullivan viewed personality as a verbal abstraction, and he believed that human behavior is determined largely by interpersonal interactions. *Dynamisms*, or habits, provide some stability of behavior from one situation to the next. The dynamism of self (including the good-me and the bad-me) is of central importance and is created in the early interactions between parent and child. A *personification* is one's concept of oneself or another person. Sullivan described the three modes of experience as *prototaxic* (primitive, unrelated sensations), *parataxic* (differentiated but highly personal images and meanings), and *syntaxic* (shared perceptions and language). The seven stages of development (infancy, childhood, juvenile, preadolescence,

adolescence, late adolescence, and adulthood) were tied to interpersonal experiences.

Among the other early theorists was Erik Erikson who stressed the *stages of development* and the crises we each must meet and resolve. An American physician-psychologist, William Sheldon, created a modern *typology* in which individuals are said to vary along three basic bodily dimensions (or *somatotypes*). These physical differences lead to differences in corresponding temperament types. Still other theorists include Alfred Adler who emphasized the *need for power* and *superiority*, Erich Fromm who stressed the importance of *freedom* and the fear with which many respond to it, and Karen Horney who emphasized *approach, avoidance,* and *aggressive* needs.

The personality theories developed by pioneers like Freud, Jung, and Sullivan have provided us with an approach to understanding human behavior. Because these theories did not have prediction as a goal, only some of their propositions are testable. With respect to application, psychotherapy tended to precede the development of theory rather than to emerge from it. Even though the early personality theories were not successful in terms of the goals of science, they represent a remarkable intellectual achievement and have had a continuing influence on psychological thought.

SUGGESTED READINGS

CHAPMAN, A. H.   *Harry Stack Sullivan: The man and his work.* New York: G. P. Putnam's Sons, 1976. A very readable biography of Harry Stack Sullivan.

HALL, C. S., & LINDZEY, G.   *Theories of personality.* New York: Wiley, 1970. An introduction to the major theories of personality, including the four that are discussed in the present chapter.

ROAZEN, P.   *Freud and his followers.* New York: Knopf, 1975. An up-to-date biography of Sigmund Freud and the group of therapists who were most directly affected by his work.

STONE, I.   *The passions of the mind.* Garden City, New York: Doubleday, 1971. A biography of Sigmund Freud written in the form of an historical novel.

WEHR, G.   *Portrait of Jung: An illustrated biography* (W. A. Hargreaves, trans.). New York: Herder and Herder, 1971. A brief biography of Carl Jung with photographs of Dr. Jung and of various symbols and archetypal figures.

Chapter Three

THEORIES OF PERSONALITY: PSYCHOLOGISTS AND RESEARCH

In this chapter you will read about the following topics:

In the decades after the Mrdlngs had made their initial explorations of the new planet, many more scientific expeditions were launched. Among the projects were those dedicated to behavioral science. The initial studies had been primarily observational and oriented toward disabled subjects, but the next wave of investigators used different methods. These new researchers shared an interest in normal as opposed to abnormal samples of subjects and a preference for empirical research over subjective speculation. Beyond that, they differed greatly among themselves and tended to divide into separate theoretical camps. The following transcripts provide some indication of how each group went about its task.

The measurement group *has collected a large body of data on the Glfln-like creatures. It has been possible to assess their bodily dimensions, weight, and other physical attributes. Of greater interest, however, are their behavioral attributes. We have had to devise some new and interesting tests, including trials of impulsivity, aggressive vocalization, and accident-proneness. Our first tests consisted of rating scales, but these have evolved into more sophisticated measuring instruments. With these tests, it has been possible to use statistical procedures to identify the basic behavioral traits that characterize these beasts. The only question dividing us at present is the precise number of factors involved. We hope to settle that matter soon and go on to use our behavioral measures in correlational and experimental research.*

The experimental group *is impatient with the methods of both the early observational scientists and the current measurement group. It is clear from the history of science that laboratory experimentation is preferable to all other approaches whenever it can be used. As a consequence, we have gathered random samples of the pseudo-Glflns from their pathways, resting places, and so forth and transported them to our satellite labs. Here we have subjected them to rigorous behavioral tests and made a surprising finding—they are able to learn only when accompanied by their soft, fleshy slaves. It seems that there is a kind of symbiotic relationship in which the slaves, lacking strength and speed, depend on the Glflns, while these creatures in turn do not seem bright enough to learn even the simplest problem when left to their own devices. There is another puzzle. We have not observed anything that could be termed mating behavior, but it is possible that they are unable to become aroused in the laboratory setting. We are at present trying to establish the pattern of life of this curious species and hope soon to be able to state a more general behavioral theory.*

In the life force group, *we never cease to be amazed by the callous attitudes of our fellow behavioral scientists. They assume that a living being can be manipulated and measured, that groups of sick and injured patients can provide important theoretical information, and that the behavior of captives in a laboratory is like that of free beings in a natural setting. Not one of these other reports even speaks of their form of worship. Though not all of the creatures engage in organized religion, a good many of them attend outdoor services in the evening, lining up in semicircular rows to pay homage to moving shadows on a screen. They simultaneously listen to some type of message on a device located at each pew. It is this spiritual dimension and individual uniqueness that must be the focus of our attention in the future. Our goal is not to measure and manipulate them but to love, respect, and understand them.*

There is a fourth report to follow soon, by the internal messages group. *It is their belief that the most important considerations are the internal thought processes of the creatures. Before any progress can be made, however, it will first be necessary to master their language.*

It can be seen that we are only at the beginning of our task of understanding the behavior of Glflns. It is not clear which is the most fruitful approach to this understanding, but we are hopeful that the final outcome will reflect the combined wisdom of our behavioral scientists.

IN THIS CHAPTER we continue the description of personality theories. The theorists to be discussed here are psychologists rather than analysts, and they differ from the earlier theorists in important ways. As psychologists, they tend to be oriented toward empirical research, whether correlational or experimental. Most recognize the importance of quantifying their constructs whenever possible and making accurate predictions of behavior. Propositions are stated in testable form, and failure to verify hypotheses leads to reformulation of the theories. We will now examine the four distinct kinds of theories that have been produced within this general framework.

TRAIT THEORIES: IDENTIFYING THE WAYS IN WHICH INDIVIDUALS DIFFER

In the previous chapter it was pointed out that type theories (from Hippocrates to Sheldon) attempted to classify people into a very limited number of categories. A more realistic and less limiting approach is to assume that people differ according to a series of dimensions or **traits.** The commonsense meaning of personality involves descriptions based on behavioral differences in traits such as honesty, sociability, and aggressiveness. Theories based on traits thus are quite appealing.

One of the earliest psychological approaches to personality theory was to identify and specify the basic traits that constitute an individual. This attempt to list and classify the domain of possibilities for human variation soon moved toward problems of measurement and statistical description. Thus the trait approach began with the everyday meaning of personality, progressed to armchair classifications or taxonomies, and moved into sophisticated statistical methodology. We will outline some of the personality theories that developed in this fashion.

Murray's Motivational Taxonomy

The First Personality Psychologist.   Henry A. Murray (1892) is a physician, chemist, psychoanalyst, and psychologist who has described his primary motivation as "a stout affection for human beings coupled with a consuming interest in their emotions and evaluations, their imaginations and beliefs, their purposes and plans, their endeavors, failures, and achievements" (1959, p. 9). Murray was born in New York City, was graduated from Harvard University as a history major, and then entered medical school at Columbia. After receiving the M.D. degree he spent two years as an intern in surgery and then five years doing research in the areas of physiology and the chemistry of embryos. This work led to a Ph.D. degree in physiological chemistry from Cambridge.

Murray's education was not in psychology, and the change in his career plans took place as a result of a number of factors. He has said that one consideration was a greater interest in the motives and thoughts of human beings than in the physiology of their bodies. In addition, he had come to believe that human personality was the major problem of our time and "not very far from proving itself an evolutionary failure" (1959, p. 11), that psychoanalysis was making great progress in the study of mental processes, and that he was temperamentally well suited to work in an area that was on the frontiers of science. His early contacts with academic psychology had disappointed him, however, and he turned instead to the medical practice of psychotherapy. A major influence on his career was his first contact with Carl Jung (Murray, 1940).

Despite his nonpsychological education, Murray became an instructor in psychology at Harvard in 1927 and the following year became director of the Psychological Clinic there. In the 1930s he and his students and colleagues at Harvard undertook a large-scale study of human personality.

Explorations in Personality.   The work of Murray's group at Harvard culminated in a book, *Explorations in Personality* (Murray, 1938), that was to have a major impact on the field of personality. In fact, it was Murray and a Harvard colleague, Gordon Allport, who created and defined the field of personality in American psychology. The American Psychological Association recently established a Henry Murray Award to honor outstanding research in personality. Murray's unusual background affected the way the group approached the study of personality. He has said that the practice of medicine taught him to arrive at a valid diagnosis by inquiring about the patient's internal sensations and emotions. Medical practice also left him with the conviction that a group of trained colleagues using many different assessment techniques on a single subject could arrive at a more accurate summary of a person than could be arrived at by a single investigator with a limited range of methods.

In studying personology, the unit Murray chose to work with was the life history of a single person (or as much of it as could be sampled). Beginning with existing personality theories, the goal was to test hypotheses, develop new methodologies, discover empirical relations, and in the process develop a new personality theory. The philosophical basis of Murray's approach to a science of personality is suggested by the following passage:

Now, at every stage in the growth of a science there is, it seems, an appropriate balance between broad speculation and detailed measurements. For instance in the infancy of a very complex science—and surely psychology is young and complicated—a few mastering generalizations can be more effective in advancing knowledge than a mass of carefully compiled data. For in the wake of intuition comes investigation directed at crucial problems rather than mere unenlightnened fact-collecting. Here we may point to the undeniable enrichment of our understanding and the impetus to further studies which has come from psychoanalytic theory. In its present stage personology seems to call for men who can view things in the broad, that is, who can apperceive occurrences in terms of the interplay of general forces. A man who has been trained in the exact sciences will find himself somewhat at a loss, if not at a disadvantage. He will find it difficult to fall in with the loose flow of psychologic thought. He will find nothing that is hard and sharp. And so if he continues to hold rigidly to the scientific ideal, to cling to the hope that the results of his researches will approach in accuracy and elegance the formulations of the exact disciplines, he is doomed to failure. He will end his days in the congregation of futile men, of whom the greater number, contractedly withdrawn from critical issues, measure trifles with sanctimonious precision. [Murray, 1938, pp. 21-22]

The project described in *Explorations in Personality* involved small groups of about 13 people who came to the clinic three or four hours per week over a period of several months. The subjects were given as many as two dozen different tests and took part in as many as 24 experiments. They wrote autobiographies; filled out questionnaires; took ability tests; were given a hypnotic test and a level-of-aspiration test; responded to projective devices; were placed in an emotional conditioning situation; and took part in experiments involving such things as cheating, frustration, and memory for success versus failure. The observations and measurements of each subject's behavior in these situations were put together by a five-person diagnostic group, and the end product was a reconstruction of the subject's personality from birth to the present.

The most important aspect of the theory that grew out of this work was the part that had to do with needs. One influence on Murray's work—dating from his medical and biological days—was his conviction that an early step in any discipline should be classifying the processes with which one is dealing. His catalog of human needs is one example of this concern.

Human Needs.   One of Murray's tasks was to identify each of the possible human motives. He divided these into the basic or **primary needs** and the learned or **secondary needs.** The primary needs were further subdivided into three major activities—taking in needed substances, expelling overabundant substances, and avoiding sources of pain. Thus, we are motivated to obtain oxygen, water, food, and various pleasant kinds of external stimulation, including relaxation and sleep. We are also driven to rid our bodies of substances that build up such as carbon dioxide, urine, feces, seminal fluid (for men), and breast milk (for nursing mothers). Avoidance behavior is evoked by painful stimulation of any sort, including cold, heat, and loud noise.

With secondary needs, Murray was able to specify a wide range of

Figure 3-1. Trait theorists such as Murray, Allport, and Cattell have emphasized the observed behavioral differences among individuals, the identification of the basic traits underlying these differences, and the construction of tests to measure the traits. (Rick Smolan, Stock, Boston)

acts that characterize learned human motivation. A summary is provided in Table 3-1. Note that each need is designated by the letter n. As we shall see in a later chapter, this notation system continues to be used in studies of n Achievement, n Affiliation, and so forth.

Other Aspects of Murray's Theory. Murray recognized that needs do not occur in a vacuum, and the role of the environment is represented by the concept of **press.** A press is an external event that helps or hinders an individual striving for a particular goal. The press may be an objectively real one ("alpha press") or a subjectively based misperception ("beta press"). A combination of a press and a need is called a **thema.** For example, rejection by a lover (p Rejection) might evoke a need to receive sympathy from a close friend (n Succorance). Individual acts (**proceedings**) are most meaningful when examined over time with respect to how they lead to a long-term goal. A succession of proceedings is known as a **serial.** Murray's theory was an eclectic one—he incorporated into it such ideas as Jung's archetypes and Freud's id, ego, and superego.

One of the most important assessment techniques developed in the Harvard Clinic was the **Thematic Apperception Test,** or **TAT.** Subjects were shown a series of pictures which served as stimuli for imaginative stories. In making up stories, the subject was supposed to reveal wishes, fears, and memories that were ordinarily hidden from awareness. Most important to the theory was that these stories could be scored for the expression of needs and for the types of press included. In a series of stories, the repeated presence of a given thema was seen as indicative of a person's unconscious concerns.

Table 3-1.   One of Murray's contributions was this taxonomy of learned human needs. He and his colleagues developed objective tests to measure each need, and a sample item from each test is shown here. (Adapted from Ewen, 1980.)

Need	Definition	Sample Test Item to Measure It
n Abasement	To submit, surrender, admit inferiority	My friends think I am too humble.
n Achievement	To accomplish tasks, surpass others	I set difficult goals for myself which I attempt to reach.
n Affiliation	To approach liked others, win their affection	I become very attached to my friends.
n Aggression	To fight opposition, attack, seek revenge	I treat a domineering person as rudely as he treats me.
n Autonomy	To seek freedom, independence, resist coercion	I go my own way regardless of the opinions of others.
n Counteraction	To overcome past failure, repress fear, master weakness	To me a difficulty is just a spur to greater effort.
n Defendance	To defend oneself against attack, criticism, blame	I can usually find plenty of reasons to explain my failures.
n Deference	To admire, praise, imitate, and support another person	I often find myself imitating or agreeing with somebody I consider superior.
n Dominance	To control others, to influence, persuade, command	I usually influence others more than they influence me.
n Exhibition	To impress, excite, amaze, fascinate, or shock others	I am apt to show off in some way if I get a chance.
n Harmavoidance	To avoid pain, injury, illness, danger, death	I am afraid of physical pain.
n Infavoidance	To avoid humiliation, embarrassment, failure	I often shrink from a situation because of my sensitiveness to criticism and ridicule.
n Nurturance	To give sympathy, support, and to console others	I am easily moved by the misfortunes of other people.
n Order	To put things in order, be neat, organized, clean	I organize my daily activities so that there is little confusion.
n Play	To seek fun, jokes, laughter	I cultivate an easy-going, humorous attitude toward life.
n Rejection	To avoid, exclude, snub disliked others	I get annoyed when some fool takes up my time.
n Sentience	To seek and enjoy sensuous experiences	I search for sensations which shall at once be new and delightful.
n Sex	To form erotic relationships, have sex	I spend a great deal of time thinking about sexual matters.
n Succorance	To have others give sympathy, support, and consolation	I feel lonely and homesick when I am in a strange place.
n Understanding	To seek answers, to enjoy analysis, theory, logic, reason	I think that *reason* is the best guide in solving the problems of life.

Though Murray's specific theory is not a major force in personality psychology today, the TAT method of measurement and his designation of needs continues to influence personality research, as we shall see in Chapter 8.

One of Murray's most distinguished Harvard colleagues was Gordon W. Allport (1897–1967). Though Murray's list of needs can easily be considered as involving a group of traits, it was Allport who first took the concept of traits as the basis of his own theory. Allport was born in a small Indiana community, and his family moved to Cleveland, Ohio, when he was six. After completing his undergraduate work at Harvard, he traveled in Europe and arranged to meet Freud in 1920. The nervous young man was surprised that Freud simply sat in silence waiting for him to speak. Not knowing what to say, he began telling about a young boy he had seen on the way to the appointment. The boy seemed to have a dirt phobia, and he suggested that perhaps this could be explained by the appearance of his "well starched" mother. Freud responded, as an analyst well might, by saying, "And was that little boy you?" Allport didn't enjoy being treated like a patient, and his negative reaction was a lasting one:

Flabbergasted and feeling a bit guilty, I contrived to change the subject. . . . This experience taught me that depth psychology, for all of its merits, may plunge too deep, and that psychologists would do well to give full recognition to manifest motives before probing the unconscious" (Allport, 1968, pp. 383–384).

Despite his negative feelings about Freud's depth psychology, Allport returned to Harvard for graduate work. He received the Ph.D. degree in psychology in 1922. He spent additional years studying in Europe and on the faculty at Dartmouth, but most of his professional career was spent at Harvard.

Personality: The Rational and Unique Individual. As with most trait theorists, Allport emphasized personality as an internal process rather than a reaction to external events. He viewed personality as something unique to each individual—a dynamic process that changes throughout life. A child, for example, was seen as being driven mainly by instinctual needs and thus as a demanding, destructive agent of the pleasure principle—an "unsocialized horror." Such selfishness could be overcome with appropriate learning as the person matures. Once one learns to think, weigh consequences, and delay gratification, it becomes possible to act in ways that may be immediately unpleasant but ultimately to one's benefit. Such mature acts as voluntarily studying in school, visiting a dentist, and completing a hard job indicate that one has moved beyond childhood. Further, Allport argued that some of these instrumental behaviors achieve **functional autonomy.** That is, we may initially read books, take a shower, or work at our occupations because we *have to.* Eventually, such acts become independent (functionally autonomous) of their origins. We *enjoy* reading, showering, and getting our work done well.

Freud's interpretive remark to him as a young man was in contrast to his own later approach to human functioning. Allport believed in a rational, conscious process whereby people were guided by their intentions and values. His emphasis on uniqueness (the **idiographic** approach) led him to the study of individuals rather than groups of subjects (the **nomothetic** approach). Nevertheless, when he developed a theory of traits, it sounded suspiciously nomothetic.

Traits and Values.   Allport felt that underlying traits are responsible for what we call personality. He conceptualized traits as falling along a continuum from the specific to the general. For example, at the most specific level—a *behavior*—we might observe a person wash a car. If this behavior occurs regularly, it can be said to be a *habit.* If this habit is consistent with other habits such as keeping belongings in place, dressing well, not allowing dishes to stack up, and so forth, it is possible to speak of a *trait* of neatness.

Allport recognized the existence of **common traits** by which most people in a given culture could be compared. Closer to his definition of personality as unique were the **personal traits** that define each individual. To describe someone's personality is essentially to describe five to ten personal traits, and that is what a good novelist or biographer tries to do. Such descriptions at their best capture the essence of a real or fictional character. Sometimes, a person is dominated by a single characteristic that forms much of his or her behavior—a **cardinal trait.** If, for example, a Don Juan's life is totally governed by the desire to seduce every female he meets, this predatory behavior represents a cardinal trait. Another example is Miss Havisham in Dickens's *Great Expectations;* her life was devoted to avenging herself on all men because she had been rejected by her groom-to-be.

In a similar way, Allport classified the **values** that give meaning to each person's life. He proposed that we are governed by some combination of the values presented in Table 3-2. Such values give meaning to our acts and to our lives. At best, they provide us with a philosophy of life.

Though few psychologists today could be identified as fullfledged adherents of Allport's theory, his influence has been considerable. Perhaps most importantly he affirmed the view of human beings as rational and conscious, and he laid the groundwork for many approaches to defining and measuring personality traits.

Cattell's Factor Theory

Of the several measurement-oriented approaches to the development of trait theory, the most notable are those of Hans J. Eysenck (1916–) and Raymond B. Cattell (1905–). Both have emphasized the importance of test construction and both have relied on the statistical procedures of **factor analysis** to identify basic traits. In factor analysis, correlational techniques are used to determine which items in a scale tend to elicit related responses.

Table 3-2. One of Allport's contributions was an emphasis on six basic values that influence people's lives. A test was devised by Allport, Vernon, and Lindzey (1960) to measure a person's value orientation. (Adapted from Ewen, 1980.)

Value	Description
Theoretical	An intellectual desire to discover truth and to fit one's knowledge into a systematic framework. An occupational choice might be science or philosophy.
Economic	A business-like concern with the useful and practical. A person guided by this value might choose to work in industry, in sales, or some other aspect of business.
Esthetic	An emphasis on the enjoyment of harmony, beauty, and the artistic for its own sake. Occupations include the world of art and design.
Social	A concern for and love of other people. Many positions in education, social work, and the helping professions satisfy this value.
Political	A love of power, not necessarily related to the field of politics. In almost any field, from science to organized religion, it is possible to become concerned with interpersonal politics and the exercise of power.
Religious	A mystical desire for unity with some higher reality. This can lead an individual into a religious vocation or into experimentation with different life styles, drugs, and religious philosophies.

These items are then grouped together to form a test that presumably measures a homogeneous trait.

Though space does not permit detailed coverage of Eysenck's (1975) system, it should be noted that he has identified three basic dimensions of personality. One, like that of Jung, is labeled **Introversion-Extroversion.** At the introverted end of this spectrum are individuals who would be described as careful, thoughtful, passive, quiet, and unsociable. At the extroverted end are personalities seen as optimistic, active, sociable, and outgoing. The **Neuroticism** dimension ranges from stable (even-tempered, calm, reliable) to unstable (moody, anxious, touchy, restless). The third dimension, **Psychoticism,** identifies the solitary, insensitive, and uncaring character at one pole and the gregarious and empathetic type at the other. The tests that measure these basic traits have been used in a great deal of personality research (see Wilson, 1978). Cattell's factor theory, to be summarized next, has generated even more research.

Cattell was born in Staffordshire, England, and did his undergraduate work at the University of London in chemistry and physics. After graduating, he made a sudden switch to the field of psychology and received the Ph.D. degree at that same university in 1929. In 1937, he crossed the Atlantic and taught at a number of universities (Columbia, Clark, Harvard) before accepting a research professorship at the University of Illinois. When he retired from that position 30 years later, he became visiting professor at the University of Hawaii in 1973.

His theoretical goal was to build an empirically based theory that permitted one to predict a person's behavior in a given situation. The observable differences in behavioral tendencies (talkative-silent, assertive-indecisive, etc.) are conceived as **surface traits.** They represent the way in which a person expresses his or her underlying **source traits.** Source traits involve sixteen basic dimensions along which people differ. These traits, as measured by the **Sixteen Personality Factor Questionnaire** (Cattell, Eber, & Tatsuoka, 1970), are summarized in Table 3–3. In this list, intelligence is an **ability trait** while the remainder are **temperament traits.** An example of the research conducted with these variables is Curran's (1973) project to match males and females as dates on the basis of similarity in source traits. It should be noted that recent research suggests that additional source traits may need to be added to the list (Cattell & Kline, 1976). Besides ability and temperament, other dimensions involve motivation, and these **dynamic traits** are divided into those that are innate (**ergs**) and those that are learned (general **sentiments** and specific **attitudes**). As with Murray's "serials," Cattell deals with chains of development that tend to extent from erg to sentiment to attitude. Thus, a person with a sex erg might express an affectionate sentiment toward her husband that leads to an overt attitude involving a desire to make love. Behavior consists of just such **subsidiation chains.** If an individual's various interlocking chains are considered simultaneously, the result is a complex motivational structure, known as the **dynamic lattice.**

Though a great deal of research and test construction forms the basis of Cattell's theory, most personality psychologists have not been to-

Table 3-3. 16 Trait Dimensions. Cattell's trait theory of personality includes the 16 basic source traits defined here. These basic dimensions are expressed overtly in surface traits. (Adapted from Ewen, 1980.)

Low Scores =	High Scores =
1. *Sizia:* reserved, detached, aloof	*Affecta:* outgoing, warmhearted
2. *Low Intelligence:* dull	*High Intelligence:* bright
3. *Low Ego Strength:* agitated, emotionally unstable	*High Ego Strength:* calm, emotionally stable
4. *Submissiveness:* humble, docile	*Dominance:* assertive, competitive
5. *Desurgency:* sober, serious	*Surgency:* happy-go-lucky, fun-loving
6. *Weak Superego:* ignores rules, immoral	*Strong Superego:* conscientious, moral
7. *Threctia:* shy, timid	*Parmia:* adventurous, bold
8. *Harria:* tough-minded, self-reliant	*Premsia:* tender-minded, sensitive
9. *Alaxia:* trusting, accepting	*Protension:* suspicious, rejecting
10. *Praxernia:* practical, down-to-earth	*Autia:* imaginative, head-in-the-clouds
11. *Artlessness:* forthright, socially awkward	*Shrewdness:* astute, socially skilled
12. *Untroubled Adequacy:* secure, self-assured	*Guilt Proneness:* apprehensive, self-blaming
13. *Conservatism:* conservative, traditional	*Radicalism:* liberal, free-thinking
14. *Group Adherence:* joins groups, follows others	*Self-Sufficiency:* independent, self-reliant
15. *Low Self-Sentiment Integration:* uncontrolled, impulsive	*High Self-Sentiment Integration:* controlled, compulsive
16. *Low Ergic Tension:* relaxed, composed	*High Ergic Tension:* tense, frustrated

tally accepting of his ideas. There are doubts that factor analysis actually permits us to identify the basic elements of personality (Anastasi, 1976). You might have noted that Eysenck and Cattell each used this procedure and yet ended up with quite different results. Royce (1979) has proposed that the conceptual framework employed to tie factors together is as important as the identification of the basic factors. Cattell's unique terminology also tends to evoke a degree of resistance. Nevertheless, Cattell and his followers have provided a tremendous quantity of research. This body of measuring devices, theory, and empirical findings represents an impressive example of where trait theory can lead.

RESEARCH CLOSE-UP

Focusing on a Specific Characteristic: Coronary-Prone Behavior

A supposedly inclusive typology, such as that of Sheldon, is appealing, but human behavior seems to be too complex to fit within a brief list of categories. The more detailed trait theories, such as those of Murray, Allport, Eysenck, and Cattell, appear much more realistic, but it is difficult to conduct meaningful research on a large number of variables simultaneously. Many personality psychologists have tried to solve this problem over the past several decades by concentrating their attention on a single trait. An example of such research is the recent study of **coronary-prone behavior.**

It has been found that people who are competitive, achievement-oriented, aggressive, impatient, and always in a hurry are most apt to develop heart trouble (Rosenman & Friedman, 1974; Suinn, 1976). At the opposite extreme are those who are relaxed, passive, lacking in ambition, and unconcerned about time pressures—these individuals tend to be free of heart disease. Though this collection of behaviors can obviously be defined as a trait dimension along which individuals can be placed, the coronary-prone characteristics have been labeled as **Type A personality,** and the others **Type B personality** (Glass, 1976, 1977).

In the earliest investigations of this trait, Type A and Type B individuals were identified by means of interviews in which people were asked if they eat too fast, if others describe them as hard-driving and competitive, and if they are easily irritated. That kind of questioning has now been replaced by a personality test, the **Jenkins Activity Survey** (Jenkins, Zyzanski, & Rosenman, 1979). Research on this trait provides an indication of the way in which detailed knowledge about a single personality dimension can constitute a solid core of predictive data. Some of the findings are summarized in Table 3-4 (see page 92). Such findings constitute not only a detailed picture of Type A and Type B individuals, they also suggest clues as to how this trait fits in with other personality traits. See, for example, the work on achievement need in Chapter 8. In addition, they provide guidelines indicating ways in which behavior might be changed. For example, there is a strong possibility that an individual who learns how to relax, avoid pressure, and generally slow down might be lessen-

Table 3-4. Research on coronary-prone behavior (Type A) and behavior associated with less risk of heart attack (Type B) is an example of current trait research. Rather than attempt to study all of an individual's traits at one time, attention is directed to single traits and the way in which they affect behavior.

Responses Typical of Type A Individuals	Responses Typical of Type B Individuals	Investigators
Prefer to work alone when under pressure	Prefer to work with others when under pressure	Dembroski and Mac-Dougall (1978)
Feel uncomfortable, awkward, and insecure with others	Feel comfortable and at ease with others	Jenkins, et al. (1977)
Work hard at a task even without a deadline	Work hard at a task only if there is a deadline	Burnam, Pennebaker, and Glass (1975)
Involved in sports and extracurricular activities in college	Not involved in sports or extracurricular activities in college	Glass (1974)
Work harder and report less fatigue	Work less hard and report more fatigue	Carver, Coleman, and Glass (1976)
Complain less about their work	Complain more about their work	Weidner and Matthews (1978)
Set high goals and often feel they failed to meet them	Set low goals and often feel successful	Snow (1978)
Have high fear of failure	Have low fear of failure	Gastorf and Teevan (1980)
Express exaggerated achievement strivings	Express lower achievement strivings	Gastorf, Suls, and Sanders (1980)
Feel very frustrated, irritated, and angry with uncontrollable task	Feel less frustrated, irritated, and angry with uncontrollable task	Levine and Moore (1979)
Ignore distractions and get task done	Respond to distractions and allow work to suffer	Matthews and Brunson (1979)

ing the possibility of becoming the victim of a heart attack (Farquhar, 1977). In one such therapy project, subjects learn to avoid situations that bring about Type A behavior, such as those involving time pressure (*APA Monitor,* February 1980, pp. 8 and 33).

It appears that this sort of concentrated research on a single trait is valuable in increasing our ability to predict behavior and in suggesting how to bring about a desired behavioral change. In Chapters 5 through 8, we will explore four other trait dimensions that have been extensively studied.

LEARNING THEORY: FROM THE COUCH TO THE LABORATORY

Other psychologists besides those developing trait theory were also interested in personality. As the twentieth century began, the science of psychology was in its early stages in experimental laboratories. Scientists interested in basic research were working on problems such as perception, learning, and cognition. Though both the psychoanalysts and these experimental psychologists were studying human behavior, they differed greatly in their methods, the kind of behavior they investigated, and the theories produced. In the 1930s, some experimentalists began to try to bridge the gap.

The Hullians: Stimulus-Response Theory

As we shall see in Chapter 7, a learning theorist named Clark Hull had a major impact on American psychology with the development of a rigorous theory of behavior. In addition, he met regularly with students and colleagues in a series of seminars at Yale that often went beyond the topic of learning theory. One of the goals of these behavioral scientists was to make sense of Freud's psychoanalytic theory in terms of established principles of learning. Some of the earliest scientific investigations of Freudian concepts were pioneered by this group. As an example of their approach, we will consider the work of sociologist John Dollard (1900–) and psychologist Neal E. Miller (1909–). One of their most influential contributions was the book *Personality and Psychotherapy: An Analysis in Terms of Learning, Thinking, and Culture* (Dollard & Miller, 1950).

Both men were born in Wisconsin. Dollard's sociological training was at the University of Chicago where he received a Ph.D. in 1931. He later traveled to Germany to obtain psychoanalytic training at the Berlin Institute. He spent his professional career at Yale where he held appointments in sociology, psychology, and anthropology. He retired in 1969. Miller received a Ph.D. in psychology in 1935 at Yale and then went to the Vienna Institute to study psychoanalysis. He also spent most of his academic career at Yale, but moved to Rockefeller University in 1966.

When these two individuals undertook the task of bringing together the brilliant insights of Freud with the hard-nosed scientific approach of the learning laboratory, the result was a **stimulus-response theory** of personality. To take one example of how Freud was translated into quite different terms, consider the "pleasure principle" (see Chapter 2). Dollard and Miller assumed that primary (biological) and secondary (learned) **drives** energize the organism to act. When a given behavior results in **drive reduction,** this is a reinforcing event. **Reinforcement** strengthens the tendency of the individual to make that particular response whenever the same stimulus conditions are encountered on subsequent occasions. The stimuli can be intense (a **drive stimulus**) and act as motivators or they can be relatively weak **cues** that allow the person to make a relevant discrimination. For example, extreme thirst is a drive stimulus whereas a soft drink machine is a cue.

How can such concepts be applied to an actual behavior problem? Dollard and Miller described a 23-year-old married woman whose neurotic behavior included the compulsive need to count her own heart beats. She was obsessed with the idea that her heart would stop if she failed to concentrate on the counting. This tendency was most active when she went out shopping alone. She mentioned that she was afraid of sexual advances being made to her when she went out, so she began staying home most of the time. It would be possible to speculate about the meaning of this behavior—the symbolic aspects of a rhythmic heart beat, an anal retentive need to control one's bodily reactions, or unresolved Oedipal fears. Instead, Dollard and Miller concluded that she was caught in a simple conflict between two drives: sex and fear. When she went out, there was the possibility of being seduced by a strange man, and such fantasies were tempting and titillating. At the same time, her values were such that she experienced guilt and was afraid of the consequences of her sexual desires. The conflict could be resolved most easily by reducing one of the drives. Reduction of the sex drive involved either staying home and thus avoiding the arousing stimuli or counting her heart beats and thus avoiding sexual thoughts. It may be seen that both staying home and counting were reinforcing behaviors, and hence she continued to engage in them. One could say that the woman "repressed" her sexual needs or that she accidentally discovered certain behaviors that were drive-reducing and hence resolved her conflict. From the viewpoint of learning theory, the latter conceptualization is preferred, being more precise, better tied to observables, and linked to a body of knowledge about drives and drive reduction.

It should be noted that one result of dealing with clinical phenomena in this fashion has been the development of therapeutic techniques based on learning theory. Many of the behavior modification procedures described in Chapter 7 have been developed over the past few decades by psychologists who viewed psychopathology in terms of learned responses. In that context, psychotherapy becomes a way to help a person unlearn maladaptive responses and learn new and more beneficial ways to behave.

Skinner's Operant Conditioning

Chapter 1 gave an example of complex animal learning in which Skinnerian principles were briefly mentioned. It was pointed out that through **shaping** (or **successive approximation**) it is possible to reinforce an organism's spontaneous responses (**operants**) and so induce it to engage in novel and uncharacteristic behaviors. Through such **operant conditioning,** pigeons have been taught to guide rockets against military targets and mentally retarded human beings have been taught to dress and feed themselves. Skinner (1953, p. 91) describes the idea as follows:

Operant conditioning shapes behavior as a sculptor shapes a lump of clay. Although at some point the sculptor seems to have produced an entirely novel object, we can always follow the process back to the original undifferentiated lump, and we can make the successive stages by which we return to this condition as small as we wish. At no point does anything emerge which is very different from what preceded it . . . An operant is not something which appears full grown in the behavior of the organism. It is the result of a continuous shaping process.

The creator of this approach to learning is B. F. Skinner (1904-). He was born in Pennsylvania and grew up planning to be a writer. He eventually turned away from this career and earned a Ph.D. in psychology at Harvard in 1931. He taught for several years at the University of Minnesota and at Indiana University, but most of his professional life has been at Harvard. In describing the invention of some of the basic techniques associated with his name, Skinner (1972) provides an interesting example of how chance events can be important in science. A "Skinner box" is designed in such a way that when the animal gives a certain response or series of responses, reinforcement is automatically provided—his original idea was simply to make things easier for the experimenter. A version of this device was later designed for the care of human infants. His work on **schedules of reinforcement** (the effect of reinforcing a given behavior only part of the time) began when he found himself running out of animal food

Figure 3-2. For learning-oriented psychologists such as B. F. Skinner, the complex behavior of human beings in natural settings is viewed as simply an extension of basic behavioral laws established in experimental laboratories with simpler animals.   (Monkmeyer)

one Saturday afternoon. His interest in **extinction** (the gradual weakening of nonreinforced responses) began when the automatic food dispenser jammed. It might be noted that his literary aspirations recurred from time to time as evidenced by a novel, *Walden Two* (Skinner, 1948a) and an autobiography (Skinner, 1976).

Though Skinner has never described himself as a personality theorist, his approach, concepts, and techniques have been applied to almost every aspect of behavior, including various forms of therapy. He has indicated repeatedly (Skinner, 1971) that most personality theories are unnecessarily mentalistic. He stresses the importance of dealing only with variables that we can observe and manipulate (Skinner, 1974). It is easy to make up some entity that is supposed to be *inside* of people (id, archetype, trait, motive, or whatever) and assume that we have succeeded in understanding the phenomenon in question, a habit reflected by statements like, "He committed that act *because of* unconscious id impulses," and "She's successful *because* she has a high need to achieve."

His focus on stimulus conditions, reinforcement, and observable behavior leads to a simple and yet predictively powerful view of human behavior. Why does an individual behave in a particular way? The answer is always the same within Skinner's framework—because he or she is reinforced for doing so. How do you change the behavior? The answer is also always the same—change the **reinforcement contingencies.** If a given behavior is undesirable, arrange the reinforcement contingencies so that it is no longer reinforced. Reinforcement is thus made contingent on the desirability of the behavior.

To illustrate where such an approach leads, consider an example. You see a man who always walks around in a circle before he sits down to eat. This unusual—perhaps "crazy"—act could be explained in many ways. From Skinner's viewpoint, it probably occurred first by accident, was reinforced (he ate after doing it), and now continues to be reinforced (the meal always follows the behavior). He was able to teach pigeons to engage in just such odd "superstitious" behavior by reinforcing them when some random behavior occurred (Skinner, 1948b). To change the behavior, the reinforcement must change: if the man is not fed when he circles but only when he sits down directly, the circling behavior will be replaced by normal activity.

One major therapeutic application of Skinnerian concepts is the **token economy** (Kazdin, 1976). Consider a mental hospital that is set up in such a way that individuals can earn tokens for engaging in desirable behaviors (making their own beds, for example) and then the tokens can later be spent for reinforcements (food, special privileges, etc.). In his novel, Skinner conceived of an entire society arranged in this way—reinforcers were sensibly arranged so that optimal behavior occurred. Some critics complain that this approach is mechanistic and potentially totalitarian.

Skinner would reply that behavior is always simply a function of rein-forcement. The question is not *whether* we are guided by reinforcing stimuli but rather *what* we are reinforced for doing and *who* decides on the rein-forcement contingencies.

Social Learning Theory

Personality psychologists interested in learning theory tended to follow the lead of Dollard and Miller by adapting Hull's principles to human be-havior. Because this theory was based primarily on data obtained in animal laboratories, some felt that the most important aspects of human function-ing were being neglected—thought, expectation, intention, imagination, and so forth. In 1954 Julian Rotter introduced a variant of the learning theory approach. His **social learning theory** was devised explicitly to deal with the complexities of human behavior.

Rotter: Expectations and Rewards.   Rotter was born in 1916 and received his undergraduate training at Brooklyn College. After a year of graduate work at the University of Iowa where he received an M.A. degree, he moved to Indiana University and earned a Ph.D. in 1941. The bulk of his academic career was spent at Ohio State University. He was actively engaged in research there and also was responsible for training an impres-sive array of personality and clinical psychologists. He currently is at the University of Connecticut.

As with all learning theory approaches, Rotter's formulation as-sumes that individuals behave in a certain way to satisfy needs, that re-warded behavior tends to be repeated when similar conditions sub-sequently recur, and that the environment is of paramount importance in influencing behavior. In addition, thought processes are an integral part of the total picture for humans. We remember past experiences and can use them to guide our current actions. We can anticipate the future and assess the consequences of a given action; we can evaluate the likely outcome, and then decide whether or not to engage in the behavior. To predict behavior, we must know what an individual has learned in the past, what his or her expectations may be, and what value each possible behavioral outcome has for that individual (Rotter & Hochreich, 1975).

Figure 3–3 presents the general outline of the major aspects of the theory. The response to be predicted in any given situation is concep-tualized in terms of **behavior potential.** This refers to the probability that the person will engage in a particular act. To predict that behavior, it is necessary to assess two internal constructs: **expectancy** and **reinforcement value.** Expectancy is the person's estimate of the probability that the be-havior will result in reinforcement. Since one usually must choose between alternative behaviors leading to different rewards, reinforcement value is a

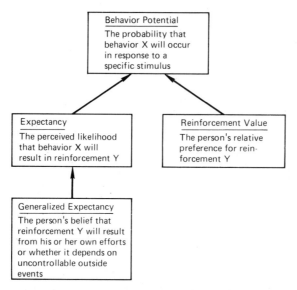

Figure 3-3. In Rotter's social learning theory, the occurrence of any given behavior in a specific situation is prompted by the person's expectations about the outcome of the behavior and his or her evaluation of that outcome. Generalized expectancies, which depend on the person's belief either that rewards and punishments are controlled personally or controlled by outside events, also exist.

person's relative preference for each one. For example, if you were interested in predicting whether Jane will go out with John or Frank, it would be necessary to know her expectancies about the kinds of reinforcement that would occur in each interaction as well as the value she places on each. Presumably her choice will represent her best guess as to how to maximize her own pleasure.

There is an additional concept posited by Rotter that involves an important personality trait—**locus of control.** Individuals learn a set of generalized expectancies about how reinforcements are obtained (Phares, 1978). At one extreme is **internality,** the belief that one can control his or her own fate. In effect, a person thinks that by skill, hard work, foresight, and acceptance of responsibility it is possible to obtain reinforcements and avoid punishments. At the opposite extreme is **externality,** the belief that what happens is due to chance, luck, the behavior of those more powerful, and complex events in one's surroundings. Sometimes good things happen and sometimes bad, and there's not much you can do about it. This trait is measured by the *I-E Scale* (Phares & Lamiell, 1975).

It might be surmised from Rotter's theory that behavior depends on external circumstances and on past experience that provides a basis for expectancies, generalized expectancies, and reinforcement value. As we shall see in Chapter 4, such a theory has led to the conclusion that it is not necessary to rely on a large number of personality traits to predict behavior.

Mischel and Bandura: Social Learning at Stanford.   Two of the most active and influential proponents of a social learning approach to personality are Walter Mischel (1930–) and Albert Bandura (1925–), both of whom are at Stanford University.

Mischel was one of Rotter's students at Ohio State. He was born in Vienna and spent his childhood there. In 1939, his family left to escape Nazism and relocated in New York City. He attended City College there and became a social worker. Disappointed by his inability to help the delinquents with whom he worked, he entered graduate school in Columbus. His first academic position was at Harvard, and he is currently at Stanford. Albert Bandura was born in the province of Alberta, Canada. His undergraduate work was done at the University of British Columbia. He came to the U.S. for graduate training and entered the clinical program at the University of Iowa. There, Kenneth Spence (see Chapter 7) had a major influence on his theoretical interests. In 1952, Bandura took a position at Stanford University where he has remained throughout his career.

These two modern personality theorists share a belief in the importance of the external situation and the role of reinforcement in determining behavior. In addition to the powerful part played by such stimuli, they each emphasize the importance of cognitive processes—"what goes on in the head." In Bandura's (1977), p. 129) words, "Theories that explain human behavior as solely the product of external rewards and punishments present a truncated image of people because they possess self-reactive capacities that enable them to exercise some control over their own feelings, thoughts, and actions."

While both theorists deny the conception of homo sapien as an externally controlled organism, the opposite view—that human behavior is governed strictly by internal forces—is also rejected. In place of either extreme view, they stress the interaction between internal processes and the environment. Mischel (1977, p. 253) describes his image of what people are like:

This image is one of the human being as an active, aware problem-solver, capable of profiting from an enormous range of experiences and cognitive capacities, possessing great potential for good or ill, actively constructing his or her psychological world, and influencing the environment but also being influenced by it in lawful ways.

Some of the specific research conducted by Mischel and Bandura on delay of gratification, person perception, modeling behavior, and aggression will be described in later chapters of this book.

HUMANISTIC THEORIES OF PERSONALITY

There is yet another approach to personality theory, one that views the work of psychoanalysts, test builders, and learning theorists as sharing a set of harmful biases about humanity. From the perspective of the **humanists,** personality theorists from Freud to Skinner have looked upon people as little more than research subjects to be analyzed and manipulated (Krasner, 1978). In this view traditional psychology robs people of their dignity and ignores their capacity for creativity and improvement. The humanists, in contrast, stress two major beliefs: the basic goodness of human beings and their natural tendency to move toward higher levels of functioning. One of the first personality psychologists to advance such ideas was Gordon Allport (1955), who expressed concern that personality theories were based primarily on the study of emotionally disturbed patients in therapy or, worse still, of laboratory rats. Out of these criticisms grew some alternative personality theories. Two of these will now be described: the work of Abraham Maslow and that of Carl Rogers.

Figure 3-4. In Maslow's humanistic theory of personality, belongingness is the first of the higher-order needs to develop. Once the lower-order physiological and safety needs are satisfied, human beings within a family unit are first able to love and be loved. (Peter Menzel, Stock, Boston)

Abraham Maslow was born in Brooklyn in 1908. He describes his child-hood as a lonely and unhappy one shaped by uneducated parents, poverty, and the anti-Semitism of neighbors (Hall, 1968). After a brief period at Cornell, he went on to finish his undergraduate work at the University of Wisconsin. He stayed in Madison for graduate studies, conducting research on the sexual behavior of monkeys under the direction of Harry Harlow in 1934. Though he began his career as a behavioristic animal psychologist, first at Brooklyn College and then at Brandeis, he changed his views dra-matically and became a leading exponent of humanistic personality psy-chology. He died in 1970.

A basic tenet of Maslow's (1970) personality theory was the **need hierarchy.** As illustrated in Figure 3–5, needs are grouped into two broad

Figure 3-5. In Maslow's theory, the need hierarchy consists of five types of human needs. Those on the bottom of the hierarchy must be satisfied first in order for the individual to be able to progress to the next highest level. The natural direction of growth is toward the top of the hierarchy and the attainment of *self-actualization*. External events can block one's progress in the hierarchy, or even cause retrograde movement.

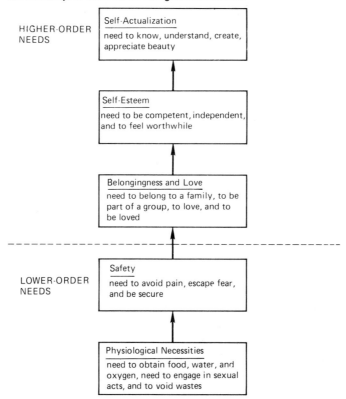

categories: lower-order needs involving physiological requirements and safety and the higher-order needs of belongingness and love, self-esteem, and self-actualization. The *physiological* needs are primary drives that must be satisfied in order for the individual and the species to survive. Since much laboratory research with animals involves the manipulation of such needs, learning theorists were thought to have a limited view of humanity. Once the basic needs are met, the individual can address *safety* needs: freedom from pain, fear and insecurity. The satiated, secure individual finds himself or herself moving toward higher-order or **meta needs** such as *belongingness and love.* The desire to identify with others and to enter a loving relationship is a higher-order need, while sex is a lower-order need. The contented, secure, loving person progresses to concerns about *self-esteem.* We need to feel worthwhile as human beings—competent, in control of our environment, free, and independent. The highest of all needs is that of **self-actualization.** This is the need to know about oneself and about one's surroundings, to be creative, and to appreciate beauty.

In a good home environment situated in a free and supportive society, each of us would naturally move upward in the hierarchy and become self-actualized. In fact, there are bad homes and bad societies, and many people never reach the highest level of human potential. In a restrictive, harsh environment, one's thoughts reflect **D-cognition** based on *deficiency needs.* People judge, condemn, and evaluate one another. In a free, healthful environment, one's thoughts involve **B-cognition** based on *being.* Here the concern is not with evaluation but with beauty and goodness. At best, these B-cognitions are **peak experiences** of insight, understanding, and awareness.

The truly self-actualized human being is realistic, unprejudiced, accepting, happy, uninhibited, problem-oriented, creative, and democratic. In an ideal world, all of us would become totally self-actualized.

TRY IT YOURSELF

Assessing Your Self-Concept and Your Ideal Self-Concept

In reading about the various personality theories described in this book, you may have noticed that the concept of **self** was mentioned in several of them. In addition to the **self-theories** such as that of Rogers (to be described next), theorists as diverse as Jung, Sullivan, Maslow, and Bandura (1974, 1978) recognize the importance of how an individual views himself or herself. The capacity to recognize and respond to oneself in a mirror is apparently limited to humans and a few higher primates like chimpanzees and orangutans (Gallup, 1977). In addition to recognition, however, we are able to attach descriptive and evaluate labels to ourselves, and these labels, in turn, influence our behavior. We also have goals and standards as to what kind of person each of us wants to be. Thus, we have a **self-concept** and an **ideal self-concept.** How would you characterize yourself? How closely does your self-image match the person you would ideally want to be? Try the following test.

Respond to the following adjective check list by reading it quickly and making a check mark beside each item that describes you. Work quickly and do not spend too much time on each one. Be as frank with yourself as possible. Next, go back through the list and make a check mark beside each item (in the second column) that describes the person you would like to be. Again, work quickly.

1. absent-minded	—— ——	24. headstrong	—— ——
2. anxious	—— ——	25. hurried	—— ——
3. artistic	—— ——	26. imaginative	—— ——
4. attractive	—— ——	27. impatient	—— ——
5. capable	—— ——	28. impulsive	—— ——
6. charming	—— ——	29. industrious	—— ——
7. clear-thinking	—— ——	30. ingenious	—— ——
8. clever	—— ——	31. initiating	—— ——
9. confused	—— ——	32. insightful	—— ——
10. courageous	—— ——	33. inventive	—— ——
11. dissatisfied	—— ——	34. irritable	—— ——
12. dreamy	—— ——	35. moody	—— ——
13. emotional	—— ——	36. nervous	—— ——
14. energetic	—— ——	37. original	—— ——
15. enterprising	—— ——	38. persevering	—— ——
16. excitable	—— ——	39. pessimistic	—— ——
17. forceful	—— ——	40. polished	—— ——
18. forgetful	—— ——	41. preoccupied	—— ——
19. gentle	—— ——	42. resourceful	—— ——
20. good-looking	—— ——	43. restless	—— ——
21. handsome	—— ——	44. tactful	—— ——
22. hard-headed	—— ——	45. wise	—— ——
23. hasty	—— ——	46. witty	—— ——

You might take a separate piece of paper and make three lists; first list those terms that you checked as characteristic of your self but not of your ideal, then those characteristic of your ideal but not your self, and finally those for which you checked both columns. The first list suggests those aspects of yourself that are not consistent with your highest standards. The second list is the way you would ideally like to be. The third list shows those traits that live up to your ideals. Do you believe this is an accurate description of your self-image?

Data from Gough, Fioravanti, and Lazzari (1979) provide a way to compare your responses with those of American and Italian males and females. In their sample, both sexes in both countries checked the following items as more characteristic of their real selves than of their ideals:

1, 2, 9, 11, 12, 13, 16, 18, 22, 23, 24, 25, 27, 28, 34, 35, 36, 39, 41, 43

The following items were more characteristic of their ideal selves than of their real selves:
3, 4, 5, 6, 7, 8, 10, 14, 15, 17, 19, 20, 21, 26, 29, 30, 31, 32, 33, 37, 38, 40, 42, 44, 45, 46

Carl Rogers: From Scientific Agriculture to Client-Centered Therapy

Personality theorists have not been intensely interested in global theories for at least twenty-five years (McWilliams, 1977). One notable exception to this general trend is the work of Carl Rogers. He is an able representative of those psychologists who feel that it is more appropriate to deal with each human being as an organized, whole person rather than in terms of isolated dimensions. The cornerstone of his theory is the **self-concept.** Self-concept is defined as the collection of attitudes, judgments, and values that a person holds with respect to his or her behavior, ability, appearance, and worth as a person. Like those of many other personality theorists, Rogers' ideas grew out of his experience as a therapist.

Carl Rogers (1967a) has described his own background in terms of early influences on his work. Born in Oak Park, Illinois, in 1902, he moved with his family to a farm near Chicago at the age of 12. He lived in a large, hard-working, conservative, Protestant household in which fundamentalist religious beliefs were the norm. As a teenager he became interested in the study of night-flying moths and scientific agriculture, which led him to appreciate the experimental method. He describes himself as having been a loner without close friends outside his family circle, living in a world of his own created by the books he read. His interest in agriculture carried over to his undergraduate work at the University of Wisconsin. It was there that he first found friendship and companionship outside of his home through membership in a YMCA group. He became a history major and after graduation spent two years at the Union Theological Seminary, where he became acquainted with clinical psychology. He transfered to Teachers College, Columbia University, and in 1931, after a clinical internship at the Institute for Child Guidance, he received a Ph.D. in educational and clinical psychology; his thesis involved the development of a way of measuring the personality adjustment of children. He then spent twelve years at the Child Study Department of a clinic in Rochester, New York. In 1938 he became the first director of the Rochester Guidance Center. His efforts to conceptualize the work of psychotherapists and to understand the behavior of their clients amounted to a quest for a theoretical model of psychotherapy and, more generally, personality.

Rogers taught courses at Columbia and Rochester, but he did not move into a university setting until 1940, when he joined the faculty at Ohio State University. During this period his ideas concerning client-centered psychotherapy were forming. His position at Ohio State was that of full professor, and he notes, "I heartily recommend starting in the academic world at the top level. I have often been grateful that I have never had to live through the frequently degrading competitive process of step-by-step promotion in university faculties, where individuals so frequently learn only one lesson—not to stick their necks out" (Rogers 1967a, p. 361). In 1945 he began an extremely productive twelve years at the University of Chicago. His work as a therapist at the Counseling Center there, his research, his development of a personality theory, and his influence on graduate students and colleagues brought him to prominence in the field of psychology. He served as president of the American Psychological Association in 1946–47, and in 1957 he became a professor of psychology and psychiatry at the University of Wisconsin. At that point his interest was directed toward more serious behavior disorders; he undertook a large-scale project to study the effects of psychotherapy on schizophrenics (Rogers, 1967b). However, there were a number of interpersonal conflicts in the department of psychology at Wisconsin and in his own research group. In 1964 Rogers decided to leave the university environment and accepted a position at the Western Behavioral Sciences Institute at La Jolla, California.

Figure 3-6. Rogers suggests that a central aspect of personality is one's self-concept. We develop a series of attitudes involving self-awareness and self-esteem. Our perceptions of ourselves and of the world around us are governed by this self-structure.   (James Foote, Photo Researchers)

His present work is centered on encounter groups and the development of a philosophy of the behavioral sciences.

As Rogers worked out his novel approach to psychotherapy, he also tried to account for the apparent success of this nondirective or client-centered method in bringing about changes in his clients. The therapeutic methods developed by Rogers and his co-workers were a clear departure from traditional procedures such as psychoanalysis. The therapist is not cast in an interpretive, judgmental role, and the process of therapy is not viewed as an intellectual enterprise in which interpretations are used to bring unconscious material into consciousness. Rather, the therapist simply facilitates the natural growth processes of the client by offering acceptance, understanding, and empathy.

Over the years such ideas were extended into a theory of personality and even more broadly into theoretical statements about behavior in a variety of situations, including education, interpersonal relations, and family life.

Self-Congruent Versus Self-Incongruent Experiences.   Several general points of Rogers' approach should be noted. It attempts to deal with the whole person. Behavior is believed to be a function of the perception of events, and the frame of reference of the theorist or researcher is *internal* rather than external. Thus, the manipulation of external stimuli, defined in the researcher's terms, might overlook the fact that the subjects are responding in terms of their own perceptions and that each subject structures the environment in a way that may well be different from the way other subjects and the researcher structure it. There is emphasis on internally directed behavior as opposed to that which is externally directed. Behavior is not seen as a response to stimuli but "*is basically the goal-directed attempt of the organism to satisfy its needs as experienced, in the field as perceived*" (Rogers, 1951, p. 491).

The most important aspect of an individual's world is that portion which consists of the perceptions of "I" or "me"—the self. The basic motive of the organism is the **actualizing tendency,** an inherent desire to develop all of its capacities in ways that serve to maintain or enhance the organism.

The **need for positive regard** is universal. We all want to be loved and respected. To satisfy this need one must depend on other human beings. This need is important enough so that the person is influenced more by it than by his or her actual experience. A child can learn that her feces are disgusting, that she does not hate her aunt, or that sexual thoughts are sinful, even though her own experiences in each instance might have provided quite different perceptions. Developing out of the need for positive regard from others is the need for positive *self*-regard. The child's self-concept is formed by means of interactions with others, and in this process the child adopts the need to be thought of positively. Children see and judge themselves as others do. And they come to judge their own experiences in terms of the values acquired from others. For example, the person who has acquired a positive self-image judges his or her performance on a task as better than someone with a negative self-image does, even when their performances are equally good (Shrauger & Terbovic, 1976).

There is almost always some lack of congruence between a person's experiences and acquired values. Some experiences are in accord with the self-concept and are accurately perceived and symbolized in consciousness: A person goes several hours without food, feels hungry, and decides to eat some potato chips. Some experiences are contrary to the self-concept and are perceived selectively, distorted, and denied to awareness either in whole or in part: A high school senior learns that her best friend is getting a new car for graduation. She is unable to perceive that she is envious of her friend or resentful about her parents' inability to provide such gifts because her self-concept does not include the possibility of envy or resentment. Instead, she feels anxious when her friend is around, is critical of her appearance, and suddenly becomes concerned about the energy inefficiency of gas guzzlers. Such defensive processes lead to rigid perception, inaccurate perception of reality, and the tendency to view experience in overgeneralized and abstract terms. Figure 3–7 shows how self-concept and experience interact.

Whenever self and experience are not in accord, there is psychological maladjustment, and the person is subject to anxiety, threat, and disorganization. For example, if feelings of dependency are not consistent with a person's self-concept, any situation that suggests the need for someone else's help is threatening, even though the person is not able to verbalize the reason why. Likewise, the person's own behavior may be consistent with his or her self-concept and may be perceived accurately, or it may be inconsistent with the self-concept and hence subject to distorted perception and lack of awareness. In the latter instance the person may feel that the behavior is not really part of himself or herself: "I'm not myself today."

If there is enough incongruence between self and experience, the repeated occurrence of such threatening experiences may lead to a breakdown of defenses, extreme anxiety, and disorganization of the self structure. There may be a severe attack of anxiety, acts that are different from the person's previous behavior, or even an acute psychotic breakdown. The person can feel overwhelmed, without direction, and unable to function as anxiety mounts. A model high school boy, described by all who know him as nice and polite, rapes and strangles a small neighbor girl after choir practice. A meek, submissive man comes home from work and shoots his wife and children. A quiet, prudish young lady picks up a stranger in a bar and has intercourse with him.

One of the major ways in which these various negative processes

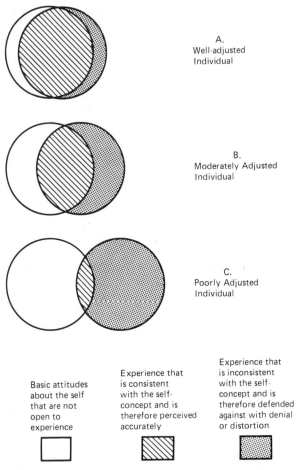

A.
Well-adjusted
Individual

B.
Moderately Adjusted
Individual

C.
Poorly Adjusted
Individual

Basic attitudes
about the self
that are not
open to
experience

Experience that
is consistent
with the self-
concept and is
therefore perceived
accurately

Experience that
is inconsistent
with the self-
concept and is
therefore defended
against with denial
or distortion

Figure 3-7. In Rogers' theory self-concept and experience can be fairly congruent, as in drawing A, somewhat incongruent, as in drawing B, or very incongruent, as in drawing C. The greater the incongruence, the more the person must defend against experiences that are inconsistent with the self-concept and, hence, the greater the maladjustment. The goal of psychotherapy is to alter the self-concept in such a way that the person can accurately perceive his or her internal and external experiences without the need to be defensive.

(inaccurate perception, defensiveness, and breakdown) may be reversed is by receiving **unconditional positive regard** from another person. This may occur in psychotherapy, marriage, or close friendship. This leads to an increase in the person's own unconditional positive self-regard. With the reduction of threat, there is less need for defense and increased potential for accurate perception. With self and experience more congruent, psychological adjustment is increased. The person functions on the basis of felt experience and not on the basis of distorted perceptions. Thus, he or she can become a fully functioning person open to experience, free of defensive distortion, and able to have a high positive regard for both self and others.

Origins of the Self-Concept.   Rogers proposed that a person's self-concept and values are acquired during early interactions with a significant other person, most often the mother. Different kinds of parent–child interactions are described by Rogers (1951) as having quite different effects on the development of the self. For all infants, the first dawning of awareness involves likes and dislikes, pleasure and pain. Being cold is disliked; being cuddled is liked. In addition to physical stimuli, judgments by others come to be perceived as pleasant or unpleasant. "You're a good boy" is pleasant to hear, while "You're a naughty boy" is not. Since judgmental statements by parents often have a greater influence than the child's own perceptions, inconsistency between them can lead to the distortions in perception and symbolization discussed earlier. For example, a little boy may enjoy hitting his baby brother but is told by his parents that he feels only love for him. To maintain the positive regard of his parents and himself, the child can come to believe that he really does feel only love for his brother. Thus, the visceral reaction is hate and the self-perception is love. The consequence of such imposed distortions, as we have seen, is maladjustment. Rogers suggests a more beneficial kind of interaction between parent and child that can have quite different consequences with respect to the child's self structure. It is possible for early experience to form the basis for a psychologically well-adjusted self. The beginning would be the same, with the child feeling various likes and dislikes. If it happened that sometimes he hated his baby brother and felt good when he hit him, parents could react in such a way as *not* to create a distorted self. The parent could (1) accept and recognize the child's satisfaction at hurting his brother, (2) at the same time accept and love the child himself, and (3) still make it clear that this kind of behavior cannot be accepted in the family. According to Rogers,

> The child in this relationship experiences no threat to his concept of himself as a loved person. He can experience fully and accept within himself and as a part of himself his aggressive feelings toward his baby brother. He can experience fully the perception that his hitting behavior is not liked by the person who loves him. . . . Because the budding structure of the self is not threatened by loss of love, because feelings are accepted by his parent, the child in this instance does not need to deny to awareness the satisfactions which he is experiencing, nor does he need to distort his experience of the parental reaction and regard it as his own. He retains instead a secure self which can serve to guide his behavior by freely admitting to awareness, in accurately symbolized form, all the relevant evidence of his experience in terms of his organismic satisfactions, both immediate and longer range. [1951, p. 502]

COGNITIVE THEORIES OF PERSONALITY

Among the ways in which personality theories differ is the relative emphasis on the role of internal versus external events. Both emphases have been represented in the theories discussed so far; an example is Jung versus Skinner. Another difference concerns the characterization of human beings as either emotional/irrational/unconscious or intellectual/rational/conscious. You might think of Freud versus Rotter. The final theoretical approach represents a special combination of these two dimensions: it propounds an internal, intellectual/rational/conscious view of humanity. It can be argued that the most distinctive aspect of our species is the ability to think symbolically and deal abstractly with past, present, and future aspects of our experience. To focus on these internal events and consider this functioning as a rational activity results in a **cognitive theory** of personality.

The Importance of Thought Processes

One of the basic assumptions of cognitive theorists is that human behavior is based on the individual's personal interpretation of events rather than on "objective" reality. Debbie likes the taste of black olives, finds Ed handsome, enjoys disco music, and believes that the government spends too much money on welfare, while Janice dislikes black olives, thinks Ed is repulsive, hates disco, and thinks more money should be spent on welfare. There is no sense in trying to deal with the "real" taste of those olives, the appearance of Ed, the aesthetics of Disco Duck, or the merits of different social philosophies. The perceptions of each person are equally valid, and their behavior will be consistent with those perceptions.

This approach to human functioning is known as **phenomenology.** The goal is to understand how each person perceives and categorizes his or her experiences. Some of the theorists we have discussed earlier have stressed the phenomenological approach in varying degrees. For example, Allport emphasized the unique individual and the idiographic approach, and Rogers stresses the importance of reality *as it is perceived.*

One of the best known early phenomenological theories was that of Kurt Lewin (1935, 1951). He proposed that behavior is determined by events in the **life space.** This consists of the person and his or her psychological environment, as shown in Figure 3–8. In his theory, Lewin dealt with the dynamic, ever-changing events of the life space and each person's attempt to structure experience.

With respect to more current psychological research, perhaps the best known example of this general approach is Leon Festinger's (1957, 1958) theory of **cognitive dissonance.** The focus of this theory is on cognitions as the unit of study. The general idea is that we strive to be consistent in our cognitive structure; inconsistency or dissonance is unpleasant, and the person is motivated to avoid or reduce it. For example, if you *know* that you smoke two packs of cigarettes each day and you also *know* that most research on the topic shows that smoking is hazardous to your health, these two cognitions are dissonant. You can approach this cognitive inconsistency in a variety of ways. You can stop smoking, you can fail to think about or

all of the other external
events in the world

Figure 3-8.   In Lewin's theory, the behavior of an individual is a function of the person (P) and his or her psychological environment (E), or *life space*. The remaining environmental events were by definition irrelevant in terms of their influence on that individual.

remember the scientific findings, you can read only the conclusions of research financed by American tobacco manufacturers, and so forth.

The basic point is that to some theorists the central concern is the way we as rational individuals interpret our surroundings and act on the basis of those interpretations.

Kelly's Psychology of Personal Constructs

A consideration of the cognitive approach brings us to a final personality theorist, George A. Kelly. This psychologist argued (Kelly, 1955) that each person behaves like a scientist who functions by generating hypotheses and devising ways to test his or her beliefs about the world. The resulting constructs are unique to each person. Kelly explicitly rejects the usefulness of such familiar concepts as learning, ego, emotion, motivation, reinforcement, and the unconscious.

Kelly was born in 1905 on a Kansas farm. After studying physics and mathematics as an undergraduate, he switched to psychology and received a Ph.D. in 1931 from Iowa State University. Like many of the other personality theorists he was involved in clinical practice in addition to his research at Fort Hays State College, in the Navy, and at the University of Maryland. The bulk of his career was spent at Ohio State University where he and Julian Rotter were colleagues, representing two important and quite different branches of personality theory. George Kelly died in 1966.

Kelly argued that if the scientist's ultimate aim is to be able to predict and control, it is reasonable to believe that each person has the same goals. To achieve that end, we create and try out our own **personal constructs** that allow us to understand, predict, and control the environment. This is an active process in which we work hard to interpret reality. There are always different ways of making sense of the same events— **constructive alternativism.** Different alternatives can lead to quite different behavior. One aspect of political rhetoric is the attempt to convince the public that one interpretation of the economy, foreign affairs, the nation's priorities, and so forth is preferable to another. If your construction of the world includes a threatening communist menace, you make different decisions than you would if your perceived world were composed of the imperialist conspiracies of capitalists.

Kelly believed that the process of devising and testing constructs was a central part of our activity. We seek meaning—"To construe is to hear the whisper of recurrent themes in the events that reverberate around us" (Kelly, 1955, p. 76). Rather than stressing *past* experiences, he indicated that the *future* was more important to most of us. We anticipate what will happen as a result of what we do.

Each person's construction of the world is organized into a structure that distinguishes degrees of generality and importance. An example of such an organization is shown in Figure 3-9. In general, there is a tendency to organize cognitions into a limited number of the most important (superordinate) constructs and then to subdivide these into subordinate constructs of lesser importance. Each of us employs only a certain number of dimensions to categorize our experiences.

People are motivated to make their system of constructs as useful as possible in order to anticipate future consequences of their acts. This can be done by narrowing one's focus to a limited number of constructs and becoming an "expert" on a few topics or by widening one's horizons to include as much as possible, thus knowing "a little bit about everything." as with a scientific theory, an individual's construction of the world can lead to inaccurate predictions and so require revision. In some instances there can be a dramatic restructuring, so that the person suddenly views the world in an entirely different way.

In interpersonal situations, each of us brings our own constructs to the interaction, and we may or may not hold congruent world views. What we try to do is to guess at one another's constructs (as in the current phrase "I know where you're coming from") and play roles that facilitate interaction (student and teacher, for example). The more roles a person can play, the more effective his or her interpersonal relationships.

Kelly outlined numerous aspects of the development and organization of constructs, but we will examine only one of these. He devised a

Figure 3-9. In Kelly's theory, each person's constructs are said to be organized in a hierarchy. Thus, designating a person as either good or bad could be the most important, or superordinate, level of conceptualization. Of less importance, might be the classification of the person as helpful rather than dangerous, clean rather than dirty, and so forth (subordinate constructs).

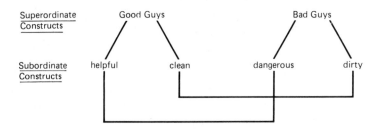

measuring device, the **Role Construct Repertory Test** (or **Rep Test**) that asks a subject to list the significant people in his or her life. Then these names are put in groups of three; the person specifies how two of them are alike and how they are different from the third. The final result is a grid that shows how that person organizes the interpersonal world. Factor analysis is used to identify the way in which constructs are grouped. One important insight into the person is whether he or she uses many constructs or only a few—the size of that person's repertory of roles. A limited repertory indicates a restricted and probably oversimplified view of others.

In describing Kelly's theory, as with those described earlier, we have been able to provide only an overview of the theorist's approach along with a sampling of specific details. A thorough understanding of any of these formulations requires more extensive contact with the original books and articles that present the theories. Nevertheless, we hope that these two chapters help establish a perspective and suggest the range of approaches to understanding personality. With these theories as background, we will now turn our attention to the kinds of research problems being investigated in the field of personality psychology.

SUMMARY

As psychologists began developing personality theories, their approaches differed considerably from those of earlier analysts. Despite the diversity of psychological theories, there has been general agreement about the importance of quantification, prediction, and hypothesis testing.

Trait theories assume that people differ along a finite series of dimensions. Henry A. Murray founded the study of personality psychology at Harvard. Among his contributions was an attempt to identify all of the basic and learned human needs. He also developed the Thematic Apperception Test to measure these needs along with other aspects of personality. Gordon Allport, one of Murray's colleagues, established the first extensive trait theory of personality, but he was most interested in the unique individual. Raymond Cattell brought test construction skills and statistical sophistication to trait theory, as did Hans Eysenck. As part of empirically based theory, Cattell has identified sixteen basic source traits. Most of today's trait research focuses on a single dimension, such as coronary-prone behavior, rather than on the total array of human traits.

The learning theory approach to personality began with the efforts of Hull's group at Yale to translate Freudian concepts into principles of learning. The stimulus-response theory of John Dollard and Neal Miller is perhaps the best example of this work. Though B. F. Skinner's principles of operant conditioning do not constitute a personality theory, they have frequently been applied to personality and to attempts to bring about personality change. Currently the most successful version of the learning-oriented approach is social learning theory as created by Julian Rotter and extended by Walter Mischel and Albert Bandura. In addition to emphasizing the importance of external events such as reinforcement, there is also recognition of the equal importance of internal processes such as expectancies and self-regulating cognitions.

Humanistic theories of personality were developed in part because some psychologists felt that both psychoanalysts and experimentally inclined psychologists treated human beings as mere research subjects. It was felt that such an approach ignored the basic goodness of people as well as their innate tendency to grow toward higher and better levels of functioning. Abraham Maslow outlined such a process in his need hierarchy which describes the potential for psychological growth and eventual self-actualization. The most influential of the theorists with humanistic interests has been Carl Rogers. In the development of client-centered therapy and a self-theory of personality, Rogers has consistently stressed the importance of the need for positive regard, the actualizing tendency that motivates each of us, and the crucial ability to be able to perceive our experiences accurately.

Cognitive theories of personality stress the role of rational thought processes and the phenomenological approach. That is, people act on the basis of their perceptions of the world rather than in response to some generally defined external reality. Examples of cognitive theorists include Kurt Lewin who emphasized the life space, Leon Festinger with his theory of cognitive dissonance, and George Kelly who built a theory of personal constructs.

SUGGESTED READINGS

CATTELL, R. B. *Personality and learning theory.* New York: Springer, 1979 (Vol. 1), 1980 (Vol. 2). A comprehensive effort to bring together the principles of personality and learning by the distinguished trait theorist. The author shows how the environmental influences stressed by learning theorists interact with personality structure as defined by trait theorists.

DEMBROSKI, T. M., WEISS, S. M., SHIELDS, J. L., HAYNES, S. G., FEINLEIB, M. (eds.) *Coronary-prone behavior.* New York: Springer-Verlag, 1978. An important review of research on coronary-prone behavior, including assessment techniques, cultural influences, childhood development, and ways to alter such behavior.

DOLLARD, J., & MILLER, N. E. *Personality and psychotherapy: An analysis in terms of learning, thinking, and culture.* New York: McGraw-Hill, 1950. Though this book was written over three decades ago, it presents what is still an interesting and informative description of a stimulus-response theory of personality. The reformulation of Freudian theory in principles of learning is an impressive achievement.

EVANS, R. I. *Carl Rogers: The man and his ideas.* New York: Dutton, 1975. A very interesting portrait of Carl Rogers, including a description of his contributions to psychology, his debate with B. F. Skinner on the control of human behavior, and a complete bibliography of his work.

EWEN, R. B.   *An introduction to theories of personality.* New York: Academic Press, 1980. This is a very readable and up-to-date summary of the major theories of personality. It includes such student-oriented features as capsule summaries of each theorist's terminology, applications of the theories, and biographical sketches of the major contributors to this field.

SKINNER, B. F.   *Particulars of my life.* New York: McGraw-Hill, 1976. An informative and revealing autobiography of a leading psychologist. In his life story, Skinner presents insights into the factors that had an influence on his career and his theoretical development.

Chapter Four

PERSONALITY RESEARCH: INTERNAL AND EXTERNAL DETERMINANTS OF BEHAVIOR

In this chapter you will read about the following topics:

MEASURING HUMAN BEHAVIOR

In a universe far away lying in other dimensions of time and space, there is a planet much like our own on which evolution has progressed in a similar way and at a similar pace. The major differences lie in some aspects of science and technology. In this other world, they are ahead of us in some respects, and they lag behind in others.

Imagine for a moment a planet on which Galileo had not constructed an open-air "thermoscope" as he did on earth in 1593. This instrument measured temperature changes by means of a glass tube dipped below the surface of a container of water. Without that beginning, Fahrenheit would probably not have devised a mercury thermometer in 1714, and Celsius would have had no reason to propose a centigrade scale to indicate how much the mercury expanded and contracted with heat and cold. In such a parallel world, the human species could develop much as we have, but without being able to measure temperature the way we do today.

In the capital of one of the most powerful nations, the staff of Senator Noxoius Ire met in his suite in the Ornate Office Building. They knew that the senator was expecting a report that would allow him to present his monthly Wool-over-the-Eyes Award to someone who was spending government funds in a manner he deemed wasteful. Among his favorite targets were the holders of research grants whose work could usually be made to look ridiculous with the right choice of words.

When the senator swept into the meeting, he was obviously pleased. This was an aspect of his job that he enjoyed. It combined almost certain public attention, the chance to make some egg-head squirm, and the virtuous appearance of being a monetary watchdog. His Emotional Index as indicated by a digital wrist band was 97.2, very high indeed. (You see, on that planet the technology for measuring many psychological variables was advanced far beyond our own.)

"What have you got for me, boys?"

One of the staff members spoke up. "Well, sir, we have looked into one project that may suit your needs. There's a professor out west who is using grant money in an attempt to measure temperature. The information I have indicates that he is using some kind of glass tube filled with liquid. When the weather warms up, the liquid expands. Supposedly, there is some relationship between how hot it is and how much liquid rises up in the tube. He plans eventually to use it to measure body temperature."

Laughing, the senator said, "That's a good one. For $60,000, this jerk is going to tell us that water can boil over. How about a headline like, RESEARCHER FULL OF HOT AIR INVENTS TUBE FULL OF HOT WATER?"

His staff laughed appreciatively. They began suggesting possible points to be included in the press release. "There are some things too vague and too personal to be subjected to scientific measurement. Our language tells us that temperature is an internally controlled aspect of our lives and not something external that can be reduced to mere numbers. Expressions such as 'She's a hot number,' 'He's a cool dude,' 'My boss is a hothead,' 'I quit cigarettes cold turkey,' and 'Come on baby, light my fire' demonstrate this conclusively."

Leaning back, the senator interrupted. "That's good, but we need to conclude with something even stronger. Let's try this. Frankly, I am appalled by this use of tax dollars in such a wasteful manner. In our hearts we know that every living being in our great land has a unique body temperature. This basic individuality cannot be

measured and assigned a number like so many rump roasts at a butcher shop.
Temperature is beyond the scope of our measuring instruments, and I for one am
glad."
The staff members stood and applauded, some with tears in their eyes.

EVEN THOUGH THERE ARE obviously no such controversies about the measurement of temperature on our planet, such doubts *have* been expressed
about the assessment of various behavioral characteristics. With respect to
intelligence, anxiety, and love, for example, there are those who would
argue as to whether they are internally or externally based. Some can even
be found who believe that these characteristics cannot or should not be
measured. It is somewhat difficult to realize that such questions were actually raised with respect to physical variables in the past. In this chapter,
we will describe the way in which behavior can be measured, and we will
deal with the general issue of internal versus external control of behavior.

MEASURING HUMAN BEHAVIOR

When you are asked to describe another person, to say what he or she is
really like, you probably respond with a series of adjectives. You indicate
where the person falls along various dimensions. In a rough way we also
tend to compare the people we describe by saying that John is smarter than
Bill or that Kathy is more outgoing than Linda. We seem to assume that
descriptions and comparisons of this kind provide useful predictive information. That is, you might decide whether to study for a test with John or
spend time at a party with Kathy on the basis of such information.

In the same general way, personality research has frequently involved efforts to identify and operationalize the important dimensions of
individual differences.

Among the requirements of any science is a set of reliable and valid
instruments with which to measure the variables under study. As any field
advances there is a steady improvement in its measuring instruments. No
advantage is gained from developing precise measuring tools in the absence of theory, but in the absence of such tools theoretical advances are
necessarily limited. Much of the history of science consists of the interplay
of theory and methodology.

In studies of human behavior the problem of measurement has
been a difficult one. Here we will examine some of the solutions that have
been developed. Bear in mind that the measurement problems of psychology are not conceptually different from the measurement problems of
other fields. Just four centuries ago the measurement of temperature really
was an unsolved mystery.

What is there about a rating scale or a device like a thermometer that makes it a measuring instrument? The primary feature of measurement is that it differentiates a variable along a scale. The differentiation may be along a simple **ordinal scale,** which defines an order of events. A few thousand years ago, temperature was assessed in ancient Egypt by having judges estimate it along a four-point rating scale that ranged from "feels like the hottest day of summer" to "feels like the coldest day of winter." Or it may be along a more precise scale with **equal intervals** as in the division marks on a mercury thermometer). Quantification occurs when we assign numbers to the points on these scales; this is a great advantage because it allows us to deal with the variable in mathematical terms. Psychologists have four main techniques to scale behavior: ranking, rating, counting frequencies, and using a physical dimension.

Ranking.   As an example of behavior measurement, let's say that you are interested in assessing sexual arousal. One of the simplest approaches is to **rank order** people along the dimension. If no other measuring instrument were available, judges could observe what a group of people say about their sexual feelings and how they behave; then they could be ranked from least to most excited. This kind of ordering of people becomes extremely difficult when the group gets larger. You can rank three people much more easily than you can rank 30 people, and ranking 300 people is almost impossible. Ranking also gives information only within a given group, and the information often has no meaning across groups. For example, the person who is ranked number one in arousal in one group may be the least excited in another group.

Rating Scales.   Another familiar way to measure behavior is to ask people to provide a **rating** of themselves or others along an ordinal scale. Thus, you could indicate whether you like or dislike a TV show on a two-point scale, or you could make finer distinctions by indicating degrees of liking–disliking along a scale with more than two levels. With sexual arousal, for example, after viewing an erotic movie you could describe your reactions by making a check mark on the following five-point rating scale:

Extremely aroused _____
Strongly aroused _____
Moderately aroused _____
Mildly aroused _____
Not at all aroused _____

In theory, such a scale could contain any number of points, but in fact people are not able to make meaningful distinctions beyond seven or nine points. With both ranking and rating, the ability to differentiate is quite limited. For finer and more precise behavior measurement, one must turn to other techniques.

Frequency Count.   When responses can occur over and over again, one way to measure behavior is with respect to the total number of times the person engaged in a given act within a specific time period—that is, a **frequency count** can be made. For example, level of sexual excitement could be measured by asking people the number of times they had engaged in intercourse during the past week. A different approach using frequency is to construct a test containing a series of related items. Thus, a sexual test might ask about a person's behavior with respect to thinking about sex, dreaming about sex, reading erotic material, attending X-rated movies, masturbating, spending time with a member of the opposite sex, engaging in intercourse, and so forth. The total number of these different activities in which the person had engaged would constitute an index of his or her level of sexual arousal. This approach to measurement is common in the field of personality and represents a potential improvement over ranking or rating. However, it is a somewhat indirect procedure that very often rests on verbal reports of attitudes, feelings, or actions.

Using a Physical Dimension.   The physical sciences had to face the problems of measuring time, distance, temperature, weight, and so forth long before there was such a thing as behavioral science. Whenever human behavior can be measured along these well-established physical dimensions, it is clearly an advantage. As we will see in Chapter 11, sexual arousal in both males and females is accompanied by an increased flow of blood in the genitals. Instruments have been developed to assess these changes by means of devices attached to the penis or inserted into the vagina. The result is an extremely objective way to measure sexual arousal. Male excitement is measured in terms of increases in the volume or length of the penis and female excitement in terms of the light reflected by the walls of the vagina.

Reliability: Is the Measure Consistent?

The consistency with which a variable is ordered along a dimension is the **reliability** of measurement. Good measurement is consistent and bad measurement inconsistent. Inconsistency in measurement is called **measurement error.** In any field, the more consistent the measuring device, the better the data. A set of numbers obtained from an unreliable instrument is partly "garbage" because such numbers reflect not only the variable under study but also random measurement errors. The lawful relationships that the scientist is seeking are often obscured by such errors. Imagine the task of attempting to work with time if one's only measuring instrument were a clock whose minute hand did not move at a regular speed.

Stimulus Consistency.   It is never possible to control all of the stimuli that are present in the testing situation. When a test is given, the test materials themselves are only one aspect of the total array of stimuli to which the subject may be responding. Figure 4-1 depicts the situation in which the test is the "central stimulus," and all other external factors are the "peripheral stimuli." Let us say, for example, that subjects are asked to write stories in response to four drawings. The central stimulus consists of those four pictures and the instructions given to the subject. Individual differences in responding to such pictures have proved to be a useful indicator of motivation, as will be seen in Chapter 8. What if the four pictures were changed in some way from one subject to another? Under these conditions individual differences in the stories might be a function of differences in the pictures. While no experimenter would make such changes on purpose, accidental changes in the peripheral stimuli (e.g., the temperature of the room, the number of subjects present, the time of day at which the pictures are shown) are always possible. Therefore, the psychologist must describe the central and peripheral stimuli in painstaking detail so that they may be reproduced as exactly as possible by anyone who wishes to measure the same variable. Ideally, all stimuli are kept constant. When this is not done, stimulus inconsistency results in less reliable measurement.

A related problem arises when different stimuli are combined in a test because they are known to be equivalent in some way. For example, in

Figure 4-1.   When a person takes a test he or she may be responding not only to the test itself but also to any number of other, peripheral stimuli. If such stimuli do not remain constant each time the test is given, reliability will suffer because the responses to the test will vary as a function of those peripheral influences.

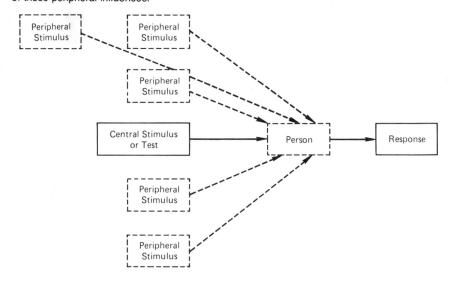

an intelligence test a series of vocabulary items are assumed to have something in common even though each specific word in the list is different. Test items are judged to be equivalent if they elicit correlated responses. This type of reliability may be determined by correlating items or groups of items with one another. The resulting correlation is known as the **coefficient of internal consistency.** When one half of the test is correlated with the other half, the result is called **split-half reliability.**

When more than one version of the test has been constructed, it is necessary to know whether the two sets of stimuli are equivalent. For example, you expect a yardstick and a tape measure to yield the same measure of distance. The correlation between two test forms is called the **coefficient of equivalence.**

Response Consistency.   Objective measurement requires that if different people judge the responses they arrive as closely as possible at the same numerical score. Without very high **interjudge consistency,** reliable measurement is impossible. Careful training of scorers is needed to obtain such consistency, especially when the judgments are subjective. Interjudge consistency is highest when response measurement is based on simple perceptual judgments such as counting black marks on a true–false answer sheet or reading a number on a dial. Such consistency is lowest when judgments must be made with respect to complex responses such as overt behavior (Bourne, 1977).

Figure 4-2. Not everyone agrees that the same stimulus is equally interesting or pleasant. One task of the personality psychologist is to develop and use techniques of personality measurement.   (Sing-Si Schwartz)

With most measures of traits and abilities, responses are expected to be stable over time. In a similar way, your bathroom scales should not show extreme variation in your weight from day to day. The **coefficient of stability** or **test–retest reliability** is the correlation between scores on tests given on two different occasions.

Validity: What Is Being Measured?

Validity refers to the "truth" of the measure, the degree to which the test is capable of achieving a predictive goal. It is sometimes defined as the extent to which a test actually measures what it is supposed to measure. As with reliability, different types of validity have been defined.

Content of the Items. The simplest form of validity is defined by the item content. A measure has **face validity** to the extent that the items are related logically or reasonably to the variable that the test is intended to measure. For example, if someone constructed an intelligence test, it would have face validity if it contained material such as vocabulary, arithmetic, reasoning, and memory. A test that required the subject to lift weights, inquired about sexual habits, or examined the subject for bad breath would not be considered a measure of intelligence.

A more sophisticated version of face validity is **content validity.** If a test is supposed to constitute a sample of a certain body of material, there should be evidence that it is in fact an adequate sample. For example, an algebra test should consist of algebra problems that represent the material covered by the course. In the field of personality we do not have a specific body of material that test items are supposed to sample. Therefore, there is usually no way to specify content validity for a personality test.

Predicting Criterion Behavior. The type of validity that is most often discussed is suited mainly to applied situations in which there is a specific criterion behavior that the test is designed to predict. For example, in a manufacturing plant employees on the assembly line must be able to perform a mechanical task quickly and accurately. An employee selection device that predicts that ability would save time and money. The validity of a test used for this purpose might be determined by the correlation between test scores and the number of parts assembled per hour without error. The higher the correlation, the more valid the test and the better the prediction of job performance; this correlation would indicate the test's **predictive validity.** It has been found, for example, that the written tests one takes in order to obtain a driver's licence have no validity as predictors of driving behavior (Conley & Smiley, 1976). That is, there is *no relation* between test scores and such criterion behavior as violating the law or being involved in automobile accidents.

A distinction is sometimes made between predictive validity and concurrent validity. Predictive validity refers to the correlation between test scores and criterion performance at a later time. **Concurrent validity** refers to the correlation between test scores and criterion performance at about the same time.

To What Are Test Scores Related?   Except for tests designed to predict a specific behavior, no single comparison or correlation can be said to indicate the validity of the test. **Construct validity,** however, involves *many* such indicators. The point is that there is no single criterion by which most personality tests can be "validated." How could you determine whether a test of prejudice is a valid one? The term *prejudice* refers to a variety of behaviors and attitudes. A valid test of prejudice would have to be related to several kinds of responses in different situations.

Construct validity, then, is determined by studying as many relations as possible. It is not quite accurate to speak of personality tests as valid or invalid. It is more realistic to say that a given test has been found to be related to certain variables. From the standpoint of validity the most meaningful question in personality is, "To what are test scores related?"

Constructing Reliable Measures of Behavior

The Intuitive Approach.   In constructing any test, the initial step is to obtain or devise a series of stimulus items that make logical sense. There are no hard-and-fast rules to follow, and there is probably a degree of both theory and art in devising any measure of behavior.

At first glance it does not seem likely that simply putting a group of items together in an **intuitive approach** would yield a reliable test. However, research in personality has shown the usefulness of this approach. The measure of anxiety (described in Chapter 7) and the measure of attraction (described in Chapter 9) were constructed in this way. In fact, Ashton and Goldberg (1973) have shown that graduate psychology students and even people with no formal training in the field are able to use the intuitive approach and construct scales as good as or better than tests based on elaborate test construction procedures.

The Internal Consistency or "Bootstrap" Approach.   Item selection can go beyond intuitive judgments by determining the extent to which each item is related to the others; in other words, the items are good if they provide **internal consistency.** Those which prove to be unrelated are discarded. In a sense the test is "lifted up by its own **bootstraps.**"

The usual procedure is to begin with the intuitive approach and then evaluate each item. The test is given to a large number of subjects, and their responses are scored according to the intuitively based scoring system. Then the relationship between the score on each item and the score on the test as a whole is determined. A good item is one that is related to the total score; that is, it is measuring the same thing. A bad item is one that is unrelated to the total score. This type of **item analysis** provides an empirical check of the test constructor's skill in building a consistent measuring device. The measure of authoritarianism described in the following chapter was developed using the bootstrap approach.

The External Criterion Approach: Correlational.   Whenever an **external criterion** exists for the variable being measured, it is a good idea to use it as the basis for selecting test items. All potential items are judged in terms of their correlation with the criterion.

With this method people who differ on the criterion variable are given the test. Those test items which distinguish among them are assumed to measure some behavioral trait on which they differ. The measure of intelligence discussed in Chapter 6 was built in this way, using age differences as the criterion. For example, if a potential item was answered correctly by more 6-year-olds than five-year-olds, it would be retained on the final test.

The External Criterion Approach: Experimental.   If it is possible to manipulate the criterion behavior in an experiment, another method of test construction may be considered. Rather than depend on correlations with other behaviors, the test builder may bring about the condition he or she wishes to measure and then determine those items which measure it best. In the test construction phase an experimental group and a control group are used. The central stimulus is kept the same for both groups, while some of the peripheral stimuli are varied in a certain way. For example, an experimenter might present two groups with a series of pictures of food items and ask the subjects to rate them on a scale from one to ten (the higher the rating, the more they like the picture). Each picture would be part of the central stimulus. The peripheral stimulus to be varied might be hunger. The experimenter would instruct one group—the experimental group—not to eat for six hours before coming to the experiment. The other group—the control group—would be tested shortly after mealtime. The experimental group represents the hunger condition and the control group the "normal" condition.

In this experiment the results would probably show that the hungry subjects rated the food pictures higher than the control subjects did. When such a test is given in the future, it can be assumed that those subjects whose responses are like those of the experimental group are hungry. By the way, it should be obvious that there is no need to construct a psychological test to measure hunger.

This approach to test construction has not been used as much as the other approaches. In part, this is a function of our inability to manipulate many of the variables we desire to measure. It is not possible, for example, to create conditions that make subjects more intelligent.

Motivational states can be manipulated, however. The use of this method to develop a measure of need for achievement is described in Chapter 8.

RESEARCH
CLOSE-UP

Constructing a Personality Test:
The Crucial Importance of Cross-Validation

In each of the methods of test construction described in this chapter, there are two essential steps in determining the items to be included in the final measuring instrument. In the first step all of the items in a given pool are evaluated. Those that meet the necessary standards (correlation with total score, correlation with criterion, etc.) are retained, and the remaining items are discarded. At that point, however, the job is only half done. It is very likely that some or perhaps all of the items are worthless. How could that be?

The problem, especially if there are a large number of items in the original pool, is that many items will meet the criterion *by chance alone*. That is, they do not actually measure what they are supposed to measure. The only way this problem can be dealt with is by going through the test construction procedure a second time with a new sample of subjects. This **cross-validation** of the test is an essential step because an item is very unlikely to meet the criterion twice on a chance basis. Thus, any item that is identified as a good one in both the original sample and the cross-validational sample is assumed to be valid.

To demonstrate the crucial nature of the cross-validation process, Blumenfeld (1972) conducted a mock test construction experiment using Art Buchwald's amusing *North Dakota Null-Hypothesis Brain Inventory* as the item pool. A group of students in an introductory management course at Georgia State University responded to the true–false test in Table 4-1. You may want to take it yourself (see page 128).

The behavior to be measured was college ability. The correlational external criterion method was used, with grade point average (GPA) as the criterion. Each item was evaluated with respect to its correlation with GPA, and nine items were found to be significantly related to the criterion. The items and their scoring key are as follows: 5-F, 6-T, 11-F, 16-T, 17-T, 18-T, 20-T, 27-T, 31-T. Scores on this new nine-item test might appear to be a good measure of college ability in that they correlate well with the criterion *in the original sample of subjects*. How well did you do? If the items were related to grades only by chance, however, they would be useless; this fact could be determined only by evaluating them a second time in a new sample of subjects.

When this step was taken, all nine items were found to be unrelated to GPA, as Blumenfeld of course expected. He points out that many tests used in business, including some used to select personnel, have been constructed in just this fashion—*without cross-validation*. Perhaps this will convince you to look very carefully at how tests are constructed. Otherwise, you may someday find yourself being accepted or rejected for a job on the basis of whether you answer "true" or "false" to items such as, "I am never startled by a fish."

Table 4-1. Art Buchwald devised a "personality test," the North Dakota Null-Hypothesis Brain Inventory, that was used by Blumenfeld (1972) to demonstrate the necessity of cross-validation in constructing a test.

North Dakota Null-Hypothesis Brain Inventory

Respond to each item by placing a check mark under the column labeled TRUE or the column labeled FALSE.

TRUE   FALSE

—— —— 1. I salivate at the sight of mittens.
—— —— 2. If I go into the street, I'm apt to be bitten by a horse.
—— —— 3. Some people never look at me.
—— —— 4. Spinach makes me feel alone.
—— —— 5. My sex life is A-okay.
—— —— 6. When I look down from a high spot, I want to spit.
—— —— 7. I like to kill mosquitoes.
—— —— 8. Cousins are not to be trusted.
—— —— 9. It makes me embarrassed to fall down.
—— —— 10. I get nauseous from too much roller skating.
—— —— 11. I think most people would cry to gain a point.
—— —— 12. I cannot read or write.
—— —— 13. I am bored by thoughts of death.
—— —— 14. I become homicidal when people try to reason with me.
—— —— 15. I would enjoy the work of a chicken flicker.
—— —— 16. I am never startled by a fish.
—— —— 17. My mother's uncle was a good man.
—— —— 18. I don't like it when somebody is rotten.
—— —— 19. People who break the law are wise guys.
—— —— 20. I have never gone to pieces over the weekend.
—— —— 21. I think beavers work too hard.
—— —— 22. I use shoe polish to excess.
—— —— 23. God is love.
—— —— 24. I like mannish children.
—— —— 25. I have always been disturbed by the sight of Lincoln's ears.
—— —— 26. I always let people get ahead of me at swimming pools.
—— —— 27. Most of the time I go to sleep without saying goodby.
—— —— 28. I am not afraid of picking up door knobs.
—— —— 29. I believe I smell as good as most people.
—— —— 30. Frantic screams make me nervous.
—— —— 31. It's hard for me to say the right thing when I find myself in a room full of mice.
—— —— 32. I would never tell my nickname in a crisis.
—— —— 33. A wide necktie is a sign of disease.
—— —— 34. As a child I was deprived of licorice.
—— —— 35. I would never shake hands with a gardener.
—— —— 36. My eyes are always cold.

INTERNAL DETERMINANTS OF BEHAVIOR: THE ROLE OF PERSONALITY TRAITS

As described in the preceding chapters, many assumptions about human behavior are based on the idea that personality traits are either genetically determined or learned at a very early age. When we describe other people we tend to imply that they always have been, always are, and always will be behaving in a manner consistent with the category in which we place them. If one of your friends is said to have a sense of humor, for example, you might guess that he was the class cutup as a youngster, that he would be equally amusing in a chemistry lab and on a camping trip, and that he will be as much fun next year as he is this year. This predictability and resistance to change is what we usually mean by the term *personality*. William James described this stability as

the enormous fly-wheel of society, its most precious conservative agent. . . . Already at the age of twenty-five you see the professional mannerism settling down on the young commercial traveller, on the young doctor, on the young minister, on the young counsellor-at-law. You see the little lines of cleavage running through the character, the tricks of thought, the prejudices, the ways of the "shop," in a word, from which the man can by-and-by no more escape than his coat-sleeves can suddenly fall into a new set of folds. On the whole, it is best he should not escape. It is well for the world that in most of us, by the age of thirty, the character has set like plaster, and will never soften again. [1950, p. 121]

Personality Measurement: Trying to Learn a Lot by Observing a Little

The assumption that behavioral traits are stable over time and from one situation to another has led to certain kinds of measurement strategies. Heine (1969) notes that in its early stages science tends to involve ideas based on intuition. It is not surprising that theories of personality first focused on those traits which are found "inside" the person (Sampson, 1977). From this perspective the ideal measuring device would be one that obtained from inside the individual a limited sample of very special information that could be used to identify his or her basic personality traits. Once these were identified, a great deal would be known about the person's past, present, and future behavior. This type of measurement and its aims are illustrated in Figure 4-3.

Typologies, Body Characteristics, and the Positions of the Planets. The simplicity of typologies has had an appeal through the centuries and has produced Jung's system (described in Chapter 2), Spranger's (1928) typology based on interests and values, and Sheldon's (Sheldon, Stevens, & Tucker, 1970) theory based on body types and associated temperaments.

Nonpsychologists have taken analogous approaches to the prediction of behavior. Phrenologists tried to use bumps on the head as indicators of personality traits. Physiognomists pursued the possibility that facial features (e.g., a strong, assertive chin or a sinister brow) are the best clues. Palmists used the creases on people's hands, and astrologers focused on the positions of the planets when the person was born. The trouble with these systems is that head bumps, noses, life lines, and birth signs have not proven useful as predictors of behavior.

Global Measuring Techniques. In the 1920s and 1930s the strategy

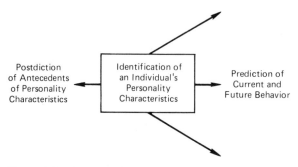

Figure 4-3. An emphasis on personality traits involves a model in which stable internal variables are of central importance. Once those traits are measured, research entails discovery of the antecedents of the personality variable and prediction of as many behaviors as possible on the basis of that variable.

of trying to predict behavior on the basis of a limited observation was pursued in the realm of **projective tests** of personality. Freud's description of unconscious processes provided the underlying rationale for this approach: If a person could be shown an ambiguous stimulus, his or her interpretation of that stimulus would be influenced by unconscious motives. The process was thought to be analogous to dreaming, in which the censoring process was relaxed, permitting unconscious material to rise to the surface in either pure or distorted form.

A Swiss psychiatrist named Hermann Rorschach (1921), felt that patients revealed much about themselves through what they perceived in blots of ink. This procedure became known as the Rorschach Ink Blot Test or Technique. This assessment device gradually became very popular among clinical psychologists and psychiatrists. The promise of obtaining extensive knowledge on the basis of a person's responses to ten ink blots was clearly an exciting one.

In the following decade psychological research at Harvard produced another projective test, the Thematic Apperception Test or TAT (Morgan & Murray, 1938). It consists of a series of pictures that are like illustrations in books or magazines. The person taking the test is asked to make up a story to go with each picture. Again, the assumption is that unconscious material will be revealed as he or she becomes absorbed in the task of creating a fantasy.

These two instruments were followed by many others, especially in the late 1940s and early 1950s. Subjects listened to ambiguous sounds, interpreted drawings of dogs, and created little plays with cardboard figures on a miniature stage set. In each instance unstructured, ambiguous tasks were supposed to encourage the person to reveal material of which he or she had no conscious awareness. The skilled tester could take this material and construct a global personality portrait that would serve as the basis for numerous behavioral predictions.

Among the side effects of the educational boom following World War II was a dramatic increase in personality tests and personality testing. Psychology was among the most rapidly growing fields in this period, stimulated partly by widespread interest in behavioral science, partly by the surge of returning servicemen attending college with financial support from the G.I. Bill, and partly by funds made available through federal research grants as well as training grants and traineeships in clinical psychology. With the influx of personnel and money, clinical psychology became a "growth industry," and its offshoot, personality psychology, was not far behind.

Personality measurement was an integral part of this burgeoning activity, and projective tests were its most popular and promising instruments. In classrooms and clinics the Rorschach and the TAT were taught and put into practice. Murray's claim that the TAT provided an "X-ray of the psyche" stimulated widespread application. Psychologists could ask people to interpret blots or pictures or whatever, and on the basis of such simple and yet mysterious activities they supposedly could peer directly into the mind, even the unconscious, and learn enough to diagnose, describe, and predict behavior. For a field less than half a century old, that would have been a truly impressive feat.

There was, however, a fly in the ointment. Clinical and personality psychology are academic disciplines in which research is stressed as an integral part of both doctoral training and later academic or applied activity. The emphasis on research meant that many of the theses, dissertations, convention papers, and scholarly articles of the postwar years dealt with correlational and experimental studies of personality tests. In the decade of such research following the end of World War II, it became painfully clear to a number of psychologists that the various tests were much less useful than had been hoped.

Julian Rotter was one of the most influential of those who perceived the warning signs in the research findings. In Chapter 3 we described his contributions to personality with the development of social learning theory. Consistent with this approach, in his research, in his training of numerous clinical and personality psychologists, and most notably in the publication of his *Social Learning and Clinical Psychology* in 1954, Rotter questioned the existing approaches to personality measurement. He concluded that there were serious deficiencies in the existing tests:

We have in this field not only many hundreds of articles dealing with research investigations of reliability and validity of personality measurement, but also many published clinical studies or clinical evaluations and many years of experience that have not been formally communicated by publication ... The very best techniques we have are of doubtful validity for predicting the specific behavior of any person in a particular situation. [1954, p. 334]

Similar reactions were soon expressed by others in the field, and it became clear to many that personality measurement had a long way to go.

A Possible Solution: Focusing on Personality Traits

One major alternative to global measures of personality was to focus on smaller segments of behavior. In other words, perhaps the major problem with the measuring devices was that too much was expected from a limited sample of behavior. Instead of trying to learn *all* about a person, why not design the test to learn a great deal about a single aspect of that person?

As described in Chapter 3, many personality psychologists assume that people differ along a series of dimensions, and these dimensions are known as personality **traits** (Hogan, DeSoto, & Solano, 1977). A trait is a fairly stable behavioral characteristic in which individuals differ. In 1936 Allport and Odbert identified almost 20,000 words in the English language that we use to describe how we differ from one another. Some of these words have the same or similar meanings, so the number of *different* trait descriptions can be reduced to 171. This suggests that the construction of 171 personality tests would allow us to measure all of the basic aspects in which people vary.

Actually, no one has undertaken such a task. Some, such as Cattell (1976), have used statistical techniques to identify those traits which form groups or clusters, as was described in the previous chapter. Another approach is to consider the different kinds of traits in terms of subcategories of behavior. For example, Wiggins (1978) has shown that traits involving *interpersonal behavior* can be reduced to eight dimensions:

gregarious-extroverted
ambitious-dominant
arrogant-calculating
cold-quarrelsome
aloof-introverted
lazy-submissive
unassuming-ingenuous
warm-agreeable.

Scales were developed to measure each characteristic, and they are useful in assessing and describing a wide range of interpersonal acts.

A more familiar attempt to assess a major subcategory of personality is the **Minnesota Multiphasic Personality Inventory** or **MMPI** (Hathaway, Monachesi, & Salasin, 1970). This instrument consists of scales whose items have been found to differentiate those with specific psychiatric diagnoses from normals. In addition to using this test to diagnose mental illness, it has been found to be useful as a personality test that predicts a variety of behaviors. For example, when college males were given the MMPI as juniors, their test scores were found to predict their marital status ten years later and whether they had completed an advanced degree (Dworkin & Widom, 1977).

A more popular approach to the measurement and study of traits has been to set aside the problem of measuring either the "total personality" or even major categories of behavior and concentrate on single traits. In the following four chapters such research will be described with respect to authoritarianism, the need for achievement, anxiety, and intelligence. The general idea is to focus on one trait at a time and leave the task of integrating all that we learn about such dimensions to the future.

Figure 4-4. Individuals who are oraphilic have very positive attitudes about food and eating. (Jean-Claude Le Jeone, Stock, Boston)

Measuring a Trait: Food, Glorious Food

BEFORE YOU READ ANY FURTHER, TURN TO TABLE 4-2 AND FOLLOW THE INSTRUCTIONS.

We all spend much of our lives engaging in behaviors related to eating. We plan meals, purchase food, prepare something to eat, and obtain food prepared by others. Most of us eat at least three times a day, not counting what we sometimes consume between meals in the form of snacks. In addition to the behavior itself, there are attitudes and feelings about the eating process. We once had a friend who considered eating a somewhat repulsive activity that one engages in only out of necessity. He preferred eating alone and felt that a group of people dining together was not much different from a group of people defecating together. At the other extreme was another friend whose whole life revolved around eating. We seldom saw him without an apple, a cookie, a banana, or something else edible clutched in his hand. At parties he quickly turned any hors d'oeuvre display into a disaster area. Most of us fall somewhere between these two extremes. Thus, there seems to be a personality trait that could be labeled **oraphilia**. Those who are high in oraphilia have extremely positive attitudes toward food and the eating process; those who are low on this dimension have negative attitudes toward food and eating.

The personality test in Table 4-2 represents an attempt to measure this general trait (Byrne, Golightly, & Capaldi, 1963). It was assumed that positive or negative attitudes toward food and eating are reflected in a variety of food-related activities and that these attitudes are based on positive or negative food-related experiences in childhood. The test is scored so that high scores represent a positive orientation to food and low scores a negative orientation.[1] Your instructor may want to combine the scores of the various members of your class in order to give each student a basis of comparison. If that is done, how do *your* scores compare with those of others in the group? Is your position on the basis of test scores consistent with your own perceptions as to how you feel about food?

Beyond attitudes toward food, there are other characteristics that could be linked with oraphilia. As you may guess from what you read in Chapter 2, since Freud's time speculation in the field of personality has centered on such concepts as the "oral personality." Similarly, Sheldon described a *viscerotonic temperament* as one that is characterized by a relaxed life style, love of comfort, sociability, and a tendency to be affectionate to others. In our research we found a small but significant relation between scores on the food test and scores on a measure of viscerotonia. What behaviors do you think might be related to oraphilia? What predictions would you make? If your instructor agrees, you might want to plan some research in which you explore the relation between scores on the Survey of Eating Habits and other aspects of behavior.

---

[1]The test was constructed using the internal consistency method, with an original sample of 200 college students and a cross-validational sample of another 200 students.

Table 4-2. The Survey of Eating Habits is a personality test designed to measure attitudes toward food. To score the test, turn this page upside down and compare your answers with the scoring key. Give yourself one point for each answer that matches the key. Note that males and females use different keys.

Survey of Eating Habits

Read each statement and decide if it is **true as applied to you** *or* **false as applied to you.**

Do not omit any of the items. Mark either true or false for every one by placing a check mark in the TRUE column or in the FALSE column.

TRUE   FALSE

I. PAST ATTITUDES AND HABITS

1. My family seldom argued at the dinner table.
2. Many different types of meals were served at our house.
3. I did not particularly care for the food served at home.
4. My mother was a good cook.
5. Our family seemed to be in a better disposition at and shortly after meals than before.
6. My mother enjoyed cooking.
7. Meals were simple but substantial in our family.
8. My mother served desserts frequently.
9. Discipline was usually enforced shortly before or after the evening meal.
10. Mealtimes were quite unhurried; in fact they took on the aspect of a social activity.
11. My father enjoyed eating.
12. I enjoyed eating.
13. Younger members of the family were requested not to talk too much at meals.
14. My family often celebrated something important by going to a restaurant.
15. Less than an average amount of conversation occurred at mealtime in my family.
16. My father tended to dampen mealtime conversation.
17. Conversation at meals was more light than serious.
18. Business matters were often discussed at meals (chores, etc.).
19. Flowers or candles were sometimes placed on the table at evening meals.
20. Sometimes my mother would give me my favorite food when I was sick or unhappy.
21. My mother used to take special precautions to avoid giving us contaminated food.
22. The emphasis was on nutritional meals in our family.
23. My mother liked cooking least of all household chores.
24. Meals were quite elaborate in our family.
25. Individuals other than my immediate family, such as grandparents, usually participated in the evening meal.
26. Following the main meal, I tended to linger about the table talking and so on, rather than leaving the table.
27. My mother enjoyed eating.
28. Sometimes I felt like leaving the table before the meal was over.

_____ _____ 29. My mother fixed my favorite foods when I was sick.
_____ _____ 30. At restaurants everything I ordered had to be eaten.
_____ _____ 31. Eating out was infrequent.
_____ _____ 32. The entire family was usually present at the evening meal.
_____ 33. On my birthdays I helped plan the menu.
_____ 34. My mother tended to dampen mealtime conversation.
_____ 35. Discipline was often applied at mealtime.
_____ 36. Family meals were more hurried than unhurried.
_____ 37. My father sometimes scolded us at the evening meal.
_____ 38. At breakfast, I often read what was printed on the cereal boxes.

II. PRESENT ATTITUDES AND HABITS

_____ 39. Mealtime is usually pleasant in my home.
_____ 40. I like to smell food cooking.
_____ 41. In general, I prefer a slow leisurely meal to a quick, hurried one.
_____ 42. I like many different types of food.
_____ 43. I tend to be underweight.
_____ 44. At a party, I tend to eat a lot of peanuts.
_____ 45. I do not care much for desserts.
_____ 46. I seldom like to try a new food.
_____ 47. I often get indigestion or heartburn.
_____ 48. If I am very busy, I may forget all about eating.
_____ 49. Shopping for groceries is unpleasant.
_____ 50. I like to eat foreign foods.
_____ 51. A good wife must be a good cook.
_____ 52. I think that going to an expensive restaurant is a good way to celebrate an important event such as an anniversary, a birthday, etc.
_____ 53. I have a tendency to gain weight.
_____ 54. Sometimes I have a craving for sweets.
_____ 55. I tend to be quiet rather than talkative.
_____ 56. If a child refuses dinner, he should be made to eat.
_____ 57. I almost never eat between meals.
_____ 58. I dislike many foods.
_____ 59. I enjoy eating at restaurants.
_____ 60. I often eat while I am watching television.
_____ 61. Watching people eat makes me hungry.
_____ 62. People who eat heartily in public have bad manners.
_____ 63. I often buy refreshments at movies, ball games, etc.
_____ 64. I sometimes reward myself by eating.
_____ 65. When depressed I sometimes eat my favorite foods.

Scoring key

Males: 2-T, 3-F, 4-T, 5-T, 7-F, 9-F, 10-T, 11-T, 12-T, 15-F, 16-F, 17-T, 18-F, 19-T, 24-T, 25-T, 26-T, 27-T, 32-T, 33-T, 34-F, 37-F, 38-T, 39-T, 42-T, 45-F, 46-F, 47-F, 51-T, 52-T, 53-T, 54-T, 58-F, 60-T, 61-T, 63-T, 64-T.

Females: 1-T, 2-T, 4-T, 5-T, 6-T, 8-T, 9-F, 10-T, 11-T, 12-T, 13-T, 14-T, 15-F, 16-F, 17-T, 18-F, 19-T, 20-T, 21-T, 22-T, 23-F, 26-T, 27-T, 28-F, 29-T, 30-F, 31-F, 34-F, 35-F, 36-F, 39-T, 40-T, 41-T, 43-F, 44-T, 45-F, 48-F, 49-F, 50-T, 51-T, 52-T, 53-T, 54-T, 55-F, 56-F, 57-F, 59-T, 61-T, 62-T, 63-T, 65-T.

THE SITUATIONAL REVOLUTION: LOOKING AT EXTERNAL DETERMINANTS OF BEHAVIOR

It may be remembered from Chapter 2 that Harry Stack Sullivan stressed that personality was only a construct. Carson (1969), among others, has extended Sullivan's concepts into current personality research, noting that we observe behavior in social situations and generate the *idea* of personality out of those observations. Once one realizes that personality variables are only ways of explaining behavior, it becomes obvious that they can easily be replaced by different constructs if they do not turn out to be useful.

With respect to the assumption that personality variables are the major determinants of behavior, it may be necessary to throw out traditional wisdom and the traditional approach of clinical and personality psychology and start afresh from a completely different set of constructs.

Is Behavior Consistent from one Situation to Another?

At Stanford one of Rotter's former students carried the criticism of personality dimensions and tests to its logical extreme. In *Personality and Assessment* Walter Mischel (1968) questioned the usefulness of broad personality dimensions that are supposed to reflect consistent behavior across diverse situations. His arguments and the evidence he presented are impressive. He did not, of course, deny that there are individual differences, but he questioned how consistent and general those differences may be. Such issues are important in personality psychology. How consistent is behavior across situations and how predictively useful is it to conceptualize behavior as though it were largely determined by personality variables? With respect to each of these questions, Mischel suggests that the answer is, "Not very." In fact, our current knowledge suggests that any simple theory of human behavior based on traits, instincts, genes, or whatever is inadequate (Mischel, 1977).

Problems with Broad, General Traits. Partly because we cannot know one another fully and partly because our cultural traditions assume that behavior is consistent, it is easy to think of others as unchanging. A shy person must be shy no matter where or with whom. A dishonest politician is just a grown-up version of a dishonest child. A person who is rude to us is likely to be rude to everyone. Such beliefs make for a seemingly predictable interpersonal world, and most people agree that the world is like that. In a 1975 interview with Mike Wallace, H. R. Haldeman pointed out that people should not have been surprised that former President Nixon was different on the White House tapes than he was in public. Those were *different situations.* In other words, the belief in behavioral consistency was an illusion (Shweder, 1975).

The operation of such illusions has been shown in research. In two experiments (Hayden & Mischel, 1976), high school students read about a person and formed their initial impressions of that person's traits. Then they received further information about the person that was either consistent with those traits or inconsistent with them. It was found that consistent behavior was perceived as representing the person's "real self" while inconsistent behavior was seen as superficial and temporary. The need to believe in consistency seems to be very strong. In addition, once we think of another person as possessing a given trait, this information biases both our perception and our memory of that person's behavior so that it conforms to that trait (Cantor & Mischel, 1977). People are found to discount deviant information when they are trying to predict how someone will behave (Levin, Ims, Simpson, & Kim, 1977). In addition, one person's expectancies about another person's traits can elicit the expected behavior, thus confirming what was expected. For example, Snyder and Swann (1978) led subjects to believe that a stranger was hostile. When they then interacted with that person, there actually *was* more behavioral hostility, presumably because the expectations led to the kind of behavior that would evoke a hostile response. All of these processes offer a stable and consistent view of human behavior; the problem, of course, is that such a view is a distorted one.

Doubts about consistency are most likely to arise when one considers oneself. Are you the same in every place and with every person? Are you the same at school as at home? Are you the same with close friends as with your parents? Are you the same on a date as in a gym class? Are you the same when you are a customer in a store as when you are an employee in a store? Do you behave the same way when you are alone as when you are with a group of strangers? If the answer is not yes in each case, what becomes of the concept of behavioral consistency, not only for you but for those with whom you interact? The surprising thing is that they, too, are different in different situations. No one really knows all the "personalities" of one's parents or children or friends, let alone those of one's acquaintances. Our son and daughter have been described by their teachers as extremely attentive and eager to learn, by distant relatives as extremely quiet and polite, by their friends as loud-mouthed extroverts, by their parents (on occasion) as nuisances, and by opposite-sex peers as love objects. All of these descriptions are accurate, yet none is complete. From the narrow perspective of an outside observer, other people seem consistent because we tend to be with them in a single situation or in a limited array of similar situations. If you are many different people depending on where you are and with whom, you can be assured that the rest of us are many different people too.

In addition to changes across situations, it is also useful to consider consistency over time. E. Lowell Kelly (1955) suggests that "because of the need to believe in consistency of one's self from moment to moment and from year to year, we tend to infer an unwarranted degree of consistency in others" (p. 659). But how consistent are we from moment to moment and year to year? One of the authors can recall a series of different people called Donn Byrne who had, for example, different interests, different tastes, different beliefs, and quite different behavioral characteristics. I no longer believe in Santa Claus. I no longer need to be tucked in before I go to sleep. I would no longer attend thirty-two consecutive Saturday matinees in order to see every episode of a Lone Ranger serial. I no longer consider sexy scenes in movies boring or embarrassing. I no longer enjoy building model airplanes or watching the Three Stooges. I am no longer uncertain about the anatomy of females and no longer feel that conspiracy theories about assassinations or other public events are imaginary. I no longer wonder what my career should be and no longer enjoy riding down the highway with a group of adolescent males while sipping cheap beer from a quart bottle. Yet at various times in my life I have been each of those people (and many others as well), with those interests and pleasures and ideas and concerns. The point is not that I have had a fascinating life but that each of us changes from year to year with respect to what we do and, hence, who we are.

In seeking research evidence for behavioral consistency over time and across situations, Mischel (1968) concluded that the tests that provide the best evidence for reasonable cross-situational generality and stability are the intellectual measures. Even here, the generality is greatest between similar tests or between a test and a very similar behavior (e.g., a mathematical ability test and grades in a math course). Altogether, academic achievement in different subjects is found to be fairly consistent in that grades from course to course substantially correlate with one another (Rushton & Endler, 1977). Thus, the specifics of the situation do not play as important a role in school performance as do characteristics of the individual.

With other kinds of trait measures, Mischel summarized a series of studies showing lack of generality of such traits as attitudes toward various authority figures, moral behavior, aggressive behavior, rigidity, and anxiety. Similar results are obtained when investigators seek consistency or stability over time. These studies are more difficult to conduct and hence are done less frequently but the evidence that does exist suggests that some variables, such as dependency, show no stability over time while others, such as need for achievement, show a very small degree of consistency. Kelly (1955) studied a group of adults over a period of twenty years and found a relatively low degree of consistency for personality and attitude variables over that time span. During a seven-year period, however, personality traits show much more stability (Schaie & Parham, 1976).

Such data have begun to influence research and thinking in personality psychology. Mischel (1968) says, "It is evident that the behaviors which are often construed as stable personality trait indicators actually are highly specific and depend on the details of the evoking situations and the response mode employed to measure them" (p. 37).

The Usefulness of Narrow, Specific Traits.   If behavior is controlled to a large extent by situations, does this imply that there is no consistency in behavior? Even from the most extreme situational viewpoint, the answer is no. Most of us encounter the same or similar situations over and over again, and we tend to react in a similar way each time. For example, you have often interacted with someone who is in a position of authority over you, such as a parent, teacher, police officer, or boss. You have probably learned to behave in a certain way in that type of interaction—politely, defensively, anxiously, or whatever. In a study of four different kinds of conflict situations, subjects were found to respond in a consistent way—presumably because each subject had learned a certain behavior to deal with such situations (Ringuette, 1976).

Pervin (1976) devised a procedure to try to get at the way people perceive situations so as to form clusters of similar interactions. College students were asked to list a series of specific situations and describe the feelings and behaviors they had experienced in each one. The answers were analyzed statistically, and groups of similar situations with similar reactions emerged. Table 4-3 presents the findings for one of the subjects as an example. Each person revealed a very different "personality" in different settings, but reacted in a characteristic way within each setting. Pervin suggested that further research of this type could lead to a way of categorizing situations and hence would allow us to identify stable, situation-specific behaviors as well as behaviors that vary across situations. For some traits, such as anxiety, there appears to be a genetic basis for the person-situation interaction (Dworkin, in press).

Sometimes the categories of situations must be quite narrow. Even within what seems to be a single type of situation, such as threat, sub-

Table 4-3. An undergraduate female's description of her traits, feelings, and behavior in four different situations. As with other subjects, her behavior was consistent in a given type of situation but quite different in dissimilar situations.

Type of Situation	Examples	Traits Associated with Situation	Feelings	Behaviors
Interacting with males	on a date; talking to a fellow student; at a friend's party	easygoing, sociable, light, friendly, intellectual	fun, OK, mature	enjoying, laughing, interested, honest, extraverted
At work or interacting with strangers	working in Washington; doing research in Boston; in a large, new group	difficult, tiring, demanding, intimidating	shy, inadequate, overwhelmed, quiet	listening, fearful, polite, cool, aloof, introverted
Interacting with supportive others	in a counseling session; in a therapy group; talking with mother	unique, special, personal, important	love, sadness, gratitude, tenderness, closeness	loving, hopeful, questioning
Family relationships	at home; being with relatives; fighting with mother; interacting with brother; drinking alone	defensive, unaware, closed, lonely, familiar	want attention, frustrated	demanding, exploding, expecting too much

(Based on Pervin, 1976, p. 470)

categories are necessary (Magnusson & Ekehammar, 1975). For example, perceptions and reactions are found to differ for threat of punishment (e.g., being caught stealing, discovered to be playing hooky), threat of pain (e.g., getting a shot, waiting in dentist's office), and inanimate threat (e.g., being lost in woods at night, being alone in a house during a thunderstorm). Stagner (1976) and Magnusson (1974) have argued that trait theory should take account of the fact that a person's responses are linked with classes of situations. This is a much more sophisticated and accurate approach than assuming that a trait somehow exists *within* the person, independent of external events. It should also be noted that some people are fairly consistent across situations while others show a great deal of variability (Bem & Allen, 1974); thus, the trait approach is effective in predicting the behavior of those who remain the same in different situations. It is also possible that some people are consistent with respect to only certain traits but inconsistent on others (Kenrick & Stringfield, 1980). To be able to predict behavior, one has to know who is consistent across situations in specific kinds of behavior.

Some Implications of a Situational Approach

Emphasis on stimulus determinants is not new in psychology and has, in fact, been traditional in experimental and social psychology. It is mainly in personality and clinical psychology that the *situation* has been treated as secondary (Mischel, 1969).

In Figure 4-3 the trait approach was depicted as one in which the behavior of a person is sampled and that information is used to predict many other responses in many other situations. A different kind of approach is depicted in Figure 4-5. Here, a given behavior is identified as the one to be predicted, and research is designed to identify the stimuli and combinations of stimuli that affect that behavior. In other words, instead of expecting one behavior to provide predictive information about many other behaviors (the trait approach), knowledge of the determining stimuli is expected to provide predictive information about a given behavior (the situational approach).

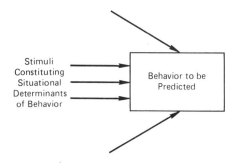

Stimuli Constituting Situational Determinants of Behavior

Behavior to be Predicted

Figure 4-5. Emphasis on situational variables involves a model in which the ability to predict a specific behavior is sought. Many different stimulus events may be studied as potential causes of that behavior.

The difference in research emphasis can be seen if we select a specific example. Let's say that you are studying rape behavior. Rape is a hostile and illegal act. If you approached the problem from the standpoint of traits, the task would be to identify the personality traits of rapists. You might begin with a clinical study in which convicted rapists were interviewed so that you could look for patterns in their attitudes or their childhood experiences or various aspects of their interpersonal behavior. You might think of a number of personality traits that would logically be a part of the rapist syndrome, such as hostility, impulsive behavior, and sexual anxieties. You might want to identify and measure the rapist personality as a specific trait, and perhaps develop a special test by finding out which items on a questionnaire differentiate rapists from nonrapists. If such a personality dimension were established, the test could be given to large numbers of males, and for each one you could predict the probability that he would ever commit a rape. Those with high scores but no history of rape would be labeled as potential rapists. If this research followed the pattern of most other studies of personality traits, researchers would find moderate correlations between the rapist scale and various other personality questionnaires, but the correlation between the rapist scale and overt behavioral acts would be very low.

Figure 4-6.   In attempting to explain behavior such as that of a criminal, the trait and situational approaches lead in quite different directions. The trait approach suggests that we should identify the characteristics of those who become criminals. The situational approach suggests that we should identify the environmental conditions that produce criminal behavior.   (Ellis Herwig, Stock, Boston)

From the situational viewpoint the question would be a different one. Instead of finding out the characteristics of rapists, research would begin by finding out the conditions under which rape occurs (Menachem, 1971). For example, you might study the settings in which rape is most likely to be committed, the time of day, the section of the city, and so forth. It might be useful to find out if there are aspects of the victim, such as attractiveness, style of clothing, or behavioral cues, that are most likely to elicit aggressive sexual responses. You might decide to examine some of the broader determinants of rape in various societies. Do cross-cultural studies reveal differences in the incidence of rape that are correlated with differences in general attitudes toward sexual behavior? Do pornography law have any effect on the incidence of rape? Does legalized prostitution have any effect on the incidence of rape? It would be possible to examine the socioeconomic level, educational level, and race of both rapists and victims. The latter study might disclose, for example, that the incidence of rape is greatest among less wealthy and less well-educated citizens. Close study might even reveal that what is called rape at one economic level would not be so labeled at another level. The young businessman who drinks too much at a country club party and is sexually aggressive with his date is not likely to be charged with rape. The young man on welfare who drinks too much at the corner bar and is sexually aggressive with a girl he picks up may very well be charged with rape. Germaine Greer (1977) points out that a poor man may apply force to a girl by showing her a knife while a rich man may apply force by telling her she can get out of the sports car and walk home. Which act do you think is more likely to be called rape? Such considerations suggest the importance of the sociocultural environment in the study of personality (Feshbach, 1978).

In any event, a situational approach to a behavioral problem tends to lead in quite different directions and to focus on quite different variables than an individual-differences approach. Peterson (1968) suggests that one of the most effective things we can do for emotionally disturbed people is to alter their social environment. In a graduate program where one of the authors taught, each student's entire career depended on the outcome of an intensive five-day series of examinations. As the exam period approached, the students scheduled to take it that year became anxious, developed symptoms of physical illness, and showed numerous signs of maladjustment. One solution would be to focus on the personality traits of these students in order to screen out those who might have problems in the future, or to recommend psychotherapy for the most disturbed. A much simpler, and probably more effective, solution was to eliminate that type of exam. When that was done, the annual outbreak of emotional problems disappeared.

Many political and social issues are different when viewed in trait terms than they are when viewed in situational terms. Most of us have learned to respond to behavioral differences with some kind of trait theory. What happened under Hitler was a function of the German character—including love of authority figures, uniforms, and war. People are on welfare because they are lazy and don't want to work. The man who commits a murder is a crazy person. Women have achieved less than men in science because they are more emotional and less intellectual. Automobile accidents are caused by bad drivers. In addition to simplicity, viewing the world in terms of inherited and learned traits has some distinct advantages. It has been suggested (Lerner, Miller, & Holmes, 1975) that we tend to believe in a **just world** in which bad things happen only to the undeserving. For example, you don't have to worry about the issues just described if you are Irish rather than German, neither lazy nor crazy, and a male who drives carefully. One can "solve" such problems in a straightforward manner by disarming the Germans, forcing welfare recipients to do an honest day's work, executing murderers, pampering the little woman so she won't have to bother her head with complex matters, and cracking down on careless drivers. The most insidious aspect of this approach is that it makes it unnecessary to examine our political or economic or interpersonal traditions to seek either the real problems or effective solutions. The atmosphere of Germany in the 1930s, the exploitation of various classes of citizens, the lack of interest in designing safe as opposed to stylish automobiles—all such disturbing issues need not even be raised. You can see that the question of trait versus situation involves more than a disagreement among personality psychologists.

WHAT DO YOU THINK?

Explaining Behavior

We have been considering two ways of explaining human behavior. The trait approach stresses the internal factors that guide our actions. Thus, well-established behavior patterns (either inherited or learned in early childhood) determine that people will respond to events in a certain way. The situational approach stresses the power of the environment to elicit certain responses. Thus, specific stimulus conditions can be expected to determine specific kinds of behavior.

Why do you think you behave the way you do? As an example, select something that you have done about which you are at least somewhat ashamed. Perhaps you lied to your parents about something, cheated on an exam, passed on a bit of gossip, or took something that did not belong to you. Whatever the act was, list on a piece of paper what you believe to be the causes of that behavior. Be as honest with yourself as possible.

Next, select another action of yours—something of which you are very proud. Perhaps you won an award, did something helpful for another person, mastered a difficult skill, or achieved a worthwhile goal. Again, list what you believe to be the causes of the behavior.

Now consider someone you know very well—a relative or a very close friend—and think of something good and something bad that that person has done. For each behavior, again make a list of the causal factors.

When you have finished all four lists, go back and classify each factor as to whether it refers mainly to an internal or an external influence. Are there different proportions of trait explanations for good acts compared to bad ones or for yourself compared to the other person? If you emphasized one type of explanation more than another, can you go back and suggest some of the opposite type? On the basis of what you have written here, do you think that as a psychologist you would stress traits more than the situation or vice versa? As you will see in the next section of this chapter, perhaps both points of view are correct.

INTEGRATING THE TRAIT AND SITUATIONAL APPROACHES

A good deal of current personality research involves the manipulation of a stimulus variable *and* the division of subjects into subgroups that differ with respect to some personality variable. In this type of research design the two major approaches to personality can be seen to merge. The next section of this book describes research on individual differences with an emphasis on establishing response–response relationships. The third section of the book describes research on the situational determinants of behavior with an emphasis on establishing stimulus–response relationships. There are obvious advantages in bringing together these two approaches (Blass, 1977).

Figure 4-7 depicts the general case of such an experiment. Though a lawful relationship may be established between the stimulus and the behavior we wish to predict, the fact that there are variations among subjects in that behavior suggests that there may also be personality differences affecting the behavior. If so, predictions of behavior will be improved by the use of a personality test (Dworkin & Kihlstron, 1978). By means of this approach we can use individual differences along a trait dimension to increase the accuracy with which we can predict responses to the situational variable (Cronbach, 1975). The personality trait measured by the test procedure can be thought of as a *moderator variable* in the stimulus–response relationship.

It can be seen that traits remain alive and well in spite of increased emphasis on situational factors. In fact, the number of experiments that include *both* situational manipulation and assessment of traits is on the increase (Sarason, Smith, & Diener, in press). People learn different re-

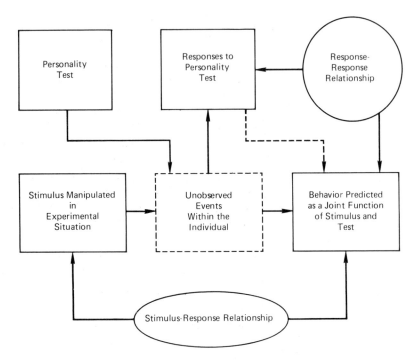

Figure 4-7. In much current personality research the trait and situational approaches are combined. That is, a personality test is given to assess a trait so that a response—response relationship can be established. At the same time, a situational variable is manipulated so that a stimulus—response relationship can be established. Behavior is often found to be a joint function of these two types of influence.

sponses in a given situation, and these differences tend to persist unless the situation is altered. Tests provide an efficient and useful way to get at such differences and, hence, to utilize them in predicting behavior. Test behavior is seen as a useful and frequently essential source of information on which to base predictions of the response in question. The trait model has weaknesses, but it should not be assumed that the whole idea is a mistaken one.

Existing tests tend to be fairly broad in scope because the aim has been to predict as much as possible from a limited sample of test responses. It now appears that we should look for consistency not in broad, general traits but in specific behaviors. For example, Wallach and Leggett (1972) found that individual children were consistent across situations in drawing figures of a given size. On the basis of such data, they argue for transsituational consistency of behavior with respect to what might be called mini-traits. When traits are defined in limited or narrow terms, they generally prove to be useful predictors of behavior. McGowan and Gormly (1976) studied "energetic behavior" as a personality trait; people who engage actively in sports and regularly swim, run, and otherwise exercise a great deal are said to be high in this trait. A great deal of transsituational consistency was found for energetic behavior as rated by peers, as revealed in interviews, and as observed in natural settings. Thus, a narrowly defined trait seems to provide fairly accurate predictions of relevant behavior. On logical grounds and on the basis of the predictive weaknesses of present tests, it could be argued that future tests need to be more specific with respect to situations. Take, for example, the following item, which is typical of those found in objective personality tests: I like to go to parties. True or false? Surely anyone who has taken such a test and thought more than five seconds about how to respond can remember a feeling of frustration. You ask yourself, "What kind of party? (A small party with conversation or a mob scene with tightly packed bodies, formal or informal, with alcohol or with tomato juice?) With whom? (Parties with close friends can be a great deal of fun whereas parties attended as a social duty can be a pain.) How frequently? (Occasional parties may be fun; nightly parties might be an inhuman torture.) What alternatives are open? (One might prefer a party to a public hanging but might prefer a Broadway play to a party.)" Turner and Fiske (1968) have shown that subjects frequently refer to a single, sometimes quite unusual, experience, or mentally qualify their answer before selecting an answer to such a question.

It quickly becomes clear that an adequate assessment of a person's general reaction to parties would require a great many questions rather than just one and a great deal of specification of situational details. The resulting tests would be longer and more time-consuming than those now in use, but their predictive utility should increase as a consequence. There is also the problem that some degree of mystery is lost. If we asked you whether you prefer a tub bath or a shower and then used your reply to predict your political attitudes, your racial views, your sexual habits, and your feelings about tapioca pudding, you might well be impressed with the magical powers of psychologists. If we asked you whether you enjoy going to small, informal, nonalcoholic parties once a week with a steady date more than you enjoy going to movies and then used your reply to predict your response to a party invitation, you might feel that our predictive feat was less than breathtaking. If the latter approach were effective and the former approach a waste of time, perhaps it would be worth sacrificing the role of witch doctor for the goal of predictive accuracy.

Another aspect of testing is the probable importance of assessing the same trait by various methods. It might be, for example, that reactions to social situations could best be measured by a series of tasks, such as a questionnaire plus a series of TAT stories plus a measure of physiological responses to various social stimuli plus observation of overt behavior in a standard social setting. One implication of both the emphasis on narrow, specific traits and the use of multiple types of assessment is that a lot of effort will be required to predict any given behavior. It should not be surprising that accurate and precise behavioral prediction is likely to be quite costly in time and effort.

SUMMARY

Much of the research in the field of personality grew out of the general cultural tradition in which we describe other people in terms of their position on various descriptive dimensions.

Among the essential requirements of any science is a set of reliable and valid instruments with which to measure the variables being studied. The primary feature of measurement is the ability to differentiate along a scale. When such differences are quantified, it becomes possible to deal with data in mathematical terms. Behavior can be measured by means of ranking a series of individuals or rating them along an ordinal scale. With these techniques, the degree of differentiation among subjects is limited. This problem can be overcome by constructing measures based on response frequency or by using a physical dimension.

The consistency with which a variable is ordered along a given dimension is the *reliability* of measurement. Measurement error can be caused by inconsistencies in the stimulus variable. When stimuli are combined to form a test, they must be equivalent in that they elicit correlated responses as determined by a *coefficient of internal consistency*. When two different stimuli or sets of stimuli are used as alternate measures of the same variable, they must yield correlated responses as determined by a *coefficient of equivalence*. Response inconsistencies occur if *interjudge consistency* in scoring the responses is low or if consistency of responses over time, as determined by a *coefficient of stability,* is lacking.

Validity of measurement is the extent to which a test measures what it is supposed to measure. *Face validity* refers to the logical connection between test materials and the variable being measured. *Content validity* refers to how well a body of material has been sampled by the test items. When the measure is designed to predict a specific criterion behavior, validity is the correlation between test scores and the criterion; depending on the time sequence of the two behaviors, this is either *concurrent* or *predictive* validity.

In personality research there is generally no single standard by which to judge a test. Instead, *construct validity* is important. The question is; To what are scores on the instrument related? Tests may be constructed by the intuitive approach, the internal consistency or bootstrap approach, and by the use of an external criterion with either a correlational or an experimental methodology. Whatever the method by which items are evaluated, it is essential to repeat the process with a new sample of subjects in order to *cross-validate* the items.

An emphasis on traits as internal determinants of behavior has a long tradition in our culture. People are assumed to behave consistently across situations and over time. This view of personality led to attempts to predict behavior on the basis of a few categories or types. Projective tests such as the Rorschach and TAT represent another attempt to gain as much predictive power as possible from a brief behavioral observation. The interest in such personality tests grew rapidly with the expansion of psychology after World War II. In the years that followed, research showed that the usefulness of the various tests was not as great as was originally hoped. In the mid-1950s Julian Rotter summarized the research literature and concluded that both the reliability and the validity of existing tests were inadequate. One solution to the problem was to turn away from global measures of personality and focus on individual personality traits.

By the late 1960s a more radical criticism of personality tests had gained numerous supporters. Among them was Walter Mischel, who questioned the utility of broad personality dimensions. He presented evidence that behavior is inconsistent when the situation is changed. It appears that behavior is fairly consistent in a given type of situation but may vary widely in different situations. Thus, many researchers began to emphasize situational influences on behavior. One implication of a situational emphasis is that problems and suggested solutions take a quite different form; that is, there is concern with identifying and altering environmental factors rather than personality factors.

A great deal of our current research integrates the trait and situational approaches. Personality tests are often designed to measure much more limited and more situationally specific response tendencies. It seems clear that accurate prediction of behavior is going to become more costly in terms of both time and effort.

SUGGESTED READINGS

BEM, D. J., & ALLEN, A.   On predicting some of the people some of the time: The search for cross-situational consistencies in behavior. *Psychological Review*, 1974, *81*, 506–20. An excellent article that explores the problems involved in establishing personality traits that remain constant across different situations. The authors indicate that there are individual differences in behavioral consistency across situations.

BLASS, T. (ed.). *Personality variables in social behavior.* Hillsdale, N.J.: Lawrence Erlbaum, 1977. A collection of original chapters covering a variety of research areas in which personality variables and situational variables are utilized together to predict behavior.

HOGAN, R., DeSOTO, C., & SOLANO, C.   Traits, tests, and personality research. *American Psychologist*, 1977, *32*, 255–64. A vigorous defense of the trait approach and the utility of personality tests.

MAGNUSSON, D., & ENDLER, N. S. (eds.)   *Personality at the crossroads.* Hillsdale, N.J.: Erlbaum, 1977. A collection of original chapters dealing with the issue of traits versus situations as the determinants of behavior. The problem and a variety of solutions are presented by experts in the field.

MISCHEL, W. *Personality and assessment.* New York: Wiley, 1968. An exposition of the weaknesses of the trait approach and of many personality tests, plus an impressive description of the importance of situational determinants of behavior.

WIGGINS, J. S. *Personality and prediction: Principles of personality assessment.* Reading, Mass.: Addison-Wesley, 1973. A difficult but thorough introduction to the field of personality assessment.

Part Two

BEHAVIOR AS A FUNCTION OF
PERSONALITY TRAITS

Bohdan Hrynewych, Stock, Boston

Chapter Five

AUTHORITARIANISM: THE FASCIST WITHIN

In this chapter you will read about the following topics:

The Horton family had assembled around the diningroom table for their Friday evening meal. William, 10 years old and the eldest of the three children, sat upright in his chair and quietly watched as his father sliced the roast beef onto each plate. Mr. Horton, still dressed in the coat and tie he wore at his job, silently passed the dishes as he filled them—first to his wife and then to each child in turn.

Beth, the 5-year-old, squealed excitedly as she spotted one of her favorite dishes—mashed potatoes.

"Settle down, young lady," Mrs. Horton said sternly. "The dinner table is a place to eat, not a playground." Beth looked suitably ashamed of her outburst.

The 8-year-old, Bob, scowled at his mother and muttered under his breath, "Why don't you get off her back?"

Mr. Horton grabbed Bob's arm roughly. "Repeat what you just said!"

"Nothin'."

"You were saying something disrespectful to your mother. That's something that no

decent person would think of doing. You can leave the table right now. Maybe next time you won't be so quick to talk back."

Bob looked even angrier as he pushed his chair away from the table. "Why?" Why can't Beth enjoy herself at dinner?"

"Because we say so," Mr. Horton announced with finality. "Look at William. He's dressed properly, and his hair is neatly cut and combed. He knows to speak only when he is spoken to. Perhaps a few evenings without supper will help you mend your ways and be more like him. Otherwise, you'll find out about good manners soon enough, at the end of my belt."

William spoke for the first time. "Sir, may I have some of Bob's meat—since he isn't going to eat it? That would be even more punishment for what he did." Mr. Horton nodded, and his older son scraped the extra meat onto his plate as Bob ran out, trying to stifle a sob.

The rest of the meal was spent mainly in silence except for a few pronouncements by Mr. Horton on the events of the day. He was clearly upset by the news that a Jewish family had bought the Baldwin house just across the street. "I don't know what the world is coming to," he complained, as his wife nodded sympathetically. "That Greek-looking real estate man will sell a house to anybody with enough cash in their hands. And you can bet that our new neighbors had cash all right. Nobody can raise a fuss, either, because some government bureaucrat will back them up. There's got to be a change. We've got to get America back to the way it was."

After dessert William asked permission to go down the street to play in the neighborhood park.

"You won't get dirty, will you?" Mrs. Horton asked.

"No ma'am, I promise. And I'll be back by nine."

Approaching the park, William was surprised to hear a great deal of shouting and the sounds of an angry crowd. When he reached the tennis courts, he was even more surprised to see an old man, wearing only a pair of scuffed shoes, spread-eagled against the wire fence, his hands and feet tied tightly.

He spotted a teen-age boy whom he knew and asked what was going on.

"We caught this pervert exposing himself over by the girls' rest room. My sister saw him and ran home crying."

William felt his anger rise as he thought of Beth or his mother undergoing such an experience. "What will you do to him?"

"We're planning to teach him a lesson. A permanent lesson."

William noticed that many of the youngsters in the park had rocks, baseball bats, chains, and other objects in their hands. The old man was whimpering now and begging them to let him go. William, with a smile of grim satisfaction, broke a thick branch from a nearby maple tree and joined the group as they advanced on their victim. He hoped that he would get his turn to strike while that scum could still feel it.

IN THIS CHAPTER we will examine some research that suggests that various aspects of the story about the Horton family are not random bits of fiction but, in fact, a series of clearly related aspects of behavior. Work on the **authoritarian personality** provides evidence that certain kinds of home atmosphere produce a very specific array of attitudes, values, and behaviors involving respect for authority, ethnic prejudice, repressive sexual standards, and the tendency to define certain targets as proper outlets for hostility and aggression. We will examine this personality dimension in some detail.

IDENTIFYING AND MEASURING AUTHORITARIAN TRAITS

The streets of our country are in turmoil. The universities are filled with students rebelling and rioting. Communists are seeking to destroy our country. Russia is threatening us with her might and the Republic is in danger. Yes, danger from within and from without. We need law and order. Yes, without law and order our nation cannot survive. Elect us and we shall restore law and order. [Adolph Hitler, Hamburg, 1932]

Research interest in **authoritarianism** owes a debt, of sorts, to Adolf Hitler. When the Nazi party gained power in Germany in 1933, the world witnessed the creation of one of the most authoritarian regimes ever to control a major nation. Authoritarian ideology and its associated behaviors pervaded every aspect of German life. Prompted in large part by the horrors of Hitler's anti-Semitism, in the 1940s the American Jewish Committee provided support for psychological research on ethnic prejudice. The committee was interested in learning the traits of people who establish authoritarian societies and of those who readily accept this ideology. Who will be attracted to a fascist leader and why? The committee hoped to be able to identify and describe the *potentially* fascistic person as well as the determinants of this behavior. It was hoped that a scientific understanding of authoritarianism would provide the means to prevent its future reappearance in Germany or any other nation. There is one thing that these investigators would not have guessed: A few decades later it is difficult to find anyone who even knows who the Nazis were or what they did (*Time,* April 26, 1976). As one Milwaukee woman said, "I've heard of Nazis, but I don't listen to the news that much." It appears that for many people the ideological aspects of World War II do not go beyond reruns of *Hogan's Heroes.*

Among the products of the research on prejudice was a classic book entitled *The Authoritarian Personality,* by T. W. Adorno, Else Frenkel-Brunswick, Daniel J. Levinson, and R. Nevitt Sanford. The work of these social scientists and their colleagues was conducted throughout the late 1940s and was published in 1950. The methods used included a unique and fruitful blend of clinical insight and empirical research. The impact of this project on subsequent psychological theory and research has been impressive. We will now examine how this aspect of personality was first studied.

Authoritarians were described as people who use repressive defenses to control their sexual and aggressive impulses and develop conforming, submissive, and extremely conventional patterns of behavior in interacting with other people. Their repressed sexuality and hostility result in the tendency to project such tendencies onto others, and they feel justified in aggressing against anyone who deviates from what they consider proper conduct.

This general conception of the authoritarian personality was based mainly on observations of people who were attracted to fascism in Nazi Germany and elsewhere, as well as on ideas derived from Freud's psychoanalytic theory. Such observations and ideas led the researchers to propose nine central traits of an authoritarian person. Once these elements had been defined, test items were constructed in an attempt to measure each of them. The nine aspects of authoritarianism and sample test items will now be described.

Conventionalism: Rigid Middle-Class Values. **Conventionalism** was proposed as a factor in the authoritarian makeup because it had been observed that (1) fascism often develops in conventional middle-class environments and (2) unconventional people tend to be free of the usual ethnic prejudices. The fact that a great many conventional individuals are democratic, tolerant, and egalitarian in outlook presented some problems. It was proposed that when conventional values are based on a well-developed superego such values are not related to antidemocratic trends. When the values are external in origin, however, a different situation exists. A person whose ideas of right and wrong are simply a function of external social pressure would be expected to be receptive to antidemocratic ideology. This difference is seen in the contrast between people who truly value the American ideals of democracy, freedom of speech, and equality and those whose values seem to represent only a shallow, flag-waving patriotism. A familiar example from the Vietnam War years was the bumper sticker reading, "America—love it or leave it." The test items that were constructed to measure this factor attempted to make such distinctions. The following is a sample item:

A person who has bad manners, habits, and breeding can hardly expect to get along with decent people.

Submission to a Strong Leader. Because the Nazi creed stressed submission to authority, desire for a strong leader, and the subservience of the individual to the state, this type of submission was included among the probable traits of authoritarian people. In writing the items, the researchers guessed that submission would characterize the authoritarian person's relationship to all authority figures—parents, older people, supernatural beings, or anyone who could be seen as a leader. "I did not question the orders. I only obeyed them." It was hypothesized that complete submissiveness occurred because of a deficiency in superego development. In addition, the fear of having any negative or hostile feelings toward authority could lead to a defensive overemphasis on the reverse, that is, submission to such authority. One of the imprisoned Watergate offenders, G. Gordon Liddy, told an interviewer that to him the leader *is* the government. It follows from such an assumption that anything the leader demands is legitimate whether it involves spying, burglary, or even assassination.

Sample item:

Obedience and respect for authority are the most important virtues children should learn.

Aggression: Punishing Those Who Express Deviant Values.   It was hypothesized that people who are *forced* to adopt conventional values and to submit to authority without complaint would inevitably experience feelings of hostility even if they were not aware of the source. The outward expression of this hostility would seem justified and safe if it could be directed not toward authority figures but toward those who violate whatever is conventional. In effect, an authoritarian says, "I don't hate my

Figure 5-1. Would a highly authoritarian person participate in a protest such as this?

Peter Southwick, Stock, Boston

father; it's the freaks who make my blood boil." Thus, hostility is displaced from the appropriate targets in the ingroup onto inappropriate targets in the outgroup. The latter, depending on the time and place, could consist of Jews, communists, sexual offenders, members of the women's movement, or any other easily identified group. If you read the letters to the editor in almost any newspaper, you can easily find examples of such prejudices. In addition, these letters reveal how indignant people can become about the hair styles, clothing, beards, or other observable characteristics of those who differ from themselves. Not only is the authoritarian person able to give vent to hostility, but he or she does so for "good" reasons based mainly on a distorted version of patriotism, "common decency", or morality.

Sample item:

Homosexuals are hardly better than criminals and ought to be severely punished.

Destruction and Cynicism: People Are No Damn Good.   In addition to directing hostility toward outgroups, authoritarian people express hostility toward the human race in general and cynicism with respect to the motives of others. Among other things, one's own hostility is more acceptable if everyone acts that way or it is seen as natural. "Everybody's out for a fast buck. People are no damn good." War is acceptable because it is part of "human nature." One of the ways of justifying political "dirty tricks" and illegal acts is to claim that "everyone does it." Those who perceive their fellow human beings in such a negative fashion assume that decent behavior will occur only when people are threatened by harsh laws, severe punishments, and the superior strength of the police and military.

Sample item:

The true American way of life is disappearing so fast that force may be necessary to preserve it.

Power and Toughness.   Because of their own psychological weaknesses, authoritarians are believed to overemphasize strength and power. It is especially important to have a leader who provides power, and to be identified with a group that has such attributes: the strongest nation on earth, the master race, the worldwide communist movement, and so forth. Authoritarians would be expected to submit completely to the orders of such power sources and, in turn, to be ruthless in their use of power when the situation arises. An example would be someone who obeyed his superiors without question but then displayed his own power over subordinates and victims. "Might makes right." We have often observed a very polite, respectful graduate student transformed into a petty tyrant upon becoming a teaching assistant. A very common example of identification with a strong group is the way most of us respond when "our" team wins. When an excited crowd begins shouting "We're number one!" it suggests that each member feels somehow better, more powerful, and more successful just because he or she is associated with the winning side.

Sample item:

People can be divided into two distinct classes: the weak and the strong.

Superstition and Stereotypy.   Among the mechanisms that may account for the authoritarian's belief in mystical and fantastic forces is the tendency to avoid responsibility for various feelings, acts, and consequences by placing the blame on outside causes rather than on oneself. If some unknowable factor is responsible for what happens, the individual is guiltless. "The war must be just—God is on our side." "It was written in the stars." **Stereotypy** refers to the tendency to think in rigid categories and resort to oversimplified, black-and-white explanations. Successful authoritarian leaders take advantage of this tendency by providing a simple rationale for past difficulties and future achievements. Such complex events as war, depression, and crime emerge as straightforward problems with straightforward solutions presented as slogans and catch phrases. In addition, such leaders do well when they attach elements of the mysterious to themselves and their regime. Authoritarian rulers may provide themselves with supernatural ancestors, as the Roman and Japanese emperors did. The ruler appears in public only rarely and then with pomp and ceremony, as in the Nazi rallies with their searchlights, banners, and gigantic stage settings. The leader's destiny is mystically linked with that of the nation; the leader is free from illness and has divine protection from assassins. It is difficult not to get caught up in the emotional power of spectacles like large political rallies complete with music, banners, and chanted slogans. Similar feelings can be aroused at a pep rally or football game.

Sample item:

Science has its place, but there are many important things that can never possibly be understood by the human mind.

Anti-Intraception: Beware of Unacceptable Thoughts and Wishes.   It was hypothesized that authoritarians tend to respond to concrete, clearly observable, tangible facts and to oppose fantasy, speculation, and imagination. "Keep your feet on the ground and your head out of the clouds." Presumably, the authoritarian is afraid of "wrong" thoughts, of basic emotions that might get out of hand. The "prying into the mind" that is typical of psychological testing and psychotherapy is viewed with great suspicion. Interestingly enough, prying by government authorities on external behavior by means of wiretapping or secret agents is viewed as acceptable. Totalitarian nations and authoritarian political groups also reject any artistic endeavor that tends to arouse frightening or dangerous thoughts and feelings. Thus, censorship of art, including books, movies, and plays, seems necessary and right to the authoritarian. The greatest perceived danger comes from creative material that is sexually arousing or critical of those in power. Authoritarian governments find it essential to censor newspapers, television, and the movies. Ideally, they would like to control what people think as well as what they say. In such a society the practical businessperson is seen as a contributor to the state, but a novelist, a poet, or any type of intellectual is viewed as a potential threat.

Sample item:

The businessman and the manufacturer are much more important to society than the artist and the professor.

Projectivity: It's Not Me, It's Them.   One of the most pervasive aspects of authoritarianism is **projectivity,** the tendency to transfer internal problems to the external world—taboo impulses, weaknesses, fears, responsibilities. Thus, authoritarians see the most unacceptable aspects of their own selves in the world around them. Especially prominent are projections of sexual and aggressive impulses. An authoritarian is surrounded by depraved people engaging in sexual excesses—outgroup members, foreigners, people in high places, college students, neighbors. Equally rampant is hostility—crime waves, subversion, plots in the government, threats from abroad. "At least half the college professors are Commies and most of the rest are pansies." Such projection shades rather easily into paranoid delusions, and the beliefs of authoritarians sometimes assume rather bizarre forms. For example, in the 1960s some groups believed reports that the government was secretly training cannibals in Georgia and that millions of Red Chinese troops were massed just over the Mexican border. In the 1970s, a syndicated columnist wrote that all of the student unrest in the United States had been planned years ago by a secret group that met outside Prague. In all honesty, however, it has become very hard to determine what is a paranoid projection and what is an accurate view of the world. Continued revelations of assorted plots and conspiracies in various parts of the world make it difficult to reject even the most farfetched ideas.

Sample item:

Most people don't realize how much our lives are controlled by plots hatched in secret places.

Sex: A Crucial Concern.   The early investigators of authoritarianism felt that sexual concerns of authoritarians warranted a prominent and separate position in their description. Authoritarians are likely to punish those who violate sexual standards, censor sexual material, and project sexual excesses onto others. It is suggested that for such people sexual impulses must be strongly attached to anxiety cues. The anxiety is reduced by projecting these impulses onto others and expressing hostility toward those who engage in "unacceptable" sexual activities. "I would never even think of having premarital intercourse, but half the kids down at the high school belong to wild sex clubs." In terms of Freudian theory, an unresolved Oedipal complex would lead to the association of incestuous fears with any sort of forbidden sexual activity. Various individuals and groups are constantly worrying about the amount of sex in television programs and movies. We were listening to a Chicago radio station when a woman called in to complain about the song, "She's Having My Baby"; she said that such lyrics lead her kids to ask questions about where babies come from. Authoritarians believe that sex should not be discussed, that sex education only serves to stir up unwholesome thoughts, and that the availability of contraception and legal abortions is a bad moral influence. As evidence for all of these bad effects, they assert that other people are constantly engaging in wild sexual orgies.

Sample item:

The wild sex life of the old Greeks and Romans was tame compared to some of the goings-on in this country, even in places where people might least expect it.

Measuring Authoritarianism: The California F Scale

Constructing the Test.   The researchers attempted to measure authoritarianism by creating test items that matched their theoretical description. The Fascist Scale (known as the **F Scale** or **California F Scale**) was to become a widely used personality test. An effort was made to write items that were indirect and not obviously irrational. As you can see from the sample items we presented, each consisted of a statement, and the subject was asked to respond by indicating some degree of agreement or disagreement.

In an effort to build a reliable measuring instrument by means of the bootstrap technique, the Berkeley group constructed three successive versions of the F Scale. Each time, they carried out an item analysis and discarded or rewrote items that were unsuccessful. The resulting test consists of 29 items and is keyed in such a way that the people with the highest score are the most authoritarian. Extremely low scores on this test indicate an **equalitarian personality,** but relatively little attention has been devoted to describing and understanding this type of personality.

It should be noted that descriptions of research with the F Scale in this book and elsewhere often refer to "authoritarians" and "equalitarians" as if they were two clearly defined groups. Actually, as with almost all personality tests, there is no agreed-upon score that identifies a person as falling into a particular category. Thus, authoritarianism is really a *dimension* along which people differ, not a *typology* that classifies a person into one of two groups.

Acquiescence Versus Authoritarianism.   Criticism has been leveled at the F Scale because of the fact that each item is worded so that agreement with the content of the item indicates authoritarianism. Thus, the scores could confound authoritarian tendencies with another personality variable: **acquiescent response set.** Acquiescence refers to the tendency of some people to indicate agreement with almost any broad generalization that is stated as a test item. One problem that arises when the F Scale is confounded with acquiescent response set is that correlations between it and other tests may be a function of an actual relation between authoritarianism and another variable *or* an artifact caused by the common element of acquiescence. On the basis of a number of theoretical and empirical factors, Samelson and Yates (1967) concluded that there is little evidence of a serious acquiescence bias. They criticize the debate over acquiescence as a blind alley that had the unfortunate effect of reducing interest in authoritarianism. However, when highly authoritarian people are separated from those who simply are high in acquiescent response set, they are found to behave somewhat differently—at least with respect to how well they persuade others to change their attitudes. Authoritarians are less able than highly acquiescent individuals to persuade others (Marquis, 1973).

Given such problems, it would seem desirable to build an F Scale that controls for response set. What is needed is the creation of reversed items that measure the same trait as the original items. It is not difficult to write an item that is logically reversed, but that is no guarantee that authoritarians will disagree with it and equalitarians agree. In one such attempt (Cherry & Byrne, 1977), a large number of reversed items were given to various samples of undergraduates along with the original F Scale. Those reversed items which correlated well with the regular ones were retained to form a new test. When eleven of these reversed statements were combined with eleven of the original F Scale items, the result was a balanced scale that controls for acquiescence. This test is shown in Table 5-1. It was found that this revised measure of authoritarianism is related to various tests and questionnaires in the same way that the original F Scale is, but with slightly lower correlations (presumably because the original relationships also involve acquiescence). In any event, it is possible to construct a balanced F Scale, and the correlation between this test and the original one is substantial. Whether or not such a test represents any improvement over the original scale is a question for future research.

TRY IT YOURSELF

Authoritarianism and Political Preferences

First, consider the following list of political figures: John Anderson, Howard Baker, Jerry Brown, George Bush, Jimmy Carter, Gerald Ford, Ted Kennedy, Walter Mondale, George McGovern, Richard Nixon, Ronald Reagan, George Wallace. Leaving aside the question of who might have the best chance to win nomination or be elected, which of these individuals would *you* most like to see as President of the United States?

Second, consult Table 5-1 and, if you have not already done so, take the test shown.

Third, score the test according to the instructions provided in the table.

Fourth, if your instructor wishes, you and each member of your class should hand in a piece of paper on which is written your presidential choice and your score. There is no need for anyone to include his or her name.

Table 5-1. A balanced F Scale designed to control for acquiescent response set. Items 1, 2, 3, 4, 5, 6, 10, 11, 14, 17, and 21 are from the original test; agreement with these statements is the authoritarian response. Items 7, 8, 9, 12, 13, 15, 16, 18, 19, 20, and 22 represent a reversal of content; disagreement with these statements is the authoritarian response.

Public Opinion Scale

The following items are part of an attempt to assess the opinions of college students about a number of important personal, academic, and social issues. The best answer to each statement is your *personal opinion.* We have tried to cover many different and opposing points of view; you may find yourself agreeing strongly with some of the statements, disagreeing just as strongly with others, and perhaps uncertain about others. Whether you agree or disagree with any statement, you can be sure that many people feel the same way you do.

Mark your opinion about each statement on the answer sheet according to how much you agree or disagree with it. Please mark every one.

1. There is hardly anything lower than a person who does not feel a great love, gratitude, and respect for his parents.
2. An insult to our honor should always be punished.
3. Books and movies ought not to deal so much with the unpleasant and seamy side of life; they ought to concentrate on themes that are entertaining or uplifting.
4. What the youth needs most is strict discipline, rugged determination, and the will to work and fight for family and country.
5. No sane, normal, decent person could ever think of hurting a close friend or relative.
6. Young people sometimes get rebellious ideas, but as they grow up they ought to get over them and settle down.
7. The findings of science may some day show that many of our most cherished beliefs are wrong.
8. It is highly unlikely that astrology will ever be able to explain anything.
9. People ought to pay more attention to new ideas, even if they seem to go against the American way of life.
10. If people would talk less and work more, everybody would be better off.
11. A person who has bad manners, habits, and breeding can hardly expect to get along with decent people.
12. Insults to our honor are not always important enough to bother about.
13. It's all right for people to raise questions about even the most sacred matters.
14. Obedience and respect for authority are the most important virtues children should learn.
15. There is no reason to punish any crime with the death penalty.
16. Anyone who would interpret the Bible literally just doesn't know much about geology, biology, or history.
17. In this scientific age the need for a religious belief is more important than ever.
18. When they are little, kids sometimes think about doing harm to one or both of their parents.
19. It is possible that creatures on other planets have founded a better society than ours.
20. The prisoners in our corrective institutions, regardless of the nature of their crimes, should be humanely treated.
21. The sooner people realize that we must get rid of all the traitors in the government, the better off we'll be.
22. Some of the greatest atrocities in man's history have been committed in the name of religion and morality.

ANSWER SHEET

	Strong Support, Agreement	Moderate Support, Agreement	Slight Support, Agreement	Slight Opposition, Disagreement	Moderate Opposition, Disagreement	Strong Opposition, Disagreement
1.	____	____	____	____	____	____
2.	____	____	____	____	____	____
3.	____	____	____	____	____	____
4.	____	____	____	____	____	____
5.	____	____	____	____	____	____
6.	____	____	____	____	____	____
7.	____	____	____	____	____	____
8.	____	____	____	____	____	____
9.	____	____	____	____	____	____
10.	____	____	____	____	____	____
11.	____	____	____	____	____	____
12.	____	____	____	____	____	____
13.	____	____	____	____	____	____
14.	____	____	____	____	____	____
15.	____	____	____	____	____	____
16.	____	____	____	____	____	____
17.	____	____	____	____	____	____
18.	____	____	____	____	____	____
19.	____	____	____	____	____	____
20.	____	____	____	____	____	____
21.	____	____	____	____	____	____
22.	____	____	____	____	____	____

SCORING KEY

	Items 1, 2, 3, 4, 5, 6, 10, 11, 14, 17, 21	Items 7, 8, 9, 12, 13, 15, 16, 18, 19, 20, 22
Strong support, agreement	7	1
Moderate support, agreement	6	2
Slight support, agreement	5	3
Slight opposition, disagreement	3	5
Moderate opposition, disagreement	2	6
Strong opposition, disagreement	1	7

(Any item that is omitted receives a score of 4.)

Fifth, your instructor can determine the mean score of those who chose each of the names on the list of possible presidents. Do the means differ greatly? Is there any relation between the political views of the possible candidates and the authoritarianism scores of those who favor them?

Several studies of this type have been conducted, usually during or just before a presidential campaign. Most often, the political figure who is preceived as having the most conservative views is chosen by the subjects with the highest scores on the F Scale while the one who is perceived as having the most liberal views is chosen by those with the lowest scores. Interestingly enough, perceptions of candidates frequently change over the years, and as a result the authoritarianism of their followers may be different in different years.

For example, just before the 1960 primaries relatively high F Scale scores were obtained by those who favored Lyndon Johnson and relatively low scores by those who favored Adlai Stevenson (Wrightsman, Radloff, Horton, & Mecherikoff, 1961). Four years later, in the 1964 campaign, the most authoritarian subjects chose George Wallace, the least authoritarian ones chose Lyndon Johnson, and the Goldwater supporters were in between (Milton & Waite, 1964). In an unpublished study conducted just before the 1968 nominations, Nixon attracted those with highest F Scale scores, Johnson's supporters fell in the middle range, and Robert F. Kennedy was chosen by those with the lowest scores.

It may be seen, then, that political choices seem to be related to authoritarianism, but perceived shifts among the candidates and in the available alternatives can affect the relationship. Note, for example, that between 1960 and 1968 Johnson attracted the most and least authoritarian voters, as well as those in the middle. at different times.

It has been argued by some psychologists that the attempt to measure authoritarian *attitudes* is a mistake and that it would be preferable to measure authoritarian *behavior*. Ray (1976) has developed a scale with such items as "Do you tend to boss people around?" and "If anyone is going to be Top Dog would you rather it be you?" Responses to such items were found to be better predictors of authoritarian behavior as rated by peers than was the usual F Scale.

THE DEVELOPMENT OF AN AUTHORITARIAN

The Differing Childhood Experiences of Authoritarians and Equalitarians

The most obvious origins of authoritarianism would seem to be one's early experiences with parents and others. Two kinds of influence appear to be likely. Most important are those factors which contribute to the development of the basic aspects of an authoritarian orientation: repression and the denial of aggressive and sexual impulses. In addition, there must be contact with the specific ideas and beliefs that form the content of authoritarian ideology.

In the original Berkeley studies a number of clinical investigations (using interviews, case histories, and projective tests) were carried out in order to provide information about the highest- and lowest-scoring subjects. These observations led to many hypotheses that were later tested in research.

Of course, when subjects talk about their parents or their childhood experiences, these memories may or may not accurately reflect what really happened. The position taken by the Berkeley group, however, was that all such material could be relevant in understanding the differences between people who are high and low in authoritarianism. On the basis of the material that was collected, several conclusions were drawn concerning the possible role of early family experiences. Subjects who were high in authoritarianism reported that their parents used relatively harsh and threatening forms of discipline. The child was expected to be submissive and to suppress unacceptable impulses. The emphasis was on rules and regulations, not on free expression of ideas or feelings. The family seemed to be anxious about status and stressed conventional values as a way to succeed socially. Such values were simply imposed by the parents and were not really integrated by their offspring. Because parents became indignant when their child failed to conform, the child learned to express indignation toward anyone who behaved according to different values. All rules and ideas seemed to represent a set of clichés to be memorized. Relations in the home were based on prescribed roles with an emphasis on duties and obligations rather than affection. Any expression of hostility toward the parents was forbidden, and the child tended to overreact by glorifying and idealizing them in a stereotyped fashion. Male authoritarians, especially, reported having a "stern and distant" father who made them feel weak and helpless. Among other things, the son would later try to become like his father by being aggressive and stressing rugged masculinity.

With respect to the equalitarian individuals on the opposite end of the continuum, family experiences were described as more or less the reverse of those just outlined. That is, less obedience is expected of the children, and parents are less status ridden, less anxious about conformity, and less intolerant of socially unacceptable behavior. Equalitarian individuals report more affection within the family, and they seem more free to express emotion.

The Ideology of a Traditional Family

Several basic aspects of family structure and functioning seemed to distinguish authoritarians from equalitarians. Levinson and Huffman (1955) labeled the general beliefs of the autocratic extreme **traditional family ideology** and predicted that the democratic–autocratic dimension of family structure would be associated with the equalitarian–authoritarian dimension of personality.

Their first step was the construction of a test to measure attitudes toward family organization: the Traditional Family Ideology Scale. The five major features of autocratic families are conventionalism (emphasis on conformity, cleanliness, practicality, and upward mobility); submission (emphasis on obedience); exaggerated masculinity and femininity (emphasis on role differences between the sexes); discipline (emphasis on rules and punishment for violating the rules); and moralistic rejection of desires (emphasis on inhibition and denial of emotions, especially if they involve sex or hostility). The test consists of 35 items; here are some examples:

A child should not be allowed to talk back to his parents, or else he will lose respect for them.

A man can scarcely maintain respect for his fiancée if they have sexual relations before they are married.

Some equality in marriage is a good thing, but by and large the husband ought to have the main say-so in family matters.

Research indicates that the Traditional Family Ideology Scale and the F Scale are highly correlated. Authoritarianism is strongly linked with traditional family ideology. The correlation between the two tests suggests that authoritarians are raised in autocratic homes, equalitarians in democratic homes. It seems likely that these very different types of interpersonal interactions are largely responsible for the resulting personality differences that characterize authoritarians and equalitarians.

Cultural Differences in Family Ideology

Descriptions of the family background of authoritarians very often contain words such as *traditional* and *conventional,* which reflect an "old-fashioned" and "old-world" way of organizing families and raising children. Such families are contrasted with the more "modern" and "progressive" American spirit of equality and permissiveness that many people associate with Dr. Spock. One implication of this contrast is that, as a group, Americans should be lower in authoritarianism than the citizens of various other countries, especially countries in which family traditions change very little over time. Likewise, the children of people who have come to this country only recently should be higher in authoritarianism than the offspring of people who arrived earlier and hence are more thoroughly assimilated.

Turkish–American Comparisons.   Kagitcibasi (1970) observed that the typical Turkish family is restrictive with respect to discipline. On the average, one would expect to find a much greater proportion of traditional, father-dominated families and, hence, a higher mean level of authoritarianism in Turkey than in the United States.

His subjects consisted of a large group of high school students in Turkey and in the San Francisco area. As expected, the Turkish students were higher in authoritarianism than the American students. In addition, the Turkish subjects scored higher than the Americans in patriotism and respect for authority.

Mexican-American–Anglo-American Comparisons.   Ramirez (1967) has pointed out the similarity between Mexican family structure and that of authoritarians in that both are characterized by dominating fathers, strict discipline, and rigid separation of sex roles. Thus, the average Mexican-American should be more authoritarian than the average Anglo-American. To test this hypothesis Ramirez obtained college students from each group to serve as subjects. They were given the F Scale and a special scale dealing with family values. As expected, the Mexican-American subjects scored significantly higher on the F Scale than the Anglo-American subjects did. Similar differences were found on the items dealing with family values. For example, the Mexican-American subjects were much more likely to agree with items suggesting that the mother should be the dearest person in existence for the child, that it helps a child in the long run if he or she is made to conform to the parents' wishes, that the word of an adult should never be questioned, and that it does no good to try to change society because the future is in the hands of God. Ramirez speculated that adherence to these values could be a source of continuing conflict for someone who is caught between the Mexican and Anglo cultures.

Discipline and Restrictiveness

Punishment Versus Loss of Love.   Contained within the description of the autocratic family are a number of specific elements. Hart (1957) focused on one of these: disciplinary techniques. It has been hypothesized that the way parents attempt to control their children's behavior during socialization is a function of their own position on the authoritarianism–equalitarianism dimension. Hart utilized the Whiting and Child (1953) conceptualization of punishment techniques: a dimension varying from love-oriented to nonlove-oriented. The former serve to maintain the child's striving for parental affection and include denial of love and threats of ostracism. Nonlove-oriented techniques, on the other hand, tend to focus on the importance of obeying rules and on punishment when the rules are violated. Included are physical punishment, threats of physical punishment, and ridicule. Hart hypothesized that authoritarian parents would punish children with nonlove-oriented techniques.

A group of mothers of preschoolers were selected for study. Each mother was asked a series of questions about her most probable response to her child's behavior in a series of situations such as not eating, handling his or her genitals, and destroying property. The mothers were also given the F Scale. It was found that the higher a mother scored in authoritarianism, the more she chose nonlove-oriented techniques to discipline her child.

How Much Freedom?   Block (1955) administered a test dealing with *restrictiveness* versus *permissiveness* in child-rearing attitudes to a group of military officers. The restrictive items included the following:

Figure 5-2. Harsh, threatening punishment of children is one the factors in the development of the authoritarian personality.

Christy Park, Monkmeyer

When adults are entertaining, a child should "be seen but not heard."

Firm and strict discipline makes for strong character in later life.

Children need some of the natural meanness taken out of them.

The permissive items included the following:

A child should be permitted to have secrets from his parents.

Jealousy among brothers and sisters is a very common thing.

Children have a right to make a mess just for the fun of it.

On the basis of their responses to the test items, the most and least restrictive fathers were selected for further study. The restrictive group was found to score much higher on the F Scale than the permissive group. Once again, authoritarianism was found to be closely associated with the way children are treated in the family setting.

Transmitting Authoritarianism Across Generations

On the basis of the various correlational findings that have been reported, one might reasonably speculate that a circular pattern of cause and effect links child-rearing practices and authoritarianism. The sequence is shown in Figure 5-3. Authoritarian and equalitarian traits lead parents to structure their families and raise their children in quite different ways. The results for the children include the development of personality traits like

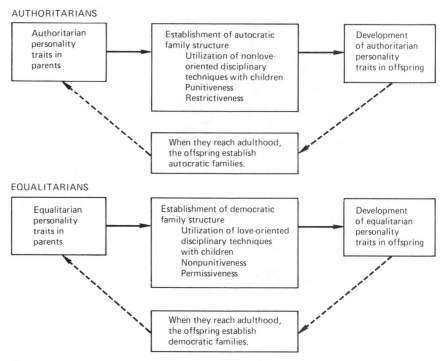

Figure 5-3. If the relation between authoritarianism and child-rearing practices were really as simple as it is often thought to be, the process would follow the sequence shown in this figure. That is, the personality traits of the parents result in their establishing a certain type of family structure. This structure results in the development of the same traits in their offspring. When they grow up, the same process is repeated in the next generation.

those of the parents. On reaching adulthood, these individuals repeat the pattern, and so it continues from one generation to another.

Two untested assumptions are built into generalizations about the effects of child-rearing patterns on authoritarianism. Husbands and wives are assumed to be similar in both authoritarianism and child-rearing practices. Even more strongly, parental authoritarianism and child-rearing techniques are assumed to lead to the development of the same characteristics in their offspring.

To test these assumptions, Byrne (1965) administered the F Scale to a group of college students and their mothers and fathers. Husbands and wives are somewhat similar in authoritarianism, but across generations the correlations are smaller. If the authoritarianism of both parents is considered, we can predict the level of authoritarianism in their offspring with a moderate degree of accuracy. It seems, however, that other variables must also be involved.

One possible clue lies in differences between the parents. While the similarity between husbands and wives was significantly greater than zero, it was not very large. When the parents were divided into high, medium, and low thirds on the basis of their authoritarian scores, all possible patterns of husband–wife combinations were found. Authoritarian offspring were found to be most likely to develop in families in which neither parent is low F and the same-sex parent is high F. Equalitarian offspring are most likely to be found in families in which at least one parent is low F and the same-sex parent is not high F.

Still another variation was reported by Baumrind (1972). In studying black families in the United States, she noted that they are higher in authoritarianism than white families. Yet authoritarian black parents produce daughters who are independent and assertive. It seems that they tend to treat their daughters in nontraditional ways in that they discourage dependent behavior and encourage the expression of emotion. Once again, it seems that the transmission of authoritarianism or equalitarianism across generations may be a complex phenomenon.

Outside Influences: The Role of the Schools

Authoritarianism Versus Education. Outside the family setting children come into contact with numerous people who have an impact on their development. The most obvious and pervasive of these outside influences—in our culture at least—is the school system. In the United States, by the time we reach college age most of us have spent twelve years in a variety of classrooms. This means six or seven hours a day, five days a week, nine months each year interacting with teachers, reading assigned material, and interacting in specific ways with our peers and with people in positions of authority. It is not at all surprising to find that our behavior is partly shaped by this experience. What effect does education have on authoritarianism?

For some time it has been known that children who are high in authoritarianism tend to do less well in school than equalitarian children (Davids, 1956) and also are likely to complete fewer years of school (Lindgren, 1962). Presumably, one reason that authoritarian children do badly is the tendency of many schools to foster the democratic ideal and emphasize student-centered concerns. It has been found that teachers who are trained to focus on the motives and wishes of their pupils can actually lower the F Scale scores of their students (Levitt, 1955). It is possible that the most authoritarian children do not do well in such an atmosphere and tend to become alienated from the school system.

Simpson (1972) proposed that education will lower authoritarianism only when the schools emphasize cognitive learning and only when nonauthoritarian teachers are employed. By contrast, a system that stresses rote learning in an authoritarian atmosphere will not lead to a reduction in authoritarianism over the school years. A comparison of the relation between authoritarianism and years of schooling is shown in Figure 5-4 for Mexico and the United States. It is clear that number of years of schooling is unrelated to authoritarianism in Mexico and strongly related in

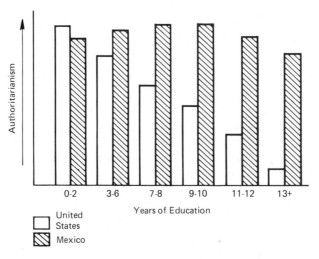

Figure 5-4. It appears that in a democratic school system like that of the United States, authoritarianism decreases as years of education increase. In a relatively autocratic school system like that of Mexico, there is no relation between authoritarianism and years of education. (Data from Simpson, 1972)

the United States. It would seem that in understanding the influence of schools on personality the type of school is crucial.

Creating a Fascist Classroom.   If authoritarian values can be influenced by the actions of teachers and by the structure of the school system, what would be the result of a deliberate attempt to create antidemocratic values? In his high school history class Ron Jones (1976) found that a Nazi ideology is frighteningly easy to create.

While studying the events of the 1930s and 1940s, Jones' students expressed puzzlement as to how it was possible for the German people to have allowed their Jewish fellow citizens to be persecuted, tortured, and murdered. How could a whole nation get caught up in Nazism? Jones gave them a demonstration. In the next class session he introduced the idea of discipline by having his thirty students sit "at attention" with their feet flat on the floor and their hands behind their backs. Then he made them stand beside their desks whenever a question was asked, start each inquiry with "Mr. Jones," and keep their remarks as brief as possible.

To his surprise, the new rules were very popular. The next day he wrote slogans on the blackboard that the students were to repeat over and over—"Strength Through Discipline" and "Strength Through Community." He also gave them a special salute: right hand to the shoulder, fingers curled. This was called the Third Wave. The students were instructed to greet each other and their teacher with this salute whenever they met, even outside the classroom. Anyone who failed to obey that rule was to be reported by an informer. By the third day, thirteen students had cut other classes to visit Jones' room to see what was going on. All of them received membership cards in the Third Wave Organization.

On the fourth day, the teacher told his enlarged class of 80 students that the Third Wave was not an experiment but a nationwide movement to identify young people who were willing to fight for political change. He said there would be a TV announcement the next day in which the leader would appear and reveal the plans of the Third Wave. On the fifth day, over 200 students showed up in the high school auditorium to receive the word of the leader. Jones gave the salute and the students returned it. They all chanted "Strength Through Discipline" over and over again and with increasing volume. When the excitement was at its peak, Jones turned on the TV set, and of course nothing happened. There was no leader and no Third Wave. He then explained to them what had been going on and the parallels between their responses and those of the German people.

The ease with which people can be carried along by an authoritarian program is perhaps a cause for concern. One hope is that those who took part in the Third Wave movement and even those of us who just read about it will be especially alert to similar happenings in real life.

One reason for concern is the finding that the opinions of many citizens do not coincide with the democratic principles on which the United States was founded. Consider the following two paragraphs and decide which one you favor:

Unrestricted free speech has threatened the foundation of the structure of democratic government. So have unrestricted criticism of the government by the press and the freedom of people nonviolently to protest their grievances to the government. Public order and welfare need to have the State ... act to limit these things. This is in the public interest.

Unrestricted free speech is a necessary foundation of the structure of democratic government. So are unrestricted criticism of the government by the press and the freedom of people nonviolently to protest their grievances to the government. Public order and welfare need to have the State ... always defend these things. This is in the public interest.

If you find yourself in agreement with the first paragraph, you are similar to the majority of respondents in Sacramento, California, who were surveyed in their neighborhoods (Samuel, 1972). Only a minority agreed with the second paragraph; it is, sad to note, a paraphrase of statements from the Bill of Rights of the U.S. Constitution. The more popular version reverses those basic rights.

Liberal Biases: Would You Want Your Family to Raise an Authoritarian?

In the theoretical description of authoritarians, a number of the proposed traits suggest psychological maladjustment. Thus, authoritarians were described as rigid, conforming, repressing, denying, projecting, and displacing. Equalitarians, on the other hand, were said to be flexible, free, aware of their impulses, and less likely to utilize unconscious defense mechanisms. Masling (1954) suggested that the primary reason for these differences was lack of objectivity in the social scientists who studied authoritarianism. His point is a good one. From the very beginning, research in this area has been influenced by the biases of relatively liberal, antifascist researchers. To most psychologists, authoritarians are bad guys and equalitarians are good guys. Masling also pointed out that only four studies had examined the relation between authoritarianism and mental health and that not one of them found any connection between them.

Sanford (1956) also pointed out that a low score on the F Scale is not a guarantee of mental health. He describes several types of people who are low in potential fascism but are also maladjusted. For example, rigid low authoritarians can be as totalitarian as those with high F scores. It is just that their compulsiveness and paranoia are expressed in support of such ideals as minority rights and in opposition to right-wing ideology. Rokeach (1960) has tried to separate the tendency to be rigidly totalitarian from the issue of right-wing versus left-wing political ideology. On his Dogmatism Scale both left-of-center groups such as communists and right-of-center groups such as extreme conservatives tend to receive high scores. Only the right-of-center groups score high on the F Scale.

Figure 5-5. Early training in conforming to right-wing ideology tends to result in later acceptance of a very conservative, rigid set of attitudes.

Bettmann Archive

It appears, then, that some of the personality traits identified with authoritarianism are not necessarily tied to a particular political philosophy and that authoritarianism is not an indicator of poor mental health.

WHAT DO YOU THINK?

Disciplining Children: The Carrot or the Stick?

Imagine for a moment that you are given a summer job as the supervisor of twenty 10-year-old children who are enrolled in a day camp in a local park. Part of your job is fairly straightforward because a schedule is provided by the Park Board. There are specific amounts of time to be spent playing table tennis, swimming, eating lunch, resting, and so forth. Problems arise, however, when some of the kids fail to do something that you expect *and* when they do something that you think is wrong. How do you respond? Consider the following situations and decide what might be the best way to deal with each of them.

1. In the middle of a table tennis game, Tony and Bobby begin arguing about the score. Before you can do anything about it, Tony throws his paddle at Bobby's head, giving him a bruise on the temple. Bobby is crying and Tony is glaring at you. What do you do?

2. At the swimming pool two of the children say they are afraid of the water. You have a note from each child's parents indicating that they know how to swim, but Mary and Rich insist that they cannot swim and refuse to go near the pool. What do you do?

3. It is time for lunch, and the children are seated at two large picnic tables. You leave for a moment to pick up the chilled cartons of milk. When you return you find chaos. All twenty children are shouting and screaming and wildly throwing bits of bread, cookies, fruit, and paper bags at one another. Most are laughing as they pelt each other and create a bigger and bigger mess. What do you do?

4. During the 30-minute rest hour you notice some unusual activity on one of the mats at the edge of the group. Carol and Ken have removed some of their clothing and are examining each other's genitals. What do you do?

After you write down your probable response to each situation, go back and consider the meaning of your behavior. Did you rely mainly on rewards or on punishments? Why do you think your methods should be effective? Did your handling of each situation suggest that you are relatively permissive or relatively restrictive with children? Are your responses more like those of an authoritarian parent or those of an equalitarian parent?

Parents, teachers, and others must respond to many such situations each day. Most of us are able to justify the way we deal with the problem of discipline, but do you think it is possible that we are simply behaving in a way that is consistent with our personality traits?

CONSERVATISM, CONFORMITY, AND CONVENTIONAL VALUES

Political and Economic Beliefs

Liberalism–Conservatism. One of the basic dimensions of political ideology is a complex set of beliefs and values concerning people and their relation to the state and to the existing social order: liberalism versus conservatism. It has been found that authoritarians are more likely to preserve arbitrary social norms across generations than equalitarians are (Montgomery, Hinkle, & Enzie, 1976). In other words, authoritarians show the conservative tendency to preserve current values and practices while equalitarians show the liberal tendency to seek change (Kopkind, 1977).

In their original series of investigations, Adorno and colleagues (1950) suggested that adherence to right-wing or conservative politics should be related to antidemocratic beliefs because fascism is the most extreme right-wing ideology. A Politico-Economic Conservatism Scale was built in an attempt to measure such trends as support of the American status quo, resistance to social change, and support of conservative values. It includes items like the following:

America may not be perfect, but the American Way has brought us about as close as human beings can get to a perfect society.

In general, full economic security is bad; most men wouldn't work if they didn't need the money for eating and living.

Conservatism, as measured by this test, is positively related to authoritarianism. Consistent with this finding is Rim's (1970) research with a group of Israeli students. Both high and low scorers on the F Scale assigned ranks to a series of values. Those who were high in authoritarianism assigned a higher rank to politeness and cleanliness than those who were low in authoritarianism; the reverse was true with respect to the importance of being ambitious, independent, and broad-minded.

Socialized Medicine, the Women's Movement, and Loyalty Oaths. Since a number of specific issues are involved in liberal–conservative differences, it is not surprising to find the F Scale related to the positions people take on many topics. For example, Mahler (1953) found that authoritarianism is linked with a negative attitude toward socialized medicine. High F's feel that compulsory health insurance would destroy the doctor–patient relationship and result in inferior medical care.

Another issue is the women's movement. Worell and Worell (1977) measured attitudes toward equality between the sexes with a test containing items such as, "Women have more to gain than to lose by asking for complete equality." As expected, they found that both male and female college students who opposed the women's movement were higher in authoritarianism than those who supported it.

Several types of political behavior have been found to be related to authoritarianism. Beginning in 1949, the University of California at Berkeley was shaken by what became known as the "loyalty oath controversy." In the summer of that year the regents of the University sent out a special noncommunist oath with the academic contracts for 1949–50. A great many people refused to sign the oath on the grounds that (1) there were no communists on the faculty and (2) the oath was a violation of tenure. Eighteen nonsigning faculty members took their case to court, while a number of nontenure employees lost their positions. Handlon and Squier (1955) located a group of the nonsigners who had been fired and selected a random sample of nontenured employees who had signed the oath. Each subject was interviewed and given the F Scale. Those who had refused to sign were significantly less authoritarian than those who had signed the oath.

Conforming to the Group

The proposed authoritarian traits of conventionalism and submission have led a number of investigators to hypothesize that those who score high on the F scale should be conformists. In the widely used conformity procedure devised by Asch (1956), subjects are given a task such as judging the lengths of lines. The subject believes he or she is one of a group of subjects who are carrying out the task. Actually, each subject is mixed in with a group of confederates who are instructed to give incorrect responses on specified trials. Conformity is defined as the number of trials on which the subject goes along with the group in making incorrect decisions.

Though there have been some inconsistent findings in this area, a number of studies (e.g., Crutchfield, 1955; Nadler, 1959) have confirmed the hypothesis that people who are high in authoritarianism tend to conform to group pressure. These individuals are also more likely to believe what they are told by media figures such as TV newscasters and newspaper columnists (Levy, 1979).

Religious Beliefs and Activities

Several aspects of religious behavior have been found to be linked with authoritarianism and ethnocentrism. Jones (1958) used two large samples of naval aviation cadets. He found that, compared to equalitarians, those who are high in authoritarianism (1) are more likely to be Protestant or Roman Catholic than to be Jewish or unaffiliated with any church and (2) are more likely to attend church regularly.

Data obtained by David Dustin and Robert K. Young using college undergraduates are consistent with these findings. In terms of religious preference, those students who were Baptists, Episcopalians, or Catholics obtained the highest mean scores, while those with no religious affiliation were the least authoritarian. In between were those who were Jewish, Methodist, Presbyterian, or members of other Protestant groups. Likewise, those who attended church more regularly (weekly or twice a month) were significantly more authoritarian than those who never or almost never attended church. Even among people with religious affiliations, those who attend church regularly are significantly more authoritarian than those who stay away from church. A study of Stanford undergraduates by the authors revealed a difference of about thirty points between the authoritarian scores of those who never attended church and those who reported weekly attendance.

If the traditional Christian values are tolerance, brotherhood, and equality, why is it that these values are held more firmly by people who are not affiliated with a church than by those who are? It has been suggested that the majority of middle-class Americans belong to a religious group as a matter of course and not because they consider the matter carefully or accept the church's ideology. Thus, for many people church membership and attendance may represent nothing more than socially acceptable behavior. Kahoe (1974) differentiated religious beliefs into those based on intrinsic motives ("My religious beliefs are what really lie behind my whole approach to life.") and those based on extrinsic motives ("The purpose of prayer is to secure a happy and peaceful life."). Only those individuals with extrinsic religious motives are high in authoritarianism.

It has also been found that authoritarian churches (Mormon, Catholic, Seventh Day Adventist, Southern Baptist) attract more converts during times of economic hardship while nonauthoritarian churches (Congregational, Northern Baptist, Presbyterian, Episcopal) are more successful when the economic situation is good (Sales, 1973). It may be that in threatening times authoritarians are motivated to turn to organized religion as a way to solve their problems.

PREJUDICE, HOSTILITY, AND AGGRESSION

Prejudice: Hating Those Who Are Not Like You

Many organizations follow authoritarian principles, and such groups almost always express strong prejudices against other nations, religions, races, and so forth. The Ku Klux Klan is one example. The Indiana grand dragon, William N. Chaney, expressed some of these bigoted ideals in a newspaper interview:

"We still believe in the superiority of the white race," Chaney said.
Chaney said to his knowledge there has never been a great civilization that was not white.

"And there has never been a great civilization in Africa," he said.

Asked about Egypt, Chaney said, "If you look at history you will find that the ancient Egyptians were white before they were mongrelized."

Chaney said, "When one race enslaves another it is a sign of superior intelligence." But, he added, "I'm not in favor of slavery, of course." [Keegan, 1975]

Ethnocentrism: My Country's Better Than Your Country.   One part of the original series of authoritarian studies dealt with **ethnocentrism.** Ethnocentrism refers to cultural narrowness, the tendency to believe that one's own culture is superior and all others are inferior. The Ethnocentrism Scale includes items like the following:

The worst danger to real Americanism during the last 50 years has come from foreign ideas and agitators.

Filipinos are all right in their place, but they carry it too far when they dress lavishly and go around with white girls.

It is only natural and right for each person to think that his family is better than any other.

Research indicates a strong positive relation between authoritarianism and ethnocentrism.

Anti-Semitism: Jews as Scapegoats.   The starting point in the Berkeley group's study of prejudice was an investigation of **anti-Semitism,** partly because the world had recently witnessed what happens when the horror of prejudice is carried to an extreme and partly because of the long, unhappy history of the Jewish people. It was suggested that organized anti-Semitism presents a major threat to democracy because it serves as a rallying cry for antidemocratic political movements.

The Anti-Semitism Scale included items like the following:

I can hardly imagine myself marrying a Jew.

The trouble with letting Jews into a nice neighborhood is that they gradually give it a typical Jewish atmosphere.

Research indicates a substantial correlation between the F Scale and the Anti-Semitism Scale. As expected, authoritarianism is positively related to anti-Jewish attitudes.

Anti-Black Attitudes.   In the United States, perhaps the most widespread prejudice among whites is directed against blacks. Probably in part because other factors (e.g., regional differences) confound the relationship, authoritarianism is not generally found to be as highly correlated with attitudes toward blacks as might be expected from the anti-Semitism and ethnocentrism findings. That is, authoritarianism is only moderately linked with anti-black prejudice (e.g., Klein, 1963).

One of the basic traits that has been ascribed to the highly authoritarian person is hostility. It is hypothesized that this hostility is directed mainly toward outgroups and those who violate cultural norms. Many of the items on the F Scale were designed to reflect this hostile component. In addition to the prejudice studies, other empirical evidence supports the hostility hypothesis.

Solving Crime with Punishment.   Both on the basis of the general description of authoritarianism and on the basis of child-rearing data, one might expect to find that authoritarians are convinced that punishment and retaliation are the best way to solve problems. It is believed that the solution to the problem of crime is to have more and more severe punishment. When President Kennedy was assassinated, Sherwood (1966) hypothesized that authoritarians would be most likely to respond with righteous indignation and to be concerned with blame and punishment. He compared this kind of response to "moral realism" in children. That is, from about 3 to 8 years of age children tend to view both rules and the punishments for violating them as givens that are unquestioned and unchangeable. Tied in with this view of the world is a conception of justice in which the wrongdoer should suffer a punishment that fits the crime. One week after the assassination, questionnaires were mailed to a group of past and present officers of various midwestern organizations that had expressed public concern with "Americanism"; the same questionnaires were also given to liberal arts college students. Not only was the organization sample higher in authoritarianism than the student sample, but the mean score of this sample was one of the highest ever reported. Table 5-2 shows some of the items on which the two groups differed.

War: My Country, Right or Wrong.   The ultimate expression of hostility is warfare. Again, it would be expected that authoritarians would differ from equalitarians in their attitudes toward war. The conflict in Vietnam provided an especially relevant topic in that opinions about various aspects of the American presence in Vietnam were sharply divided and strongly expressed. It was a time when many people totally rejected those who disagreed with them. Students chanted, "Hey, hey, L.B.J., how many kids did you kill today?" An elderly man was interviewed on a television news program. He said that he was 100 percent behind the commander-in-chief; though he was too old to fight, he said he was willing to go to Vietnam, tie tin cans to his body, and run out in front of the troops so as to draw enemy fire. Supporters of the war tended to reject dissenters as cowards or traitors. These attitudes were identified with various visible symbols—the peace sign versus the American flag, long hair versus short

Table 5-2. When authoritarians and equalitarians were questioned about their reactions to the assassination of President Kennedy, the authoritarian subjects expressed the greatest concern with punishing whoever was guilty.

Questionnaire Items	Authoritarians	Equalitarians
The assassination of the President was part of the communist conspiracy.	4.51	1.95
The most important consideration facing the nation after President Kennedy's death was finding who was guilty and punishing him.	5.32	2.44
Lee Harvey Oswald got what was coming to him when he was shot.	6.03	3.31
The important thing is that the wrongdoer should suffer.	4.81	2.21
Rewards and punishments should be decided by those in charge, even if it means unequal punishments for the same crime.	5.05	2.63
We spend too much time worrying about being just and fair when we know all the time that someone is guilty.	4.87	2.12

On each item, 7 = strongly agree and 1 = strongly disagree.
(Data from Sherwood, 1966)

hair, pot versus booze. Is it possible that such deeply felt and widely different viewpoints were related to authoritarianism?

Izzett (1971) predicted such a relation in that anti-Vietnam War attitudes amounted to a break with authority. On October 15, 1969, a large number of people took part in a moratorium on the war. Izzett predicted that students who observed the moratorium by refusing to attend classes on that day would have significantly lower F Scale scores than students who did attend classes. In addition, a paper-and-pencil questionnaire dealing with attitudes about the war was expected to show that authoritarians were more in favor of the war than equalitarians. A large group of students at the State University of New York at Oswego were administered the F Scale and a series of items dealing with the Vietnam War. Before the Vietnam moratorium day it was announced that classes would be held as usual but that students should follow the dictates of their own beliefs with respect to coming to class on that day. It was found that the students who observed moratorium day by staying away from class had significantly lower F Scale scores than those who attended class. On the questionnaire items, authoritarianism was positively related to responses indicating that the United States should invade North Vietnam, resume the bombing of North Vietnam, and send more troops and supplies to South Vietnam. Authoritarianism was negatively related to responses indicating that the United States should withdraw its troops immediately and press for a coalition government in South Vietnam that included the Viet Cong.

In other research, people scoring low in authoritarianism have also been found to be more likely to engage in protest actions against the war, such as signing petitions, writing letters to political leaders, and attending antiwar rallies (Granberg & Corrigan, 1972). Thus, both in questionnaire responses and in overt acts, authoritarians and equalitarians responded quite differently to U.S. military involvement in Southeast Asia.

Aggression: Inflicting Pain

Experimental research has shown a general tendency of authoritarians to respond with punishment. For example, Dustin and Davis (1967) placed subjects in a setting that was supposedly designed to measure their leadership ability. The "follower" had to perform a simple task, and the leader was to maximize that person's performance. After each trial the subject could choose one of various sanctions to communicate to the follower: awarding money, taking money away, saying the follower had done well or poorly, or simply telling the follower to go on to the next trial. The equalitarian subjects used the negative sanctions significantly less often than the authoritarians. Since the follower's performance was the same for all subjects, the findings suggest that people who score high and low in authoritarianism differ in their beliefs concerning the effectiveness of different kinds of sanctions. That is, authoritarians seem to think that people will work best if they are punished or scolded, while equalitarians feel that performance is enhanced by rewards or praise.

Experimental studies have also dealt with the proposed relation between authoritarianism and aggressive responses. Epstein (1965) pointed out that authoritarians are supposed to be sensitized to power relations such as strong–weak or superior–inferior and hence should feel that aggression is justifiable against low-status rather than high-status persons. It is as if weakness and lower status confer a permit or license to aggress. This is one explanation, for example, of the fact that harsh repressive measures are more likely to be directed against minority groups, the victims of poverty, or "hippie types" than against members of the majority group, wealthy persons, or members of the establishment. Epstein selected high and low authoritarians on the basis of a pretest. As in many of the experiments to be described in Chapter 10, a version of the Buss aggression machine was used. The subject is supposedly teaching another subject (the victim) a verbal learning task by giving shocks for incorrect responses. Actually, the experimenter is interested in the strength of the shocks that the subject believes he or she is administering.

In Epstein's experiment, the victim was either low status (old clothes, family making under $1,500 a year, planning to drop out of school, unemployed parents who have a grade school education) or high status (well dressed, planning to obtain a graduate degree in business administration, family making $20,000 a year, parents who have a college education, father a vice president in an advertising firm). There was an interaction between the authoritarianism of the subject and the status of the victim. That is, authoritarian subjects gave more intense shocks to a low-status victim than to a high-status victim, while the reverse was true for the equalitarian subjects. It was suggested that perhaps high and low scorers both tend to express differential aggression on the basis of status, but in opposite directions. It was suggested that some people who score very low on the F Scale may represent "authoritarianism of the left." These people express hostility toward those who are wealthy and powerful. Right-wing authoritarians, in contrast, are hostile toward the poor and disadvantaged.

RESEARCH CLOSE-UP

Personality in the Courtroom: Authoritarian and Equalitarian Jurors

Neither theory nor research suggests that authoritarians are *always* hostile and aggressive. Instead, it is proposed that authoritarians must justify their punitive behavior by aggressing only against those who "deserve" it. In that way hostility can be freely expressed against those who deviate from society's moral code, against the enemies of one's country, and against anyone who breaks the law.

Given this tendency to seek justifiable reasons to punish others, authoritarians would be expected to find a great deal of satisfaction in serving on a jury. They are more likely than equalitarians to reach a guilty verdict, and they impose more severe punishment on those convicted (Bray & Noble, 1978). In addition, they seem to be especially sensitive to the biases of a judge and are willing to follow his or her lead (Landewehr & Novotny, 1976). In the courtroom a person can be a good citizen and at the same time be in favor of acting against a very acceptable victim—the defendant. Among people serving on actual juries, authoritarians are found to be more likely to convict a defendant and more punitive in assigning penalties afterward (Jurow, 1971). In an experiment dealing with this tendency, (Mitchell and Byrne, 1973), college undergraduates were asked to respond to a court case in which a student had been seen stealing an examination. The task of the jurors was to decide how severely to punish the thief. The description of the defendant was manipulated so that he was a very likable person for half of the subjects and very unlikable for the other half. Also, half of the subjects were relatively high and half relatively low in authoritarianism. The effects of these variables on their decisions are shown in Figure 5-6. You can see that the equalitarian jurors were more or less able to ignore their feelings about the defendant and recommend roughly the same degree of punishment, regardless of whether they liked him. The authoritarians, on the other hand, clearly allowed their feelings to determine their judgments. They recommended a very severe punishment for a disliked defendant and a very mild one for a defendant they liked.

That and similar research led to doubts about the fairness of having authoritarians on juries and to the suggestion that tests might be used to screen such

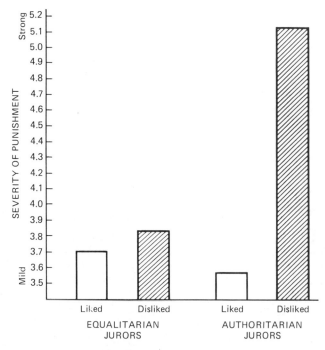

Figure 5-6. In an experimental study of authoritarians as members of a jury, those high on the F Scale were found to be punitive toward a student defendant they disliked and very lenient toward one they liked. Equalitarian jurors responded with similar recommendations regardless of their personal feelings about the defendant.

(Data from Mitchell & Byrne, 1973)

people out of prospective jury panels (Lamberth & Kirby, 1974). Procedures have even been devised to lower the authoritarianism of prospective jurors through verbal conditioning just before the trial begins (Griffitt & Garcia, 1977). It has been reported that authoritarians pay more attention to information about guilt and personal qualities (Berg & Vidmar, 1975). They also tend to recall the evidence presented by the prosecution more readily than that presented by the defense (Garcia & Griffitt, 1978). In most experiments of this type, however, the defendant was a fellow student or an average citizen. We have seen, however, in the research on aggression that authoritarians tend not to express hostility toward someone who has high status or is an authority figure. In fact, against a target of that sort, it seems that the equalitarians are the aggressive ones. What if the defendant in a jury trial were someone other than an ordinary person? Is it possible that under certain conditions an equalitarian juror can be as unfair and biased as an authoritarian juror?

In a test of this possibility Mitchell (1979) created a courtroom situation based on an actual incident. A trial transcript described a riot that had broken out at a

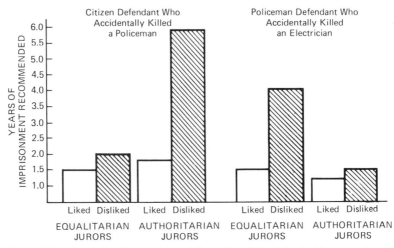

Figure 5-7. In another jury experiment the status of the defendant in a manslaughter trial was varied. When an ordinary citizen had accidentally killed a policeman, authoritarian jurors behaved as in previous studies and responded much more punitively to a disliked defendant than to a liked one. When the situation was reversed, however, it was the equalitarians who responded much more positively to a disliked policeman defendant than to a liked one, while the authoritarians were able to ignore their biases.

(Data from Mitchell, 1979)

summer rock concert. In the chaos that followed, a policeman and an electrician's apprentice scuffled briefly; one was knocked down and died a few hours later as a result of internal injuries. In the experiment, half of the subjects were told that the electrician had accidentally knocked down and killed the policeman and half were told that the reverse had happened. Again the defendant was made to appear either likable or unlikable, and the subjects were either high or low in authoritarianism. As depicted in Figure 5-7, it was found that when the electrician was the defendant, authoritarians once again were punitive toward someone they disliked while equalitarians were fair and unbiased. In contrast, when the policeman was the defendant, the equalitarians were punitive toward a disliked person while the authoritarians were unbiased. Among other things, this experiment shows that some of the personality traits of authoritarians may depend on the specifics of the situation and also, in Mitchell's words, that "the good guys don't always wear white hats."

SEXUALITY AND AUTHORITARIANISM

Concern with sexuality and sexual "goings-on" was given an important place in the proposed description of authoritarians. Studies of the relation between F Scale responses and attitudes toward sex have consistently verified that authoritarians respond negatively to many aspects of sex.

In an unpublished study of undergraduates at the University of Texas, John McCoy found that authoritarians were more likely than equalitarians to feel that children should not be given frank explanations about sex until they are old enough to have some self-control. Likewise, it has been found that authoritarians are more likely than equalitarians to judge stimuli with sexual content as pornographic. Eliasberg and Stuart (1961) presented color slides of works of art showing nudes, such as Chabas' "September Morn," to male and female students. Subjects were asked to judge each as pornographic or not pornographic. The higher the subject's score on the F Scale, the more paintings were judged to be pornographic. One of the basic traits of authoritarians in the proposed description was the tendency to utilize repressive defenses. One of the best-designed studies testing this hypothesis was an experiment by Kogan (1956). If the repression hypothesis was accurate, it was suggested, authoritarians would find it more difficult to recognize threatening aggressive and sexual material than equalitarians would. Kogan selected 42 sentences to be recorded on tape, partially masked by white noise to make recognition difficult. Subjects were given 14 neutral, 14 aggressive, and 14 sexual sentences in random order. Samples of the three types of sentence follow:

NEUTRAL
You like to go swimming during the summer season.
The thought of a good meal increases your appetite.
AGGRESSIVE
Only your death would be a just punishment for you.
Your mother is to blame for your worst faults.
SEXUAL
You have been unable to break your ugly sex habits.
You would have loved to share your father's sex life.

The subjects were male undergraduates. Each sentence was played, the tape stopped, and the subjects asked to write down what they had heard; then the next sentence was played. Because of the white noise, it was difficult to perceive the sentences accurately. Recognition of the threatening material was measured in relation to recognition of neutral material to control for differences in hearing ability. It was found that as the authoritarian scores increased, ability to perceive the threatening material decreased.

Another study of authoritarian projection was undertaken by Griffitt (1973). He presented slides depicting explicit sexual themes to a group of unmarried undergraduates. In addition to providing self-ratings of their responses to the erotic stimuli, the subjects were asked to guess how a member of the opposite sex would respond. Authoritarianism in both sexes was associated with projection of negative responses to members of the opposite sex. Thus, members of the opposite sex were seen as angry, disgusted, and restrictive about erotica by those who were high in authoritarianism. In addition, female authoritarians had interesting perceptions of the responses of males. They differed from equalitarian females in guessing that undergraduate males would be relatively more aroused by themes of female homosexuality and oral–genital sex and relatively less aroused by conventional heterosexual intercourse. Griffitt noted that the themes that were projected as producing arousal in males involved traditionally more unacceptable acts. Thus, female authoritarians seem to assume that males are most aroused by taboo behavior.

When authoritarians are found to repress or project in response to sexual stimuli, it is reasonable to assume that such stimuli bring about negative emotional responses. That is, authoritarians and equalitarians may not differ in the extent to which erotic stimuli are sexually stimulating, but they may very well differ in whether such arousal is perceived as pleasant or unpleasant, a source of enjoyment or a source of concern. In an experiment with married couples, explicit erotic materials were presented (Byrne, Cherry, Lamberth, & Mitchell, 1973). As expected, authoritarianism was unrelated to sexual arousal, but it was consistently related to negative feelings about being aroused. As authoritarianism increased, self-ratings of disgust and depression increased. In addition, authoritarianism was linked with the judgment that the sexual stimuli were pornographic and the belief that there should be legal restrictions on the production and sale of such material. It may be seen, then, that the crucial variable in the response of authoritarians to sexual material is their attitudes and emotional reactions to sexuality. For them, sexual arousal is a negative experience and one that should be severely limited and controlled. Legal restrictions on erotic stimuli would serve as a protection against such arousal. A picket outside of the theater showing Monty Python's *Life of Brian* expressed the authoritarian viewpoint quite clearly when he said that "anybody civilized tolerates a certain amount of censorship" (*Albany Times-Union*, Sept. 29, 1979, p. 16).

One clue to the origin of these negative attitudes is provided by Kelley (1977). She presented college students with slides depicting heterosexual acts, members of the subject's own sex masturbating, and members of the opposite sex masturbating. In both male and female authoritarians strong negative feelings were aroused by the same-sex masturbation pictures but not by the other photos. It seems quite possible that masturbation was an especially taboo topic, and perhaps a forbidden activity, in authoritarian homes. If this hypothesis were confirmed, it would help explain why sexual concerns and conflicts are associated with authoritarianism.

Because authoritarians are extremely negative toward any sexual behavior they consider deviant and because they tend to aggress against those who violate social norms, Garcia and Griffitt (1977) hypothesized that a person's willingness to punish a sex offender would be a function of his or her level of authoritarianism. They created a jury situation and presented college students with simulated court material dealing with a case of incest. A 35-year-old male teacher was accused of exciting his 13-year-old offspring by showing her obscene photographs and then engaging in mutual genital fondling with her. Both high and low authoritarians thought the defendant was guilty, but those with high scores gave him a longer prison sentence and decided to permit him fewer visits per year with his child, as may be seen in Figure 5-8. It was also found that the authoritarians rated the defendant as less good and more unpleasant than equalitarians rated him.

Interestingly enough, in a parallel case involving child abuse (hitting the child with fists, beating her with a belt until her body was covered

Figure 5-8. When authoritarian subjects were presented with the case of a sex offender (a father who committed incest), those with high F Scale scores were found to be more punitive than those with low scores. Presumably, a sex offense is seen as especially bad by authoritarians.

(Data from Garcia & Griffitt, 1977)

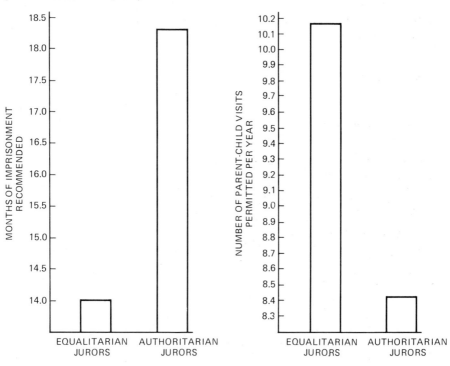

with bruises) it was found that authoritarians were no more punitive than equalitarians. It took a sexual offense to bring out this difference in willingness to punish the guilty person.

SITUATIONAL FACTORS: MAYBE ANYONE CAN BE AN AUTHORITARIAN

Despite several decades of research on authoritarianism as a trait, the situational approach suggests the possibility that authoritarian behavior may be brought about in most of us if the conditions are "right." When we see extreme examples of authoritarianism, it is difficult to believe that we ourselves—or even most of the people we know—could do such things. For example, would you be brutal toward a group of prisoners if you had total authority over them? Would you follow whatever orders were given to you even if it meant making someone else suffer? Could you have worked at a Nazi extermination camp? Could you have killed women and children at the Vietnamese village of My Lai? There is, of course, no way for any of us to know for sure what we would do unless we were to find ourselves in such a situation. People with antidemocratic ideologies may not ever put them into action unless the right situation arises (Sanford, 1973). Some research in recent years provides evidence that most people can easily be induced to behave in ways that one might expect only from extreme authoritarians.

Brutality in Prison: The Stanford Experience

The story of prisoners receiving brutal treatment is a sadly familiar one around the world. Whether they are prisoners of war, common criminals, or political dissidents, those who are locked up usually find themselves at the mercy of someone in a position of total power. You might assume that the resulting brutality is a function of the kind of people who are attracted to the work of military police, prison guards, and so forth. A study done at Stanford University by Philip Zimbardo (1971, 1974) provides evidence that personality factors may not be the main variable in such behavior.

The subjects were 21 college students who volunteered to take part in an experiment for which they were to be paid $15 a day. Ten were randomly assigned to play the role of prisoner and eleven the role of prison guard for the next two weeks. The "prisoners" were picked up at their homes by police cars, taken to the station house, and put through the usual arrest routine. Then they were blindfolded and taken to the basement of the psychology building, which would serve as their "jail." There they were stripped and provided with a loose-fitting smock with a number printed on the front and the back, rubber sandals, a chain and lock on one ankle, and a stocking cap. They were placed in small three-person cells.

The students who were to be the guards were given complete power over the inmates, except that physical punishment was forbidden.

They were furnished with uniforms, reflecting sunglasses, billy clubs, whistles, handcuffs, and keys to the cells. There were sixteen arbitrary rules that the prisoners were supposed to obey, and the guards were supposed to enforce those rules. For example, toilets could not be used after 10 P.M.; no one could smoke or write a letter without permission; and the prisoners had to address one another by number rather than by name.

Because this was only playacting, you might think that the students would react to the situation as a game for which they were being paid. Instead, the guards were very strict in enforcing the rules. They also seemed to take delight in making the prisoners do useless work, sing or laugh on command, and curse one another. The guards were insulting, aggressive, and threatening. None of them tried to help the prisoners or interfere with the other guards. The prisoners became outwardly servile, but they hated the guards and plotted ways to escape. The situation became so bad, in fact, that the experiment was stopped after six days rather than the planned two weeks. It was becoming too real for the students involved, and much too unpleasant (at least for the prisoners). The guards were disappointed when the experiment was stopped and reluctant to give up their power.

Afterwards most of the student subjects were shocked when they looked back at what had happened. One guard expressed the feelings of those in his group; "I was surprised at myself . . . I made them call each other names and clean the toilets out with their bare hands. I practically considered the prisoners cattle." (Haney, Banks, & Zimbardo, 1973).

Obedience and Respect for Authority

Though the possession of authority over others seems to bring out very unpleasant forms of behavior, at least none of the "guards" caused any physical harm. What if they had been ordered to do so? Would they obey blindly and harm a fellow human being just because someone told them to do it? College students were asked what they would do if an experimenter told them to give a strong electric shock to a stranger who protested and gave signs of being in pain. Most said that they would refuse to follow such orders and would terminate the experiment.

In reality, however, Milgram (1974) has found that in an experimental situation most people will continue to do what the researcher tells them. The subjects were seated before a simulated shock generator on which were a series of switches labeled with voltages from 15 to 450. Their task was to deliver a shock to another person (actually a confederate, who of course received no shock) each time that person made a mistake on a learning task. The shock was to be increased after each mistake. The "mistakes" were prearranged so that the subject would have to either keep on shocking the victim all the way to the highest level on the machine or disobey the experimenter and stop. It was found that even after the victim pounded on the wall and then lapsed into silence, about two-thirds of the subjects continued to deliver the supposedly painful electric shocks to him. These results are shown in Figure 5-9.

Like the prison guards, the subjects in Milgram's experiment were very uncomfortable about what they had done; some were almost hysterical in their emotional reactions. Still, most of them *did* continue to do as the authority figure commanded them.

It seems, then, that most people tend to respond to an authority figure and are able to play such a role fairly easily. It should be noted, however, that some people did not obey the authority in Milgram's experiment and that some of Zimbardo's guards were more humane than others. Such differences suggest that personality factors may be operating. As you might expect, when the authoritarianism of the subjects was examined in the obedience study (Elms & Milgram, 1966), those subjects who had defied the experimenter's orders were found to have much lower scores on the F Scale than those who had obeyed. These obedient authoritarians even

Figure 5-9. Subjects were told to give what they thought were increasingly painful electric shocks to an innocent victim. Even when the victim seemed to be in pain and stopped responding, almost two-thirds of the subjects obeyed the experimenter and continued the shocks. (Data from Milgram, 1963)

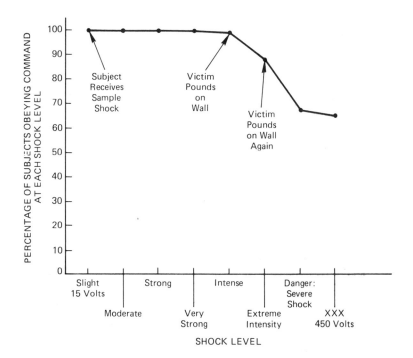

praised the researcher and said negative things about the victim to a greater extent than the defiant equalitarians did. It appears that both the situation *and* authoritarianism influence authoritarian behavior.

SUMMARY

Authoritarianism is a personality dimension that consists of a number of interrelated antidemocratic attitudes. Research on this variable was pioneered by Adorno, Frenkel-Brunswick, Levinson, and Sanford just after World War II.

The proposed description of the authoritarian personality was drawn from observation and from Freudian concepts. Authoritarians were hypothesized to be conventional, submissive to authority, aggressive toward "justifiable" targets, destructive and cynical, concerned with power and toughness, superstitious, distrustful of ideas and emotions, and overconcerned about sexuality. They were also said to have stereotyped beliefs and use projective defenses. Questionnaire items were written to tap each of these nine traits. The bootstrap technique was used, with item analyses of successive versions of the test, and the final product was the California F Scale. Because the items are worded so that agreement indicates authoritarianism, test scores may involve a confounding of authoritarianism and acquiescent response set. Balanced scales have been constructed in an effort to avoid this problem.

Research on the development of authoritarianism has dealt with child-rearing attitudes and practices and with educational influences. Authoritarian parents hold a traditional family ideology that includes expectations of obedience from their children, overconcern with status, the desire to conform, and intolerance of socially unacceptable behavior. There is a higher level of authoritarianism in traditional Turkish and Mexican-American cultures than among Anglo-Americans. Authoritarianism is also related to the use of non-love-oriented disciplinary techniques and restrictiveness. When mothers, fathers, and their offspring are studied together, it is found that the best predictors of authoritarianism in the offspring is authoritarianism in the parents. School experiences are also found to affect this personality trait; in a democratic school system authoritarianism decreases as years of schooling increase, but this does not happen in an autocratic school system. It has been found that students can easily be induced to behave in an authoritarian fashion. Though the biases of many researchers have led them to describe authoritarians as psychologically maladjusted, research suggests that adjustment is not related to this dimension. Also, totalitarianism can be found on either the political left or the political right.

With respect to political and economic beliefs, authoritarians are found to be conservative, to oppose socialized medicine, to oppose the women's movement, and to be more likely to sign a loyalty oath. Authoritarians are more likely to conform to group pressure than equalitarians. Compared to people with low scores on the F Scale, high scorers are more likely to be Protestant or Roman Catholic than to be Jewish or unaffiliated, and they are more likely to attend church regularly.

Authoritarianism is positively related to prejudice, as is shown by studies of ethnocentrism, anti-Semitism, and anti-black attitudes. Hostility is also typical of authoritarians in that, compared with equalitarians, they are more concerned with the punishment of wrongdoers and were more supportive of the American role in the Vietnam War. Authoritarians prefer punishment as a way to motivate others, while equalitarians prefer reward. Those who are high on the F Scale are found to respond with greater aggression toward low-status victims than toward high-status victims, whereas equalitarians respond in the reverse way. In the courtroom, authoritarians are punitive toward an ordinary defendant whom they dislike while equalitarians are more fair; when the defendant is an authority figure, it is the equalitarians who make biased judgments.

In research on defense mechanisms authoritarians have more difficulty perceiving sexual and aggressive stimuli. Authoritarians believe that members of the opposite sex respond negatively to erotic material, and they themselves react to such stimuli in a negative and restrictive fashion. Authoritarians are especially willing to punish someone who has committed a sexual offense.

The situational approach to personality suggests that authoritarian behavior may be brought about in most people under the right conditions. In a role-playing study of prison behavior, the subjects assigned to the role of guard quickly became insulting, aggressive, and threatening to the "prisoners." Studies of obedience indicate that most people tend to obey the commands of an authority figure even if it results in apparent pain to an innocent victim. The fact that authoritarians are more obedient than equalitarians in this experimental setting indicates that both the situation and the personality dimension operate to influence authoritarian behavior.

SUGGESTED READINGS

ADORNO, T. W., FRENKEL-BRUNSWICK, E., LEVINSON, D. J., & SANFORD, R. N.   *The authoritarian personality.* New York, Harper & Row, 1950. The classic description of the theoretical rationale of the California F Scale and the original research on this personality dimension.

CHERRY, F., & BYRNE, D.   Authoritarianism. In T. Blass (ed.), *Personality variables in social behavior.* Hillsdale, N.J.: Lawrence Erlbaum, 1977. Pp. 109–33. Review of research on the F Scale, including studies showing interaction between this personality variable and situational variables.

DIXON, N. F.   *On the psychology of military incompetence.* New York: Basic Books, 1976. An interesting and controversial book in which it is proposed that authoritarians are most likely to become our military leaders. It is then argued that such personality traits as overcontrol, obedience, antiintraception, and ethnocentrism cause the generals of all nations to be incompetent in responding to the emergencies of actual warfare.

MILGRAM, S. *Obedience to authority.* New York: Harper & Row, 1974. A very readable summary of the obedience experiments, describing the factors that increase and decrease the likelihood of a person's defying an authority figure.

ORWELL, G. *Nineteen eighty-four.* New York: Harcourt Brace Jovanovich, 1949. An absorbing fictional account of a world totally controlled by three authoritarian nations. The characteristics of such a world include total obedience to a leader, repressive sexual attitudes, punishment of those who deviate from acceptable behavior, and the channeling of hate and aggression against external enemies.

WILKINSON, R. *The broken rebel: A study in culture, politics, and authoritarian character.* New York: Harper & Row, 1972. The author takes the general empirical and theoretical descriptions of the authoritarian personality and applies them to specific individuals and specific cultures. For example, historical figures such as Heinrich Himmler and Martin Luther, events such as the Salem witch trials, and cultures such as that of the American South are each examined with respect to the role played by authoritarianism.

ZIMBARDO, P. G. On the ethics of intervention in human psychological research: With special reference to the Stanford prison experiment. *Cognition,* 1974, *2*, 243–56. A discussion of the ethical issues involved in conducting research, such as the prison study, that has a powerful emotional impact on the participants.

Chapter Six

INTELLIGENCE:
THE BASIC ABILITY

In this chapter you will read about the following topics:

Special Inserts

TRY IT YOURSELF

Culture and Intelligence: What Do IQ Tests Measure?

WHAT DO YOU THINK?

Intelligence and Grades: What Is Their Role in Our Society?

RESEARCH CLOSE-UP

What Is It Like to Be Gifted?

The living quarters of the faculty group were cramped, but the thirty residents were not really uncomfortable. The alien conquerors provided them with sufficient food, and the library was amazingly complete. The professors were not happy about being confined here, and they missed their families. Most of them also missed their work and hoped to be back in their laboratories and classrooms in the near future. Their major complaint, however, centered on the PERFORMANCES. Almost every day one member of the group was taken to the auditorium to lecture before an enthusiastic audience of aliens.

Professor Rostan had not yet been summoned, and he was very curious about what went on in the mysterious auditorium and exactly why the whole process was taking place. He realized that each of the faculty members was famous in his or her specialty. There were a biochemist, a psychologist, an engineer, an astronomer, a mathematician, and others—but only one member of the humanities faculty, a philosopher. He himself was a theoretical physicist. In thinking about the possible reasons for what was happening to them, Professor Rostan had tentatively concluded that the aliens were trying to educate themselves by forcing these professors to teach them what they knew. Perhaps it was sort of a crash course in the accumulated knowledge of the human race.

One confusing factor, however, was the reaction of his colleagues after returning from a PERFORMANCE. Some sat quietly as if in a daze, a few cried, and Broderick, the economist, was furious. No one would talk about what had happened except to reassure him that no physical torture was involved. Why, then, the intense reactions? What could possibly happen up there?

Abruptly the metal door slid open and an alien guide crept across the room to Professor Rostan's desk. An elongated blob of flesh beckoned him to follow, and the two of them left quickly. An elevator that seemed to consist only of light beams whisked them upward from the dark living quarters and suddenly onto a bright and dazzling stage. In the audience, row upon row of rounded seats formed a series of semicircles, and the professor found himself facing more aliens than he had ever seen gathered in one place.

He was led to a podium at the center of the stage and handed a note. It read, "Please explain to us what you know about the theory of relativity." At the same time, his guide squeaked a series of shrill noises to the audience, informing them of the subject

199

matter of the talk. There was a stir as each alien placed a small metallic disc on one side of its body. The professor knew that this was some sort of translating device. The onlookers settled their grotesque bodies into their basket-like seats and watched him intently.

Clearing his throat, Professor Rostan settled into what was for him a familiar classroom manner. "Though I wish that I had been warned to bring my notes on this topic, I believe that I can give you some basic information without too much trouble. Perhaps we should begin with Einstein's 1905 paper, in which he dismissed the problem of absolute motion as a stumbling block to the Lorentz-FitzGerald hypothesis by denying its existence. That is, there is no object in the universe that can serve as a stable frame of reference. Thus, it is as correct to say that a station is moving past a train as to say that the train is moving past the station. It may be seen that all motion is relative. Einstein went on to state that the relative rate of motion between any observer and any ray of light is always the same—186,000 miles per second—and therefore . . ."

He stopped. The aliens were making an unusual sound, first somewhat subdued and gradually louder and louder. He realized with a sinking feeling deep in his being that they were laughing. Great waves of hysterical and uncontrollable laughter rolled upward toward the stage. Professor Rostan was puzzled at first; then he knew. The PERFORMANCE was the alien's cruel idea of entertainment. It was as if a human audience had gathered to watch trained chimps ride motorcycles or to see dogs run through a series of clever tricks. They were laughing at him! They were amused by his simple ideas, as adults are when they laugh at a very young child's explanation of something that is too complex for him or her really to understand. How could he communicate with these creatures if they perceived him in that way—as someone or something so stupid as to be mocked like a cheap carnival act?

The professor motioned to his guide. He wanted to go back to the living quarters. The guide gently placed a piece of chocolate in Rostan's mouth. His shoulders slumped sadly as he left the stage, and his ears rang with the high-pitched laughter until the elevator had made its descent.

IT IS DIFFICULT TO IMAGINE the existence of some other species that might be so much brighter than ours that the most intelligent human beings would be objects of amusement, though they probably exist in the universe (Justrow, 1978). We also know that different animal species vary greatly in **intelligence:** the ability to learn, to remember, to understand, to form concepts, to think effectively. It is obvious that gnats are less intelligent than chickens, chickens less intelligent than cats, and cats less intelligent than monkeys by almost any standard you can name. Human beings, of course, are the smartest species on this planet. At least, this is what we tell ourselves. And there are vast differences in mental ability among humans. In this chapter we will examine this trait and the way it is measured, as well as the determinants of intelligence, how individual differences influence behavior, and some of the controversies over intelligence and its origin.

Individual differences in intelligence were observed and discussed at least 2,000 years before anyone made an attempt to measure this trait (McNemar, 1964). Intelligence is strongly related to social desirability. It is good to be bright, smart, and wise, and bad to be dull, dumb, and stupid. But a precise definition of this dimension has been elusive. The most concrete and least theoretically useful suggestion is that "intelligence is what intelligence tests measure." A more abstract definition specifies that *intelligence is the capacity of the individual to understand his or her environment and the ability to cope with its challenges* (Wechsler, 1975). With a few exceptions (e.g., Sternberg, 1979), there has been more interest in measuring this trait and using test scores as predictors than in understanding it in a theoretical sense.

We each know that *we* are intelligent, at least with respect to things that matter. In a personality class we once asked 95 undergraduates to estimate (anonymously) their intelligence relative to the rest of the group. That is, the person who thought he or she was the smartest should indicate a percentile of 100, the one who was least intelligent a percentile of 0, and so forth. Their responses are shown in Table 6-1. You can see that almost two-thirds of the group felt that they were in the upper one-third, and no one placed himself or herself in the lower 40 percent. Males tended to overestimate their intellectual ability slightly more than females. Do you, or does anyone you know, respond any differently?

One reason that we place such a high value on intellectual skills is because they have proven to be of great value in terms of survival. Sagan

Table 6-1. When 95 undergraduates were asked to estimate their intelligence relative to that of other members of their class, most felt that they were in the upper third and none felt that they were in the lower 40 percent. It seems that we tend to value intellectual ability and to think of ourselves as possessing it.

Intelligence Level in the Group, by Percentiles	Percentage of Students Actually Falling in Each Category	Percentage of 42 Males Estimating That They Fall in Each Category	Percentage of 53 Females Estimating That They Fall in Each Category
91–100	10	21.4	7.5
81–90	10	26.2	24.5
71–80	10	33.3	28.3
61–70	10	14.3	13.2
51–60	10	2.4	20.8
41–50	10	2.4	5.7
31–40	10	0.0	0.0
21–30	10	0.0	0.0
11–20	10	0.0	0.0
1–10	10	0.0	0.0

(1977) notes that our tree-dwelling ancestors had to be smart to survive. If a squirrel falls off a branch, it is light enough to be unhurt by the fall. Our primate forebears, on the other hand, would be badly injured or killed by a similar fall, so only those who understood and remembered the danger, only those who grasped spatial relationships (as well as tree limbs) would survive to pass on their intellectual ability to their offspring. It has also been pointed out that primate intelligence developed in a social context (Jolly, 1966). As crude societies came into being, it was essential that the young learn the rules of that society, whether they were gorillas, baboons, or human beings. Those who were most successful at comprehending the rules and devising ways to avoid danger and obtain an adequate diet were most likely to survive. Thus, intelligence was a biological necessity for several relatively weak and helpless species. Later, as human societies came into being, it was no less important to be able to learn, understand, and remember. It seems obvious that some very basic skills are involved, but how can we measure them and make them an integral part of a science of behavior?

Measuring Intelligence: Simple Versus Complex Responses

Simple Behavioral Skills.   The earliest attempts to measure individual differences in intellectual functioning focused on very simple responses. In the latter half of the nineteenth century, Galton worked with such factors as hearing and the ability to form mental images. James McKeen Cattell studied psychology in Germany and returned to the United States in 1890 with a series of such tests, including sensory measures and strength of grip. This general approach to measurement was largely abandoned when Wissler (1901) correlated the scores on numerous simple tasks with college grades. The results were very discouraging: There was *no relation* between grades and these measures of ability.

It is interesting to note that recently more sophisticated approaches *have* found physiological differences among individuals differing in intellectual ability (Ahern & Beatty, 1979). While performing a mental task, a person's pupillary dilations are smaller as his or her intelligence level increases. This suggests that those who are high in intelligence possess more efficient cognitive structures for processing information.

Binet: Identifying the "Feebleminded."   Alfred Binet (1857–1911) was born in Nice, France, into a family of physicians; his father and both grandfathers practiced medicine. His parents separated during his childhood, and at the age of 15 Binet was taken by his mother to Paris to attend the Lycée Louis-le-Grand. He then tried both law school and medical school.

At the Bibliothèque National he became interested in psychology, and he avidly read the works of writers like John Stuart Mill. He published his first paper in 1880 while still an armchair psychologist. Like Freud, Binet was interested in the work of Charcot, who was using hypnosis in both medical treatment and experimental investigations. In 1891 Binet took a position (apparently without pay) at the Laboratory of Physiological Psychology at the Sorbonne, the first French psychological laboratory.

His specific interest in hypnosis shifted to a more general concern with complex mental processes. Between 1893 and 1911 he worked with and reported on the numerous types of tests used to explore individual differences in the intellectual ability of children. In 1903 he published *The Experimental Study of Intelligence.* With only a general notion of what kinds of behavior might be useful indicators of intelligence, Binet tried out such tests as recall of numbers, moral judgment, and mental addition. In working with various children, including his daughters, he found that ability on simple tasks was unrelated to ability on more complex tasks, such as those involving memory, comprehension, and mathematics.

In 1904, while this work was in progress, a problem was raised within the Paris school system. The school administrators wanted to be able to identify "feebleminded" children so that they could be removed from regular classes and placed in special schools. Teacher ratings might be used for this purpose, but the administrators were afraid that the teachers would make too many mistakes in classifying the children. For example, they could rate bright troublemakers as dull in order to get rid of them and dull but wealthy children as bright so as to avoid offending their parents. What was needed was an objective, accurate way of measuring intelligence, and the schools asked Binet if his research was applicable to the problem.

In 1905 Binet announced the formation of the Laboratory of Experimental Pedagogy within one of the primary schools. It was designed to help teachers learn how to identify and teach retarded children (Wolf, 1973). In 1905, putting together the most successful of the various tests that he had been studying, Binet and a medical colleague, Theodore Simon, created the **Binet-Simon Scale;** it was revised in 1908 and again in 1911, the year of Binet's death.

From the very beginning, the concept of intelligence was of greatest use in solving a practical problem in an applied setting, and test items were selected on an empirical and practical rather than a theoretical basis. Individual tests in the Binet-Simon Scale consisted of the same types of items as those in use in such tests today. This measurement technique had a great impact on psychologists and nonpsychologists alike, as is suggested by such statements as that by Goddard (1912), who felt that the Binet-Simon Scale "would one day take a place in the history of science beside Darwin's theory of evolution and Mendel's law of heredity" (p. 326). While this statement seems overenthusiastic from our present perspective, it is true that the history of psychology, at least, has been closely intertwined with the history of intelligence testing.

Terman: a Test for Americans.   Lewis M. Terman (1877–1956) became interested in Binet's work while still in graduate school; later he adapted the French test for use with American children.

Terman was born on a farm in rural Indiana, the twelfth of fourteen children. He has said that his family was not very well educated and that his initial educational experiences in a one-room schoolhouse were somewhat limited. He did, however, have an early interest in individual differences:

Whatever the cause, almost as far back as I can remember I seem to have had a little more interest than the average child in the personalities of others and to have been impressed by those who differed in some respect from the common run. Among my schoolmates or acquaintances whose behavior traits especially interested me were a feebleminded boy who was still in the first reader at the age of eighteen, a backward albino boy who was pathetically devoted to his small sister, a spoiled crippled boy given to fits of temper and to stealing, a boy who was almost a "lightning calculator," and a playmate of near my own age who was an imaginative liar and later came into national prominence as an alleged swindler and multimurderer. I am inclined to think that the associations which I had with such schoolmates were among the most valuable of my childhood experiences. [1932, pp. 300–301]

Terman did well in his classes and was promoted from the first to the third grade after six months in school. Between the ages of 11 and 18, he spent half of each year working on the farm and half in school. He then attended Central Normal College in Danville, Indiana, where he received the B.S. degree in 1896. Interspersing his college work with teaching in rural schools, he later received the A.B. degree at the Danville school. He married a fellow teacher in 1899, and in 1901, after two years as a high school principal, he entered Indiana University to study psychology. There, in two years, he received another bachelor's degree and a master's degree. Obtaining a fellowship at Clark University, he moved there in 1903 for two years of graduate study.

At Clark he first learned about Binet's work in detail from students returning from Europe and by reading Binet's publications. His dissertation dealt with an experimental study of mental tests. He selected two groups of subjects of about the same age, one bright group and one dull group, and devised tests on which he believed they would perform differently. These tests consisted of the kind of vocabulary, arithmetic, and comprehension items used by Binet in France. After receiving the Ph.D. degree at Clark, Terman, who had tuberculosis, accepted a job as principal of the high school in San Bernardino in the hope that the California climate would be healthful. After a year there he became a professor at the Los Angeles State Normal School. In 1910 he accepted a position at Stanford University in the School of Education. There he immediately began an experimental study of the Binet tests. This work culminated in the publication in 1916 of

The Measurement of Intelligence, which contained the first **Stanford-Binet Scale,** a model for the many intelligence tests developed later.

During World War I Terman served under Yerkes on the committee that devised the first group intelligence tests for the armed forces. Their test was used to select the men who would make the best officers (Cronbach, 1975). His later work at Stanford involved the development of a number of other tests, the study of gifted children, and continued work on the Stanford-Binet and its revisions.

Constructing the Stanford-Binet

Selecting Items. In selecting items for the 1916 Stanford-Binet, Terman used ninety tests of the type that Binet had employed, chiefly those involving "the more complex mental processes." Though it was highly useful, the 1916 test had several drawbacks. In 1937 it was revised by Terman and Maud Merrill, a clinical psychologist on the Stanford faculty. The items in the 1937 revision were similar to the earlier ones and included such subtests as analogies (Brother is a boy; sister is a —————.); comprehension (What makes a sailboat move?); vocabulary (What is an orange?); similarities and differences (In what way are a baseball and an orange alike, and how are they different?); verbal and pictorial completions (What is

Figure 6-1. The measurement of intelligence involves the use of stimuli such as these, which are designed to assess the child's verbal and reasoning capabilities. The youngster is being asked to identify and discriminate pictures of common objects.   (Sybil Shelton, Monkmeyer)

gone in this picture? What isn't there?); absurdities (One day we saw several icebergs that had been entirely melted by the warmth of the Gulf Stream. What is foolish about that?); drawing designs; and memory of digits and verbal material. From a large initial sample of such items, the final test consisted of those items which (1) were passed by a higher percentage of children at successive ages and (2) were positively correlated with the total score on the test. Subtests were arranged in age levels, and the test scores obtained were reported in terms of **mental age** or MA. A more recent version of the Stanford-Binet (Terman and Merrill, 1960) was designed to bring the test content up to date.

Intelligence Quotient. In the 1937 Stanford-Binet, the **intelligence quotient** or **IQ** consisted of the mental age obtained on the test divided by the subject's chronological age (CA), with the quotient multiplied by 100. Thus, the average 10-year-old obtains an MA of 10 which is divided by the child's CA of 10; the quotient is 1. This multiplied by 100 equals 100, or an average IQ. A score below 100 indicates a test performance below average for the person's age level, while scores above 100 indicate above-average test performance.

The MA/CA × 100 = IQ approach runs into various problems, especially in late adolescence and adulthood. Mental age as measured by the test items does not continue to show yearly increases after the mid-teens. In the 1937 revision the IQ formula could not be utilized in its pure form beyond age 13 because MA increases become smaller and smaller. After age 16 no further yearly increases occur.

To get around this problem, the 1960 Stanford-Binet defines IQ in terms of how well one does in relation to the average performance of one's age group, as was suggested by David Wechsler. The test is arbitrarily arranged so that a score of 100 still means an average performance.

DIFFERENCES IN INTELLIGENCE: INHERITED OR LEARNED?

A great deal of research interest has centered on the origins of individual differences in intellectual ability. Much of this research has led to a continuing debate between two theoretical camps—heredity versus environment or nature versus nurture. Disagreements on this issue began almost as soon as intelligence tests were created:

By intelligence, the psychologist understands inborn, all-around, intellectual ability. It is inherited, or at least innate, not due to teaching or training; it is intellectual, not emotional or moral, and remains uninfluenced by industry or zeal; it is general, not specific, i.e., it is not limited to any particular kind of work, but enters into all we do or say or think. [Burt, Jones, Miller, & Moodie, 1934, pp. 28–29]

Some recent philosophers appear to have given their moral support to the deplorable verdict that the intelligence of an individual is a fixed quantity. . . . We must protest and act against this brutal pessimism . . . A child's mind is like a field for which an expert farmer has advised a change in the method of cultivating, with the result that in place of desert land, we now have a harvest. It is in this particular sense, the one which is significant, that we say that the intelligence of children may be increased. One increases that which constitutes the intelligence of a school child, namely, the capacity to learn, to improve with instruction. [Binet, 1909, pp. 54–55]

Genetic Influences: Is Intelligence Determined at Conception?

Resemblances Among Family Members.   One of the ways to study the genetic determinants of human behavior is to examine behavior similarity as a function of genetic similarity, that is, closeness of family relationships.

If intelligence tests were given to a group of adults and to a group of unrelated children, the correlation between the members of random adult–child pairs would be .00. That is, there is no relation between their scores. If on the other hand, the adult-child pairs consisted of grandparents and their grandchildren, the IQs would correlate about .33 (Jensen, 1974); for parents and their offspring, the correlation is about .50 (Conrad & Jones, 1940). The problem with interpreting such findings as showing that intelligence is inherited is that grandparents, parents, and children are more similar than random strangers in environment as well as genes.

Another approach is to compare siblings who differ in genetic closeness. Again, random pairs of unrelated children should have IQ correlations of .00. When unrelated children are reared together, their IQ scores are found to correlate .25 (Burt, 1958). Thus, environmental factors lead to some similarity in IQ. With pairs of siblings, IQs have been found to correlate about .50 (Conrad and Jones, 1940; Matarazzo, Wiens, & Shealy, 1978). The greater genetic similarity between siblings than between unrelated children reared together seems to make them more similar in IQ. Given a sibling relationship plus *identical* genetic structure—in other words, identical twins—greater IQ similarity further indicates the influence of heredity on intelligence. Intelligence scores of identical twins are found to correlate in the .80s (Gottesman, 1963), about as high as twins correlate in such physical traits as height and weight (Newman, Freeman, & Holzinger, 1937). Among infants, the mental development of twins is similar enough so that it can be assumed to rest almost entirely on genetic factors (Hurd, Mellinger, Wolf, & McNaughton, 1972).

These findings seem clear, but there is a methodological weakness in comparing twin pair similarity with sibling pair similarity. The twins are the same age when they are tested; the siblings are not. If half of the siblings are 4 and the other half 9, they do not correlate as highly with each other as pairs of 4-year-old twins or pairs of 9-year-old twins. But we know that the 4-year-olds are likely to be somewhat different in IQ by the time they are 9, and possibly more similar to their siblings in test scores. A way out of this dilemma is to compare fraternal twins with identical twins; here the pairs are the same age but differ in degree of genetic similarity. Fraternal twins have been found to have IQ correlations of about .60 (Gottesman, 1963). Thus, fraternal twins are similar in IQ, but not as similar as identical twins. Also, it appears that the only reason fraternal twins are more similar than nontwin siblings is that they are the same age. When fraternal twins are tested at different ages, their IQ scores are no more similar than those of other siblings (Richardson, 1936). These various relations are shown in Figure 6-2.

In summary, twin studies confirm that intellectual ability is partly a function of genetic factors.

"Experiments of Nature."   With respect both to twin and parent–

Figure 6-2.   Studies of family resemblances indicate the effects of both genetic and environmental factors on intelligence. It seems clear, however, that the more similar two people are with respect to heredity, the more similar they are in intelligence. In addition, the more similar the environments in which two individuals are reared, the more similar their IQs.

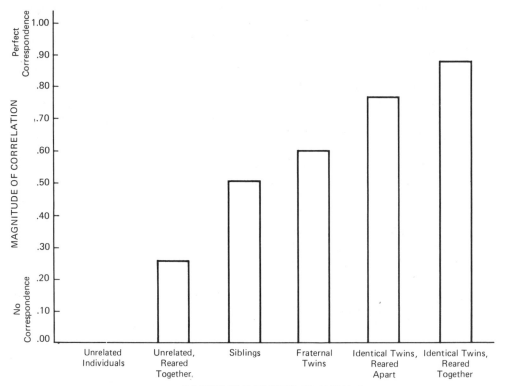

child comparisons, further evidence concerning genetics and IQ has been provided by "experiments of nature."

Newman and colleagues (1937) studied fifty pairs of identical twins who had been reared together and nineteen pairs of identical twins who had been separated in infancy or early childhood and reared apart. The correlation between IQ scores for those reared together was .88, while for those reared apart it was .77. The homes of the separated pairs were rated in terms of several variables, including educational level. It was found that the greater the difference in their environment, the greater the difference in intelligence of twins reared apart. Thus, the great similarity of identical twins indicates the role of genetics, and the clear effect of educational level indicates the role of environment.

Studies of adopted children provide the chance to examine parent–child similarity in IQ with respect to natural parents who do not actually raise their children (genetic influence but no environmental influence) and with respect to foster parents (environmental influence but no genetic influence). Skodak and Skeels (1949) obtained a sample of children who had been placed in their adoptive homes before they were six months old. The children were given the Stanford-Binet at various times, beginning when they were about 2 and continuing until they were about 13. As an estimate of parental IQ, educational level was determined for both the true parents and the foster parents. In addition, the Stanford-Binet was given to the true mothers. The results were somewhat surprising. Beginning when the children were 4 years of age, their IQ scores correlated significantly with the educational level and IQ of their *true mothers*. At age 13, the children's scores correlated .32 with their true mothers' educational level and .44 with their true mothers' IQ. For the true fathers whose educational level was known, this estimate of intelligence correlated .44 with the child's IQ at age 13.[1] In contrast, no correlation existed between children's IQ and foster parents' educational level. At age 13, the children's scores correlated .00 with foster fathers' education and .02 with foster mothers' education. The effect of genetic factors is obvious in that the only significant parent–child correlations are with the natural parents.

Even the Skodak and Skeels data, however, offer no either– or answer for the question of heredity and environment. The correlations indicate that the *ordering* of the children along a dimension of intelligence is related to the *ordering* of their true mothers and fathers along the same dimension; it says nothing about *level* of intelligence. For the true mothers, the mean IQ was 85.7, while the mean IQ of their children at age 13 was 106. The children were clearly brighter than their mothers. Since the true mothers were predominantly girls from inferior socioeconomic back-

---

[1] Computed from raw data reported by Skodak and Skeels (1949).

grounds, and since the foster homes were relatively high in educational opportunity and socioeconomic level, this last finding probably indicates that the foster home environment had a positive effect on the children's IQ. Research like that of Skodak and Skeels has led to the hypothesis that genetic factors set some sort of limit or maximum with respect to the development of intellectual ability, with environmental factors determining the extent to which development takes place within those limits. Figure 6-3 shows how both variables seem to operate in this study of adopted children.

A fairly recent survey of several studies of adopted children confirms these early findings (Munsinger, 1975). It is consistently found that the intelligence of adopted children is closely related to the intelligence and educational level of their biological parents. In addition, IQ is affected to a small but significant degree by the quality of the adoptive home environment.

Science Versus Belief: Were Some of the Data Faked?   Perhaps the most serious charge against a scientist is that data have been deliberately faked. The search for lawfulness, the standards of objectivity and control, the goal of predictability—all of these concepts are meaningless if research results are simply created by the scientist to support a strongly held belief.

Figure 6-3.   Studies of adopted children reveal the influence of both genetic and environmental factors. The *relative intelligence* of the adopted children is a function of the relative intelligence of their true parents (genetics), but their *level of intelligence* was closer to that of their foster parents (environment).

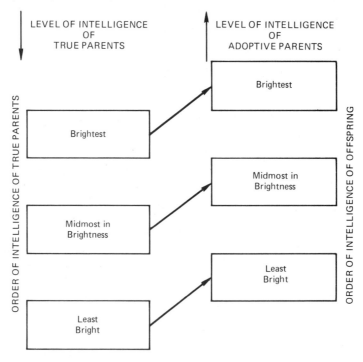

When strong feelings are aroused by differing theories, there is the greatest temptation to claim empirical support for one's position even when it does not really exist. Perhaps the earliest example is provided by the astronomer Ptolemy who appears to have invented some data and distorted others in order to confirm his theory that the earth was the center of the universe (Wade, 1977). Work on the genetic versus environmental determinants of IQ has also aroused very strong feelings, and the labels "fascist," "racist," and "communist" have been applied to one researcher after another in the heat of argument. The most startling charge, however, was made against the English psychologist Sir Cyril Burt. The first psychologist to receive a knighthood has been accused of committing scientific fraud (Dorfman, 1978; Wade, 1976).

Burt was a strong proponent of the belief that intelligence is inherited, and his work on identical twins is often cited as evidence for the genetic basis of IQ. His work even had profound applied effects, because he was largely responsible for the establishment in the 1940s of the English system in which children are tested at age 11 and then assigned to one of three educational levels on the basis of that all-important test score.

His research was difficult to replicate in that much of it involved the study of twins who had been separated and raised in different families, (e.g., Burt, 1966). It is very hard to locate a suitable number of such cases in order to study them. After Burt's death a reporter for the *London Sunday Times* discovered that two of Burt's "co-workers" apparently did not exist. It appears that he even used their names as a cover to write book reviews of his own work (Gillie, 1979). At best the data were handled in a very sloppy way, and some were destroyed. Burt often failed to provide critical information about his subjects, referring readers to obscure theses that did not actually exist (Kamin, 1977). Some psychologists noticed that his statistics remained exactly the same even when he claimed to have gathered additional data from other subjects. Though Burt continued to publish his "findings" until his death in 1971, Hearnshaw (1979) provides evidence that no new data were actually gathered after 1950. His defenders claim that his critics are unfair and inaccurate and are motivated only by the desire to cast doubt on the entire genetic viewpoint (Jensen, 1977, 1978). Whatever the final resolution of this case, the chance that a distinguished scientist may have "faked the data" is a profoundly disturbing one (Evans, 1976).

Environmental Influences: Is Intelligence Learned?

Intellectual functioning seems to have a long period of development, stretching at least from conception to adolescence. In a relatively "standard" middle-class environment a regular and steady increase in mental age occurs from infancy to middle or late adolescence. Given the limits or boundaries set by genetic factors, intellectual functioning shows a typical growth pattern and IQ remains more or less constant over the years. The fact that all environments are not the same leads to striking departures from this pattern. Some investigators have examined the negative effects of the earliest environment—the uterus—and found that such factors as cigarette smoking by the mother can have a negative effect on the infant's birth weight and even on the amount of brain protein present at birth (Fechter & Annau, 1977). Most of the research involving environmental influences on intelligence has dealt with environmental deprivation or enrichment during the period of development.

Living in a Deprived Environment. One way of creating a relatively poor environment is by isolating a group from the cultural mainstream. For example, Gordon (1923) tested a group of English canal-boat children. These youngsters attended school only when the boats were being loaded or unloaded; their parents were illiterate, and they had little contact with anyone outside the family. Instead of the usual average of 100, the mean IQ of these children was 69.6. More important, however, is the finding that IQ and age were negatively correlated. The youngest children (4–6 years of age) had a mean IQ of 90, while the oldest children (12–22 years of age) had a mean IQ of 60. In other words, intelligence seemed to decline as the children grew older. Findings consistent with these have been reported for children living in isolated mountain areas in the United States, in rural communities, in slum areas, and in homes that are socioeconomically deprived.

Another type of environmental deprivation is life in an institution. Goldfarb (1945) has emphasized the probable importance of parent–child contacts as a source of constant stimulation for young children. The child's motor and verbal responses are of interest to its parents; the parents sing and talk to the child and encourage it to babble, talk, sit, stand, walk, and climb. The child receives toys, is taken to see interesting things, and is encouraged to perform a variety of acts. In contrast, a child in an institution is one of a large group, and even under the best of conditions the amount of contact between the child and any adult figure is not great. Goldfarb selected a group of children who had been placed in an institution in early infancy, had remained there for three years, and had then been placed in foster homes. A control group consisted of children who had been placed in foster homes in early infancy. The Stanford-Binet was administered just before the institutional group left the orphanage and again after seven months in the foster homes. The control group was tested at the same intervals. On the first testing, the control group had a mean IQ of 96 while the institutional group had a significantly lower mean IQ of 68. After seven months in the foster home, there was still a 26-point IQ difference between the two groups. Even after early separation from parents and placement in an institution, however, intelligence is not adversely affected if there is an opportunity to develop an affectionate relationship with adults or older children in that institution (Wolins, 1969).

Living in an Enriched Environment.   Positive effects on IQ scores are likely to occur among children who are raised in well-educated families, presumably because such families provide above-average intellectual stimulation. It has also been found, incidentally, that children who show signs of high intellectual ability cause their mothers to become more involved and to provide additional play materials for them (Bradley, Caldwell, & Elardo, 1978). Not only does environment influence the child's IQ, but the reverse holds true as well. However, "enriching" experience has been defined mainly in terms of the child's schooling. Intellectual stimulation in nursery school, primary and secondary schools, and even in college has generally been found to lead to higher IQ scores.

Though there is some controversy about the effects of nursery school on IQ, there is much evidence for a positive effect. Kirk (1958) studied groups of retarded children over a number of years. The children who went to nursery school showed a significantly greater increase in IQ than those who did not have the school experience. Most of the nursery school group showed IQ gains of ten points or more. Likewise, Wellman and Pegram (1944) compared below-average orphanage children who went to preschool with a matched orphanage group who did not. Those in the

Figure 6-4. The preschool experience can be an enjoyable initiation to the school environment. Such early stimulation of cognitive activity facilitates intellectual development. (Mimi Forsyth, Monkmeyer)

preschool group showed gains in IQ, and the gains were greater for those who attended regularly than for those who missed class frequently. Part of the impetus for the Head Start Program, in which deprived children may attend preschool classes, was provided by studies like these. It should be noted that the effect of a school experience depends on the quality of the setting; the better the school, the more positive the effect on IQ (Worbois, 1942). There is some evidence that participation in art classes is especially important in raising the intellectual level of children (Williams, 1977).

Finally, several studies have reported that college attendance has a positive effect on IQ. For example, Charles and Pritchard (1959) tested students at Iowa State when they entered and again four years later. A significant increase in IQ scores occurred for both male and female students over the four-year period. In a more convincing test of the same idea, Lorge (1945) obtained IQ scores of boys who had been tested in the eighth grade and then again thirty years later. The increase in IQ on the second test was a function of the number of years of schooling between the two testings. The more years of school, the higher the adult IQ.

Some researchers think intelligence is a skill that can be learned (Whimbey, 1976). That is, low-IQ individuals simply have never been taught to reason, seek answers to problems, and pay attention to relationships. Research has shown that intelligence test scores are increased simply by practicing such things as tests and puzzles and engaging in reasoning whenever one reads a book, magazine, or newspaper. It is suggested that social-class or racial differences in IQ may rest not on innate factors but on differences in how children learn how to learn. Related studies show that simply providing feedback *during* an intelligence test as to which answers are right and wrong produces significantly higher IQ scores (Kratochwill & Brady, 1976).

INTELLECTUAL DIFFERENCES IN SOCIETY: OCCUPATIONAL STATUS, SOCIAL CLASS, AND RACE

It is easy enough to view the research on the origins of intelligence as an academic exercise that is of interest mainly to those who are directly involved in the research. Thus, they can quietly examine twins and canal boat children and then politely argue about the meaning of their findings in scholarly journals. There is, however, a flaw in that description. Intelligence has come to be regarded as a highly valued indication of personal worth *and* as the major way in which people are evaluated with respect to educational and occupational opportunity. Though it is possible for a few people to succeed through luck—to inherit money or win a lottery—or through special talents or skills (e.g., in art or athletics) or physical attractiveness, most individuals must rely on a system that classifies us according to intellectual ability.

Given the psychological meaning of intelligence plus the practical value attached to it, the arguments about its origins take on great importance. When we add questions of social-class or ethnic differences, the debate over genetic versus environmental origins leads to issues that affect us all. Let's examine some of the relevant research and the sometimes violent disputes that have arisen as a result of that research.

Intelligence and Socioeconomic Factors

Occupation. Intelligence is one of the major factors that determine the likelihood that a person will obtain a specific level of education and enter a specific occupation. Those who are below average in intelligence are not likely to become corporation lawyers, while those with very high IQs are not usually employed as unskilled laborers. Large-scale studies in both World War I (Fryer, 1922) and World War II (Stewart, 1947) found a substantial relation between occupational level and scores on Army intelligence tests. Since parent–child IQ scores are related, we would expect children from different socioeconomic levels to differ in their performance on intelligence tests. A number of studies have confirmed this expectation (Firkowska, Ostrowska, Sokolowska, Stein, Susser, & Wald, 1978), and social-class differences among mothers are clearly related to the IQ of their children as early as age 4 (Broman, Nichols, & Kennedy, 1975). More surprising perhaps is the fact that a child's IQ as measured in the second grade is a good predictor of that person's occupational status as an adult (McCall, 1977).

Occupational Status of Parents. The members of Terman and Merrill's standardization group for the 1937 revision of the Stanford-Binet were divided in terms of the *occupations* of their fathers. The IQ variations across groups for preschool children are shown in Table 6-2. The higher the father's occupational level, the higher the IQ of the children. It is even found that when sons are more intelligent than their fathers, they tend to achieve a higher socioeconomic level as adults (Jensen, 1978; Waller, 1971).

Another approach is to obtain socioeconomic ratings of an entire community in order to compare those ratings with the IQ scores of the children residing there. Maller (1933) found that the value of home rentals in a neighborhood correlated .50 with the mean IQ of the schoolchildren living in that neighborhood. Thorndike and Woodyard (1942) found that per capita income for thirty cities correlated .78 with the mean IQ scores of the sixth-graders in those cities.

Interpreting the Socioeconomic Findings. The rather well-established relation between socioeconomic status and IQ has been interpreted in a number of different ways.

For example, it is possible that hereditary factors are operating, in that genetically brighter people do better in school, obtain better jobs, select

Table 6-2. The relation between fathers' occupations and the IQs of their preschool children as measured by the Stanford-Binet. The higher the occupational status of the father, the higher the intelligence of the offspring.

Father's Occupation	Child's IQ
Professional	116.2
Semiprofessional and managerial	112.4
Clerical, skilled trades, and retail business	108.0
Semiskilled, minor clerical, minor business	104.3
Rural owners	99.1
Slightly skilled	95.1
Day laborers, urban and rural	93.6

mates of similar intelligence and pass on these "good" genes to their offspring. Likewise, those who are genetically less bright do worse in school, obtain lower-level jobs, select less bright mates, and pass on these "bad" genes to their offspring.

The other major explanation involves differences among socioeconomic groups in the amount of intellectual stimulation available to the child in the home. As socioeconomic status increases, the vocabulary of parents becomes larger, the amount of reading material in the home becomes greater, and the opportunity for intellectual enrichment (e.g., music, art, and theater) increases. It is found that a child's future educational level can be predicted better from the educational level of the father than from the child's own IQ scores (McCall, 1977). Also, upper-class children live in wealthier neighborhoods where higher taxes pay for better schools. Given the same genetic structure, wide differences in environment should produce different levels of intelligence. One rather convincing finding with respect to the role of the environment is provided by studies of adoptions across social-class lines. When infants from a working-class background are adopted by upper-middle-class parents, their performance in school and on IQ tests is considerably better than that of children who are raised by working-class parents (Schiff, Duyme, Dumaret, Stewart, Tomkiewicz, & Feingold, 1978).

Within families, there is a great deal of evidence to suggest that as family size increases, intelligence decreases (Belmont & Marolla, 1973; Zajonc, 1976). Further, the firstborn child tends to be brighter than the second, the second brighter than the third, and so on. Zajonc suggests that one reason for such effects is that the average intellectual level of the family drops each time a new infant enters the household. When there are long intervals between the births, this effect is diminished, but firstborns still are found to be higher in IQ than secondborns, regardless of spacing (Belmont, Stein, & Zybert, 1978). External influences, such as the quality of the school system, can also erase these effects (Davis, 1977). Social class is relevant because large families with little spacing between children are more common in lower than in higher socioeconomic groups.

There is another environmental factor that could explain social-class differences in intelligence. Studies of both rats (Vore & Ottinger, 1970) and human beings (Kaplan, 1972; Lloyd-Still, 1976) indicate that a poor diet during pregnancy can have negative effects on the offspring's ability to learn. Thus, the poorest members of society may be at a disadvantage even before they are born. Malnutrition during the early years of infancy also tends to impair mental development (Lester, 1977). It should be noted, however, that the negative effects of early malnutrition can be at least partly overcome by a later switch to a good diet (Winick, Meyer, & Harris, 1975). The earlier something is done about malnutrition and bad health, the greater the chance cognitive ability will be improved (McKay, Sinisterra, McKay, Gomez, & Lloreda, 1978). We will now turn to the question of racial differences in IQ and examine how the genetic versus environmental arguments are applied to this complex problem.

TRY IT
YOURSELF

Culture and Intelligence: What Do IQ Tests Measure?

Though you have probably taken a great many tests that measure intelligence, you might enjoy trying your luck at one more such instrument. Mark your answers to each of the following items.

DOVE'S SOUL FOLK CHITLING TEST*

Your age: _____   Your sex: _____   Your race: _____

Size of community in which you grew up:
  Rural or small town (up to 100,000) _____
  Medium-sized town (100,000 to 500,000) _____
  Large City (500,000 to 1,000,000) _____
  Very large city (over 1,000,000) _____

1. "T-Bone Walker" got famous for playing what?
   a. trombone   d. guitar
   b. piano   e. "hambone"
   c. "T-flute"
2. Who did "Stagger Lee" kill (in the famous blues legend)?
   a. his mother   d. his girlfriend
   b. Frankie   e. Billy
   c. Johnny
3. A "gas head" is a person who has a
   a. fast-moving car   b. stable of lace

*Copyright 1980 by *Newsweek, Inc.* All rights reserved. Reprinted by permission.

   c. "process"   e.   long jail record for arson
   d. habit of stealing cars

4. If a man is called a "blood," then he is a
   a. fighter   d.   hungry hemophile
   b. Mexican American   e.   American Indian
   c. black

5. If you throw the dice and 7 is showing on the top, what faces down?
   a. seven   d.   little Joes
   b. snake eyes   e.   eleven
   c. boxcars

6. Jazz pianist Ahmad Jamal took an Arabic name after becoming famous.
   Previously he had some fame with what he called his slave name.
   What was his previous name?
   a. Willie Lee Jackson   d.   Fritz Jones
   b. LeRoi Jones   e.   Andy Johnson
   c. Wilbur McDougal

7. In "C. C. Rider," what does "C. C." stand for?
   a. Civil Service   d.   Country Club
   b. Church Council   e.   Cheatin' Charlie (Boxcar Gunsel)
   c. Country Circuit preacher

8. Cheap "chitlings" (not the kind you purchase at a frozen-food counter)
   will taste rubbery unless they are cooked long enough. How soon can you
   quit cooking them to eat and enjoy?
   a. 15 minutes   d.   1 week (on a low flame)
   b. 2 hours   e.   1 hour
   c. 24 hours

9. "Bird" or "Yardbird" was the jacket that jazz lovers from coast to coast
   hung on
   a. Lester Young   d.   Charlie Parker
   b. Peggy Lee   e.   "Birdman of Alcatraz"
   c. Benny Goodman

10. A "hype" is a person who
    a. is always sick   c.   uses heroin
    b. has water on the brain   d.   is always ripping and running

11. "Hully Gully" came from
    a. East Oakland   d.   Harlem
    b. Fillmore   e.   Motor City
    c. Watts

12. What is Willie Mae's last name?
    a. Schwartz   d.   Turner
    b. Matauda   e.   O'Flaherty
    c. Gomex

13. The opposite of square is
    a. round   d.   hip
    b. up   e.   lame
    c. down

14. Do the Beatles have soul?
    a. yes   c. gee whiz
    b. no   d. maybe
15. A "handkerchief head" is
    a. a cool cat   d. a hoddi
    b. a porter   e. a preacher
    c. an Uncle Tom
16. What are the "Dixie Hummingbirds"?
    a. a part of the KKK
    b. a swamp disease
    c. a modern gospel group
    d. a black Mississippi paramilitary strike force
    e. deacons
17. Jet is
    a. a motorcycle club
    b. a gang in the West Side Story
    c. a news and gossip magazine
    d. a way of life for the very rich
18. "You've got to get up early in the morning if you want to _____"
    a. catch the worms
    b. be healthy, wealthy, and wise
    c. try to fool me
    d. fare well
    e. be the first one on the street
19. "Money don't get everything it's true _____"
    a. but I don't have none and I'm so blue
    b. but what it don't get I can't use
    c. so make with what you've got
    d. but I don't know that and neither do you
20. "Bo Diddley" is a
    a. camp for children   d. new dance
    b. cheap wine   e. Mojo call
    c. singer
21. Which of the following words is out of place?
    a. splib   d. spook
    b. blood   e. black
    c. gray
22. A "pimp" is also a young man who lays around all day.
    a. true   b. false
23. If a pimp is up tight with a woman who is on the state, what does he mean
    when he talks about "Mother's Day"?
    a. second Sunday May   d. first and fifteenth of every month
    b. third Sunday in June e. none of these
    c. first of every month

24. Many people say that "Juneteenth" (June 19) should be made a legal
holiday because this was the day when
a. the slaves were freed in Texas
b. the slaves were freed in the USA
c. the slaves were freed in Jamaica
d. the slaves were freed in California
e. Martin Luther King was born
f. Booker T. Washington died

As you have undoubtedly realized, this test is not like those based on the white
middle-class culture. Rather, it was developed by a Watts social worker, Ad-
rian Dove, with items representing a lower-class black culture. After you have
scored yourself according to the key below, your instructor may want you to
determine how well you did in comparison to the rest of your class.

Scoring Key

1-d, 2-e, 3-d, 4-c, 5-a, 6-d, 7-c, 8-c, 9-d, 10-c, 11-e, 12-d, 13-d, 14-b, 15-c,
16-c, 17-c, 18-e, 19-b, 20-c, 21-c, 22-a, 23-c, 24-a.

Racial Differences in IQ: Are Whites Smarter Than Blacks?

The study of individual differences in intelligence has led to the question of racial differences (Humphreys, Fleishman, & Lin, 1977). Most often, American psychologists have asked whether there are differences between blacks and whites in mean IQ and how any such differences may be explained (Loehlin, Lindzey, & Spuhler, 1975). Controversial as those questions are, still greater concern is generated by the implications of such issues for educational, social, and legal policies.

It is hoped that racial questions will seem meaningless to future generations except as historical curiosities. Up to the present time, however, much research effort has been devoted to seeking information about racial differences, and a great deal of emotion is aroused by whatever conclusions are drawn from this research.

The Myth of Race and the Reality of Racism. Though the following discussion involves some common assumptions about race as a subject of study, it should be noted that many social scientists find the concept not very meaningful. That is, race is a descriptive term that can be used as a way of grouping people, just as we could group them by eye color or height or the shape of the ear lobe. Gottesman (1968) points out that even the number of races is a matter of debate; that no objective answer exists. Thus, race tends to be a social rather than a biological concept (Baughman, 1971). One problem with any racial classification scheme is that the resulting groups are not "pure" (mating behavior has not been limited to same-race pairs), and there are more similarities than differences across groups (Nei & Roychoudhury, 1972).

Another problem with racial classification is that there is a strong tendency to place groups along a superior–inferior dimension. For example, for centuries the Chinese have considered all non-Chinese to be barbarians. American Indians believed that when God created people by baking them in an oven, some were removed too soon (whites), some were left too long and overcooked (blacks), and some came out just right (native Americans). The notion that one's own racial or ethnic group is superior seems to be almost universal and has been expressed in varying degrees by Germans, Jews, French, Americans, Russians, and many others.

Racial prejudice is not really different from religious prejudice, class prejudice, age prejudice, or nationality prejudice, but the use of genetic differences to explain behavioral differences and justify discrimination seems logical only with respect to race. Thus, efforts to find a genetic link between race and IQ can easily be interpreted or misinterpreted as racist activities. In the nineteenth century, a Philadelphia physician named Samuel Morton collected over 1000 human skulls and measured their cranial capacity. He reported racial differences consistent with the beliefs of his day—whites were at the top and blacks at the bottom. When his data were recently reexamined, it became clear that bias had consciously or unconsciously affected Morton's conclusions—all races were found to have approximately equal-sized skulls (Gould, 1978). Kamin (1974) points out that indications of racial differences in intelligence test scores were first noted in World War I, and the findings were quickly used to influence U.S. immigration laws and support the racist beliefs of the times. He quotes writers of that period who concluded on the basis of test findings in the armed services that the Nordic race is composed of self-reliant rulers and organizers and the Alpine race of unstable slaves and peasants, much like the Jews. The notion of inherited inferiority was so strong that in 1918 a California law provided that orphans, tramps, and paupers were subject to compulsory sterilization if it was approved by a board of Ph.D.'s in clinical psychology.

Interestingly enough, the conclusions drawn from studies of black–white differences are found to be linked with the backgrounds of the researchers (Sherwood and Nataupsky, 1968). The investigators who conclude that blacks are intellectually inferior because of their genetic makeup tend to come from higher socioeconomic backgrounds than those who attribute racial differences to environmental factors.

We will now examine some of the known facts about black–white intellectual differences, the arguments favoring genetic and environmental explanations, and the possible meaning of this research for other aspects of black–white interaction.

American Blacks and American Whites: Is There an IQ Dif-

ference?   Studies stretching over half a century consistently report IQ differences between these two groups; white subjects obtain significantly higher mean IQ scores than black subjects (e.g., Bruce, 1940; Humphreys, Lin, & Fleishman, 1976; Kaufman, 1973; Shuey, 1966; Yerkes, 1921). Shuey (1958) estimated that the mean for blacks is 85 (compared with 100 for whites). Figure 6-5 shows some typical score distributions comparing white and black children from different sections of the country. Before we turn to the various attempts to explain these racial differences, two points should be understood.

First, even with group means differing by fifteen points, a large overlap occurs between groups. Those who stress racial differences often speak of there being *only* a 20 or 30 percent overlap between the groups. The overlap, however, refers to the percentage of blacks falling *above the midpoint* of the white group. Thus, a 30 percent overlap indicates that about one-third of the blacks are brighter than one-half of the whites. It also indicates that 99 percent of blacks are as smart as or smarter than some

Figure 6-5.   IQ scores of children in four research groups showing differences related to race and geographic location.
A = white children in a national sample obtained by Terman and Merrill (1937)
B = white children in rural North Carolina
C = black children in rural North Carolina
D = black children in five southeastern states
(Adapted from Baughman and Dahlstrom, 1968)

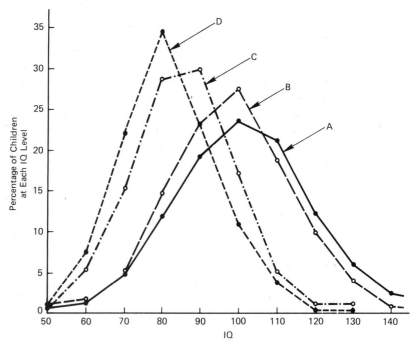

whites. If the connection between race and IQ were as strong as it is some-times claimed to be, it would be possible to use these variables for predic-tion purposes. Obviously, however, the fact that a given person is black or white does not provide the kind of information that would enable you to predict his or her IQ. Dreger and Miller (1968) make the point even clearer by noting that knowledge of a person's IQ does not tell you his or her race.

Second, intelligence tests ask questions that are drawn from a spe-cific culture, and the testing is carried out under certain conditions. For the most part, the questions are verbal ones based on aspects of the white middle-class culture, and the tests most often are given by whites. It is interesting to note that blacks perform better on verbal tests given by a computer than on verbal tests given in the usual way (Johnson & Mihal, 1973). If the person being tested comes from a subculture in which the language patterns and social surroundings are quite different from those represented by the test and the tester, a poor performance may be due to factors other than innate intelligence. Kagan (1971) concludes that "the IQ test is a seriously biased instrument that almost guarantees middle-class white children higher IQ scores than any other group of chil-dren" (p. 93). Though the effects of the tester's race do not seem to be consistent (McClelland, 1974; Sappington & Grizzard, 1975), the relevance of the test content to the subject's cultural background is clearly a crucial issue. What if intelligence tests had been developed by ghetto blacks rather than middle-class whites?

When Robert L. Williams (1974), a black psychologist, was 15, an IQ test showed that he had an IQ of 82. He was advised by his school counselor to become a bricklayer, but he decided to pursue an education anyway. A few years later he received the Ph.D. degree from Washington University in St. Louis. His experience convinced him that the usual tests were unfair to minority group members. He points out that even instruc-tions are in a language that is unfamiliar and confusing to many black children. "Show me the toy that is behind the sofa" is all right for a white child, but blacks do better when the item is phrased as "show me the toy that is in back of the couch." He went on to develop the **Black Intelligence Test of Cultural Homogeneity** (the BITCH), which is somewhat like Dove's test. For example, select the right answer to this item:

Running a game means
  a. writing a bad check.
  b. looking at something.
  c. directing a contest.
  d. getting what one wants from another person or thing.

With 100 black and 100 white teenagers, Williams (1972) found that the mean score of blacks was 30 points higher than that of whites. If you did not know that the correct answer is (d), does that make you feel intellectually inferior? If such tests were used to determine who could and could not go to college, would that be fair? Are the current white-oriented tests fair to nonwhites?

The type of problem faced by Williams is still with us. In October 1977 a trial began contesting the use of white IQ tests to make decisions about blacks. The suit was brought on behalf of six black children who had been placed in classes for the mentally retarded because of their scores below 75 on an IQ test (Shapley, 1978). When they were retested by psychologists using a black-oriented test, they scored 17 to 35 points higher, thereby qualifying for regular classes. The federal judge who ruled on the case concluded that IQ tests discriminate against black children and that those who used them should have known better (Opton, 1979).

If Whites Have Higher IQs, Is It Because of Genetic Superiority?   In recent years an electrical engineer at Stanford, William Shockley, and an educational psychologist at Berkeley, Arthur Jensen, have been at the center of the controversy over the meaning of racial differences in IQ. Shockley claims that "the major cause for American Negroes' intellectual and social deficits is hereditary and racially genetic in origin and thus not remediable to a major degree by improvements in environment." (*Playboy,* August 1980, p. 69). Jensen (1969a,b,c) has presented the best-documented case for interpreting the data in terms of racial genetic differences. After the publication of these views, Jensen was not only the subject of scientific criticism but was personally attacked as well. A sound truck cruised the Berkeley campus broadcasting such messages as "Stop racism. Fire Jensen!" Though one may not agree with Jensen's conclusions, his freedom to speak should not be open to question. He has made five major points.

1. He began with a review of the studies of the effects of compensatory education on the intelligence of disadvantaged children. It was concluded that well-meaning efforts such as the Head Start program did not result in higher IQs or in better scholastic performance.

2. He also examined the data showing that intelligence is inherited and concluded that environmental factors play a minor role in individual differences. Specifically, 80 percent of the variance in IQ scores was attributed to genes (Jensen, 1973). In 1980 such beliefs led to the establishment of a sperm bank supplied by winners of the Nobel Prize to be made available to selected women. The goal is to increase the proportion of genetically superior individuals in our society. So far, only William Shockley has made a public announcement that he is a depositor at that bank.

3. The firmly established relationship between social class and intelligence was attributed largely to genetic differences in that brighter people tend to be successful in school and obtain better jobs. Herrnstein (1971) pushed this argument further and predicted that society will become a "meritocracy" with bright people at the top of the social structure and dull people at the bottom.

4. Though Jensen regards the whole matter as open to further research, he believes that the data on racial differences in IQ strongly suggest that blacks are less well endowed genetically than whites with respect to intellectual ability. In England, Eysenck (1971) agrees with these general points but argues that they hold only for *American* blacks in that the slave traders selected the dullest and strongest to work the plantations; highly intelligent

slaves would have been a disadvantage. He adds, incidentally, that other ethnic groups in the United States are also "poor samples of the original populations" (p. 43).

5. Finally, Jensen feels that if society continues to ignore this difference between the races because of wishful thinking, we will actually do harm to blacks by not providing "appropriate" educational opportunities.

In the storm of criticism and debate that followed Jensen's original article, many psychologists sought to refute the various points made by Jensen. Among their arguments are the following:

1. The notion that special educational programs have not succeeded is not consistent with achievements in other places such as the Israeli *kibbutzim* (Vernon, 1970). It should also be noted that even a clearly inherited trait can be modified by environmental forces. For example, Japanese-Americans are taller than their counterparts in Japan, presumably because of their richer and better-balanced diet (Greulich, 1957). Analogous changes in IQ could be expected in response to an enriched intellectual environment (Eysenck, 1971). It has been pointed out that the original Head Start projects were set up on the basis of what we know about the task-oriented middle-class child and that much work is needed to discover *how* best to reach the disadvantaged (Anastasiow, 1969; Zigler & Trickett, 1978). For example, it is found that some lower-class preschool children need to be taught to verbalize their experiences and to communicate. In an operant conditioning approach instructors use M&M candies to reward each such behavior.

2. Many statisticians have questioned Jensen's conclusion attributing 80 percent of the variance in IQ to genes (Jacobson, 1978; Layzer, 1974). The percentage of variance that can be attributed to genetic factors depends in part on child-rearing conditions (Scarr-Salapatek, 1971b), and it is questionable to base variance estimates obtained in white samples and generalize them to black samples. This conclusion seemed obvious and important enough to the Genetics Society of America for it to issue a resolution that included the following message:

> It is particularly important to note that a genetic component for IQ score differences *within* a racial group does not necessarily imply the existence of a significant genetic component in IQ differences *between* racial groups; an average difference can be generated solely by differences in their environments... In our views, there is no convincing evidence as to whether there is or is not an appreciable genetic difference in intelligence between races.   [Edlin & Prout, 1977, p. 6]

The example presented in Figure 6-6 may make this issue clear.

3. There are many other variables besides IQ that account for success and social status. For example, success can result from hard work, luck, a special nonintellectual talent, or inheriting a relative's money.

4. The assertion that blacks are genetically inferior to whites in intelligence glosses over the complexity of this trait. For example, Jinks and Fulker (1970) conclude that at least twenty-two genes control IQ. Another weakness is that in most studies race is defined by the researcher in terms of skin color or what the subject says his or her race is. Dreger and Miller (1968) point out that "investigations presuming to assess the effects of genetic differences on performance but failing to take obvious steps to identify genes ... would be laughed out of court in any other field of genetic investigation" (p. 25).

5. A tentative and probably incorrect conclusion concerning inborn genetic differences would do a great disservice to blacks. It has been said that "to assert, despite the absence of evidence, and in the present social climate, that a particular race is genetically disfavored in

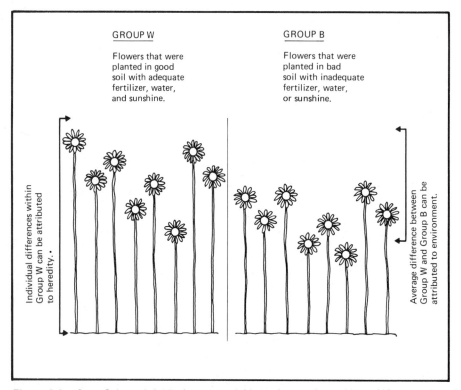

Figure 6-6. Scarr-Salapatek (1971a) suggested this analogy to the problem of IQ and racial differences. Assume that you have a large box of flower seeds and randomly divide them into two groups, W and B. You plant the group W seeds in good soil with adequate fertilizer, water, and sunshine. You plant the group B seeds in bad soil with inadequate fertilizer, water, and sunshine. When they bloom, the group W flowers turn out to be superior to the group B flowers. The reason, obviously, is a matter of environmental differences. If a scientist were to do research only on group W, however, individual differences among the flowers would be found even though they had all grown in a good environment. It could be correctly concluded that such differences were due to genetic factors; perhaps even as much as 80 percent of the variance could be attributed to heredity. The scientist asserts that "the differences within group W are hereditary, so it follows that the differences between W and B must also be hereditary." Is that reasoning correct?

intelligence is to scream 'FIRE . . . I think' in a crowded theater" (Scarr-Salapatek, 1971a, p. 1228).

If Blacks Have Lower IQs, Is It Because of Environmental Deprivation? On a great many bases, the most likely explanation for racial differences in IQ is the different environments encountered by blacks and whites. The history of blacks in the United States has been a tragic one. From slave quarters to modern ghettos, in both the North and the South, blacks have been underprivileged educationally, economically, socially, and occupationally. In other words, all of the environmental factors that are known to affect intelligence have operated to make the average black IQ test score lower than the average white score. It has been found, for example, in both races that the absence of a father in the home is linked with a lower IQ; a higher proportion of black children are raised in homes without fathers than is true of white children (Dreger & Miller, 1968). As prosegregationist writers are quick to point out, the existence of negative influences does not demostrate that the removal of such influences would cancel black–white IQ differences. There is, however, more convincing evidence.

First, black and white infants are found not to differ in intelligence (Lewis, 1976). Even among preschool children, racial differences in intelligence are absent (Anastasi & d'Angelo, 1952; Pasamanick & Knobloch, 1955). Only as children grow older do the black and white groups begin to diverge (Osborne, 1960). Some of the most convincing evidence for the negative effects of environment on the IQ of blacks has actually been provided by the leading proponent of genetic factors. Jensen (1977) examined the IQs of children in rural Georgia and found that blacks show a decline between the ages of 5 and 16 while whites do not. Since blacks in California do not show a similar decline, he concluded that "poor environment has contributed, at least in part, to the relatively low average IQ in the present sample of blacks" (Jensen, 1977, p. 191).

Second, given better schooling, black IQs go up. A study by Klineberg (1935) in New York City and one by Lee (1951) in Philadelphia each showed that the IQ scores of black children from the South increase as a function of the number of years of schooling they have had in the North. Lee found the highest IQs for black children born in Philadelphia, the next highest for black children born in the South but entering the first grade in Philadelphia, somewhat lower IQs for black children born in the South but entering the second grade in Philadelphia, and so forth. In London, the IQs of immigrant children from the West Indies and elsewhere is directly related to the length of time they have lived in the city (Vernon, 1969). Consistent with such findings, after two years of integration in Louisville, Kentucky, black IQs at every grade level increased (Stallings, 1959). It should be noted, however, that integration is not helpful to any minority group unless teacher attitudes are positive (Gerard & Miller, in press). The newly integrated student also does much better in school if he or she forms friendships among the white students (Lewis & St. John, 1974). Even more convincing evidence for the effects of schooling is the fact that blacks from New York, Ohio, and Illinois score higher than whites from Arkansas, Kentucky, and Mississippi (Benedict & Weltfish, 1943; Tyler, 1956). Presumably, the difference in ability is based on differences in the quality of education.

Third, if racial differences are genetic, interracial mating should lead to a mean IQ in the offspring below that of the "superior" race, regardless of who raises the children. In contrast, Willerman, Naylor, and Myrianthopoulos (1970) proposed that if racial IQ differences are dependent on environmental factors, the race of the mother should be a crucial

Figure 6-7. The nurturance of intellectual skills depends on environmental factors such as whether the youngster is encouraged to develop his or her talents. Racial differences in IQ tend to disappear when such environmental experiences are equalized.   (Mimi Forsyth, Monkmeyer)

factor because she has the greatest amount of contact with the child. From a large national sample of black–white pairs, they obtained groups in which the mother was white and the father black and in which the mother was black and the father white; each pair had a 4-year-old child who could be given the Stanford-Binet. As may be seen in Table 6-3, interracial matings lead to lower IQ scores when the mother is black but not when she is white. It would again seem that environmental factors play the major role in black–white differences in intelligence.

Fourth, when black children are adopted by financially secure

Table 6-3. A study of black-white parents indicates that the children (at age 4) have a higher IQ when the mother is white (and the father is black) than when she is black (and the father is white). This finding suggests that racial differences in intelligence are not due to genetic differences between the races but, rather, to cultural or environmental differences such as type of mother–child interaction.

Race of Mother	Race of Father	Mean IQ of Child
White	Black	100.9
Black	White	93.7

(Data from Willerman, Naylor, & Myrianthopoulous, 1970)

white families, their IQ scores and school performance are superior to those of the average white child (Scarr & Weinberg, 1976). In addition, the children adopted before the age of 1 were brighter than those who were adopted after that age.

Racial Differences and Discrimination. "Martin Luther King had a dream—a beautiful, eloquent dream of an American society without barriers between black and white. If he had lived, he might have brought us a little closer to its realization" (Klineberg, 1971, p. 127). Even if racial differences were greater than they are and even if genetic factors could account for all of the differences, there still would be no justification for prejudging *all* blacks as intellectually inferior and hence not capable of attending certain schools or holding certain jobs. There would be no justification for prejudging *any* black as unqualified to vote or eat in a certain restaurant or sit in the front of a bus. "The science of psychology can offer no support to those who see in the accident of inherited skin color or other physical characteristics any excuse for denying to individuals the right to full participation in American democracy" (Klineberg, 1963, p. 202). It should be noted that Jensen himself cautioned that "the full range of human talents is represented in all races of man and in all socioeconomic levels. . . . It is unjust to allow the mere fact of an individual's racial or social background to affect the treatment accorded to him" (1969a, p. 78).

WHAT DO YOU THINK?

Intelligence and Grades: What Is Their Role in Our Society?

We are tested from early childhood all the way through the school years and beyond. IQ tests are used by most institutions in our society, perhaps overused (Brody & Brody, 1976). Tests determine whether we can enter college, and which ones we can enter. Tests determine whether we can pursue a graduate education, enter certain professions, and do certain jobs (Kondracke, 1978). This is of great personal importance because, at least for males, self-esteem is a function of the status of one's occupation (Bachman & O'Malley, 1977). It is reasonable, then, to ask *why*. Why do we rely on intelligence tests, entrance tests, screening tests, and even classroom exams?

You will remember that IQ tests were devised to predict how well children would do in school. It is not surprising, therefore, to find a positive relation between IQ scores and school grades, with intelligence accounting for about 25 percent of the variation in grades. The remaining 75 percent can presumably be attributed to motivation, work habits, anxiety, and errors of measurement (see, e.g., Battle, 1966; Dielman, Schuerger, & Cattell, 1970). It should also be noted that the correlations are highest and the predictions best in elementary and high school (Frandsen, 1950); they drop with respect to college grades (Spielberger & Katzenmeyer, 1959), and are very low when we consider performance in graduate school (Marston, 1971; Willingham, 1974). The reason for the lower correlations at the highest levels of education is that the least intelligent students are excluded from that part of the educational system, and correlations drop when one of the variables (IQ in this instance) is restricted in its range. In any event, IQ scores allow us to predict grades with varying degrees of success. Why do we want to predict grades? Let's consider two possible reasons. Then you can decide which one makes more sense to you.

The traditional view is that intelligence tests indicate mental ability. On the basis of test results the schools could be tailored to the student's ability (e.g., classes arranged according to reading level, math skills, etc.), or the schools could admit only those who are able to benefit from the education experience (some private elementary and high schools, most colleges, and all graduate schools do this). It is assumed that intelligence testing is a democratic and equalitarian way to ensure that anyone with ability can rise to the top through education and hard work. It is not possible for everyone to go to college, enter the profession of his or her choice, or become a top executive. In other societies such selection has at one time or another been based on social class, income, inherited rights, or political ideology. We, in contrast, rely totally on ability, so that anyone may qualify and only the most able people become physicians, lawyers, engineers, professors, executives, and so forth. Surely a meritocracy is the fairest of societies.

A much more radical and perhaps cynical view is that the entire testing process has other uses and other goals.

1. It can be granted that IQ tests predict grades, but what exactly do grades tell us? A simple pass-fail system would separate those who learned *something* in each course from those who did not. Besides, we all forget most of the details of what we learn unless we continue to use the knowledge in a regular way. Even when forgetting does not occur, it can be argued that much of what is learned in school is useless in later life because it is either outdated or irrelevant after a few years. In 1784 an American Indian chief used this argument in rejecting the offer of the colonial government to educate his people:

   Several of our young people were formerly brought up at the Colleges of the northern provinces; they were instructed in all your sciences; but, when they came back to us, they were bad runners, ignorant of every means of living in the woods, unable to bear either cold or hunger, knew neither how to build a cabin, take a deer, nor kill an enemy, spoke our language imperfectly and were therefore neither fit for hunters, warriors, nor counsellors; they were totally good for nothing. [quoted by Berman, 1975, p. 18]

2. Detailed grading and intelligence test distinctions would be useful if grades actually predicted surgical skill, scientific ability, effectiveness as a teacher, or any other real-life attainment. In fact, tests seem to be poor predictors of how well one will do after leaving school (DeMott, 1974). Intellectual measures are most useful in predicting school grades, and grades are useful mainly in predicting still other school grades.

3. The entire measuring—grading—screening process can be viewed as a device to fill the higher positions in our society with people who will fit in best and not rock the

boat (von Hoffman, 1977). It is the view of Thomas Haskell (1977, p. 28), for example, that "Everyone already knows that the university—whatever loftier purposes it may also serve—earns its keep by catering to middle class students and acting as gatekeeper for the professions." We have seen that tests favor those who come from the dominant white middle-class culture and/or from upper socioeconomic levels. Further, those who have the ability to do well in school (whatever their social background) are not likely to have done so unless they have the personality traits that are most desired by existing institutions. That is, a record of good grades through seemingly endless years of school means that the person is highly motivated, works hard, conforms to established demands, is willing to delay gratification for long periods, is not obviously disturbed emotionally, and wants to please people in positions of authority.

What do you think? Are tests and school grades a fair system for building a society based entirely on merit, or are they a hypocritical system that admits those who are most likely to maintain the status quo?

INTELLIGENCE AS A PREDICTOR OF BEHAVIOR BEYOND THE CLASSROOM

Ability to Learn

Since intelligence tests were developed to predict ability to learn in a school setting, we might expect to find a large number of learning experiments focusing on the IQ of subjects. Actually, there are relatively few such studies (Estes, 1970, 1974).

One of the early experiments of this type was carried out by Kenneth Spence and a fellow student as an undergraduate project (Spence & Townsend, 1930). On the basis of an IQ test, high-scoring and low-scoring subjects were selected. The learning task was a finger maze that had to be learned by the blindfolded subjects. Each trial was timed and the number of errors recorded. The subjects with the highest IQs took fewer trials to learn the maze, made fewer errors, and mastered the task more quickly than those with low IQ scores. Other research (e.g., Koch & Meyer, 1959) also indicates, that, in general, IQ is an important factor in predicting how quickly and how well a person can learn something new.

Ability to Change: Response to Psychotherapy and Persuasion

Therapy as Learning.   One situation in which IQ has a good deal of relevance is psychotherapy. Therapy most often consists of a verbal interchange between therapist and patient. Changes in the patients' behavior may be viewed as learning. Murray (1964) proposed that therapy, like all learning, involves the acquisition, performance, and elimination of responses. It follows that response to psychotherapy should be in part a function of ability to learn, as measured by intelligence tests.

Active participation in group psychotherapy was studied by McFarland, Nelson, and Rossi (1962). It was found that the brighter the patient, the greater the participation. It was suggested that IQ tests might be used to select patients who would benefit most from such treatment. In their group, a cutoff IQ of 100 would maximize the chances of excluding patients who would not participate and including those who would.

Another therapeutic problem is that of predicting which patients will continue in therapy and which ones will decide to terminate it. Hiler (1958) found that those who remained in therapy were more intelligent than those who dropped out within the first five sessions. Again, an IQ of 100 was found to be the best cutoff point; most of those with IQs below 100 dropped out, while most of those with IQs above 100 remained in treatment.

Opinion Change: Comprehension of Factual Arguments. When someone listens to persuasive arguments about any issue, weighs whatever factual information is provided, and then alters his or her opinion, we are likely to describe that person as open-minded and responsive to change. Eagly and Warren (1976) predicted that intelligence would be a factor in such change. That is, intelligent people should be able to comprehend the information better, and it has been found that the better a person's comprehension of information, the more likely he or she is to be persuaded by it (Chaiken & Eagly, 1976).

High school students were given messages about penicillin and toothbrushes, either with supportive factual arguments or without such support. It was found that the most intelligent subjects were more likely to remember the content of the messages. When there were supporting arguments, the most intelligent students showed the most opinion change; without such arguments, the least intelligent subjects changed the most.

Creative Ability

Much has been made of the fact that among bright people there is little relation between creativity and general intellectual ability (e.g., Getzels & Jackson, 1962). Ripple and May (1962) rightly point out that the magnitude of this relation would necessarily be low in groups that do not vary much in IQ. They studied several groups of seventh-grade students and gave them various creativity tests. With groups that were homogeneous in intelligence (either all fairly high or all fairly low), IQ and creativity were found to be unrelated. In heterogeneous groups, IQ and creativity were highly related. In the general population, then, IQ is positively related to creativity.

It can be assumed that a fairly high level of intelligence is necessary for creative achievement (Nicholls, 1972). In addition, it has been found that the most creative members of a society are brighter than those who become the leaders of that society (Simonton, 1976).

Ability to Delay Gratification

Mischel and Metzner (1962) hypothesized that ability to delay gratification involved a transition from immediate wish-fulfilling types of behavior to those that require delay and reality testing. Since learning to delay is related to thinking, cognitive ability should be positively related to ability to delay. A group of elementary school children served as subjects. They were given a choice between two candy bars; the children could receive a small Hershey bar now or a bar twice as big at a later time. Those who chose the delayed reward were significantly brighter than those who chose the immediate reward.

Consistent with such laboratory results is the finding that rapists are less intelligent than violent criminals who do not commit rape (Ruff, Templer, & Ayers, 1976). Presumably, one element in this crime is the inability of the rapist to postpone the satisfaction of his needs.

IQ OVER THE LIFE SPAN

Childhood and Adolescence

In a number of studies children and adolescents have been tested at one age and retested when they are older. Typical of the findings are those reported by Kangas and Bradway (1971) dealing with the stability of IQ over a 38-year period. As might be expected, the longer the interval between testings, the lower the correlation. Also, the older the person when first tested, the higher the correlation between successive testings.

Tests of IQ in infancy are usually found to be unrelated to later measures of intelligence (Lewis & McGurk, 1972). Nevertheless, when the performance on the infant test is *extremely* low (bottom 5%), it is possible to predict low IQ and poor school performance in childhood (Rubin & Balow, 1979). In fact, later IQ can be predicted better on the basis of the parents' socioeconomic level than on the basis of a direct test of an infant's "IQ" (McCall, Hogarty, & Hurlburt, 1972). After infancy, IQ is fairly stable over time, especially from adolescence on (Bradway, Thompson, & Cravens, 1958; McCall, 1977).

Adulthood and Old Age

Cross-Sectional Research: IQ Peaks and then Declines Slowly. The first studies of the effects of aging on intelligence utilized a **cross-sectional design.** That is, people of various ages were tested, and comparisons of different individuals in different age groups were made. The findings were fairly consistent and somewhat disheartening. For example, a World War I study found that Army Alpha scores decreased steadily from young (under

20) groups to older (51–60) groups of officers (Yerkes, 1921). Jones and Conrad (1933) found the same trend among people living in nineteen villages in New England.

The conclusions drawn from such studies are depicted in Figure 6-8. We see that intellectual growth seems to reach a peak by late adolescence or early adulthood, remain fairly constant through the 20s, and then begin a sharp decline. Wechsler, for one, concluded that

every human capacity after attaining a maximum begins an immediate decline. . . . The age at which the maximum is attained varies from ability to ability but seldom occurs beyond 30 and in most cases somewhere in the early 20s. [1944, p. 55]

Longitudinal Research: Continued Growth of Intellectual Abilities.   More recent studies have employed a **longitudinal design** to examine intelligence over the life span. In this approach *the same individuals* are retested at various ages, and a quite different picture emerges. For example, Owens (1953) compared the test performance of a group of subjects in middle age with their own test performance as college freshmen thirty years earlier. On every subtest except the arithmetic items, their performance was better in middle age. Such data have led some investigators (Baltes & Schaie, 1976; Schaie, 1974) to label the idea of intellectual decline in old age a myth, though others feel that there is *some* decrease in ability if one lives long enough (Horn & Donaldson, 1976, 1977).

As we have noted previously, one of the important variables in the effect of aging on IQ seems to be amount of education. Swanson (1952) retested men on a college entrance test after a 20-year interval. Those who

Figure 6-8. Cross-sectional studies of the effect of aging on IQ seemed to indicate that intellectual ability increases from infancy to late adolescence or early adulthood, reaches a peak, and then declines slowly over the remaining years. This theoretical curve describes these general findings.

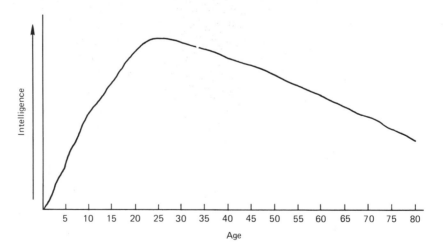

Figure 6-9. Development of one's intellectual skills can continue into old age. With continued stimulation, IQ actually tends to increase over the life span. (Tyrone Hall, Stock, Boston)

had graduated from college gained a mean of 35 points; those who attended college but did not graduate gained 9 points; and those who did not attend college gained 7 points. Even in old age, however, people can be *taught* to be more intelligent (Plemons, Willis, & Baltes, 1976). Not only can training increase ability to perform on intellectual tasks, but this improvement is found to generalize to other tasks and to be maintained over time. It seems that you *can* teach an old dog newer and better tricks; it is sad when we mistakenly assume that such improvement is impossible.

Why was there a difference between the results of the cross-sectional and longitudinal studies? In the cross-sectional studies, each group is different not only in age but in life experiences. Many things change from one generation to the next—schools are different, technology improves, communication broadens. The reported decline in IQ apparently was caused by differences in life experiences across generations rather than by the aging process. The results of the longitudinal research have led to the view of intellectual ability shown in Figure 6-9. In sum, intelligence can remain constant over the life span or even continue to grow.

Interference with Intellectual Growth. Despite the fact that longitudinal studies present an optimistic picture of intellectual functioning during old age, it is obvious from common observation that some people show a dramatic decline in mental ability as they grow older. What are the causes of such declines? Even though age itself may not impair intellectual

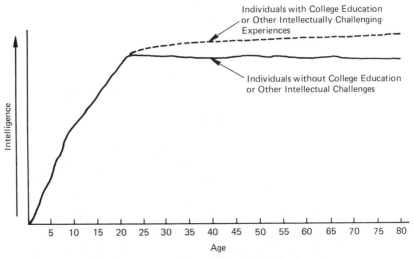

Figure 6-10. As shown in this theoretical curve, longitudinal studies of the effect of aging on IQ indicate that intellectual ability increases from infancy to late adolescence or early adulthood and then either remains constant or shows an increase over the remaining years. Increases are most likely to occur if the person has a college education or engages in other intellectually challenging experiences.

functioning, there may be some physical or psychological conditions that cause a decline in mental ability in *some* older people. One condition that occurs more frequently as one grows older is hypertension (high blood pressure). Wilkie and Eisdorfer (1971) hypothesized that as blood pressure increases, intelligence decreases. As part of a long-term study, both variables were measured among a group of older subjects over a 10-year period. As predicted, the presence of hypertension was associated with intellectual loss over the years.

In addition to high blood pressure in old age, there are other factors that can lead to a decrease in intellectual functioning. Examples are brain damage (Satz, Richard, & Daniels, 1967), mental illness (Schwartzman, Douglas, & Muir, 1962), and some infectious diseases such as Rocky Mountain spotted fever (Wright, 1972). Temporary negative effects can be brought about by intoxicants such as liquor; after about 10 ounces of 86-proof alcohol, memory functions very poorly (Rosen & Lee, 1976).

RESEARCH CLOSE-UP

What Is It Like to Be Gifted?

In 1921 Lewis Terman began a study of the characteristics of very bright people. His plan was to determine the "physical, mental, and personality traits" of gifted children and follow them as they developed into young adulthood and beyond. The study extended over the remainder of Terman's life and was continued by his colleagues (Burks, Jensen, & Terman, 1930; Terman, 1925; Terman & Oden, 1947, 1959).

On the basis of their performance on the Stanford-Binet, over 1,500 children with IQs of 140 or more were selected; the mean IQ of the group was 151. One major research interest was in the physique and health of the gifted children. A common myth is that those who are bright must "pay for it" by being weak and sickly; in *Richard III* Shakespeare wrote, "So wise so young, they say, do never live long." Terman found, however, that these very bright children were both taller and heavier than others of the same age. Compared with normative groups they walked earlier, talked earlier, and reached puberty at a younger age. The gifted children were found to have a lower incidence of physical defects and abnormal conditions of almost every kind than ordinary schoolchildren.

In high school, the gifted children continued to do well, and they were still superior to their classmates in such things as size, health, social interests, and leadership. As young adults, they were found to be no different from the nongifted with respect to mental illness, alcoholism, homosexuality, and marital adjustment. They were clearly superior, however, with respect to educational attainment and the status of their occupations. About 15 years later, they were still like the general population with respect to mental illness, though they were less likely than the nongifted to be alcoholic or imprisoned. Their death rate was also lower than that of the general population. The big differences were in such areas as education, occupation, and achievement.

Among others of their generation, only about 8 percent graduated from college; about 70 percent of the gifted did so. Over half of the men and about one-third of the women went on to obtain at least one advanced degree. Their income tended to be well above average, and with respect to achievement they were unusual. In terms of such honors as listing in *American Men of Science,* election to the National Academy of Sciences, listing in the *Directory of American Scholars,* and listing in *Who's Who,* the group did exceptionally well. They wrote 60 books and monographs and 2,000 technical and scientific articles, and were granted 230 patents. Their other writings included 33 novels, 375 short stories, and 265 miscellaneous articles. A great many members of the gifted group became prominent in various fields; several are internationally known. Included are physical scientists, biological and social scientists, members of the U.S. State Department, and a motion picture director.

The most recent study of Terman's "children" focused on the males, whose average age was then 62 (Sears, 1977). It was found that those who were happiest with their jobs had been satisfied, ambitious, and in good health thirty years earlier. Those who were happiest with their family life had been socially well adjusted as children and had positive attitudes toward their parents. Thus, happiness and satisfaction with life seem to result from a number of psychological factors, and a high IQ neither guarantees such an outcome nor acts against it. Once again, however, it can be seen that IQ is very important with respect to education and occupational status in our society. A good education and a successful occupation, in turn, can probably explain why these people were able to avoid committing crimes or becoming alcoholics.

IS INTELLIGENCE PARTLY A MATTER OF BELIEF? PYGMALION AND GALATEA IN THE CLASSROOM

While most of the research on intelligence and intellectual performance is based on the assumption of a very stable level of a more or less fixed ability, there is another element to consider. Since academic performance is affected by many factors, is it possible that the *expectations* of parents and teachers can influence how well a person does? For example, if a child does very well on his or her first couple of tests in a class, others tend to label that person "smart." It seems quite possible that there would then be some degree of pressure (from others and from the child as well) to live up to that label. Also, the authority figures who provided the label in the first place might be inclined to give more support to the person who is believed to be very bright, to offer more encouragement, and even to give the intelligent student the benefit of the doubt in grading test responses.

Rosenthal and Jacobson (1968) tested this possibility. They reasoned that, as in *Pygmalion,* the expectations of one person could influence and perhaps transform the behavior of another. The title of Shaw's play (on which *My Fair Lady* was based) was taken from the ancient Greek legend in which a sculptor, Pygmalion, was able to mold the behavior of a statue, Galatea, who had come to life. In a field experiment, teachers were given false information about the intellectual ability of some of the students in their classes. It was found that when the teachers expected a child to do well, those children actually showed an increase in IQ compared with children about whom they had no special expectations.

As with much of the work on intelligence, these research methods and results were the targets of sharp criticism (e.g., Cronbach, 1975; Elashoff & Snow, 1971). However, Zanna, Sheras, Cooper, and Shaw (1975) were able to replicate and extend the original findings. In a summer program for mostly black, inner-city students who had just finished the sixth, seventh, or eighth grade, the teachers were told that some of their pupils could be expected to "bloom" intellectually, but no predictions were made about the remaining students. At the end of the program the students' academic achievement was measured. Compared to scores on tests given during the previous spring, there was a tremendous improvement in test scores among the students whose teachers expected them to do well but not among those whose teachers had not received the false information.

Zanna and his colleagues also gave some of the students false feed-back indicating they could be expected to improve; others were given no information. As in the case of teacher expectations, the students who believed they would do well actually showed a dramatic increase in test scores by the end of the summer compared with those who had not been given positive expectations. In other words, students perform better intellectually if they expect to, and they perform better if their teachers expect them to. Strangely enough, if *both* teachers and students were given the positive expectations there was less improvement. Improvement depended on either the student *or* the teacher's believing that the student had academic ability.

In general, then, these experiments suggest that ability can be increased to a surprising extent just on the basis of expectation. They also add further support to the idea that intellectual performance is not an unchangeable index; at least in part, it is a flexible response to external conditions.

SUMMARY

Intelligence is the ability to learn, remember, understand, form concepts, and think effectively.

The earliest attempts to measure individual differences in intellectual functioning involved very simple responses, but these tests were unrelated to such criteria as school grades. Alfred Binet, a French psychologist, successfully developed complex verbal tasks to measure intellectual differences among children. In 1905 he produced the first intelligence test, and it was used in the Paris school system. An American psychologist, Lewis M. Terman, became interested in Binet's work and in 1916 published the Stanford-Binet Intelligence Scale, which set the pattern for all subsequent measures of intelligence. The items used on this test were those that (1) were passed by a higher percentage of children at successive ages and (2) correlated with the total score on the test. IQ was defined as the mental age obtained on the test divided by the subject's chronological age and multplied by 100. Today IQ is simply a score that indicates how well a person does relative to others of the same age. An IQ of 100 indicates an average performance.

Research on the origins of individual differences in intelligence has involved a controversy between those who stress genetic factors and those who stress environmental factors. Genetic research shows that the more closely related two people are, the more similar they are in IQ. Identical twins raised apart are more similar than siblings raised together but less similar than twins raised together. Among adopted children, differences in IQ are correlated with the intelligence of their true parents, but their level of intelligence tends to be more like that of their adoptive parents. A recent scientific scandal surrounds the possibility that one of the leading proponents of genetic effects, Sir Cyril Burt, falsified his data in order to support his arguments.

Environmental studies indicate that people raised in intellectually deprived surroundings do less well on IQ tests. Intellectually enriched environments have a positive effect on ability. College attendance also has a positive effect, and it has been shown that people can be taught to do better on such tests.

It is well known that IQ is highly correlated with occupational status. In addition, the occupation of a father is a good predictor of the IQ of his offspring. Such findings have been interpreted as showing that genetically superior people succeed in society or as showing the effect of enriched surroundings plus such related variables as family size and nutrition. Studies of black–white differences in IQ tend to ignore the problems involved in defining race, and they are a subject of heated debate. Whites obtain a higher mean score on IQ tests than blacks, but there is a large overlap between the groups. A few scientists have concluded that the evidence shows that whites are genetically superior, though most social scientists disagree with that conclusion. The most likely explanation for racial differences in IQ appears to rest on different environmental factors. Black and white infants do not differ in intelligence; the IQ of blacks goes up with improved schooling; the IQ of interracial offspring depends on the race of the parent who raises the child; and when black children are adopted by affluent white families their IQs are higher than those of the average white child.

IQ tests are good predictors of school grades, especially at the lower levels. Beyond the classroom, IQ is found to be related to ability to learn, ability to change in response to psychotherapy, and the tendency to be persuaded by factual arguments. Intelligence is positively related to creativity and the ability to delay gratification.

Measures of IQ in infancy are unrelated to later test scores. In general, IQ becomes fairly stable by adolescence and can be used to predict adult IQ very well. Cross-sectional research suggested that intelligence reaches a peak and then declines slowly with age. In contrast, longitudinal research has shown that intelligence tends either to remain the same over time or (with stimulation) to show an increase. Impairment of IQ can be brought about by high blood pressure, brain damage, mental illness, and some diseases. A long-term study of gifted children has revealed that they are much like the nongifted in many respects but are clearly superior in educational attainment, occupational success, and many types of achievement.

Research has shown that school performance can be positively influenced by beliefs about IQ. If either the teachers or the students themselves are led to believe that certain pupils are bright, academic ability actually increases. Such research provides evidence that intelligence is, in part, a flexible, changeable response to external circumstances.

SUGGESTED READINGS

BLOCK, N. J., & DWORKIN, G. (eds.) *The IQ controversy: Critical readings.* New York: Pantheon, 1976. A comprehensive collection of readings that traces the nature–nurture arguments about intelligence from the gentlemanly debates of the 1920s to the current heated exchanges concerning race and IQ.

HEARNSHAW, L. S. *Cyril Burt, psychologist.* Ithaca, New York: Cornell University Press, 1979. This is a sympathetic biography of the respected British psychologist whose work influenced theories of intellectual development and the practices of intelligence testing in his nation's school system. The author presents convincing evidence that in Burt's later years, he resorted to the use of false data in an attempt to support his theories.

JENSEN, A. R. *Bias in mental testing.* New York: Macmillan, 1980. A presentation of the data on the inheritance of IQ and on racial differences, which are interpreted in terms of genetics.

KAMIN, L. J. *The science and politics of IQ.* Hillsdale, N.J.: Lawrence Erlbaum, 1974. A spirited and often biased attack on the idea that intelligence is genetically determined, a view that the author equates with right-wing extremism.

LEWIS, M. (ed.) *Origins of intelligence.* New York: Plenum, 1975. A fascinating collection of papers dealing with the development of intelligence in infancy, including such topics as early learning, cross-cultural differences, the role of social class, and how the intelligence of infants is measured.

LOEHLIN, J. C., LINDZEY, G., & SPUHLER, J. H. *Race differences in intelligence.* San Francisco: Freeman, 1975. A comprehensive and fair review of the issues involved in the debate over racial differences in IQ.

RESNICK, L. B. (ed.) *The nature of intelligence* Hillsdale, N.J.: Lawrence Erlbaum, 1976. A collection of twenty chapters by researchers who are active in this area.

SAGAN, C. *The dragons of Eden: Speculations on the evolution of human intelligence.* New York: Random House, 1977. An extremely interesting and thought-provoking account of how the human brain evolved and the way it functions as a "living computer."

SEAGOE, M. V. *Terman and the gifted.* Los Altos, Calif.: Kaufmann, 1975. An interesting biography of the man who developed the Stanford-Binet and devoted his career to the study of intelligence.

WOLF, T. H. *Alfred Binet.* Chicago: University of Chicago Press, 1973. The biography of the man who developed the first intelligence tests and also conducted research on such diverse topics as hypnotism, education, and abnormal behavior.

Chapter Seven

MANIFEST ANXIETY: THE EFFECTS OF EMOTIONALITY

In this chapter you will read about the following topics:

Susan woke up in her cluttered dormitory room, and her first thought was that something dreadful was about to happen. Her clock radio had just come on, and a bland voice was reading a series of news bulletins that dealt with an apartment house fire, a train derailment, and a shooting at a local bar. Susan made a mental note to reset the time so as to wake up to music instead of the newsbreak. As she walked sleepily down the hall to the communal bathroom, a wave of fear washed over her—she remembered this morning's examination. At 10:00 she would be one of thousands of students across the country taking the test that would determine whether she would be able to go on to graduate school. Her hand trembled as she sought the right mix of hot and cold water in the shower.

Thinking about the exam was bad enough, but her memory of last night's date was even worse. Maybe she was imagining it, but Mike had seemed distant and vaguely irritated with her in a way that she hadn't seen before. Everything he talked about appeared to be leading toward something—toward letting her down easy. Whenever she said something about the two of them, he became noncommittal. They both drank too much beer, and that only made things worse. This morning her head throbbed with pain. Was their love really coming to an end after all these months? Did she really care, or did she just hate the thought of being rejected? This wasn't the first time, but it was getting more and more difficult to explain away her failure to get involved in a relationship that lasted.

Later, after breakfast, she hurried across campus to the Chem Building, where the test was being given. With each step her tension grew. Her hands were clammy with perspiration, and she was acutely aware of the spreading damp splotches under her arms. As she entered the auditorium she felt dizzy, and her mouth was so dry that she wanted to avoid having to talk to anyone she knew. She took a seat near the back. A monitor handed her a newly sharpened pencil and the test forms. Susan read the bold print, DO NOT OPEN TEST BOOKLET UNTIL INSTRUCTED TO DO SO, and this sounded somehow ominous. If only the headache would go away.

By the time the testing was to begin, her thoughts were a jumble. It was difficult to hear the instructions being given by the test administrator. He said something about erasing an answer if you change your mind, or did he say not to erase? There would be two separate sets of questions, and each was to last no longer than an hour. First there would be a measure of general verbal ability, then a quantitative test. It was time to begin; the signal was given. Susan could see some of the students sitting near her rapidly marking their answers to the first questions while she was still fumbling to open the test to the first page. If everyone would just slow down! She began to panic. If she really bombed the test, what would her father think? He had always been so proud of his daughter, and now she could imagine his look of disappointment when he found out how badly she had done.

She tried to throw off these thoughts and concentrate on the first question. It was a vocabulary item:

  1. EMINENT
     a. remote
     b. distinguished
     c. impending
     d. mountainous

Oh lord! The answer was either (b) or (c), but she always got eminent *and* imminent *mixed up. She marked (b) and then quickly erased it. Was it (c), or had she been right the first time? Just then the queasy feeling in her stomach increased and she felt a sharp, cramping pain. She had to get out of that room! Her world was collapsing, and she wanted to escape. Susan hurried toward a rear exit, half blinded by tears.*

WE HAVE ALL FELT ANXIETY and the unpleasantness that goes with it, though our anxiety may not have been as extreme as Susan's. Who has not worried about an examination or the chance of being rejected by someone we care about or the reactions of our parents to what we do? **Anxiety** and **fear** are very similar emotions that are characterized by an unpleasant state of arousal or tension, dread of some object or event, and the desire to avoid the source of these feelings. There are often physiological responses such as a faster heart rate, a dry mouth, and the tendency to perspire heavily; in addition, there may be such symptoms as headaches, nausea, and diarrhea. The major difference between fear and anxiety is that fear usually refers to a specific source—such as your dental appointment next Friday afternoon—while the cause of anxiety is vague and abstract. Most often, as in Susan's case, there are both specific fears and a generalized anxiety whose roots are more difficult to identify.

In this chapter we will deal with anxiety as a trait and show how it has been measured; the effects of individual differences in anxiety will be examined with respect to several kinds of behavior, including college grades. Next it will be shown that anxiety can be considered as a temporary state as well as a more or less stable trait, and some of its specific sources will be discussed. Finally, we will consider the ways in which anxiety can be reduced and controlled.

ANXIETY AS A TRAIT

Hull-Spence Theory

Hull and Spence: Building a Science of Behavior. The life and career of Clark L. Hull (1884–1952) overlapped that of Freud, but their background, training, and approach to a theory of behavior were markedly different. Hull was born on a farm near Akron, New York; a few years later the family moved to another farm in Michigan. He went to a one-room rural school, with attendance often interrupted by farm work in the spring and autumn. He attended Alma College, where he took courses in mathematics and science to prepare for a career as a mining engineer. He was working as an engineer in Minnesota when he was suddenly stricken with polio, which left him a partial invalid for a year. At this point he decided that he must change his occupational plans; he considered the ministry but decided on psychology.

With two years of teaching, Hull saved enough money to enter the University of Michigan. After receiving a bachelor's degree in psychology, he taught for a year in Kentucky, earning $75 a month. He was rejected for fellowships at both Cornell and Yale, but was given a teaching assistantship at the University of Wisconsin. He received the Ph.D. degree in 1918 and remained at Wisconsin until 1929. His original research interests were varied and included a study of the effects of tobacco on mental efficiency, work on aptitude testing, a dissertation dealing with concept formation, and a series of experimental studies of hypnosis. Hull's belief in **behaviorism** was already well developed at Wisconsin, and in his seminars he would ask students to explain various psychological phenomena in behavioral terms, that is, by using concepts that did not involve hypothetical mental states. Once, after a guest lecturer had gotten an audience very excited about psychical research, Hull rose and said, "It is very strange that every time phenomena of this sort are reported or observed, a poet, or a philosopher, or some other sort of nonscientific person is involved" (Gengerelli, 1976, p. 687). This kind of skepticism was unpopular with many psychologists at the time.

Moving to Yale in 1929, Hull found that experiments with hypnosis met with medical opposition, and he was forced to give up this line of research. John B. Watson's work on conditioning was of interest to him, so Hull soon focused on the field of learning. He died in 1952, the year in which the following statement of his beliefs was published:

As the result of the considerations of these behavioral problems over a number of years, probably influenced considerably by my early training in the physical sciences, I came to the definite conclusion around 1930 that psychology is a true natural science; that its primary laws are expressible quantitatively by means of a moderate number of ordinary equations; that all the complex behavior of single individuals will ultimately be derivable as secondary laws from (1) these primary laws together with (2) the conditions under which behavior occurs; and that all the behavior of groups as a whole, i.e., strictly social behavior as such, may similarly be derived as quantitative laws from the same primary equations. With these and similar views as a background, the task of psychologists obviously is that of laying bare these laws as quickly and accurately as possible, particularly the primary laws. This belief was deepened by the influence of my seminar students, notably Kenneth W. Spence and Neal E. Miller. It has determined most of my scientific activities ever since, and the longer I live the more convinced I am of its general soundness. [Hull, 1952, p. 155]

As mentioned, one of his early associates was Kenneth Spence (1907–1967), who entered Yale in 1930 after receiving his undergraduate education and a master's degree at McGill University. He was awarded the Ph.D. degree in 1933 and worked briefly in Florida and in Virginia. At that point he began a long, productive, and very influential career at the University of Iowa. From 1964 until his death in 1967, he held a professorship at the University of Texas (Kendler, 1967).

Anxiety as a Theoretical Construct.   To provide a sample of **Hull-Spence theory** and indicate the impetus for the development of the **Manifest Anxiety Scale** (MAS), one type of learning situation (**classical conditioning**) will now be described.

An **unconditioned stimulus** is one that regularly evokes an observable response (called an **unconditioned response**). For example, a sudden loud noise will evoke a fear response. A **conditioned stimulus** is one that does not evoke that response until after it has been paired with or associated with the unconditioned stimulus. For example, if a sudden loud and frightening noise occurs when a person is in an elevator, the elevator can become associated with the noise. Once conditioning has taken place, the conditioned stimulus evokes the response, which is then labeled the **conditioned response.** A person who has undergone such conditioning is now likely to exhibit fear when he or she approaches an elevator.

Even in such a relatively simple situation, a great many variables have been found to influence the relation between the conditioned stimulus and the conditioned response. For example, the probability that

Figure 7-1. Anxiety about heights was the subject of Alfred Hitchcock's 1958 thriller, *Vertigo.* (Bettmann/Springer Film Archive)

the stimulus will elicit the response has been found to be influenced by the number of trials in which the conditioned and unconditioned stimuli were associated; the more such pairings, the greater the probability that the response will follow the stimulus. Another influence is the strength of the unconditioned stimulus; an intense stimulus (such as a very loud noise) has a greater effect on performance than a weak one. There are individual differences in **emotional responsiveness,** and this has an effect on simple conditioning. There are also a number of variables that have been found to inhibit performance.

Now, one could simply catalog these variables and indicate that they have such and such an effect on performance. It would be an obvious advantage, however, to have a theoretical system that enabled us to conceptualize all of the variables in an integrated way, could be generalized to different situations, and would generate predictions about quite different kinds of behavior. Hull (1943) proposed such a system. His approach involved a set of hypothetical factors that were each defined in terms of observable variables like those just described. The relation between the conditioned stimulus and the conditioned response is seen as a function of a series of lawful relations. Several independent variables influence the strength of whatever habits are activated in a given stimulus situation, while other independent variables influence the strength of an emotional response, which in turn influences the strength of the total generalized **drive** state. In Hull's system the strength of a response is determined by **habit strength** multiplied by drive; any inhibiting factors are then subtracted from this product.

This theoretical system uses only constructs that can be defined in operational terms, and relatively precise relations between and among variables are specified. Where does the concept of anxiety fit into such a system? Spence (1958) wrote that if there were a way to measure individual differences in emotional responsiveness, the theory would allow one to predict how a person would perform in a classical conditioning situation. The solution was the Manifest Anxiety Scale (see box), which led to predictions of behavior in a great many laboratory and real-life situations.

TRY IT YOURSELF

Anxiety and Fear

Respond to the following personality scale by circling T for true or F for false beside each statement:

T   F   1. I do not tire quickly.

T   F   2. I am troubled by attacks of nausea.

T   F   3. I believe I am no more nervous than most others.

T   F   4. I have very few headaches.

T F 5. I work under a great deal of tension.

T F 6. I cannot keep my mind on one thing.

T F 7. I worry over money and business.

T F 8. I frequently notice my hand shakes when I try to do something.

T F 9. I blush no more often than others.

T F 10. I have diarrhea once a month or more.

T F 11. I worry quite a bit over possible misfortunes.

T F 12. I practically never blush.

T F 13. I am often afraid that I am going to blush.

T F 14. I have nightmares every few nights.

T F 15. My hands and feet are usually warm enough.

T F 16. I sweat very easily even on cool days.

T F 17. Sometimes when embarrassed, I break out in a sweat which annoys me greatly.

T F 18. I hardly ever notice my heart pounding and I am seldom short of breath.

T F 19. I feel hungry almost all the time.

T F 20. I am very seldom troubled by constipation.

T F 21. I have a great deal of stomach trouble.

T F 22. I have had periods in which I lost sleep over worry.

T F 23. My sleep is fitful and disturbed.

T F 24. I dream frequently about things that are best kept to myself.

T F 25. I am easily embarrassed.

T F 26. I am more sensitive than most other people.

T F 27. I frequently find myself worrying about something.

T F 28. I wish I could be as happy as others seem to be.

T F 29. I am usually calm and not easily upset.

T F 30. I cry easily.

T F 31. I feel anxiety about something or someone almost all the time.

T F 32. I am happy most of the time.

T F 33. It makes me nervous to have to wait.

T F 34. I have periods of such great restlessness that I cannot sit long in a chair.

T F 35. Sometimes I become so excited that I find it hard to get to sleep.

T F 36. I have sometimes felt that difficulties were piling up so high that I could not overcome them.

T F 37. I must admit that I have at times been worried beyond reason over something that really did not matter.

T F 38. I have very few fears compared to my friends.

T F 39. I have been afraid of things or people that I know could not hurt me.

T F 40. I certainly feel useless at times.

T F 41. I find it hard to keep my mind on a task or job.

T F 42. I am usually self-conscious.

T F 43. I am inclined to take things hard.

T F 44. I am a high-strung person.

T F 45. Life is a strain for me much of the time.

T F 46. At times I think I am no good at all.

T F 47. I am certainly lacking in self-confidence.

T F 48. I sometimes feel that I am about to go to pieces.

T F 49. I shrink from facing a crisis or difficulty.

T F 50. I am entirely self-confident.

Now try a second test. The following items refer to things and experiences that may cause fear or other unpleasant feelings. Beside each item write the number that describes how much you are disturbed by it.

1 = not at all; 2 = a little; 3 = a fair amount; 4 = much; 5 = very much

_____	1. Noise of vacuum cleaners	_____	20. Worms
		_____	21. Imaginary creatures
_____	2. Open wounds	_____	22. Receiving injections
_____	3. Being alone	_____	23. Strangers
_____	4. Being in a strange place	_____	24. Bats
_____	5. Loud voices	_____	25. Train journeys
_____	6. Dead people	_____	26. Bus journeys
_____	7. Speaking in public	_____	27. Car journeys
_____	8. Crossing streets	_____	28. Feeling angry
_____	9. People who seem insane	_____	29. People in authority
		_____	30. Flying insects
_____	10. Falling	_____	31. Seeing other people injected
_____	11. Automobiles		
_____	12. Being teased	_____	32. Sudden noises
_____	13. Dentists	_____	33. Dull weather
_____	14. Thunder	_____	34. Crowds
_____	15. Sirens	_____	35. Large open spaces
_____	16. Failure	_____	36. Cats
_____	17. Entering a room where other people are already seated	_____	37. One person bullying another
		_____	38. Tough-looking people
_____	18. High places on land	_____	39. Birds
_____	19. People with deformities	_____	40. Sight of deep water

_____ 41. Being watched working

_____ 42. Dead animals

_____ 43. Weapons

_____ 44. Dirt

_____ 45. Crawling insects

_____ 46. Sight of fighting

_____ 47. Ugly people

_____ 48. Fire

_____ 49. Sick people

_____ 50. Dogs

_____ 51. Being criticized

_____ 52. Strange shapes

_____ 53. Being in an elevator

_____ 54. Witnessing surgical operations

_____ 55. Angry people

_____ 56. Mice

_____ 57. Human blood

_____ 58. Animal blood

_____ 59. Parting from friends

_____ 60. Enclosed places

_____ 61. Prospect of a surgical operation

_____ 62. Feeling rejected by others

_____ 63. Airplanes

_____ 64. Medical odors

_____ 65. Feeling disapproved of

_____ 66. Harmless snakes

_____ 67. Cemeteries

_____ 68. Being ignored

_____ 69. Darkness

_____ 70. Missing a heartbeat

_____ 71. Nude men

_____ 72. Nude women

_____ 73. Lightning

_____ 74. Doctors

_____ 75. Making mistakes

_____ 76. Looking foolish

The first of these measures is the Manifest Anxiety Scale, which was developed by Janet Taylor Spence as a measure of emotional responsiveness (Taylor, 1951, 1953). Items from the Minnesota Multiphasic Personality Inventory were given to five clinical psychologists, who were asked to judge which ones showed chronic anxiety. Those on which they agreed were then put through an internal consistency item analysis (Bechtoldt, 1953), and the fifty items that survived the analysis constitute the MAS that you took.

The second test is the **Fear Survey Schedule** (FSS), which was developed for use by behavior therapists in identifying specific patient fears (Wolpe & Lang, 1964). As you may have noticed, it deals with several types of fear cues such as animals, illness and death, and social stimuli.

If your instructor wishes, hand in a piece of paper giving your sex, your MAS score, and your FSS score. Names are not necessary. With this information, your instructor can show you how to find out whether the general trait of anxiety is associated with specific fears and whether males and females differ in either anxiety or fear. Do you think responses to the two tests will be related? Why?

Test keys:

FSS: Simply add the numbers you wrote beside the 76 items.

MAS: 1-F, 2-T, 3-F, 4-F, 5-T, 6-T, 7-T, 8-T, 9-F, 10-T, 11-T, 12-F, 13-T, 14-T, 15-F, 16-T, 17-T, 18-F, 19-T, 20-F, 21-T, 22-T, 23-T, 24-T, 25-T, 26-T, 27-T, 28-T, 29-F, 30-T, 31-T, 32-F, 33-T, 34-T, 35-T, 36-T, 37-T, 38-F, 39-T, 40-T, 41-T, 42-T, 43-T, 44-T, 45-T, 46-T, 47-T, 48-T, 49-T, 50-F.

EFFECTS OF ANXIETY ON BEHAVIOR

Learning and Performance

The initial reason for constructing the Manifest Anxiety Scale was the need for a measure of individual differences in emotional responsiveness in laboratory conditioning experiments. As Taylor (1956) has pointed out, the Iowa group was not interested in the trait of anxiety but in the role of drive in learning.

The influence of drive level (including differences in MAS scores) on behavior depends in part on the complexity of the task. Hull (1943) proposed that the response strength of all habits activated in a given stimulus situation increases as drive state increases. Using this and certain other ideas from Hull's system, Spence predicted that, in a situation which evokes one habit that is stronger than any competing ones, high drive results in greater response strength. Thus, a strong, well learned correct response (such as stepping on the brake pedal in an emergency) is very likely to occur and in a speedy and vigorous fashion. When there are several habits of approximately equal strength evoked in a situation, high drive adds to the probability of each habit occurring. Here, the response strength of correct *and* incorrect responses in increased by drive. An inexperienced driver may well respond to an emergency badly in that competing responses such as stepping on the brake, honking the horn, and shifting gears may each be evoked strongly. With someone experienced behind the wheel of the car, high drive would thus improve performance. With someone inexperienced, high drive would interfere. Thus, anxiety or drive should help performance in some situations and interfere with it in others.

The research conducted to test these hypotheses shows both the role of a strong theory in stimulating research and the value of including a personality variable in research in experimental psychology.

Classical Conditioning. A typical classical conditioning experiment using human subjects (e.g., Spence, 1953) involves eyelid conditioning. Subjects are placed in a fixed position in a dental chair. The unconditioned stimulus is a puff of air that is directed at one eye, eliciting an eyeblink (the unconditioned response). The conditioned stimulus is an increase in the brightness of a circular disk made of milk glass. In each conditioning trial the puff of air is closely followed by the conditioned stimulus. The dependent variable is the number of conditioned responses (eyeblinks in response to the brightness changes) made during the test trials. One would predict that high drive would lead to better performance in this situation and, hence, that subjects with high scores on the MAS would give more conditioned responses than subjects with low scores on the MAS.

The typical procedure has been to select subjects with extremely high or extremely low MAS scores. A typical finding is that of Spence and Taylor (1951). With an air puff intensity of two pounds per square inch, the anxious group gave significantly more conditioned responses than the relatively nonanxious group, as shown in Figure 7-2. When subjects with scores in the middle range of the MAS are included in the sample, their conditioning performance tends to fall between those of the two extreme groups (Spence, 1964).

Serial Learning. Spence and Spence (1966) predicted that when the habit strength for the correct response is low (e.g., when the task is difficult and learning has just begun), anxiety would *interfere* with performance. As learning progressed, however, the habit strength for the correct response should increase until it was stronger than the habit strength for any competing response. At that point (e.g., late in learning) anxiety should have a *positive* effect on performance. Spielberger and Smith (1966) examined the effects of anxiety on performance at different stages of a **serial**

Figure 7-2.   In an eyelid conditioning task a puff of air on the eye is the unconditioned stimulus and an eyeblink is the unconditioned response. When the air puff is repeatedly paired with increased brightness of a circular disk (the conditioned stimulus), the lighted disk will then elicit eyeblinks (the conditioned response). People who are high in manifest anxiety perform better in such a situation than those who are low in anxiety in that they give more conditioned responses on test trials.

(Data from Spence, 1960)

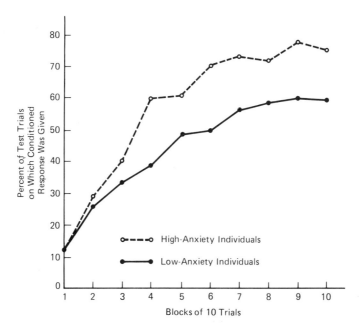

learning task. Undergraduates had to learn a list of twelve nonsense syllables, and they were told that there is a relation between ability on such a task and intelligence. Under these conditions, as may be seen in Figure 7-3, the hypothesis was confirmed. The high-anxious subjects did less well than the low-anxious subjects early in learning, while the reverse was true late in learning.

Paired-Associates Learning. In **paired-associates learning** subjects are presented with a stimulus word and required to learn the response word associated with it. The experimenter can control the variables related to response strength more precisely than is possible when the task is learning a list of words in serial order.

Figure 7-3. Consistent with theoretical predictions, the effect of anxiety on performance is found to be different at different stages of the learning process. In a verbal learning task, high anxiety interferes with performance at the beginning of a series of trials when right and wrong answers are more nearly equal in habit strength. In later trials, when the habit strength of the right answers is much stronger, high anxiety actually leads to better performance than does low anxiety.

(Data from Spielberger & Smith, 1966)

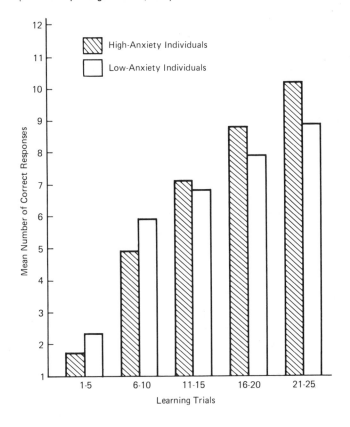

Two experiments were reported by Spence, Farber, and McFann (1956). The word pairs are shown in Table 7-1. In one experiment the correct stimulus–response connections were made strong, thus minimizing the presence of competing responses. The stimulus words were very different from one another, and each was strongly associated with its response word (e.g., roving—nomad.) As hypothesized, high-anxious subjects were superior to low-anxious subjects in learning the associations. In the other experiment an attempt was made to include stimulus-response pairs with low association (e.g., arid—grouchy) that also had high associations across stimulus words (e.g., desert), thus involving strong competing response tendencies. As hypothesized, high-anxious subjects made more errors than low-anxious subjects under these circumstances.

Anxiety and Interfering Thoughts.   The way anxiety interferes with performance can be explained in other ways besides Hull-Spence theory. Sarason and Stoops (in press) gave high- and low-anxious college students an intellectual task, but there was a four-minute waiting period between the instructions and the test itself. When subjects were asked to estimate how long the waiting period had been and how long the test had lasted, the high-anxious students made higher estimates than the low-anxious students. Those who were high in anxiety also performed less well on the task.

When subjects were asked about their thoughts during the experiment, the most anxious ones were more likely to say that they had wondered how badly they were doing, how others were doing, and what the experimenter would think about them. The authors suggested that such thoughts tend to increase the stressfulness of the situation, interfere with how well subjects can perform, and make it seem that more time is passing than is actually the case.

Table 7-1.   When subjects are asked to learn pairs of words, the effect of anxiety on performance depends on whether there is initially a clear association between the two words (high initial habit strength) or no association (low initial habit strength). Subjects who are high in anxiety make fewer errors on word pairs like those on the left and more errors on word pairs like those on the right. Can you explain why? There is something else about the stimulus words on the right that makes the task more difficult and, hence, a problem for those who are most anxious. What is it?

Pairs of Words with High Initial Habit Strength		Pairs of Words with Low Initial Habit Strength	
Stimulus Word	*Response Word*	*Stimulus Word*	*Response Word*
barren	fruitless	arid	grouchy
little	minute	desert	leading
roving	nomad	petite	yonder
tranquil	placid	undersized	wholesome

(Information from Spence, Farber, & McFann, 1956)

There is a widely accepted belief that people who become anxious in situations that involve intellectual skills will perform less well than people whose anxiety level remains fairly low. A study conducted in Greece indicated an inverse relation between educational level and anxiety, as shown in Figure 7-4 (Vassiliou, Georgas, & Vassiliou, 1967). It could be that people who do badly in school are especially prone to anxiety, but a more likely explanation is that anxiety interferes with performance and hence only the least anxious ones succeed.

Since both academic ability and anxiety would be expected to influence grades, Spielberger (1966) proposed that both variables should be considered at the same time. In a study of a large group of male undergraduates at Duke University, high- and low-anxious subjects were divided into five levels on the basis of scholastic aptitude. Grade point averages were obtained for the semester during which each subject took the MAS. The combined effects of anxiety and ability on grades may be seen in Figure 7-5. For those students with the highest and lowest aptitude scores, grades were unrelated to anxiety. At the middle levels of aptitude, however, the

Figure 7-4. In a study conducted in Greece, anxiety was found to be related to level of educational attainment. The further an individual had progressed in school, the lower that persons' anxiety level. (Data from Vassiliou, Georgas, & Vassiliou, 1967)

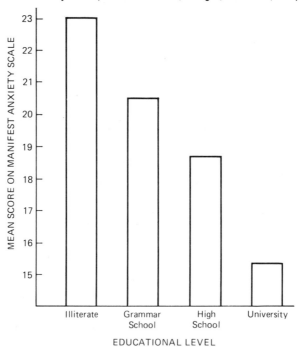

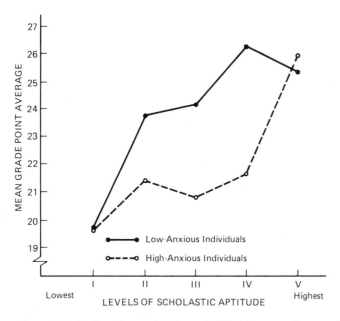

Figure 7-5. Both anxiety and intellectual ability influence college grades. It is clear that grades are poor at the lowest aptitude level and good at the highest level. For all of the other aptitude levels, low-anxious students do better in college than high-anxious students. (Adapted from Spielberger, 1966)

low-anxious students consistently obtained better grades than the high-anxious students. A follow-up study of these students three years later provided dramatic evidence of the effect of anxiety on college performance. For each of the five levels of scholastic aptitude, the percentage of students who had dropped out of the university for academic reasons was determined. At every level except the highest, the high-anxious students were much more likely to have failed in college than the low-anxious students. (The data are shown in Figure 7-6.) Such findings led Spielberger to suggest that anxiety tests could be used to identify those who were likely to have trouble in school. Then therapy could be provided in order to prevent the tragedy of anxiety-based failure.

Maladjustment

Taylor (1953) administered the MAS to neurotic and psychotic patients who were undergoing psychiatric treatment. Their median score of 34 is much higher than the median of 13 obtained by Iowa college students. Half of the patients had scores that were higher than those of 98 percent of the students. Figure 7-7 compares the two groups.

When psychiatric patients are compared with college students, the two groups are different in many respects besides maladjustment. For example, the students tend to be younger, brighter, and better educated. A

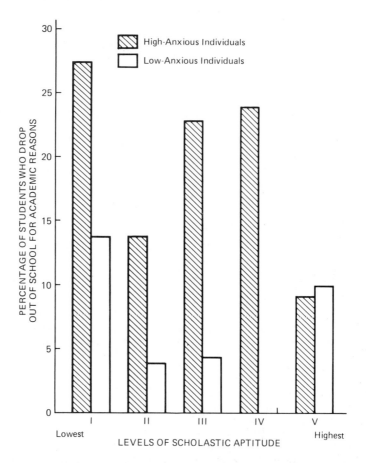

Figure 7-6. Except at the highest level of academic ability, high-anxious students are much more likely to drop out of college for academic reasons than low-anxious students.

(Data from Spielberger, 1966)

study of the MAS scores of psychiatric patients and medical patients who were matched for age and intelligence was conducted by Matarazzo, Guze, and Matarazzo (1955). The psychiatric patients obtained much higher scores (mean = 26) than the medical patients (mean = 13). It seems, then, that maladjustment and anxiety are linked.

Interpersonal Behavior

It has been found that people tend to seek out others—to affiliate—when they are anxious (Schachter, 1959). Presumably, it is comforting and anxiety reducing to be with others when one is in a stressful situation.

Because people differ in their characteristic anxiety level,

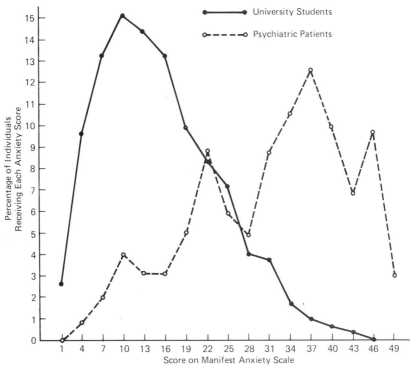

Figure 7-7. When university students are compared with psychiatric patients on the MAS, the patients report a much higher level of anxiety than the students. It seems that anxiety can be associated with psychological maladjustment.

(Data from Taylor, 1953)

Teichman (1974) proposed that those who are highly anxious should show even stronger **affiliative behavior** than those with low anxiety scores. The experimental subjects were told that the research dealt with the physiological assessment of their problems and innermost secrets. For the control subjects, a neutral, nonthreatening experiment was described. There was a waiting period before the experiment began, and subjects were asked whether they would prefer to spend this time alone or with other subjects.

Those who were low in anxiety responded to the stressful situation by wanting to be with others. High-anxious subjects responded in the opposite way—those in the neutral condition wanted to be with others, but under stress the anxious subjects preferred to be alone. Thus, the original hypothesis was wrong. It seems that characteristic high levels of anxiety lead to affiliative behavior under normal conditions; when further stress is present, the resulting anxiety level is so high that the person wants to avoid contact with others. Consistent with this is the finding that at high levels of anxiety, people tend to disclose less about themselves (Post, Wittmaier, & Radin, 1978).

Should Instructors Use Humor to Help Anxious Students?

If anxiety interferes with performance on difficult tasks and with performance in the college classroom, it follows that any mechanism that would reduce anxiety should be helpful to high-anxious students. Smith, Ascough, Ettinger, and Nelson (1971) pointed out that most theories of humor include the notion of tension reduction. In various experiments (e.g., Singer, 1968) emotional arousal has been shown to decrease when subjects are exposed to humor. Smith and his colleagues reasoned that the use of humor in a testing situation should reduce stress and hence improve the performance of those who were anxious.

The subjects (whose anxiety had been measured early in the semester) were Purdue undergraduates who were taking a regular multiple-choice classroom examination in a psychology course. Two test forms were prepared. On the humorous form the stem of every third item was written in a humorous way. The corresponding items on the regular, nonhumorous form contained an equal number of words and had the same four alternative answers. Examples:

HUMOROUS

Three years ago Prudence Sigafoos met and became enamored of Errol Raunch, who had a thin mustache. But, alas, one night Errol snatched her purse and jewelry, bound her hands and feet with baling wire, and tossed her into a passing circus wagon, where she was assaulted three times by a playful orangutan. Since that night, Prudence has claimed that men and women who have thin mustaches can't be trusted. Her reaction is an example of:

NONHUMOROUS

Three years ago as a freshman Janet took a course from a college professor who had a beard. This professor was quite unreasonable in many respects. His lectures were disorganized and largely irrelevant to the goals of the course, his examinations contained many trick questions, and he gave over half of the class, including Janet, failing grades. Since then Janet has refused to take any courses from professors having beards. Her reaction is an example of:

ANSWERS
   a. a stereotype
   b. an archetype
   c. an effectance motive
   d. a projection

Did the presence of humor have any effect on test scores? The results are shown in Figure 7-8. Students who were high in anxiety did less well than those who were low in anxiety on the regular test, but this difference was eliminated when the test contained humorous material. It was concluded that the funny items acted to reduce anxiety, and that anxiety reduction improved the performance of the high-anxious individuals.

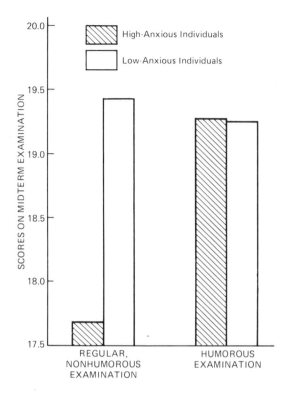

Figure 7-8. When high- and low-anxious students were given a regular examination in a psychology class, those who were low in anxiety received higher test scores. When the instructors attempted to reduce anxiety by constructing an examination with several humorous items in it, those who were high and low in anxiety did equally well.
(Data from Smith, Ascough, Ettinger, & Nelson, 1971)

When the students in a personality class read about this experiment, some became angry because the tests had not included humorous items. They felt that such tests would be more fair to those students who were high in anxiety. Others argued that grades based on a humorous test would not be good predictors of future performance on ordinary tests given in other classes by other instructors. Still others argued that very anxious students should simply study harder; then their anxiety would actually improve their performance on classroom exams.

What do you think? Should instructors take anxiety into account and try to help anxious students in some way? Are humorous exams more fair than regular exams? Could anxious students create their own humor and raise their test scores by thinking of jokes during a test?

ANXIETY AS A STATE

An important development in this research area has been the differentiation of two types of anxiety. On the one hand, there is **trait anxiety,** which refers to fairly stable individual differences in anxiety level; this is the construct measured by the MAS. In addition, there is **state anxiety,** which refers to a temporary condition that fluctuates over time in response to situational changes. Spielberger (1972) points out that anxiety states are characterized by subjective feelings of apprehension and tension plus activation of the autonomic nervous system. Trait anxiety refers to a motive system or acquired tendency that predisposes a person to respond with an anxiety state reaction to numerous situations that are each perceived as threatening. As with many personality variables, this distinction may be seen simply as a way of saying that anxiety is both a dimension along which people characteristically differ *and* a reaction to certain aspects of the immediate situation (Bartsch & Nesselroade, 1973; Shedletsky & Endler, 1974).

In an effort to provide a reliable and easily administered measure of the two aspects of anxiety, Spielberger, Gorsuch, and Lushene (1970) developed the **State-Trait Anxiety Inventory.** The A-Trait scale asks subjects to describe how they generally feel with respect to such statements as "I feel like crying," "I lack self-confidence," and "Some unimportant thought runs through my mind and bothers me." the A-State scale asks subjects to indicate how they feel right now, at this moment, with respect to such statements as "I feel calm," "I am jittery," and "I am worried."

Research using this instrument suggests that trait anxiety involves cognitive factors in that people report many interfering worries, thoughts, and concerns. State anxiety, on the other hand, reflects current feelings such as being nervous, as well as denial of pleasant emotions such as calmness or joy (Kendall, Finch, Auerbach, Hooke, & Mikulka, 1976).

Effects of General Stress

State and trait anxiety were studied by Johnson (1968). The subjects, male psychiatric patients, were interviewed. In the control condition, subjects were asked to talk about nonstressful topics such as their favorite hobbies or sports. In the stress condition, subjects were asked to indicate their bodily reactions to fear and to describe in detail the most frightening experience of their lives. The anxiety measures were given before and after the interview.

There was a significant increase in state anxiety following the stressful interview, but there was no change in trait anxiety. It appeared that the trait measure, which reflects individual differences in characteristic anxiety, is not affected by changes in the situation.

Reactions to Surgery and Dental Treatment

A very real stress that would be expected to arouse anxiety is the knowledge that one is going to undergo surgery (Auerbach, 1973). Besides the actual physical danger, there is a feeling of helplessness and uncertainty about

Figure 7-9. One of the common sources of anxiety in our current society is the stress of living with the possibility of another accident at a nuclear power plant. (U.P.I.)

one's fate. Spielberger, Auerbach, Wadsworth, Dunn, and Taulbee (1973) proposed that state anxiety would be aroused prior to surgery and would decline afterwards; trait anxiety was expected to be uninfluenced by these changes in the situation.

The State-Trait Anxiety Inventory was given to a group of male patients before and after surgery. The first testing took place 18 to 24 hours before surgery, and the second took place three to nine days after the operation. It was found that state anxiety was quite different before and after the stressful event while trait anxiety remained constant. However, the investigators were also interested, in the effect of trait anxiety on the level of state anxiety. That is, even though state anxiety should decrease for everyone after the stress is over, its absolute level should be higher for those who are chronically anxious than for those who are not. This relationship is shown in Figure 7-10. Such research also shows that the higher the state anxiety, the more pain the person reports after surgery (Martinez-Urrutia, 1975).

In a similar way, it is found that response to dental treatment is affected by trait anxiety in that people with high scores report greater state anxiety while waiting for the dentist, during treatment, and afterwards than people with low trait anxiety scores (Lamb, 1972). The situational nature of state anxiety is shown by the fact that it is highest when

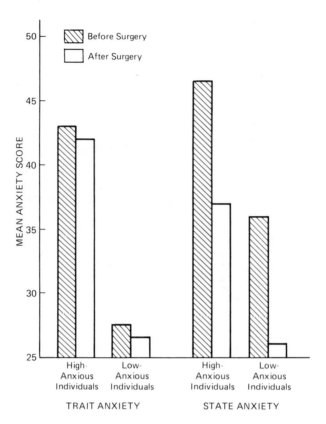

Figure 7-10. Research with surgical patients shows how both state and trait anxiety function. State anxiety is much higher before surgery than afterwards, while trait anxiety remains fairly constant. The absolute level of state anxiety (both before and after surgery) is much higher for people who are high in trait anxiety than for those who are low in trait anxiety.

(Data from Spielberger, Auerbach, Wadsworth, Dunn, & Taulbee, 1973)

the person is actually sitting in the chair and lowest when the treatment is over.

Specific Types of Anxiety

As with many types of personality measures now in use, the MAS may well be superseded in the future by instruments designed to measure the variable in question more specifically. Even though the concept of a general, multisituational anxiety trait appears useful, one of the basic properties of anxiety is the ease with which it can be attached to specific cues. The specific anxieties experienced by students were assessed by Thurman, Baron, and Klein (1979) who kept a record of the problems indicated by University of Texas students who telephoned the counseling center for help. A list of the fifteen most frequently stated problems is presented in Table 7-2. Tests that attempt to measure differences in specific types of anxiety may turn out to have greater predictive value than a measure like the MAS, which attempts to cut across many different situations (Kendall, 1978). Zuckerman (1977) has developed a trait-state anxiety measure that assesses responses to very specific situations such as the following:

You make a comment in class which the teacher ridicules, implying you are stupid for saying such a thing.

You face a dental or medical treatment which you know will be painful. You are sitting in the reception room waiting to be called in to see the doctor. The nurse calls your name.

Research indicates that this instrument is better than more global measures of anxiety at predicting responses to specific situations.

Because of the many possible sources of anxiety, Endler and Okada (1975) developed the **S-R Inventory of General Trait Anxiousness,** which deals with a variety of situations in which anxiety may be experienced. It is found that there are two main types of situations that arouse this emotion—interpersonal interaction and physical danger—and two major ways of responding to such situations—with symptoms of physiological distress and by trying to approach the danger. People appear to be quite consistent with respect to the situations to which they react and in the way they react (Cartwright, 1975). It has also been found, however, that some people are either anxious or nonanxious across many different situations

Table 7-2. The University of Texas counseling center receives about 70 telephone calls per day from students with problems. The varied nature of student anxieties is revealed in this list of the fifteen most frequent concerns.

Student Problem	Number of Monthly Calls to Counseling Center
Timing difficulties in male sexuality	71
Love vs. infatuation	61
Dating skills	55
How to have fun despite lack of cash	51
Relaxation exercises	47
Male homosexuality	42
Female homosexuality	40
Human sexuality	39
How to say "No"	38
Physical intimacy	37
How to cope with anxiety in general	37
Self-esteem and self-confidence	33
Broken relationships	33
How to meet people	32
Dealing with loneliness	32

(Data from Thurman, Baron, & Klein, 1979)

while others are inconsistent from one situation to another (Magnusson & Ekehammar, 1975).

Fear of Electric Shock. In a typical manipulation of stress a relatively unpleasant situation is created and subjects are expected to respond with increased anxiety. As just discussed, there are individual differences in how threatening a given stressor might be, so it should be helpful to determine such differences. Hodges and Spielberger (1966) gave high- and low-anxious subjects a verbal conditioning task in which they were told that they would be given several shocks. It was found that heart rate increased under these conditions, but there was no difference between the responses of people who scored at different extremes on the MAS.

The subjects had been given a fear-of-shock question two months before the experiment. This was a single item on which people indicated how much concern they would feel about taking part in a psychology experiment in which they received an electric shock. When subjects were divided into high and low groups on the basis of their responses concerning this specific kind of threat, there was a marked difference in the heart rates of the two groups, as shown in Figure 7-11. Thus, the *general* measure of anxiety was not a predictor of physiological responses in this stressful situation, whereas the measure of anxiety that dealt with this *specific* type of situation was a very good predictor. Similarly, measures to get at specific fears such as reactions to snakes is a better predictor of how a subject will feel when asked to pick up a snake than a general measure of anxiety (Mellstrom, Cicala, & Zuckerman, 1976).

Stage Fright. A familiar source of anxiety is having to speak before a group of people. Some people respond to such situations with **stage fright.** For them, having to stand up in front of a class, appear in a play, speak into a microphone, or perform in front of a camera can be an awesome experience. Even many well-known entertainers report "butterflies" in their stomachs, sweaty palms, and nausea just before facing an audience. Mulac and Sherman (1974) have devised a behavioral measure of such reactions. There seem to be four major factors that can be observed in the behavior of a person who is frightened before an audience; these are described in Table 7-3. You might notice some of these factors in your classmates, guests on television talk shows, political figures, your instructors, or even yourself. A paper-and-pencil measure of stage fright has been developed, and people who are high in this specific trait show the greatest increases in state anxiety when asked to give a speech (Lamb, 1973).

When people are taught to relax in such situations and have a chance to practice the behavior with helpful feedback, stage fright and the behaviors that go with it can be greatly reduced (Sherman, Mulac, & McCann, 1974).

Test Anxiety. The most widely used measures of a specific type of

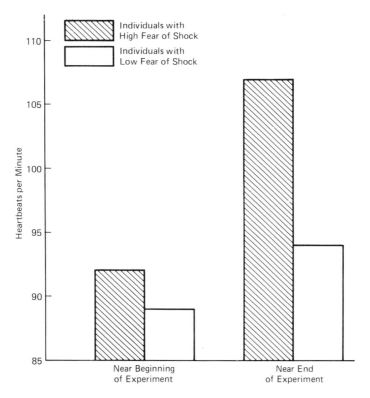

Figure 7-11. A physiological indicator of anxiety such as heart rate can be predicted on the basis of a specific measure of anxiety. When subjects are told that they will receive an electric shock, those who score high on a fear-of-shock scale show a much faster heart rate than those who score low on that scale.

(Data from Hodges and Spielberger, **1966**)

anxiety focus on **test anxiety** (Sarason, in press, a). A typical scale has items such as "While taking an important examination I perspire a great deal" and "I freeze up on things like intelligence tests and final exams." Because this type of anxiety clearly interferes with effective performance on many kinds of tests, much research has been directed at the problem of trying to devise ways to alter test-related emotions. For example, **cognitive therapy** has been shown to reduce anxiety, improve performance on a simple task, and improve grade point average (Holroyd, 1976). In this type of therapy, efforts are made to alter the kind of thoughts a person has during tests because it is believed that these cognitive responses distract attention from the task and, hence, lower the person's performance (Goldfried, Linehan, & Smith, 1978). This preoccupation with performance not only results in cognitive interference, but test anxiety also makes time seem to pass more slowly during an exam (Sarason & Stoops, 1978). When people who are

Table 7-3.   The four aspects of stage fright. Research indicates that those who are most anxious when appearing before an audience tend to reveal that state in these four types of behavior.

Stage fright is characterized by the following:

1. *Rigidity*

   The arms and hands are rigid and tense; the person is motionless and doesn't use appropriate gestures; there are grimaces or twitches in tense facial muscles.

2. *Inhibition*

   The voice is monotonous and without emphasis; there is a deadpan facial expression; the person speaks too softly.

3. *Disfluency*

   The person blocks in his or her speech and has to hunt for words; the voice is quivering or tense; speech is stammering or halting; breathing is heavy.

4. *Agitation*

   The person fidgets, sways, paces, shuffles his or her feet, avoids eye contact with the audience.

(Data from Mulac & Sherman, 1974)

high in test anxiety are exposed to someone with the same problem who tells them how to cope with it (e.g., stop thinking about yourself, think about interesting aspects of the task, don't think about how others are doing), performance is improved (Sarason, in press, b).

It is possible that test anxiety is fairly widespread because of the way most courses are taught. That is, students attend lectures, read assignments, and take tests—all according to the instructor's schedule. However, a different approach, **personalized system of instruction** or **PSI** (Keller, 1968; Kulik, Kulik, & Carmichael, 1974), is gaining acceptance in college classrooms. With this technique, students set their own pace, hear only a few lectures, take tests when they feel ready, and retake them if necessary until the material is mastered. Dziadosz, Curran, and Santogrossi (in press) proposed that students in a PSI course would have lower levels of test anxiety than students in a traditional lecture course. In a child psychology course they tried both methods of teaching. As predicted, test anxiety was consistently lower among students exposed to the PSI method.

What Are the Origins of Anxiety?

It seems reasonable to assume that individual differences in trait anxiety would be a function of how much stress a person undergoes during childhood. Research indicates, however, that it is the *type* of stress that is critical. For example, it is difficult to imagine a more frightening and dangerous environmental event than war. Yet observations of children subjected to air raids in World War II suggest that such situations do not result in increased anxiety (Solomon, 1942). More recently, Ziv and Israeli (1973) examined the anxiety of Israeli children living in *kibbutzim* that were shelled frequently; their test scores did not differ from those of children living in *kibbutzim* that had never been under fire. A child's relation with his or her mother appears to be a much more important determinant of anxiety than external danger.

Early Separation from Mother and Anxiety during Pregnancy.   Clinical studies have provided convincing evidence that children who are separated from their mothers show a number of adverse symptoms, including anxiety. Many sorts of maladjustment in children seem to result from the mother's death, illness, or absence. Further, children who undergo such experiences become sensitized so that similar separations that occur later are frequently traumatic to them (Yarrow, 1964).

Experimental studies of such effects are obviously not possible with human subjects, but research with monkeys has confirmed the importance of an infant's contact with its mother. For example, when infant monkeys are taken away from their mothers even for a short time, they make cooing noises and act afraid and depressed (Kaufman & Rosenblum, 1967). As much as a year later, subjects who are given such experiences in infancy still show fear reactions (Mitchell, Harlow, Griffin, & Moller, 1967).

There is also evidence from animal research that when mothers undergo stress during pregnancy there are lasting effects on the offspring who react to stress with anxiety. The mother's fear seems to affect the hormone balance of her unborn offspring (Herrenkohl, 1979). In mice, even a mild stress such as being picked up and handled gently during pregnancy results in offspring who show increased susceptibility to seizures when exposed to unexpected sounds (Beck & Gavin, 1976).

It should be possible to show that human beings who undergo early separation from their mothers or whose mothers underwent stress during pregnancy have unusually high manifest anxiety scores, but such a study has not yet been reported.

The Power of Anxious Thoughts.   Much of the research on anxiety seems to indicate that a person's thoughts are a powerful source of anxiety. Right now, if you were to spend a few moments thinking about things in your life that worry you, your past failures and embarrassments, or uncertainties in your future, you might well experience an increase in your anxiety level. Hypnosis is a dramatic way of demonstrating such effects.

Hypnotic induction of anxiety was attempted by Grosz and Levitt (1959). A group of medical and nursing students took the MAS three times: in an ordinary waking state, in a hypnotic trance without special instructions, and in a hypnotic trance with anxiety instructions. The anxiety instructions were as follows:

I suggest to you that you will begin to feel in a certain way, that you will have certain definite feelings which I am going to suggest to you. You will begin to feel these feelings and emotions so vividly that your whole person, your whole body, every fiber of yourself, will feel that way—at first slightly, then gradually stronger and stronger. These feelings will last until I suggest to you that they are no longer there. The feelings and emotions which you will begin to experience are those of anxiety—feelings of anxiety, more and more intensely, more and more vividly. You will become more and more anxious. At first, there will just be a feeling of apprehension. Then, gradually you are beginning to feel more and more afraid but you do not know what it is that makes you feel so afraid and so anxious. You just feel that way without knowing why. You feel more and more afraid and anxious all the time, as if something dreadful is going to happen to you. Yet, you do not know what this dreadful thing is. I suggest that you will gradually begin to experience a state in which you feel really panicky, where you are so fearful that you feel an almost unbearable dread, fear, and panic. In fact, you are most likely already feeling this way and you will continue to feel this way more and more strongly. [Grosz & Levitt, 1959, p. 282]

In the waking state and the no-instruction trance state, the mean MAS score was a little over 12; in the anxiety trance state, the mean score was 25. Clearly, the "right" instructions can bring about a dramatic increase in anxiety. In everyday life we can also give ourselves "anxiety instructions" and cause ourselves to become anxious.

RESEARCH
CLOSE-UP

Dating Anxiety: Reducing Interpersonal Fears

Interpersonal situations evoke anxiety in most of us. Perhaps the most stressful of these situations occur when we are trying to impress others and make them like us, for example, when we are trying to make a sale, participating in a job interview, or interacting with a potential friend. A familiar example is the dating situation, and a person who is not successful in forming a close relationship with someone of the opposite sex often experiences unhappiness and loss of self-esteem.

Worries about failure as a date are fairly common, and 10 percent of the college students in one study reported anxiety that was severe enough to make them avoid interactions with the opposite sex (Calhoun, 1977). When students who took part in a computer dating study were asked about such feelings, 30 percent reported that the degree of anxiety they felt on dates was high enough so that they would like to have some help in overcoming the problem (Curran, 1977a). This type of anxiety has two somewhat different causes. There is realistic anxiety among those who lack the necessary interpersonal skills (Wessberg, Mariotto, Conger, Farrell, & Conger, 1979), and there is conditioned anxiety among those who have experienced or even simply anticipated failure in dating situations. In many people, both kinds of anxiety may be operating.

What can be done about these problems? Curran (1977b) carried out an experiment in which people with dating anxiety were either given training in interpersonal skills or helped to become desensitized to this type of anxiety. Compared to control groups, both experimental groups showed reduced anxiety.

Subjects were recruited by means of ads in a college newspaper and dormitory handouts describing an experiment designed to reduce anxiety in the dating situation. The students who reponded to the ads reported physiological symptoms and impaired social skills while on dates. For some, this was so strong that they tended to avoid dating.

The subjects were randomly divided into experimental and control groups. The "skills" subjects received instructions about dating behavior, and they had a chance to practice dating skills and receive feedback on how well they did. The "desensitization" subjects were given **relaxation training** for several sessions. Then they received a **counterconditioning** treatment in which anxiety-evoking dating cues were presented while they were totally relaxed; this technique is used to help people respond in a calm way to cues that formerly caused them to feel anxious. As control groups, some subjects were either put on a waiting list (receiving no treatment) or given a series of placebo treatments unrelated to dating anxiety.

Observers watched videotapes of each subject role-playing a dating interaction before and after the experiment, and each subject was rated as to interpersonal skills and anxiety. Both the "skills" group and the "desensitization" group showed improvement after the experiment, while the two control groups remained unchanged. The experimental subjects also reported that they found the treatment program useful, that they were less anxious about dating than before, and that they would recommend the program to others.

Generally, we tend not to think of dating behavior as involving a series of skills that should be taught, or to think of anxiety about dating as a problem that can be treated. Still, this experiment suggests that a great deal of interpersonal unhappiness could be relieved by fairly simple procedures.

REDUCING AND CONTROLLING ANXIETY

Lowering the Anxiety Level with Psychotherapy

Effective psychotherapy should bring about a reduction in anxiety. Gallagher (1953) proposed that **client-centered therapy** lowers MAS scores. After therapy mean scores were significantly lower than before therapy began: 13.76 versus 17.28.

It also seems that the specific type of therapy is a crucial factor. Using group psychotherapy Kilmann and Auerbach (1974) again found that the client-centered approach led to a decrease in anxiety. With directive therapy—a procedure that is highly structured and involves a set of psychological "exercises"—the opposite effect occurred: Anxiety actually increased following therapy. It seems that a directive style of therapy can be threatening to those who are prone to react with anxiety.

Behavior Modification Techniques

In contrast to traditional forms of psychotherapy, **behavior modification** techniques apply learning theory to the treatment of specific symptoms such as a particular type of anxiety. Perhaps the simplest and most direct approach is to treat the anxious person as one who is in need of specific information to replace vague and often unfounded fears. For example, patients about to undergo dental surgery were found to be less anxious if they listened to a detailed tape recording that explained the procedures to be used in the operation (Auerbach, Kendall, Cuttler, & Levitt, 1976).

Most behavior modification approaches, however, are designed to deal directly with emotional responses rather than provide information about the situation. It has been found, for example, that test anxiety can be reduced by having subjects watch a videotape of someone dealing success-fully with the same problem (**modeling**). This is followed by a **role playing** session in which the subjects try out the techniques they have observed (Malec, Park, & Watkins, 1976). Such rehearsal is quite effective in reduc-ing anxiety (McCordick, Koplan, Finn, & Smith, 1979).

In the dating anxiety experiment described earlier, systematic de-sensitization was used. In this procedure subjects are taught to relax and then are exposed to cues related to their fears, beginning with mild ones and working up to the most frightening ones. This technique has also been used successfully to reduce fear of public speaking (Slutsky & Allen, 1978) and test anxiety (Zemore, 1975). Interestingly enough, treatment that was designed to help one of these problems was found to reduce the other type of anxiety as well. It is possible that when one becomes desensitized in a particular problem area this effect tends to generalize to other situations in which anxiety is aroused.

Using Filmed Models to Reduce Anxiety About Surgery

The prospect of an operation is unpleasant for anyone, but for children it is especially likely to produce anxiety. Besides the surgery itself, there are all the unknown and unfamiliar aspects of hospital procedures and the activi-ties of doctors and nurses. Most children who are hospitalized for surgery become upset to some extent, and for a few the emotional reaction can be extreme (Cassell, 1965).

We have already noted that, with respect to various types of fears and anxieties, modeling is an efficient and effective method of treatment. In one study fear of dogs was eliminated by having children watch a series of movie scenes in which other children gradually played more and more actively with a dog (Bandura & Menlove, 1968). Likewise, fear of snakes can be overcome by exposure to films in which others touch, pick up, and handle snakes (Bandura, Blanchard, & Ritter, 1969).

Melamed and Siegel (1975) applied these modeling techniques to hospitalized children who were about to undergo surgery. Experimental subjects were shown a 16-minute movie, *Ethan Has an Operation,* in which a 7-year-old boy is admitted to a hospital, has a blood test, undergoes an operation, and so forth. Control subjects saw *Living Things Are Everywhere,* a film about a boy who takes a nature trip in the country. Several state measures of anxiety revealed that the experimental film was very effective as an anxiety reducer. Compared to the control group, those who saw the hospital film were less anxious the night before the operation and several weeks later as well. The parents of those in the control group reported an increase in behavior problems after their children had left the hospital, but this was not true for those who saw the filmed model.

It seems clear that the children's ward in every hospital would do well to show such films to young patients—and perhaps to older ones too. Research on hospitalized adults indicates that simple information provides some help but that they also need to learn to cope with the anxieties evoked by a forthcoming operation (Kendall, Williams, Pechacek, Graham, Shisslak, & Herzoff, 1979; Langer, Janis, & Wolfer, 1975). For example, it is helpful if they are taught to think about the stress in positive as well as negative terms (being in the hospital is a chance to rest, relax, and lose weight), to calm themselves down, and to shift their attention from unpleasant fears to something interesting. Not only do such techniques lower anxiety before and after an operation; they even reduce the number of pain relievers and sedatives requested during the recovery period. In more general terms, it is literally possible to "talk yourself out of pain" (Girodo & Wood, 1979). Talking to oneself in the appropriate way can not only reduce fears but can actually provide a way to manage anxiety when emergencies arise (Girodo & Roehl, 1978).

Being able to view a model is as helpful for adults as for children. When patients are shown a videotape of an unpleasant medical procedure they must undergo, anxiety about it is reduced. Such a tape provides both information about what to expect *and* a model whose behavior can be imitated. Shipley, Butt, Horwitz, and Farbry (1978) examined responses to an endoscopy examination. This involves the insertion of a flexible tube through the mouth and into the gastrointestinal tract. Air is then pumped into the gut, and the physician is able to view the tract lining. The patient must remain awake during the 15 to 30 minute examination, and it tends to be an anxiety-evoking experience. When such patients were shown a videotape of another patient having an endoscopy examination, their anxiety level was greatly reduced. Three viewings provided the greatest positive effect, presumably because the repeated exposures made it possible for their fears to extinguish. For some patients (those who tend to repress their fears), a single viewing of the videotape actually made their anxiety increase. The scenes reminded them of something they were trying to forget. With two more showings, however, they too were able to relax and cope with the situation.

Alcohol: Anxiety Reduction in a Bottle

A common way to reduce anxiety in our culture is by means of alcohol. At parties, on dates, after work, in restaurants, on picnics, at wakes, aboard airplanes, in bed, at wedding receptions—in short, almost everywhere and on almost all occasions, alcohol has become for many people the chosen means to reduce tension and, presumably, enhance pleasure. There is obviously a dark side to alcohol; consider the embarrassing and dangerous things that are said and done by those who overdrink—their crying jags, drunken arguments and fights, automobile accidents, and in many cases, lives destroyed by alcoholism.

Research provides evidence to support both the positive and the negative effects of alcohol consumption. Williams (1966) noted that in spite of the large number of physiological and clinical studies of drinking behavior, little attention had been paid to the emotional effects of alcohol. He was interested in the relation between alcohol and emotional reactions in a social situation. His study took place at a series of stag cocktail parties held in fraternity houses at two colleges. The parties lasted an hour or so. The subjects were told that they could do whatever they liked, and gin, scotch, bourbon, and mixers were available at the bar. Drinks could be obtained free of charge by handing in a name card to the bartender—this provided a record of how much each person consumed. Measures of anxiety and depression were taken on the evening before the party, at the party after two drinks (4 ounces) and at the end of the party after various amounts of consumption (4 to 28 ounces).

The first comparison was between the pre-experimental measures and the measures taken after two drinks. There was a decrease in both anxiety and depression at this point. Such findings verify the common observation that after a couple of drinks the people at a party become more relaxed and happier. With strong positive reinforcement of this sort, it is not surprising that the behavior would be repeated, so many people continue drinking. Subjects in Williams' experiment varied a great deal in how many drinks they ordered, so the second comparison (between the 4-ounce condition and the end-of-party condition) was made separately for those who had consumed different amounts of alcohol. Among those who had only one more drink, there was a further reduction of anxiety and depression. Among those who had two additional drinks or more, Williams found the opposite effect: Anxiety and depression *increased*. Those who had more than five drinks were found to express the most negative feelings.

Despite the fact that alcohol reduces anxiety, it is found that the presence of anxiety does not affect the amount of alcohol a person drinks (Higgins & Marlatt, 1973). When subjects were told that an experiment involved the effect of drinking on response to an electric shock, they drank no more alcohol than those who thought that no pain was involved. Also, scores on an anxiety test were found to be unrelated to the amount of alcohol consumed. Such findings have led Marlatt (1975) to conclude that the basic idea that alcohol is used as an anxiety reducer is incorrect. He believes that drinking is arousing rather than relaxing and that it leads the person to feel that he or she has increased control over what is going on.

In any event, alcohol can be seen as having paradoxical effects on anxiety. It is a powerful and very pleasant means of feeling relaxed and happy, but used to excess it can become a cause of unpleasant emotions. A socially acceptable drug that had the former effect without the latter danger would clearly be preferable to alcohol. Many people believe that marijauna is the solution, but research on its long-term and even short-term effects is still a subject of controversy. Interestingly enough, anxiety can be reduced simply by eating food. Pines and Gal (1977) found that test anxiety was lowered when subjects were given peanut butter sandwiches to eat.

Figure 7-12. People use alcohol and other drugs to relieve social anxiety. One or two drinks are found to reduce anxiety and make people feel relaxed and happy. Additional drinking, however, leads to an *increase* in anxiety and depression. (Irene Springer)

One aspect of response to stress is the person's ability to control his or her autonomic reactions. When we face a psychological stress such as a course final, our bodies may respond as if we faced a physical danger. Since we are not going to run away at top speed or engage in hand-to-hand combat with the instructor, we would clearly be better off if we could bring our physiological responses under control. Even with physical danger, if there is a complex task to perform, those with the most experience learn to control their autonomic responses so that they can function without disruption at the time when the action must occur (Fenz & Epstein, 1967). Auto racing involves such requirements. In the June 1972 issue of *Playboy,* Grand Prix racing champion Jackie Stewart was asked by an interviewer, "Aren't you at least *nervous* before a race?" He replied,

Of course I am, and the intensity of the nervousness is like that of a person about to go in for major surgery. But by the time the race actually starts, I see things through absolutely cold, crystal-clear eyes, without fear or apprehension of any kind. It's a strange feeling of being totally removed from the scene and looking at it from the outside, as though I'm no longer a part of my body. But this is an acquired talent it's taken a long time to perfect, and it helps me immensely.

To determine the relation between manifest anxiety and autonomic control, Fenz and Dronsejko (1969) selected extreme scorers on the MAS and measured their physiological responses during conditions of real and imagined shock. It was found that the responses of the medium-anxious group were more adaptive than those of either the high- or the low-anxious group. When shock was expected, medium-anxious individuals reacted with increasing physiological activity until just before the time specified for the shock; then their activity decreased. Thus, they controlled their autonomic responses in time to handle the real danger. Low-anxious subjects were also able to some extent to control their physiological responses at the proper time. Subjects who were high in anxiety were the least adaptive in that they showed strong physiological responses at the moment of danger; they also responded in exactly the same way to real and imaginary stress. Thus, people with high levels of trait anxiety respond physiologically to their thoughts as strongly as to external danger, and they have not learned to control these responses when they must actually deal with the threat.

Is it possible for anyone to learn how to respond as effectively as race car drivers and medium-anxiety individuals? It has been found that people can learn to increase or decrease their heart rate when they are rewarded for a certain reaction, provided that they receive feedback as to how well they are doing (Sirota, Schwartz, & Shapiro, 1974). Once subjects have been taught this skill, they report that an unpleasant stimulus such as an electric shock seems less painful (Sirota, Schwartz, & Shapiro, 1976). Long-standing fears can be reduced or eliminated in this way (Gatchel, 1977). Thus, it appears that it is possible through proper training to learn how to control both anxiety and pain by learning to control the appropriate physiological responses.

Such research, plus research on control of the cognitive and emotional factors that elicit anxiety, suggests that we can all learn to avoid or reduce severe anxiety in response to stressful events in our lives.

SUMMARY

Anxiety and *fear* are similar states characterized by unpleasant arousal or tension, dread of some object or event, and the desire to avoid the source of these feelings. Both are accompanied by physiological reactions; fear is directed at a specific source, while the source of anxiety is vague and abstract.

Some of the research interest in anxiety grew out of the learning theory of Clark Hull and Kenneth Spence. One of their theoretical constructs involved individual differences in emotional responsiveness. The personality test designed to measure this variable is the Manifest Anxiety Scale or MAS.

According to Hull-Spence theory, in a situation in which one strong habit is evoked, the higher the drive the greater the response strength. Thus, the performance of high-MAS subjects should be superior to that of low-MAS subjects in such situations. With a task in which several competing incorrect responses are evoked as strongly as the correct one, high drive interacts with each habit to increase its response strength. Thus, the performance of low-MAS subjects should be superior to that of high-MAS subjects in these situations. These predictions have been confirmed in research using classical conditioning, serial learning, and paired-associates learning. High anxiety has been found to be associated with thoughts that may interfere with performance. Educational level and manifest anxiety tend to be negatively related. When academic ability and anxiety are considered together, grades are found to be negatively influenced by anxiety only at the middle levels of scholastic aptitude. Humor is found to reduce anxiety and improve the test performance of people who are high in MAS. Psychiatric patients obtain higher scores on the MAS than normal control subjects. High-anxious individuals desire to affiliate with other people under ordinary conditions but not under conditions of stress.

Trait anxiety refers to stable individual differences in anxiety level, whereas *state anxiety* refers to a temporary condition that fluctuates in response to situational changes. Various types of stress are found to raise the level of state anxiety, and the removal of the stress lowers it again. In contrast, trait anxiety remains relatively unchanged across such situations.

Measures of specific types of anxiety have been found to increase predictive accuracy in research on fear of electric shock, stage fright, and test anxiety. The level of anxiety seems to be highest among people who have undergone early separation from their mothers. A person's current anxiety level is very much affected by his or her thought processes.

Anxiety can be reduced by psychotherapy (especially client-centered therapy) and behavior modification techniques such as modeling, role playing, and desensitization. A small amount of alcohol appears to reduce anxiety and elicit pleasant emotions, but increasing amounts have the opposite effect. Recent research indicates that anxiety can be controlled when people are taught to regulate their autonomic responses.

SUGGESTED READINGS

BOLLES, R. C. *Theory of motivation.* New York: Harper & Row, 1975. A fairly advanced book that covers in detail the research and theory on motivation, including the effect of anxiety on performance.

DAVIDSON, P. O. (ed.). *The behavioral management of anxiety, depression, and pain.* New York: Brunner/Mazel, 1976. A set of papers that stress the use of behavior modification techniques to alter maladaptive responses such as anxiety.

SARASON, I. G., & SPIELBERGER, C. D. *Stress and anxiety.* Washington, D.C.: Hemisphere, in press. A series of volumes describing the latest theoretical and empirical advances in anxiety research.

SPIELBERGER, C. D., & DIAZ-GUERRERO, R. *Cross-cultural anxiety.* New York: Halsted, 1976. A review of anxiety research in several parts of the world.

ZUCKERMAN, M., & SPIELBERGER, C. D. (eds.). *Emotions and anxiety: New concepts, methods, and applications.* Hillsdale, N.J.: Lawrence Erlbaum, 1976. A collection of chapters by a series of investigators dealing with many important aspects of negative emotional states and their origins.

Chapter Eight

NEED FOR ACHIEVEMENT: STRIVING FOR SUCCESS

In this chapter you will read about the following topics:

As the space shuttle touched down on the dry, dusty surface of Mars, the three troubleshooters from Amalgamated Earth Unigov began adjusting their ties and smoothing the wrinkles from their acetate suits. The delta-winged airship rolled across the grayish desert sand toward the gleaming domes of the largest colonial city in the solar system.

The project coordinator, Frank Cowan, summarized the basic problem for his two assistants one last time. "Remember that the Chairman himself will be keeping tabs on our every move here. Our investment on Mars has run into billions, but the return has averaged less than two percent a year. Our job is to find out why, to recommend productive changes, and to transform this fiasco into something the company can point to with pride. Remember that the future of the entire Behavioral Engineering Division may depend on what we do here. Any final questions?"

Matthews looked up. "What are our chances?"

Cowan smiled and patted his briefcase. "Based on the company's past experiences with the moon colony as well as the pilot project in the Amazon basin, the best we can hope for is a 50–50 shot at it."

"What can we expect from the chief if we manage to pull it off?" asked Laughton, the other assistant.

Cowan looked at each man intensely. "If we turn the Mars colony into a profitable venture, the sky's the limit—no pun intended. All three of us will move several rungs toward the top of the corporate ladder. And don't forget, that's the way it's going to be, so we won't even speak about the chance of failure." The craft moved smoothly into the air lock that was the entrance to the colony. "Let's go get 'em!"

Ten months later the transportation process was reversed and the space shuttle moved out of the city toward the takeoff strip. Inside the plane there was laughter and excitement. "We did it!" Cowan's booming voice filled the passenger section, and he gave each assistant a resounding slap on the back. "This calls for champagne. As soon as we get up to the spaceship, I'll break out the two bottles I brought along for just this occasion."

"The only thing that puzzles me," said Matthews, "is how the counterproductive pattern of behavior ever got started. The schools were a hotbed of lazy contentment—no grades, no competition, no sports, no awards or prizes. I asked one teacher to organize a race to identify the fastest runner. Do you know what she said? 'What does it matter if one child is better coordinated than another?' We'll be changing that kind of talk soon enough."

"You should have seen the factories," said Laughton. "One worker tried to give me the old song and dance about pride in craftsmanship as he turned out one transistor telecommunicator every couple of days. I'd like to see his face when he finds out that from now on the pay system will be based on piecework. He'll be surprised at the way his craftsmanship suddenly speeds up."

Cowan leaned back in his bucket seat. "You fellows did a fine job with the schoolchildren and the workers. I am recommending, however, that the corporation really hit hard on the family structure. We have to instill ambition and the old get-up-and-go right in the home. All that touchy-feely emphasis on love and affection has to be jazzed up with a strong dose of hard-hitting competitive spirit. Right in the *nursery those kids have to learn that this universe isn't made for losers. Don't worry, when our detailed reports reach headquarters the behavior programmers will take care of these details in short order."*

As the two assistants settled down to a three-dimensional chess game to pass the time, Cowan looked at the ancient motto inscribed on the wall at the front of the cabin: "Winning Isn't Everything; It's the Only Thing." He gazed out the window, distractedly biting his lower lip. He thought, "I wonder what the next assignment will be?"

ACHIEVEMENT NEED IS A LEARNED MOTIVE to strive for success and excellence. Because almost any activity from gardening to managing a corporation can be perceived as a challenge, the need to achieve may underlie many different kinds of behavior. And because it is a *learned* motive, individual differences in past experiences result in vast differences in achievement motivation.

MEASURING THE NEED FOR ACHIEVEMENT: FANTASIES AND MOTIVES

McClelland and the Wesleyan Project

In 1947, building on Murray's work, David C. McClelland (1917–) began a research project at Wesleyan University that resulted in an extremely fruitful approach to the study of the need to achieve. He had received the B.A. degree from Wesleyan in 1938, the year in which *Explorations in Personality* was published. He went to Missouri for an M.A. degree and then entered graduate school at Yale, where he received the Ph.D. degree. He later spent a very productive fourteen years at Wesleyan, where his initial work on *n* Ach was carried out. In 1956 he joined the faculty at Harvard.

The first systematic research on the achievement motive was summarized in book form in 1953 by McClelland, John W. Atkinson, Russell A. Clark, and Edgar L. Lowell. Interestingly enough, though they utilized Murray's concept of *n* Ach and used Murray's TAT as a measurement technique, their approach to the study of personality was in dramatic contrast to Murray's:

We have discovered that concentration on a limited research problem is not necessarily narrowing; it may lead ultimately into the whole of psychology. In personality theory there is inevitably a certain impatience—a desire to solve every problem at once so as to get the "whole" personality in focus. We have proceeded the other way. By concentrating on one problem, on *one motive*, we have found in the course of our study that we have learned not only a lot about the achievement motive but other areas of personality as well. So we feel that this book can be used as one basis for evaluating the degree to which a "piece-meal" approach to personality is profitable, an approach which proceeds to build up the total picture out of many small experiments by a slow process of going from fact to hypothesis and back to fact again. [McClelland et al., 1953, p. vi]

The TAT was chosen as a measuring device because fantasy appeared to be a good place to look for the effects of motivation. As a first step, Atkinson and McClelland (1948) took a motive about which a good deal is known—hunger—and tested the effects of food deprivation on thematic apperception stories. Sailors at a submarine training school were divided into groups that had been without food for one hour, four hours, or sixteen hours. Seven thematic apperception pictures were projected on a screen, and the subjects wrote stories in response to each. Significant relationships were found between their level of hunger and the content of the stories; for example, there was an increase in the number of stories about hunger and an increase in the number of plots about obtaining food. Given this success in measuring "n Food" with fantasy material, the experimenters moved on to the construction of an n Ach scoring system.

Scoring Stories for n Ach

As reported in 1949 by McClelland, Clark, Roby, and Atkinson, the test construction procedure involved having groups under achievement-arousing conditions and other groups under nonarousing conditions each write thematic apperception stories. These stories were scored for a number of achievement-related categories, and statistical procedures were used to determine which categories were reliable indicators of aroused n Ach. For reasons that will be discussed later in this chapter, only male students were used.

The four pictures consisted of the following themes:

1. Two men in a shop working at a machine, often seen as inventors.
2. Boy in checked shirt at a desk, with an open book in front of him.
3. An older man and a younger man, often seen as father and son.
4. Boy, with vague operation scene in background.

The subjects were told that the test was intended to determine their ability to imagine things creatively. One of the pictures of the type used by McClelland and the questions asked of each subject are shown in Figure 8-1.

Several procedures were used to arouse the achievement motive, and both the aroused and nonaroused groups were given the TAT cards immediately afterwards. The story content was scored by judges, and then the frequency of each content category in the experimental conditions was compared with its frequency in the control conditions. Each scoring category that yielded significant differences was then defined as a fantasy response that indicated the presence of n Ach. You will recognize this type of test construction procedure as an experimental use of an external criterion, as described in Chapter 4.

Of the twelve categories that were found to vary across experimental conditions, two examples follow:

Figure 8-1. In the TAT-type measure used to determine *n* Ach, subjects are shown pictures like this one and instructed to answer the following questions in creating a story to go with it:
1. What is happening? Who are the persons?
2. What has led up to this situation? That is, what has happened in the past?
3. What is being thought? What is wanted? By whom?
4. What will happen? What will be done?
(From McClelland, Atkinson, Clark, & Lowell, (1953)

1. Achievement imagery is scored for stories in which an achievement goal is included.

Example: A group of medical students are watching their instructor perform a simple operation on a cadaver. A few of the students are very sure they will be called on to assist Dr. Hugo. In the last few months they have worked and studied. The skillful hands of the surgeon perform their work. The instructor tells his class *they must be able to work with speed and cannot make many mistakes.* When the operation is over, a smile comes over the group. Soon they will be leading men and women in the field.

2. Instrumental activity is scored if the activity of at least one of the characters in the story indicates that something is being done to attain an achievement goal, whether successfully or unsuccessfully.

Example: James Watt and his assistant are working on the assembly of the first steam engine. They are working out the hole for a slide valve of the first successful steam engine . . . All previous experiments have failed. Successful use of steam has not been accomplished. If the slide valve works, the first compound steam engine will be harnessed. *James Watt is pulling the pinion in place for the slide valve.* His assistant is watching. The purpose is to make a pinion to hold the yoke in place which will operate the slide valve. If the slide valve works satisfactorily, they will perfect it for use in factories and for use on the railway. *It will work.*

To construct the test, the achievement motive was manipulated in order to identify those aspects of fantasy material which are affected by motive arousal. In later research on individual differences in this motive, the thematic apperception pictures usually have been given and the subjects' stories written under nonarousing conditions. The assumption is that differences in achievement fantasy in a neutral situation reflect differences in the characteristic level of this motive for each individual. Those who obtain very high n Ach scores in a nonarousing condition are assumed to function ordinarily at the level attained by the experimental subjects when the drive has been purposely aroused. Individual differences in a neutral situation constitute the personality variable called need for achievement. This trait measure of n Ach is *not*, by the way, predictive of state n Ach in an arousal situation (Patrick & Zuckerman, 1977).

With training and practice, judges can learn to use this scoring system with a high degree of agreement. Though internal consistency is not as high as one would ordinarily expect in a test (Entwisle, 1972), it has been shown that measures of this type can have construct validity even without that type of reliability (Atkinson, Bongort, & Price, 1977). Other research shows that a person's level of achievement motivation is moderately stable over time (Murstein, 1963). It should be noted that those who receive medium scores (neither very high nor very low in n Ach) are the most inconsistent in their achievement behavior (Sorrentino & Short, 1977).

Objective Tests of Achievement Need

Given the difficulty of administering sets of TAT pictures, the subjectivity of the scoring system, and the amount of scoring time required per subject, it would be an obvious advantage to be able to use a simple, objective measure of n Ach. Several early attempts to construct such tests were found not to correlate with one another or with the TAT measure of achievement need (Atkinson & Litwin, 1960; Weinstein, 1969). When a series of n Ach measures were found to be uncorrelated in a study at the University of Oregon, Weinstein (1969) concluded that "scales with 'achievement' labels do not appear to tap the same construct, and should not be used interchangeably" (p. 170).

After reviewing many of the studies that have tried to relate the TAT measure and alternate objective measures, McClelland (1958) stated that "*the conclusion seems inescapable that if the n Achievement score is measuring anything, that same thing is not likely to be measured by any simple set of choice-type items*" (p. 38). Further, he suggested that a fantasy measure of motivation is "purer" than a questionnaire measure. In a questionnaire, the subject is asked to describe himself or herself, and numerous factors influence such responses. In the fantasy measures, the emphasis is on what people spontaneously think about. For example, when LeVine (1966) asked members of high- and low-achieving African tribes to write about how to become a successful man, they did not differ. When he asked them to write down their dreams, those from achieving groups produced a much higher n Ach content.

More recent work, however, provides evidence that objective measures may be able to do as well as the TAT (Nygard & Gjesme, 1973; Pomerantz & Schultz, 1975; Weiner, 1970). Mehrabian (1968) built two objective tests to measure male and female achievement need. On a seven-point scale of agreement–disagreement, subjects respond to items like the following:

I more often attempt difficult tasks that I am not sure I can do rather than easier tasks I believe I can do.

I think more of the future than of the present and past.

Scores on these tests were found to be stable over time, to correlate fairly well with the TAT measure, and to predict performance on an achievement-related task. Holmes (1971) described n Ach to subjects and asked them to rank themselves on this dimension with respect to their fraternity brothers or sorority sisters. For both sexes, self-rankings were correlated with grade point averages, even when the rankings were made early in their first semester of college, prior to the actual report of college grades.

Some of these objective measures have shown that achievement motivation is composed of several dimensions. For example, Jackson, Ahmed, and Heapy (1973) built a test to measure this motive and discovered six factors that are related to somewhat different aspects of achievement, as may be seen in Table 8-1. They suggest that the way achievement

Table 8-1.   Achievement need has been found to consist of several independent factors, as is shown by the work of Jackson, Ahmed, and Heapy (1973).

Factor	Sample Test Item
Wanting to have high status with experts	I only accept a reliable authority's criticism of my work.
Desire for financial gain	I enjoy feeling that my job pays well enough to allow me to get ahead.
Wanting to achieve in an independent way	I would like a job where I could depend on my own efforts to get me ahead.
Wanting to have high status with peers	I enjoy displaying my ability on certain tasks to other people.
Competitiveness	On the whole, I like the idea that only the strongest survive.
Desire for excellence	I set my standards high and work hard to achieve them.

needs are expressed in behavior is a function of the relative strength of these six factors. That is, one person might achieve mainly in situations involving competition; another might strive for success only if money were the reward; and still another would be driven only if status were at stake.

THE DEVELOPMENT OF A HIGH NEED ACHIEVER

The development of individual differences in the achievement motive has been of great interest to those working with this variable. McClelland and colleagues (1953) hypothesized that motives are learned on the basis of the emotional experiences connected with specific kinds of behavior. A child is primarily dependent upon adults to judge the value of achievement outcomes by way of the rewards they provide for success (Ames, Ames, & Felker, 1977). With n Ach, the relevant behavior should be that which occurs in situations involving standards of excellence and striving to attain those standards. If a child is raised in such a way that rewards are provided for doing well and no reward is provided for failure, the child's motive to achieve should be fairly strong. On the other hand, if there is little pressure to compete for standards of excellence, and if parents are equally accepting of success and failure, a strong achievement motive is unlikely to develop.

It should be noted that the primary achievement goal is that of doing well and thus living up to one's standards of excellence. Competition itself is generally aversive, and most people find it rewarding to avoid having to compete (Steigleder, Weiss, Cramer, & Feinberg, 1978). Despite its unpleasant qualities, competition does serve to arouse a person's general drive level (see Chapter 7) and so to affect performance either positively or negatively, depending on the relative strengths of the correct and incorrect habits (Steigleder, Weiss, Balling, Wenninger, & Lombardo, 1979).

Loving or Dominant Fathers = Low n Ach Sons

One background factor is the way fathers interact with their sons. Somewhat surprisingly, it has been predicted that a warm, accepting father would produce low n Ach—because he would be too accepting and comforting with respect to the son's failures.

McClelland and colleagues (1953) obtained data dealing with family background. It was found that the higher a male's n Ach score, the more his parents tended to be described as rejecting, unprotective, unsolicitous, and tending toward neglect and rigidity. The highest single correlation was between n Ach and perceived rejection by the father. At the opposite extreme, the more the sons felt loved and accepted by their fathers, the lower their achievement need.

Bradburn (1963) suggested that boys with low n Ach had dominant fathers who tended to interfere with their sons' attempts to achieve. Since families in Turkey tend to emphasize male dominance, he hypothesized that Turkish men should be lower in achievement need than American men. He writes,

Almost universally, the Turks interviewed described their fathers as stern, forbidding, remote, domineering, and autocratic. Few of them had ever argued with their fathers, and those who had had done so at the price of an open break . . .

One man reported that even after he was married and had his own family, he did not dare smoke or even sit with his legs crossed in his father's presence or in any way contradict him. [Bradburn, 1963, pp. 464–65]

To test the effect of such a family structure, junior executives from Turkey were compared with junior executives in the United States. The groups were alike in age and educational background, but as predicted, the American group was found to score much higher in n Ach than the Turkish group. Bradburn also hypothesized that since father dominance is linked with low n Ach, Turkish males who were separated from their fathers at an early age would be higher in n Ach than those who remained under their fathers' influence. His subjects were students in a teacher-training college in Ankara. About half of them had lived apart from their parents since the age of 14 in village institutes. Life in these institutes is free of the repressive family influence that would be expected to stifle the development of need for achievement. The hypothesis was confirmed. For those who had been separated from their parents by the age of 14, 67 percent were high in n Ach and 33 percent were low. For those who had remained with their parents, 35 percent were high and 65 percent were low in n Ach.

Independence Training

Children must master a series of skills at some point in their development. They must learn to walk, talk, feed themselves, dress themselves, and urinate and defecate in specific places under specific conditions. There are differences among families, however, with respect to how early the child is expected to master a given behavior. It has been hypothesized that parental insistence on early mastery leads to higher achievement need and greater independence.

Winterbottom (1958) obtained n Ach scores on a group of elementary school boys. In addition, the mothers of the boys were interviewed in order to obtain their attitudes toward **independence training.** For example, each mother was asked to indicate the age by which she expected her son to learn such things as how to find his way around the neighborhood and how to undress and go to bed by himself. The mothers whose sons were high in n Ach expected such independence at a significantly younger age than the mothers of low n Ach sons. For example, the mothers of high *n* Ach sons expected 60 percent of the behaviors to be learned by age 7, whereas the mothers of those with low scores expected only 33 percent of the behaviors to be learned by that age. Winterbottom also asked the mothers how they responded when the child was trying new things for himself or entering competitions. Mothers who reported that they responded with physical affection (kissing or hugging) had sons with higher *n* Ach scores. Thus, not only do the mothers of sons with high need for achievement expect and demand independent behavior at an early age, they provide reinforcement in the form of affection when the achievement demands are met.

Other research (Teevan & McGhee, 1972) has extended these findings by distinguishing between positive and negative attitudes toward achievement. For example, a person who is highly concerned about achievement can be motivated largely on a positive basis in that he is hoping for success, or largely on a negative basis in that he is afraid of failure. Fear of failure is expressed in TAT stories in which a person's needs or goals are threatened. Such concerns in an individual's fantasies, labeled "hostile press", are related to an unwillingness to volunteer for an achievement-oriented task and to a defensive reaction when such tasks must be undertaken (Ceranski, Teevan, & Kalle, 1979). It is found that fear of failure develops when mothers respond in a neutral way to satisfactory behavior and with punishment when behavior is unsatisfactory. When there are rewards for satisfactory behavior and a neutral response to unsatisfactory behavior, a positive achievement motive is developed.

Achievement Training

Rosen and D'Andrade (1959) suggested that **achievement training** (doing things well) should be distinguished from independence training (doing things by oneself). They studied family groups composed of a father, a mother, and their son (age 9 to 11). Boys who were high and low in *n* Ach were matched for age, race, IQ, and social class. Two investigators visited the home. The parents and their son sat a table, and the researchers explained that the boy would be asked to perform certain tasks as part of a study of factors related to success in school and later success in a career.

The goal was to create a situation in which visitors could observe the behavior of parents while their son engaged in achievement-related behavior. The experimenters were interested in parental behavior with respect to the demands they placed on their son, the way the demands were enforced, and the amount of independence the child revealed in interacting with his parents. The five tasks involved building block towers with one hand while blindfolded, solving anagrams, making patterns out of blocks, tossing rings at a peg, and constructing a hat rack using two sticks and a clamp.

A number of comparisons were made between the parents of sons with high and low need for achievement. When asked how well their sons would do in stacking blocks, the parents of the high n Ach boys gave higher estimates than the parents of low n Ach boys. In the ring toss, parents were asked to decide how far away from the peg their son should stand; those with high n Ach sons selected a greater distance than those with low n Ach sons. In general, the parents of high need achievers seemed to be more competitive and more involved, and to feel more positive about the experimental tasks. They were more interested in their son's performance and more concerned about how well he did. They were also more likely to express approval of success and disapproval of failure.

The high and low n Ach boys also *performed* differently. Those with high n Ach built higher block towers, constructed patterns faster, and thought of more anagram words than those with low n Ach. Boys who were high in achievement motive asked for less aid, were more likely to reject offers of help from their parents, and showed less negative and more positive affect than those who were low in achievement motive.

It may seem that independence training and achievement training should be related to one another because each is found to influence the development of n Ach. Smith (1969) has provided evidence suggesting that these two aspects of child rearing are relatively independent and that when both are present high n Ach is most likely to develop. Parents of sons with high need for achievement say, "Do it well" *and* "Do it on your own."

Father's Occupation and Son's Need for Achievement

Middle-class families are most likely to engage in the kind of child-rearing practices that produce high need for achievement in their offspring. Turner (1970) proposed that the nature of the father's occupation was the crucial factor accounting for that fact. He examined occupational roles across different social classes. It was proposed that the more a father worked with people rather than with things and the more freedom and less supervision he had at work, the more he and his wife would stress achievement, independence, and self-reliance in dealing with their children.

Subjects were seventh- and eighth-grade males who were given a questionnaire about their father's occupation and the TAT measure of n Ach. The questionnaire information was used to classify the occupations as **entrepreneur** or **nonentrepreneur** in each of two social-class levels. White-collar entrepreneurs consisted of managers for bureaucracies and owners of businesses while blue-collar entrepreneurs were managers in industries or factories. Nonentrepreneurs were engaged in a routine white-collar or blue-collar job in which there was minimal authority or independence for the worker.

The relation between the father's occupation and the son's

achievement need is shown in Figure 8-2. Sons of entrepreneurial fathers are much higher in achievement need than sons of fathers with routine jobs. The reason other investigators have found a social-class effect is that there is a much higher proportion of entrepreneurial occupations among white-collar workers than among blue-collar workers.

Turner proposed two kinds of child-rearing influences that could stem from differences in occupation. First, when the occupation calls for responsibility, decision making, competition, and aggressiveness, an achievement ideology develops that is shared by both the husband and the wife and influences their child-rearing practices. Second, a father who is supervised and has little authority or decision-making power develops frustrations that can be expressed only at home. Thus, nonentrepreneurial fathers exercise authority and express aggression toward their sons because only in their family life is it possible for them to behave in this independent way and tell someone what to do. The results of these two occupational influences on fathers lead to quite different levels of achievement motivation in their sons.

The behavior of fathers has also been studied in relation to their age. Since younger fathers are more likely to see themselves as teachers and older fathers as benevolent overseers (Nydegger, 1973), it follows that the offspring of young fathers would be higher in achievement need than the offspring of older men. Flabo and Richman (1979) found precisely this difference.

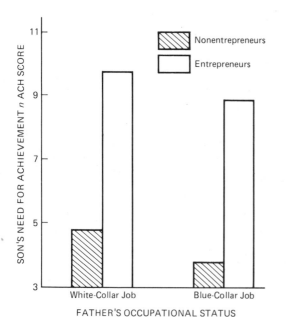

Figure 8-2. Research indicates that the nature of a father's job, rather than its status, influences the achievement need of his son. Boys whose fathers were in entrepreneurial jobs (managers, owners of businesses) were much higher in need for achievement than boys whose fathers were employed in nonentrepreneurial positions (routine jobs lacking in authority).

(Data from Turner, 1970)

Is Success Worth the Price?

Our society has long placed a very high value on hard work, competition, and success. American history is usually presented to young people as a record of constant struggle against the environment (the Pilgrims in Massachusetts), hostile Indians (the cavalry making the West safe for railroads and homesteaders), and the frontier (wagon trains heading up the Oregon Trail or toward the California gold fields). Our most famous legendary hero was Paul Bunyon, who destroyed mile after mile of forests to clear land so that farms and towns could be built. The payoff was a new nation carved out of the wilderness in which the settlers and pioneers became wealthy landowners and businesspeople by virtue of their own persistent efforts.

In more recent times financial success has remained the goal of a great many people, and it is sometimes said that anyone who works hard enough can make it. The competitive spirit is encouraged from our earliest school days by means of contests ranging from spelling bees to athletic events. The late Green Bay Packer coach Vince Lombardi said, "Show me a good loser and I'll show you a loser," and President Carter wrote a book entitled *Why Not the Best?*

Even so, some observers have begun to detect a shift in the values and motives of our society. During the 1960s there was a growing tendency to question the value of material success. Some people began to stress cooperation in place of competition and self-awareness in place of financial gain. Reich (1970) wrote of the "greening" of America and how the "youth revolution" was trying to make our country more livable; many people began truly to accept the slogan, "It's not whether you win or lose; it's how you play the game." Alcohol and arm wrestling were replaced by pot and Frisbee throwing. There is a New Games Foundation in San Francisco whose aim is to replace the competitive aspects of traditional sports such as baseball with noncompetitive games in which no one wins and no one loses. For example, the goal of "new volleyball" is simply to keep the ball from hitting the ground rather than trying to score points by making those on the other side of the net miss (*Time,* September 11, 1978, p. 54). Some say that the 1970s began to reverse this trend and that college students are returning to a culture characterized by hard work, concern with grades, and desire for good jobs and financial rewards.

The achievement motive expresses the traditional values of our society, and many behavioral scientists appear to accept such values. They imply that it is desirable to be driven to achieve—thus, ways should be developed to raise children with high need for achievement, to alter adults whose achievement need is low, and even to alter nations in the direction of high *n* Ach. Those who question such values would argue that success is often empty and satisfies for only a short time, that the price one pays is the sacrifice of quiet contentment and close interpersonal relations. It is suggested that we stop and smell the roses. Harry Chapin's song tells us that the father who is too busy to spend time with his small son will eventually find that his grown son is too busy for him—"just like you, Dad."

What do you think? What do you want for yourself? Which would you choose—hard-driving achievement and material success or a relaxed, noncompetitive life style? Which would you choose for your sons and daughters? What is the best kind of future for your country? And is it necessary to choose? Is it possible to have success *and* contentment at the same time? Is it possible to fight one's way to the top of the heap and still pause from time to time to sniff the fragrance of a rosebush?

ACHIEVEMENT NEED AND PERFORMANCE: SUCCESS IN SCHOOL AND ELSEWHERE

Academic Performance

Grades and IQ.   The importance of "motivation" among the factors that influence academic performance is widely accepted, but efforts to obtain relevant empirical evidence run into problems. For one thing, a great many variables affect academic performance, and they include many different motive systems. Still, one of the variables should be n Achievement, and research confirms this expectation. Positive relations have been reported between n Ach scores and school grades (Schultz & Pomerantz, 1976) and between n Ach and IQ (Robinson, 1961). One behavioral characteristic necessary for success is *persistence* (Nygård, 1977). The longer a

Figure 8-3. Evidence of a strong need to achieve scholastically is obvious in some youngsters. In general high n Ach results in a high gradepoint average. (Owen Franken, Stock, Boston)

person continues working at a task, the more likely it becomes that the goal will be attained.

Relevance of Grades to Future Success.   The possibility of a more complex relation between achievement need and grades was proposed by Raynor (1970, 1974). First, he considered both need for achievement and test anxiety. The former was termed **motivation to attain success** (M_s) and the latter **motivation to avoid failure** (M_f). It was expected that when M_s is greater than M_f, a person should be more strongly motivated to achieve and hence should attain good grades. Second, he considered the meaning of a given grade with respect to the person's future career. Presumably, the *relevance* of a course will be a factor in determining whether achievement need will influence performance in that course. It was hypothesized that for people in whom the motive to achieve success is stronger than the motive to avoid failure, course grades would be higher if the course is related to their future career than if it is not. Students with the reverse pattern of motivation ($M_f > M_s$) would not be expected to show this difference between career-relevant and career-irrelevant course grades.

Students in the introductory psychology course at the University of Michigan were given the TAT measure of *n* Ach and a test anxiety questionnaire. To determine the relevance of the course to their future career, another questionnaire was given.

Figure 8-4 shows the effects of achievement motivation and course relevance on grades for the course. As predicted, when $M_s > M_f$, grades

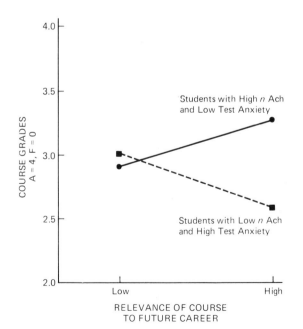

Figure 8-4.   Students who are high in achievement need and low in test anxiety (motivated to attain success) get better grades in courses that are relevant to their future careers. Students with the opposite pattern (motivated to avoid failure) actually get worse grades in career-relevant courses. (Data from Raynor, 1970)

were higher if the course was relevant for the person's future career than if it was not. When $M_f > M_s$, there was a tendency toward the reverse relationship.

Longitudinal research based on those ideas provides evidence that it is possible to measure the motives of high school sophomores and predict the likelihood of their obtaining some form of higher education. Students who were high in achievement need and low in test anxiety were much more likely to continue in school than those with low n Ach and high test anxiety (Atkinson, Lens, & O'Malley, 1976). In addition, those who perceived education as relevant to their career goals were more likely to continue past high school. Combining the three predictor variables, the investigators found that 58.6 percent continued in school if they had high achievement need, low anxiety, and perceived relevance. Among those with the reverse pattern, only 27.1 percent pursued higher education.

Laboratory research in which task relevance has been manipulated reveals the same kinds of relationships. When success in one activity is necessary to obtain success in a subsequent activity, subjects who are high in the motive to attain success do better than those who are high in the motive to avoid failure. On unrelated tasks, this difference disappears (Entin & Raynor, 1973; Raynor & Rubin, 1971).

Risk-Taking Behavior

Motives, Expectancies, and Incentives. Atkinson (1957) proposed three variables as determinants of behavior. (1) A *motive* such as n Ach consists of a disposition to strive for certain kinds of satisfaction. There are avoidant as well as approach motives. Avoidant motives refer to individual differences in the painfulness of specific negative consequences of behavior. In achievement-related situations one may assume that both the motive to achieve success and the motive to avoid failure are aroused. (2) An *expectancy* is the anticipation, usually aroused by situational cues, that a given behavior will lead to a specific consequence. (3) In addition, there is an *incentive* variable, which is the relative attractiveness of a specific goal or the relative unattractiveness of the consequences of a given goal-directed behavior. Atkinson proposed that the strength of the motivation to perform an act is a function of the strength of the motive, the expectancy that the act will be successful, and the value of the incentive.

Without going into all of the details of Atkinson's theory or of more recent extensions of it (e.g., Heckhausen, 1977), a few general points can be summarized. Whenever the success and failure motives are of equal strength, the resultant motivation is zero. The person is caught between a tendency to approach the task and a tendency to avoid it; he or she is "frozen" in the middle and does nothing. When the achievement motive is stronger than the fear-of-failure motive, the resultant motivation is positive. The person tends to approach the task, and the motivation is strongest when the expectancy (chance of success) is .50. With a 50–50 chance of success, such people are more highly motivated than they are when faced with either very easy or very difficult tasks. When fear of failure is stronger than the achievement motive, the reverse is true. That is, the resultant motivation is negative, and it is most negative when the chance of success is .50. These people prefer a very easy or very difficult task. We will now see how experimental findings have confirmed these predictions. Would you have guessed that high n Ach (low fear of failure) individuals prefer an intermediate risk while low n Ach (high fear of failure) individuals prefer either very low or very high risk?

Too Easy, Too Hard, or a Challenge?   McClelland (1958) asked a group of kindergarten children to engage in a ringtoss game. Those who were high in n Ach selected an intermediate range of difficulty; that is, they chose a moderate distance from which to throw the ring at the peg. Those who were low in n Ach selected an extreme in terms of difficulty; they stood either right on top of the peg or so far away that success was almost impossible. Over a series of trials, the low need achievers stop alternating between very easy and very difficult tasks and begin to choose only the easy ones (Kuhl & Blankenship, 1979).

When people are given a task that is described as difficult, those who are high in achievement need perform better than those who are low in achievement need; with an easy task, the reverse is true (Kukla, 1974). Strong achievement motives seem to be related to responding well to a challenge. Those who are high in achievement need even remember their failures better than those whose need is low (Tuder & Holmes, 1973). Presumably, they have learned to overcome past problems by focusing on their weaknesses.

Another sort of situation was utilized by Clark, Teevan, and Ricciuti (1956), who asked college students to estimate their final exam grade (the highest and lowest grade it could possibly be) and to indicate what grade they would be willing to settle for if they could skip the final. Those who settled for an intermediate grade were significantly higher in n Ach than those who settled for a grade near either their maximum or their minimum estimate.

In a group situation in which there are people with both high and low need for achievement, more risks are taken when those with high achievement need are in the majority (Goldman, 1975). Within limits, then, a strong motive to achieve seems to lead people to "take a chance" *if* there is a reasonable chance of success. It is also found that those with high need for achievement overestimate the chance of success—the harder the task, the greater the tendency to overestimate (Schultz & Pomerantz, 1974). Thus, achievement need is related to confidence in one's own abilities.

An interesting, though very speculative, extension of these findings has been proposed by Dixon (1976). He presents a series of case histories of generals whose poor decisions led to defeat. One reason, he proposes, is that such men are usually low in need for achievement and are motivated by fear of failure. Therefore, they either choose to take very low risks and thus miss out on crucial opportunities or go for very high-risk actions and thus stumble into terrible disasters. Whether or not this is an accurate description of military decision making, you can probably think of historical examples that are consistent with these ideas.

The Situation Can Make a Difference.   Zander and Forward (1968) examined the effects of achievement motivation on behavior in a group situation. Motivation to achieve success or avoid failure can presumably be aroused with respect to the activity of a group as well as personal activity. In a group, however, all the members are not equally involved in decision making and, hence, in the responsibility for success or failure. The individual's motivational pattern and role in the group would be expected to interact to determine his or her response to the group's activity. Specifically, a person in a central, decision-making role was expected to respond differently than a person in a peripheral role.

The TAT measure of n Ach and a test anxiety questionnaire were given to a large group of eleventh-grade boys; subgroups differing in success and failure motivation were selected. The experiment itself was described as a study of teamwork. Groups of three were to work on a task for a series of trials to see how fast they could complete it. Their performance was to be compared with that of other groups, and they were asked to do their best. The task involved completing a design with dominoes. Only the central person knew the design to be made; the other two were to slide the required dominoes under a partition when the central person asked for them. No talking was allowed, and communication was by means of written messages. Clearly, the responsibility for success fell on the central person. Each subject played different roles on different trials. The response that was of interest was the estimate by each group member as to how long they believed it would take to complete the next trial; examples were given to specify easy, average, and difficult goals.

It was found that intermediate group aspirations are preferred by individuals for whom $M_s > M_f$ and not for those with $M_f > M_s$ when they are in the peripheral position. Such findings are consistent with those described earlier. What happens to people who are placed in the decision-making role? The demands of the central position were so great that groups with both motivational patterns had intermediate aspirations when they were placed in that role. Another way to view the same findings is to say that the success-motivated people were equally likely to chose intermediate aspirations regardless of their role whereas the failure-motivated people did so only when they were in the central position. It appears that some people are success oriented whatever the situation. For others it takes a particular kind of situation to bring forth such behavior.

CHARACTERISTICS OF AN ACHIEVER

The Importance of Time

The person who is high in *n* Ach is described as one who is concerned with using time efficiently, planning ahead, being on the move, and so forth. Several studies of the achievement motive have dealt with such factors.

Delay of Gratification. If high need achievers are planful and forward looking, they may be expected to be able to delay gratification in order to obtain greater rewards. Mischel (1961) has suggested that achievement fantasies in part reflect the person's hope for rewards in the future. For one thing, those who are high in *n* Ach presumably have learned to tolerate the waiting period between expenditures of effort and later rewards.

The subjects were black 11- to 14-year-olds in Trinidad who were given a TAT measure of *n* Ach. One measure of delay preference involved a choice between a small 10¢ candy bar that was available immediately and a much larger 25¢ candy bar that would be available in a week. Two verbal items were also used to determine preference:

1. I would rather get ten dollars right now than have to wait a whole month and get thirty dollars then.
2. I would rather wait to get a much larger gift much later rather than get a smaller one now.

The children who chose the delayed reward on the behavioral measure and on both verbal measures were significantly higher in *n* Ach than those who chose the immediate reward on all three. It seems that achievers tend to delay immediate gratification when it is possible to obtain greater rewards by waiting.

"Time Is Like . . ." Knapp and Garbutt (1958) assumed that high achievement need leads to a desire to manipulate one's surroundings and to acute awareness of time and its value, and, hence, the perception that time moves rapidly. Phrases such as "Time is money, don't waste it" seem to describe this general attitude. Male undergraduates were asked to rate each of twenty-five metaphors in terms of its appropriateness in evoking a good image of time. Those who were high in need for achievement found metaphors involving speed and directness most appropriate for describing time, while those who were low in need for achievement responded to slow or static metaphors as most descriptive. Table 8-2 gives the six metaphors that correlate most positively and the six that correlate most negatively with *n* Ach scores. The metaphors chosen by subjects high in *n* Ach seem to represent a much greater sense of speed and action than those chosen by the low *n* Ach subjects.

Table 8-2.   People who are high in need for achievement are found to think of time in terms of metaphors involving speed and rapid movement. Those who are low in need for achievement prefer metaphors that stress slow, static qualities.

Metaphors Preferred by High n Ach Subjects	Metaphors Preferred by Low n Ach Subjects
A dashing waterfall	A devouring monster
A galloping horseman	A quiet, motionless ocean
A bird in flight	A stairway leading upward
A winding spool	A string of beads
A speeding train	A vast expanse of sky
A fleeing thief	A large, revolving wheel

(Data from Knapp & Garbutt, 1958)

Time Flies When You're Having Fun Achieving.   McClelland (1961) reports a simple behavioral test of attitudes toward time. After checking his watch carefully an investigator announced the correct time to a class of senior high school boys. Then he said, "Please raise your hand if your watch is fast by any amount. Now please raise your hand if your watch is slow." Of those who were high in achievement need, 87 percent reported that their watches were fast, compared with 44 percent of those who were low in achievement need. High need achievers would seem to be most likely to get where they are going on time.

We all know that there is not a constant relation between the passage of time as measured by clocks and our subjective perception of time. For example, an hour spent studying for an exam for a dull course can seem like four hours while an hour spent on an enjoyable date can appear to rush by in a few minutes. Meade (1966) proposed that achievement need is one of the factors that influences time perception. "Time for the high need achiever is regarded as a commodity not to be wasted, while it is of much less importance to the low need achiever" (Meade, 1966, p. 578). The subjects were male college students; their watches were removed so that they had no external means of measuring time. There was a fifteen-minute maze task, which the subject was to complete while blindfolded. Each subject had twelve trials, and the experimenter gave false feedback after each trial, saying either that the subject was making poor progress at reaching the goal or that he was making good progress. After fifteen minutes the task was ended, and the subject had to estimate how long it had taken. Figure 8-5 shows the time estimates. As predicted, the subjects with high need for achievement overestimated the time when they thought they were not doing well and underestimated it when the feedback was positive. The low *n* Ach subjects were much less responsive to these situational changes. Presumably, those who were high in achievement need were more involved

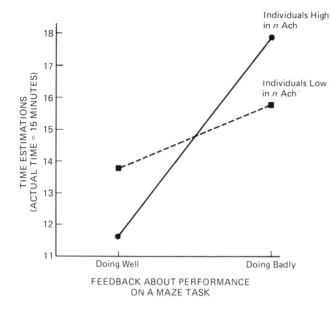

Figure 8-5. When subjects were given false feedback about how well they were doing on a maze task, their estimates of time were affected. In general, time was overestimated when subjects thought they were doing badly and underestimated when they thought they were doing well. This difference was much greater for those who were high in achievement need than for those who were low in that need.
(Data from Meade, 1966)

in and challenged by the task, and information about their performance had a greater impact on them than on the subjects who were low in *n* Ach.

Time is also a factor in the way people perform as they get closer to a goal. Gjesme (1974) found that those who are high in achievement need tend to work harder and faster as a goal approaches in time while those who are low in that need tend to slow down. Again, it is as if time is more valuable to those whose achievement need is high.

How to Succeed in Business

Perhaps occupation, more than any other factor, is linked with our culturally defined standards of success, prestige, and status. If *n* Ach is measuring the sort of motive that involves striving for such goals, occupational aims should be a function of *n* Ach.

Status as the Goal. A person's occupation plays a major role in his or her life, and the most desirable jobs are those with a high salary, heavy work load, and high prestige (Gray & Levin, 1978). Minor and Neel (1958) suggested that the occupation a person chooses indicates the role he or she wants to play in life. Male veterans were asked to indicate their occupational preferences. The occupations were ranked for prestige by a group of judges. At the upper end of the prestige scale were such jobs as mechanical engineer, retail sales manager, high school teacher, and news reporter. At the lower end were such jobs as barber, order filler, longshoreman, and guard. When the subjects were divided into high and low *n* Ach groups, the prestige of their occupational choices was found to differ. In the high *n* Ach group, 88 percent preferred high-status occupations while only 12 percent preferred low-status ones. In the low *n* Ach group, 54 percent preferred low-status and 46 percent preferred high-status occupations.

There's No Business Like Business. The Strong Vocational Interest Blank yields scores that compare a person's test response with the responses of people who have achieved success in various occupations. Among a group of college freshmen, the responses of those who were highest in *n* Ach were compared with the responses of those who were lowest in *n* Ach. The only jobs on which the two groups differed significantly were those of stockbroker, real estate salesperson, advertiser, buyer of merchandise, and factory manager. Each of these jobs is related to business, and in each instance subjects who were high in *n* Ach responded more like people in the field than subjects who were low in *n* Ach (McClelland, 1961).

It was reported earlier that fathers in entrepreneurial jobs had sons

Figure 8-6. Outstanding achievement tends to be rewarded. In rare instances, the reward can be spectacular—five gold medals from the Olympics. (U.P.I.)

who were high in n Ach. Such jobs involve making decisions and being responsible for their consequences. They also involve receiving objective feedback of the success of those decisions, and taking risks. Meyer, Walker, and Litwin (1961) selected managers in several manufacturing plants who held positions of this type. A group of nonentrepreneurial specialists was also chosen, and the two groups were matched for salary or status, age, years of education, and length of time with the company. As expected, the mean n Achievement score of the entrepreneurial managers was found to be significantly higher than that of the specialists.

The fact that there is relation between n Ach and entrepreneurial work does not necessarily show that n Ach is responsible for choice of occupation. Among other things, the demands of such jobs could well influence the test scores. However, this interpretation can be ruled out on the basis of a longitudinal study conducted by McClelland (1965a). A group of male students had taken the n Ach measure while in college, and a fourteen-year follow-up was made to determine the types of occupations they eventually entered. It was found that 83 percent of those in entrepreneurial occupations had received high n Ach scores while in college; only 21 percent of those in nonentrepreneurial occupations had received high scores. Thus, achievement need in adolescence can be used to predict later occupational choice.

Achievement Need and Success in an Organization.   Andrews (1967) sought to trace the relation between a person's achievement level and performance in the business world. Since high achievement motivation leads a person to engage in hard and effective work, this would seem to ensure success in a business firm. But what if the values and judgments of one's superiors involve elements other than achievement, productivity, and success? Here, achievement need might be expected to hinder success.

In Mexico, two firms that were quite different in value orientation were identified. One (firm A) was highly achievement oriented, progressive, expansive in its policies, and successful in economic terms. The other (firm P) was power oriented, conservative, traditional, and less successful. The subjects were Mexican executives working for the two firms. The executives' TAT stories were scored for need for power as well as n Ach. Success in each firm was defined in terms of the status of the person's job and the number of promotions received.

First, a strong trend was found for the executives in firm A to be higher in n Achievement and lower in n Power than the executives in firm P. Second, the relation between the motivations of the executives and their success depended on the type of firm for which they worked. In firm A, achievement need was positively related to success and need for power was negatively related to status in the firm. In firm P, need for power was positively related to success and n Ach was negatively related to status.

Andrews concluded that the pattern of status and achievement in the two firms was the outcome of a mutual adjustment process between men with different motives and firms with different values. He also suggested that business is attractive to people with high need for achievement only when business firms value n Ach.

Physiological Correlates of Achievement Need

It has been found that, for males, achievement-oriented behavior is positively related to the level of uric acid in the system (Brooks & Mueller, 1966). Those with the highest levels were rated as higher in drive, achievement, and leadership.

This finding was replicated by Mueller and French (1974), who suggested that uric acid tends to affect the person's general level of activation. Thus, a high level of uric acid would lead to alertness and striving. Achievement is simply one of the ways in which this general activity can be expressed. It is also possible that those most concerned with achievement behave in ways that lead to an increased production of uric acid.

TRY IT YOURSELF

The Case of the Mysterious Surgeon

Before you ask anyone else to attempt to solve the following riddle, see if you can solve it:

A father and his son were driving along the interstate highway when the father lost control of the car, swerved off of the road, and crashed into a telephone pole. The father died instantly, and his son was critically injured. An ambulance rushed the boy to a nearby hospital. A prominent surgeon was summoned to provide immediate treatment. When the surgeon arrived and entered the operating room to examine the boy, a loud gasp was heard. "I can't operate on this boy," the surgeon said, "He is my son!"

Can you explain this? The father died in the crash, so how could the boy be the surgeon's son? Write down as many explanations as you can.

Now try a second version of the same riddle:

A father and his son were driving along the interstate highway when the father lost control of the car, swerved off of the road, and crashed into a telephone pole. The father died instantly, and his son was critically injured. An ambulance rushed the boy to a nearby hospital. A prominent surgeon was summoned to provide immediate treatment. When the surgeon arrived and entered the operating room to examine the boy, the surgeon burst into tears and became hysterical. "I can't operate on this boy," the surgeon sobbed, "He is my son!"

Now can you solve it more easily? The surgeon, of course, is the boy's mother. Our stereotypes about males and females seem to be so strong that "a prominent surgeon" is usually assumed to be a male. Only when the female-stereotyped behaviors of crying and hysteria are added do most people find the riddle easy to solve (Gorkin, 1972).

Try the two riddles on a few friends. Ask five males and five females to solve the first one and then ask the same number of people to solve the second version. Are the males and females alike in their responses, and is the second riddle easier to solve than the first? In one study (Goldberg, 1974) only 12 percent of the males and 17 percent of the females could solve the original riddle. Does your sample do any better? What do you think such findings indicate about our views concerning males and females? For example, is it possible that most people are somewhat sexist even if they don't realize it?

FEMALES AND THE NEED TO ACHIEVE

Among the most puzzling aspects of the early research on achievement was that males and females differed greatly in this motive. In general, the first studies found that the relations established among male subjects did not hold true for female subjects. For this reason for about two decades most of the research on achievement concentrated almost entirely on males and ignored females (Alper, 1974). Attempts to create special tests with female pictures rather than scenes showing males did not succeed—females actually responded with more achievement-oriented stories to male pictures than to those depicting females (Lesser, Krawitz, & Packard, 1963). Attempts to explain these sex differences and to understand female achievement behavior have led to some intriguing research.

Learning the "Right" Roles: Males Are the Achievers

It seems to be generally agreed that sex differences in the achievement motive, in achievement-related behavior, and in actual success in our society result from what we are taught about male and female roles. Traditionally, this learning has begun in the preschool years and continued throughout life. Various studies have shown, for example, that the male and female characters in children's books are usually portrayed as stereotypes in which the males are active and achievement oriented while the females are passive helpers who tag along (Weitzman, Eifler, Hokada, & Ross, 1972). Most of us can remember reading such stories—Dick builds a tree house while Jane stands by to hand him a hammer and admire his skill.

In an attempt to show how these **sexist** stories affect behavior, McArthur and Eisen (1976) wrote a stereotyped story about two 4-year-olds—a boy and a girl. The boy constructs a model ship while the girl paints a picture; the girl is frightened by a goat and is saved by the boy; and the boy puts the model ship in a bottle with much effort while the girl watches and suggests asking an adult for help. The experimenters also wrote the same story in reverse, with the girl as the active character and the boy as the passive one. Nursery school children heard either the regular, stereotyped story or the one in which the roles of the boy and girl were reversed. Afterwards they engaged in a task involving an attempt to get some plastic flowers to stand upright in a bottle. It was found that boys tended to work at the task longer and more persistently after the regular story than after the reversed one, and that girls tended to do the opposite. The children tended to like and identify with the character of their own sex and then to behave as that character had behaved in the story.

Such differences in the portrayal of males and females have been pervasive in our society and tend to be consistent with the way most children are raised (Stein & Bailey, 1973). Those females who *do* develop achievement-oriented behavior are those with nontraditional, permissive parents who reinforce and encourage their achievements. The mother apparently plays a crucial role; for example, tenth-grade girls who feel most competent have mothers who place a high value on their daughter's being independent, ambitious, and doing well in school and a low value on their daughter's being self-controlled and responsible (Baruch, 1976). The girls who felt most competent, by the way, also had higher career goals and a desire for fewer children than those who felt least competent.

One effect of the prevailing stereotypes is that those females who develop high achievement need and feelings of competence tend to be perceived as more "masculine" than those who adopt more traditional roles. Interestingly, women who receive low femininity scores on a measure of role orientation write TAT stories in which women are successfully engaged in important tasks; those with high femininity scores write stories about women seeking a husband in order to, in the words of one subject, "live satisfiedly ever after" (Alper, 1973).

Role Pressures in Adulthood: The Achieving Female

Television and Female Achievement.   It might seem that the pressures and influences of stereotypes would be reduced as one reaches adulthood. A study of prime-time television programs by Manes and Melynk (1974) suggests that the preschool storybook models continue to operate throughout our lives, though in more subtle ways. For example, on television an achieving female is one who does not have good social relations with males; only the low-achieving women tend to be happily married. It was found that male jobholders on TV are most often married, while jobholding females are shown to be unmarried or stuck in an unhappy marriage. Good marriages tend to be reserved for housewives. Think of career women like Phyllis (widowed), Rhoda (divorced), and Charlie's Angels (variously single and divorced) versus secure wives and mothers like Marion Cunningham (*Happy Days*), Olivia Walton, and Kate Lawrence (*Family*). Mary Tyler Moore has convincingly played both types of woman—the happily married housewife Laura Petrie and the successful and single Mary Richards. Television tends to tell women that female achievement is a pitfall to be avoided and that happiness is reserved for the wife and mother who stays home.

One result of such pressures is the all too common view that females who achieve have, in a sense, "failed" as women. Swertlow (1977) pointed out that Barbara Walters is a world-famous television personality who became the first anchorwoman on a network news program, earns a reported million dollars a year, and was voted Woman of the Year by United Press in 1976. Despite all this, even she is pressured not to relax and enjoy her success. In an interview she said, "I just wish my mother would get more pleasure from my life. She would be happier if I were at home, married, with a couple of kids" (p. 18). In a similar way, when actress Julie Harris was nominated for the third of her four Tony awards she said, "If I had to do it again, I would like to have met a man and just been his helpmate and nothing else" (*Time*, May 9, 1977).

How Do Women Achieve? Not surprisingly, the bias against women who achieve has resulted in less female than male achievement in most aspects of our society (Maccoby & Jacklin, 1974). In part, this difference can be attributed to cultural stereotypes that encourage women to have lower expectations with respect to success (Deaux, 1976). There are, however, other ways in which female achievement can be expressed. For example, it is possible to achieve in a social sense, and females seem more likely than males to equate success with popularity and acceptance by others (Field, 1951).

The expression of female *n* Ach through the success of one's husband was studied by Littig and Yeracaris (1965). Married females in an upstate New York community were interviewed and given a TAT measure. The topic of interest was the occupational mobility of the women's husbands. If a woman's father and husband were both white-collar workers or both blue-collar workers, there was no mobility. If the father was blue collar and the husband white collar, there was upward mobility. If the father was white collar and the husband blue collar, there was downward mobility. Mobility was found to be significantly related to *n* Ach. Upward mobility was more typical of high *n* Ach females and downward mobility of low *n* Ach females. It seems possible either that their choice of a husband was influenced by their *n* Ach in relation to the males' occupational potential or that their n Ach led them to exert an influence on their husbands' choice of occupation.

What Happens to Female Achievers After Graduation?   Baruch (1967) suggested that during the school years and immediately afterwards women should be high in achievement motivation. Women obviously perform as well as men and often outperform them while in school. When women marry and become concerned with home and children, however, achievement motivation might be expected to decline markedly. The woman's culturally assigned role is to be nurturant and affiliative rather than to achieve. Baruch also expected that in women's later years there would be a return of n Ach. Her subjects were Radcliffe alumnae, who constitute a highly selected and achievement-oriented group. The subjects had graduated from college 5 to 25 years prior to the study. Figure 8-7 shows the percentage of each age group that was high in n Ach. It seems that shortly after graduation high need for achievement is characteristic of the majority of the group; there is a dramatic decrease in subsequent years. Later the proportion of subjects with high levels of achievement motivation rises again, but not quite to the level of college and postcollege days. The time at which the decline occurs corresponds to the time when most of the subjects were having children. The later rise in n Ach was attributed to a growing interest in work and returning to a career. Subsequent findings with a noncollege sample present a more dismal picture. Among poorly educated women there is a steady decline of n Ach with age.

The career of a married woman has been found to be influenced by the motives and attitudes of her husband. Winter, Stewart, and McClelland (1977) studied a group of males who had graduated from an Ivy League school over a decade earlier and had taken the TAT when they were freshmen. Information about the careers of their wives was also obtained. It was found that the husbands' need for power (measured prior to marriage) was negatively related to the wives' career level. The higher the husband's need for power, the less likely it was that the wife would have a career. It was also found that husbands who were politically conservative and were employed as business executives had wives who avoided careers. Further research will be necessary to determine whether certain kinds of males actively discourage their wives' career aspirations or whether women who are destined for successful careers select mates who are low in power needs, relatively liberal, and headed for a job outside the ranks of business executives.

A Special Barrier: Fear of Success

A special barrier to female achievement—**fear of success**—has been suggested by Horner (1972). She proposes that women have learned that successful competition and achievement actually have negative conse-

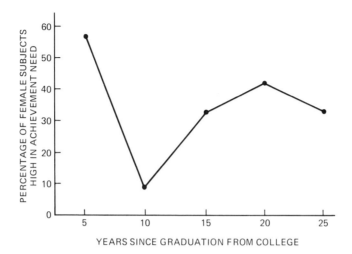

Figure 8-7. Female college graduates were found to be highest in achievement need shortly after graduation. Ten years later very few could be so classified, but fifteen years later achievement motivation showed an increase. The drop in *n* Ach is presumably a function of involvement in marriage and motherhood, and the later increase occurs when the children are old enough to permit the woman to return to her career.

(Data from Baruch, 1967)

quences. women learn to avoid success so that they will not be rejected as unfeminine (Tresemer, 1977). How many mothers have warned their daughters not to reveal how intelligent they are or beat their dates at tennis? When a woman sees success as likely or even possible, anxiety is aroused and efforts to achieve are thwarted. An example of such reactions is the finding that college males indicate feeling high self-esteem when they obtain grades of A or B while females indicate such a feeling when they are getting C's (Hollender, 1972). Perhaps fear of success is one reason female college students rate paintings by female artists higher than those by males when they are described as work to be entered in a competition but the opposite way when the paintings were described as winners (Honig & Carterette, 1978). Each painting, by the way, was identified as having been done by a male for half the subjects and by a female for the other half.

Sad Anne, Happy John. To measure feelings about female success, Horner (1970, 1972) asked female students to complete a story that began with the sentence, "After first-term finals, Anne finds herself at the top of her medical school class." Over one-third of the subjects wrote stories suggesting that this success was unfortunate in that no one would like Anne or that Anne's achievement showed masculine traits. Some of the stories also suggested that Anne did well by accident, that the computer made a mistake, or that she won't be able to perform consistently at this high level.

In later samples as many as 85 percent of the subjects wrote anti-achievement stories about Anne. When the name *John* was substituted for *Anne,* only 10 percent of the subjects reacted to the success in a negative way. How do expectations about the bad effects of female success influence achievement need? It has been found that for females, the higher they score in fear of success, the lower they score in need for achievement; for males, there is no relation between these variables (Karabenick, 1977).

Horner has also found that women indicate much greater fear of success than men, especially if they also *desire* to do well. An interesting sidelight is that this sex difference is reversed for blacks, and fear of success is lower among black college women than among white (Puryear & Mednick, 1974). Though many black women *do* have an internalized fear of success (Fleming, 1977), this actually seems to facilitate their performance, at least among middle-class blacks (Fleming, 1978). In our culture black men are more anxious than black women about the effects of success. Horner suggests that the roles of white women and black men in American society have much in common. In both instances it appears that white males have the most to gain from maintaining such motive systems. It is a tragic waste for the people concerned and for society as a whole that in a large segment of the population achievement potential is discouraged and, hence, scarcely tapped.

In recent years there have been dramatic changes in the attitudes of females in our society. There is increasing support for the ideal of equal opportunity for the two sexes. Despite their verbal support of equality, males actually seem to want women to be bright—but not too bright (Komarovsky, 1973). Even so, today a larger percentage of college females are planning careers than was true of previous generations (Cross, 1971). One personality trait that makes it possible for either males or females to achieve is masculinity (Sadd, Miller, & Zeitz, 1979). It was found that traditionally masculine characteristics such as assertiveness and competition for success were negatively related to fear of success. However, continuing research (Hoffman, 1974) indicates that fear of success continues to be expressed by the majority of female college students. A new finding is that fear of success is also increasing among males (Alper, 1974). The content of the antisuccess stories differs, however. Anne is in trouble because she won't be liked; the stories about John are more likely to question the basic value of achievement.

Women who express high fear of success are found to react quite differently in real life than those who do not write such stories. When they find themselves about to succeed relative to their husbands or boyfriends, they become pregnant (Hoffman, 1977). In one group of women who were succeeding or about to do so (entering graduate school, obtaining a better job, etc.) and then became pregnant, over 90 percent had written fear-of-success stories when they were undergraduates, nine years earlier!

Both males and females respond to Anne's success differently than to John's success (Monahan, Kuhn, & Shaver, 1974). It seems to be an accepted stereotype of our culture that a female who succeeds in the traditionally masculine world is likely to face special problems. Males, however, are especially likely to respond to Anne's achievement in a very negative way (Spence, 1974). For example, they say that the female has sought a career out of loneliness or some personal limitation; males (but not females) also tell stories in which Anne has an illness or accident that ends her career or even her life. Such stories can be interpreted as meaning that some males strongly resent evidence of success in females.

One aspect of fear of success has to do with the setting in which it occurs. Cherry and Deaux (1978) proposed that part of Anne's perceived problem was that she was described as being in the male environment of *medical school*—remember the riddle about the prominent surgeon? They asked subjects to respond to a story in which John or Anne is at the top of the class in *nursing school.* Here, fear of success was reversed, and John was described as facing negative consequences. It appears that success in an out-of-role behavior is a crucial factor in bringing forth negative expectations. Presumably, it is all right for a female to succeed as long as she stays away from traditionally masculine areas of achievement.

Why? It Starts in Elementary School.   One way in which fear of success seems to be instilled in children is through experiences in the school setting. The Carnegie Commission on Higher Education (1973) reports that successful women tend to be graduates of colleges that do not admit men, perhaps because they can take an active part in campus life and assume leadership roles without worrying about male competition or rejection. Laboratory research indicates that women, at least those with traditional attitudes toward male and female roles, do better on a verbal task when working *with* their boyfriends than when competing *against* them (Peplau, 1976a). Also, women with high fear of success perform less well on a masculine task only when they are in the presence of a male competitor (Marshall & Karabenick, 1977).

To pursue the possible effects of different school experiences, Winchel, Fenner, and Shaver (1974) compared the fear-of-success stories of female high school seniors who had gone to all-girl schools at the elementary or high school level with those of females who had attended coeducational schools. The rather dramatic results are shown in Figure 8-8. Those with only female classmates responded with much less fear of success to the Anne story than those who had been in coeducational schools. It also appears that the elementary school experience is the most powerful determinant of such responses.

For males, by the way, type of school had no effect on fear-of-success stories. The authors suggest that though non-coeducational schools would seem to provide a way to reduce fear of success among women, a

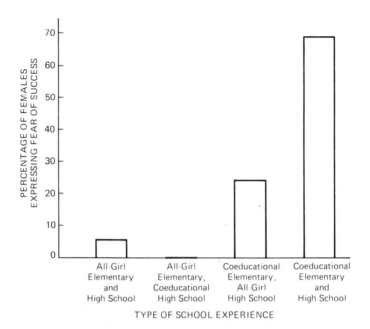

Figure 8-8. When female high school seniors were asked to respond to the story about Anne's success in medical school, the amount of fear of success they expressed was clearly a function of the type of school experience they had had. Fear of success was much higher in those who had attended coeducational schools, especially coeducational elementary schools.

(Data from Winchel, Fenner, & Shaver, 1974)

restructuring of our school system is not likely to occur. A more practical solution may be to develop ways of reducing male–female competition in the earliest years of school.

At the other end of the educational spectrum, among candidates for the Ph.D. degree, sex composition has also been shown to be important. The question was whether the sex of one's major professor has any effect on scientific achievement after leaving school. Goldstein (1979) compared the number of publications by new Ph.D.s in psychology in their first four years after receiving the degree. Both males and females performed better if their major professor had been a member of their own sex. Among these same-sex pairs, the new psychologists averaged two publications each. When the major professor was of the opposite sex, both males and females averaged only about half a publication each. Though there are other explanations that could explain this finding, the one preferred by the investigator is that a major professor of one's own sex serves as a role model for the new Ph.D. If so, the historic preponderance of males in academic positions would help explain any male-female differences in achievement in varous research fields.

Motivating People to Achieve

An unusual approach to bringing about a change in *n* Ach was undertaken by Burris (1958). A group of college students who were enrolled in a self-improvement course wrote thematic apperception stories that were scored for achievement need. Then, in a series of eight weekly sessions, they met to discuss the type of achievement imagery in their stories. In effect, they were directed to engage in fantasy centering on achievement behavior and achievement goals. One matched control group of students in the same course met for counseling on how to study, while a second control group did not meet for any special sessions.

After eight weeks the test was given a second time. As predicted, the subjects in the experimental group who had discussed achievement showed a significant increase in *n* Ach. This finding alone is not very surprising. Burris went further, however, and compared the grade point averages for the following semester of those who had shown an increase in *n* Ach and members of the control groups. He found a significantly greater increase in grade point average for those who had undergone the experimental treatment than for the controls.

Kolb (1977) designed a training program intended to increase concern for academic achievement in a group of underachieving high school boys. The program was carried out at Brown University during a six-week summer school session for high school boys. Underachievement was defined as an IQ of 120 or higher coupled with school grades of C or lower. The boys were divided into an experimental group that received the achievement training along with an academic summer school program and a control group that received only the summer school program. It was hypothesized that need for achievement would be enhanced by the presence of effective role models, positive expectations about the effects of the program, learning and practicing the *n* Ach scoring system, and participation in games simulating various life situations that are relevant to achievement. In addition to extensive testing throughout the experiment, the subjects were contacted for follow-up tests at various times up to a year and a half later.

Increases in *n* Ach were shown by the experimental subjects, but improvement in school grades was the crucial variable. At the six-month follow-up, the experimental and control groups showed no differences. By the one-and-a-half-year follow-up, however, the grade point average of the experimental group had improved significantly more than that of the control group. Thus, training in achievement imagery seemed to have a lasting effect on school performance.

When the subjects were subdivided in terms of social class, the improvement was found only for those who were of fairly high socioeconomic status. The differential social-class effect did not appear to be a difference in reactions to the program or ability to perform in it. Rather, it was suggested that the difference arose when the boys returned to their home environments. Boys of higher socioeconomic status probably received more support and encouragement for their achievement-oriented behavior. Can you suggest possible ways to make such a program work for those at lower socioeconomic levels?

THE ACHIEVING SOCIETY

One of the most unusual aspects of the n Ach scoring system, in contrast to most other personality measures, is the fact that any written material can be scored the same way TAT stories are scored. Thus, unlike IQ tests or the California F scale or almost any other widely used measure, n Ach scores may be obtained for individuals who lived centuries before this scoring system was even developed. In addition, an entire culture can be assessed for n Ach on the basis of a sample of its written material. The possibility of using the n Ach scoring system in this way led to an ambitious project by McClelland and his colleagues. It was an unusual type of research for psychologists in that it invaded the domains of history, economics, and sociology. The general background for this research is given in *The Achieving Society:*

From the top of the *campanile*, or Giotto's bell tower, in Florence, one can look out over the city in all directions, past the stone banking houses where the rich Medici lived, past the art galleries they patronized, past the magnificent cathedral and churches their money helped to build, and on to the Tuscan vineyards where the *contadino* works the soil as hard and efficiently as he probably ever did. The city below is busy with life. The university halls, the shops, the restaurants are crowded. The sound of *Vespas*, the "wasps" of the machine age, fills the air, but Florence is not today what it once was, the center in the 15th century of a great civilization, one of the most extraordinary the world has ever known. Why? What produced the Renaissance in Italy, of which Florence was the center? How did it happen that such a small population base could produce, in the short span of a few generations, great historical figures first in commerce and literature, then in architecture, sculpture and painting, and finally in science and music? Why subsequently did Northern Italy decline in importance both commercially and artistically until at the present time it is not particularly distinguished as compared with many other regions of the world? Certainly the people appear to be working as hard and energetically as ever. Was it just luck or a peculiar combination of circumstances? Historians have been fascinated by such questions ever since they began writing history, because the rise and fall of Florence or the whole of Northern Italy is by no means an isolated phenomenon. [McClelland, 1961, p. 1]

McClelland's research was undertaken in an attempt to understand the economic growth and decline of cultures as a function of changes in the achievement motive. The general scheme developed by McClelland (1971) and his colleagues to link n Ach with the achievements of a society is outlined in Figure 8-9.

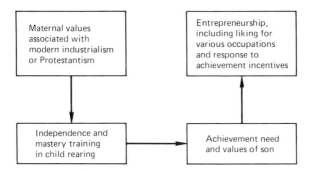

Figure 8-9. McClelland proposed a series of links among the values of a society, the way children are raised, the personality traits that are developed, and the resulting achievement behavior, which moves the society forward.

(Adapted from McClelland, 1961, p. 58)

The Protestant Reformation

The German sociologist Max Weber described the new character type brought about by the Protestant Reformation—a shift toward self-reliance and the new capitalistic spirit in Western Europe. In other words, it could be said that the Protestant Reformation brought about the development of a group of people with high need for achievement.

If this general idea is valid, a number of specific predictions follow. For example, given the findings of the child-rearing studies, Protestant parents should engage in independence training earlier than Catholic parents. McClelland, Rindlisbacher, and de Charms (1955) obtained samples of Protestant, Irish Catholic, and Italian Catholic parents, matched them for socioeconomic level, and gave them Winterbottom's scale of expectancies and demands concerning independent behavior. The differences between the groups were significant and in the predicted direction, with the Protestant parents expecting independence earlier than the Catholic parents. Another prediction was that among male children a higher n Ach would be found for Protestants than for Catholics. With a group of German boys, the mean n Ach of Protestants was significantly higher than that of Catholics.

A still more general prediction was that Protestant countries should be more economically advanced than Catholic countries. As a measure of economic development McClelland (1955) used consumption of electricity (in kilowatt-hours per capita, or kwh/cap). Since advanced economies tend to be found mainly in the temperate zone, and since a number of Catholic countries are located near the equator, nations located in the tropics were omitted in order to make the test more fair. The Protestant countries (Norway, Canada, Sweden, United States, Switzerland, New Zealand, Australia, United Kingdom, Finland, Union of South Africa, and Denmark) were found to consume an average of 1,983 kwh/cap in 1950. A significantly lower average of 474 kwh/cap was found for the Catholic countries (Belgium, Austria, France, Czechoslovakia, Italy, Chile, Poland, Hungary, Ireland, Argentina, Spain, Uruguay, and Portugal). Even when the findings are corrected for differences in natural resources, the Protestant countries do better than expected and the Catholic countries worse than expected.

Predicting the Economic Growth of Nations

Children's Stories and Kilowatt-hours.   To assess a nation's mean n Ach, children's readers used in the second to fourth grades were scored according to the n Ach scoring system. Such readers are fairly standardized within a country, are read by nearly all schoolchildren of a given age, and represent what the culture considers acceptable for its young people. By going back in time one generation and obtaining n Ach scores, McClelland (1961) hoped to be able to predict the subsequent economic growth of various countries. Stories from 23 countries were collected from the period 1920–29 and scored for n Ach. Subsequent economic growth was measured as changes in kwh/cap between 1929 and 1950 in terms of deviation from expected growth. McClelland found that the achievement need expressed in the children's stories correlated well with this index of economic growth. Children's stories for 1950 were also scored for n Ach, and no correlation was found between achievement scores and previous economic growth. It was proposed that this measure of a culture's n Ach level is linked with subsequent growth because the n Ach was *responsible* for the growth.

The Rise and Fall of Achievement Need.   A study by de Charms and Moeller (1962) sampled children's readers used in the United States from 1800 to 1950. At least four books from each twenty-year period were scored for the achievement motive. To obtain an index of achievement in the society, the researchers divided the number of patents issued by the U.S. Patent Office in each twenty-year period by the population during that period. They found that the amount of achievement imagery in the readers rose rapidly from 1800 to 1890 and declined steadily after that period. As shown in Figure 8-10, achievement imagery and the patent index show remarkably similar patterns. The two measures are strongly related. Affiliation imagery in the stories was also scored, and this motive revealed a steady increase over the same period. We seem to have been concerned more with affiliation than with achievement since about the turn of the century. Current novels and movies also appear to stress interpersonal relationships rather than success. It is difficult to think of current fictional heroes who are not unhappy with their achievements (fear of success?) or whose success is not based on violence.

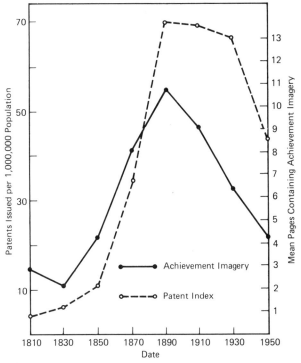

Figure 8-10. When the stories in U.S. children's readers in various decades were scored for *n* Ach, a steady increase was found until the end of the nineteenth century; at that time a sharp decline began. A remarkably similar pattern is found for the number of patents per capita issued to inventors during the same period.

(From de Charms and Moeller, 1962, p. 139)

An interesting follow-up to such data and observations was provided by Anderson (1978). Examining colleges where students took part in demonstrations and riots that led to the overthrow of the Greek government, he found an interesting pattern. In colleges where the outbreaks occurred, males had higher affiliation need and lower achievement need than in colleges where the student body remained quiet. Once again, it appears that personality variables may help explain behavior that influences all of society.

In further research the McClelland (1961) group examined the relation between *n* Ach as estimated from various types of written material and the historical record of economic growth in numerous countries. Space does not permit a full description of these studies, but one of the findings provides a general picture. For England from the time of the Tudors to the industrial revolution, a relation is found between *n* Ach in English literature and rates of gain in coal imports at London fifty years later (McClelland, 1961). The connection between *n* Ach and economic activity in England is shown in Figure 8-11.

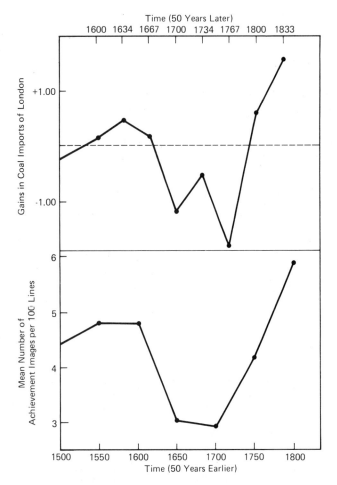

Figure 8-11. When English novels were scored for achievement motivation, the scores were found to predict that nation's economic activity fifty years later.

(Adapted from McClelland, 1961, p. 139)

Achievement, Ulcers, Hypertension, and the Movies. Rudin (1968) proposed that there are also negative consequences when a society stresses achievement. In contrast to the general belief that high levels of achievement need have positive effects, he suggested that *n* Ach could also produce undesirable psychological effects. He hypothesized that hard-driving achievers are likely to suffer from psychologically based ailments such as ulcers and hypertension.

The 1925 *n* Ach scores for sixteen countries were obtained and compared with the 1950 death rates in those countries. It was found that the *n* Ach index correlated highly with the death rates for ulcers and hypertension.

Another proposal was that people in countries with high *n* Ach would seek escapist types of recreation and avoid forms of recreation that are intellectually demanding. In support of this hypothesis the 1925 need achievement scores were found to be positively related to per capita movie attendance in 1955–58 and negatively related to per capita book production in 1955–58. Thus, high need for achievement in a culture has been shown to be linked with hard work, economic growth, psychosomatic illness, and nonintellectual forms of recreation.

What Changes the Achievement Level of a Nation?

Life Without Father. Drawing on some of the developmental studies discussed earlier, McClelland suggested that if dominant fathers are responsible for low *n* Ach, their absence would have the reverse effect. It is interesting to discover that a person is much more likely to become famous for his or her achievements if there is a loss of the father at an early age (Eisenstadt, 1978). Even father's absence from the home can affect the achievement needs of offspring. For example, fathers are taken away from their families when they serve in the armed forces. Therefore, "wars may well have a marked and sudden effect on *n* Achievement by removing authoritarian fathers from the scene" (McClelland, 1961, p. 404). McClelland notes that *n* Ach showed a significant increase in both France and Germany between 1925 and 1950. From this standpoint the marked economic growth and seemingly high level of *n* Achievement since World War II in those countries which were most involved (most of Western Europe, Russia, the United States, Japan, China) compared to those which were relatively isolated (Latin America, Africa, Ireland, Portugal, Turkey) is intriguing.

Father absence can also be caused by certain occupations. If a father's job is such that he is away from the home for extended periods, the *n* Ach of his offspring should be affected in a positive direction. McClelland points out that, historically, many seafaring nations showed abrupt increases in economic growth. He notes as examples the Greeks, early Etruscans, British, Japanese, Scandinavians, and Genoese, and one might add the New Englanders in this country. Thus, when large numbers of dominant fathers go to sea, the achievement need of later generations seems to increase. What do you suppose might be the effect on future generations of our commuter culture, in which the father leaves for work in the early morning and returns home at the children's bedtime? In many respects these fathers are as far removed from their children's lives as if they had gone to sea. A high rate of divorce—with child custody going to the mother—could be expected to have similar effects.

Child Rearing by Slaves and Servants. Throughout history, as nations have become powerful they have engaged in slavery. One of the tasks often assigned to slaves is the rearing of the master's children. McClelland hypothesized that the slave and the slave's children should be oriented toward dependence on the master, obedience, and compliance—precisely the kind of atmosphere that is likely to foster low achievement motivation. He points out that in this country black slaves developed child-rearing practices that stressed nonachievement factors. Their descendants, though free, should still show these effects, and it has been found that lower-class blacks have the lowest average n Ach scores of any minority group tested. Those blacks who have moved into the middle and upper classes, by contrast, are very high in n Ach.

If these general statements about slavery are accurate, it follows that the slaveholders should also tend to develop low n Ach over the generations because their children are raised by slaves. The slave would be expected to respond to the master's child by indulging every whim. Those who founded the southern plantations were probably high in n Ach, but the subsequent generations showed a different pattern. Business enterprise in the United States has been associated with the North and even with the non-slaveholding portions of the South, such as North Carolina. McClelland writes,

What is most fascinating about such a possibility is that it suggests a rather simple, if ironic, account of the rise and fall of many great civilizations in the past. The argument runs as follows: A people with a higher level of n Achievement tend to pursue business enterprise more rigorously and ultimately to become more wealthy. Nearly always in the past such wealth has been used to support slaves. Certainly this was the case in ancient Greece. Beginning around 525 B.C. when a much larger proportion of Athenian families were wealthy enough to support slaves, each child of good family was ordinarily assigned two slaves—a nurse and a pedagogue to go to school with him . . .

Furthermore, in our sample of preliterate cultures, 45 percent of twenty cultures with high n Achievement versus only 19 percent of 21 low in n Achievement had slaves . . . In short, high n Achievement leads to increased wealth, which leads to more household slaves. But in Greece the more general use of such slaves preceded by a generation or two the marked drop in n Achievement . . . Is it unreasonable to infer that the slaves undermined the achievement training of their masters' children, although probably not consciously? So, ironically, the masters were undone by the very instrument that demonstrated, they thought, their mastery—namely, their enslavement of those they had conquered. The irony lies in the fact that what happened was certainly not *intentional* on either side. Explanations of the decline of civilizations in terms of the "decay of moral fibre," although vague and *ad hoc,* do have at least this kernel of truth in them: The institution of slavery in all probability undermined achievement training, which in turn lowered general n Achievement level and made civilizations less enterprising in business and more vulnerable to economic decline and ultimately attack and destruction from without. [McClelland, 1961, pp. 377–78]

An analogous effect could be proposed in modern societies when low n Ach servants, drawn from lower socioeconomic levels, are assigned major child-rearing tasks by families that can afford this luxury. As with the slave cultures, the pattern could involve economic activity leading to wealth and the employment of servants, leading in turn to lower n Ach and less business enterprise in succeeding generations.

It has been suggested (Maehr, in press) that McClelland's approach to the cross-cultural study of the achievement motive is biased toward the values of our society and toward the definition of achievement in terms of money and property. He proposes that achievement motivation is involved in any behavior in which there is a standard of excellence, personal responsibility for the outcome, and a degree of challenge. It is clear that these qualities can apply to other things besides economic success in the world of business.

As a strong proponent of achievement-oriented values, McClelland 1965b) began a large-scale project designed to increase *n* Ach in business executives. Presumably, if enough people were motivated in this direction an entire society could be altered. Groups were brought together for one to three weeks of interaction centered on acquiring a high achievement motive. The general procedure includes training and practice in the production of achievement fantasies, group activities involving goal setting and risk taking with achievement-related tasks, role-playing activities (such as portraying a democratic father with high *n* Ach standards for his son), and interpretation of cultural demands, values, and folklore in terms of *n* Ach. Such training sessions have been carried out in the United States, Mexico, and India.

McClelland and D. G. Winter (1969) reported the results of an international study attempting to alter the need for achievement. This applied research was undertaken to find out whether one could bring about a change in the spontaneous fantasies of a small segment of a nation's population and, potentially, bring about far-reaching economic changes. In each of two Indian cities (Kakinada & Rajahmundry), comparable groups of businessmen were chosen either to receive or not receive achievement training. Those who received the training were required to leave their work and attend a special workshop in Hyderabad. The subjects, whose average age was 36, were engaged in industry, commerce, and several professions.

To evaluate such an ambitious endeavor, it is necessary to look at many possible kinds of changes that could be attributed to achievement training. Table 8-3 summarizes some of the variables studied during a two-year follow-up period. The effects of achievement training may be seen when the behavior of the participants is compared with that of nonparticipants. The achievement training course appeared to influence an impressive number of business and economic activities.

It was concluded that the training program worked best by strengthening self-confidence among those who wanted to feel effective. It also taught them concrete ways to reach their goals. The authors point out that the growing belief in social determinism has undermined the belief that it is possible to bring about social change. They suggest an optimistic picture in which we are not hopeless victims of external forces:

Table 8-3. Indian businessmen selected to take part in achievement training were compared with a control group that did not receive the training. In a number of ways the subsequent achievement-oriented behavior of the experimental group was found to exceed that of the control group.

	Subjects with Achievement Training		Subjects in Control Group	
	Before (1962-64)	After (1964-66)	Before (1962-64)	After (1964-66)
Entrepreneurs classified as active	18%	51%	22%	25%
Entrepreneurs working longer hours	7	20	11	7
Entrepreneurs starting new businesses	4	22	7	8
Entrepreneurs in charge of firm making specific fixed capital investment	32	74	29	40
Entrepreneurs in charge of firm employing more people	35	59	31	33
Entrepreneurs in charge of firm having large gross income increases	52	61	43	38

(Data from McClelland & Winter, 1969)

If man's confidence in himself derived from his former conviction that he was created, looked after, and guided by an all-powerful God, where will it come from now that in popular terminology, "God is dead"? Where will he get the confidence to believe that he can act and change the course of events when he is told almost daily by the social scientists that he is not free to act, that his every reaction is predetermined by his personal and social history? Two experiences point the way to an answer to these questions. First, it is a curious paradox that the most deterministic of contemporary psychologists—namely the neo-behaviorists, followers of B. F. Skinner—are the most confident that they can create a new Utopia. The more they think they know about man, the more they think he is capable of anything. It is true that they talk in terms of creating an environment that will shape man's behavior optimally according to deterministic laws. Yet someone must act, must make the decision to create the environment and design the environment that will predetermine the best response from individuals who live in it. Where does the creator, the prime mover, get his confidence to act? From science, of course. Knowledge is the new source of power. Somehow, by thoroughly understanding how we are determined, we gain the confidence to act so as to transcend determinism. . . .

Scientific knowledge is the new God, the new source of man's conviction that he has the competence to act. Yet in another sense, of course, it is a very old God, a conviction that there are certain immutable laws which exist outside of man in the universe and which, if known and obeyed, give man the power to shape his destiny. [McClelland & Winter, 1969, pp. 377-78]

SUMMARY

Achievement need is a learned motive to compete and to strive for success and excellence.

David McClelland and his colleagues utilized the TAT to construct an experimentally based measure of *n* Ach. In subsequent years several objective measures of this motive were constructed, but none has been utilized as much as the fantasy measure.

It is theorized that a child develops the need to achieve if the parents tend to reward success. Fathers who are extremely loving and accepting *or* autocratic and domineering produce sons who are low in achievement need. High *n* Ach is linked with early independence and achievement training. Fathers with entrepreneurial jobs tend to have sons who are higher in *n* Ach than sons of fathers in nonentrepreneurial jobs.

Need for achievement is positively related to success in school, especially in courses that are perceived to be relevant to the person's future career. High *n* Ach (plus low fear of failure) is connected with preference for a challenging task and intermediate levels of risk; people with the opposite set of motives prefer tasks at which they are almost certain to succeed or almost certain to fail. When people are placed in a position of authority that requires them to make decisions, both high and low *n* Ach individuals select goals that are intermediate in difficulty.

People who are high in achievement need are found to be better able to delay gratification in order to obtain a larger reward in the future. They also tend to think of time as something that speeds by, to have watches that run fast, to overestimate the passage of time when they are not succeeding, and to work faster when approaching a goal. High *n* Ach is also linked with desire for a high-status occupation, interests like those of successful businesspeople, a tendency to seek entrepreneurial occupations, and the ability to succeed in business *if* the organization stresses achievement. High achievement need is also linked with high levels of uric acid.

Females were largely omitted from the earlier research on need for achievement because their behavior did not parallel that of males. Cultural stereotypes stressing achieving males and passive females are reflected in children's stories, child-rearing practices, and television programs. Females have been found to equate achievement with social success and to achieve through their husbands' upward mobility. In college-educated women achievement need is found to drop after graduation, when they become involved in home and motherhood, and to rise after the children grow up. One problem for women is fear of success—the assumption that female achievement in the masculine world reflects nonfeminine traits and elicits rejection by others. Girls who attend elementary and high schools with students of their own sex are much less likely to express fear of success than those who attend coeducational schools.

One of the most ambitious areas of research on *n* Ach is the attempt to explain the economic rise and fall of nations on the basis of changes in this personality variable. McClelland and his colleagues have shown that Protestantism is linked with achievement need and economic success and that national economic growth or decline is linked with increases and decreases in *n* Ach in children's readers, novels, and other written material in many nations across many centuries. Other studies suggest that a highly achieving society is also characterized by ulcers, hypertension, and escapist entertainment. Nations are believed to show a sudden increase in achievement need when large numbers of dominant males are removed from the parent role, as in wartime or by the nature of their occupations. Decreases occur over generations when a successful, achieving society uses slaves or servants to raise its children. Since it has been found that the achievement need of individuals can be increased by special training in the use of fantasy and role playing, this technique has been utilized to raise school grades and increase business success in several countries. Such techniques have the potential to bring about changes in entire nations.

SUGGESTED READINGS

ATKINSON, J. W.   Motivation for achievement. In T. Blass (ed.), *Personality variables in social behavior.* Hillsdale, N.J.: Lawrence Erlbaum, 1977. A summary of the research and theory dealing with the achievement motive and its effect on behavior.

ATKINSON, J. W., & RAYNOR, J. O.   *Personality, motivation, and achievement.* Theory and research involving the way in which personality differences affect motivation and the way in which motivation, in turn, affects behavior.

DEAUX, K.   *The behavior of women and men.* Monterey, Calif.: Brooks/Cole, 1976. An excellent summary of the ways in which the behavior of males and females is similar or different, with a section covering the achievement motive and fear of success.

McCLELLAND, D. C.   *The achieving society.* Princeton, N.J.: Van Nostrand, 1961. An impressive and original application of the methods and theories of personality research in an attempt to explain historical differences in achievement among nations.

McCLELLAND, D. C., & WINTER, D. G.   *Motivating economic achievement.* New York: Free Press, 1969. An interesting account of the proposal to apply knowledge of the achievement motive to bring about behavioral change in various less developed countries.

SMITH, C. P. (ed.).   *Achievement-related motives in children.* New York: Russell Sage, 1969. A collection of original chapters summarizing various ways in which children develop and express the need for achievement.

TRESENER, D. W.   *Fear of success.* New York: Plenum, 1977. A thorough summary of research on fear of success and the way in which males and females respond differently to the possibility of succeeding.

WEINER, B.   *Achievement motivation and attribution theory.* Morristown, N.J.: General Learning Press, 1974. A summary of a program of research in which attribution theory and achievement motivation have been brought together.

Part Three

BEHAVIOR AS A FUNCTION
OF THE SITUATION

Mimi Forsyth, Monkmeyer

Chapter Nine

ATTRACTION: LIKING AND LOVING

In this chapter you will read about the following topics:

Tom was somewhat anxious as he entered the clinical psychologist's office for the first time. He was sweating profusely and obviously used no deodorant. The gray-haired man smiled and motioned him toward the overstuffed chair beside the desk.

"Mr. Bower, I'm Dr. Greeley. Why don't you tell me what brings you here?"

Tom bit his lip and began hesitantly, warming to the topic as he got under way. "Nobody likes me, especially girls. None of the guys in my dorm want to spend any time with me. They go to the movies or out for a beer and never even ask me if I want to go along. Girls are the worst, though. I go out with some chick once, if I'm lucky, and that's the end of it. I can't understand it. I'm sharper than most people on this campus—maybe the dummies are just envious of me."

"You think you're not popular because others envy you?"

"Brilliant! That's what I just said. Are you a real therapist or some kind of parrot act?" Amused by his own joke, Tom—all 250 pounds of him—shook with laughter.

Dr. Greeley smiled blandly and asked, "Why don't you just tell me about what happened the last time you took out a young lady?"

"I don't know about the 'lady' part. All the birds around here are too busy dropping their pants to be called anything that nice. Anyway, last Saturday I zeroed in on this kinda ugly broad who sits next to me in my math class. She's got this chest you wouldn't believe, but a face that belongs in a kennel. I figured she was so hard up, she wouldn't dare say no. I think her name was Glenda or something like that. I asked her if she wanted to do herself a favor and go with me to the basketball game. She said 'Why not?' and I gave her a great time. We had dinner at my favorite place, even though with "energy conservation" it felt like 180° in there. I was very patient in straightening her out about her dumb political ideas. During the game I told her all about myself and my plans for the future. She didn't say much, just yawned every now and then—talk about a drag! Afterwards, when we were in my car, I made my move. I told her that old Tom Bower had the perfect cure for up-tight girls like her—I said a horizontal love session with me would be the best thing that ever happened to her. That was the only time she laughed all evening. Can you imagine? I took that dog right home. Who needs a girl like that?"

"You don't have any ideas as to what you might be doing that is causing other people to turn off?"

"Are you kidding? I wouldn't be paying good money to some dummy like you if I had the answers. Is psychology a total waste of time or can you help me?"

Dr. Greeley sighed. "It won't be easy, Tom, but yes, I think I can help. Let's begin."

THOUGH ALMOST EVERYONE wants to be liked, to have friends, and to be loved by at least one other person, many people behave in ways that make interpersonal relations difficult. Perhaps you have known someone who is similar to Tom in at least some respects. You might want to make a list of his characteristics that you think could make others dislike him. After you have read this chapter, go back to Tom's story and see if you can add to the list.

Attraction refers to the evaluation of other people along a dimension that includes such interpersonal attitudes as hate, dislike, indifference, liking, and love. In this chapter we will examine some of the research that has been conducted to identify the variables that determine how we react to one another. We will look at how we tend to meet one another, the aspects of individuals and situations that lead to positive or negative interactions, and why the same person tends to be liked by some people and disliked by others. Finally, we'll take a look at some recent work on an aspect of behavior that is an important part of our lives—love.

POPULARITY

From our earliest experiences with our peers, it is obvious that a few people tend to be liked by almost everyone and a few to be disliked by almost everyone. It is as if likability were a trait—or a combination of traits. Those with the "right" traits are liked by their teachers, elected as officers by their classmates, and generally have more than their share of friends. Later in life, those with the special charisma of **popularity** continue to be sought after, to make friends easily, and even to be elected to public office. It is not surprising, then, that much of the early research on attraction was designed to determine exactly what traits are related to popularity.

For one thing, those children and adolescents who are popular tend to be intelligent and to have high socioeconomic status (Bonney, 1944; Grossmann, & Wrighter, 1948). They are likely to be only children or to have few siblings (Bonney, 1942, 1949). When there are several children in the family, those born later are more popular than those born earlier, perhaps because they have to develop social skills to deal with older and stronger siblings (Miller & Maruyama, 1976). In adulthood, the higher a person's income (Loomis & Proctor, 1950) and the more education he or she has had (Stewart, 1947), the better liked that person is found to be.

Studies of popularity among subjects ranging from preschool children to college students have been fairly consistent in reporting that certain personality characteristics distinguish the most popular from the least popular. Popularity tends to be linked with good psychological adjustment (Bonney, 1944; Grossmann & Wrighter, 1948; Kuhlen & Bretsch, 1947; Mills, 1953), good health (French, 1951), and high self-esteem (Turner & Vanderlippe, 1958). Those who are unpopular tend to be neurotic (Thorpe, 1955), agressive (Dunnington, 1957), discourteous (Bleda, 1978), and anxious (McCandless, Castaneda, & Palermo, 1956; Trent, 1957). Unpopularity is also related to dependent, withdrawn, and depressed behavior (Winder & Rau, 1962).

In general, studies have found that popularity is linked with positive interpersonal behaviors such as generosity, enthusiasm, and being affectionate (Lemann & Solomon, 1952). There are two major routes to behaving in an unpopular way. General unpopularity is linked with egotistical, overconfident, sarcastic, and domineering behaviors or with a timid, quiet, retiring interpersonal style (Kidd, 1953). The former traits lead to rejection and dislike while the latter lead to isolation (Krebs & Adinolfi, 1975).

In many respects these attraction studies were interesting in suggesting that people with positive attributes are liked while those with negative attributes are disliked. People generally seem to like individuals who are healthy, wealthy, wise, and nice; dislike is reserved for those who are too aggressively obnoxious; while shyness leads to being ignored. Where do these findings lead us? The predictive power of the personality variables is not very high, partly because of wide variations among individuals with respect to the people they like and dislike. Even the most unpopular person may have a few friends, and even the most popular one may have a few enemies. Beyond these extreme groups, predictions of liking based on traits is quite poor.

Partly for these reasons, the focus of attraction research began to shift to another question: Under what conditions is attraction most likely to occur? Even more interest was directed to a somewhat different question: Why does a given person like or dislike another specific person? In other words, the interest in attraction shifted from a trait approach to a situational approach.

The process of getting to know another person well takes place in three stages as two people become acquaintances, then friends, and finally best friends (or lovers). We will discuss the positive and negative factors operating at each stage. Positive factors keep the process going while negative factors stop or even reverse the process.

BECOMING ACQUAINTED

Propinquity: The Power of the Environment

The first meeting of two people can take many forms. There are introductions by mutual friends or relatives. There are meetings arranged by a computer dating service. Accidents can occur—one of the authors once met a girl by answering a dormitory telephone; the boy she was calling was out, and we decided to get together. The majority of our initial contacts, however, are determined in a very regular and predictable way by an obvious and often overlooked factor—the structure of our everyday environment. **Propinquity**, or physical closeness, is the key. People tend to become aware of one another because their houses or apartments are located close together, because they use the same hallways or the same sidewalks, or because they sit near one another in a classroom or on a bus. This awareness leads to recognition, and recognition leads to some level of interaction—

even if they only say "Hi" when they see each other. Once that lowest level of acquaintanceship develops, the stage is set for conversations and the possibility of a friendship, provided that a variety of other factors are also operating. We will first examine propinquity along with other factors in initial acquaintance.

Chance Encounters of a Close Kind.

Two types of propinquity were described by Festinger, Schachter, and Back (1950). There is the actual *physical distance* between dwellings, classroom seats, and so forth, and there is the *functional distance* between them. Functional distance refers to factors that determine whether two people are likely to come into contact. For example, two houses can be functionally distant if a high fence separates them, even though they are physically close (Whyte, 1956). In a classroom, side-by-side seats are functionally closer than seats in adjacent rows, even though the physical distance between them may be the same— it is easier to talk to someone who sits beside you in class than to someone in the row behind you (Byrne & Buehler, 1955).

In studies of married-student housing (where strangers are assigned randomly to apartments on a first-come, first-served basis), the distance between dwellings is found to be the major factor determining who knows whom (Caplow & Forman, 1950). In a cluster of apartment buildings, tenants are much more likely to know the people in their own building than those in other buildings. In fact, Festinger and colleagues (1950) reported that if two families live within 22 feet of one another, they are very likely to know each other; if they are separated by as much as 88 feet, they are very unlikely to know one another. The intensity of the relationship is also influenced by propinquity. In a condominium complex, not only does distance between residences determine the probability of friendship but *best friends* are found to live closer than other friends (Ebbeson, Kjos, & Konečni, 1976).

In a building that has two or more stories, friendships are most likely to form between people living on the same floor (Nahemow & Lawton, 1975). If two people live more than one floor away from one another (e.g., on the first and third floors), they are very unlikely to meet (Evans & Wilson, 1949).

Classroom studies show very clearly that when regular seats are assigned, students sitting beside one another tend to meet and to learn one another's names. Presumably this is why, in such situations, people are most likely to have friends whose last names begin with the same or adjacent letters in the alphabet (Segal, 1974). In an attempt to *create* friendships in such a situation, Byrne (1961a) randomly shifted the assigned seats in sections of an introductory psychology course. The more the students were shifted, the more friendships they formed. Thus, students who had the same seats all semester met an average of 4.78 classmates; those who were reassigned seats at midsemester met an average of 5.50; and those with three different seating assignments met an average of 6.12.

The study just described suggests one of the reasons that an obvious variable like propinquity may be more important than would appear at first glance. That is, propinquity can be *manipulated* to determine who knows whom and how many contacts each person is likely to have. When an architect is deciding where to place sidewalks or stairways, friendship patterns are also being decided. When a person is assigned to an end apartment or even to a classroom seat on the end of a row, he or she will meet fewer people than if the apartment or seat were in a middle position. In public housing projects such decisions can lead to more or fewer interracial contacts and, hence, to increased or decreased interracial tolerance (Deutsch & Collins, 1951).

It should also be clear that dormitory assignments, room seating charts, and the location of office desks can determine whom you are likely to meet, know, date, and marry. In other words all relationships start somewhere, and that starting place very often is simply a matter of propinquity.

Familiarity Breeds Liking.   Though it may seem "natural" that people who are thrown into contact by their environment should become friendly, the reason is not apparent. You don't *have* to talk to the people you pass regularly in the hallway or those who sit near you in class; you also don't *have* to ignore everyone else. What makes the difference?

An explanation is provided by Zajonc's (1968) theory of **repeated exposure**. Zajonc suggests that when we first encounter anything new (a word, clothing style, a person, etc.), our first reaction ranges from indifference to a slightly negative feeling. With repeated exposure, the negative response is gradually extinguished and is replaced by increasingly positive feelings. For example, repeated exposure to a particular piece of music leads to greater liking for it (Brickman & D'Amato, 1975). In general, then, we respond more favorably to something familiar than to something new and strange (Moreland & Zajonc, 1976, 1979; Stang, 1975). Advertisements take advantage of this effect by presenting a product or a political candidate over and over again so that we will come to like whatever or whoever is being sold (Grush & McKeough, 1975; Stang & Crandall, 1977). Familiarity is so important that we even prefer mirror-image photographs of ourselves to true images because we are used to seeing reflections of ourselves; when it comes to friends, we prefer the true image because that is the way we are used to seeing them (Mita, Dermer, & Knight, 1977).

Experimental studies of repeated exposure to people are very convincing in showing how propinquity can lead to positive interpersonal responses. For example, subjects exposed to photographs of strangers respond more and more positively as the number of exposures increases

(Wilson & Nakajo, 1965). In an experiment closer to real life, Saegert, Swap, and Zajonc (1973) showed that casual contacts lead to liking. Their subjects thought they were taking part in a study of the sense of taste. Each subject entered a small room, tasted a liquid, recorded the reactions, and went on to the next room on the list. The schedule was carefully arranged so that each taste session involved two subjects in a room at the same time in a complex pattern ensuring that any two subjects would be with one another ten times, five times, twice, once, or not at all. When the subjects were asked to rate their fellow subjects for likeability, amount of exposure was positively related to liking, as shown in Figure 9-1. Thus, strangers who had not been seen before or had been seen only once were given a neutral rating, but those who had been seen more often received more positive ratings as the number of contacts increased.

The positive effects of repeated exposure on attraction seem to be most effective if the other person is either initially neutral or somewhat liked. If there is reason to dislike a stranger, increased familiarity has very little effect on attraction (Brockner & Swap, 1976). Thus, coming into contact with someone you dislike over and over again will not necessarily cause you to like that person. There is even some evidence that repeated exposure to a negative stimulus will lead to increasingly negative evaluations (Grush, 1976; Swap, 1977).

The first step in the acquaintance process, then, is simple contact

Figure 9-1.   In an experiment it was arranged that each subject would have zero to ten brief contacts with various strangers. As the theory of repeated exposure would predict, as the number of interactions with a person increased, liking for that person also increased.

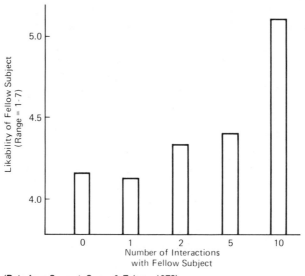

(Data from Saegert, Swap, & Zajonc, 1973)

between two people. Contact and repeated interaction usually lead to attraction (Insko & Wilson, 1977). Such contact is very likely to be a function of propinquity, which permits each person to become familiar with the other and, hence, to react positively.

How Strong Is Your Need to Affiliate?

Individual differences in need for affiliation seem to account for some differences in interpersonal behavior. How would you describe yourself with respect to this kind of motivation?

To compare your responses with those of others, first answer the following questions:

1. What is your position in your family in terms of birth order?
   Only child_____Firstborn_____Later born_____Twin_____

2. How many friends would you say you have?
   _____ : _____ : _____ : _____ : _____ : _____

   Less than   An   More than
   most people   average   most-people
                      number

3. How many students in this class do you know by name?_____

4. How self-confident are you?
   _____ : _____ : _____ : _____ : _____ : _____

   Not at   Self-confident   Extremely
   all self-   to an average   self-confident
   confident   degree

5. If you found yourself alone in a situation with an extremely attractive stranger of the opposite sex, what would you be likely to do?
   _____ : _____ : _____ : _____ : _____ : _____

   Remain silent   Start a conversation
   except to   and try to get to
   answer   know the person
   questions

6. If you were in an experiment and were told that you were going to receive a somewhat painful electric shock, how would you want to spend the waiting period?
   ____ : ____ : ____ : ____ : ____ : ____

   Alone   No   With other
                      preference   subjects

Affiliative Tendency Test

Now respond to the following test according to the instructions.

   9 = very strong agreement
   8 = strong agreement
   7 = moderate agreement
   6 = slight agreement
   5 = neither agreement or disagreement
   4 = slight disagreement

3 = moderate disagreement
2 = strong disagreement
1 = very strong disagreement

_____ 1. I think that fame is more rewarding than friendships.

_____ 2. I sometimes fall into conversations with strangers.

_____ 3. I prefer independent work to cooperative effort.

_____ 4. When I see someone I know walking down the street, I am usually the first one to say hello.

_____ 5. Having friends is very important to me.

_____ 6. I prefer individual activities such as crossword puzzles to group ones such as bridge or canasta.

_____ 7. I would rather serve in a position to which my friends had nominated me than be appointed to an office by a distant national headquarters.

_____ 8. When making an important decision, I feel more certian if I read up on the subject than if I rely on the advice of friends.

_____ 9. I don't care whether or not the people around me are my friends.

_____ 10. I have very few close friends.

_____ 11. I think that any experience is more significant when shared with a friend.

_____ 12. I like people who have many other friends besides myself.

_____ 13. I would rather read an interesting book or go to the movies than spend time with friends.

_____ 14. I join clubs because it is such a good way of making friends.

_____ 15. I would rather travel abroad starting my trip alone than with one or two friends.

_____ 16. I don't really have fun at large parties.

_____ 17. I would rather have a committee meeting to solve a problem than work out the correct solution by myself.

_____ 18. When traveling, I prefer meeting people to simply enjoying the scenery or going places alone.

_____ 19. If I had to choose, I would rather have strong attachments with my friends than have them regard me as witty and clever.

_____ 20. I would rather go right to sleep at night than talk to someone else about the day's activities.

_____ 21. I would rather express open appreciation to others most of the time than reserve such feelings for special occasions.

_____ 22. I don't care whether I'm surrounded by friends or strangers.

_____ 23. At parties, I prefer to talk to one person for the entire evening instead of participating in different conversations.

_____ 24. I prefer a leader who is friendly and easy to talk to over one who is more aloof and respected by his or her followers.

_____ 25. I don't spend much time talking with the people I see every day.

_____ 26. I enjoy a big party more than a good movie.

_____ 27. I don't believe in showing a lot of overt affection toward friends.

_____ 28. I like to make as many friends as I can.

_____ 29. When I'm not feeling well, I would rather be with others than alone.

_____ 30. I prefer the independence which comes from lack of attachments to the good and warm feelings associated with close ties.

_____ 31. If I had to choose between the two, I would rather be considered intelligent than sociable.

If your instructor wishes, you can turn in your scores and your responses to the six questions on a sheet of paper. No names should be used, but indicate whether you are male or female.

The test is a measure of the tendency to affiliate and was developed by Mehrabian (1970). The questions were based on some of the findings in research on affiliation behavior. As described in this chapter, there is a relation between birth order and desire to wait with others in a frightening situation. In other research, Crouse and Mehrabian (1977) found that males who received high scores on the affiliation measure are more talkative with an attractive female stranger and rate themselves as more self-confident; for females, the less affiliative subjects were most likely to talk to an attractive male.

When your instructor has combined the responses of the members of class, you can compare your results with those of the subjects in these various studies.

Scoring Key

: Add the numbers you wrote beside the following items:
2, 4, 5, 7, 11, 12, 14, 17, 18, 19, 21, 24, 26, 28, 29

Affiliative score total _____

Add the numbers you wrote beside these items:
1, 3, 6, 8, 9, 10, 13, 15, 16, 20, 22, 23, 25, 27, 30, 31

Nonaffiliative score total _____

Subtract the second total from the first.

Net score _____

Add 129

Your test score _____

Need for Affiliation

Though propinquity is a common first step in the acquaintance process, some people who come into contact with one another never go on to interact. Why not? There are several variables that either increase or decrease the likelihood of interpersonal interaction. The first of these is a motivational variable—the need for affiliation.

Individual Differences in an Affiliative Trait. Have you ever noticed that on a bus or an airplane, or waiting in line, some people remain quietly isolated while others strike up a conversation with whomever happens to be near them? Those who initiate such contact are described as having a strong motive to affiliate with others. This **need for affiliation (n**

Aff) has been studied using procedures very much like those described in Chapter 8 in discussing n Ach. Like the concept of achievement need, this concept was borrowed from Murray's early work, and a scoring system for the TAT was developed using an experimental criterion of motive arousal (Shipley & Veroff, 1952).

Research on n Aff has shown that interpersonal behavior in many situations varies as a function of the strength of this motive. For example, when there is pressure to conform in a group, people who are low in affiliation need are not greatly affected—it would seem that they are more or less unconcerned about the reactions of others, while those who are high in n Aff want very much to be liked (Hardy, 1957). It is also found that the higher the need for affiliation, the more anxious people are when others are making judgments about their interpersonal skills and attractiveness (Byrne, McDonald, & Mikawa, 1963). Thus, this dimension involves a desire to be accepted and liked by other people versus a relative indifference to others.

It follows from the research that has been conducted in this area that people who are high in affiliation need are more likely to initiate contact with those around them, seek the company of others, and attempt to establish friendships (Crouse & Mehrabian, 1977).

Situational Constraints: How Many Friends Do You Need?

In addition to overall trait differences with respect to affiliation, there are situational factors that can make the same person desire to seek friends and acquaintances at one time and not to feel this desire at other times. In other words, affiliation need varies as a state as well as a trait.

For example, if someone has just entered a new school or moved to a new city, he or she is very likely to want to meet people and form some friendships. Someone who is well established in an interpersonal setting has less need to seek new relationships. Likewise, with respect to the opposite sex, someone who is deeply involved with a partner is less likely to respond to a potential new love object than someone who has no close attachment.

As an analogy, it might be helpful to think of need for affiliation in terms of a file cabinet. Differences in the trait of n Aff are represented by the number of file drawers; some people need very few relationships and some need a great many. State differences are represented by the number of folders (relationships) currently stored in the file; at one time a person may have more friends than he or she can handle, while at other times the friendship file is empty.

Situational Instigation: Misery Loves Company.

One of the reasons that people want to be with one another is to talk, compare ideas, and validate their own perceptions of the world around them. You have probably noticed that when there is an important news event, unusual weather conditions, or the like, people tend to seek out others, even strangers, to comment on what happened and "compare notes."

Schachter (1959) proposed that anxiety or fear is an important determinant of affiliation. In experiments designed to test this hypothesis, subjects were informed that they would be receiving painful electric shocks. Others were led to expect only mild, nonpainful stimulation. While the apparatus was supposedly being set up, subjects could choose between spending the waiting period either alone or with other subjects. As may be seen in Figure 9-2, those who were most fearful were most likely to want to be with others; when fear was low, subjects either preferred to wait alone or did not care. Later research showed that waiting with others actually does make subjects feel less fearful (Wrightsman, 1960).

The major reason for the relation between fear and affiliation, according to Schachter, is the desire to communicate to others about one's feelings and make interpersonal comparisons. Subsequent research found, for example, that anxious people have no desire to wait with others *unless* those others also expect to receive a shock. What exactly do people do when they are together and expect something fearful to occur?. In one experi-

Figure 9-2. When subjects were afraid because they expected to receive a painful electric shock, most wanted to spend the waiting period with other people. When fear was low, most preferred to wait by themselves or had no preference. In other words, as fear level increases, need to affiliate increases also.

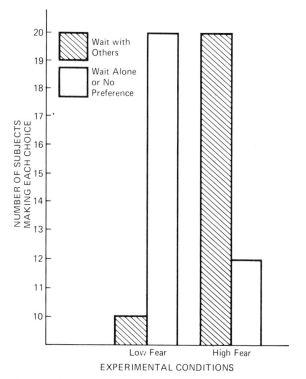

(Data from Schachter, 1959)

ment, groups of four to six college students were observed through a one-way mirror as they waited for an experiment that supposedly involved reactions to electric shock and sexual stimuli (Morris et al., 1976). Compared to subjects waiting for nonfearful experiments, these subjects interacted more and actively discussed their upcoming experience.

There are strong individual differences in the tendency to respond to fear with affiliative behavior—it holds true mainly for firstborn and only children. A plausible explanation of this difference is that a firstborn or only child has the undivided attention of parents who offer comfort when anything goes wrong; thus, these children learn to seek interpersonal help when they are hurt or afraid. Later-born children have more competition for the parents' time and have siblings who may not be sympathetic to the "crybaby."

In general, then, the research on affiliation suggests that when people are brought into contact by such factors as propinquity, they are most likely to interact if one or both is high in n Aff, if one or both currently lacks interpersonal relationships, and (especially if one or both is a firstborn or only child) if something frightening is going on at the time (Fish, Karabenick, & Heath, 1978).

Physical Attractiveness

Other determinants of attraction are various physical features to which we have learned to respond in a positive or negative way. Before we know another person or have a chance to learn much about him or her, our response to that person is often determined by such things as body build, height, weight, hair color, race, clothing style, accent, hair length, and numerous other factors that can arouse feelings in us. In addition, an unpleasant characteristic such as body odor leads others to assume that the individual has negative personality traits (unsociable, unintelligent, unattractive) and that he or she is dirty, poor, and unhealthy (McBurney, Levine, & Cavanaugh, 1977). In our culture, physical attractiveness is positively valued and influences our liking of others, however irrational this reaction may be (Dion, 1980). There is a clear belief that "beautiful is good" (Dion, Berscheid, & Walster, 1972). Not only do people seek attractive friends, but the positive effects seem to "rub off." At least for males, being seen with an attractive partner leads others to evaluate the man more favorably; it's as if "he must be good to attract a woman like that" (Sigall & Landy, 1973).

Many investigators have reported a relation between attractiveness and liking. Byrne, London, and Reeves (1968) conducted a study in which subjects responded to a stranger whose attitudes were given along with a photograph of that person. The picture had been prejudged as attractive or unattractive by another group of students. Both males and females responded to physical attractiveness; they liked an attractive stranger better than an unattractive one, regardless of sex. When there is an actual interaction between males and females, as in a computer dating situation, physical attractiveness takes on even greater importance. The more attractive the partner, the more he or she is liked (Byrne, Ervin, & Lamberth, 1970; Curran, 1973; Curran & Lippold, 1975).

Though most of the studies of physical attractiveness have focused on college students, it seems that people tend to respond more positively to attractive others than to those who are unattractive, regardless of age. Thus, very similar findings are reported with respect to the way children respond to one another (Dion, 1977; Dion & Berscheid, 1974) and in the responses of elderly people (Adams & Huston, in press).

It is interesting to note that people tend to have spouses who are similar to themselves in physical attractiveness (Cavior & Boblett, 1972; Murstein & Christy, 1976). In fact, when we see "mismatched" couples we tend to look for an explanation. For example, when college students viewed slides of supposedly married couples in which the males were unattractive and the females attractive, they assumed that the male had a high income, high occupational status, and high IQ (Bar-Tal & Saxe, 1976). It is as if there was equity in the marriage because the female's greater attractiveness was balanced by the male's greater financial and intellectual assets (Walster & Walster, 1978).

BECOMING FRIENDS

If the initial factors are positive, the odds are that two people will begin to interact verbally. What they say and how they say it will determine whether the relationship continues toward a deeper level or is ended abruptly. Sometimes, for example, a person can try *too* hard. When a couple converse for the first time, it is found that males who use the female's first name repeatedly are perceived as trying to make a good impression but as phony; use of that tactic leads to less desire on the part of the female to converse with the male in the future (Kleinke, Staneski, & Weaver, 1972). While such first impressions can be important, the most crucial aspect of such "getting-to-know-you" conversations seems to be the exchange of attitudes and beliefs.

Similarity of Attitudes

If You Think Like Me, I Will Like You.   It is commonly observed that when two people express dissimilar views about the government or about moral standards or even about the quality of a television program their interaction grows unpleasant and increasingly negative. The expression of similar views about such topics tends to lead to a pleasant and

Figure 9-3. Progressing through the beginning stages of an interpersonal relationship depends on such factors as the similarity of attitudes communicated to each other.   (Ellis Herwig, Stock, Boston)

increasingly positive interaction. Not only may such responses be observed among people who are actually interacting, but one of the parties may be physically absent and still elicit positive or negative responses; we can respond strongly to newspaper columnists or televised political candidates on the basis of whether we agree or disagree with what they say. It is very easy to arouse anger by expressing attitudes with which someone disagrees, as an insurance company in Indianapolis discovered. The firm tries to entertain passing motorists by placing a humorous message on a signboard outside its building, and one Monday the sign read, "To Be an Atheist Is a God-Given Right." By the end of the day the company had been barraged by angry phone calls, written messages, and a visit from an irate woman in an American Legion uniform; the sign was removed the next morning. Most people seem to perceive attitude similarity in the same manner as a Vancouver politician who pledged to settle disagreements about the censoring of art exhibits by setting up a committee "of open-minded people who agree with me" (*New Yorker*, August 30, 1976). Not only do we respond positively to those who agree with us, we also tend to overestimate the extent to which those around us believe as we do (Goethals, Allison, & Frost, 1979).

Long before there was a field of psychology, similar observations were made and reported by a number of people, including philosophers and novelists, in many different parts of the world. There is an ancient (perhaps 700 years b.c.) Hebrew reference to a saying, "Every fowl dwells near its kind and man near his equal."[1] Five hundred years later, Aristotle noted more specifically that friends tend to have similar attitudes.

In 1870 Sir Francis Galton published a report that included empirical data on the marriage patterns of eminent men and members of their families. He concluded that his findings "establish the existence of a tendency of [like to marry like] among intellectual men and women, and make it most probable, that the marriages of illustrious men with [equivalent] women ... are very common" (Galton, 1870, p. 375).

In subsequent decades a great many field studies were conducted following Galton's general procedure. It was soon well established that with respect to attitudes, beliefs, and values, husbands and wives were much more similar than could be expected by chance (e.g., Newcomb & Svehla, 1937; Schuster & Elderton, 1906). Other researchers (e.g., Winslow, 1937) studied pairs of friends and found that they, too, showed greater-than-chance agreement about numerous topics. These very consistent findings were extended in further research such as that of Terman and Buttenweiser (1935a, b), which showed that the greater the similarity between husband and wife, the more successful their marriage.

Cause and Effect: Similarity Leads to Attraction. A question that went unanswered in all of these studies was the direction of the relation. That is, does attitude similarity lead to attraction, friendship, and marriage or does a close personal relationship lead people to greater and greater agreement? Newcomb (1961) provided an answer to this question by measuring the attitudes of a group of transfer students before they moved to the University of Michigan to live together in co-op housing; their developing friendship patterns were studied during the following semester. Attitude similarity was found to be one of the determinants of friendship formation.

Whenever possible, scientists turn to the experimental method because there are great advantages to isolating, manipulating, and controlling the variables under study. During the 1950s a number of psychologists (e.g., Schachter, 1951; Smith, 1957) became interested in conducting experiments in which attitude similarity was manipulated and attraction measured. In each instance the evidence showed that attraction is a positive function of attitude similarity.

The move from this empirical finding toward the statement of a behavioral law was described in some detail by Byrne (1971). The initial

---

[1]This reference was kindly supplied by Paltiel Lifshitz from the Hebrew-English edition of the *Babylonian Talmud, Baba Kama* (London: Soncino Press, 1964), p. 92b).

step was to create an experimental situation in which attitude similarity could be easily manipulated, other factors in attraction could be controlled, and attraction responses could be reliably measured (Byrne, 1961b). The subjects were given an attitude scale and simply asked to express their opinions on each issue. A few weeks later each subject was given another copy of this attitude scale, already filled out. They were told that students in another class had responded to the same scale and were asked to examine each other's responses, supposedly to determine how much they could learn about one another from this information alone. The subjects actually received a scale that had been filled in by the experimenter. For half of the group, the "stranger" expressed opinions just like those of each subject on all twenty-six items; for the remaining subjects, the stranger had opposite opinions on all of the items. The response measure, the **Interpersonal Judgment Scale**, consisted of rating scales dealing with opinions about and evaluations of the stranger. Attraction could range from 2 (extreme dislike) to 14 (extreme liking).

It was found that the subjects responded more positively to a stranger with attitudes similar to their own than to one with dissimilar attitudes. A similar stranger is liked better and is evaluated as being more intelligent, better informed, more moral, and better adjusted than a dissimilar one.

Attraction and Similarity: A Low-Level Empirical Law.   To move beyond an empirical finding such as the effect of similarity on attraction, one must expand the stimulus dimension to more than two points (i.e., similar and dissimilar attitudes). A follow-up study (Byrne, 1962) created eight such stimulus conditions using seven issues and all possible combinations of agreement and disagreement. It was found that as *degree* of attitude similarity increased, attraction increased. Such a functional relation between a stimulus and a response suggests the possibility of a law.

Combining data from a series of attraction studies, Byrne and Nelson (1965) plotted the relation as shown in Figure 9-4. A straight-line function was found to yield the best description of the relation. The information shown in Figure 9-3 can be expressed by the formula $Y = 5.44X + 6.62$. That is, the attraction response (Y) of any subject toward a stranger can be predicted by multiplying 5.44 times the proportion of attitudes (X) expressed by the stranger that are similar to those of the subject, and then adding a constant of 6.62. This relation between attitude similarity and attraction is a low-level empirical law.

Though the effects of attitude similarity were first observed in real-life interactions, the laboratory findings are sometimes questioned. That is, the effect is so regular and predictable that it has been suggested that it must somehow be a mistake, something that could only occur under artificial conditions! Despite these doubts, when researchers venture beyond the

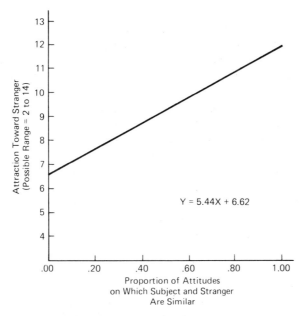

Figure 9-4. Data from several similarity–attraction experiments were combined in order to establish the functional relationship between the two variables. The result was a low-level empirical law that can be expressed by the formula Y = 5.44X + 6.62. This means that attraction responses (Y) increase in a linear fashion as the proportion of similar attitudes (X) increases. To predict the precise attraction response that a person is likely to give on the interpersonal judgment scale, multiply the proportion of similar attitudes by a constant (5.44) and then add another constant (6.62).

laboratory it is clear that attitude similarity influences attraction among males confined in a fallout shelter for ten days (Griffitt & Veitch, 1974), toward a computer date (Byrne, Ervin, & Lamberth, 1970), and between husbands and wives (Byrne, Cherry, Lamberth, & Mitchell, 1973). It may safely be concluded that people respond to attitude similarity both inside and outside the laboratory.

RESEARCH
CLOSE-UP

The Threat of Disagreement

"Reasonable men may be allowed to differ where no one can reasonably be positive."

Ideally, we would each be able to accept and live by this statement, made by Hume in the *Dialogues*. If you believe in God and I don't (or vice versa), we should be able to accept calmly the fact that we differ. If you are a Republican and I a Democrat (or vice versa), that disagreement should be equally tolerable. In fact, however, neither sort of disagreement tends to be tolerated very easily. Over and over again, research indicates that dissimilar views about these and almost every other issue, large and small, important and trivial, lead to negative emotional responses and to dislike. Why?

It has been proposed (Byrne, 1971; Byrne & Clore, 1967) that human beings have a drive to be logical, consistent, and accurate in interpreting their world—this is called the **effectance motive**. For most of our beliefs and values, there is no objective way to obtain validation. There is no way to prove, for example, that there is or is not a God or that the Republican or Democratic party offers the best solutions to our problems. How, then, do we determine whether we are being logical, consistent, and accurate? The only way is by finding out what others think. Thus, if others agree with us, it is a positive experience because the effectance motive has been satisfied. If they disagree, it is a negative experience because the effectance motive has been frustrated.

The effect of disagreement on our feelings is strong enough to elicit a physiological response. For example, Clore and Gormly (1974) found that skin conductance levels are higher during an interaction when there is disagreement than when there is agreement. In other words, just hearing a statement that disagrees with your beliefs or saying something that you know another person does not agree with results in physiological arousal. Thus, there is evidence that frustration of the effectance motive has direct and measurable effects on the autonomic nervous system.

Pursuing this idea more directly, Baugher and Gormly (1975) proposed that people would feel threatened by disagreement only if their minds were made up about the issue in question and they felt competent to discuss it. (If you know nothing about the major political movements in the Sudan, try to guess what they are, and then find that someone disagrees with you, there is little reason to feel threatened. Your effectance motive need not be aroused, because the issue is beyond your realm of competence. On the other hand, if you have a firm and well-thought-out opinion about communism, disagreement *is* threatening because it suggests that you are not logical, consistent, or accurate in making sense of the world.) The experimenters obtained the attitudes of male subjects on a variety of topics and their judgments as to how competent they were to discuss each topic. When these subjects heard another subject state his opinion on an issue, their skin conductance was raised mainly by disagreement on issues about which they felt most competent. In other words, effectance frustration occurs only when there is disagreement about something that directly involves a person's attempts to make sense of his or her world.

Affect: The Crucial Variable

According to one major theory of interpersonal attraction (Clore & Byrne, 1974), the variables that influence attraction do so because they bring about changes in a person's affective state. That is, positive or negative emotions are aroused, and it is these emotions that lead us to like or dislike another person. For example, in the research discussed so far, repeated exposure to a stranger results in more *positive feelings;* the affiliation motive is *pleasantly satisfied* when interpersonal contact is made; physical attractiveness elicits *positive affect*; and learning that another person's attitudes are similar to ours makes us *feel good*. Negative emotions are aroused by unfamiliar strangers, frustration of affiliative needs, ugliness, and dissimilar attitudes. Such positive or negative feelings become associated with other people through a simple conditioning process like that described in Chapter 7 in the discussion of anxiety. Thus, we learn to like or dislike others on the basis of the feelings they evoke in us *or* the feelings evoked by other sources when we happen to be together. Because of such "conditioning trials," another person becomes a conditioned stimulus for positive or negative affect, and we translate these feelings into positive or negative evaluations such as like or dislike. This is the reason, in theory, that a person who succeeds at a task or in a competition likes his or her teammates better than a person who fails (Blanchard, Adelman, & Cook, 1975; Lott & Lott, 1960).

Physical Comfort or Discomfort.   One of the more intriguing implications of this model of attraction is that anything that influences a person's affective state will influence his or her evaluative responses. An experiment that is important not only for the theoretical model but also for its potential applications was conducted by Griffitt (1970). He selected increased temperature and humidity as a way to arouse negative feelings. In a special laboratory at Kansas State University, temperature and humidity can be precisely controlled. Subjects were given the attitude scales of either a similar or dissimilar stranger under either normal or uncomfortable temperature conditions. As hypothesized, the subjects' feelings were quite negative in the hot condition, and attraction was negatively influenced as a result. As may be seen in Figure 9-5, the subjects respond to both attitude similarity and temperature.

Movies and Mood.   In a related test of the power of affect, Gouaux (1972) utilized movies to arouse different emotions in the viewer. Would such emotions influence how subjects reacted to a stranger? Female undergraduates were shown either a slapstick comedy, to make them feel happy, or a documentary about the death of President Kennedy, to make them feel sad. Measures of mood showed that these films were effective in bringing about the intended emotions.

The subjects then took part in what seemed to be a completely different experiment. They were shown a series of attitude responses that were supposed to be those of another student and asked to indicate how much they like that person. As usual, the greater the similarity, the greater the liking. However, the emotions induced by the movies also influenced attraction. Those who felt elated after seeing the comedy film were more

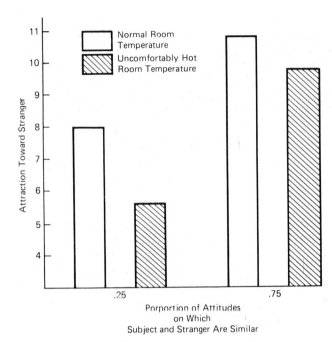

Figure 9-5. Any stimulus conditions that influence a person's affective state will have an effect on his or her attraction responses. Griffitt (1970) manipulated both attitude similarity and room temperature and found that each variable had an effect on attraction. Strangers are liked better when they express similar attitudes and when the room temperature is at a comfortable level.
(Data from Griffitt, 1970)

positive toward the stranger than those who felt depressed after seeing the documentary.

Play It Again, Sam. In our society music is almost omnipresent—on our car radios, on phonographs and tape decks, on Muzak recordings wherever we go, in movies, at concerts, and when we dance. Especially when a male and a female go out together, music in one form or another seems to be an integral part of the interaction. What effect does music have on attraction?

May and Hamilton (1977) proposed that music has a powerful effect on feelings, and our folklore supports this idea in ways ranging from romantic seranades to the mood music in a "bachelor pad," which is supposed to be essential to seduction. The experimenters tested the influence of music on interpersonal responses. First they found that rock music elicits more positive affective responses among college students than avant-garde classical music. Female subjects were asked to look at photographs of male strangers and make several ratings of them. During this procedure there was either rock or avant-garde music playing in the background, or no music at all. As shown in Figure 9-7, music had a pronounced effect on their reactions to the males in the pictures. Rock music led to the most positive responses in terms of attraction and even perceived physical attractiveness, while the avant-garde music led to the most negative ratings. In addition, there were similar findings with respect to ratings of the stran-

Figure 9-6. Any source of positive or negative mood state, including comic relief, influences our emotional reactions to those around us. (Ellis Herwig, Stock, Boston)

gers' intelligence and morality—rock in the background was linked with higher ratings. It appears that music may play an extremely important role in our interpersonal lives.

The Six O'Clock News. One influence on our emotions that is often overlooked is our knowledge of events in the world around us. We listen to our car radios or watch our TV sets and learn about murders, tax increases, kidnappings, drownings, inflation, wars, riots, terrorism, and occasionally something nice that has happened. Is it possible that our feelings, and hence our interpersonal responses, are influenced by such information?

Veitch and Griffitt (1976) proposed that good news leads to good feelings and to positive interpersonal responses while bad news has the opposite effect. The subjects were asked to spend a few minutes in a waiting room "before the experiment began." In the background there seemed to be a radio playing, but it was actually a cassette recorder that contained a five-minute broadcast of either good or bad news. For example, it was announced that local food prices were going down (good news) or that food prices would go up substantially (bad news).

At this point the experimenter returned and conducted an attitude similarity study in the usual way. It was found that the brief news broadcast was sufficient to alter the mood of the listener, and that the positive or negative feelings were strong enough to influence attraction toward a

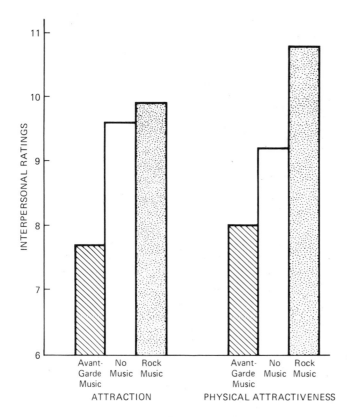

Figure 9-7. When female students rated male strangers on the basis of photographs, background music had a very strong effect on their responses. In each instance ratings were most positive when rock music was playing and most negative when avante-garde classical music was playing. (Data from May & Hamilton, 1977)

stranger. The other person was liked more if the subject had just heard good news and was liked less following a bad news announcement. Considering the fact that much of the news reported in the papers and on the air focuses on bad events, one can only wonder about the day-to-day effect of negative happenings around the world on our interpersonal relations.

Other Kinds of Similarity

It is clear that in a wide variety of situations most people tend to prefer others who express attitudes, beliefs, and values that correspond with their own (Davison & Jones, 1976). What should we expect when we examine other characteristics of individuals? There is nothing in the theory of affect and attraction that says that similarity should always be positive or dissimilarity always negative. And the general folklore of our culture contains at least some support for the idea that "opposites attract." Many investigators have proposed that with personality traits there should be a law of **complementarity**; for example, dominant people should like submissive ones and vice versa, and sadists and masochists should get along well with one another. Though there is some support for such a relation (Wagner, 1975), most attempts to establish complementarity have not been very successful (Meyer & Pepper, 1977; Nakazato, Inoue, & Tanaka, 1975). Festinger's (1954) **social comparison theory**, on the other hand, suggests that we should respond most positively to similar others on most traits. With a few scattered exceptions, research findings tend to support Festinger and to show that even with nonattitudinal traits similarity is a powerful determinant of attraction. It is even found that children like those who are similar to them in such tasks as selecting a crayon of a certain color to draw a simple picture (Thelen, Dollinger, & Roberts, 1975).

Personality Similarity.   One of the personality variables that have been studied in this way is **repression–sensitization**, a continuum of defense mechanisms varying from denial and avoidance at one extreme to intellectualization and approach at the other. Byrne, Griffitt, and Stefaniak (1967) gave a measure of defenses to a large group of subjects and some weeks later presented them with a scale that had supposedly been filled out by a stranger. The material they examined was not the stranger's attitudes but responses of "true" or "false" to such behavioral descriptions as "Once in a while I think of things too bad to talk about" and "At times I feel like picking a fist fight with someone."

It might be expected that attraction would be most positive toward strangers who gave the most socially acceptable or least neurotic responses. It was also possible that subjects would like strangers whose responses were opposite (or complementary) to those of the subject. Instead, there is a very strong and clear similarity effect. Subjects who give repressive responses themselves like repressers best, and sensitizing subjects like strangers who give sensitizing responses. In an analogous study Lombardo, Steigleder, and Feinberg (1975) found that even though subjects may describe a given personality trait in very negative terms, if they themselves possess that trait they prefer similar others.

It has also been found that different personality traits play different roles as a relationship progresses. Duck and Craig (in press) studied forty previously unacquainted subjects after they had known each other one month, three months, and eight months. Personality similarity was related to attraction, but with respect to different traits at different points in time. Certain kinds of similarity (such as values) seem to be important early in a relationship while other kinds (such as the way the person perceives the world) are important as two people get to know one another better.

Economic Similarity.   Most of us feel that it's better to be rich than to be poor. So those who are rich should be admired and liked. In contrast, one might guess that envy would operate and cause the deprived to hate those who are well off. The rich, of course, would not envy those who are poor and would have no reason to dislike anyone just because that person has less money. Byrne, Clore, and Worchel (1966) found, however, that similarity of economic status operates to determine attraction much as other characteristics do.

Economic level was determined by asking a group of Texas undergraduates to indicate their monthly spending on entertainment, miscellaneous purchases, and clothing. When they were later given similar or dissimilar economic data about strangers, it was found that the attraction of subjects who were either low or high in economic status was most positive toward a stranger of similar status and least positive toward one of dissimilar status. Subjects were also asked to state their relative preference for their own economic standing versus that of the stranger. High economic status was preferred in each case. Thus, subjects agreed that it is better to be rich than to be poor, but attraction was once again found to be greatest toward someone like oneself.

Personal Evaluations

The large amount of research on the similarity effect should not be taken to mean that similarity is the most powerful aspect of attraction. Similarity is simply one of the variables to which we respond. One of the results of discovering similarity between yourself and someone else is not only a feeling of attraction, but the tendency for one or both of you to *say* that you like the other person. Similar attitudes not only lead you to think that the person is smart, but to *express* that judgment. What effect do these evaluations have on attraction?

Attraction has been found to be most strongly affected by personal evaluations. When someone tells you that he or she likes you or can't stand you, that you are very attractive or unbelievably ugly, that you are really bright or hopelessly dull, your attraction toward that person tends to correspond closely to how positive these judgments are. We like those who like and admire us, and we dislike those who see us in a negative light. We even like someone who says positive things about *other people* better than someone who is evaluating others in a negative way (Falkes & Sears, 1980).

Flattery Will Get You Everywhere.   Byrne and Rhamey (1965) presented subjects with the attitudes of a stranger and with a series of evaluations that the stranger was supposed to have made about the subject. Both variables influenced attraction, and it was found that each evaluation had three times the effect of each attitude item. The effects of such personal evaluations last over time, and they tend to generalize to others who are "innocent bystanders" (Wyant, Lippert, Wyant, & Moring, 1977).

Evaluations also influence attraction toward groups. Bleda (1976) divided subjects into three two-person teams. It was arranged that each team would receive evaluations from one of the other teams that was either positive ("those two are very open-minded, thoughtful, likeable, etc.") or negative ("those two are very narrow-minded, thoughtless, unlikable, etc.").

There was no feedback from the third team. As expected, subjects liked the team that gave them a positive evaluation and disliked the one that gave them a negative evaluation. In addition, attraction toward the third team ("innocent bystanders") was influenced in a similar way, as a conditioning model would predict. That is, the second team gave evaluations that caused the first team's affective state to be positive or negative. The third team said nothing, but they were present during the affect arousal. Thus, they served as conditioned stimuli for the affect aroused by the evaluations (the unconditioned stimuli).

Evaluations and Affect.   In theory, the reason personal evaluations influence attraction more strongly than attitudes is that they evoke more intense positive or negative feelings. Research indicates that this is correct: Negative evaluations result in more negative affect than dissimilar attitudes, and positive ones yield more positive affect than similar attitudes (Singh, 1974). Interestingly enough, these emotional responses influence performance on a learning task in a parallel way. As in the anxiety research described in Chapter 7, drive level is higher after a person receives evaluations than after he or she receives attitude information, as shown by performance in paired-associates learning (Davis & Lamberth, 1974).

In another experimental approach to these general phenomena, subjects were led to believe that their feelings were stronger than they actually were. As they read agreeing or disagreeing attitude statements, false feedback of their physiological functioning was provided. This feedback indicated high arousal (Piccione & Veitch, 1978). Compared to subjects who did not receive such feedback, the experimental subjects reported greater attraction in the agreeing condition and greater dislike in the disagreeing condition. Thus, both intensity of feelings and *perceived* intensity of feelings are related to intensity of attraction.

FALLING IN LOVE

In the process of friendship formation most of the variables that have been found to lead to attraction or dislike are equally important in same-sex and opposite-sex friendships. When two people are of the opposite sex, however, and form a close relationship, something different is likely to occur— **love.**[2] Only recently have psychologists begun to conduct research on this familiar yet mysterious phenomenon.

---

[2]This portion of the chapter is written as though only heterosexual couples fall in love. One reason is that the research on this topic has dealt almost exclusively with heterosexual relationships. Nevertheless, male and female homosexuals also fall in love, and it seems very likely that such relationships would be affected by the same variables in the same way as described here. Until there is an extensive research literature on gay love, however, we will necessarily concentrate on male-female interactions.

What we experience as love is an intense emotional state in which one feels an overpowering desire to be with, talk to, look at, and touch the object of one's affection. Often what seems to be love might better be labeled **passionate infatuation**. In either case, the person who falls "head-over-heels" for another person undergoes an intense and frequently unrealistic emotional reaction. Under what conditions does this state occur? For a person to cross the line between a close friendship and either romantic love or passionate infatuation, three conditions seem to be required. These are (1) belief in love, (2) an appropriate love object, and (3) emotional arousal.

Cultural Factors: It Begins with Cinderella. It has been pointed out that the concept of love is not universal. At other times and places love has been unknown. Marriage, for example, may be arranged by parents on the basis of economic and social factors. Sexual relations may be based simply on physical attraction. However, the notion of marriage and sex based on love is very much a part of our culture. Our ideas of love may be our heritage from the days of chivalry in Western Europe. Love in its purest form was felt for an unobtainable love object to whom one swore undying devotion, willingness to undergo hardships and make sacrifices, and a reverence that was clearly religious in tone. When the *Man of La Mancha* idolized Dulcinea, it was worship of an idea, an image of feminine perfection on a pedestal; the fact that she was actually a promiscuous scullery maid did not matter.

Over time, love in western culture became something that could be fulfilled sexually, and it was considered necessary (especially by females) before sexual intercouse and marriage could take place. According to Udry (1971), we begin to learn the "myth" of love from fairy tales. Cinderella is saved from her cruel living conditions because she and the prince fall in love. Sleeping Beauty is awakened from her otherwise endless nap by the kiss of another prince who is infatuated with her beauty; Snow White is awakened in the same way for the same reason. As we grow up, our stories, movies, songs, and television programs continue to tell us that the ideal is for two people to meet, fall in love, and live more or less happily ever after. From Andy Hardy to Annette Funicello and Frankie Avalon to *Love Story* and the *Goodbye Girl*, we are told and shown over and over again that love is the ultimate emotional state for a male and a female. Research suggests that the more one thinks about love in general and love for a given person, the more one reports being in love (Tesser & Paulhus, 1976). In part, the thought seems to lead to the emotional state.

The point is that we are all taught to believe in love, but we are seldom instructed as to how to identify it when it occurs. "If you have to ask, it isn't love." Thus, many people wait for the mystical experience to occur, for bells to ring and birds to sing. The outcome is either intense disappointment that this peak experience was missed *or* the conviction that the miracle *has* in fact occurred. You yourself probably fit into one of these two categories. Have you ever fallen in love? Do you expect to fall in love in the future?

Despite the widespread acceptance of the general stereotype of love, it should be noted that there are individual differences in attitudes toward love. Dion and Dion (1975) asked over 200 undergraduates to respond to a series of questionnaires that included questions about romantic love. As shown in Table 9-1, four quite different attitudes were expressed by these students. It is interesting to consider the way these attitudes could interfere with a relationship if a male and a female were mismatched with respect to their conceptions of love.

Table 9-1. Dion and Dion (1975) found that undergraduates express four quite different sets of attitudes toward love. Which of these comes closest to your own views?

Attitude Toward Love	Beliefs Associated with Attitude
Idealistic	Any previous love affair before the present one must not have been *true* love. It is not possible to love two people at the same time.
Stereotypic	True love is known at once by the two people involved. Sex destroys romantic love.
Anti-Romance	There's no room in modern marriage for the old idea of romance. Romantic love is an outmoded and unrealistic concept.
Cynical	True love doesn't last forever. Love doesn't lead to perfect happiness. Love goes out of a marriage after a few years.

Interestingly enough, there are sex differences in attitudes and beliefs about love. In a sociological study, Hobart (1958) developed a Romanticism Scale that appears in Table 9-2. You might want to take it yourself before reading any further. In a study of almost 1,000 men and women who took that scale, a significant sex difference emerged. The male average was five romanticism responses on those items, while the female average was four. How does your score compare with the way those subjects responded? In another investigation, some supporting evidence was found with respect to sex differences. When a couple begins going together regularly, more men than women say that they fall in love before the fourth date (Kanin, Davidson, & Scheck, 1970).

An Appropriate Love Object. A necessary component of love as defined by our culture is an attractive member of the opposite sex (Berscheid & Walster, 1974b). As in the fairy tales with the handsome

Table 9-2. Hobart's (1958) Romanticism Scale was designed to tap individual differences in attitudes and beliefs about love. Men are found to score slightly higher than women on this test.

On items 3,5,6,7,8,11, give yourself one point for each agree response. ____

On items 1,2,4,9,10,12 give yourself one point for each disagreement. ____

Total Score ____

Romanticism Scale

Indicate your agreement or disagreement with each item by making a check mark in the appropriate column.

	Agree	Disagree
1. Lovers ought to expect a certain amount of disillusionment after marriage.	____	____
2. True love should be suppressed in cases where its existence conflicts with the prevailing standards of morality.	____	____
3. To be truly in love is to be in love forever.	____	____
4. The sweetly feminine "clinging vine" girl cannot compare with the capable and sympathetic girl as a sweetheart.	____	____
5. As long as they at least love each other, two people should have no trouble getting along together in marriage.	____	____
6. A girl should expect her sweetheart to be chivalrous on all occasions.	____	____
7. A person should marry whomever he loves regardless of social position.		____
8. Lovers should freely confess everything of personal significance to each other.	____	____
9. Economic security should be carefully considered before selecting a marriage partner.	____	____
10. Most of us could sincerely love any one of several people equally well.	____	____
11. A lover without jealousy is hardly to be desired.	____	____
12. One should not marry against the serious advice of one's parents.	____	____

(Test items from Hobart, 1958. Copyright by The University of North Carolina Press.)

prince and the beautiful maiden (or the beautiful princess and the handsome young man (who is temporarily a frog), the ideal love situation is one in which two highly attractive people both like each other and desire each other sexually. Research with college students indicates clearly that physical attractiveness is equated with sexual attraction, desirability as a date, *and* desirability as a marriage partner (e.g., Byrne, Ervin, & Lamberth, 1970).

Belief in love and the presence of an appropriate love object may sometimes be enough to trigger the feeling of love. We speak of "love at first sight" and hear songs about responding to a stranger "across a crowded room." This stereotype of romantic love was studied by Averill and Boothroyd (1977). They asked subjects ranging in age from 18 to 54 to read the following newspaper account of a couple who fell in love: .

On Monday, Cpl. Floyd Johnson, 23, and the then Ellen Skinner, 19, total strangers, boarded a train at San Francisco and sat down across the aisle from each other. Johnson didn't cross the aisle until Wednesday, but his bride said, "I'd already made up my mind to say yes if he asked me to marry him." "We did most of the talking with our eyes," Johnson explained. Thursday the couple got off the train in Omaha with plans to be married. Because they would need to have the consent of the bride's parents if they were married in Nebraska, they crossed the river to Council Bluffs, Iowa, where they were married Friday. [Pp. 237–38]

After reading this, the subjects were asked to indicate how closely their most and least intense experiences of love conformed to that romantic ideal. Almost half reported having had an experience of that sort. Males and females did not differ in this respect, nor was age a factor in predicting whether love at first sight might occur. When asked to specify the circumstances surrounding their experience, these subjects were most likely to mention the other person's appearance and meeting that person by chance. As an example of how love is reported to feel, consider one subject's description; he said that this intense experience

left me completely enraptured with the person. Nothing else seemed to matter. She was everything I have ever hoped and looked for in another person. It was very beautiful, mystical, encompassing most of my thoughts, feelings and actions. I was extremely happy, after being lonely and forlorn, but I hadn't been looking for anyone else. I had wanted to be alone for a while, but just couldn't help myself. I fell in love with her after talking to her once. [P. 244]

Emotional Arousal: "It Must Be Love."   Though love at first sight can and does occur under a variety of conditions, Berscheid and Walster (1974a) suggest that a third element is usually present—intense emotional arousal. The basis of this suggestion is provided by Schachter (1964): All emotional states are simply a combination of physiological arousal and the label the person places on this arousal. With respect to love, aroused individuals who find themselves with an appropriate love object tend to label their emotional state "being in love." Even in a brief laboratory situation, males who are exposed to sexually arousing photographs in the presence of a female confederate perceive her as more sexual and more likable than control subjects (Istvan & Griffitt, 1978). False feedback showing arousal has the same effect. Female college students interacted with male interviewers, and half were told that their heart rates were significantly higher than those of other subjects. Compared with controls, these students were more attracted to a pleasant male interviewer and more turned off by an unpleasant one (Walsh, Meister, & Kleinke, 1977).

An interesting feature of this theoretical description is that the arousal can actually be based on any kind of excitement (sexual stimulation, fear and anxiety, joy, or whatever) and still be interpreted as love. Various studies have shown that people in an anxiety-arousing setting find themselves strongly attracted to a stranger who is present in that setting if that stranger is a member of the opposite sex (Dutton & Aron, 1974). For example, males in a laboratory experiment who thought they were going to receive a strong electric shock were more inclined to ask a female confederate for a date and had a greater desire to kiss her than was true of subjects expecting a weak shock. The same general effect was also found outside the laboratory. Males walking across a narrow, wobbly suspension bridge high above a rocky canyon were more attracted to a female experimenter (as evidenced by telephoning her later) and more sexually aroused (as evidenced by the sexual content of their TAT stories) than males walking across a wide, solid, low-lying bridge. It should be noted that such findings have also been interpreted as representing interpersonal reinforcement, in that the stranger serves to reduce the subject's fear and anxiety (Kenrick & Cialdini, 1977; Kenrick & Johnson, 1979).

For a variety of good and bad reasons, parents often feel that their son or daughter has made a terrible mistake in choosing a partner. Parents may criticize their offspring's choice, provide arguments showing that the match is unsuitable, and try to keep the lovers apart. They may try to forbid their offspring to continue the relationship. What is the outcome of these parental efforts? Driscoll, Davis, and Lipetz (1972) found that parents who try to interfere have exactly the opposite effect from that which they intend. In what was labeled the **Romeo and Juliet effect**, lovers who undergo that kind of pressure from parents actually feel closer and more in love. Perhaps the lover's reaction is due partly to the fact that the parents are increasing their level of physiological arousal (guilt, fear, resentment, etc.), which is interpreted by the couple as increased love.

It appears, then, that love is a combination of a learned set of beliefs and expectancies plus a state of physiological arousal in the presence of an appropriate partner who is sexually attractive. It may be obvious that such factors are not likely to form the basis of a lasting relationship. Is there a deeper and more meaningful sort of love?

Love as a Special Kind of Friendship

When a male and a female find that they like each other very much, have a great deal in common, enjoy being with one another, and find each other sexually desirable, it is possible for love to develop in a slower, quieter, and more lasting form than passionate infatuation.

How Do I Love Thee?   In an attempt to measure love, Rubin (1973) developed a **Love Scale** that asks each member of a couple to respond to a series of questions about his or her partner in terms of the truth of each statement. It contains items such as, "I would do almost anything for _____." In Rubin's initial research with this test at the University of Michigan, dating partners obtained mean scores of about 90. When these students were asked to estimate the probability that they would marry one another, the higher their score on the Love Scale, the higher their estimated probability of marriage. Other research has shown that scores on the Love Scale are much higher for couples who are married, engaged, or dating each other exclusively than for those who are only dating casually (Dion & Dion, 1976).

Love seems to be defined by this test as a very close and very special friendship. Is there anything about two people in love that is not true of two people who are simply dating? Rubin (1973) studied several possible correlates of love. For example, in a laboratory setting, two people who had high scores on the Love Scale made more mutual eye contact than two people whose scores were low. In addition, when others observe a couple gazing at each other a great deal, it is assumed that they are strongly attracted to one another (Kleinke, Meeker, & La Fong, 1974).

It is worth noting that a relationship may begin with passionate infatuation and grow into a more realistic and mature sort of love. As people get to know one another better, blind "love" can be transformed into feelings of deep attachment, mutual caring, and positive evaluation of each other's intelligence and judgment (Rubin, 1974). As in other phases of the acquaintance process, even the most loving relationship involves learning more and more about each other and, if all goes well, becoming better and better friends. It should be noted that the distinction between unrealistic and realistic love has been made by others. For example, Landers (1975) differentiates infatuation from love according to the criteria shown in Table 9-3.

A person who feels that he or she is in love usually believes that the feeling will always be there and that the relationship is "forever." The lack of realism in that belief is suggested by Dorothy Parker:

Oh, life is a glorious cycle of song
A medley of extemporanea
And love is a thing that can never go wrong
And I am the Queen of Rumania.

Table 9-3. Advice columnist Ann Landers (1975) makes distinctions between infatuation and love that are very similar to those emphasized by psychologists studying these phenomena.

Infatuation	Love
Occurs suddenly.	Grows slowly over time.
Feelings of uncertainty; thrilled when together and miserable when apart.	Feelings of security; warmly happy when together and calmly confident when apart.
Afraid of losing the other person so must rush into marriage or living together.	Cautious about rushing into any permanent commitment until the two people are sure of one another.
Sexual excitement is the major driving force. Lovers are not necessarily friends.	Mature friendship is the major driving force. Friends can become lovers.
Leads you to do things that you later regret.	Makes you a better person than you were before.

Sadly enough, love can turn sour or even be transformed into hate; couples break up, and marriages all too frequently end in divorce. We will now look briefly at what can happen to love.

Breakin' Up Is So Hard to Do.   Rubin's research on love included a follow-up study of the relationships after six months had passed. In this period one-sixth of the pairs had broken up. A "more intense relationship" was reported by 60 percent of the couples. On a short-term basis at least, these dating couples were more likely to grow closer than to grow apart.

In order to gain a more detailed understanding of the end of a love affair, Hill, Rubin, and Peplau (1976) undertook a two-year study of dating relationships among college students. They began with 231 couples; two years later 103 of these pairs had broken up. The others either were still dating or had become engaged or married. Those whose relationships did not last were contacted and asked the reasons for the breakup and their reactions to it.

Though more than half of the separated couples had felt that they were "in love" when the study began, it is interesting to note that those who stayed together had higher scores on the Love Scale than those who broke up. As we might expect from all of the research on similarity and attraction, the couples who broke up were less similar in a number of ways—age, degree plans, SAT scores, and physical attractiveness, than those who stayed together. The timing of the break-ups seemed to be determined in part by the beginning and end of the semester in this college population—the peak times for a relationship to end were June, September, and December. When the separated couples were asked why the relationship had ended, it was found that the breakup often had been instigated by one member of the pair: The man or the woman desired independence; one or the other became interested in someone else; or there was pressure from his or her parents. Interestingly enough, the breakup was more likely to be the woman's idea than the man's. Other factors involved both parties, as shown in Figure 9-8. Note that general boredom and differences in interests were mentioned by the majority of these subjects.

One special feature of this study involved sex differences in the emotional reaction to breaking up. Breaking up was much more traumatic for males than for females. Men were more likely to report feeling depressed, lonely, and unhappy. In interviews, men revealed that they found it very hard to believe that the other person no longer loved them and that the relationship was truly over. Women, on the other hand, were more realistic in accepting the fact that love had died and the relationship had actually ended.

Other research suggests that some of these effects are based on what appear to be striking differences between males and females in general interpersonal behavior. Wheeler and Nezlek (1977) studied the social interactions of college freshmen of each sex early in the fall semester and

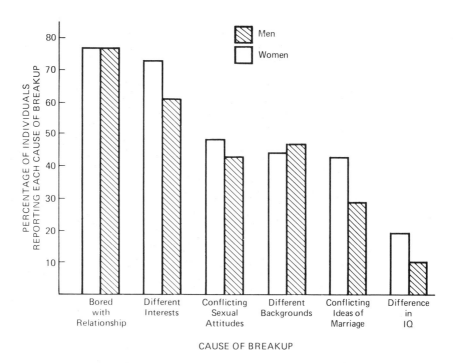

Figure 9-8. When college couples who had broken up were asked to state the reasons, men and women were in fairly good agreement. The most commonly stated causes were boredom with the relationship and the discovery that the couple had different interests.
(Data from Hill, Rubin, & Peplau, 1976)

late in the spring semester. Even with same-sex friends, females showed a marked decrease in interactions over that period. Males were much more consistent over time in interacting with friends. It seems that females react to a new and exciting situation such as college with intense socialization, and then tone down or break off the relationships when things calm down. As one female subject said,

We were all very anxious and excited that first semester and wanted to be friends with everyone. We had a lot of freedom and a lot of fun. Over the Christmas vacation, we had time to take stock of what we were doing and realized that we were spending a lot of time with people we didn't have much in common with and didn't really like. We made a conscious decision to drop these people and not spend all of our time socializing. We came back from vacation and looked for the library. [Wheeler & Nezlek, 1977, p. 751]

WAYS TO MAKE INTERPERSONAL INTERACTIONS MORE POSITIVE

Much of the research on attraction has emphasized the tendency to reject and dislike others who are different from oneself. What can we do with this knowledge to make the world a more pleasant place in which to live? One possibility is to accept the basic tendency to prefer similar others and make it operate as well as possible by selecting dates, marriage partners, and co-workers on the basis of similar attitudes, values, beliefs, personality traits, abilities, and habits. With sufficient knowledge and a good computer matching system, it might be possible to sort the world into increasingly homogeneous groups of similar and probably more harmonious people. Despite the somewhat chilling aspects of that suggestion, it actually represents a deliberate and probably more effective version of what most people ordinarily try to do. That is, we *already* tend to sort ourselves into homogeneous groups. A quite different and perhaps more difficult approach would be to determine ways to increase tolerance for dissimilarity. If there is no realistic reason for us to be threatened by and hostile toward a dissimilar idea or person, it is clearly in our best interests to find ways to neutralize or defuse that threat. How can that be done?

Open-Minded Expression of Opinions

We might begin by considering why dissimilar attitudes elicit negative affect. We seem to feel threatened and are afraid of being incorrect and made to look like fools. It is easy to recall childhood experiences in which errors in use of words or in reasoning or understanding were met with ridicule by parents, older siblings, classmates, relatives, or teachers. Think of Charlie Brown in a classroom surrounded by HA HA HA's as the other kids laugh at his mistakes. One result of such experiences is a strong tendency to try to be correct, to hold onto whatever we believe, and to say something bad about those who differ from us. Hodges and Byrne (1972) proposed that if the flavor of dogmatic certainty could be removed from the expression of attitudes, there would be less implied ridicule and rejection of those who disagree; therefore, there should be a less negative reaction to those whose attitudes seem open-minded. For example, one can express a belief in God dogmatically: "There's no doubt in my mind. There *is* a God." The same belief can be expressed in an open-minded way: "Personally, I strongly believe there is a God, but this is purely a matter of faith, rather than knowledge." The belief is the same, but there is a great difference in the implied acceptance of or tolerance for the opposite belief. In two experiments it was determined that open-minded disagreement elicited a less negative response than dogmatic disagreement. The results of both studies are summarized in Figure 9-9.

Perhaps one reason disagreement with an open-minded person is less unpleasant is that it seems possible to talk to such a person, to communicate, and perhaps even to convince him or her of one's own point of view. When Brink (1977) presented subjects with a disagreeing stranger and then allowed them to communicate a reply to this person, attraction was much higher than when no reply was possible.

Such findings raise the possibility that people could be taught to

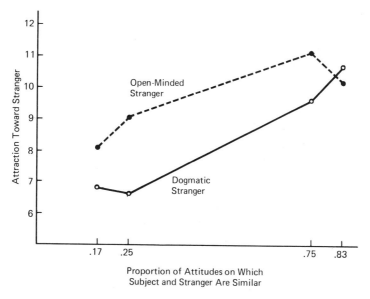

Figure 9-9. Attitudes can be expressed in either a dogmatic or an open-minded fashion. Degree of agreement has an effect on attraction in both instances, but there is a much less negative response to open-minded disagreement than to dogmatic disagreement. (Data from Hodges & Byrne, 1972)

express their views in such a way as to be less threatening and to encourage open exchanges of opinion that need not be hostile and negative. If children, for example, could be taught not to express themselves dogmatically, wouldn't their future interpersonal interactions be quite different from those that are common to most of us?

Experiencing the World as Others Do

Smith, Meadow, and Sisk (1970) conducted research in which subjects who had watched a stranger receive electric shock in a learning task were asked to indicate how painful the shock was to that person. Those who believed the stranger was similar to themselves rated the shock as more painful than did those who were told the stranger was dissimilar. Our compassion for others seems to decrease the more they differ from us. In a similar way such activities as torture, warfare, and murder appear to be facilitated when one perceives the victims as different from oneself. What if a person is induced to take the place of the potential victim and to see the world from his or her point of view? Clore and Jeffery (1972) presented a number of examples of the way in which role playing is used to induce a perception of the world from the perspective of someone else—a policeman spending a night in jail, a writer dying his skin black and traveling through the South, a teacher segregating students into "inferior" and "superior" groups on the basis of eye color. The result in each instance was an increase in empathy for others.

Physical handicaps represent something that can set a person apart from others, something that makes the person "different." It is even found that such handicaps tend to elicit negative responses, perhaps in part because the person is different from the majority (Noonan, Barry, & Davis, 1970). Clore and Jeffery asked University of Illinois undergraduates to role-play the part of a handicapped person. Some of the subjects were instructed to go across the campus in a wheelchair, have a cup of coffee at the student union, and return. This was a rather difficult task involving an uphill sidewalk, two elevator rides, several ramps and doors, and a complex procedure to obtain coffee. Many subjects found this an emotional experience, and they remarked on the way other people responded to them—glancing out of the corners of their eyes, sneaking a look at their legs, and so forth. Other subjects were placed in a vicarious role-playing group (they followed those in the wheelchairs as observers) or in a control group that had no contact with the wheelchair conditions.

Afterwards, those in the role-playing group expressed the most positive attitudes about facilities for the handicapped; those in the control group were least positive. The experimenter was in a wheelchair, and at-

Figure 9-10.   Concern about the handicapped can be increased by experiencing some of the trials they must undergo in everyday life. In general, people become more tolerant of those who differ from themselves if they are induced to view the world through their eyes.   (David S. Strickler, Monkmeyer)

traction toward this person was most positive for the role-playing subjects and least positive among the controls. A telephone survey taken four months later showed that both the role-playing and the vicarious role-playing groups were more willing to spend money on facilities for the handicapped than members of the control group. If situations could be arranged so that each of us had similar chances to experience the world from other person's perspectives, it seems very likely that interpersonal tolerance would increase.

Sharing Emotions and Interacting

In discussing affiliation need we noted the role of fear or anxiety. That is, people who are afraid tend to affiliate. Observations of a number of seemingly quite different events suggest a more general phenomenon. For example, during the "blizzard of '78" many parts of the country were more or less paralyzed for several days by heavy snow and high winds. How did these terrible conditions affect interpersonal interactions? There were many newspaper reports of people helping one another, rescuing those who were stranded in cars, providing shelter for travelers, and so forth. We saw a less dramatic example of the same kind of behavior. In West Lafayette, Indiana, the streets were piled high with snow and there was no way to obtain food except to struggle to the grocery store on foot. Three of us struck out on this surprisingly difficult walk of a couple of miles through deep drifts, dragging a sled on which to bring back our purchases. Despite the bitter cold, the physical exertion, and the unpleasant weather conditions, everyone we encountered on our trek seemed to be in a friendly, almost exhilarated mood. People spoke to strangers, made jokes, and helped one another when help was needed. It was as though the snowstorm was an occasion for a party atmosphere—the town had temporarily become a slightly bizarre amusement park.

You can read similar accounts of strangers interacting in a friendly and mutually helpful fashion during power failures in a large city; even looting tends to be done in a carefree fashion as if it were a neighborhood scavenger hunt. An oil spill in California during the Vietnam War was followed by stories of pro-war blue-collar workers and anti-war college students working happily together to clean up the beach and save the birds. There are also happy occasions such as football games, Mardi Gras festivals, and the Indianapolis 500 in which there is a widespread excited friendliness, a coming together of strangers, and a feeling of general good will. Even work can sometimes bring out these reactions. When people have to rush to meet a deadline, spending extra hours on the job and losing sleep, again a feeling of camaraderie is likely to develop; those involved feel good about the experience and positive about one another. A cast party after the opening or closing of a play is an example.

Why? What do blizzards, Mardi Gras, and an extra effort to complete a job have in common? Analysis of such situations led Byrne, Allgeier, Winslow, and Buckman (1975) to propose three crucial factors that result in unexpectedly positive interpersonal responses. First, there has to be an emotionally arousing situation, and it does not matter whether the emotion is positive or negative. Second, people have to share the emotional state; an onlooker at a disaster, for example, does not share the "we-feeling" of those who are directly affected, and tends to be resented. Third, there has to be some activity, preferably unusual activity, so that the people involved have something to do together. It was predicted that the creation of such conditions in the laboratory would lead even people who had reason to dislike one another to express interpersonal acceptance.

An unpleasant emotion was created by having subjects act out something, as in charades, in front of a video camera. A pleasant emotion was created in other subjects by having them examine a "laughing bag" that emitted the loud, hearty sound of laughter whenever it was picked up. To test the three-factor hypothesis, all combinations of emotion versus no emotion, sharing versus not sharing, and being active versus having nothing to do were compared. It was found that only when all three factors were present did interpersonal harmony result—people felt positive enough so that strangers with dissimilar attitudes were actually liked as much as strangers with similar attitudes.

In the real world, it would be to the advantage of each of us if similar interpersonal conditions could be created regularly. Without waiting for a natural disaster or the like, we might do well to find ways to arrange analogous situations on purpose. The goal is an important one: more positive interpersonal interactions and increased tolerance of the people with whom we share this planet.

SUMMARY

Attraction refers to one's evaluation of other people along a dimension that includes such attitudes as hate, dislike, indifference, liking, and love.

Some of the first studies of attraction dealt with popularity. In general, the people who are most liked are intelligent, nice to others, and well off. Dislike is associated with unpleasant interpersonal behavior. People who are shy and reserved tend to be ignored.

The initial contact in the process of becoming acquainted is often determined by propinquity. One explanation for this is that repeated exposure to others leads to more favorable attitudes toward them. The next step seems to be determined by affiliative needs. There are fairly stable individual differences in n Aff, and there are temporary situational factors that affect this motive, such as the number of relationships one already has and the threat of a frightening occurrence. There is a general tendency to respond positively to people who are physically attractive; this variable is especially important in responding to members of the opposite sex.

Once the initial steps of acquaintance have been completed, the relationship may move on toward friendship. Attitude similarity is consistently found to be an important factor, and the similarity–attraction relationship is strong enough so that it can be expressed as a low-level empirical law. Disagreement seems to be threatening and even causes a physiological reaction. In theory, this is due to our need (the *effectance motive*) to be logical, consistent, and accurate in interpreting the world. All of the variables that influence attraction are found to involve the arousal of positive and negative affect. Through conditioning, these emotions become associated with other people, and our evaluations of them are based on the affect they arouse. There is scattered evidence of a complementarity effect for a few personality traits, but most of the time we prefer others who are like ourselves in most respects, including personality and economic status. One of the most powerful influences on attraction is a personal evaluation; strong emotions are aroused by positive and negative evaluations, and attraction responses are therefore intense.

Passionate infatuation should be distinguished from a more mature loving relationship, but usually both states are interpreted as love. Unrealistic love is likely to occur if one is taught that such an emotion exists, an appropriate love-object is available (sometimes leading to love at first sight), and there is intense emotional arousal. A more realistic type of love is based on a very close friendship, sexual attraction, and mutual concern. Lovers break up when they discover that they are too dissimilar, when one partner desires greater independence, when someone else comes along, or when there is just general boredom in the relationship. Men appear to react more strongly to breaking up than women.

Suggestions for making interpersonal interactions more positive include open-minded expression of views rather than dogmatic statements, opportunities to experience the world as others do, and the creation of special circumstances in which people can share their emotional reactions while interacting. The goal is more positive reactions toward and increased tolerance for others.

SUGGESTED READINGS

BERSCHEID, E., & WALSTER, E. *Interpersonal attraction*. Reading, Mass.: Addison-Wesley, 1978. A very readable overview of research on attraction, rejection, courtship, and love.

BYRNE, D. *The attraction paradigm*. New York: Academic Press, 1971. A research monograph presenting a detailed summary of attraction studies within the framework of the reinforcement–affect model.

CLORE, G. L. *Interpersonal attraction: An overview*. Morristown, J.J.: General Learning Press, 1975. A well-written brief summary of attraction research.

DUCK, S. *The study of acquaintance.* Westmead, England: Saxon House, 1977. An excellent summary of the acquaintance process from the initial meeting to the development of love.

DUCK, S., & GILMOUR, R. (eds.) *Personal relationships.* London: Academic Press, 1980. A collection of original chapters by experts in the field. The topics include friendship, marriage, and both heterosexual and homosexual relationships.

HOBART, C. W. The incidence of romanticism during courtship. *Social Forces,* 1958, *36,* 362–367.

HUSTON, T. L. (ed.). *Foundations of interpersonal attraction.* New York: Academic Press, 1974. A collection of original chapters by some of the major investigators of attraction, affiliation, and love.

HUSTON, T. L., & LEVINGER, G. Interpersonal attraction and relationships. In M. R. Rosenzweig and L. W. Porter (eds.), *Annual review of psychology,* vol. 29. Palo Alto, Calif.: Annual Reviews, 1978. A thorough review of research on interpersonal relations ranging from first impressions to romantic and sexual partnerships.

KANIN, E. J., DAVIDSON, K. D., & SCHECK, S. R. A research note on male-female differentials in the experience of heterosexual love. *Journal of Sex Research,* 1970, *6,* 64–72.

Chapter Ten

AGGRESSION:
HATING AND HURTING

In this chapter you will read about the following topics:

Lieutenant Diandro dressed quickly as his wife busied herself in their small kitchen, preparing coffee. He was pleased with his woman—with their lovemaking and with their two young sons. As soon as his country's political unrest settled down, life would be as it should be . . . more money for everyone and better homes and schools and . . .

These thoughts reminded him of the guerrillas that plagued his land, and of his job at the Interrogation Center. He took a quiet pride in his work and in the contribution he was making to the success of the new government. When the last pockets of resistance were eliminated, everything would be for the better. Why couldn't those stupid revolutionaries see that? That last batch, now being held for questioning, was unbelievably stubborn. They wouldn't reveal the whereabouts of their leader or the source of their ammunition and other supplies. At least, they wouldn't part with such information without a good bit of persuasion. Lieutenant Diandro and others had been sent abroad for special training in encouraging reluctant prisoners to talk. Today that training would be put to good use.

In the kitchen he accepted a steaming cup of black coffee and sipped it slowly. He savored the taste and the way its odor blended with that of the flowering trees growing in the tiny yard. His wife was putting together a more substantial breakfast for the still-sleeping children. He thought with grim satisfaction of the program scheduled for the prisoners this morning. They had been kept awake all night in brightly lit cells, naked and without toilets so that they must relieve themselves like animals on the floor. According to the instructors at training school, their combined fatigue and humiliation would make them more vulnerable to the alert and crisply dressed interrogators.

Each questioning team was equipped with the necessary hardware, some as old as recorded history and some invented only recently. There were the thin, flexible riding crops for beating the soles of the feet until a man or woman was unable to stand up without screaming in pain. There were the electrodes to be attached to the genitals to deliver increasingly stronger surges of electricity whenever a prisoner refused to answer a question. Another device requiring electric power was the "grill"; the prisoner was attached spread-eagled to iron bedsprings and the current turned on. The "parrot's perch," a horizontal beam across the room, was used to suspend prisoners upside down, with all their weight pressing on the undersides of their knees. One of the newer technologies was a metal helmet that clamped around the head so that the resounding noise of the prisoner's screams echoed painfully in his or her ears. Then there were the drugs supplied by the doctors, drugs that induced painful constipation or sleeplessness. Out in the field, of course, cruder methods were necessary—beatings, violations of a man's wife or daughters, dropping one or two prisoners from a helicopter until the remaining ones decided to talk . . .

He glanced at his watch. If he didn't hurry, he would not get there by nine, when the session was to begin, and there was much work to be done. A busy day ahead. It was good to have an important role to play in building a new and better nation. He kissed his wife and walked out into the bright, sunlit street, humming softly to himself.

THE UNPLEASANT SCENES suggested by a fictional Lieutenant Diandro are, sadly enough, based on grim reality. The torture of political prisoners has been an all-too-familiar part of human history, and continues today. The small cell without food, water, or toilets is used in Guinea. The soles of the feet were beaten in Spain, (where this technique is known as the *bastinado*), and the electrified grill was an Iranian specialty. The parrot's perch is of Brazilian origin, while the drugs are popular in Russian "hospitals" for dissidents. Sexual violation of prisoners or members of their families has been widely reported in many countries, including Chile. Prisoners were dropped from helicopters in Vietnam. Pain from electric generators has been administered all over the world, from an Arkansas prison farm to British barracks in Northern Ireland. Brutal beatings are routine from South Africa to North Korea.

Torture, of course, is not the only form of aggression. By **aggression** is meant any act intended to harm or injure another person. In this chapter we will examine some of the many forms aggression takes and explore some of the possible causes of this behavior. Variables that influence aggression will be described and various ways of controlling or reducing aggression discussed.

THE MANY FACETS OF HUMAN AGGRESSION

It is obvious that aggression is a depressingly familiar aspect of human behavior. One cannot read history, keep up with current news, or even turn to fiction without learning about aggression, hostility, and cruelty. An exhibit in a New York zoo has the title, THE MOST DANGEROUS ANIMAL IN THE WORLD. It is actually a mirror, and the visitor can look at himself or herself and read the caption, "You are looking at the most dangerous animal in the world. It alone, of all the animals that ever lived, can exterminate (and has) entire species of animals. Now it has achieved the power to wipe out all life on earth, including its own." Before reading about psychological research on aggression, you might consider an overview of such behavior as part of our everyday lives.

Organized Aggression: Cooperating to Cause Harm

War: Political Aggression. War is the most organized of the human activities that are designed to harm others. For most of us, history consists largely of revolutions within nations and wars between and among them. The best-known events in a nation's past seem to be those that involve violence. List the most important happenings in American history. You might include the writing of the Constitution, the Emancipation Proclamation, or the landing of the Pilgrims at Plymouth. Even more likely is a list that includes the American Revolution, the War of 1812, the Battle of New Orleans, the Battle of the Alamo, the Civil War, Custer's Last Stand, World Wars I and II, and the wars in Korea and Vietnam. And our country is certainly not unique in our parade of internal and external battles. Political decisions have led almost all nations to the glories of uniforms, marching troops, military bands, and waving flags—and to the realities of pain, mutilation, and death. Only the details have changed as technology has transformed the tools of organized killing from crude hand weapons to nuclear devices. To pick a random "incident," consider the following attack by Cambodian troops on a Vietnamese village as reported by Hanoi radio on January 12, 1978:

> All of the houses were surrounded by Cambodian soldiers who immediately opened fire and used machetes, axes, sabers and sharpened sticks to slay the villagers . . . A fleeing child was caught by a soldier who cut off his leg and threw him into the flames. All seven members of Mrs. Truong Thi Rot's family were beheaded. Rot was disemboweled and had a seven-month fetus placed on her chest.
>
> All the eight members of Nguyen Van Tam's family were beheaded and the heads were put on a table for amusement. All eight persons in Nguyen Thi Nganh's house were disemboweled, the intestines piled in one shocking heap. Mr. Quang's wife was also disemboweled. The killers took out her five-month fetus, then cut off her breast and chopped her body in three parts. Her 2-year-old boy was torn in two and dumped into a well.

It should be pointed out that aggression, even in war, does not always involve hostile emotions or feelings of hate. The enemy *may* be despised and there *may* be righteous indignation and a desire to destroy those who are viewed as evil. There may also be fear and the demands of self-defense or the defense of one's homeland. There may also be the simple feeling that one is doing one's job and obeying orders. In modern warfare skilled technicians often deal only with advanced equipment that may be miles or even continents away from unseen targets. The resulting destruction of property and lives becomes a somewhat unreal abstraction.

Organized violence may also occur in a fashion short of full-scale revolution or war. There are terrorist groups (called "freedom fighters" if you are on their side) with political goals using such tactics as bombing, kidnapping, highjacking, and assassination. Leaders are shot down, hostages are held, buildings are occupied, and random citizens become innocent victims. During the late 1960s and early 1970s, opposition to the Vietnam War led to many anti-war demonstrations and rioting and often to violent responses from government forces. When members of the Ohio National Guard wounded ten students and killed four during a demonstration at Kent State University on May 4, 1970, the nation's sentiment ran 38 to 1 *against* the students. As one woman said, "I would rather see my sons dead, dead in their caskets, than to see them tear down the flag or insult their country like those kids at Kent" (Goodman, 1977).

It is a fairly safe, though tragic, bet that during the week in which you read this paragraph there will be more than one incident of organized aggression that you can read about in your newspaper or watch on the evening news.

Torture: The Ultimate Cruelty. Perhaps the worst example of deliberate aggression is the centuries-old use of torture to punish, intimidate, extract confessions, and obtain information from prisoners. No part of the world and no racial group can claim to be innocent of such behavior. Torture is common to communist countries, the nations of the third world, and the industrialized nations of the West. The latter countries, by and large, have had the best record in this respect in the twentieth century, but there are notable exceptions, such as Nazi Germany in the 1930s and 1940s and France in its struggle to maintain control of Algeria. As of March 1977, there were 82 nations receiving aid from the United States, and torture was routinely used in 32 of them. During the past decade torture was officially practiced in 60 nations (*Time*, August 16, 1976).

Throughout history much human effort has been devoted to devising ways to create physical and psychological pain for helpless captives. Almost always, attempts are made to justify the activity, whether for religious reasons, as in the Inquisition, or for the protection of the state. Both war and torture seem to be more acceptable if the perpetrators define themselves as the "good guys" and the enemies as both bad and not quite human.

A brief sample of such practices in four quite different parts of the world does not make pleasant reading.

THE PHILLIPINES

Stripping, sexual abuse, electric shock, and the use of "truth-serum" drugs are . . . standard procedures. Hot irons are sometimes pressed against the bare soles of a prisoner's feet; cigarettes and cigarette lighters are often used to burn genitals, mouths, and eyelids. Faces are pushed into toilet bowls; heads are held under water until victims pass out.

Perla Somonod, pregnant at the time of her arrest, was made to lie clasping a block of ice on her stomach until her baby died. [*The New York Times*, October 30, 1976]

IRAN

During the Shah's reign, [according to **Reza Baraheni**, an Iranian professor of English and literature,] not every prisoner goes through the same process, but generally this is what happens to a prisoner of the first importance. First he is beaten by several torturers at once, with sticks and clubs. If he doesn't confess, he is hanged upside down and beaten; if this doesn't work, he is raped; and if he still shows signs of resistance, he is given electric shock which turns him into a howling dog; and if he is still obstinate, his nails and sometimes all his teeth are pulled out, and in certain exceptional cases, a hot iron rod is put into one side of the face to force its way to the other side, burning the entire mouth and the tongue . . . At other times he is thrown down on his stomach on the iron bed and boiling water is pumped into his rectum by an enema. [*New York Review of Books*, October 28, 1976]

GREECE

[Under the now-deposed military dictatorship,] the most ominous sign of the new repression is the reopening of the ancient prison on Yiaros, a bleak Aegean island 75 miles from Athens that has been used as a penal colony since Roman days. The island is legendary for its monstrous rats and vipers and a unique torture: jailers tossing a naked prisoner into a sack with a frightened cat and then dumping them into the chilly waters of the Aegean. Many a Greek has borne the scars produced by that experience. [*Time*, April 29, 1974]

UGANDA

When Idi Amin was in power [a young Ugandan schoolmaster] described how one of the prisoners complained to the guards that he was hungry. The prisoner and one other were called forward by the guard and beheaded. Then the blood from the bodies was collected in a bucket and two more prisoners were ordered to butcher the corpses. The meat from the bodies was cooked over a fire.

"We were hungry, angry, and ashamed," the teacher said in his statement, "but because of the guns we had to do it. One soldier announced the food was ready and we ate shamefully." Those who vomited were kicked and beaten with rifle butts. [*New York Review of Books*, September 16, 1976]

Such examples are easy enough to find, despite the impressive efforts of Amnesty International, a human rights organization based in London. This group brings publicity to bear on offending nations in order to stop such practices and save the victims. But there is still widespread failure to observe a 1948 United Nations Declaration of Human Rights: "*No one shall be subjected to torture or to cruel, inhuman, or degrading treatment or punishment.*"

Aggression by Individuals

Despite the drama and horror of war, terrorism, and political torture, there are other forms of aggression that occur even more frequently and are perhaps more to be feared in our daily lives. We are never far from news of muggings, beatings, stabbings, and shootings, and we know that such events could involve any one of us without warning. We will examine two aspects of such aggression: murder and family violence.

Murder: A Special Problem for Americans?   H. Rap Brown once suggested that "violence is as American as cherry pie." The United States clearly holds no monopoly on aggression, but we do lead the economically advanced Western nations in the rate at which we murder one another— currently about one killing every thirty-three minutes. The extent of our problem can be seen when we compare ourselves with others. For example, Philadelphia, with 2 million citizens, has the same number of homicides as England, Scotland, and Wales combined, with 54 million citizens. In 1979, New York City set a new record in the number of people murdered with 1,733 homicides (Buder, 1980). In the course of a normal lifetime, more than one in 200 Americans can expect to be murdered (Lunde, 1975). For black males in this country, homicide is the fourth leading cause of death following cancer, heart disease, and cerebrovascular disease (*UPI*, April 25, 1980). You might be interested in the safest and the most dangerous times with respect to the probability of becoming a murder victim. In New York City, the greatest number of murders take place during December, on Fridays, and between 9 and 10 p.m.; the fewest killings occur during February, on Tuesdays, and between 9 and 10 a.m. (Buder, 1980). Aggression is sufficiently familiar in our country that American children express more hostile fantasies than children in the neighboring country of Mexico (Laosa, Lara-Tapia, & Swartz, 1974).

On any given day you can open your morning newspaper and read about such incidents as the murder of four teenage boys in their mobile home in Hollandsburg, Indiana; the killing of a policeman and four fellow workers by a furniture mover in New Rochelle, New York; the attempted murder of a sex magazine publisher in Lawrenceville, Georgia; and the shooting of a woman in the Great Smoky Mountains National Park. Murders of store clerks by robbers, shootings and stabbings among friends in bars and at neighborhood parties each weekend, and the killing of police officers on duty are so common that they are unlikely to be reported except as local news. Nationwide reporting tends to concentrate on the most unusual cases. Multiple murders seem to be special favorites, especially if a colorful name can be attached. As this is being written, for example, the admitted Son of Sam is in jail in New York while the Trash Bag Killer has confessed in Los Angeles. Still at large and finding victims are the Georgia Strangler and Wichita's BTK ("bind, torture, kill") Strangler. Efforts to create personality profiles of such murderers have not been successful, and often it appears that people who are otherwise quite ordinary are the ones who become mass killers (Campbell, 1976).

Though it is easy to assume that such a dismal picture is something new in the world, violent crimes have characterized much of our history. In 1751, a London magistrate wrote the following:

The innocent are put in terror, affronted and alarmed with threats and execrations, endangered with loaded pistols, beat with bludgeons and hacked with cutlasses, of which loss of health, of limbs, and often of life, is the consequence, and all this without any respect to age or dignity or sex (Hughes, 1979, p. 3).

Secret Aggression: Violence in the Family.   In recent years it has gradually become known that the American family is all too often the scene of violent acts against wives, against children, among siblings, against parents, and sometimes against husbands (Steinmetz, 1977; Walker, 1979). According to testimony before a House subcommittee in 1978, more than 1.8 million wives are beaten by their husbands each year. This adds up to about 28,000,000 wives who have been physically abused by their husbands, according to data gathered by Roger Langley and Richard Levy (*Playboy*, July 1978, p. 242). The same investigators estimate that about 12,000,000 men have been beaten by their wives. During the past year about one million children suffered from abuse and neglect, and 2,000 of them died as a result (National Committee for Prevention of Child Abuse, 1978). Among children aged 3 to 17, 1.2 million are attacked by their parents with a lethal weapon at some point in their young lives. Almost twice that many are attacked by a brother or sister using a knife or gun. It should be noted in connection with the high American murder rate discussed earlier that in over 20 percent of the cases the killer is related to the

Figure 10-1. Battered wives are increasingly the victims of violence within the family. (Bettye Lane, Photo Researchers)

victim (Boudouris, 1971). A disturbing finding is that such behavior is showing a steady increase. There were 280 cases of violent child abuse per million population in 1972, 348 in 1973, and 380 in 1974, according to the National Center for the Prevention and Treatment of Child Abuse and Neglect.

In general, family members do not complain to outsiders, and any bruises or injuries tend to be ascribed to "accidents" (Bell, 1977). Neighbors and relatives may suspect what is going on but can do nothing about it as long as the family raises a wall of silence. Often police are called; they try to stop a husband from beating his wife; and at that point both parties become angry at the outsiders for "interfering." It is reported that 25 percent of the police officers killed in the line of duty and 40 percent of police injuries occur when police intervene in disputes between family members or friends (Bard & Zacker, 1976).

Though battered wives are a matter of increasing concern, small children present an even more tragic and heart-rending problem. Besides the tragedy of a helpless, abused child, such treatment has a long-term effect as well. Abused children are likely to grow up as violent, abusive adults (Restak, 1979). Even in a controlled laboratory situation mothers who experience stress respond by becoming more punitive toward their children (Passman & Mulhern, 1977). In the privacy of the home, the actions against a helpless child can be much more aggressive. Children have no way of knowing how to seek help. Usually people outside the family become aware of the problem only if the abuse is great enough to require medical treatment or the child dies. One such case, which occurred in Cleveland, Tennessee, in 1976, provides an extreme example of abusive behavior:

A four-year-old girl named Melisha had difficulty sleeping on Monday night and wet her bed. This angered her stepfather, who forced the girl to lie on a cold floor without covers, wearing her urine-soaked clothing. The next morning, the stepfather decided to "get the stiffness and laziness out of her." She was forced to walk from the bedroom to the kitchen and back, over and over again; she received a slap each time she passed her tormenter. The man then forced her to swallow a tablespoon of hot sauce; after she vomited, the walking was resumed. Beginning to slow down after two hours of this treatment, she was made to speed up, being told to trot on her toes. After stopping for the family meal, the stepfather then beat the girl's feet with a stick, fed her more hot sauce, and the walking was begun again; this time he struck her with the stick each time she passed. Finally, the child was allowed to go to bed—by the following morning, she was dead.

When one considers the horror of such scenes, it is clear that we *must* seek the causes of aggressive behavior and discover ways to prevent it. It may be that war, torture, murder, and child abuse are very different phenomena that have different causes and will require different means of prevention. The research on aggression, to which we now turn, tends to assume that all aggressive acts have something in common—the desire of one person to harm another.

WHY DO HUMAN BEINGS AGGRESS?

There is a widespread belief that human beings are aggressive by nature, that we are only partly civilized descendants of a "killer ape." This idea was first proposed by a South African anatomist, Raymond Dart, and was popularized in Robert Ardrey's *African Genesis*. In a strange way the idea seems to be a comforting one—we can't help being aggressive because violence is part of our nature (Rensberger, 1977). However, modern research on the behavior of primates and archaeological evidence concerning the behavior of early human beings simply do not support such notions. Even more dramatic evidence that our genes do not compel us toward violence has been provided by anthropologists. The most recent example is the discovery of a primitive group, the Tasaday, hidden away in the mountain jungles of Mindanao (Nance, 1975). These gentle people have no weapons and lead seemingly happy lives filled with love and affection. Their language contains no words for "bad," "enemy," "war," or "kill." These and other peaceful societies in various parts of the world suggest that aggression must be explained on the basis of external rather than internal causes.

Genetic Factors: The Criminal Mind and the XYY Male

Even though *all* human beings may not be aggressive by nature, perhaps *some* of us have a genetic heritage that makes us violence-prone. That idea, too, is an old one, dating back to the nineteenth-century Italian criminologist Caesare Lombroso, who wrote of the "criminal mind." Recently, psychiatrist Samuel Yochelson and psychologist Stanton Samenow have concluded after a fourteen-year study that there really *is* a criminal personality, that hard-core criminals are inherently different from other people (Holden, 1978). Though this proposal runs contrary to what most psychologists believe about aggression, those authors suggest that violent behavior is observable from earliest childhood, when aggressive individuals can be seen to reject their parents' love and respond to the world with anger and antisocial activities.

Others report that such childhood behaviors as impulsiveness and aggressiveness can be predicted from certain physical features of the new-born infant (e.g., abnormal head circumference, ears that are not symmetrical, and a wide gap between the first and second toes). These features and the aggressive behavior could be due to genetic factors or to something that occurs during the early weeks of pregnancy (Waldrop, Bell, McLaughlin, & Halverson, 1978). If further research were to support such proposals, it would obviously have a profound effect on how society tries to deal with violent criminals.

A related line of research on the causes of extremely violent behavior has sought an explanation in specific genetic factors. It has been found that in a small percentage of the male population there is an extra male chromosome (Owen, 1972). That is, sex is determined at conception, when there is either an X chromosome from each parent (XX = female) or an X from the mother and a Y from the father (XY = male). By accident, some males (known as **XYY males**) receive an extra Y chromosome. Various studies suggest that such males are taller than average, are more aggressive, and are overrepresented among criminal populations (Jacobs, Brunton, Melville, Brittain, & McClemont, 1965).

The role of this genetic accident in various behavior problems has been noted by comparing the frequency with which it occurs in different groups. Among adult males, it is estimated that the XYY pattern occurs in one in eighty tall men. This pattern is found with a much greater frequency among juvenile delinquents (one in fourteen), mentally defective delinquent adults (one in fifteen), adult criminals (one in twelve), and the criminally insane (one in eight) (Jarvik, Klodin, & Matsuyama, 1973; Telfer, Baker, Clark, & Richardson, 1968). More recent data suggest that while XYY males do have a higher crime rate than normal XY males, the crimes are not of an aggressive nature (Witkin et al., 1976). Since there is a tendency for those with an XYY pattern to have a lower IQ, even the nonaggressive crime rate may not be different from that of normals—such men simply are not bright enough to avoid getting caught.

The Frustration-Aggression Hypothesis

For some decades the most widely known and generally accepted explanation of aggression has been the **frustration–aggression hypothesis** as proposed by Dollard, Doob, Miller, Mowrer, and Sears (1939). This proposition states that when a behavior directed toward a goal is blocked, there develops a motive to injure whomever or whatever was the source of the frustration. Miller (1941) softened this hypothesis soon afterward by saying that frustration leads to various types of behavior, aggression being only one form. For example, frustration may lead to withdrawal or depression or to constructive efforts to overcome it. Likewise, it can be argued that some extremely aggressive acts occur without any preceding frustration. An executioner, for example, may electrocute a convicted murderer without having suffered any interference with a goal-directed activity. It seems, then, that frustration does not always lead to aggression and that aggression cannot always be attributed to frustration.

A newer version of the frustration–aggression hypothesis has been proposed by Berkowitz (1969), who conceptualizes frustration as one of several possible determinants of aggression. Berkowitz suggests that a frustrating event will increase the probability of aggressive behavior. Much of the relevant research on this type of behavior has used an experimental procedure known as the **Buss aggression machine** (Buss, 1961; Hynan, Harper, Wood & Kallas, 1979). The subject is told that he and another individual (actually a confederate) will interact in a study involving the effect of punishment on learning. By means of a rigged drawing, the subject is assigned the role of teacher and the other person that of learner. The learning task is prearranged so that some responses are correct and others incorrect. The subject is supposed to respond to correct responses by giving a simple signal and to incorrect ones by giving the learner an electric shock. The latter response is the measure of aggression, in that the subject chooses to push one of a series of buttons indicating different degrees of shock. A second aggression measure is the duration of the shock—how long the subject presses the button. No shock is actually delivered to the confederate, of course.

In one test of the effect of frustration, Buss (1963) attempted to create three levels of motivation to reach a goal in different groups of subjects. The subjects were prevented from reaching the goal, and then they took part in the "learning task" involving the aggression machine. The subjects were supposed to perform as well as possible in teaching the other person. In one group a good performance was described as a sign of intelligence, in a second group as a way to win money, and in a third group as a way to raise one's grade for the course. Subjects in all three groups were frustrated because the learner did not master the task in the specified number of trials. Frustration was found to have only a weak effect on aggression in the experimental groups when compared to a control group, and the three levels of frustration did not greatly differ from one another in their effects. Thus, the results did not provide very strong support for the frustration–aggression hypothesis.

Though frustration has been found to affect aggression under specific conditions, the general conclusion is that it is not a powerful or consistent factor. One condition in which aggression is very likely to occur is when the frustrating situation takes away a person's freedom to act (Worchel, 1974). If frustration blocks the satisfaction of a very strong motive, aggression becomes more probable. For example, when children are involved in a competitive tower-building game in which only the winner will receive a prize, they respond with both verbal and physical aggression against their opponents (Rocha & Rogers, 1976). In this and other situations aggression can serve a useful function in that it is *instrumental* in removing the frustration (Thompson & Kolstoe, 1974).

Instigation: Aggression as a Response to Physical and Verbal Attacks

Though a number of variables influence aggression, as we will see shortly, it seems that the most reliable **instigation** to aggressive behavior is an attack by another person (Buss, 1961). When you are attacked you tend to aggress in a counterattack, and most other animals respond in the same way. In fact, the most potent stimulus for aggression in an animal is an unknown member of its own sex and species that comes into close physical contact with it, causing pain (Marler, 1976). Human beings seem to react in similar ways. In March 1978 an Associated Press story from New York told of a secretary who accidentally stepped on another woman's foot while waiting for a subway train. The woman reacted by pushing her onto the tracks in front of the next train that came along. Another person pulled the secretary to safety, and the aggressing woman was charged with attempted murder.

Striking back appears to be an automatic, almost involuntary response; it can even lead us to aggress against inanimate objects such as doors and hammers when they cause us pain. It is interesting to note that when an isolated animal is given a shock, it will attempt to escape from the situation. When an animal is given shock in the presence of a second animal, the two will attack one another in whatever manner is usual for their species (Ulrich, 1966).

Physical Attack: An Eye for an Eye. An experimental situation devised by Stuart Taylor and his colleagues provides a way to study reactions to attack. In the **Taylor interaction task** subjects are presented with a situation in which they believe they are competing with another subject on a reaction time problem. On each trial the slower of the two players receives an electric shock from the other, and the one giving the shock determines how strong it will be. Actually, there is no opponent and the task is rigged so that the subject will be the loser on a predetermined number of trials. As these trials progress, the subject receives stronger shocks from the "opponent." There are five shock levels that the subject may use when it is his turn to respond. The measure of aggression is the strength of the shock level selected by the subject.

This general procedure has been used to test the effects of different kinds of frustration on aggression. Though the frustration had little effect on the subjects' aggression, there was a clear effect for the level of shock received from the opponent. As the intensity increased, the subject set higher and higher levels in response. The relation between shock received and shock returned is shown in Figure 10-2.

When students are asked about their perceptions of such interactions, they don't label the behavior as aggressive (Kane, Joseph, & Tedeschi, 1976). When a person is attacked and responds by doing harm to the attacker, this is seen as justified behavior. Students express dislike of someone who is labeled as aggressive, and they avoid that label when they approve of the behavior. When the retribution is delayed, however, it is a different story. Under these conditions, the aggression is seen as premeditated and so the person responding in that way is blamed for his actions (Harvey & Enzle, 1978).

Perceived Intent.   Though aggression clearly occurs in response to attack, the intent of another person is an important determinant of one's response to that person. We may not like the pain caused by the dentist when we have a tooth filled, but we do not usually strike him or her

Figure 10-2.   When subjects are exposed to stronger and stronger levels of electric shocks from an opponent in a competitive task, they respond by counterattacking with increasingly stronger shocks. Thus, aggression is easily instigated when one person causes another to experience pain.

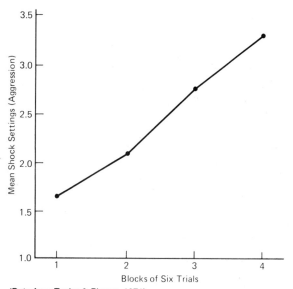

(Data from Taylor & Pisano, 1971)

whenever the drill touches a nerve ending. A much less intense pain caused by someone with harmful intent can result in an overtly aggressive response.

Using Taylor's procedure, Greenwell and Dengerink (1973) created a clever way to separate the actual physical attack from the perceived intent of the attacker. In addition to the shock received from the opponent in the interaction task, subjects were given visual feedback on each trial that supposedly showed the intensity of the shock. It was assumed that this feedback would constitute evidence of the opponent's intention to harm the subject. If intent is a powerful determinant of aggression, the subject's responses should be a function of information about intent rather than a function of the actual physical pain caused by the shock. It was found that when the information and the pain were discrepant, the subjects responded to the intent rather than to the pain caused by the electric shock.

It was concluded that while attack is an important determinant of aggression, the actual pain delivered in the attack is less important than the perceived intent of the attacker. In other words, it's not what you do to me so much as what you *mean* to do to me (Dyck & Rule, 1978).

Verbal Attack. Given the importance of language in human affairs, it is not surprising to find that verbal attacks also instigate aggressive responses. Thus, insults, threats, or comments about a person's character can arouse as much anger as a physical attack, partly because the intent is usually made quite clear by what is said. Once an insult occurs and a person labels his or her emotions as anger, aggression can be increased even more by the presence of frustration, a loud noise, or some other negative stimulus. Without the label, however, these other factors do not increase aggression.

We learned in Chapter 9 that personal evaluations have a very strong effect on attraction because they arouse intense feelings. In addition, such evaluations can function as deliberate insults. For these reasons, aggression research often utilizes such evaluations as a way to arouse anger and facilitate aggressive behavior among experimental subjects.

The effect of personal evaluations on both feelings and subsequent aggression was studied by Miller, Byrne, and Bell (1978). A subject and a confederate (supposedly a second subject) met and then wrote and exchanged self-descriptions. Each then rated the other on a series of personality traits. The ratings from the confederate were either positive (the subject was said to be intelligent, mature, likable, sincere, etc.) or negative (the subject was rated as unintelligent, immature, unlikable, insincere, etc.). Afterwards the subject had a chance to aggress against the confederate, using the Buss aggression machine.

Self-ratings of anger showed that subjects who received negative evaluations felt more anger than those receiving positive evaluations. On the aggression machine, more intense shocks were given by those receiving negative evaluations than by those receiving positive ones. Other research indicates that the person who is insulted is less aggressive if he or she must remain anonymous while getting back at the insulter—it's as if the retaliation doesn't count unless the other person knows who did it (Worchel, Arnold, & Harrison, 1978). Considering the fact that we are often evaluated by teachers, parents, employers, friends, and others, it seems likely that whenever such verbal behavior is negative it contributes to angry feelings and, potentially, to aggressive behavior.

WHAT DO YOU THINK?

Are Males More Aggressive Than Females?

Aggression seems to be one aspect of behavior in which there are clear differences between the sexes. Animal studies, sociological data, research with children and adults, and common observation attest to the greater aggressiveness of males than of females (Maccoby & Jacklin, 1974). For example, aggression is greater in boys than in girls among preschool children (Pedersen & Bell, 1970) and those in elementary school (Feshbach & Feshbach, 1969). It is also true that even one-year-old males are more independent, engage in more gross motor activity, and play more vigorously than one-year-old females (Goldberg, Godfrey, & Lewis, 1967).

Not only are males more aggressive, but they also receive more aggression from others. In the Taylor interaction task, for example, among both college students (Taylor & Epstein, 1967) and sixth-graders (Shortell & Biller, 1970) it is found that males respond with more aggression toward their opponent than females do and that opponents who are identified as females receive less punishment than opponents who are identified as males. Even females are more aggressive toward a male opponent than toward a female one. Similar results are reported when the aggression machine is used (Buss, 1966). In a real-life setting, when a female cuts in front of someone standing in line less aggression is directed toward her than toward a male doing the same thing (Harris, 1974). It is interesting to note that these sex differences in aggressiveness extend even to extremely aggressive acts such as murder:

> Men kill and are killed between four and five times more frequently than women. When a woman kills, a man is most likely to be her victim. She kills him with a butcher knife in the kitchen. If a woman is killed, her husband or "other close friend" is the murderer. He beats her to death in the bedroom. [Edmiston, 1970, p. 31]

Male–female differences could occur because aggression is a sex-typed behavior in our culture (Maccoby, 1966). That is, boys are expected to be aggressive, and to some extent they are rewarded for aggressiveness and punished for passivity. The opposite pattern is applied to girls. Females, given a choice, are more likely to aggress verbally while males tend toward physical aggression (Shope, Hedrick, & Geen, 1978). When adolescent males do aggress against their peers, this behavior does not detract from their popularity (Olweus, 1977). It is possible that in the long run cultural changes in sex roles will erase these differences between the sexes (Deaux, 1976). Even the role models have shown some changes—consider Policewoman, Wonder Woman, the Bionic Woman, and even Charlie's Angels. One bit of support for the idea that changes are taking place is the reported existence of gangs of teenage girls in England who engage in violent attacks on random victims. In a Piccadilly Circus incident a group of young women in their teens and early 20s beat and robbed a business executive, attacked another man who tried to help him, and knocked unconscious a policeman who came upon the scene. In the United States, the crime rate for women is increasing much more rapidly than the rate for men (Adler, 1975). Even in the laboratory some recent studies report no sex differences in the strength or duration of the shocks delivered to a victim (Baron & Bell, 1976).

To the extent that aggression is a learned behavior and to the extent that expectancies for males and females are becoming more similar, differences in aggressive behavior may disappear completely. What do you think? Is there a basic, built-in sex difference in aggressiveness? Is learning the key? If so, will females "catch up" to males in aggressive behavior or will males be taught to respond more like females?

LEARNING TO AGGRESS

Many experiments have been based on the idea that aggression is a learned behavior. One of the most comprehensive theoretical formulations outlining this approach has been made by Bandura (1971).

Acquiring Aggressive Responses

Albert Bandura has proposed that aggressive responses are learned in two somewhat different ways. New behavior is acquired through observational learning. That is, the aggression of others is observed, and we model our behavior on theirs. The effects of violence in television and movies may be seen as examples of this kind of modeling or imitation of aggression by others. It has even been found that the widespread publicity given to such incidents as a spectacular murder or assassination leads to an upsurge in similar crimes, presumably as a function of observational learning (Berkowitz, 1970b). Children also probably learn specific modes of physical or verbal aggression by noting how adults, peers, and older siblings respond to threat and attack. One of the reasons cultures can differ greatly in the amount and type of overt aggression they express is that they differ in the presence of various kinds of models on which behavior can be patterned.

Even in a brief interaction the presence of a nonaggressive model can serve to inhibit the amount of aggression expressed (Baron, 1971).

The other type of learning involves the possible rewards that follow an aggressive act. Aggressive behavior can be reinforcing in that it may be successful in stopping an attack on oneself, can lead to other types of satisfaction such as praise or the attainment of goal objects, and can reduce tension. One can increase the frequency and intensity of an aggressive response by simply reinforcing that response.

Therefore, Bandura views the acquisition of aggression as based on modeling (when we observe the aggression of others) and direct reinforcement (when we try out the behavior ourselves). As we have seen, the most reliable instigator of aggression is an attack or at least the perception of an attack. Once there are well-learned aggressive responses in a person's repertory of behaviors, an attack will serve to evoke such responses.

Learning Aggression from Parents.   Aggression and hostility seem to be inevitable childhood behaviors. The process of socialization (training children to become members of even a simple society) involves frustration, discomfort, and imposed constraints. The child cannot eat right away when he or she is hungry, cannot defecate or urinate whenever or wherever the urge arises, cannot do as he or she pleases with the property of others. When the child responds to such constraints with aggression, that behavior

Figure 10-3.   Aggressiveness is a highly valued masculine trait in our society.   (David S. Strickler, Monkmeyer)

also must be socialized to some extent, but the way this is done and the limits placed on aggression differ greatly across families.

A large-scale study by Sears, Maccoby, and Levin (1957) involved interviews with mothers of kindergarten children. When the mothers were asked about the amount of aggression shown by the child in the home, the replies ranged from none to highly aggressive. Presumably, the amount of aggression shown was in part a function of the way the parents responded to aggressive behavior. Two variables were studied. First, mothers differed greatly in the amount of aggression they permitted. Those who were not permissive at all believed that the behavior should not be allowed to occur under any circumstances and should be stopped the moment it begins. At the other extreme were mothers who were entirely permissive—the child has a right to hit parents or shout angrily at them; children should fight it out if they quarrel because that is a "natural" part of growing up.

The second variable studied was the severity of parental punishment for aggression. At some point even the most permissive parent stops aggression in some way (no one allows a child to maim or kill others, for example). Again, there are vast differences in what parents do. Aggression was treated by some parents with only very mild punishment and disapproval. Parents with the opposite beliefs responded with anger, hostility, beatings, and removal of privileges. What effects do these differences in permissiveness and punishment have on the aggressiveness of children?

The greatest percentage of highly aggressive children had mothers who were highly permissive about aggression and also punished it severely. The smallest percentage of highly aggressive children had mothers with the opposite pattern: they were nonpermissive about aggression and used mild punishments.

Another study of parental determinants of aggression was carried out by Bandura and Walters (1959). They interviewed a large number of adolescent boys and their parents. Half of the boys had histories of aggressive antisocial behavior; the other half were nonaggressive. The aggressive subjects had each been in trouble with the law or school authorities because of antisocial, aggressive acts. There was a clear pattern of hostility and use of punitive types of discipline in the families of the aggressive teenagers.

The effects of parental punishment on aggressive behavior have been verified in numerous studies, including research with animals. When rhesus monkeys are raised by punitive mothers, they are more aggressive toward their peers than monkeys raised by nonpunitive mothers (Arling & Harlow, 1974; Mitchell, Arling, & Moller, 1967). It seems that this aggressiveness gets worse with age, and the experimenters reported that the two most highly punished males "severely aggressed against a female cage-mate and bit off several fingers. After this incident had occurred, these males were removed from the group living cage but were mistakenly returned for one weekend, during which they killed another female" (Mitchell et al., 1967, p. 210).

The Overcontrolled Personality.   It was noted by Megargee (1966) that a great many newspaper and magazine reports of violent acts included a description of the person who committed the crime as gentle, mild, easygoing, and good natured. Relatives and friends consistently express great surprise that such a quiet person could have committed violence. A typical incident was reported by the Associated Press on November 29, 1976:

A freshman cadet at a military academy, described as "a good kid" by his minister, had been charged with killing his parents and two younger brothers while he was home for Thanksgiving . . .

A woman neighbor who asked not to be identified said the youth was "a quiet, studious kid who always was very cordial."

Megargee developed a theoretical description of these seemingly gentle people who engage in assaultive criminal acts. The **overcontrolled personality** is extremely inhibited about expressing aggression toward anyone in any situation. When such people receive instigation to aggress, they refrain from doing so. Thus, they "store up" aggression over a long period, and never learn how to express an acceptable level of aggression. The result of these two factors is that any aggression from such people is likely to be sudden, violent, and out of all proportion to whatever triggered it.

The utility of this description has been shown in a series of successful investigations. It has been found, for example, that groups of extremely assaultive delinquents are actually less aggressive and more controlled than groups of either moderately assaultive or nonassaultive delinquents (Megargee, 1966). A scale has been developed to identify overcontrolled hostility (Megargee, Cook, & Mendelsohn, 1967). It includes items like the following:

At times I feel like swearing. (False)
I do not mind being made fun of. (True)

Extremely high scores on this scale are found in groups as diverse as conscientious objectors and overcontrolled delinquents imprisoned for violent crimes (Megargee, 1969). In general, the most aggressive criminals are low on measures of hostility and high on measures of control (Dieker, 1974). In an experimental situation an overcontrolled person is found to report less anger after being frustrated and to engage in less overt aggression (Vanderbeck, 1972). This general line of research suggests that it is essential that children learn to express some degree of aggression in an appropriate manner rather than being taught to suppress all aggressive impulses. It is found, for example, that athletes are less aggressive than nonatheletes when provoked, presumably because they have learned to cope with provocation in an acceptable yet aggressive manner (Zillmann, Johnson, & Day, 1974).

Maintaining Aggressive Responses

Bandura's theory also deals with the conditions that make it likely that aggressive responses will continue to be part of a person's usual behavior. It is generally assumed that aggressive behavior will continue if it is associated with rewards. Thus, children can find that aggression brings them respect on the playground; criminals can obtain financial rewards; soldiers can become heroes; officers can win promotions; and aggressive spouses can get their own way. In addition, aggression can serve as protection against the aggression of others.

In theory, aggression will cease to occur if it is not rewarded. For example, if a person's surroundings are such that cooperation and kindness lead to social approval and material gains whereas aggression leads to disapproval and failure, one would expect less aggression and more cooperation and kindness from that person. It would seem possible that aggression could be eliminated even more effectively and quickly through punishment than through nonreinforcement, but this is probably not the case. Punishment serves both as a model for aggression and as an instigator to further aggression. Thus, aggression by parents or police or military forces may be successful in controlling the immediate overt aggression of others, but such tactics are by no means successful in decreasing the likelihood of future aggression. In fact, the result is just the opposite.

It would be expected that the reinforcement or nonreinforcement of an aggressive response would determine whether or not its strength increased. Geen and Pigg (1970) utilized the Buss aggression machine with male undergraduates. For half of them, the experimenter said "That's good" or "You're doing fine" whenever the subject gave the stranger a more intense electric shock. Half of the subjects received no verbal reinforcement for their aggressive behavior. The effect of reinforcement may be seen in Figure 10-4; the intensity of the aggressive responses increased when they were reinforced.

A second aspect of the Geen and Pigg study dealt with generalization. After the aggression task the subjects were given a word association test. After each word the subject was to write his first five associations. The stimulus words were *wash, choke, travel, walk, murder, relax, stab, sleep, torture,* and *listen.* The experimenters were interested in the number of aggressive associations given by each subject. The subjects who had been reinforced

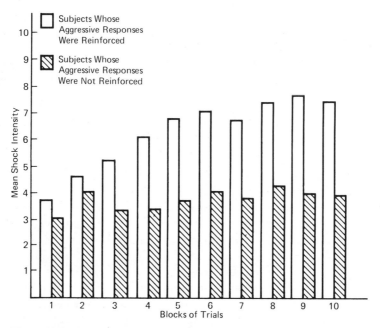

Figure 10-4. When aggressive responses on the Buss aggression machine were reinforced by such statements by the experimenter as "That's good," subjects gave stronger shocks on subsequent trials. Without such reinforcement, the level of aggression did not increase. (Data from Geen & Pigg, 1970)

for aggressing against the confederate gave more aggressive associations than the nonreinforced subjects. Thus, reinforcement not only increased physical aggression but had a similar effect on later verbal aggression as well.

Generalization also occurs in the opposite direction—from reinforced verbal aggression to later physical aggression. Gentry (1970) gave male undergraduates a projective test and reinforced half of them whenever they gave a hostile response by saying such things as "Very good." Afterwards each subject served as the teacher on the aggression machine. It was found that those whose hostile verbal responses were reinforced gave more intense shocks to the victim than those whose responses were not reinforced.

Reinforcement does not have to be direct. If a person *expects* approval for engaging in aggression, such behavior increases. For example, Borden (1975) placed male subjects in an aggression experiment with an observer. If the observer wore a jacket indicating membership in the university's karate club, subjects were more aggressive than if the jacket showed membership in a world peace organization. Even without the jacket, the presence of a male observer led to more aggression than the presence of a female one, presumably because males are generally thought to be more approving of such behavior than females.

Sexual Arousal: Increasing and Decreasing Aggression

Berkowitz (1969) proposed that general arousal contributes to aggressive behavior. For example, it would be predicted that in any situation that evoked aggression (e.g., being attacked), a high drive level (anxiety, hunger, or whatever) would lead to a more intense aggressive response. Thus, subjects who are exposed to noise are found to respond more aggressively than subjects who are not aroused in this way (Donnerstein & Wilson, 1976). Even physical exercise leads to increased aggression (Zillmann, Katcher, & Milavsky, 1972). Diener (1976) aroused subjects by having them throw rocks and bottles against a concrete wall as fast as possible; control subjects painted an ecology sign. Afterwards each subject was placed in a darkened room with another person sitting on the floor. The subjects were told that they could hit that person with foam swords or throw newspaper balls at him; the aroused subjects were much more aggressive toward the stranger than the nonaroused controls. Zillmann (1978) has conducted extensive research showing that arousal of various kinds increases later aggression *only if* the person misinterprets the arousal state as anger. One of the strangest sources of arousal that has been studied is the full moon. Lieber and Sherin (1972) found that laboratory hamsters increase their running activity soon after there is a new moon but calm down again when the moon changes phase. The murder rate among human beings (as recorded in Florida and Ohio) shows the same pattern, with an increase starting twenty-four hours after a new moon and continuing throughout the following twenty-four hours.

Sexual arousal presents special problems in this respect. It could be argued, for example, that sexual arousal should act like any other drive state and increase aggressive responses. Freud (1933), among others, emphasized more specific connections between sexual and aggressive behavior. It was proposed that aggression and sex are often blended together and that each enhances the other. An opposing contention is that sex and aggression are incompatible. For example, male mice tend to attack an intruding male quite viciously, but their response to an intruding female is to mount her sexually (Mackintosh, 1970). So rather than sexual arousal enhancing aggressive behavior, sex can function as an alternative or incompatible response and hence interfere with aggression. With respect to human subjects this might be thought of a the "make love, not war" effect. Strangely enough, research on aggression provides support for both ideas—sexual arousal both increases aggression and interferes with it.

Zillmann (1971) tested the general-arousal hypothesis by exposing male subjects to portions of a neutral, aggressive, or erotic movie (a journey through China, a violent prize fight, or a young couple engaged in intimate foreplay). After the movie the subjects performed in the teacher–learner task on the Buss aggression machine. The results may be seen in Figure 10-5. The erotic movie strongly increased the amount of aggression, even more than the aggressive movie. It was concluded that arousal of sexual feelings can intensify aggression. Other research has confirmed this relation (Jaffe, Malamuth, & Feingold, 1974; Meyer, 1972).

Support for the opposite hypothesis has been provided by Baron (1974a). Male subjects were either angered or not angered and then exposed to one of three types of pictures. Some saw erotic stimuli (nude females); others saw human stimuli that were not erotic (fully clothed females)l and still others received stimuli that were neither human nor erotic (scenery, furniture, abstract paintings). Afterwards the subjects performed the aggression machine task. Though the erotic stimuli were rated as arousing, less aggression was expressed by angry subjects who had just seen the pictures of nude or clothed females than by those who had been exposed to neutral stimuli. The mild sexual arousal seemed to counteract the effects of anger arousal. Again, subsequent research has also shown that sexual arousal reduces later aggression (Baron, 1974b; Baron & Bell, 1973; Frodi, 1977).

When several studies provide opposite findings, it is important to seek the reasons for the discrepancy. Malamuth, Feshbach and Jaffe (1977) suggest that there is a difference between hostile aggression and assertive aggression; sexual arousal is incompatible with the former but closely linked with the latter. An examination of the erotic stimuli used in the research provides a different kind of clue. The investigators who found that arousal increased aggression tended to use extremely explicit films or literary passages, while those who found the opposite effect tended to use mild, *Playboy*-type stimulus material. Donnerstein, Donnerstein, and Evans (1975) proposed that mildly erotic stimuli are distracting and take the person's attention away from any aggressive attacks they have experienced; highly erotic stimuli, on the other hand, add to their general state of arousal and serve to increase aggression. They confirmed their hypothesis by showing that exposure to *Playboy* nudes reduces aggression while explicit pictures from X-rated magazines does not. Other research using both mildly and strongly erotic stimuli has also provided evidence supporting this general idea (Baron & Bell, 1977).

Actually, erotic stimuli are found to have one of *three* effects on aggression. Mild erotica tends to inhibit aggression, quite possibly because they reduce feelings of annoyance (Zillmann & Sapolsky, 1977). Explicit erotica tend to increase aggression *or* to have no effect on such behavior. White (1980) proposes that the crucial variable is the positive or negative feelings aroused by the sexual material. He found that mild cues such as nudes and petting elicit positive feelings. More explicit pictures can arouse either very negative feelings (photos of male masturbation) or a mixture of positive and negative feelings (photos of oral sex). Aggression responses tend to be inhibited by the material that arouses positive feelings; increases in aggression occur as the level of negative feelings rises. The latter effect is called *annoyance summation* (Zillmann, Bryant, & Carveth, 1980). These experimenters found that any arousing *and* displeasing erotica (such as sex with animals or scenes of sadism) increases a person's tendency to retaliate against someone who hurts them. The two sources of unpleasant affect somehow add to one

Figure 10-5. Young television viewers intently observe lessons for life from an electric box. When the lessons involve aggression and violence the viewers model this kind of behavior. (David S. Strickler, Monkmeyer)

another to influence an aggressive response. An additional finding with disturbing implications is that males exposed to an erotic film are more aggressive toward female than toward male victims (Donnerstein & Hallam, 1978). It is now clear that the relation between sexual arousal and aggression is quite predictable and that it is much more complex than was once supposed.

FACTORS THAT INFLUENCE AGGRESSIVE BEHAVIOR

Exposure to Violence and Aggression: TV and the Movies

One topic that is guaranteed to generate strong opinions from social scientists, parents, educators, and executives in the entertainment industry is the effect of violence in movies and television on the aggressiveness of viewers. The average American child from age 2 to 11 spends over 24 hours each week watching the material shown on the family's television set (Moody, 1980). Anyone who watches TV or attends movies can observe countless aggressive acts, including beatings, knifings, shootings, and hangings. By the age of 18 the average American has watched 18,000 TV murders (*Time*, October 10, 1977). Even TV characters who are supposedly on the side of law and order are shown routinely engaging in violent and illegal acts such as beating and threatening suspects (Arons & Katsh, 1977). As technology improves, the violence we see on the screen becomes more realistic. In addition, actual violence and real blood are an almost daily feature of television news, and we are all familiar with pictures of genuine battle casualties, assassinations, and riots. What is the effect of such scenes on our behavior? What is the effect on children? Is it possible that watching violence tends to make us less aggressive (the **catharsis effect**) or does it teach us to be aggressive ourselves (the **modeling effect**)? These are hardly trivial questions, and the answer could have a major influence on future television programming and movie making as well as on the amount of real-life violence with which all of us are threatened.

Important as the questions are, the answers are not easy to obtain. Three general approaches to the study of this problem have been taken. (1) Survey studies have sought the correlation between television and movie viewing habits and aggressive behavior. (2) Experimental investigations have exposed subjects to specific scenes of violence and observed their subsequent behavior. (3) Longitudinal studies have examined viewing habits at one point in time and aggressive behavior at a later time. We will consider examples of each kind of research to see if any general conclusions can be drawn.

Aggressive Kids Watch Aggressive Shows.   Eron (1963) pointed out that although television is frequently described by editorial writers and

Figure 10-6.   It has been found that subjects exposed to an explicit erotic movie behave more aggressively afterwards than subjects exposed to either an aggressive or a neutral movie.

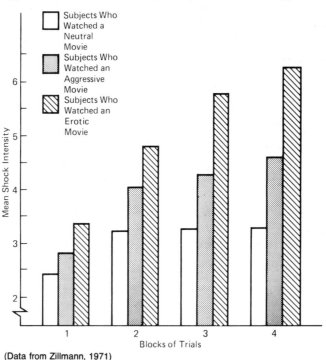

(Data from Zillmann, 1971)

others as the cause of increased rates of crime and delinquency over the past several decades, in earlier times, radios, movies, dime novels, and comic books were singled out as the cause of violence. To determine the connection between television viewing and aggression, he conducted a study involving hundreds of third-grade students in New York State. The parents of the children were interviewed to determine the frequency of TV viewing by their offspring and each child's favorite programs. Aggressiveness was measured in the schools by asking each child to rate every other child in the class.

The TV programs were rated by independent judges with respect to the amount of violence typically shown. For example, *The Lone Ranger* and *Perry Mason* were rated as nonviolent while *Have Gun—Will Travel* and *77 Sunset Strip* were judged to be violent. Viewing habits were classified with respect to the number of violent shows that were included in the child's three favorites.

For male third-graders, a strong positive relation was found between the level of violence in their favorite programs and their classroom aggressiveness as rated by their peers. This relation may be seen in Figure 10-7. It was also found that spending many hours viewing TV is not associated with aggression (the relation is actually in the opposite direction); it is the aggressive *content* of the programs watched that is the important variable.

There is a built-in weakness in this and other studies like it; there is no way to determine whether viewing violence leads to aggressive behavior, whether aggressive habits lead to a preference for violent television programs, or whether some third factor is responsible for both behaviors. To determine cause and effect, experimental research was needed.

Aggressive Shows Bring Result in Aggressive Behavior. Bandura, Ross and Ross (1963) utilized real-life, film, and cartoon models to determine the effects of viewing aggressiveness on the way children behaved afterwards. The subjects were 3- to 5-year-olds in nursery school. One group observed an adult acting aggressively; another group observed the same person in a film; and a third group watched a movie depicting an aggressive cartoon character. A control group did not see an aggressive model. The aggressive behavior of the model involved hostility toward a five-foot inflated Bobo doll—sitting on it, punching it, hitting it with a mallet, tossing it in the air, and kicking it, with appropriate words and exclamations. The children were tested for aggressive behavior in a different room after receiving a mild frustration. Among the available toys was a Bobo doll. Subjects in all three experimental groups were found to be more aggressive toward the Bobo doll than subjects in the control group. There was not much difference in the effects of the three types of models.

There was a certain amount of criticism of this experiment and others like it. The "aggressive" behavior was against a plastic toy rather

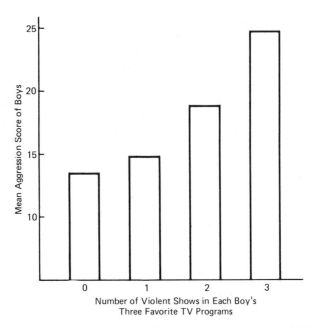

Figure 10-7. It is found that the more violent programs a child likes to watch on television, the more aggressively the child behaves. Such research can only inform us that a connection exists between TV viewing habits and aggressive behavior, not whether there is a cause-and-effect relationship.

(Data from Eron, 1963)

than another person; the stimulus was not really like ordinary TV programs with characters involved in a story; and it was possible for the aggression of the children to be just like that of the models even though such precise imitation is seldom possible with respect to what is seen on TV or in movies. In an attempt to get around such criticisms, Liebert and Baron (1972) exposed children of two different ages to a three-and-a-half-minute excerpt of violence from an actual television program, *The Untouchables*. These subjects watched a simple story involving a chase, two fist fights, two shootings, and a knifing. Other children were shown a nonviolent program, an exciting race taken from a sports show involving athletes running around a track and jumping hurdles. Right after viewing the program, the children took part in a game that was essentially a child's version of the Buss aggression machine. A subject could supposedly hurt another child by pushing the appropriate button. As may be seen in Figure 10-8, children of both sexes who had seen the violent program aggressed more against their supposed victim than those who had watched the nonviolent program.

It has recently been found that viewing aggressive shows has the greatest effect on behavior if the person is angered just *after* seeing the film (Donnerstein, Donnerstein, & Barrett, in press). Also, watching a violent

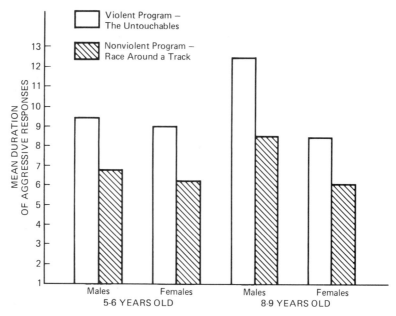

Figure 10-8. When children were exposed to a violent TV scene, they were consistently more aggressive afterwards than children exposed to a nonviolent scene involving a race. This effect was found for both males and females ranging in age from 5 to 9.
(Data from Liebert & Baron, 1972)

film such as a prize fight leads to more aggressive behavior if the viewer identifies with the winner than if he or she identifies with the loser (Perry & Perry, 1976). Still another finding is that people are angered and become more aggressive when watching violent films if there are pauses for commercials (Worchel, Hardy, & Hurley, 1976). Thus, TV violence may have a greater effect on behavior than filmed violence in a movie theater simply because there are commercials.

In research with college students, subjects were found to be more likely to attack a fellow student after exposure to a model who behaved aggressively (Diener, Dineen, Endresen, Beaman, & Fraser, 1975). Their behavior included throwing balls of paper, shooting rubber bands, shooting ping pong balls from a gun, and hitting the person with a styrofoam sword. The subjects who engaged in such aggression did so with feverish intensity, and the session had to be stopped when one subject started hitting the victim extremely hard on the ears and face.

In an experiment involving delinquent high school boys, aggressive behavior was observed and recorded before and after a week during which movies were shown each evening (Leyens, Camino, Parke, & Berkowitz, 1975). Some of the boys viewed aggressive movies such as *Bonnie and Clyde* and *The Dirty Dozen;* others saw nonaggressive films such as *Lily* and *Daddy's*

Fiancée. Those who saw the aggressive films showed an immediate increase in physical aggression and a longer-lasting increase in verbal aggression. The boys who saw the neutral movies interacted more as a consequence, and there was even some tendency for them to *decrease* their usual level of physical and verbal aggression.

Children Who Watch Aggressive Shows Become Aggressive Adolescents.

One type of study makes it possible to untangle the cause-and-effect relationship obscured in the survey studies while bypassing the argument that laboratory experiments are artificial. Eron, Lefkowitz, Huesmann, and Walter (1972) carried out a follow-up study of the third-graders studied by Eron in the survey research described earlier. The subjects were 19 years old when they were rerated by their classmates. The most important finding was that the boys' preference for violent television programs while in the third grade was related to the aggressiveness of their behavior ten years later. It was concluded that a preference for violence on TV is a cause of aggressive behavior. Television habits established by the age of 8 influenced aggressive behavior both at that age and a decade later.

Conclusion: We Are What We Watch.

If movie and TV violence leads to increased violence among viewers, why don't the producers provide something different? The usual answer is that the audience likes violence and is only getting what it wants and demands. A study by Diener and DeFour (1978) suggests that this position is simply untrue. First, they correlated the amount of violence in 62 television episodes with the Nielson ratings of those shows and found no relation; thus, violence and popularity were unrelated. Second, they conducted an experiment in which subjects viewed *Police Woman* in its original violent version or in a nonviolent cut version. The programs were liked to an equal degree; again, violence was found not to enhance audience response to a show. It would seem, then, that violence on the screen cannot be blamed on the desires of viewers. Parents can also play a crucial role in the effect of TV violence on their offspring. Children who watched a violent show with an adult who made negative comments about the violence were faster in summoning help to stop "real" violence afterward than were children who saw the same show without the adult comments (Horton & Santogrossi, 1978).

The consistent research findings across several different kinds of studies lead us to the conclusion that exposure to violence on television and in movies has both a short-range and a long-range effect on behavior (Bryan & Schwartz, 1971). Those who view violence in real life are also likely to react by behaving in the same way. Cheren (1980) reports that when the players in an athletic contest start to fight, the fans then begin fighting among themselves. Well-publicized aggressive acts also have a tremendous impact on the audience. For example, twelve years after the assassination of President Kennedy, 90 percent of a large group of American subjects could remember in great detail what they were doing, the people they were with, and where they were when they first received the news (Yarmey & Bull, 1978). It might be noted that newspaper publicity has also been found to affect behavior. For example, suicides increase as a function of how much publicity a famous person's suicide receives in newspaper stories; during the month after Marilyn Monroe killed herself, the U.S. suicide rate rose 12 percent (Phillips, 1977). In a similar way, well publicized murder-suicides are followed by a significant increase in fatal crashes of private and business-owned airplanes (Phillips, 1978). It is proposed that many of these airplane "accidents" are actually disguised murder-suicides. Part of the impact seems to come from the fact that real as opposed to fictional acts are involved. When subjects are shown a videotape of a fight, they are more aggressive afterwards if they believe it was an actual fight than if it was described as actors playing roles (Geen, 1975).

One of the more disturbing effects of viewing aggression is that the audience becomes desensitized to aggression and violence. Both children and college students who were exposed to a violent police drama were less aroused (compared to those who watched a nonviolent volleyball show) afterwards when viewing a film of real aggression (Thomas, Horton, Lippincott, & Drabman, 1977). It was also found that the more violence they normally watched on TV, the less responsive they were to real aggression.

One final point should be made. *Violence that cannot be imitated does not necessarily lead to aggressive behavior*. For example, violence by the shark in *Jaws* and similar movies does not serve as a model for the audience. And violent action like gunplay does not lead to such behavior where guns are not available (e.g., in Japan and Great Britain). When the violence *can* be imitated, exposure to such material can and does lead to acts of aggression.

Other Determinants of Aggression

It appears that aggressive feelings can be aroused quite easily. For example, customers standing in a line in a supermarket behave more aggressively toward a rude confederate when the confederate wore a sweatshirt with the words "Drop Dead" on it than when he wore a plain sweatshirt (Harris, 1977). In a quite different setting, Goldstein and Arms (1971) found that hostility increased as a function of watching the Army–Navy football game, regardless of whether the subject's preferred team won or lost. What other aspects of our surroundings increase the likelihood of aggressive responses?

Hostile Humor.   Berkowitz (1970) noted that it is sometimes proposed that when observed aggression is disguised as humor it might serve to "drain off" aggressive feelings. In part, this is the sort of reasoning used to defend television programs like *All in the Family*, in which bigoted hostility was depicted humorously. Despite such arguments, Berkowitz hypothesized that aggressive humor brings about aggressive behavior in the same way that filmed violence does.

Female students were placed in a situation in which they were supposed to evaluate another student who was applying for a dormitory job. The applicant either provoked their anger by saying something insulting, or else was bland. Afterwards the subjects listened to one of two tape recordings. Half of them heard George Carlin with a nonaggressive, humorous routine, and half listened to Don Rickles, whose routine involved insults to various members of his audience. At that point the subjects rated the job applicant. If the applicant had been insulting and the subject had been listening to Don Rickles, a great deal of hostility was expressed by the subject. It was concluded that hostile humor leads to increased aggressiveness for those who are ready to act aggressively.

Aggressive Cues.   Berkowitz (1969) has stressed the importance of aggressive cues in eliciting aggressive behavior. Such cues include any aspect of the environment that suggests aggression, such as the "Drop Dead" sweatshirt. Other research indicates that when subjects are exposed to a violent boxing film, aggression toward a stranger is greater if that person is somehow linked to that film by such cues as being identified as a college boxer (Berkowitz, 1965), having the same name as one of the actors in the film (Berkowitz & Geen, 1966), or having the same name as the film character who is the victim of aggression (Geen & Berkowitz, 1966). Even an impersonal stimulus associated with aggression (such as a flashing light) can serve as a cue and thus increase aggressive behavior (Swart & Berkowitz, 1976). It seems that whenever someone or something has been associated with aggression, that person or object acquires cue value in eliciting aggressive responses. The same phenomenon is true of other species. When a pigeon has been taught to attack in a specific enclosure, that environmental setting becomes a conditioned stimulus for the bird to attack (Looney & Dove, 1978).

Taking this idea one step further, Berkowitz and Le Page (1967) proposed that the presence of objects that have been associated with violence should facilitate aggressive behavior simply by being there. Since there are approximately 115 million privately owned guns in the United States and 65 percent of the killings in this country are committed with guns, this weapon represents an obvious cue to aggression. In an experiment male students were either angered or not angered by another person and then were given a chance to aggress against him by giving him an electric shock. When the subjects were pushing the buttons on the aggression machine, there were a .38 caliber revolver and a 12-gauge shotgun on a nearby table. Compared to control groups for which there were no objects in view or there were badminton rackets on the table, those who were angered and were in the presence of guns delivered more shock to the confederate.

Subsequent research on this phenomenon has been somewhat confusing in that the weapons effect is sometimes difficult to replicate (Buss, Booker, & Buss, 1972); weapons have even been found to inhibit aggressive behavior under certain conditions (Ellis, Weinir, & Miller, 1971). Berkowitz (1971) agrees that it is a weak effect and that other variables can interfere with it. He maintains, however, that whenever weapons are associated with aggressive ideas and feelings, they may be expected to act as aggression-eliciting cues.

Further support for this idea is provided in a field study by Turner, Layton, and Simons (1976). Males who were driving late-model cars were blocked at a signal light by an older-model pickup truck for twelve seconds after the light turned green. Horn honking was taken as an aggressive response directed toward the driver of the truck. More honking was found to occur if there was a rifle in the truck's gun rack than if there was not. The greatest amount of honking took place when there was a further cue—a bumper sticker with the word *Vengeance*. In a laboratory study it was found that aggression is increased if subjects were previously involved in a learning task involving aggressive words such as *fist, gun, punch,* and *smash* (Turner & Layton, 1976).

A Dehumanized Victim. One way to justify aggressive behavior is to decide that the victim is not quite human. In wartime, for example, enemies are almost always described as vicious, subhuman beasts who deserve whatever is done to them. As Feshbach (1971) has noted, people tend to dehumanize any target of their aggression and invent names (e.g., "pig" or "Gook") that suggest inferiority and differentness. Bandura, Underwood, and Fromson (1975) were able to create laboratory conditions in which the victims had been described in humanized terms (perceptive, understanding, etc.) or in dehumanized terms (animalistic, rotten, etc.). Compared with a control group, subjects were much more aggressive toward the dehumanized victims and much less aggressive toward the humanized ones. It appears that the way a victim is labeled plays a crucial role in the amount of aggression directed toward him or her.

Some of the same effects can result from less obvious "dehumanization," for example, when the victim is simply perceived as different from the aggressor. Members of a different race can rather easily be placed in a separate category. They are not like us, and therefore aggression toward them is somehow more acceptable. When white subjects interact with a black victim in the laboratory, aggression toward that victim is greater than toward a white victim as long as the subject has no fear of retaliation (Donnerstein, Donnerstein, Simon, & Ditrichs, 1972). Interracial aggression occurs in both directions, of course. Black subjects are found to aggress more toward white victims than toward fellow blacks (Wilson & Rogers, 1975).

It is interesting that an individual who gives someone else the orders to shock a victim sets a higher level of intensity than someone who must act directly against the victim (Gaebelein & Mander, 1978). It seems that those who are "one step removed" from the person being attacked find it easier to aggress.

As you might guess from the studies of attitude similarity and attraction, the fact that a person disagrees with the subject on a variety of topics might be grounds for aggression. Surprisingly, several early studies failed to find such an effect. One problem was that when people are insulted or physically attacked, the resulting aggression is very strong, regardless of the victim's attitudes. Kelley and Byrne (1977) reasoned that aggression *would* be greater toward a victim with dissimilar attitudes if the strength of the instigation were low enough. In an experiment using the Buss aggression machine, subjects had a chance to aggress against a similar or a dissimilar victim under conditions of no instigation, after observing someone else aggress, or after receiving very negative evaluations. As may be seen in Figure 10-9, aggression was greater toward a dissimilar victim than toward a similar victim chiefly in the no-instigation condition. That is, dissimilarity alone seemed to act as a stimulus for an aggressive response. When the attraction manipulation is strong enough (e.g., with increased contact between subject and victim), aggression is increased by attitude dissimilarity even when a strong instigation such as pain is used (Shuntich,

Figure 10-9. Aggression is greater toward a victim who expresses dissimilar attitudes than toward one who expresses similar attitudes when other instigations to aggression are not present.

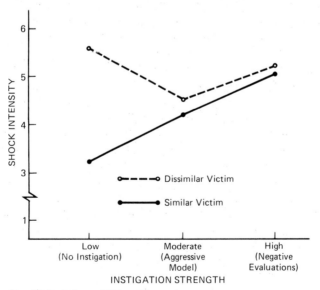

(From Kelley & Byrne, 1977, p. 35)

1976). It is interesting to note that when attitude similarity and race are included in the same study, white aggression toward blacks is greatly reduced when the black victim's attitudes are similar to those of the white subject (Donnerstein & Donnerstein, 1975).

The Curvilinear Effects of Heat.   From research on attraction we know that many external factors influence a person's affective state and that the more negative the person's feelings, the less he or she likes anyone who is present at the time. Could such feelings be negative enough to enhance aggressive behavior? We will look at one variable that has been studied with respect to both attraction and aggression: temperature.

It is obvious that very high temperatures are uncomfortable, and it was often suggested that the urban riots of the late 1960s and early 1970s were in part a result of "long hot summers." When Baron (1972a) compared the aggressive responses of subjects in a comfortably cool room (72–75° F) with those in an extremely hot room (91–95° F), he was surprised to find the reverse of what he had expected: High temperature *reduced* aggression!

When subjects were asked about their reactions to the unpleasant temperatures, they said that the room was so hot that they felt strongly motivated simply to complete the experiment and get out of there. Such clues led Baron and Bell (1976) to propose that negative affect (such as that brought about by high temperatures) might have a curvilinear influence on aggression. That is, as negative feelings increase, aggression increases—up to a point. When the feelings become intensely negative, subjects are motivated mainly to escape or avoid the unpleasant conditions, and aggression should decrease. When affect was varied from extremely positive to extremely negative levels, just such a curvilinear effect was found (Bell & Baron, 1976). This finding leads to some unusual predictions. For example, when the temperature is very hot and uncomfortable, aggression decreases; if subjects in that situation are given a cooling and refreshing drink, they feel somewhat better, and at that point aggression *increases* (Baron & Bell, 1976). In other words, going from extreme discomfort to moderate discomfort leads to increased aggression, just as the curvilinear model predicts.

One major implication of the curvilinear model is that real-life aggression should be affected in a similar way. Thus, violent acts should increase as the temperature rises and then, as the discomfort level goes even higher, should decrease. Baron and Ransberger (1978) identified 102 incidents involving collective violence in the United States between 1967 and 1971. Such violence was defined as an incident in which the setting of fires, looting, and rock throwing persisted for at least a day and required action by a law enforcement agency. Then the investigators determined the temperatures that had been recorded on those days in those locations. The

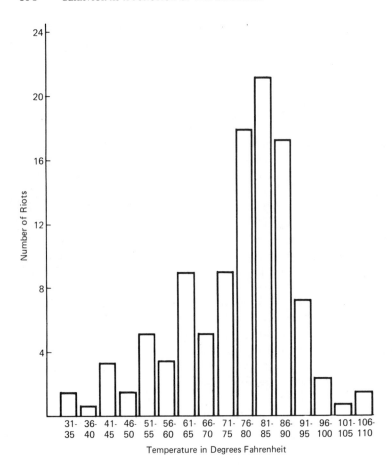

Figure 10-10. The curvilinear relation between temperature and aggression has been found with respect to both laboratory responses and real-life aggression. The number of riots in the United States between 1967 and 1971 increased with the temperature up to 81–85° F and then decreased as the temperature rose to more uncomfortable levels.

(Data from Baron & Ransberger, 1978)

results are shown in Figure 10-10. To an amazing extent, the curvilinear relation between heat and aggression established in laboratory experiments is also found with respect to actual aggressive acts such as rioting.

It should be noted that the conclusions on riots and temperature have been questioned by Carlsmith and Anderson (1979). They argue that a greater number of riots occurred in the 81° to 85° F range because there are *more* such days than there are 91° to 95° F days. When the number of days on which a given temperature occurs are taken into account, the probability of a riot was found to increase as the temperature increases. Whatever the precise nature of the relationship, it is agreed that heat leads to aggressive behavior both in the laboratory and in natural settings.

Alcohol and Marijuana.   One of the frequently observed effects of alcohol is an increase in aggressive behavior. It seems that the depressant properties of alcohol decrease feelings of anxiety and fear. Under these conditions aggression is more likely to be expressed (Tucker, 1970; Zeich-

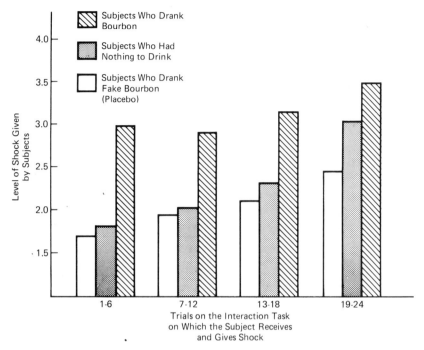

Figure 10-11. Subjects who consumed two drinks of bourbon behaved more aggressively than either control subjects who drank nothing or placebo subjects who consumed two nonalcoholic drinks disguised as bourbon.

(Data from Shuntich & Taylor, 1972)

ner & Pihl, 1979). Considerable evidence indicates that violent crimes are most often connected with the consumption of alcohol (Jones, Shainberg, & Byer, 1973).

An experimental study of this relationship was conducted with male undergraduates by Shuntich and Taylor (1972). The subjects were given either two bourbon drinks, two nonalcoholic drinks that appeared to be bourbon (a placebo), or nothing to drink (control group). Thirty minutes after drinking, the subjects performed Taylor's interaction task, in which they received shocks from an imaginary opponent and had a chance to respond by giving him shocks. It may be seen from Figure 10-11 that, as in previous studies, all subjects showed an increase in aggression over trials as the opponent gave stronger and stronger shocks, but the subjects who had consumed alcohol beforehand responded with the greatest amount of aggression at each point during the interaction.

It should be noted that alcohol leads to aggression only if the person who is drinking feels threatened or provoked (Taylor, Gammon, & Capasso, 1976). Other research has shown that a very small amount of alcohol—half an ounce—leads to less aggressive behavior (Taylor & Gam-

Figure 10-12. The effects of smoking marijuana and drinking alcohol can influence social behavior. Aggression is found to increase when alcohol is consumed and to decrease with pot.   (Mimi Forsyth, Monkmeyer)

mon, 1975). You may remember that alcohol had a similar effect on anxiety and depression—a small amount reduced these negative feelings while a large amount increased them.

In contrast to the aggression-increasing effects of alcohol, marijuana is found to have a slightly inhibiting tendency. Thus, high doses of alcohol lead to more aggression while high doses of the major active ingredient of pot lead to less aggressive responses (Taylor, Vardaris, Rawtich, Gammon, Cranston, & Lubetkin, 1976).

PREVENTING AND CONTROLLING AGGRESSION

Catharsis: Getting It Out of Your System

Freud (1920) proposed the idea of catharsis; he thought in terms of a hydraulic model in which the expression of aggression was seen as "draining the reservoir" and lowering the level of aggressive motivation. Hokanson (1970) has analyzed this hypothesis into two components: (1) Aggressive behavior will reduce subsequent overt aggression and (2) aggressive behavior will reduce the level of physical energy.

In pursuing these ideas experimentally, Hokanson and Shetler (1961) began by seeking the autonomic indicators of aggression. Subjects were harassed and insulted while they worked on an intellectual task. Blood pressure was found to increase under these conditions. When half of the subjects were given a chance to aggress against their attacker, their blood pressure quickly returned to normal; the blood pressure of the control group remained high.

This work was expanded in another experiment (Hokanson & Burgess, 1962), in which harassed subjects were found to respond with both increased blood pressure and increased heart rate. This time, several aggressive responses were compared—physical aggression (giving a shock to the attacker), verbal aggression (rating the attacker), and fantasy aggression (writing a TAT story). There was also a control group that did not have a chance to aggress in any way. Both physical and verbal aggression were found to have a cathartic effect as shown by the two physiological measures, but the fantasy and control subjects showed no decrease in physiological excitement. In general, catharsis occurs if the activity the person engages in is aggressive; nonaggressive activity may even add to the amount of aggression (Murray & Feshbach, 1978).

Konecni (1975b) has reported that the mere passage of time between instigation and the chance to aggress will reduce the amount of aggression. If people are given an absorbing activity (working on math problems) during that period, aggression is reduced even more. Even so, the chance to aggress against the person who attacked them was found to have the greatest aggression-reducing effect. In addition, Nezlek and Brehm (1975) found that just being *informed* that there would be a chance to aggress against the person who had caused pain acted to reduce the hostility felt toward that person.

It should be noted that under some conditions the chance to aggress actually leads to an *increase* in aggression (Goldstein, Davis & Herman, 1975). Thus, over a series of trials on the Buss aggression machine subjects tend to give stronger and stronger shocks. Once an aggressive act is under way, it seems to disinhibit the person and lead to an escalation of the behavior. In line with this possibility, Geen, Stonner, and Shope (1975) found that even though the chance to aggress led to a "physiological catharsis," there was still an increase in overt aggression—just the opposite of what the catharsis hypothesis would predict. On the other hand, Konecni and Ebbesen (1976) suggest that catharsis is the more usual effect of aggression; it is believed that disinhibition occurs only under very special conditions (Ebbesen, Duncan, & Konecni, 1975).

Retaliation

Is aggression inhibited by punishment or the threat of punishment? Many procedures in our society are based on this idea; examples include the way we frequently treat children, the laws dealing with crime, and belief in Hell. It is assumed that those who fear retaliation for aggressive behavior will not engage in such acts. A series of studies suggest that this general assumption may be incorrect.

In research with the Taylor interaction task, it was found that aggression was actually greater when the subject could be counterattacked on half of the trials than when a counterattack was possible on only one trial out of six (Merrick & Taylor, 1970). Such findings indicate that there is not a direct relation between retaliation and inhibition of aggression. In a more extensive study of inhibitors, Pisano and Taylor (1971) compared different strategies for their effectiveness in reducing physical aggression. On the interaction task some subjects had a passive opponent who always responded with the lowest shock level; other had a matching opponent who set the same shock level that they did; and still others had a punitive opponent who always responded with the highest shock level. Instead of punitiveness acting to stop aggression, subjects were found to respond with the greatest amount of aggression toward the highly punitive opponent. The most effective strategy for reducing aggression was matching responses; passivity yielded intermediate effects. The authors concluded that the use of punishment by the opponent proved ineffective in intimidating the subject and reducing aggression. Though later research has not always supported the effectiveness of matching as a strategy, it is clear that increasingly strong counteraggression is the *least* effective way to reduce aggression (Kimble, Fitz, & Onorad, 1977).

Threats may be more effective than actual retaliation. It is found that subjects aggress less toward someone who will later be in a position to counterattack than against someone who will not be in such a position (Bond & Dutton, 1975). Research on interracial aggression suggests that threats of retaliation may reduce direct acts of aggression but give rise to indirect forms of such behavior (Donnerstein & Donnerstein, 1976). Much more effective reduction strategies involve informing subjects of the similarity of their attitudes to those of the other person or letting them observe nonaggressive interracial interactions.

Incompatible Responses

In describing the way mildly erotic stimuli tend to inhibit aggressive behavior, it was proposed that the pleasant response aroused by such material is incompatible with aggression. In a more general way, it has been hypothesized that whenever positive feelings are aroused, they will interfere with aggressive responses.

Several studies have found that when subjects are exposed to something amusing they will aggress less than control group (Mueller & Donnerstein, 1977). For example, Baron and Ball (1974) angered subjects and then asked them to rate some stimulus material before performing the aggression task. Some rated neutral pictures of such things as furniture and scenery. Other rated cartoons—for example, the Lone Ranger is wearing a Groucho Marx mask; he turns to Tonto and says, "Next time, I'll get the mask myself." The subjects exposed to the cartoons were much less aggressive toward the victim than those who had rated neutral stimulus material.

Outside the laboratory, incompatible responses are also found to reduce aggressive behavior (Baron, 1976). At a busy intersection a confederate managed to annoy male motorists by not starting his car after the light turned green. Horn honking plus hostile gestures and verbal expressions served as indications of an aggressive response by the delayed drivers. About 90 percent of the frustrated drivers behaved aggressively in this situation. Could such a common reaction be prevented by arousing nonaggressive responses? Three different procedures were used. Just before the light turned green, a female confederate passed by. She created either empathy (bandaged leg and crutches), amusement (wearing a clown mask), or mild sexual arousal (wearing a very brief, revealing outfit). In each instance the number of drivers responding aggressively was reduced by almost 50 percent.

An important aspect of these various situations seems to be that they cause the angered person to *think about* something else. For example, Baron (in press) found that some types of sexual humor, which he labeled nonexploitive, do *not* reduce aggression; only exploitive sexual humor had that effect. Examples of the two types of cartoon are the following:

NONEXPLOITIVE: A young woman is sitting across the table from a physician. She says, "Have I had any side effects from the Pill? Only promiscuity."

EXPLOITIVE: A young woman and an executive, both partially dressed, are shown in the man's office. The young woman is beginning to put her clothes back on when the executive, speaking on the phone, turns to her and says, "Don't get dressed yet, Miss Collins . . . I'm not through hiring you!"

The two types of cartoon were rated as equally amusing. Each involved sexual themes, but only the second type interfered with aggression. Why? A follow-up study revealed that the exploitive cartoons lead people to think and fantasize about the situation much more than the nonexploitive ones do. It appears that this change in cognitive activity is crucial in interfering with subsequent aggression.

In a more general way we can learn to control our responses to a great degree by learning to think differently about ourselves and about the potential objects of our aggression. For example, in a therapeutic setting clients can be taught to focus on nonaggressive activities when they are provoked, to cope with situations in nonviolent ways, and to think about relaxing rather than arousing scenes when attacked. Thus, cognitive self-control can regulate anger (Novaco, 1976). As with other types of behavior, aggression is controlled in part by our thought processes and in part by external events.

SUMMARY

Aggression is defined as any act designed to harm or injure another person.

Human aggression is a very real and frightening aspect of our lives. In highly organized ways human beings engage in war, revolution, and terrorist activities; in addition, in a great many nations torture is routinely used to punish, intimidate, extract confessions, and obtain information. Individual aggression includes murder (with the United States "leading" the advanced Western nations in murder rate) and, increasingly, abuse and violence within families.

The suggested causes of human aggression include the idea that such behavior is part of human nature, but cross-cultural evidence argues against this. There is some indication that people may be predisposed to aggression by genetic or prenatal factors, but XYY males do not seem to be more aggressive than normal XY males. Under some conditions frustration can lead to aggression. The most reliable instigator of aggression is a physical or verbal attack, especially if the attacker is perceived as *intending* to do harm. There is a great deal of evidence that males are more aggressive than females, but there is also some evidence that females are "catching up" to males in this respect.

Most psychologists who conduct research on aggression assume that it is a learned behavior. Bandura proposes that we learn aggression responses by observing and modeling the behavior of others and through direct reinforcement of successful acts of aggression. Children are most aggressive if their mothers are very permissive toward such behavior and severely punitive. When a person learns no appropriate aggressive responses, the result can be *overcontrol*; such people may suddenly break loose with an extreme act of violence. Once aggression is learned, it is maintained by reinforcement.

The relation between sexual arousal and aggression is fairly complex; mild arousal inhibits aggression while strong arousal either has no effect or actually increases aggression. A great deal of research in the field and in the laboratory provides convincing evidence that exposure to aggression and violence (especially if it is real) in movies, on television, and even in newspapers leads to increases in aggressive behavior. Aggression is more likely to occur when a person has been exposed to hostile humor or to aggressive cues. A dehumanized victim is seen as a proper target for aggression, and even dissimilarity of race or attitudes elicits more aggression than similarity in these respects. Temperature is related to aggression in a curvilinear fashion—in both laboratory and real-life settings, aggression increases as temperature increases up to about the mid-80s and declines at higher temperatures. A very small amount of alcohol reduces aggression, but larger amounts lead to a sharp increase in aggressive behavior.

There is some evidence that engaging in an aggressive act reduces tension (the catharsis effect), but whether such behavior increases or decreases subsequent aggression varies with the situation. Retaliation is not an effective way to deter aggression, though the *threat* of retaliation sometimes works. When there are incompatible responses such as amusement, empathy, or mild sexual arousal, aggression is reduced. One of the reasons for this seems to be that people tend to think about something other than their anger.

SUGGESTED READINGS

BANDURA, A. *Aggression: A social learning analysis.* Englewood Cliffs, N.J.: Prentice-Hall, 1973. A detailed account of the causes of aggression and procedures for controlling it.

BARON, R. A. *Human aggression.* New York: Plenum, 1977. An up-to-date and very readable survey of psychological research on human aggression.

GEEN, R. G., & O'NEAL, E. C. *Perspectives on aggression.* New York: Academic Press, 1976. A collection of chapters by specialists in the field covering a variety of topics in current aggression research.

MONTAGU, A. *The nature of human aggression.* New York: Oxford University Press, 1976. An interesting anthropological presentation of the view that aggressive behavior in human beings is based entirely on learning.

MOYER, K. E. *The psychobiology of aggression.* New York: Harper & Row, 1976. A clear and concise presentation of research on the neurobiological basis of different types of aggressive behavior in animals and human beings.

NOVACO, R. W. *Anger control: The development and evaluation of an experimental treatment.* Lexington, Mass.: Lexington Books, 1975. A brief monograph describing an emotion modification program in which people can learn to regulate and control chronic anger.

ZILLMANN, D. *Hostility and aggression.* Hillsdale, N.J.: Lawrence Erlbaum, 1978. An excellent scholarly account of the major issues and findings in current research on aggression.

Chapter Eleven

SEXUALITY:

PLEASURE AND PROCREATION

In this chapter you will read about the following topics:

Daughter: *If a woman's menstrual periods are fairly regular, when is it safe to engage in sexual intercourse with contraception?*

Mother: *According to some medical authorities, the rhythm methods of contraception have a major negative side effect: unwanted pregnancy. Even when a woman's menstrual cycle seems to be fairly regular, it can be difficult to ascertain the exact date of ovulation because many factors such as illness or stress can change it. A fairly "safe" time to engage in heterosexual intercourse without contraception is during the menstrual period itself, since **ovulation** is unlikely then, and about 70 percent of American women ovulate between 11 and 15 days after the cycle has started. A less safe time is during the two weeks preceding and following the menstrual period. Finally, sperm can live in a woman's vagina for at least three days, making the risks of unwanted pregnancy even higher if intercourse occurs close to the date of ovulation.*

Daughter: *Is it harmful to engage in heterosexual intercourse during a woman's menstrual period?*

Mother: *It is not. There is even a physiological basis for suggesting that the woman's orgasm may help relieve, at least temporarily, some of the discomfort due to cramps felt by many women during the early part of their menstrual period. The **genital vasocongestion** is released during orgasm, producing a relaxation effect and possibly fewer severe cramps for a time. However, either partner's negative psychological reaction to sexual activity during the menstrual period could result in a less than enjoyable experience.*

Daughter: *After sex, I remain interested in having additional orgasms while my boyfriend would rather have a pizza. What is the reason for this sex difference?*

Mother: *A man's responsiveness to sexual stimulation is reduced after orgasm, producing a refractory period. A woman remains responsive to stimulation and thus can have more orgasms.*

Daughter: *Why would a woman have an orgasm only during masturbation or oral–genital sex, but not during heterosexual intercourse?*

Mother: *She may not be receiving adequate clitoral stimulation during sexual intercourse. Early learning experiences in which orgasm occurred during other forms of sexual activity but not during intercourse may also have produced anxiety about her performance, which further prevents her from achieving orgasmic intercourse. Thus, a woman may evaluate her behavior during sexual intercourse negatively, and the resulting anxiety can inhibit orgasm.*

Daughter: *Is it undesirable to have sexual fantasies about other partners during sexual intercourse? Is such fantasizing a sign of lack of love for or disinterest in the partner?*

Mother: *Many people have reported in studies of sexual fantasies that they use them to heighten their own sexual arousal. The use of such fantasies doesn't usually indicate negative feelings about the partner. However, some persons report that their fantasies can enliven an otherwise adequate but unexciting sexual experience.*

Daughter: *If a gay or lesbian has sexual fantasies about members of the opposite sex, does this indicate a desire to engage in a heterosexual experience?*

Mother: *It is common for people to have sexual fantasies about members of the same or the opposite sex. However, whatever the content of the fantasies, there may not be a direct correspondence between the products of imagination and the actual desires of the person having the fantasies. For example, women's fantasies about rape don't indicate a desire to be raped. There may be some correspondence between the subject matter of fantasies and matters that are of concern to the person.*

Daughter: *I find it difficult to tell my partner what I know will excite me sexually. How can I change this?*

Mother: *Communication is one of the most important elements of healthy sexuality, yet it can be one of the most elusive in practice. Telling your partner what you find sexually pleasurable can increase enjoyment for both of you, and neither of you can read the other's mind. If you cannot bring up the topic directly, perhaps indirect comparison of your partner's and your own erotic responses to different forms of stimulation might alleviate some of the embarrassment or threat that may be implied by a more direct approach. Mutual pleasuring of each other's sexually sensitive areas can also be used in this way, if each partner guides the hand of the other.*

As YOU MIGHT GUESS, a mother-daughter conversation such as this (or any other parent-child combination) is *extremely unlikely*. In most families, both the parent and the offspring would feel much too uncomfortable to communicate about sex in this way, and most parents do not have the necessary knowledge, even if communication were possible. Nevertheless, these are the kinds of things that young people (and many older people) want and need to know. These were actually some of the questions posed to the authors by members of undergraduate sexuality classes. In this chapter you will read more about the bases for these answers and recent findings in related areas. Each of these aspects of sexuality can result in inmense pleasure or great difficulty for the people involved. Psychologists currently are very much interested in the study of sexuality and have produced many intriguing findings that will be described in this chapter.

EMOTIONS AND SEXUALITY: INDIVIDUAL DIFFERENCES

Human sexuality differs from that of other animals in that humans have greater cognitive control of their sexual responses. Our emotional evaluations of sexual stimuli influence our responses to them, producing an array of differing attitudes about sexual matters in any given culture. Every aspect of sex, from prostitution and pornography to homosexuality and contraception, elicits a variety of evaluations. Because sexual functioning can result in positive and/or negative, or even neutral, outcomes, differences exist among people in their overall evaluation of sexual stimuli. These differences become reflected in individual characteristics such as personality traits and even apparent differences between males and females.

Considering sexual behavior as a reproductive act with the reinforcing by-product of release of sexual tension, one would expect that engaging in it should lead largely to positive outcomes. Sexual intercourse, for example, would help preserve the human species by leading to the conception of offspring. The pleasurable aspect of sexual activity would bolster the reward value of the behavior. However, most societies have placed restrictions on certain types of behavior, including homosexual sex, masturbation, and intercourse in various positions. This form of social control generalizes to the personal level, where beliefs about sexuality are taught as expectations regarding one's own sexual behavior. Violations of these standards have been punished by various tactics such as ostracism, hostility, or ridicule from a social group or one's parents, and internal punishment of oneself in the form of guilt. On a societal level such means actually control the usually private sexual behaviors of individuals as well as public displays of sexuality.

The connection between emotional responses to sexual stimuli and the related behavior is not a perfect one, but emotions do influence sexual behavior. For example, negative emotions become linked with a tendency to avoid situations in which stimulation and sexual activity might occur. On the basis of what is learned about sexuality in childhood and adolescence, positive or negative attitudes develop into fairly stable emotional orientations to sex. These orientations persist at least throughout early adulthood, as research on the personality traits of **erotophobia** and **sex guilt** has shown. Because of expectations about what is appropriate sexual behavior for males and femals, gender also makes a difference in one's emotional and behavioral responses to sexual urges. The sex of a person influences his or her erotic feelings, attitudes, and subsequent behavior, but research on changes in sexuality has shown that this effect is determined largely by what is learned in a given society.

Negative Emotions: Fear and Guilt

Liberalism-Conservatism.   The evaluative responses to sexual behavior are either positive or negative and lead to a general tendency to seek out or avoid sexual cues. One can accept or reject sexual information and welcome or dislike arousal, for example. A person's orientation to sexuality may be classified as **sexual liberalism** (positive) or **conservatism** (negative). Wallace and Wehmer (1972) studied sexual attitudes among Detroit residents and found a tendency to respond to sexual arousal in ways that could be predicted from their opinions about sex. These subjects looked at a series of erotic photographs and were aroused as a result of viewing them. But the two groups varied in how they labeled this arousal. The sexual conservatives considered the most arousing pictures unentertaining and offensive, while the liberals considered the same pictures very enjoyable. Thus, the general tendency to label one's arousal defensively by devaluing the source, or to enjoy both the source and the arousal, are the result of a person's orientation to sexuality.

TRY IT
YOURSELF

Positive-Negative Sexual Attitudes:
The Sexual Opinion Survey

The Sexual Opinion Survey was developed to measure evaluative responses toward sexual topics (White, Fisher, Byrne, & Kingma, 1977). It asks subjects to indicate on a seven-point scale the extent to which they agree or disagree with a set of statements concerning sexuality. You can measure your own sexual attitudes by responding to the survey. To do this, simply place an "X" in the space on the scale that describes your feelings about each statement:

1. I think it would be very entertaining to look at hard-core pornography.

I strongly agree ____ : ____ : ____ : ____ : ____ : ____ : ____ I strongly disagree

2. Pornography is obviously filthy and people should not try to describe it as anything else.

I strongly agree ____ : ____ : ____ : ____ : ____ : ____ : ____ I strongly disagree

3. Swimming in the nude with a member of the opposite sex would be an exciting experience.

I strongly agree ____ : ____ : ____ : ____ : ____ : ____ : ____ I strongly disagree

4. Masturbation can be an exciting experience.

I strongly agree ____ : ____ : ____ : ____ : ____ : ____ : ____ I strongly disagree

5. If I found out that a close friend of mine was a homosexual it would annoy me.

I strongly agree ____ : ____ : ____ : ____ : ____ : ____ : ____ I strongly disagree

6. If people thought I was interested in oral sex, I would be embarrassed.

I strongly agree ____ : ____ : ____ : ____ : ____ : ____ : ____ I strongly disagree

7. Engaging in group sex is an entertaining idea.

I strongly agree ____ : ____ : ____ : ____ : ____ : ____ : ____ I strongly disagree

8. I personally find that thinking about engaging in sexual intercourse is arousing.

I strongly agree ____ : ____ : ____ : ____ : ____ : ____ : ____ I strongly disagree

9. Seeing a pornographic movie would be sexually arousing to me.

I strongly agree ____ : ____ : ____ : ____ : ____ : ____ : ____ I strongly disagree

10. Thoughts that I may have homosexual tendencies would not worry me at all.

I strongly agree ____ : ____ : ____ : ____ : ____ : ____ : ____ I strongly disagree

11. The idea of my being physically attracted to members of the same sex is not depressing.

I strongly agree ____ : ____ : ____ : ____ : ____ : ____ : ____ I strongly disagree

12. Almost all pornographic material is nauseating.

I strongly agree ____ : ____ : ____ : ____ : ____ : ____ : ____ I strongly disagree

13. It would be emotionally upsetting to me to see someone exposing himself publicly.

I strongly agree ____ : ____ : ____ : ____ : ____ : ____ : ____ I strongly disagree

14. Watching a go-go dancer of the opposite sex would not be very exciting.

I strongly agree ____ : ____ : ____ : ____ : ____ : ____ : ____ I strongly disagree

15. I would not enjoy seeing a pornographic movie.

I strongly agree ____ : ____ : ____ : ____ : ____ : ____ : ____ I strongly disagree

16. When I think about seeing pictures showing someone of the same sex as myself masturbating it nauseates me.

I strongly agree ____ : ____ : ____ : ____ : ____ : ____ : ____ I strongly disagree

17. The thought of engaging in unusual sex practices is highly arousing.

I strongly agree ____ : ____ : ____ : ____ : ____ : ____ : ____ I strongly disagree

18. Manipulating my genitals would probably be an arousing experience.

I strongly agree ____ : ____ : ____ : ____ : ____ : ____ : ____ I strongly disagree

19. I do not enjoy daydreaming about sexual matters.

I strongly agree ____ : ____ : ____ : ____ : ____ : ____ : ____ I strongly disagree

20. I am not curious about explicit pornography.

I strongly agree ____ : ____ : ____ : ____ : ____ : ____ : ____ I strongly disagree

21. The thought of having long-term sexual relations with more than one sex partner is not disgusting to me.

I strongly agree ____ : ____ : ____ : ____ : ____ : ____ : ____ I strongly disagree

To score your responses, code your opinions about each item in the following way:

1. Depending on your response to each item, assign it a numerical value from 1 to 7. For example, "I strongly disagree" would receive a value of 7. "I strongly agree" receives a 1.
2. Add the scores for the following items: 2, 5, 6, 12, 13, 14, 15, 16, 19, 20.
3. Then subtract from this total the sum of the scores for the following items: 1, 3, 4, 7, 8, 9, 10, 11, 17, 18, 21.

4. Add 67 to this difference.
5. The sum is your score of the Sexual Opinion Survey.

To interpret your score, consider the following breakdown. The sum you obtained in step 2 of the preceding instructions indicates your positive affect toward the opinion statements. The sum from step 3 indicates your negative affect toward the sexual topics. Individual scores can be high or low on both, one, or neither of these affective dimensions.

Lowest possible score; extremely erotophobic; negative attitudes about sex	Average score; neither extremely erotophobic nor extremely erotophilic; mixed positive and negative attitudes about sex	Highest possible score; Extremely erotophilic; positive attitudes about sex
0	53	126

Erotophilia-Erotophobia.   Individual differences in responses to sexual topics can also be measured by the Sexual Opinion Survey (White, Fisher, Byrne, & Kingma, 1977), as described in the box. The two major categories that result from responses to this survey consist of people with largely positive or largely negative attitudes about sex. **Erotophobes** report mainly negative opinions while **erotophiles** indicate generally positive opinions about sex. Between these two extremes, the scale identifies individual scores as ambivalent, consisting of fairly high levels of both positive and negative elements. Ambivalence about sexuality would indicate a tendency to have conflicts about sexual matters and to vacillate between approaching and avoiding sexual behaviors.

Important differences appear between people who are classified as erotophobic or erotophilic (Fisher & Byrne, 1978). With respect to erotophobes, they say that sex was not discussed in their families and they gained inadequate knowledge about it. Erotophiles, on the other hand, experienced more positive training in sexuality, which contributed to their more liberal or permissive attitudes toward it. Negative attitudes also occurred more often among those college students who attended church frequently, had fewer premarital sexual partners, and had less experience with sexual intercourse. The sexual backgrounds and history of erotophobes and erotophiles appear to involve a general tendency to approach or avoid related behaviors.

General attitudes about sex also distinguish these two groups in other ways. In comparison to the negative erotophobes, the erotophiles consider sex an important aspect of their lives and not an embarrassing topic. They approve of premarital sex for themselves, saying that love does not have to be linked to it, and they like performing behaviors about which the erotophobes express dislike, such as oral–genital sex. According to the erotophobes, legal measures should be used to regulate sexual behavior and pornography.

When these two groups watch an explicit erotic film of heterosexual activity, they have quite different reactions to it. The positive feelings of the erotophiles generalize to their evaluations of the actors in the 12-minute movie, since they perceive them as normal and moral instead of abnormal and immoral (the evaluations expressed by the erotophobes). Those with mainly negative responses to the film also recommend that such movies be banned, and indicate that they would not want to see another one. The one—both for themselves and for other people.

Some recent research with the Sexual Opinion Survey adds still further information about the differences between erotophobes and erotophiles (Fisher; Byrne, & White, 1981). The approach-avoidance tendencies lead to different grades in a college course on human sexuality—erotophiles do better than erotophobes. Female erotophiles also take better care of themselves when health involves sexual matters. They are more likely than erotophobes to engage in breast self-examination and to undergo regular gynecological check-ups. Finally, some as yet unpublished research by David Przybyla indicates that, when asked to make drawings of nudes, erotophiles draw males with a larger penis and females with larger breasts than do erotophobes. It appears that these different sexual orientations have pervasive effects on diverse aspects of sexual behavior.

Sex Guilt.   In addition to sexual liberalism–conservatism and erotophobia–erotophilia, a third measure of responses to sexual topics is sex guilt (Mosher, 1968). This measure of the tendency to feel guilty about sex asks subjects to express their reactions to their own sexual behaviors and thoughts. Mosher has defined **sex guilt** as the general expectation of punishment for violating sexual standards either in fantasy or actual behavior.

Self-punitiveness for sexual responsiveness affects several types of related behaviors. Sexually guilty males, for example, avoid exposure to erotic publications. Schill and Chapin (1972) asked male college students to amuse themselves by looking at a pile of magazines while they waited for an experiment to begin. The pile contained some magazines that were sexual in content, such as *Penthouse,* and others that were nonsexual, such as *Newsweek.* Subjects who were low in sex guilt were observed (through a one-way mirror) to choose the sexually oriented publications to look at during the five-minute period, while those who were high in sex guilt avoided those and chose the nonsexual ones. Even if sexually guilty males are exposed to sex-related material, they sometimes interpret it in a different way than the nonguilty men would. Galbraith and Mosher (1968) found that sex guilt can lead to a tendency to misperceive words with sexual meanings as nonsexual, especially following exposure to erotic pictures. Therefore, sex guilt can produce avoidance of sexual cues and misperception of such cues when they are encountered. The person can avoid the expected guilty feeling elicited by coming in contact with forbidden stimuli by staying awa- from such stimuli or by misinterpreting them as nonsexual.

Guilt is a way to punish one's own wrongdoing with anxiety, thereby preventing future occurrences of the forbidden behavior. What happens when a sexually guilty person is confronted with erotic material that is explicit and unmistakable in its sexual content? Does such a person continue to avoid the material or surrender to temptation and enjoy it? In one study male undergraduates watched erotic slides that they were to rate for degree of obscenity. The least obscene slides depicted bikini-clad women and the most offensive ones showed explicit heterosexual acts like intercourse. As the slides became more obscene, subjects who were low in sex guilt were observed to double the amount of time they spent viewing each slide until they spent about 40 seconds viewing the most explicit slides (Love, Sloan, & Schmidt, 1976). The sexually guilty subjects, as expected, spent less time viewing the slides regardless of their degree of obscenity. Thus, they maintained their avoidance tendencies.

Internal imaginative events also vary with sex guilt. Erotic fantasies from a book by Friday (1973) were shown to undergraduate females in a study by Moreault and Follingstad (1978). When these subjects were asked to write their own fantasies afterward, level of sex guilt influenced several aspects of their fantasy behavior. Even though the two groups of women reported equal degrees of sexual arousal due to their fantasizing, their fantasies differed greatly. Those who were high in guilt wrote stories that used fewer words, contained fewer references to sexual organs or erotic acts, and showed more embarrassment and less vividness or variation. On the basis of such findings, it seems probable that less guilty women would be more likely to use erotic fantasy to arouse themselves sexually in ways that they found pleasant.

Sexual activity is also influenced by guilt feelings. Less guilty male and female undergraduates engage in overt sexual behavior more frequently than guilty ones. Specific sexual acts are also more likely to be performed by people who are low in guilt; these include intercourse, connilingus (oral-genital stimulation of the female), and petting to orgasm (Mosher & Cross, 1971). In general, sex guilt indicates negative attitudes toward sexual topics, thoughts, and behaviors. When sex guilt is lacking, these internal and external erotic stimuli function as rewards that are sought rather than as punishing events to be avoided. (Griffitt & Kaiser, 1978).

Gender Differences in Sexuality

The traditional view of men as highly sexual and women as almost asexual has persisted for centuries. The notion that women have a much weaker sex drive, if any, has been believed in many different cultures. When a few women expressed sexual needs, they were labeled as degenerates and possibly nymphomaniacs and were encouraged to seek help for their troubles. For example, Barker-Benfield (1976) has documented the work of early gynecologists, who in the late nineteenth century routinely performed sexual surgery. One such procedure, called clitoridectomy, relieved women who were said to be oversexed of their insatiable sexual appetites by cutting off their clitorises. Women, it was believed, have or should have interests other than sex, while men, who are easily aroused, are keenly interested in it. Consistent with the idea that a revolution in sexual attitudes and behaviors has occurred, research shows that such differences are being replaced by similarity in the sexual patterns of men and women.

The traditional view of sex for women emphasized what they could achieve by enduring it in order to obtain greater rewards such as marriage, children, and financial support. Survey studies conducted twenty-five years ago supported the notion that sex had very different meanings for males and females. Women reported less interest in performing various sexual acts including intercourse and masturbation, having an orgasm, or being exposed to pornography, and indeed they engaged in such activity less frequently than men (Kinsey, Pomeroy, & Martin, 1948; Kinsey, Pomeroy, Martin, & Gebhard, 1953). Surely, if women described themselves as lacking interest in sex, then the traditional expectations about them were proven to be accurate. If biological differences between the sexes dictated that only men would be truly sexual beings, who could argue?

More recent data indicate the basic similarity of the sexes in sexuality. Given the expectations of both men and women about the latter's unresponsiveness to erotic stimuli, it was surprising to find that in the 1970s men and women equally aroused and responsive to erotica. Investigators in both the United States and West Germany reported that males and females experience similar levels of sexual arousal in response to erotic stories, photographs, and movies (Byrne & Lamberth, 1971; Fisher & Byrne, 1978; Griffitt, 1973; Schmidt, Sigusch, & Schafer, 1973). Despite their excitement in response to erotic stimuli, women still reported that they avoided and disliked such material (Kenrick, Stringfield, Wagenhals, Dahl, & Ransdell, 1980).

While some of the traditional gender differences in sexuality may persist, it is also clear that such behaviors are easily learned. For example, in the United States marital sexual activity still tends to be initiated by the male (Crain, 1978), but females can learn to play the masculine role, suggesting that these contrasts -etween male and female behavior are based on learning. Money and Erhardt (1972) have provided the most convincing evidence for this in their work on rare sexual anomalies. Sometimes a mistake is made in labeling a newborn infant as male or female on the basis of underdeveloped male or overdeveloped female genitalia. In other cases a male infant's penis has been accidentally removed during circumcision. Even though these individuals are genetically female or male, they are raised as members of the opposite sex. The results of studies on their social and personality development show that they learn to behave in typically masculine or feminine ways, depending on how they are raised rather than on their genetic sex. At puberty these persons are usually given hormones to reduce the appearance of secondary sex characteristics such as facial hair or breasts, which would contradict their learned gender. Thus, it has been shown that anyone could learn to be masculine, highly sexed, and dominant or feminine, uninterested in sex, and passive, regardless of biological sex.

Despite male–female similarities in general responses to explicit sexual stimuli, certain erotic themes can influence men and women differently. Aggression and dominance, which are present in some sexual stimuli, produce different feelings that depend on the observer's sex. Both sexes are more aroused when the victim of the aggression is not the same sex as themselves, whether the stimulus is sexual exploitation in a short story (Herrell, 1975) or sadism in a photograph (Byrne & Lamberth, 1971). Presumably, it is more threatening to observe aggression of a sexual nature toward a victim like oneself, with whom one can identify more easily than with an opposite-sex victim. An exception to this finding occurs in the case of rape. After subjects watched a film showing a male gang-rape of a female, observers of both sexes said that they had been aroused by the rape film. While generally angry and anxious feelings about the film were expressed by both sexes, there were certain differences in their moods. Men's responses to the rape scene included guilt, while women's reactions consisted of feelings of helplessness (Schmidt, 1975).

Males and females also react differently to another sexual topic that is still taboo to many people: masturbation. Negative reactions to films and pictures of masturbation are common, especially when the masturbator is the same sex as the observer. This effect occurs with respect to both arousal and reported affect. For example, Schmidt (1975) found that subjects who watched films of masturbation were more aroused after seeing someone of the opposite sex than after seeing someone of the same sex as themselves perform it. Males reported greater arousal levels in response to watching a woman stimulate herself than women reported after observing a man do the same. The effect of masturbation stimuli on *feelings* also depends on the sex of the person in the scene. Watching a member of the opposite sex masturbate produces positive feelings, but more negative moods result from viewing same-sex masturbation (Hatfield, Sprecher, & Traupmann, 1978; Mosher & Abramson, 1977).

Changes in Sexuality

In addition to studies of responses to erotica, recent changes in sexual attitudes and behavior also contradict the traditional assumptions about inborn gender differences in sexuality. The Kinsey studies contained important descriptions of the sexual behavior of American men and women (Kinsey et al., 1948, 1953). Because of their careful methods of population sampling and data collection, they have often been used as standards for subsequent surveys. Hunt (1974) attempted to update this information about sexual beliefs and practices. It was found that there have been consistent changes in our general willingness to tolerate others' sexual practices. While the respondents to Hunt's survey might not necessarily want to engage in extramarital sex, anal intercourse, or homosexuality themselves, fewer of them claim that the sexual practices of others are of concern to themselves than was the case when the Kinsey studies were conducted. Thus, Hunt (1974) found that sexual attitudes have become much more permissive among Americans. More positive attitudes are found among

Figure 11-1. Changes in sexual permissiveness have done away with taboos that influenced behavior only a generation ago. An adolescent today is more likely to engage in premarital intercourse and at an earlier age than was true of his or her parents. (Stan Wakefield)

younger males and females of college age than among middle-aged or elderly people about such topics as masturbation and oral sex.

Similar changes in sexual behavior have introduced a new element into the old debate about gender differences in sexuality. Men and women are showing more similarity than difference in sexual behavior as permissiveness has increased. For example, women have caught up with men over the last few decades in the frequency with which they engage in premarital sex. Today females born since the 1940s are about as likely as males to have premarital sex (Hunt, 1974). While the rate of increase in coital experience before marriage has increased slightly among males (Finger, 1975), the parallel changes among women have occurred at a much higher rate (Curran, 1977).

SEX EDUCATION

The Role of Parents

While the sexual behavior patterns of adult men and women have converged in many areas, the younger age groups have also joined the sexual revolution. In line with the more positive attitudes toward sex found among adolescents today than in earlier decades, American teenagers become sexually active at a younger age and with more variety in their early erotic practices. Parents may be shocked by their grade school youngster asking such questions as, "How do you spell *cunnilingus*?" Sexual references are part of the culture of children and adolescents today, and the contrast between the parent's "When I was a child . . ." may clash with their offspring's retort, "Well, I *am* one now, and . . ."

A parent's response to this difference between themselves and their children can have lasting effects on the development of their offspring's responses. The parental attitude toward such topics as masturbation and gender differences provides a basis for the child's emotional responses to his or her own sexual behavior. Partly because of the changes in sexuality over the decades, parents may find it difficult to respond to questions or to initiate discussions about sex. This problem may have its roots in several possible orientations to sex education, ranging from reluctance to inform the youngster about forbidden topics to embarrassment about revealing oneself as sexually active to confusion about how to teach children about sex. By late adolescence, college students who report that their parents had negative attitudes toward sexuality also express more sexually guilty feelings and expect more punishment for engaging in such behavior (Kelley, 1979b, 1981). Compared to those who describe their parents' attitudes as positive, they tend to express more negative affect about many aspects of their own sexual behavior and to use contraceptives less effectively.

Since parental attitudes toward sexuality can have a great impact on youngsters' sex education, what aspects of parents as models for attitudes and behavior produce this effect? The effectiveness of models depends partly on the presence of a warm, friendly relationship that includes an effort to teach what the model practices in actual behavior. The important factors in parental instruction about sexuality involve these aspects of effective modeling. Parents with positive attitudes toward the topic were described as showing little disgust about the biology of sex or negative feelings about its emotional aspects (Kelley, 1981). The presence of positive affect toward sex should generalize to the parents' actual teaching about it, and the most effective models were found to display such responses. Parents who were described as negative toward sex were seldom physically affectionate to their spouse in their offspring's presence. They also encouraged general family discussion of sex less often than parents who were described as positive about it.

If parents know that they have some negative attitudes that might have an unwanted, harmful effect on their youngster's sexuality, what can they do to correct this potential problem? The motivation for change might be to protect their offspring from learning a generalized aversion to sexuality. The task of changing established habits can involve a difficult process of substituting new behaviors for them. Other possibilities include using neutral sources like books designed for the purpose of introducing youngsters to sexual material. In this way, damaging parent–child interactions might be avoided by parents who are truly concerned about the undesirable effects of their reluctance to use a direct approach.

Effects of Formal Education

To the extent that the schools are responsible for sex education, their efforts might be expected to have mainly positive results. Studies showing the effects of such instruction have been performed mainly at the college level. In this age of sexual openness one might predict that enlightened, intelligent college students would believe few of the myths about sexuality that have persisted across many generations. Mosher (1979) studied the attitudes of college students toward such false statements as "Women ejaculate when they experience orgasm" and "Most men have had at least one sexual experience with a prostitute." About one-third of the students tested at the University of Connecticut believed 13 of 41 such myths, suggesting a high rate of sexual misinformation among people who are assumed by others to be knowledgeable about sex. Such erroneous beliefs were expressed most often by people who also felt sexually guilty and had little sexual experience. On average men believed three more myths than women; this may be a sign that adolescents who use the male peer group as a source of sexual information may not find totally accurate information there.

Assuming that college-level courses in sexuality convey accurate information, they may affect students' emotional orientation to the topic. Most studies report that sexual attitudes become more liberal or permissive after such a course. Story (1979) measured the attitudes of students before and after a human sexuality course and found that after taking the class they expressed more comfortable, accepting attitudes about others' sexual behavior. This effect persisted in a follow-up survey two years later. Students in a control group that did not take the course expressed more conservative,-negative opinions about the same topics. However, sexual *behavior* does not usually change much as a result of such a course. A minority of male students report slightly more frequent masturbation or heterosexual intercourse, but in most cases they had already engaged in such behaviors before the course began (Zuckerman, Tushup, & Finner, 1976). According to the few studies conducted so far, the effects of formal sex education at the college level seem to be mostly positive with respect to attitudes but minimal with respect to behavior.

THE PHYSIOLOGY OF SEXUAL RESPONSE

Sexual behavior is based partly on a physiological need. Biological processes do play a role in people's responses to erotic stimulation. Only recently have the roles of various internal, physiological factors in human sexual functioning been revealed through research. First we will describe the findings with respect to hormonal impact on sexual arousal. Then we will turn to a discussion of the physiological processes of sexual arousal and functioning.

Hormones and Sexual Responsiveness

In contrast to many other species, humans and other primates have the capacity for continuous sexual responsiveness. Readiness to respond sexually is not confined to yearly or monthly cycles. Primates do not have to be in a certain hormonal state to become sexually aroused in response to external stimulation. In recent generations of humans there has been a lengthening of the period of life in which sexual interest and arousal are possible. This change is due to two factors: the lowering of the age of puberty and an increase in life expectancy. Females become able to conceive offspring at puberty because of glandular changes, and they can do so after their first ovulation whether a menstrual period has occurred or not. Pubertal youngsters go through several obvious changes during this period, including increased sexual interest and activity. In the developed nations, because of improvements in nutrition and health care, the average age of puberty among females has dropped from 17 to 12 in the last 150 years (*Playboy,* April 1979, p. 280).

In spite of the important role played by hormones in the behavior of lower animals, research has shown no apparent relation between hormonal blood levels and any aspect of adult human sexual functioning (Kraemer, Becker, Brodie, Doering, Moos, & Hamburg, 1976). Hormonal variation caused by the menstrual period in women (Griffith & Walker, 1975) or by testosterone injection in men (Evans & Distiller, 1979) does not influence responses to external stimuli such as erotic pictures.

There is one period in our lives during which hormone levels indirectly influence sexual responsiveness. In elderly people the levels of the hormones estrogen and testosterone decrease and certain aspects of sexual functioning are affected. Although the ability of aged persons to engage in sexual intercourse or to have orgasm are not usually affected, other effects may occur. These include less lubrication of the woman's vagina and slower erection and a longer refractory period in the man. If these events are interpreted as problems to worry about rather than as natural processes, they may inhibit enjoyment of sexual activity.

The Process of Physiological Arousal

The physiology of sexual excitement has been described by Masters and Johnson (1966). Through the cooperation of hundreds of subjects who volunteered for their pioneering laboratory studies, they produced descriptions of the observable changes that occur when the sex drive is aroused. The details of this process emerged as the volunteers masturbated and engaged in other forms of sexual activity such as intercourse. Of course, each of us can experience either erection or vaginal lubrication and use these signs to label ourselves as sexually aroused. What are the other elements of this process?

Masters and Johnson described four phases of the **sexual response cycle.** The first three phases are quite similar in both men and women. The **excitement phase** is created by sexual stimulation and results in **genital vasocongestion,** an increase in the blood supply to the genital area, where the tissues swell, redden, become warmer, and lubricate. Additional sexual stimulation heightens arousal during the **plateau phase.** With more intense stimulation, lubrication and nipple erection increase and a sex flush may appear as a slight reddish rash on the chest, face, and inner thigh. When excitement reaches a peak, the **orgasm phase** occurs. This releases sexual tension and the vasocongestion that produced it. It consists of brief, muscular contractions lasting only a few seconds, and can vary in both intensity and duration for both sexes. Ejaculation of seminal fluid usually occurs along with orgasm in men, but it may be absent because of the recent emptying of the seminal vesicles during a prior orgasm. The **resolution phase** completes the cycle with a slow decrease in sexual tension during which men become temporarily unresponsive to further stimulation. This

refractory period typically ends when the level of sexual excitement is zero, an average of 10–15 minutes after orgasm among young adult males. Females do not have a refractory period during the resolution phase. They respond to stimulation after an orgasm with renewed arousal and can reach additional orgasms of greater intensity and duration than the first one.

Measuring Sexual Excitement

Arousal has often been measured by asking people to respond to self-rating scales, but direct measures of physiological responses are also possible. A number of devices have been used to measure various aspects of sexual arousal. The size of penile erections has been measured by the **penile plethysmograph,** which uses a strain gauge to detect changes in the size of the penis during sexual excitement (Freund, Sedlacek, & Knob, 1965). Chemical rather than mechanical measures have also been used; an example is the amount of urinary acid phosphatase in male urine (Barclay, 1970). The greater difficulty of measuring female excitement led to the development of more imaginative devices to detect changes in the less exposed female genitalia. The balloon-like kolpograph recorded vaginal expansion and contraction (Jovanovic, 1971). Geer and his colleagues (Geer, 1975; Sintchak & Geer, 1976) developed the **vaginal photoplethys-mograph,** which uses a vaginal probe the size of a tampon. The plastic probe contains a light-sensing device that detects reflections from its own light source and measures the degree of sexual arousal by the amount of light reflected from the walls of the vasocongested vagina of a sexually excited female. The arousal indicated by vaginal photoplethysmography reliably corresponds to women's reports of their own sexual excitement while watching an erotic film (Henson, Rubin, & Henson, 1979). Finally, researchers at UCLA have introduced another measure, **thermography** (Seeley, Abramson, Perry, Rothblatt, & Seeley, 1979). This method detects changes in the temperature of bodily surfaces, including changes produced by sexual arousal. Changes in the skin temperature in the genital area parallel the excitement phases described by Masters and Johnson. However, a combination of physiological measurement and subjective rating scales is probably a better measure of sexual arousal than either method alone (Hatch, 1979).

SEXUAL FANTASY

Imagination can be a powerful sexual stimulus. It can function independently of the situation, removing physical barriers to excitement that exist in the real world. Cognitive processes—as opposed to hormonal ones—play an important role in human sexual behavior compared to that of lower animals. External stimuli such as erotic pictures or a willing partner are not necessary to excite us sexually, since we can easily achieve the same result by imagining a favorite passionate scene or even a novel bit of erotic activity.

Functions and Effects of Erotic Fantasy

Compared to the effort required to obtain erotic pictures or persuade someone else to have sex, one's imagination can furnish a simple, easy way to become aroused. The internal fantasy can be more exciting than external reality. For example, Byrne and Lamberth (1971) conducted a study of married couples who were asked to view erotic pictures, to read erotic literary passages, or simply to think about sexual scenes. Compared with the effects of pictures or words, imagined scenes produced higher levels of sexual arousal. It appears that creating one's own sexual fantasy can heighten the arousal level produced by external stimuli. The "sex drive" of people who fantasize about sexual activity may be greater than that of people who avoid this form of mental behavior. This means that we have considerable power to control our level of sexual desire.

The power of sexual fantasy has been relatively neglected in research until now, but current findings indicate that it plays an important role in controlling and motivating behavior. Geer and Fuhr (1976) have provided some interesting information about the influence of imagination on males' responses to an erotic stimulus. To the extent that people can identify with sexual cues and role play in their imaginations the behavior depicted in a picture, film, or whatever, they should find the cues more arousing. The researchers tested this hypothesis by increasing the difficulty involved in cognitively processing such a stimulus. As the interference with fantasy about erotica increased, they expected to find that sexual arousal would be reduced. To provide a conflict between sources of neutral, nonsexual information and sources of sexual information, they gave the males a cognitive task to perform while listening to an erotic tape of a sensual female voice explicitly describing sexual intercourse, oral–genital sex, and other forms of sex play. Some subjects simply listened to the tape without being given any task to perform, and these became the most highly aroused according to plethysmograph measurements of penis size. Other subjects were required to copy numbers from a tape, to add pairs of them, or (at the highest level of interference) to classify the sums as above or below 50 and as odd or even. These subjects experienced less arousal as the level of interference with fantasy rose. In this study thought processes dramatically interfered with the experience of arousal due to erotic stimuli. The group with the most difficult cognitive task were not aroused by the story. Thus, a person's own thoughts can function as a barrier to sexual excitement.

Erotic fantasy can also be used to improve sexual functioning and, hence, to increase enjoyment. The involuntary use of fantasy occurs during sleep; both males and females can become sexually aroused during erotic dreams and experience orgasm—including ejaculation by males. People also use voluntary fantasies to heighten arousal during masturbation (Campagna, 1976). They can apply the same technique to sexual intercourse, either using the same fantasies utilized while masturbating (Nims, 1975) or inventing new ones. In contrast to the general assumption that fantasizing during sexual activity shows dissatisfaction with one's partner or one's relationship, the evidence suggests that no such conclusions can be drawn. In fact, a higher frequency of richer and more enjoyable sexual fantasies used during intercourse is linked with greater satisfaction with a variety of marital sexual activities in both sexes (Carlson & Coleman, 1977). In the absence of effective chemical aphrodisiacs, we can use erotic fantasies for the same purpose at no cost and with no side effects.

The Content of Erotic Fantasies

Males and females use erotic fantasies for very similar reasons, ranging from heightening their sexual arousal to increasing their partner's attractiveness (Sue, 1979). Some gender differences exist in the content of the fantasy material that is considered arousing. For example, Barclay (1973) found that male undergraduates at Michigan State University wrote sexual fantasies resembling hard-core pornography, including vivid visual images of unemotional, sexually driven characters. Females in the sample created a contrast to this finding with their highly emotional fantasies about love or sex by force.

Hunt (1974) studied the content of sexual fantasies during masturbation. A number of sex differences were found. While masturbating, a person is behaving without external constraints on fantasy and can choose the sexual topic that is most interesting at the time. Members of both sexes commonly reported the use of masturbation fantasies about a person they love. Males more frequently reported imagining group sex with several partners of the opposite sex, forcing someone to have sex, and having intercourse with a stranger. Women more often reported using their imaginations to create sexual situations that they would avoid in reality, such as being forced to have sex or engaging in homosexual activities.

Sexual intercourse differs from solitary masturbation in that a partner is required. Does this difference create a need for a different set of fantasies to heighten arousal? Sue (1979) has provided some evidence for the basic structure of fantasy during intercourse, and some of these results are presented in Figure 11-2. The kinds of fantasy that were most common in both males and females concerned a former lover, oral-genital sex, and being sexually irresistible. A few sex differences occurred in the content of intercourse fantasies, namely, in men's focus on imaginary lovers and women's thoughts about homosexual activities or being forced to engage in

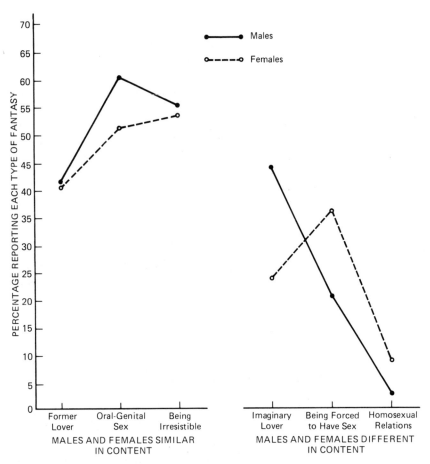

Figure 11-2. Gender differences occur in the content of erotic fantasies used during sexual intercourse.
(Sue, 1979)

sex. When the content of fantasies during masturbation and intercourse is compared, it is found that during intercourse there is more concern with a partner's participation in the activity or acceptance of oneself as a lover.

People often report that they use sexual fantasies partly to enhance arousal. Thus, there may be a relation between specific fantasies and overt behavior. For example, imagine your favorite kind of cake, a tempting, mouthwatering morsel of the best cake you ever ate. Would this scene help you decide to choose that type of cake in a restaurant, or even to arrange to eat it at the next opportunity? Would the same sort of relation exist for sexual fantasies, making certain acts more likely after you have fantasized them? In the case of acceptable, nondeviant forms of sexual behavior such as intercourse and oral–genital stimulation, such an effect would be welcome. But when deviant behavior enters the picture and another person may be forced to have sex or be harmed by a sexual act, the potential becomes a source of concern. Both college students and sexual offenders often report having fantasies involving themes of sadism or exhibitionism. Thus, it is clear that simply having such a fantasy does not mean that the imagined behavior will or will not occur in real life. A strong majority (81.5 percent) of the college students in Sue's (1979) study considered their fantasies to be normal aspects of their sexuality; the rest expressed uneasiness or shame about their fantasies. It would be interesting to know how sex offenders evaluate their fantasies.

Clearly, much remains to be learned about the impact of imagination on sexual functioning and deviance. Fantasy has some positive effects on sexual behavior, but little is known about the exact relation between the two; we cannot yet determine what, if any, aspects of behavior can be predicted from fantasy. It is argued that some types of sexual fantasy focus on hostility and domination (Dunn, 1978), and these may have negative effects on behavior. The implication of this argument would be that certain kinds of sexual fantasizing should be discouraged. On the other hand, some people suggest encouragement of all kinds of sexual fantasies regardless of their content. None of the evidence collected so far definitely supports either side of this argument. Do fantasies facilitate sexual behavior, including behavior of a deviant, antisocial nature, or does it provide a safe outlet for impulses that otherwise might be acted out in real life? Such a question must be answered on the basis of future research.

PORNOGRAPHY AND BEHAVIOR

Exposure to erotica has generally been assumed to have harmful effects that can be prevented by censorship. Because some persons—such as children or the emotionally disturbed—are thought to be led into sexual immorality by these stimuli, drastic measures must be used to protect both them and society as a whole (Frank, 1979). A total ban on sexually explicit material would accomplish this. Most adults in the United States favor such a ban, in spite of the fact that they themselves have been exposed to erotica at some time in their lives (Wilson & Abelson, 1973). Erotica can stimulate the imagination and lead to arousal in both sexes, as described earlier. However, does such arousal influence later behavior by eliciting either ordinary sexual activity or antisocial behavior? **Pornography** is often defined as material created with the intent of stimulating sexual excitement. The design and distribution of this material is a handy target of preventive legislation, yet the need for these antipornography measures is contradicted by the information currently available about the behavioral effects of erotica.

Figure 11-3. Despite fears that exposure to pornography will lead to immorality and aggressiveness, research shows that it has mild, temporary effects on those exposed to it. (Geoffrey Gove, Photo Researchers)

Effects on Sexual Activity and Interpersonal Behavior

Studies have shown the effects of exposure to erotica on subsequent sexual behavior to be surprisingly weak. This contradicts the expectation that such material might make viewers oversexed because of drive arousal or persuade them to try out the scenes themselves because of a modeling effect. Neither prolonged increases in excitement nor modeling of sexual activity seems to occur as a function of the arousal elicited by pornography. Among volunteers for experimental research, sexual and sometimes interpersonal reactions are usually compared before and after exposure to explicit erotica. Or, the behavior of an experimental group is compared to a non-pornography control group. Subjects typically show an increased tendency to engage in sexual behavior during the few hours following the viewing of pornography. Unmarried students are more likely to masturbate (Amoroso, Brown, Pruesse, Ware, & Pilkey, 1971), while married ones engage in sexual intercourse (Cattell, Kawash, & DeYoung, 1972; Kutchinsky, 1971). Even these mild effects decline following continued exposure (Mann, Berkowitz, Sidman, Starr, & West, 1974). Perhaps because erotophobes have less practice with erotica, they show more interest in subsequent sexual activity than erotophiles (Fisher & Byrne, 1978).

The arousal elicited by erotic material also influences perceptions of the opposite sex. The effect depends on whether the person (e.g., a potential date) is physically attractive or not. Sexual arousal seems to cause us to perceive a beautiful or handsome person as even better looking. Unattractive members of the opposite sex are seen as less pleasing by aroused male or female college students than by nonaroused ones (Istvan & Griffitt, 1978; Weidner, Istvan, & Griffitt, 1979). A further effect of erotica on males is to make their expressions of love for a female partner more intense (Dermer & Pyszczynski, 1978).

Sex Crimes

The assumption that sex crimes are committed by viewers of pornography is not supported by research. Exposure to erotica before the age of 14 does not seem to produce sexual deviance. It is found that early erotic experience in males is correlated with more variety and higher levels of activity in their sexual life as adults (Davis & Braught, 1973). However, sex offenders report *less* contact with erotic stimuli during adolescence than nonoffenders (Goldstein, Kant, & Hartman, 1974). Sex offenders generally report less experience with erotica of all types than other males. The experiences they do have are described as negative, repressive, and restrictive. Whereas most males have seen a picture of sexual intercourse by the age of 14, this event takes place an average of four years later among sex offenders (Eysenck, 1972).

   If restriction of erotic material can create sexual problems, as the findings just mentioned suggest, then free access to such material would be predicted to lower the incidence of antisocial sexual behavior. Chances to study behavior in a laboratory the size of a whole country are rare, but such an opportunity arose in Denmark in the 1960s, when restrictions on the availability of pornography were lifted. Following the suspension of censorship, a marked decrease in the frequency of sex crimes occurred for several years. This decline occurred in all classes of sex crimes, including child molestation (Kutchinsky, 1973), rape, and voyeurism (Commission on Obscenity and Pornography, 1970). Instead of encouraging such crimes, erotic material may *discourage* them by providing an outlet for aggressive impulses through harmless fantasy and masturbation. Erotic stimuli may have definite prosocial advantages, especially for some people, instead of the evil effects popularly attributed to it.

THE SEXUAL BEHAVIOR SEQUENCE

The Theory

Many descriptions of the physiological, emotional, and deviant or dysfunctional aspects of sexuality have been proposed. However, despite hundreds of studies on human sexual behavior, no comprehensive theory explaining this behavior has yet been generally accepted. Byrne (1977) has outlined a framework designed to bring together this collection of facts; it is called the **sexual behavior sequence.** It organizes the determinants of sexual behavior into external events and internal stimuli. The person responds to outside stimuli such as erotic material or the presence of a partner with such internal reactions as emotions, fantasy, and physiological arousal. Beliefs, attitudes, and expectancies are based in part on the positive and negative outcomes that the person experiences as rewards or punishments for sexual behavior. This sequence also includes the possibility of modification of each of its elements on the basis of subsequent sexual experiences.

In their earliest experiences with sexuality, for example, youngsters often learn that masturbation has negative interpersonal effects even though it feels good. Of course, there is nothing inherently negative about masturbation. A positive activity that is engaged in from infancy (Kelley, 1981), masturbation can quickly become linked with feelings of disgust and dislike when such reactions are learned from others. Such an affective basis for sexuality persists at least into the adult years, when it can influence later reactions. While there are social limits to the acceptability of masturbation in children in certain contexts and situations (for example, one needn't masturbate in public), such training does not have to include a negative orientation to sexual behavior. Evidence now shows that the effects of early negative teachings about sexual activity encourage feelings of sex guilt that may persist into the adult years. Abramson and Mosher (1975) found that college students' fantasies about masturbation included expectations of punishment for that activity, and that a majority of the students believed statements about its harmful effects.

An Example: Contraception

Since the theory of the sexual behavior sequence is a new one, it has been applied to only a few areas of sexuality. One of those concerns the psychological aspects of contraceptive behavior, especially the factors involved in the current epidemic of adolescent pregnancy (1 million a year in this country alone). Besides the emotional trauma of unwanted pregnancy and early parenthood, adolescents who become pregnant have other problems. They are more likely than the general population to abuse their children, commit suicide, or get a divorce (Cvetkovich, Grote, Bjorseth, & Sarkissian, 1975). Modern forms of contraception could easily prevent this problem, yet even the majority of sexually active *college students* fail to use them effectively, if at all (Fisher, Byrne, Edmunds, Miller, Kelley, & White, 1979).

Byrne (1981) has analyzed this psychological puzzle in terms of the sexual behavior sequence. Variations in the accuracy of knowledge about sex and contraception can influence this behavior, for example. If one thinks that conception cannot occur if intercourse is performed standing up, the maladaptive aspect of this belief would become evident with the "surprising" finding that the woman is pregnant. A. R. Allgeier (1981) has reported that the more knowledgeable college students also favor the use of birth control and delay the age at which they first have intercourse. Other beliefs that interfere with contraception include the notion that planning to have sex or use contraception is sinful and unromantic (Oskamp & Mindick, 1981).

Just as emotions influence sexuality in general, they also affect contraceptive behavior. Sex guilt and erotophobia help keep people from taking steps to prevent an unwanted pregnancy. These negative responses to sexuality are associated with difficulty in learning about birth control (Schwartz, 1973). Effective action, such as visiting a clinic for contraception (Fisher et al., 1979) or avoiding intercourse without it (Allgeier, Przybyla, & Thompson, 1979), occur less often among people who are predisposed to have negative reactions to such topics. One result of this chain of behavior is higher rates of unwanted pregnancy and requests for abortion among adolescents who are negative rather than positive about sex (Gerrard, 1977).

The existence of few positive models for contraceptive behavior in our media (Byrne, 1981) adds to problems adolescents face in learning how to engage in responsible sexual behavior. Existing models tend to encourage noncontraceptive fantasies about love and sex. Not a frequent topic of conversation in the early stages of an uncommitted sexual relationship (DeLamater, 1981), contraception is more likely to be ignored by those individuals who are least willing and prepared to cope with parenthood. Modifications of each of these elements, including beliefs and expectancies, emotions and attitudes, and fantasies, could help solve this troubling social problem (Fisher, 1981; Fisher, Byrne, & White, 1981).

HOMOSEXUAL BEHAVIOR

Stereotypes

Perhaps no aspect of sexual activity has involved more firmly held beliefs and fewer solid facts than sexual activity between members of the same sex. Most heterosexuals probably have little, if any, contact with people who overtly identify themselves as gay or lesbian. Fear of the unknown or mysterious can be threatening, and it is easy to solve this problem by using shorthand labels for groups that one doesn't wish to understand more fully. The stereotypes about homosexuality include descriptions of gay males as feminine and of lesbian females as masculine. These stereotypes are so strong that casual observers often think a person's sexual orientation is shown by occupation or looks. However, only a small minority (less than 10 percent) of homosexual men have "feminine" jobs such as hairdressing or decorating (Bell, 1978). Homosexual women may role-play the masculine part of a heterosexual relationship, but this usually occurs only in the early stages of a relationship while more natural forms of interaction are developing (Martin & Lyon, 1972). Yet many heterosexuals still believe in these stereotypes, often to such a point that they develop **homophobia,** or fear of anything connected with homosexuality. Lumby (1976) described some aspects of homophobia. He showed, for example, that heterosexuals are more willing than gays and lesbians to believe that these people would be a security threat as employees of an intelligence organization.

A common mistake in thinking about homosexual behavior is to confuse gender identity with sexual preference and sex roles. **Gender identity** refers to the labeling of a person as male or female. Young children usually realize their biological gender by the age of 2½ to 3 (Money & Erhardt, 1972). **Sexual preference** refers to the choice of male or female sexual partners, a choice that can vary during a person's lifetime. One's **sex role** consists of the degree of socially defined masculinity or femininity found in one's description of oneself and in one's social behavior. Most people consider themselves male or female, depending on their biological sex, and this includes gays and lesbians. With respect to sexual preference, only about one in ten homosexuals have exclusively same-sex partners, with the rest having varying frequencies of heterosexual experience as well (Kinsey, 1953). As with heterosexual men and women, either gays or lesbians can display stereotypically feminine or masculine sex role behavior, or a combination of both sex roles known as **androgyny.** Sex preference does not depend on a person's psychological sex role, as the research on gay and lesbian behavior shows.

Our society punishes homosexual behavior in many ways. In many states laws declare sexual activity between people of the same sex illegal and forbid the employment of homosexuals in many types of positions. Even though the American Psychiatric Association no longer considers homosexuality a mental disturbance, discrimination against homosexuals continues. For example, the U.S. Immigration and Naturalization Service currently enforces a legal ban on the admission of homosexual aliens to this country, whether they openly declare their sexual preference or it is discovered by accident (Pear, 1979).

Causes of Homosexual Behavior

Whatever one's evaluation of homosexual behavior, the conditions that cause and maintain this sexual activity would be of interest. Several hypotheses have received a little research support, but there is not yet a definite answer to the question of what causes it. It appears that several routes to a totally or partially homosexual life style exist. One explanation focuses on biological factors, such as genetic heritage, hormonal imbalance, or neurological conditions (Acosta, 1975). Since one might question the evolutionary value of homosexual behavior in continuing the existence of the human species, it is not surprising that there is little evidence that it has a biological basis.

Interpersonal problems during sexual development are another possible source of a homosexual orientation. Several investigators have focused on the idea that disturbed parent–child relations somehow result in a defensive preference for members of the same rather than the opposite sex as sexual partners. However, most studies of this possibility have used samples of volunteers who are in therapy. Finding that a disturbed person, homosexual or not, had problems as a child probably is not of great value in explaining this aspect of sexuality (Acosta, 1975; Bell, 1978).

There is more evidence to support a social learning account of the development of homosexual behavior. That is, sexual thoughts or sexual acts involving members of one's own sex can be pleasant and hence reinforcing. Such reinforcement increases the tendency to engage in similar behaviors on subsequent occasions. In addition, sexual behaviors with members of the opposite sex can be unpleasant, and punishing experiences can result in avoidance of heterosexual cues and heterosexual acts. It should be noted that this view leads to the conclusion that *anyone* could learn to be homosexual—*or* heterosexual. Kohlberg (1966) proposed a theory of sex typing that describes the child as learning to behave in masculine or feminine ways on the basis of his or her gender identity. If sex roles are learned as part of one's gender identity, one's sexual preference could develop in a similar way. Saghir and Robins (1973) found that romantic fantasies and repeated thoughts about members of the same or the opposite sex during childhood and early adolescence corresponded to the later sexual preference of homosexuals and heterosexuals of both sexes. Whether or not different family patterns or childhood experiences occur among people who become homosexuals, the explanation of the development of homosexuality is likely to be as complex as that of the development of heterosexuality.

Activity and Adjustment

Despite the stereotypes about gays and lesbians, they differ greatly among themselves with respect to both sexual activity and social–psychological adjustment. For example, a minority of gay males fit the description of gays as cruising promiscuously through gay bars. Many enter into serious relationships with their partners and live a socially well adjusted, productive life (Bell, 1978). Fewer lesbians have many partners for sexual activity, and compared to the males more of them develop long-term, committed rela-

Figure 11-4. Homosexual behavior appears to be learned, and there are many different ways in which an individual can come to sample such behavior, find it rewarding, and adopt a gay sexual orientation. In effect, it is believed that anyone could learn to satisfy sexual needs with a same-sex or an opposite-sex partner.   (Jan Lukas, Photo Researchers)

tionships. Like heterosexuals, homosexuals sometimes face such problems as jealousy, infidelity, and trying to deal with simultaneous relationships. The added pressure of guilt and social discrimination may result in a higher frequency of maladjustment among homosexuals. Bell (1978) has shown that failure to cope adequately with these problems characterized the minority of homosexuals who were labeled as dysfunctional in his study.

A recent large-scale study by Masters and Johnson (1979) compared the sexual behaviors of male and female heterosexuals and homosexuals. These researchers observed couples having sex in their St. Louis laboratories. The homosexual couples engaged in more frequent communication about ways to satisfy their partner sexually than the heterosexual couples. Only one group—heterosexual females—consistently expressed dissatisfaction with sexual activity and experienced less intense physiological arousal and orgasm. Lesbian couples made a definite effort to ensure that stimulation of their partner and themselves resulted in increased enjoyment; their communication was more effective than that of male–female pairs. With respect to actual sexual interactions, then, the differences between homosexuals and heterosexuals seem to favor the former as more sensitive, communicative lovers.

SUMMARY

Individual differences in sexual response indicate wide variations in attitude toward sex-related stimuli. Some of these variations have been identified as *sexual liberalism* and *conservatism, sex guilt,* and *erotophobia-erotophilia.* A tendency to avoid sexual cues and activity corresponds to a negative orientation to sex. Other differences have been attributed to gender. The traditional belief that females have a lower sex drive and less interest in sex compared to males has been contradicted by changes in female behavior. Similarities between the sexes and the role of learning in the development of sex differences have been shown in studies of physiological responses, reactions to erotica, and children raised as members of the opposite sex. Changes in attitude and behavior have produced greater permissiveness and tolerance of others' sexual behavior as well as earlier, more frequent, and more varied sexual activity by members of both sexes.

Teaching about sex occupies an important but controversial place in the education of children. Positive or negative attitudes toward sex are communicated by parental behavior. The attitudinal effects of sex education are shown in research at the college level—students become more permissive.

With respect to the physiology of sexual response, cognitive effects play a greater role in human sexuality than hormonal variables, even during the later years of life. Masters and Johnson described the sexual response cycle as consisting of four phases—*excitement, plateau, orgasm,* and *resolution*—based on changes in *genital vasocongestion.* Males go through a *refractory period* after orgasm, while females remain receptive to stimulation and can have more orgasms. Sexual arousal can be measured by a penile plethysmograph, a vaginal photoplethysmograph, or thermography.

Sexual fantasy has the function of heightening arousal. Studies of the contents of erotic fantasy show both similarities and differences between males and females.

Longstanding fears about the effects of erotic material have resulted in censorship laws. Erotic stimuli do have mild effects on normal sexual behavior, but these are of short duration. Interpersonal behavior is also influenced by erotica, in the form of increased responsiveness to attractive members of the opposite sex. A repressive and restrictive attitude toward erotic stimuli at either the societal or the individual level seems to be related to a higher frequency of sex crimes.

The sexual behavior sequence describes sexual responses as a function of external stimulation and internal processes such as emotions, cognitions, and fantasies. It has been applied to the adolescent pregnancy epidemic by exploring the effects of beliefs and emotions about sex and contraception.

Homosexual behavior is the subject of many stereotypes that act to deal with the fear of an unknown or threatening stimulus. Homosexuality is more likely to result from social learning processes than from biological influences, but no definite cause has been identified. There are wide individual differences in both homosexual activity and adjustment. Recently Masters and Johnson have described gay and lesbian sexual interactions as more satisfying and exciting than those of heterosexual couples, probably because of better communication in the homosexual pairs.

SUGGESTED READINGS

BYRNE, D., & FISHER, W. A. (eds.). *Adolescents, sex, and contraception.* New York: McGraw-Hill, 1981. A collection of original chapters by individuals in psychology, sociology, and health education. The emphasis is on explaining the reasons for the current teenage pregnancy epidemic and suggesting ways to solve the problem.

HYDE, J. S. *Understanding human sexuality.* New York: McGraw-Hill, 1979. An up-to-date, readable introduction to the field of human sexual behavior. The coverage ranges from anatomy and physiology to interpersonal behavior, conception, VD, and sexual deviancy.

MASTERS, W. H., & JOHNSON, V. E. *Homosexuality in perspective.* Boston: Little, Brown, 1979. A report of the laboratory studies of the sexual behavior of homosexual and heterosexual couples. Topics include physiological functioning, communication between partners, and fantasies.

WOLMAN, B. B., & MONEY, J. (eds.). *Handbook of human sexuality.* Englewood Cliffs, N.J.: Prentice-Hall, 1979. A comprehensive collection of original chapters by experts representing widely ranging interests in the field.

Chapter Twelve

MORALITY: DOING THE RIGHT THING

In this chapter you will read about the following topics:

Special Inserts

TRY IT YOURSELF

Do You Believe in a Just World?

RESEARCH CLOSE-UP

The Effects of Being Helped

At a large midwestern university joggers passed a young man slumped in a corner of an elevated track. Twenty minutes later, trying to awaken him from an apparent rest or fainting spell, they discovered that he was dead.

At least twelve persons in a New York City subway station watched and failed to help Claudia Castellana as she fought a mugger who repeatedly stabbed her with a large knife. Police reported that some of the passengers on an incoming train chased her attacker but did not catch him ("New Yorkers watch," Journal and Courier, *1977).*

The townspeople of Le Chambon in southern France accepted thousands of stranded European Jews and rerouted them to neutral countries during the days of the Nazi purges. The rescuers risked deportation and death for their courageous actions, but they did not refuse the desperate fugitives ("Heroes," New York Review of Books, *1979).*

Endangering his own life, surgeon Charles Haseltine attempted to rescue a critically wounded youngster caught in sniper's fire in Ann Arbor, Michigan. Haseltine was wounded himself and underwent several operations attempting to repair the damage to his right arm. His career as a surgeon has ended ("It takes all kinds," Life, *1979).*

Three timber wolves mauled toddler John Colorio after he slipped through their cage bars in a Worcester, Massachusetts, zoo. The animals retreated only when an unidentified man tossed a railroad tie at them so that rescuers could free the boy ("Zoo's wolves maul toddler," Journal and Courier, *1976).*

STORIES OF HEROISM become especially vivid when they are compared to accounts of callousness and brutality toward one's fellow human beings. Faced with threatening conditions and several alternatives for action, some people show bravery and kindness while others disappear into anonymity and guilt.

Refusal to help someone in need appears in many forms, but always with the same result—someone suffers. Lack of generosity, failure to report a crime, and cheating on an exam could bring immediate rewards but delayed punishment for those involved. How can psychologists explain why people sometimes behave according to rules of morality and ethics and sometimes do not? We will examine several possibilities.

CHARACTER AND CONSCIENCE: INDIVIDUAL DIFFERENCES

When we act in ways that maximize our rewards and minimize our punishments, we are acting according to enlightened self-interest. The world would be even more cruel than it already is if everyone actually behaved in such a way as to gain the greatest possible immediate pleasure. In Freud's view of human psychological development, discussed in Chapter 2, the reality principle places constraints on the functions of the id, which are based on immediate gratification of all needs. Through the process of ego functioning, the human infant learns to delay need fulfillment and rewards. Gradually this learning expands to the social world, with its rules, laws, sanctions, prohibitions, incentives, and punishments designed to restrain and restrict behavior in socially acceptable ways.

Many behaviors would be difficult to explain by either the pleasure principle or the reality principle alone. What prevents people from performing actions that are beneficial to themselves when the behavior is physically possible and cannot be detected by anyone else? Some other factor must be operating when a person returns a valuable lost item to its rightful owner or refuses to cheat on an important test or helps a stranger in distress. Freudian theory also suggests that the internal rules and constraints that produce such outcomes are functions of the superego, or **conscience.** At first the conscience is dependent on external influences for direction. Then it begins to operate on the basis of guilt—an uncomfortable feeling about having disregarded its own dictates. Among people who reach this developmental stage, guilt would result if they stole, cheated, or failed to help a threatened stranger, thereby going against the instructions of their internal values.

Writers throughout history have discussed the concept of conscience. Aronfreed (1968) pointed out that in the time of Plato and Aristotle rational judgments were valued above what we think of as conscience. Later philosophers, including Bentham and John Stuart Mill, still emphasized the intellectual instead of the affective or feeling component of morality. The idea that moral behavior is determined by feelings and internal compulsion can be traced from Sts. Augustine and Thomas Acquinas through Locke, Hume, and Kant. Modern traces of these different themes appear in the cognitive (intellectual) theories of Piaget and Kohlberg and the affective theory of Freud.

Piaget (1948) proposed a theoretical model in which children develop a conscience or morality in terms of a set of rules. This cognitive model describes different stages in which children first evaluate behavior with respect to the wishes of authority figures and the consequences of acts, regardless of intent. They take rules in a literal sense and are concerned with the letter of the law, not with its spirit. As the child matures, moral evaluations become more relative to situations and intentions.

Kohlberg (1963a,b) developed a method for assessing the level of moral judgment as it proceeds from avoidance of punishment to social conformity to an autonomous and internalized set of values. At the lowest level, the **preconventional level,** the young child is influenced mainly by the consequences of behavior. In the first stage of this level, the youngster learns that powerful adults can and will punish him or her for undesirable behavior. In the second stage of this level, the child begins to adapt to the relation between power and punishment by trying to behave in such a way as to obtain rewards rather than punishment. Regular performance of behaviors expected by others characterizes the **conventional level** of moral judgment, usually reached in middle childhood. The major task of the first stage of this level is to strive for others' approval by being a "good" boy or girl, however goodness is defined. In the second stage these influences contribute to the development of ideas about what is right and proper as a standard for behavior. In some cultures these notions may include doing one's duty, respecting authority, and preserving social order.

The following **postconventional level** consists of progress toward the ability to abstract moral values from circumstances. A person who reaches this level (usually in adolescence or adulthood) can identify and act on what he or she believes to be right. In the lower stage of this level, the person thinks about the rights of others in an empathic way, asking how their general welfare is promoted by laws adopted by the majority. In the higher stage of this level, conscience consists of self-chosen standards of justice; one's own morality becomes more important than society's rules and laws. Attainment of this most advanced level of morality does not necessarily imply disregard for cultural expectations; it simply means that decisions about morality are made independently of those expectations. Not everyone reaches the higher stages of morality, but in order to attain them a person must have passed through the earlier ones in the sequence outlined in Kohlberg's theory.

The developmental sequences of Piaget and Kohlberg are rejected by Hogan (1973) in favor of a five-factor theory of moral conduct. Hogan's model rests on the general assumptions that our behavior is governed largely by a system of manmade rules and that morality is a natural phenomenon that makes evolutionary sense. Moral development is based on two cognitive and three affective dimensions. Cognitively, a person has to learn the rules of conduct and moral reasoning. Affectively, certain interactions are necessary if one is to become socialized by internalizing the rules, if one is to feel empathy for others, and if one is to develop a sense of autonomy. An interesting feature of the model deals with the effects of differences in the development of these dimensions. Consider socialization and empathy as an example. A person who is low on both dimensions will tend to become a delinquent. A highly socialized person who is low in empathy will follow the rules rigidly without concern for the welfare of others. One who is low in socialization but high in empathy will be unconcerned about conventional rules and will feel free to break the rules (e.g., to smoke marijuana or to engage in unusual sexual behavior) as long as they cause no harm to others. A person who is high on both dimensions will be "morally mature" in that his or her compliance with social rules will be

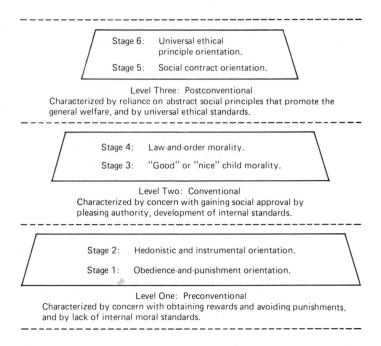

Figure 12-1. Kohlberg's stages in the development of moral judgment.

tempered by concern for other people. Hogan has developed measures for each of the five dimensions, and their usefulness has been shown in a number of studies.

To date, Freud's concept of guilt has had the greatest influence on psychological research and theorizing. The general outlines of the psychoanalytic conception of the development of conscience were discussed earlier in this chapter and also in Chapter 2. When various instinctual motives such as sex and aggression are renounced, any impulse toward satisfying them triggers guilt, and it is this feeling that induces the person to behave in ways that satisfy the internalized moral code.

Now that the major theories of morality development have been outlined, we can examine some studies of this behavior. A typical approach to studying moral judgment involves presenting stories or case studies designed to measure the subject's reasoning level. The subject is asked to read or listen to a story or watch a film involving a dilemma or conflict. Usually a main character is faced with making a decision about how to treat, help, or ignore the plight of others. The solutions recommended vary according to their content and the reasons the character should act in the recommended manner. For example, youngsters might be presented with an account of townspeople who are cut off from their food supply by a flood and farmers who could donate their hard-won crops to them. But the farmers would

Figure 12-2. Moral values and feelings of social responsibility help determine our responses to appeals for aid. (Mike Mazzachi, Stock, Boston)

then suffer because their food stocks would be depleted. Subjects could solve the dilemma in terms of the rewards or standards involved, saying that the farmers shouldn't help because they would be hungry or that they should help because it would be nice. Nancy Eisenberg-Berg (1979) compared the responses of elementary and high school youngsters to such stories and found that the responses of the younger ones were of this sort. In contrast, the older students' responses were more often based on empathy, or feeling sorry for the needy, and internalized values such as expectations of guilt and the rights of others. Note that similar solutions could be reached using both sets of reasons; it is the reasoning content of the solution that indicates the subject's level of moral maturity.

One implication of the presence of different levels of moral maturity in youngsters is that the intellectual processes used to arrive at such judgments will also vary. Piaget has described a sequence of intellectual development. The hallmark of this sequence is complexity of thought. More complex thought is characterized by attending to and processing several aspects of incoming information at once. With moral judgment, changes in the processing of information correspond to changes in intellectual capacity. Children below the age of about 10 are more influenced by the outcome of a situation in judging it as good or bad. Older children also consider the intent to do harm or good in judging people's actions (Salili, Maehr, & Gillmore, 1976). That younger children may judge behavior in a deficient way, not considering all the appropriate factors in such decisions, has persuaded some religious educators to reconsider the traditional belief that they are responsible for personal sin ("When to confess," *Time,* Sept. 3, 1973). In the Roman Catholic Church, for example, the age of 7 is regarded as the "age of reason."

The degrees of moral reasoning suggested in Kohlberg's theory have been studied, and some of the research is aimed at finding ways to change people's judgment styles. For example, it is possible to have adolescents with the appropriate reasoning skills role-play responses typical of the next-higher stage of moral judgment; as a result, they have been observed to solve moral dilemmas at the higher stage one week later (Walker & Richards, 1979). Group discussion of the possible alternatives for solving such dilemmas has produced higher-level responses than those obtained from subjects who did not have the benefit of discussion sessions (Maitland & Goldman, 1974).

There is also evidence that when the persons involved in the moral conflict are important in the lives of the subjects being studied the solutions are characterized by lower stages of moral reasoning. Levine (1976) asked college students to indicate what someone should do if a friend needed a life-saving drug that was too expensive to buy. The sick person was identified as either a stranger or a person important to the decision-maker. When the dilemma involved a person who was important to the student, a lower stage of moral reasoning was used in its solution than when it involved a stranger. As Figure 12-3 shows, when a total stranger was involved, the solution was more likely to involve stage 4 reasoning: perhaps the authorities would jail someone who stole the medicine, so it shouldn't be stolen. More stage 3 reasoning was found when a valued person faced a problem, with some students saying that such a person would try to pay for the drug in order to keep the approval of others. More sophisticated moral reasoning occurs when the problem involves a stranger rather than a valued person.

When people approach middle and later life, it is reasonable to question whether their judgment styles have changed. As they age, they may or may not become preoccupied with the concerns of everyday living and ignore the needs of others. Schaie and Parham (1974) studied the attitudes of adults ranging in age from 21 to 70. The questionnaire they used included such statements as, "It is all right to get around the law if you don't actually break it." While they found no major differences in attitude due to the age or sex of the persons they studied, they found slight differences between certain groups. Years younger males felt more responsible than older ones, while females' social responsibility did not decrease with age. As they age, males become less socially powerful and are displaced from their roles by retirement, so that a decrease in their social responsibility would be understandable. Females often continue to work at jobs or some

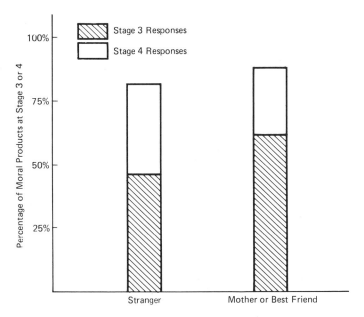

Figure 12-3. Results of a study on moral reasoning among college students in which a primary person, the student's mother or best friend, had a friend who was involved in a dilemma. A lower stage of reasoning was produced under these conditions than when the person with the problem was a total stranger.

form of the mothering or housewife role well into old age, producing little change in their feelings of responsibility. In the case of males, major changes in life style also produce predictable differences in their attitudes toward society and their roles in it.

So far we have focused mainly on the cognitive or intellectual aspects of morality. Its behavioral aspects also change over time, beginning with empathetic, caring responses in young children. Child psychologist Marian Yarrow has found evidence of infants becoming distressed by the crying of others (Pines, 1979). Signs of generosity and helping behavior in these infants persisted five years later, so that the infant empathizers in effect became young altruists. Studies have found that generosity increases in middle childhood (Rushton & Wiener, 1975). Among youngsters whose level of moral judgment is lower than that of their age mates, less generous, more socially aversive behavior has been observed. This may, for example, take the form of racist, prejudicial comments about minorities, which 7–13-year-olds made spontaneously during an experimental game (Davidson, 1976). Thus, moral development strongly affects a person's level of social understanding and empathy, with a corresponding greater likelihood that antisocial tendencies like prejudice will develop.

TRY IT YOURSELF

Do You Believe in a Just World?

Before reading the following section, respond to this scale about your opinions of the degree of justice found in the world. Indicate your degree of agreement or disagreement with each statement by placing an "X" in the space that most nearly describes your feelings:

The Just World Scale*

1. Basically, the world is a just place.

   I strongly disagree ___ : ___ : ___ : ___ : ___ : ___ I strongly agree

2. The political candidate who sticks up for his principles rarely gets elected.

   I strongly disagree ___ : ___ : ___ : ___ : ___ : ___ I strongly agree

3. I've found that a person rarely deserves the reputation he has.

   I strongly disagree ___ : ___ : ___ : ___ : ___ : ___ I strongly agree

4. People who find money in the street have often done a good deed earlier that day.

   I strongly disagree ___ : ___ : ___ : ___ : ___ : ___ I strongly agree

5. It is a common occurrence for a guilty person to get off free in American courts.

   I strongly disagree ___ : ___ : ___ : ___ : ___ : ___ I strongly agree

6. Movies in which good triumphs over evil are unrealistic.

   I strongly disagree ___ : ___ : ___ : ___ : ___ : ___ I strongly agree

7. Students almost always deserve the grades they receive in school.

   I strongly disagree ___ : ___ : ___ : ___ : ___ : ___ I strongly agree

8. Crime doesn't pay.

   I strongly disagree ___ : ___ : ___ : ___ : ___ : ___ I strongly agree

9. When parents punish their children, it is almost always for good reasons.

   I strongly disagree ___ : ___ : ___ : ___ : ___ : ___ I strongly agree.

10. Although there may be some exceptions, good people often lead lives of suffering.

    I strongly disagree ___ : ___ : ___ : ___ : ___ : ___ I strongly agree.

11. It is often impossible for a person to receive a fair trial in the United States.

    I strongly disagree ___ : ___ : ___ : ___ : ___ : ___ I strongly agree.

12. In almost any business or profession, people who do their job well rise to the top.

    I strongly disagree ___ : ___ : ___ : ___ : ___ : ___ I strongly agree.

*Source: Rubin & Peplau, 1973.

13. Although evil men may hold political power for a while, in the general course of history good wins out.

    I strongly disagree ____ : ____ : ____ : ____ : ____ : ____ I strongly agree.

14. By and large, people deserve what they get.

    I strongly disagree ____ : ____ : ____ : ____ : ____ : ____ I strongly agree.

15. American parents tend to overlook the things most to be admired in their children.

    I strongly disagree ____ : ____ : ____ : ____ : ____ : ____ I strongly agree.

16. It is rare for an innocent man to be wrongly sent to jail.

    I strongly disagree ____ : ____ : ____ : ____ : ____ : ____ I strongly agree.

Score your responses to the scale by coding them in the following way. First number each of your responses from 1 to 6, depending on where you placed the X on the continuum of agreement for each item. For example, an answer of "I strongly agree" would be numbered 6. Add the scores for items 1, 4, 7, 8, 9, 12, 13, 14, and 16. Then subtract from that sum the scores for items 2, 3, 5, 6, 10, 11, and 15. The difference is your score on the Just World Scale. Scores above the arithmetic mean of 7 indicate the belief that justice prevails, while scores below 7 indicate the belief that injustice wins out. The possible range of scores is −33 to +47, with the more extreme scores showing greater agreement with the proposition that the world is just or unjust.

In a world filled with ambiguous definitions of morality and made complex by a high rate of change, some people still expect that the unfortunate will be treated justly. Psychologist Melvin Lerner has explored the **"just world" hypothesis,** which states that because of people's need to believe in a just, orderly environment they expect that people generally get what they deserve. One of the few stable aspects of interpersonal relations may be that people begin to anticipate that they and others will receive rewards that they think have been earned (Lerner, 1977). On a very simple level, this belief appears in the tendency of young children to rate negatively story characters who were physically hurt (Suls & Kalle, 1979). Their thinking becomes more complex in middle childhood, when the characters are not rated negatively simply because they were harmed.

As adults, we continue to blame or admire others for deserved rewards. One can easily make sense of a seemingly senseless, random event by blaming, derogating, or even punishing the victim. For example, victims of rape are often blamed for being at least partly responsible for the attack. Whan a rape victim in one study was described as a Catholic nun rather than as a nude dancer, she was blamed less for the attack (Smith, Keating, Hester, & Mitchell, 1976). This suggests that the social roles occupied by such victims modify their place in the just world on the basis of whatever stereotypes exist for them. If the victim of a crime is described as suffering severely because of the attack, subjects acting as mock jurors believe the assailant deserves a stiffer jail sentence (Kerr & Kurtz, 1977).

What are the reactions of the person who is responsible for someone else's misfortune? Less derogation of a victim results when there is less guilt about the person's suffering. By describing a person negatively one can rid oneself of blame for being involved in his or her difficulty. When subjects were told that they had not caused another person to receive electric shock, they rated her more positively than when they were informed of their complicity in the shock delivery (Cialdini, Kenrick, & Hoenig, 1976). If they were given a chance to compensate the victim monetarily, they again did not derogate her.

Belief that the world operates justly also encourages trust in people and institutions. High levels of this belief are correlated with less suspicion about both the deception involved in a study using social-psychological variables and about the promise of a free gift (Zuckerman & Gerbasi, 1977). Subjects with this belief also trusted the basic position of the government on such issues as complicity in the fuel crisis. The world appears to be a rosier place to those who believe that justice prevails.

SITUATIONAL FACTORS IN MORAL BEHAVIOR

The definition of moral behavior varies with the situation. When faced with a choice between right and wrong, one would perform such actions as helping someone in distress, refraining from breaking moral codes, and interfering when another person is doing wrong. The classic studies by Hartshorne and May (1929) on the consistency with which people perform these types of behavior indicate the variability of morality across situations. The same person may cheat on an exam, donate to charity, fail to help a stranded motorist, and report a shoplifter—all in the same day. These pieces of information about moral choice have led to the study of the situational aspects of moral behavior, with emphasis on the factors that produce or inhibit it.

Reinforcement Theory

Can anyone's behavior be bought? How much would it take for you to stand in front of a lecture class and dance in the nude? Is $1,000 enough compensation? How about $1 million, tax free? Proponents of reinforcement theory consider moral behavior to be under the control of rewards and punishments. Skinner (1971), for example, suggests that we turn to a concept such as conscience only when the rewards and punishments are not obvious. Many studies indicate the powerful influence of reinforcement on altruism. For example, cocktail waitresses receive higher tips from customers at whom they flash a broad smile with their teeth showing rather than a minimal smile without the teeth showing (Tidd & Lockard, 1978). After male college students were thanked for agreeing to serve as substitutes for a female who was about to receive electric shocks, they continued to help her on later tasks (McGovern, Ditzian, & Taylor, 1975). Unthanked students refused to help her upon subsequent requests.

      Punishment for misbehavior also influences later helping behavior. In one study zoo visitors were reprimanded either mildly or severely for giving "unauthorized" food to animals. A severe punishment was the comment, "Hey, don't feed unauthorized food to the animals. Don't you know it could hurt them?" while a milder one was, "Please don't feed the animals unauthorized food." People who received a severe reprimand from a passer-by were more likely to help a woman confederate pick up the spilled contents of her handbag than people who were not punished or received a mild reprimand (Katzev, Edelsack, Steinmetz, Walker, & Wright, 1978). It appears that being caught and punished for one type of misbehavior reminds one of one's moral duty to help others in need, making it more rewarding to help another person and soothing a guilty conscience at the same time.

      The chance to help someone in need seems to have rewards of its own, even without measures designed to reward or punish the potential helper directly. Robert F. Weiss and his colleagues have shown that people will learn to make an instrumental response to relieve another's suffering. Students watch a peer supposedly receive an electric shock being delivered by an experimental apparatus; they then have a chance to push buttons that supposedly terminate the shock. Subjects cannot control the onset of the shock, but they significantly speed up their response of turning the shock off as a function of the vicarious reward of providing relief to the victim (Weiss, Boyer, Lombardo, & Stich, 1973).

      The feelings of the altruist in this situation determine his or her response to the chance to aid the victim. Kelley (1979) used the same basic procedure to study the combined effects of gender differences between helper and victim and the helper's mood on the tendency to terminate the shock. The experimenter changed the subject's mood in a positive or negative direction by having the subject read happy or sad statements. Then the subject watched a victim receive electric shock on a television monitor. As Figure 12-4 shows, the slowest termination of shock delivery occurred among male college students who had read sad statements and then watched a female receive the shock. In that group, the subjects said that they experienced negative moods after reading the statements. However, they also said that they were pleasurably excited by being able to watch the woman suffer when they felt bad themselves. For this group, a negative

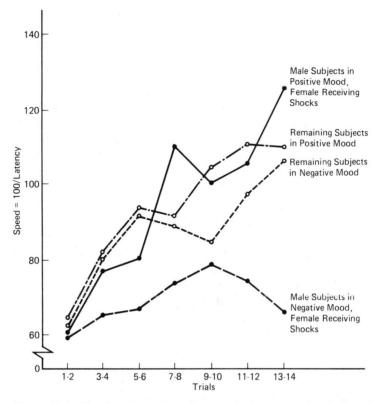

Figure 12-4. Results of a study on the speed of responses terminating shock delivery to another person. When male subjects read sad statements and then watched a female suffer from electric shock, they significantly slowed their termination of shock delivery (Kelley, 1979). The remaining groups consisted of female subjects watching a male or a female suffer, and of male subjects watching a male suffer.

mood and the chance to watch a woman suffer produced a tendency to delay relief of her discomfort. For the remaining groups in the study, terminating the victim's shock more quickly was highly reinforcing.

When punishment or positive reinforcement follows an altruistic act, it influences future helping responses. Boys aged 8 to 11 received a powerful reward or punishment—social approval or disapproval—for generosity in donating prizes to an orphaned boy. When the experimenter rewarded their kindness by calling it good-hearted rather than silly, they continued to donate to the youngster as much as two weeks later (Rushton & Teachman, 1978). The ability to empathize with the orphan's plight helped make altruism rewarding to these boys. Understanding his troubled situation required the youngsters to understand another person's perspective so that they concluded that he would benefit from their donation. Children who demonstrate this ability to empathize with others also display more altruistic behavior, and both tendencies increase with age from early through middle childhood (Buckley, Siegel, & Ness, 1979). Among youngsters who have a tendency to ignore others' needs, empathy is less common (Campagna & Harter, 1975).

Social learning theorists point out the value of models in showing observers the behavior that is appropriate in many types of situations. Seeing a model donate blood, for example, encouraged observers to do likewise in response to a request for donations (Rushton & Campbell, 1977). The model's behavior influences altruism in observers more strongly and for longer periods than preaching by the model (Rushton, 1975). In studies comparing the model's actual behavior to verbal opinions about helping, children asked to donate to charity choose to emphasize the deeds rather than the words as guides to their own behavior. Watching an adult donate to charity produced even more generosity when the youngsters were further rewarded by being told that they donated because they enjoyed helping others rather than because they were expected to do so (Grusec, Kuczynski, Rushton, & Simutis, 1978). Other variables increase the reinforcing value of the model's behavior, such as the emotional warmth of an adult model toward a child. Friendly rather than aloof adult models increased children's tendency to report another child's accident to an experimenter (Weissbrod, 1976). Making models' performance more reinforcing increases the effectiveness of their examples.

No one would dispute the fact that people in Western societies often find television viewing to be a reinforcing, pleasure-producing pastime. Whether television programs provide effective models for moral behavior is another question. Recent studies have found that the television diet of both children and adults can influence several aspects of their behavior. With respect to helpfulness and aggression, a steady stream of studies has shown that television modeling of these behaviors produces corresponding tendencies in the viewers. For example, Collins and Getz (1976) compared the effects of watching an aggressive solution or a prosocial solution to an intense conflict on a 22-minute police drama on the subsequent behavior of fourth-, seventh-, and tenth-grade youngsters. Compared to the aggressive group or to a control group that saw a neutral documentary, the youngsters who saw the prosocial version were more likely to choose to help a peer by turning off a noxious noise rather than give electric shocks to that person. The viewers who saw the physical fight preferred to behave aggressively and delivered significantly more shocks to the peer. With adult viewers, Loye, Gorney, and Steele (1977) found that a week of exposure to evening shows containing violence significantly increased hurtful behavior among husbands being observed by their wives. When they viewed aggressive television shows, these husbands were more likely to lose their tempers, for example, rather than spend time with the children.

Another, perhaps more powerful, determinant of **prosocial behavior** concerns socialization practices. Parents provide models for their offspring in ways that influence their internalization of rules and values. At least one parent usually communicates altruistic values, and one or both parents discipline their youngster (Hoffman, 1975). Of course, many variations of parental treatment of the child's transgressions and good deeds are possible. The optimal combination of socialization practices for moral development appears to involve parent-child interactions characterized by warmth, nurturance, and affection, with definite limits on the youngster's behavior (Staub, 1978). Not surprisingly, positive rather than punitive forms of control promote more prosocial activity in children. These forms of control include reasoning with the child about his or her misbehavior so that the child can correct it in the future.

If the development of prosocial tendencies depends on the reinforcements associated with related forms of behavior, then direct training in those characteristics which seem to produce it might be effective. Training programs for moral behavior have had some success. For example, learning how to perform prosocial acts can produce a change in the frequency of helping in other situations. Staub (1978) has described techniques for training youngsters to help others with first aid or with puzzle solutions that increased the children's willingness to write letters to sick children or donate to the poor. Such methods seem to be more effective with young girls immediately after the training, while boys seem to resist the effects of the training for a short time. Sex differences in independence training and values may help produce this difference in the effectiveness of the training. On delayed tests of prosocial behavior both boys and girls benefited from prosocial training given several weeks earlier. Some educators have advocated the development of "humane education" by integrating altruistic principles into schoolwork, with promising results showing that more empathy and altruism among youngsters can result from such a program ("Kind kids," *Times-Union,* 1979).

Cost-Benefit Theory

The likelihood that a person will engage in prosocial behavior varies with the rewards and punishments that become associated with it. Reinforcements for helping produce an increased tendency to aid others. Punishments reduce the likelihood of extending help to others. But what is socially reinforcing or punishing may differ from one person to another. From the viewpoint of the person concerned, the situation must be analyzed to determine the nature of both the costs and the benefits of helping.

Piliavin and Piliavin (1976) have constructed a model that attempts to predict the incidence of helping on the basis of a cost–benefit comparison. The theory arose from a study of the factors present in an emergency situation, which usually produces in its observers a high level of physiological arousal and unpleasant emotion. Such stress reactions seem to provide a motive for altruism, since they correlate with the tendency to help in highly arousing situations (Dovidio & Morris, 1975). Subjects were found to be more likely to help someone who was about to receive an electric shock if they had just received a shock, and less likely to do so when they themselves had not received a shock. Doing something to relieve stress therefore minimizes the punishments or costs of helping while maximizing the benefits of the action. According to the Piliavins' theory, the costs of helping range from continued stress to risk of injury to loss of time and expenditure of energy on a possibly disgusting experience. The rewards of helping may include social approval from the victim and others and a resulting increase in self-esteem. Failing to help can produce its own costs, such as criticism from others and guilt within oneself. Each person weighs and compares these potential costs and benefits in the decision to help.

The potential helper faced with an emergency uses what is called **bystander calculus** in assessing the costs and benefits that are perceived to result from giving aid to a needy person (Walster & Piliavin, 1972). Help is most likely to be given when the helper perceives that the costs are low and the rewards high. In a situation that produces a similar level of arousal, the person may attempt to escape altogether if he or she perceives that costs are high but the rewards are low.

Piliavin and Piliavin (1972) compared these two factors, costs and benefits, as responses to an emergency. They staged the following emergency in the Philadelphia subway system: A "victim" with a cane entered a subway car. On his way to the other end, he suddenly collapsed on the floor. During half of the enactments of this scene, blood appeared to trickle from his mouth. The costs of helping the collapsed, crippled man would be amplified by the appearance of blood (actually red diet liquid concealed in his mouth). As predicted, significantly more of the subway riders helped the victim and helped him more quickly when he did not bleed than when he bled. Even though the bleeding victim might need help more acutely, the dangers and messiness of getting involved deterred the bystanders from stepping in.

In nonemergency situations too the potential helper calculates the costs and rewards involved. Of course, the person doesn't usually make an explicit comparison of the exact rewards and punishments to be gained or avoided by helping. The calculation of payoffs is done implicitly, by comparing them in general terms according to the benefits to the potential helper. It wouldn't take much calculation, for example, to decide that the costs of completing a mail survey are lower than the costs of agreeing to return to an office to complete the survey. In one study the low costs of helping by mail instead of by an office visit increased compliance rates among college students (Gross, Wallston, & Piliavin, 1975).

The process of responding to the high costs of helping in nonemergency situations was described in a study by Tims, Swart, and Kidd (1976). Male college students were contacted by telephone to determine whether they would respond to an attitude survey on current issues. The cost of helping was indicated by the amount of time required to complete the survey, which ranged from 20 minutes to three hours. The greater the cost, the more likely a subject was to refuse to help. Those who refused to help responded to the request with some information about themselves, such as having a test to study for. On the other hand, those who agreed to help generally asked questions about the survey before they committed themselves. When the requester showed extreme dependence on the potential helper because failure to complete the study would mean inability to graduate from college on schedule, the subjects were even more likely to give information about themselves and their excuses for not helping before turning down the request. It appears that the tendency to offer excuses for not helping is an early sign that such a request will not result in compliance.

Bystander calculus operates in nonexperimental situations. Cowan and Inskeep (1978) studied the responses of past clients of a vocational rehabilitation agency to an appeal to help current clients. The potential helpers were asked to talk to the current clients about their own rehabilitation. Low costs of complying consisted of being able to telephone the person for the talk. High costs involved having to make a visit to the home of a client who had no telephone. For some of the former clients the prospect of helping was expected to be highly satisfying, with greater rewards for complying. Both low cost and greater expected satisfaction increased the tendency to comply with the request for help. This suggests once again that both factors—rewards and costs—affect decisions about helping.

A person chooses to help on the basis of perceived rewards and punishments, but different combinations of costs and benefits produce different styles of response. Hake and Schmitt (1979) have outlined the effects of receiving just or unfair rewards in interpersonal interactions. When a person interacts with others in an equitable fashion, that person expects to receive rewards in line with his or her investment in the interaction. Inequitable results consist of unbalanced states in which one receives more or fewer rewards than expected. From the subject's point of view, one is expected to give or take in such interactions. As Figure 12-5 shows, when people perceive themselves to be taking rewards from an interaction, they can either share and receive equitable, just rewards or compete and receive inequitable, disproportional rewards. When they consider themselves to be giving benefits to an interaction, they can cooperate to produce equity or

DISTRIBUTION OF REINFORCEMENTS

	Equitable	Inequitable
Taking from Relationship	Sharing (Equitable-Taking)	Competition (Inequitable-Taking)
Giving to Relationship	Maximal Cooperation (Equitable-Giving)	Altruism (Inequitable-Giving)

PERSON'S PERCEPTION OF ROLE IN RELATIONSHIP

Figure 12-5. Hake and Schmitt (1979) have classified interpersonal relationships on the bases of the distribution of reinforcements and the person's perception of his or her role.

behave altruistically to produce inequity. Sharing and cooperating for the attainment of rewards are attractive alternatives, since research has shown that people consider either one a suitable way to distribute rewards (Brickman & Bryan, 1976). However, these two forms of reward distribution can easily turn a relationship from one of trust into one of mistrust if the naturally alternating cycle is broken (Hake & Schmitt, 1979). Then the relationship may evolve into an inequitable one in which either competition or altruism becomes the dominant style, with one party at an advantage over the other. Attempts to regain equity then occur, especially when one of the parties is strongly motivated to maintain a relationship in which there is a fair exchange of rewards (Clark & Mills, 1979).

Cognitive Theory

Since altruism is usually a voluntary response, the internal, cognitive reactions of the potential helper must play an important role in the actual delivery of aid. The cognitive theory proposed by Latané and Darley (1970) has described the steps involved in the decision as to whether to help in an emergency. Before a prosocial response can occur, several things must go on in the mind of the potential helper. To help an accident victim or report a theft, a series of decisions must be made. These decisions are determined by several aspects of the situation and the person's past experiences with the factors involved. In the next section we will describe the research dealing with these factors. Several forms of helping behavior involve the same kinds of steps, which are shown in Figure 12-6. Many studies have found that a potential helper's failure to decide in favor of helping indicates that a negative decision was made at one of the necessary steps.

Notice Something Is Happening. Before help can be given, the person must notice that something is happening by perceiving it and at-

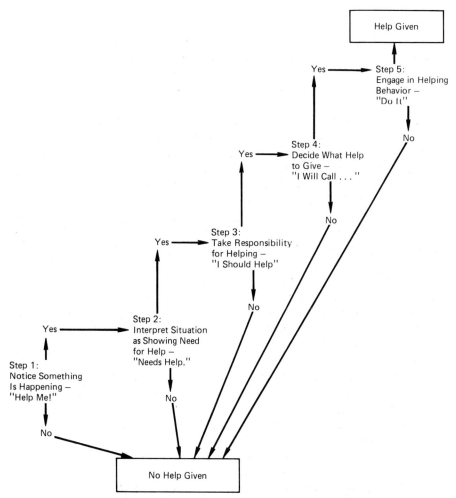

Figure 12-6. This flow diagram shows the steps involved in helping behavior according to a cognitive analysis by Latané and Darley (1970).

tending to it. Attention to oneself rather than to the concerns of others may block such a response at the earliest stage. Fear of embarrassment or social anxiety can cause a person to ignore the needs of others while avoiding the threatening aspects of getting involved with someone else. Such a reaction is more likely in an ambiguous situation that might turn out badly. McGovern (1976) studied the role of social anxiety in helping behavior. Social anxiety is the tendency to avoid unpleasant situations that might result in embarrassment or anxiety. People who are socially anxious might, for example, say on a paper-and-pencil test of this construct that they would rather clean out a cesspool than be seen picking their nose. In McGovern's study male college students who were high in social anxiety refused to help a female (by receiving an electric shock meant for her) significantly more often than nonanxious males. The socially anxious subjects agreed to help after the "victim" requested them to do so, but they still helped less often than the nonanxious males. It appears that to someone who is high in social anxiety helping means risking embarrassment.

Interpret Situation.   At the next step in the decision process, the person interprets the situation as one that requires help or one that does not. For example, there may be alternative logical reasons for a person to fall to the ground. An icy sidewalk suggests an accident. A dry sidewalk in front of a bar suggests a drunk. The interpretation of whether help is required also depends on who the victim is. Two characteristics of persons in need seem to emphasize the need for aid, especially in the view of males in the United States. These are female sex and black skin color. Males rate females as weaker and more dependent than themselves, and help them more often in various ways, such as diverting an electric shock from them by taking it themselves (McGovern, Ditzian, & Taylor, 1975). Black males were also perceived to be more dependent and deserving of help than white males when whites were asked to complete a telephone survey of racial attitudes. White males with highly racist attitudes tend to consider blacks as appropriate recipients of aid (Katz, Cohen, & Glass, 1975).

Take Responsibility.   Once the potential helper has perceived and attended to the situation as one requiring aid, he or she must cope with whether to assume responsibility for taking on the helper role. A study of this problem was conducted in a shopping center. A male confederate asked women shoppers to watch his packages while he looked for either his lost wallet or a $1 bill dropped in a store. The shoppers in the $1 condition would be expected to believe that the reason for their agreeing to watch his belongings was their own helpfulness (internal attribution). Those in the wallet condition would be expected to believe that they helped mainly because of the man's need to recover a lot of lost money (external attribution). The internal attribution was expected to produce greater helping when subsequent situations arose. After the lost-money incident was resolved, a female confederate passed by, dropping a package. Subjects in the $1 condition helped by informing her that she had dropped a package or returning it to her, while those in the wallet condition did so less often (Uranowitz, 1975). Other studies show that stating one's intent to help, especially in situations about which one has positive rather than negative attitudes, also increases the tendency to deliver aid when confronted with an opportunity to do so (Zuckerman & Reis, 1978). Thus, both internal attributions for one's altruism and an explicit commitment to be helpful lead to a greater sense of responsibility.

Decide What to Do.   After taking responsibility for the act, the potential helper must decide what to do. He or she must consider each alternative and decide which one is the most reasonable. Knowledge of which actions are appropriate will improve the chances of taking the right one. For example, knowledge of first aid would be valuable in providing such help. Professional experience with social welfare applicants might also affect the helper's perception of the type of help that would be best. Batson (1975) compared the judgments of seminary students who had experience in helping people with problems of unemployment, drug use, or psychological problems with the judgments of inexperienced college students. The subjects listened to case studies of persons who had approached a social welfare agency for aid, and then recommended remedial action. The experienced seminary students were more likely to judge the clients as the source of the problems and to refer them to institutions designed to change the individual, such as mental hospitals or residential treatment centers. The inexperienced college students, on the other hand, more often attributed the problems to the social situation and referred the clients to institutions, such as social services and employment agencies, designed to change external aspects of the client's life. Thus, expectations about aid seekers and the best courses of action to take depended on the helper's experience and familiarity with such situations.

Provide Help.   In the last step of the helping response, the person must actually carry out the behavior decided on in step four. This final step depends on the preceding series of cognitive decisions. Research has shown the value of knowing about the steps involved in behaving altruistically. College students enrolled in an introductory psychology course at the University of Montana watched or listened to a film or lecture on the factors that affect the decision to help or to ignore the needs of others (Beaman, Barnes, Klentz, & McQuirk, 1978). Control subjects observed a lecture on the emotional factors involved in obesity. Two weeks later the students took part in a second phase of the study in which each of them joined a student confederate on the way to another experiment. They encountered another person, a male, lying on the floor in one of the campus buildings. Compared to the control group, the groups that had been instructed in altruism helped the "victim" more often (42.5% vs. 25%) by calling out to him, indicating the need for help, or reporting his condition to someone. This is impressive evidence that knowledge of the factors that can hinder altruism can influence behavior in a prosocial way. It is quite possible that after you read this chapter you will behave more altruistically than before.

HELPING OTHERS: A STRANGER IN DISTRESS

In the studies on helping behavior described so far, the rates of helping that actually occurred have not been 100 percent. On the contrary, even under conditions in which an altruist can expect to be strongly rewarded for that behavior, a sizable minority of those present will not provide help. Some have suggested reasons for the failure of bystanders to help a victim,

Figure 12-7. A stranded motorist may receive aid, depending on the outcome of the decision process which a potential helper undergoes. In addition, a female motorist is more likely to receive help than males or couples.   (Irene Springer)

including apathy and unwillingness to get involved in others' problems. Often this seeming indifference is cited as evidence of the alienation and helplessness of millions of strangers living in urban areas. Loss of moral values (for a variety of possible reasons) is also named as a source of callousness toward the needs of fellow human beings. These commentaries on our way of life place the blame for lack of helpfulness in the individual. On the other hand, it is possible that the responses of the individual to factors that are present in the situation contribute to this apparent callousness. Several investigators have studied this idea by creating "emergencies" in which actors, tape recordings, and other such devices are used to simulate an accident, illness, or personal hardship.

The idea that individual differences and situational factors both contribute to altruism has received wide support. Motivational and situational factors seem to interact, so that helping behavior can be predicted more accurately from both aspects together rather than from either one alone. Wilson (1976) found that the effect on helpfulness of observing an altruistic or passive model depends on the social orientation of the observer. Undergraduates were classified as being concerned mainly with safety or with esteem in social relations on the basis of their responses to a projective sentence completion test. Safety-oriented subjects express more anxiety and less trust of their own competence and others' reliability. Those who are concerned with esteem motives, on the other hand, display feelings of personal competence and achievement need. Safety concerns might be indicated by completing the phrase, "If I could only . . ." with "find security." Esteem motives might be indicated by completing it with, "be successful as soon as possible." While subjects responded to a medical questionnaire in a laboratory, the experimenter appeared to have an accident in an adjacent room—the sound of breaking glass was followed by his calls for

RESEARCH CLOSE-UP

The Effects of Being Helped

It is sometimes assumed that a person in need of help naturally *wants* to be helped and will be appreciative of any aid that is received. In some situations, neither of these reactions holds true. Think of some time when you were in need of help. Let's say that your car would not start and you were unable to fix it. At that point, a stranger comes by, offers help, and has your car running smoothly a few minutes later.

Do you feel good about the situation or bad?

Are you grateful that this person lent a helping hand or envious and resentful that someone possessed skills that you lack?

Do you feel good about yourself, humiliated by your deficiencies, determined to learn more about auto mechanics, or what?

Research suggests that any of these responses *can* occur, depending on various aspects of the particular situation and the characteristics of the individuals involved.

It may seem surprising, but offers of help can produce distinct negative feelings in those to whom it is directed. People would generally prefer to have help offered to them than to request it (Broll, Gross, & Piliavin, 1974), but the personal traits of the potential donor influence the effect of the offer. A person who receives aid on a task may feel less intelligent and self-confident, especially when the helper was similar rather than dissimilar in such characteristics as experience with the task involved (Fisher, Harrison, & Nadler, 1978). When a wealthy donor contributed to their success in an experimental game, male college students both perceived themselves less positively and took steps to improve their deficient condition by learning how to help themselves (Fisher & Nadler, 1976). There are threatening aspects to having to be helped out of a tough situation by someone like oneself or someone with great wealth.

Cross-cultural research in the United States, Japan, and Sweden shows that affluent donors, compared to poor ones, will receive repayment less often (Gergen, Ellsworth, Maslack, & Seipel, 1975). These studies suggest that self-help and reciprocation of aid are less likely when the offer creates feelings of inability to help oneself.

help. Whether the subjects listened to this emergency alone or with two confederates in the room, esteem-oriented subjects attempted to help the victim more often than safety-oriented subjects (85% vs. 50%). The behavior of the bystanders influenced the response of the latter group. When one of the bystanders entered the adjacent room, thus serving as a model for altruism, these subjects helped. But a passive bystander inhibited such a response among these more anxious subjects. This study indicates that the effects of social influence on helping depend to some extent on observers' motivations. For some, the rewards of altruism provided the esteem they desired. For others, the stance of taking cues from others was more rewarding because it provided safety.

People who are alone in an emergency situation behave differently from people who are with a group. As the number of bystanders increases, the probability of help decreases. Intuitively, it would make sense to expect that as group size increases, so does the likelihood that a victim will be helped. In a larger group someone would surely notice another person's need and act on that perception. But a phenomenon known as **diffusion of responsibility** occurs in groups faced with an emergency. According to Darley and Latané (1968), the responsibility to provide help is shared among the bystanders and does not clearly apply to any one person. When helping involves potentially negative consequences, this diffusion is especially likely to develop (Mynatt & Sherman, 1975). Because of the inhibiting effects of multiple bystanders, then, as their number increases, the likelihood that any of them will engage in prosocial behavior decreases.

Diffusion of responsibility occurs in many settings. Remember the study described in Chapter 1, in which tipping by restaurant diners varied inversely with the size of the party (Freeman, Walker, Borden, & Latané, 1975)? As the size of the party increased, the proportion of the bill representing a tip became smaller. In another study, elevator riders could help themselves to free coupons for cheeseburgers, but they were less likely to take the coupons when other riders were present than when they were alone (Petty, Williams, Harkins, & Latané, 1977). In still another study, students evaluated an editorial and a poem either alone or in groups. In the alone condition they not only rated the writings more positively but also reported putting more effort into their work than the students working in groups (Petty, Harkins, Williams, & Latané, 1977). In general, then, behavior is altered by the presence of others.

People in groups have different expectations regarding rewards and punishments for altruism than persons by themselves. One of these differences concerns a lower expectation on the part of group members to be singled out for their performance as long as it resembles the group's typical responses. Such feelings of anonymity in a group, or **deindividuation,** apply to the helping situation. Wegner and Shaefer (1978) found that focusing on oneself as the observer of someone's need and as an individual rather than as a group member affects the helping response. They varied both the number of potential helpers and the number of victims. It was found that people responded positively to requests for help when there were fewer bystanders or more victims. Responsibility for helping apparently was diffused among members of a larger group of bystanders, but there was "more to be shared" when there were several persons in need. When the experiment required group members to introduce themselves to each other and thus reduce their feelings of group anonymity, they helped a student who fainted on his desk during the study. Students who wore hoods to hide their faces and did not introduce themselves helped less often (Solomon & Solomon, 1978).

Just as a lack of clear responsibility for helping can inhibit its occurrence, ambiguity in the perception of the situation can have the same effect. For example, college students who were responding to an attitude survey in a laboratory saw an experimenter have an accident while they watched a closed-circuit television monitor. Some subjects both saw and heard the accident; others only heard it, since the experimenter left camera range before a file cabinet supposedly fell on him or he pretended to faint. When the observers could both see and hear the accident, so that its ambiguity was reduced, they helped the "victim" significantly more often than subjects in the audio condition (Solomon, Solomon, & Stone, 1978). Lowest rates of helping occurred among subjects who heard the event in groups rather than alone.

Other ways of studying the effect of ambiguity on helping have involved the creation of a conflict about what action would be appropriate. Shotland and Straw (1976) attempted to pinpoint the reasons for the finding that male observers fail to intervene in a physical attack by a man on a woman. They found that the attitudinal response to this scene among observers resolved some of the ambiguity in the attack—the bystanders typically defended nonintervention in what they considered a "lovers' quarrel." When subjects of both sexes were informed that the pair were strangers rather than married to each other, the helping rate increased. These observers also interpreted the situation to be more rewarding and less costly, since in this case they thought the woman was in greater danger from the stranger's attack and needed more help. They also expected the stranger to run away and the husband to stay and fight, suggesting that the subjects' reason for nonintervention was the perception of a potentially negative outcome.

Conflict about helping is also introduced by a task that competes with the helping response. Being too busy to help someone in need may seem callous and uncaring, but a prior commitment may outweigh the importance of prosocial behavior. A study exposed male undergraduates to an emergency—another young man slumped in a doorway—while they were on their way between two buildings to take part in an experiment. Half of the subjects were instructed to hurry to meet a deadline and the other half were told they had sufficient time so they did not need to hurry. Their participation in the experiment was also described as either very important or not essential. As Figure 12-8 shows, both the instruction to hurry and the alleged importance of participation in the experiment decreased the incidence of attempts to help the victim. The hurrying, preoccupied subjects had already made a commitment to aid the experimenter; they decided to carry out what they considered their responsibility and ignore the victim's need more often than those who did not feel such a conflict (Batson, Cochran, Biederman, Blosser, Ryan, & Vogt, 1978).

Social variables in the environment are critical in determining people's reactions to emergencies. A person in a position of authority can place demands on potential helpers that interfere with their prosocial responses. What happens when an authority figure is present? Does the authority of a leader, for example, produce effective functioning in emergency situations? A study by Firestone, Lichtman, and Colamosca (1975) indicates that leaderless groups operate less effectively under such conditions. Groups of students were led by people who were either highly qualified or unqualified to help the group reach consensus because they were very skillful at communication and persuasion. After a period of group

Figure 12-8.   Male undergraduates stopped to help someone slumped in a doorway when they were not in a hurry or when their task was unimportant.

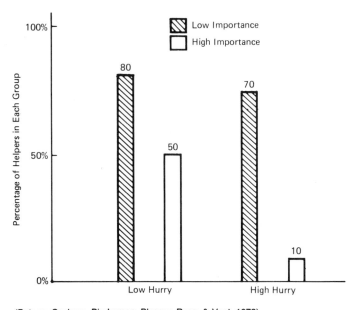

(Batson, Cochran, Biederman, Blosser, Ryan, & Vogt, 1978)

functioning under one of the two types of leaders, a group member suddenly seemed to experience insulin shock and appealed for help. Groups with more effective discussion leaders responded to the crisis more frequently and faster than those with less competent leaders, who often had to be replaced during the crisis while valuable time was lost. Thus, the failing leader did not "rise to greatness" during the group reaction to the emergency. Effective leaders, on the other hand, improved the victim's chances of getting help by setting a clear course of action to which the followers readily responded.

An emergency creates an unpleasant emotional reaction in bystanders who observe it, some of whom may be unwilling captives of events that are beyond their control. Preoccupation with another task or reliance on a leader's competence can be used to justify inaction. In the absence of excuses like these, though, people appear to take other steps to escape from an unwanted source of bothersome arousal. For example, observers' responses to an emergency that they could hear but not see depended on the victim's race and the number of other bystanders. If they could diffuse the responsibility for helping to others, they discriminated against black victims who had supposedly fallen. When the bystanders could attribute their negative emotional responses to a sugar placebo instead of to witnessing an accident, the black victim again received less help (Gaertner & Dovidio, 1977). This suggests that whites take advantage of opportunities to misattribute the arousal they feel in an emergency in order to direct their prosocial responses toward white rather than black victims. These results were independent of white bystanders' racial attitudes, implying that the social desirability of nonracist opinions may not extend to interracial helping.

By manipulating observers' opinions about their own levels of arousal in response to emergencies, it should be possible to examine directly the role of empathy in such situations. Coke, Batson, and McDavis (1978) asked college students to listen to a radio broadcast about the plight of Katie, a senior in college whose parents had recently been killed in an automobile accident. Then they were informed that they could help Katie reach her goal of graduation by babysitting for her siblings and doing household chores for her. Some of the students' level of empathic emotional arousal to this story was reduced by allowing them to misattribute their emotions to the effects of a drug (actually a placebo) taken during an unrelated memory experiment. Others' arousal level was increased by false feedback about their physiological reactions. Compared to those whose arousal levels were caused only by hearing Katie's story, higher levels of empathic emotion increased the amount of helping and lower levels reduced it.

The benefits for helping emanate from the expectation of vicarious reinforcement by an improvement in the victim's situation. Mood manipulations like those used in the studies just described influenced helping by increasing the amount of emotional arousal felt as a result of the victim's need. Other studies have manipulated moods in situations unrelated to one requiring aid to test their effects on later altruism. For example, Isen, Clark, and Schwartz (1976) manipulated the moods of Lancaster, Pennsylvania, residents in a positive direction by means of a gift of stationery from a door-to-door salesperson. After they received the gift, the telephone rang. The caller was an experimenter who asked the resident to make a phone call for her, since she had called the wrong number and had no more change. Subjects who had just received the gift were more likely to comply with the request to convey a phone message. The effect of this mood manipulation on altruism was only temporary, however, since no improvement in helping resulted among subjects who received the gift twenty minutes before the phone call. The prosocial effects of a good mood on this form of helping seem to dissipate quickly. Mood may increase helpfulness because of the tendency to evaluate situations more positively when one is in a good rather than a bad mood, as discussed in Chapter 9. A prosocial reaction to someone else's need may be enhanced by the expectation that a good mood can be maintained by relieving the other person's distress.

Bystander intervention in emergencies depends partly, then, on how the situation is evaluated. Witnesses are especially likely to consider an event an emergency if it is an accident rather than some natural or deliberate event such as war, a severe storm, or a rape. In a survey of attitudes toward such events, college students displayed a high degree of consistency in their perception of certain events, such as an accident victim's bleeding or a child's being poisoned, as emergencies. In contrast, other events, such as a cat's getting stuck in a tree, or someone needing a match, were considered as everyday problems and not as emergencies. Emergencies were distinguished from less serious events and everyday problems by the perception that the harm to the victim could worsen and that the solution might require outside help. The tendency to perceive the harm as less threatening and serious resulted in a lower probability of labeling it as an emergency requiring immediate help from bystanders, who were more willing to help when the victim's need was obvious to them (Shotland & Huston, 1979). As we have seen from several studies in this section, however, bystanders commonly find various ways to misperceive the need of a victim.

RESISTING TEMPTATION

An important part of moral behavior consists of resisting the temptation to acquire forbidden rewards. Helping oneself to another student's answers on a test, keeping quiet when a clerk gives too much change, or keeping money that one has found are examples of ways to reward one's luck without apparently hurting anyone else. A Gallup Youth Survey reported in 1978 that six out of ten adolescents admit to having cheated on a test but only a small minority report having been caught. They consider cheating to be common, and the frequency of cheating is only slightly lower among students with higher grades (57 percent) than among those with lower ones (67 percent) (Gallup Youth Survey, 1978). Breaking the moral code in order to help oneself is common. Is it possible to identify people who are likely to cheat on the basis of personality traits?

Need for Approval, Religiosity, and Lying

A high **need for approval** by others of one's own performance can lead to cheating. In one experiment college students had a chance to change their scores on a test of intelligence, supposedly without the change being detected. Among those with a strong, defensive need to avoid social disapproval and failure as shown on a paper-and-pencil test, cheating was significantly higher than among those who were low in that need (Millham, 1974).

Religiosity would be expected to reduce cheating, but the evidence indicates otherwise. Smith, Wheeler, and Diener (1975) classified college students in terms of their attitudes, values, and self-reported behavior with respect to the Christian religion. Four groups of students were identified: highly or moderately religious, nonreligious, and atheistic. These four groups did not differ in amount of cheating on an examination or in willingness to donate time to a program for mentally retarded children. Training in and adherence to religious doctrine does not always produce the expected increase in moral behavior.

Once a person has cheated or otherwise defied standards of morality, he or she often lies about the act. Deceiving others about one's own behavior seems to require certain interpersonal skills that improve the chances of getting away with the lie. In a study of lying, college students were videotaped while misrepresenting their true feelings about another person. Successful liars, who were not detected by students watching the videotapes, used an interesting tactic to achieve the effect they intended. They "hammed" their false statements of like and dislike by expressing more extreme feelings in these cases than when they expressed their true feelings (De Paulo & Rosenthal, 1979). Highly manipulative persons were especially likely to use this strategy, and their lies were seldom detected by observers. It is interesting to note that skill at lying did not generalize to the ability to determine when others were lying.

Delay of Gratification

Civilization is built on a foundation of impulse control in which such drives as hunger, sex, and elimination are satisfied in specific ways at specific times in specific contexts. One of the greatest tasks facing children and their parents is the development of behavior that involves delay and post-ponement of drive satisfaction. The success of this teaching varies—there are vast differences among individuals in willingness to delay gratification. For example, consider the student who attends college and goes through graduate school in order to obtain advanced scientific or professional training. The entire process revolves around delay and at least partial nonsatis-faction of primary and secondary needs in the expectation of greater future rewards. By way of comparison, consider the person who drops out of school, commits minor burglaries to obtain money, and joins a gang in a sexual assault on a young woman. Is there any way to study this range of differences in gratification as a personality variable?

Many studies have utilized a technique in which subjects must choose between a small immediate reward and a larger reward that will be available after a certain amount of time. For example, children are asked to choose between a small notebook now and a larger one in a week or between 15 cents now and 30 cents in three weeks.

Mischel and Gilligan (1964) hypothesized that people who are unable to postpone gratification in order to receive a larger reward would be likely to give in to temptation and to cheat in situations in which success was important to them. The subjects in their study were sixth-grade boys in Boston. The boys were asked to make seventeen choices between immediate and delayed rewards. They then had a chance to cheat on a game involving hitting a moving target with shots from a toy ray gun. To win the game the boys had to cheat by covertly adding extra points to their scores. The boys who cheated more on this game also preferred more immediate rewards. Those who were not willing to delay gratification in order to get a larger reward also were not willing to resist the temptation to cheat.

Young children gradually learn how to delay gratification and how to tolerate the delay more easily. Yates and Mischel (1979) compared the responses of preschoolers to those of older children in coping with the delay before they received a reinforcement. The children chose between receiving one pretzel (or some other item such as a poker chip) immediately or three in ten minutes. Those who chose the larger delayed reward had another decision to make: whether to view the item chosen, a picture of it, or another item during the waiting period. Viewing the chosen reinforcement makes the delay more difficult and frustrating than watching an unrelated object. However, the younger children consistently chose to view the real item during this period, whereas the older ones helped themselves tolerate the delay by viewing some other scene. The younger children made the self-imposed delay even more difficult for themselves by increasing their desire for the promised reward, as is shown by the fact that they more frequently terminated the delay in order to receive an immediate smaller reward. At about the age of 7, children began to realize that taking one's mind off the attractive choice makes delay of gratification easier to tolerate.

Failure to develop the appropriate responses to the prospect of a delayed reward can have serious effects on moral development. Defective impulse control is often found among delinquent adolescents and adult criminals. Roberts and Erikson (1968) studied incoming inmates in an institution for delinquent male adolescents. Those who created more nuisances among the inmates by fighting also had difficulty planning to save money rather than spend it, and preferred the immediate reward of one cigarette over a delayed reward of a whole pack one week later. Their poor tolerance for delay of gratification seemed to make it difficult for them to respond with more impulse control in the correctional setting.

People who are deficient in conscience are likely to have lower levels of moral reasoning, prefer immediate gratification, and choose delayed over immediate punishment. Each of these characteristics contrasts with the moral reasoning and preferences for delay found among more highly socialized individuals. Psychopathic delinquents are found to be more immature in moral reasoning and less empathic in role taking compared with other delinquents and with adolescents in general (Jurkovic & Prentice, 1977). That is, they tend to be unresponsive to social situations that would normally create concern for others, and they show little guilt about their unusual reactions. The lack of self-control that is found in the tendency to prefer immediate gratification can be increased by exposure to prestigious models who delay their own gratification, as was shown in a study of prison inmates. Young convicts with little tolerance for delay of gratification observed the money-saving behaviors of older inmates who held the valued positions of photographer or X-ray technician in the prison. After they observed these models planning to save money, their own plans to save rather than spend reflected more long-term saving than before, and the effect persisted one month later (Stumphauzer, 1972). Finally, psychopathic subjects in prison chose to receive delayed rather than immediate doses of painful electric shock compared with their nonpsychopathic peers and normal subjects, who choose the immediate aversive stimulus (Hare, 1966). Future punishment is less emotionally significant to psychopaths than to normal individuals.

Learning to Resist Temptation

If it can be assumed that moral behavior is learned, the study of how such learning takes place is important, both in theory and in practical terms. Children are rarely, if ever, purposely taught to be devoid of feeling for others and indifferent to all values. Yet almost all societies, including our own, regularly turn out their full quota of murderers, sadists, cheats, liars, and thieves.

Aronfreed (1968), among others, views the development of conscience in terms of **internalization.** That is, a given value is internalized to the extent that its maintenance has become independent of external outcomes; internal reinforcement, rather than external reward and punishment, keeps the behavior going. An important research task, then, is to identify the crucial factors in parent–child interactions and other childhood learning situations that lead to internalization.

MacKinnon (1938), in early work on this research problem, created a setting in which subjects were tempted to do something about which they would feel guilty. One by-product of that research was an intriguing hint of a relation between child-rearing practices and resistance to temptation. By disguising the study as a study of the steps used in problem solution, MacKinnon gave subjects a chance to cheat by looking at solutions to some problems (but not others) in a booklet. An experimenter observed the behavior of the subjects through a one-way mirror. The cheaters tended to verbalize anger toward the problem ("You bastard"), whereas none of the noncheaters did so. The cheaters also engaged in a destructive, aggressive kind of behavior in scuffling their feet, stamping on the floor, kicking the table, and pounding their fists. The noncheaters tended to behave with restlessness and fidgeting—crossing and uncrossing their legs or hunching their shoulders. The most striking difference between those who peeked at forbidden solutions and those who didn't was in oral activity (touching the mouth, biting fingernails), which was twice as frequent among the noncheaters as among the cheaters. Likewise, the noncheaters engaged in nose picking and hair twisting more often than the cheaters. MacKinnon interpreted these differences in psychoanalytic terms, suggesting that the cheaters directed aggression externally while the noncheaters aggressed against themselves.

The two groups were asked various questions about their parents, and again there were notable differences. The fathers of cheaters were described as using physical punishment in disciplining their children, while the fathers of noncheaters used methods that made the child feel that he or she "had fallen short of an ideal or was not worthy of the parent's love." When asked how they had reacted to punishment, subjects who had received physical punishment said that they had become angry, sulked, disliked the punisher, and sometimes secretly repeated whatever they had been punished for. Psychological punishment led to feelings of shame, sorrow, and resolutions to be good and behave as expected.

The themes emerging from MacKinnon's research have influenced much of the subsequent research and theorizing on this problem. Since moral behavior appears to be socially learned, observation of models who resist temptation should influence children to do the same. When the nature of the temptation and the model's behavior both clearly suggest to children a possible transgression and the best solution to it, models have a strong influence on their subsequent moral behavior. In one study Canadian kindergarteners were asked to help an experimenter sort colored cards into piles. The adult introduced them to Charlie, the friendly table, located in the same room and covered with attractive toys. Charlie, she added, sometimes talked and tried to persuade youngsters to play with his toys. After the experimenter left, an adult model joined the child in working on the card-sorting task. Charlie the table urged the model to play with his toys by means of a tape-recorded message attached to his underside. For half of the children, the model resisted this temptation; for the other half, the model yielded and played with the toys. Later the child was left alone to work. At that point Charlie the talking table attempted to distract him or her from the card sorting by saying,

Hey! Listen to me. I've got lots of nice toys over here. Any of my toys is more fun than sorting those cards. You could bounce my ball or read my books or play with anything you want. Who cares about cards anyway? Enjoy yourself. [Grusec, Kuczynski, Rushton, & Simutis, 1979, p. 235]

Children who had seen the model resist Charlie's enticement were more likely to continue to resist it themselves and for longer periods than children who had witnessed the yielding model. It appears that learning to resist temptation occurs partly as a function of the self-restraint exercised by agents of socialization.

Peers as sources of social influence can also encourage youngsters to overcome or yield to temptation. Trick-or-treaters in Seattle, Washington, were observed in several homes to determine whether they would take forbidden extra candy after the first child in their group did so. When the youngsters entered the homes each was invited by an adult to take one piece of candy from a bowl. An experimenter recorded their behavior from behind a backdrop through a peephole. After the first child in the group took extra candy, each of the others usually disobeyed the adult's instructions and took more as well (Diener, Fraser, Beaman, & Kelem, 1976). The presence of an adult, either a parent or the resident experimenter, greatly reduced the incidence of this transgression. It appears that the presence of an adult served to remind the children of the standards of behavior and the prospect of punishment.

Several questions about the process of resistance to temptation have been raised. One interesting line of research has focused on the levels of internal arousal to which subjects respond and the label they apply to their internal state (Nisbett & Schachter, 1966). For example, the concept of guilt arousal implies various internal events, both physiological and psychological. When the person perceives these internal events, the feeling must be labeled as guilt for subsequent behavior to be affected. If anything interferes with either the arousal or the labeling process, the effects of guilt are less powerful.

Following this reasoning, Dienstbier (1972) hypothesized that it is not simply emotional arousal that causes one to avoid an immoral act such as cheating but, rather, one's interpretation of that arousal. When there is temptation to commit such an act, there should be emotional arousal. The person can interpret this arousal as a sample of how bad either the guilt for committing an immoral act or the fear of getting caught will be. Either label should inhibit the immoral behavior. If, however, the person believes the emotional state has some other, quite different, cause, there should be no inhibition.

The study supposedly involved the effect of a vitamin supplement on vision. Male college students were given a pill (a gelatin) and told either that it induced symptoms of *arousal* such as pounding heart and sweaty palms, or symptoms of *fatigue* such as tired eyes and a tendency to yawn. It was assumed that any arousal of the sympathetic nervous system caused by the temptation to cheat would resemble the effects attributed to the vitamin pill in the arousal group but not in the fatigue group. The temptation was in the form of a very difficult vocabulary test that was said to be highly predictive of success in college. They were also told that if they scored lower than average for college freshmen, a college board would examine them to determine the reasons for subnormal performance. The subjects all failed to meet the criterion. When they were alone, they had access to the correct responses and had a chance to cheat by changing their answers to the test items. Through the use of a special pressure-sensitive paper, it was possible to detect changed answers. The percentage of cheaters in each condition is shown in Table 12-1. When the arousal could be attributed to the drug, many more subjects cheated than when the arousal could only be attributed to guilt or fear. One's interpretation of one's internal state can have a substantial effect on one's subsequent moral behavior.

Some people constantly get themselves into trouble, while others generally obey the law. Heisler (1974) conducted a study that compared the cheating behavior of college students who had or had not broken the law. To assess the number of crimes, misdemeanors, and behaviors like skip-

Table 12-1. When male college students were placed in a situation in which they were tempted to cheat, their physiological arousal could be perceived in one of two ways. If the arousal were the result of guilt or fear, they were expected to refrain from cheating. If the arousal were the result of a drug, they were expected to be more likely to engage in cheating. By means of different information about the effects of a vitamin pill, the experimenter was able to induce these two different perceptions of arousal. The pattern of cheating confirmed the hypotheses.

Perceived Reason for Emotional Arousal	Cheaters	Noncheaters
Drug side effects (Vitamin-arousal)	71%	39%
Guilt or fear (Vitamin-fatigue)	45%	55%

(Based on data from Dienstbier, 1972.)

ping school committed by each subject, the students were asked to respond to an anonymous scale of offenses. Surprisingly, these 123 introductory psychology students at Southern Illinois University in rural Carbondale, Illinois, had committed a large number of offenses. Fully 50 percent had broken the law. For example, 37 percent had sold narcotics. Other violations included grand larceny (17 persons); auto theft (11); forgery (5); nonstatutory rape (3); assault with intent to kill (3); and burglary (7). Only 1 student reported having been apprehended for a crime. Those who had violated laws reported having committed an average of 2 major offenses. Each of these students also admitted having committed an average of 8 misdemeanors such as running a red light, compared to an average of 4 lesser offenses reported by each of the generally law-abiding students.

When these students were given a chance to cheat on an achievement test, law violators were more apt to cheat than those students who had not broken the law. They were asked to report their scores on the test in front of other subjects. The tests had already been scored by the experimenter, who thus could determine the rate of misreporting. Consistent with the idea that the risk of danger can be exciting to an offender, the announcement that cheating could be punished by suspension from school actually resulted in *more* cheating by violators. If they witnessed a model being caught cheating, however, cheating was reduced. Deterrence of this type of behavior obviously must be manipulated carefully in order to produce a prosocial rather than antisocial effect.

INTERFERENCE: STANDING UP FOR WHAT IS RIGHT

When a person becomes aware that someone else has committed a theft, the problem is in many ways quite different from the kinds of emergency created in the studies described earlier. There is no physical threat to the subject or anyone else, and the only harm done is the loss of money or property. In fact, a bystander who reports the crime is bringing harm to the thief and facing the possibility of retribution. Even so, the moral and legal issues are quite clear. Theft is wrong, and thieves should be reported, caught, and punished. An interesting research question is whether the situational factors that affect response to theft are the same as those that affect responses to emergency situations. For example, does the presence of multiple witnesses to a theft inhibit the tendency of any one of them to report the crime?

Latané and Darley (1970) attempted to answer this question by staging a theft of money during an experiment. While male undergraduates waited to be interviewed, they saw another subject (who was actually a confederate) steal about $40 from a receptionist's desk. The subject was either the sole witness of the theft or one of two witnesses, either of whom had a choice between reporting the crime or remaining silent. Even when they were the only witnesses, most said nothing about the theft after the culprit left the room. However, more subjects in the alone condition reported the theft than subjects in the two-witness condition. Those who remained silent about the crime tended to deny having seen it or to deny knowing what exactly had occurred. This kind of illegal act is easily tolerated, especially when more than one witness is present.

Failure to report a theft also occurs when it involves stolen property rather than money. Latané and Darley (1970) staged a beer heist from a discount store during the prearranged absence of a clerk from that part of the store. Witnesses of the theft did not attempt to interfere with it, but the majority mentioned it to the clerk later. As in the helping experiments, the presence of another witness in addition to the subject reduced the frequency of reporting the crime. In this and other studies of theft (Howard & Crana, 1974), the presence of more than one bystander inhibited prosocial behavior.

The real victims of shoplifting are the consumers, who are forced to pay higher prices to compensate for the merchants' losses. Retailers pass the cost of this crime along to them, and in 1978 the bill totaled a staggering $7 billion in the United States ("Shoplifting loss," *The Indianapolis Star,* 1979). On an individual level, that cost averaged at least $200 per person for added consumer costs. Because of this social cost of shoplifting and its importance as an aspect of moral behavior, several studies have examined the factors determining how observers respond to it.

The response of one bystander can act to encourage or discourage another observer's report of shoplifting. When ambiguity about the interpretation of the theft and uncertainty about responsibility for reporting it can be reduced, a bystander responds more prosocially. Bickman and Rosenbaum (1977) studied behavior in a large supermarket in which a confederate stuffed several items into her handbag while waiting in the checkout line. In one condition of the study, a second accomplice, standing directly behind subjects, made remarks designed to encourage reporting of the theft ("We should report it. It's our responsibility.") In a second condition, she made remarks designed to discourage such behavior ("It's the store's problem. They have security people here.") Compared with subjects who heard discouraging remarks (or no remarks in a control condition), subjects of both sexes who were encouraged to take action reported the shoplifting to store personnel more often. Thus, the effect of perceiving that one has little responsibility for such a response can be counteracted by an explicit statement from a bystander.

A prior commitment by potential helpers to intervene and assist a victim also increases feelings of responsibility. Moriarty (1975) conducted field studies of the hypothesis that a previous commitment to assume responsibility can increase the likelihood of intervention if the need arises. On a crowded beach near New York City, a confederate asked another

Figure 12-9. Shoplifting is a crime costly to the consumer, but few shoppers report it when they observe such an occurrence.   (Mimi Forsyth, Monkmeyer)

sunbather either to give him a match (control) or to watch his belongings (experimental) during a brief absence. A second accomplice entered the scene while he was gone, stole the confederate's radio, and hurried off. Since the experimental subjects had agreed to watch the stranger's property, they felt a prior commitment to stop the thief and 95 percent did so. Only 20 percent of the control subjects who had been asked for a match did anything about the theft.

As the studies on commitment show, people who live in a large urban center can and do behave prosocially. In general, though, what does research show about the effects of big-city versus rural life on moral behavior? It seems possible that people raised in a community like the one depicted on the TV program "The Waltons" would be less likely to ignore a crime or a victim's need than people raised in a more impersonal city environment. Some have placed the blame on city life itself. It has been suggested that people who live in such environments somehow become accustomed to an atmosphere of crime and brutality.

To test these predictions, Gelfand and colleagues (1973) conducted a study in which a female confederate caught the attention of a real shopper by dropping something and then stuffed her handbag full of merchandise. After the shoplifter hurried out of the store without paying for the item, the shopper was observed to determine whether the theft would be reported, and was interviewed before leaving the store. In line with the predictions about the effects of big-city or small-town life, persons reared in cities of 100,000 or more reported the shoplifter much less often than those reared in small towns or rural areas.

These results and others (e.g., McKenna, 1976) indicate that the size of the community in which a person is reared may strongly influence his or her willingness to call attention to illegal acts. Other studies have shown that current residence (i.e., large city or small town) has a similar effect on helping behavior. For example, when children appeared to be lost and asked strangers for help, it was provided much more often by residents of small towns than by big-city dwellers (Takooshian, Haber, & Lucido, 1977).

Since population size appears to influence various aspects of moral behavior, the next step is to determine what it is about small-town or rural life that encourages prosocial behavior. House and Wolf (1978) compared residents of these two types of environment with respect to their degree of trust in other people and their helping behavior. There were no major differences between urban and nonurban residents in the trust expressed toward other people, which was measured between 1952 and 1972. Studies of presidential candidate choices were conducted among the people who were questioned about their trust in others, but some had refused to permit an interview for this purpose. Significantly higher rates of refusal were observed among urban residents than among rural ones, supporting the proposal that city dwellers are less helpful. However, rather than degree of trust in others being correlated with these refusal rates, another factor emerged as a possible reason for this result. Those who most often refused to help with the voting survey lived in areas with a high crime rate. This suggests that fear of negative consequences from helping is one factor in the lower helping rates observed among urban residents. Opening your door to a stranger in a big city can be dangerous—what if the person turns out to be a criminal intruder rather than someone who honestly needs help?

SUMMARY

Freud and Piaget described the development of moral conscience from the perspectives of emotion and intellectual skills, respectively. Kohlberg has presented a theory of the development of moral judgment that includes descriptions of the levels through which it progresses. The main steps in this progression are the *preconventional level*, the *conventional level*, and the *postconventional level*. The understanding of moral dilemmas reflects progress in intellectual skills. Empathy also serves as a basis for *prosocial behavior*.

The situational factors in prosocial behavior include the reinforcement value of vicarious pleasure in another person's relief from distress. Social learning factors in the helping situation include positive reinforcement, punishment, and modeling of this behavior. A second major theory of the costs and benefits of helping describes a form of *bystander calculus* in which a bystander gauges the favorable and unfavorable outcomes of an act to determine whether to perform it. A third, cognitive theory, proposed by Latané and Darley (1970), describes the steps involved in the decision to help. Failing to notice the event, or to interpret it as one requiring help, or to accept responsibility as a potential helper, can all hinder the delivery of aid to a needy person. Various situational and personality characteristics facilitate the delivery of help, often by preventing the diffusion of responsibility among bystanders who experience feelings of *deindividuation* in a group.

Two other components of moral behavior received attention in this chapter. Resistance to the temptation to acquire a forbidden reward can be strongly influenced by the ability to delay gratification. This trait varies at different stages of development, improving with growth of intellectual and emotional skills. Psychopathic delinquents and adult criminals show a markedly reduced ability to delay rewards, and choose immediate reinforcement instead. The second component, interference in antisocial behavior such as stealing, seems to depend on situational factors, including prior commitment or encouragement to help, and fear of negative effects of helping due to high crime rates in cities.

SUGGESTED READINGS

HORNSTEIN, H. A.   *Cruelty and kindness: A new look at aggression and altruism.* Englewood Cliffs, N.J.: Prentice-Hall, 1976. In an unusual approach, the author compares the research and theories dealing with aggression and altruism.

LICKONA, T. (ed.).   *Moral development and behavior: Theory, research, and social issues.* New York: Holt, Rinehart and Winston, 1976. A collection of chapters that cover many aspects of the developmental aspects of moral behavior and their practical implications.

MUSSEN, P., & EISENBERG-BERG, N.   *Roots of caring, sharing, and helping: The development of prosocial behavior in children.* San Francisco: Freeman, 1977. This book describes the childhood experiences that form the basis of prosocial behavior.

WISPÉ, L. (ed.).   *Altruism, sympathy, and helping: Psychological and sociological principles.* New York: Academic Press, 1978. A comprehensive set of chapters by psychologists and sociologists dealing with the emotional bases of helping behavior.

Part Four

BACK TO THE INDIVIDUAL

Cary Wolinsky, Stock, Boston

Chapter Thirteen

PERSONALITY: THE DEVELOPMENT AND FUNCTIONING OF AN INDIVIDUAL

In this chapter you will read about the following topics:

As Ned Woods drove his press car through the iron gates of the research institute, he still wasn't sure whether he was working on a legitimate story or being sent on a wild-goose chase. If this was the old man's idea of a practical joke . . .

The memo had been stuck in his typewriter, and it was the first thing he had seen when he sat down at his desk that morning. "Ned—check lead on artificial human story. Interview set with Professor Tobor for 10:00 A.M. at the Android Research Institute. We have info that they recently constructed a mechanical man that duplicates all human functioning. Will send photographer later if you decide it's worth it. Good luck—Sam."

Ned parked the car in a section marked "Visitors." Thirty minutes later he found himself in a plush carpeted office waiting for the professor to complete a telephone call. "Don't give me that line of bull. Just tell the senator for me that we will deliver the goods at the committee hearing. If he makes any premature statements about wasting taxpayers' money, we'll make a laughingstock of him in time to hit the network news and 50 million viewers. . . . You got the idea. . . . Fine. Let's get together for lunch soon." He winked at the reporter as he hung up the phone.

The balding, slightly paunchy professor sighed. "These politicians hate the possibility of ridicule more than anything. That strikes fear into their hearts." He laughed jovially and extended his hand. "You must be Mr. Woods, from the Ledger.*"*

"Yes, sir, and I'm here to check on a story that, frankly, seems a bit fishy. We hear you have a machine that is something like a human being."

"Not something *like one,* exactly *like one. Once a general theory of behavior was developed to its present state of precision, the rest was a snap—a mere exercise in engineering. Our humanoid will astound you* and *the senator whose committee is responsible for our continued funding. Get your editor to assign you to cover the hearing. It'll be a combination of science and razzmatazz and a guaranteed byline for you."*

Ned looked skeptical and asked, "Just what does this 'humanoid' do? What does it look like?"

"It does anything and everything that you or anyone else does. It responds to outside stimulation, it thinks and feels, it has dreams and wishes, it becomes emotionally aroused, and its behavior is quite within the normal realm. It could have been made with any combination of characteristics that you could name, but it was decided that certain ones should be stressed. For example, our creation is extremely bright, is not overly anxious, is highly motivated to achieve, has good interpersonal skills, is never cruel, . . . "

"Yes, yes, I'm sure it's a marvel, but what does this talking erector set look like?"

"Appearance was not an essential consideration, of course, but our technicians decided to make it look like a human as well as behave like one. Bit of showmanship on their part as well as pride of craft. It's amazing that such old-fashioned virtues are still to be found."

"I admit that you've aroused my curiosity, Professor. Can I get a look at your Frankenstein monster in action? No matter how good your mechanics are, I don't expect to be as overwhelmed as you seem to anticipate."

"My dear boy, I had hoped you might be just a tad impressed. You see, you have already had a sneak preview of the monster. I am the object of this conversation, and you have been interviewing a robot."

THIS STORY IS SET in the future, of course, because we do not yet know enough about the way in which people function psychologically to attempt to program a machine to behave as we do. Even so, the goal of predicting behavior carries with it at least the possibility that such knowledge will be available someday. Even today it is possible to construct electronic machines that duplicate (and sometimes improve on) specific aspects of human behavior. Thus, once the decision-making steps involved in the game of chess were known, chess-playing computers could be constructed. In addition, computers have been programmed to make medical diagnoses, going through the same process that a physician goes through. In the behavioral sphere, robots have been constructed that can clean a house and deliver the morning mail to each desk in an office. The "secret" in each instance is that when enough is known about the behavior in question, it is possible to duplicate it in a computer or robot. There is still a tremendous gap between duplications of single aspects of human behavior and an android that could carry out all the complex behavior of an actual person. Such an achievement would represent not the goal of personality theory but simply an interesting engineering offshoot of such a theory.

What do we know *now* about human behavior? What does the study of personality tell us about the way each of us develops and functions? Is there any useful way of tying together the bits and pieces of the human puzzle that we have examined in earlier chapters of this book? This chapter represents an attempt to do just that.

DESCRIBING AND PREDICTING HUMAN BEHAVIOR

Earlier, personality was defined as the combination of the enduring dimensions of individual differences. Most definitions of personality stress this combination of traits and the way they function as a unified whole. As we learned in Chapters 2 and 3, most personality theories have tried to deal with this wholeness.

Personality research, in contrast, tends to deal with one small segment of the person at a time. As we study authoritarianism, intelligence, the need to achieve, interpersonal attraction, and so forth, what happens to the *person*? Many people object to such a variable-by-variable approach and suggest that "personality as such evaporates in a mist of method" (Allport, 1961, p. 27). Carlson (1971) examined a year's worth of personality research articles and found that "*not a single published study attempted even minimal inquiry into the organization of personality variables within the individual"* (p. 209). In other words, it appears that there is much interest in specific personality variables but little interest in the total personality of an individual (Runyan, 1978).

There are at least two answers to such criticisms. On the one hand, many of us assume that the *only* way we are ever likely to understand how a specific person functions is by isolating the dimensions of individual differences and formulating the laws governing behavior in various situations. Such knowledge will allow us to "reconstruct the individual." Thus, detailed analytical research will permit us to reach the point at which we can understand, predict, and control human behavior. On the other hand, Allport, Carlson, and others have a valid point in noting the general tendency to ignore this reconstruction process and to believe that someone, somehow, someday will take care of the problem. It's as if we are waiting for a theorist on a white horse to ride into town and save the field of personality. Rather than simply hope that a research-based personality theory will emerge from the data, psychologists should probably attempt to build comprehensive general theories with the full realization that most such efforts will not be totally successful. In that spirit, an effort will be made in the following pages to suggest the tentative outlines of such a theory. It might be helpful first to consider just what we want a modern personality theory to do; that is, what is our goal?

Personality Description: Painting Word Portraits

One aspect of the person that seems to be lost when we move from the personality theories of the past to the personality research of the present is a satisfying description of the individual. Beyond scores on personality tests or responses to known stimulus conditions, what is the person *really* like? Such a question seems to take us back to an earlier problem: When do we *understand* a phenomenon? In our culture we believe we understand another person when we can describe that person's most salient characteristics.

The Approach of the Artist.   In fiction, characters are displayed clearly so that we know something about their behavior, motives, abilities, and emotions. In books, movies, and plays as well as on TV, we come to know vast numbers of imaginary people and some of them seem more real than the people with whom we associate in real life. Think of Scarlett O'Hara, Dagwood Bumstead, Ebenezer Scrooge, Archie Bunker, Jane Eyre, Lucy Ricardo, Marshal Dillon, and Charlie Brown. Compare your knowledge of them with what you know about your neighbors down the block or even some of your cousins. How do the creators of fiction manage it? In fiction it is possible to exaggerate the consistency and, hence, the predictability of human behavior:

It was necessary to establish for the time being a somewhat rudimentary psychology, on general and sharply defined lines, as a preliminary to the construction of a classical art. Lovers had to be nothing but lovers, misers wholly misers, and jealous men a hundred percent jealous, while good care had to be taken that no one should have a share of all these qualities at once. [Gide, 1946, p. xxxi]

The Case History: Blending Medicine and Art.   As psychiatry and psychoanalysis developed, their practitioners were faced with a problem similar to that of the novelist. To replace the traditional medical report focusing on physical symptoms, they developed the **case history**—a detailed, sometimes insightful description of personality. Not too surprisingly, the descriptions of patients by physicians interested in behavioral disorders resembled the productions of artists. In 1884 Freud wrote to his fiancée that he was "becoming aware of literary stirrings when previously I could not have imagined anything further from my mind." Somewhat later, in *Studies on Hysteria*, he wrote, "It still strikes me as strange that the case histories I write should read like short stories and that, as one might say, they lack the serious stamp of science." The tendency to stress the consistency of human behavior was still present, but the demands of scientific accuracy made it necessary to include a degree of inconsistency as well.

With the development of clinical psychology, the conflict between the novelistic demands of the case history and the scientific goal of predictive accuracy began to be felt more acutely. The reports of clinicians often have a literary flavor, but they also tend to contain data—test scores, comparisons with normative groups, and specific behavioral predictions.

The next question is whether it is now possible to abandon entirely the role of novelist and yet be able to describe people in a way that provides us with the kind of "understanding" that science demands.

Describing an Individual with Prediction as the Goal

Unlike a writer of fiction, the behavioral scientist does not have to be entertaining or arouse the reader's emotions. The task of description is to communicate something meaningful about a person that permits prediction of that person's behavior. The importance of prediction versus understanding (see Chapter 1) is more than just a scientific bias. In the practical world of clinics, schools, industry, politics, and courtrooms, there is a real need for precise predictions about the specific behavior of certain people. Word pictures that provide a vague feeling of understanding are of little or no use.

Consider the following description and see whether you would find it useful if you were a therapist, teacher, businessperson, candidate, or judge:

Some of Sue's aspirations tend to be pretty unrealistic. At times she is extroverted, affable, and sociable, while at other times she is introverted, wary, and reserved. She has found it unwise to be frank in revealing herself to others. She prides herself on being an independent thinker and does not accept others' opinions without satisfactory proof. She prefers a certain amount of change and variety and becomes dissatisfied when hemmed in by restrictions and limitations. At times she has serious doubts as to whether she has made the right decision or done the right thing. Disciplined and controlled on the outside, she tends to be concerned with worries and insecurities on the inside. Her sexual adjustment has presented some problems for her. While she has some personality weaknesses, she is generally able to compensate for them. She has a great deal of unused capacity that she has not turned to her advantage. She has a tendency to be critical of herself. She has a strong need for other people to like and admire her.

What has been said about Sue? Does she sound a lot like anybody you know—or *everybody* you know? Nothing appears in this description beyond what could be found in random selections from a newspaper horoscope column, but most people tend to feel that such descriptions provide them with useful information (Snyder, 1974). Snyder and Larson (1972) gave the kind of statements made about "Sue" to each of a large number of undergraduates, supposedly as a description of themselves. They had previously been measured on what was described as a "personality profile test." Each subject was asked to rate how accurately he or she had been described. The mean response was between "good" and "excellent." People place great faith in the results of psychological tests and accept what they are told about themselves as true (Snyder, Shenkel, & Lowery, 1977). The problem is that many such descriptions consist of general propositions that can apply to people in general. They are generalizations that are applicable to almost all of us and therefore tell us nothing of any value (Greene, 1977).

General truths say no more about a given person than a simple sentence indicating that he or she is a human being raised in America in the second half of the twentieth century. Of course, general truths that involve behavioral laws that apply to all people would be *extremely* useful for predictive purposes. There is no reason, however, to include them in the description of a *specific individual.* It is as if you asked someone to describe his new Oldsmobile and he responded by telling you about Newton's laws of motion and the principles of the internal combustion engine. The answer might be an accurate one, but it would not tell you what you want to know.

Perhaps there is a way to describe a person and yet not stray from the goal of prediction. The best possible descriptions and predictions are likely to be based on a combination of factors ranging from personality traits to situational factors to knowledge of past behavior and whether it led to reward or punishment (Alker & Owen, 1977). The remainder of this chapter will take such an approach to personality.

BIOLOGICAL ASPECTS OF PERSONALITY DEVELOPMENT

Almost all theories of personality stress the way in which personality traits are formed. They differ in many respects, of course. In Chapter 2 of this book, for example, we saw that Freud stressed a series of sexually toned interactions between the child and its surroundings, Jung stressed built-in tendencies and predispositions, and Sullivan stressed interpersonal relations. In Chapter 3 we saw that Rogers stressed the way a person is evaluated by his or her parents and others while learning theorists stressed rewards and punishments. In our description of personality in this chapter, all such potential influences are acknowledged, and the stress is on how fairly broad response characteristics come into being.

Inherited Traits

A detailed description of human genetics is beyond the scope of this book, but it may be helpful to indicate some of the ways in which our biological heritage underlies and influences human behavior.

It is obvious, first of all, that our anatomical structure and physiological functioning are necessary preconditions for human behavior. Our ability to stand upright, grasp tools and weapons, think in complex ways, and communicate are among the essential qualities of humankind. The evolution of these abilities—especially our intricate brain structure—constitutes the basis of personality (Sagan, 1977).

Some inherited characteristics, such as height, coordination, certain specific talents, and physical appearance, are of psychological importance because of the way other people respond to them. For example, there is a great deal of evidence that attractive people are treated better than unattractive people; the behavioral result is that those who are attractive tend to be more socially secure, more self-confident, more sexually active, and so forth (Adams & Huston, 1975; Clifford & Walster, 1973; Curran & Lippold, 1975). This interaction between biological characteristics and interpersonal responses is one way in which genetics plays an important, though indirect, role in personality development.

It is more difficult, however, to attempt to identify specific inherited behavioral traits that play a direct role in individual differences. For many thousands of years the idea of genetic transmission of anatomical and behavioral traits has been a truism. The concept of breeding dogs, for example, in order to obtain certain qualities is at least 10,000 years old. The same concept was easily generalized to human beings, as when Plato, in *The Republic*, proposed that the best men in the nation should mate with the best women in order to improve the quality of the citizenry.

One problem with applying such assumptions to human beings is that it is easy to assume that people are the way they are because they were

Figure 13-1. Inherited characteristics form part of the overall personality structure of an individual. (Mimi Forsyth, Monkmeyer)

born that way. This leads to a *tautology* (also known as circular reasoning) in which we can say that a certain person is aggressive *because* he inherited such a trait, and we know that he inherited the trait *because* he behaves aggressively. Such statements "explain" everything and tell us nothing. These ideas are also easily—and wrongly—applied to groups, as when it is asserted that Germans are by nature authoritarian, blacks are by nature less bright than whites, and females are by nature less sexually motivated than males.

In order to deal meaningfully with the possibility of innately determined behavior, we need to know the mechanisms of inheritance. Such knowledge would allow us to make predictions that could be confirmed or disconfirmed. Even Darwin (1859) was puzzled about exactly how inheritance works, and he had no idea why a given trait is sometimes inherited and sometimes not. Not until the work of Gregor Mendel, who bred pea plants in a Moravian monastery, was the concept of genes advanced to explain the transmission of characteristics from one generation to another. The leap from pea plants, which involve fairly simple genetic determinants, to animal behavior, which involve complex genetic determinants, is a broad one. Even so, with many organisms behavioral genetics has provided impressive evidence of the way in which even fairly complex behavior can be innately determined. Familiar examples include the dance used by bees to communicate the location of pollen-bearing flowers, the nest building of birds in a species-specific style even if they have never observed such nests, and the behavior of salmon, which are impelled to go from the freshwater streams in which they are hatched to the sea and eventually back again to the streams when it is time to spawn.

Further problems arise when we turn to mammals because of their amazing ability to learn—to be influenced by environmental factors. However, studies employing selective breeding are able to show that certain broad behavioral traits must be genetic in origin because animals can be shown to "breed true." For example, rats can be bred to do well or poorly in learning a maze by letting the best performers mate only the best performers (and the worst with the worst) over several generations (Tryon, 1940).

Studying the genetics of human behavior is even more difficult. Not only is our learning ability greatly superior to that of other animals, but selective breeding would be morally and ethically objectionable. As a substitute, investigators tend to look at family resemblances (as in studies comparing the IQs of identical twins, fraternal twins, etc.) and similarities between human behavior and that of our animal relatives (as in studies of male–female differences in aggressiveness across species).

In the research described in this book, some traits appear to have a genetic basis. Among human beings, this simply means that there is a general predisposition for people to be relatively likely or unlikely to behave in a certain way, for example, to respond at a given level of anxiety or show a given level of intelligence. Our responsiveness to situational factors is such, however, that these predispositions may never be expressed or may be greatly altered or even brought under external control. Thus, our species does not engage in complex reflexive behavior; there is no human analogy to the behavior of ants constructing an intricate underground home or cats mating in a specific position following an unvarying pattern of ritual foreplay—all genetically determined.

On the other hand, we should be sensitive to our general biological heritage and not try to mold behavior in ways that are totally divorced from it. For example, what are the long-term disruptive effects of our type of tree-dwelling primate's trying to adapt to crowded city environments or to the demands of outer space? In addition, we should be aware of specific genetic factors in behavior whenever they are discovered, and should recognize that some aspects of individual differences may be partly genetic in origin. At the same time, we should be cautious about the easy—and probably false—assumption that human behavior is simply an expression of inherited tendencies over which we have no control.

Prenatal Determinants of Behavior

One of the most persistent and widespread beliefs concerning human development has been the idea that what happens to a pregnant woman determines various aspects of her offspring's appearance and behavior. It was suggested, for example, that a frightening episode could leave its mark on an unborn child; a mother who was terrified at the sight of a gorilla in a zoo would be likely to give birth to an especially hairy child. At one time a great many people believed that it was possible to influence an infant's future interests and attitudes through the activities of its pregnant mother; women attended concerts and read the classics for the sake of the child's later cultural tastes. In the last several decades these colorful beliefs disappeared rapidly.

For many years, probably partly in a reaction to such false ideas, medical schools taught that the fetus is well insulated in the uterus and hence is not affected by events occurring on the outside (Montagu, 1959). However, even though the mother's exposure to Beethoven may not turn the fetus into a lover of classical music, it is equally wrong to assume that whatever occurs during the nine months of pregnancy has no effect on the child's future.

The developing infant is bathed in a chemical environment and is wholly dependent on the mother for the intake of nourishment and the elimination of wastes. Therefore, it would seem reasonable to suppose that the mother's physiological functioning is of great importance in the way the fetus develops. We learned earlier that the mother's diet can have a measurable effect on her child's IQ as much as four years after birth (Harrell, Woodyard, & Gates, 1955). When a mother's inadequate diet leads to low birth weight in the infant, the consequences over the next ten years (compared to those of normal weight) are increased likelihood of mental retardation, visual defects, poor school performance, and death (Wright, 1972). In addition, the fetus can be adversely affected by the mother's smoking (Frazier, Davis, Goldstein & Goldberg, 1961), use of psychoactive drugs (Kato, Jarvik, Roizin, & Maralishvili, 1970), or even excessive use of aspirin (Kelsey, 1969). Studies with rats show that when pregnant mothers are exposed to frightening events their young offspring are more anxious than normal—even when they are raised by nonfrightened foster mothers (Ader & Belfer, 1962). Hormonal deficiency or overabundance during the nine months of gestation can have profound effects on the sexual anatomy and functioning of the offspring (Money, 1974).

As more research examines the role of maternal experience and behavior during pregnancy, we may come to place increased emphasis on these first nine months of each individual's life.

PSYCHOLOGICAL ASPECTS OF PERSONALITY DEVELOPMENT: THE BEHAVIOR SEQUENCE

Given a genetic and prenatal base, how can we best describe the subsequent psychological development and functioning of human beings? What follows is an outline of a personality theory—the **behavior sequence.** Though the description of behavior as a series of sequences is a somewhat arbitrary one, it is interesting to note that people *do* tend to perceive ongoing behavior as consisting of just such sequences or units (Newtson, Engquist, & Bois, 1977). The purpose of presenting this theory is to provide a way of organizing and bringing together what is currently known about personality and to suggest directions in which future research might proceed. Throughout this book various **empirical findings** were presented, and some of these were developed in sufficient detail to constitute **empirical laws.** In a few instances several such laws were brought together in the form of **generalized laws.** Now, as the next step in the theory-building process, a **comprehensive theory** of personality is being suggested. It should be noted that this model had its origins in the empirical and theoretical work of a great many psychologists in various areas of research interest. An outline of a theory is just that, and much still remains to be done to determine in detail the various kinds of laws that must eventually fit within it. It should, however, provide you with a way to think about personality—both in the abstract and with respect to a specific individual—as a total system rather than as a series of unrelated relationships.

Stage 1: Infancy

Infancy will be defined as the period between birth and the acquisition of language—roughly, the first twenty months of life.

Initial Reflexive Behavior.   A human being entering the world can be viewed as a reservoir of potential. There is the potential for physical growth and development (Meredith, 1970), and there is the potential for learning (Mussen, Conger, & Kagan, 1974). Realization of the former depends on the adequacy of the physical environment (e.g., adequate nutrition, protection from external dangers, opportunities to exercise, etc.), while realization of the latter depends on the almost limitless variations in the individual's interpersonal interactions, on events occurring in his or her surroundings, on innate perceptual and cognitive abilities, and on the person's exposure to the symbolic world (including language, literature, myths, and ideas).

Initially, the human infant is dependent on the care of parents or parent substitutes and is equipped with only a few reflexive responses. A way of thinking about behavior at this stage is depicted in Figure 13-2. Infant responses are brought about by two sorts of events. Internally, there is the physiological arousal that occurs when a **need state** arises. These needs take the form of unpleasant deficits such as lack of food, lack of liquid, and lack of oxygen; there are also unpleasant internal surpluses such as a full bladder and a full colon.

These needs bring about fairly primitive, generalized, unlearned instrumental activity—crying and undirected movements of the hands and legs. Such behavior is usually followed by a goal response. Some of these

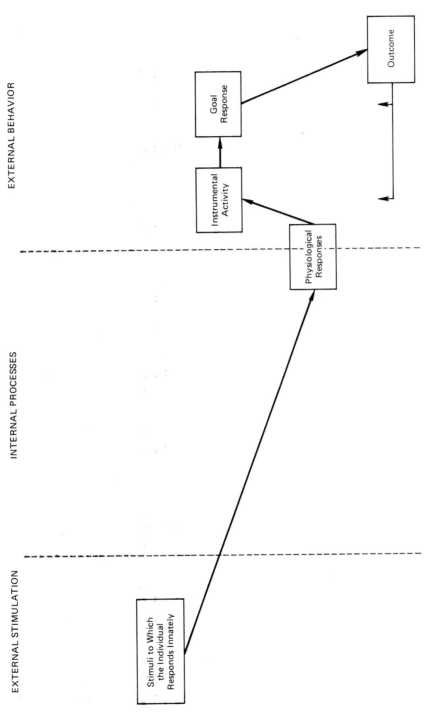

EXTERNAL STIMULATION

INTERNAL PROCESSES

EXTERNAL BEHAVIOR

Stimuli to Which
the Individual
Responds Innately

Physiological
Responses

Instrumental
Activity

Goal
Response

Outcome

Figure 13-2. In infancy the behavior sequence consists of a limited number of instrumental acts and goal responses that are initiated by external and internal stimuli. The rewarding and punishing events that accompany such behavior affect its future expression.

responses require no external help (e.g., urination and defecation), while others can occur only if an older person is present (providing nutrition, removing a blanket covering the baby's face, etc.). The outcome of these simple activities is rewarding, and the behaviors are therefore more likely to occur whenever the same internal stimulation occurs again. If such needs are temporarily unsatisfied, the outcome is punishing, and the behavior may be altered as a consequence (e.g., the baby may become silent, motionless, and seemingly apathetic). Prolonged failure to satisfy these basic needs, of course, results in death.

The other way in which behavior is instigated is by certain classes of external stimulation. Pain and other sources of discomfort are examples. Thus, a pinprick, a loud noise, the sensation of falling, or extremes of heat or cold will lead to arousal, instrumental activity, and, if those who care for the infant are available and responsive, a goal response. There are other kinds of stimulation that may or may not involve innately determined responses, but they clearly occur in very early infancy. Included here are positive stimuli such as a soothing voice, cuddling and rocking, and rhythmic sounds such as music or a ticking clock. Of special importance to human beings and other primates is the chance to rub, touch, and cling to soft objects such as a mother, a Teddy bear, or a blanket (Harlow & Harlow, 1966; Provence & Lipton, 1962). The physiological response to all such stimuli tends to involve reduced activity and what seems to be increased attention to the stimulus. The instrumental activity includes such responses as cooing and other indications of contentment. The goal response is continued contact with the stimulus, and discontinuation of the stimulus can result in physiological arousal and activity that suggests distress.

It should be mentioned that there are a few other reflexive responses that are useful in maintaining life. For example, when an infant's cheek or lips are touched, instrumental activity in the form of the sucking reflex occurs, thus making it possible to obtain milk from breast or bottle. Likewise, the gag reflex tends to protect against choking, and the blink reflex protects the eye from injury. Other reflexes were much more useful to our ancestors than to ourselves, yet they survive in our response repertory. For example, a touch on an infant's palm produces a grasping response that presumably was useful to primate infants, who were thereby saved from falling out of trees; now this response is simply a source of pleasure to relatives and friends, who stick out a finger and are happy to find that the baby responds.

Associational Learning.   The process of classical conditioning was described in Chapter 7. Because very simple organisms can be conditioned to respond to new stimuli and because such learning has been shown with fetuses still in the uterus, it is not surprising that infants are found to learn by association (Black & Prokasy, 1972), as depicted in Figure 13-3.

Thus, if the infant associates being fed or cuddled or having its

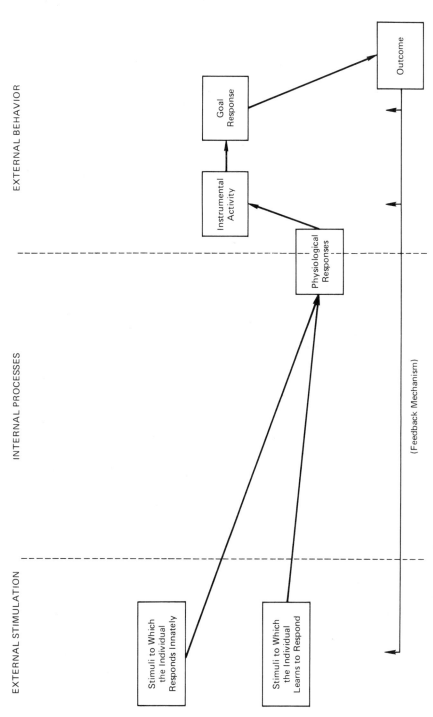

EXTERNAL BEHAVIOR

INTERNAL PROCESSES

EXTERNAL STIMULATION

Goal
Response

Outcome

Instrumental
Activity

Physiological
Responses

(Feedback Mechanism)

Stimuli to Which
the Individual
Responds Innately

Stimuli to Which
the Individual
Learns to Respond

Figure 13-3. By the process of classical conditioning, human infants can learn to respond to any discriminable stimulus that is associated with some other stimulus to which they respond innately.

499

diapers changed with the sound of its mother's voice, the blurry image of her face, or the smell of her perfume, such stimuli can easily come to evoke a quieting, comforting effect. In a similar way, if the infant is often hungry, cold, or lonely at night when the lights are out, darkness can come to evoke agitated arousal, complete with wriggling and crying. By means of such associations the child's world expands, and he or she becomes responsive to more and more aspects of the environment. Such learning can take place because perceptual skills develop rapidly during the first weeks after birth (Fantz, 1965; Trehub & Rabinovitch, 1972). Experiments have shown, by the way, that infants are more responsive to human stimuli than to other aspects of the environment (Haaf & Bell, 1967). Newborn babies quickly learn to differentiate their mother's voice from that of other females and to prefer it (De Casper & Fifer, 1980).

The behavior elicited by this growing array of both human and nonhuman stimuli frequently leads to goal responses that are reinforced. For example, an infant cries when left alone in the dark, and its mother comes in to hold, rock, and comfort it. Such reinforcement increases the probability that crying will occur whenever the room is dark. In a similar way, an infant makes contented sounds and reaches out when its mother approaches the crib, and this behavior induces the mother to pick it up, make pleasant noises, and so forth (Rheingold, Gewirtz & Ross, 1959). Again, such reinforcement strengthens the connection between the mother's face and the baby's "affectionate" behavior.

Emotional Responses and Basic Attitudes.   So far, the behavior of a human infant has been described as not really different from that of other animals with physiological needs, a few preprogrammed responses to certain stimuli, and the ability to learn by association. The rapid development of several classes of internal processes results in something quite different, however, and the eventual result is the combination of factors that constitutes personality.

The most important of these processes in infancy, as shown in Figure 13-4, involves **emotional responses.** Though there have been many attempts to classify our emotional reactions into multiple categories (Baron, Byrne, & Kantowitz, 1980), it is suggested here that there are really only two basic emotional states: positive and negative. Positive emotions are linked with positive stimuli, satisfaction of needs, and rewards that result from successful goal responses. Negative emotions are linked with negative stimuli, frustration of needs, and punishments that may accompany instrumental activity and goal responses. Positive emotions are felt as pleasant and lead to approach behavior. Negative emotions are unpleasant and lead to avoidance behavior. Thus, emotional states can add to or subtract from the influences of external stimuli and physiological arousal in influencing instrumental activity. As we learned in the discussion of attraction, emotional responses very often consist of a mixture of positive and

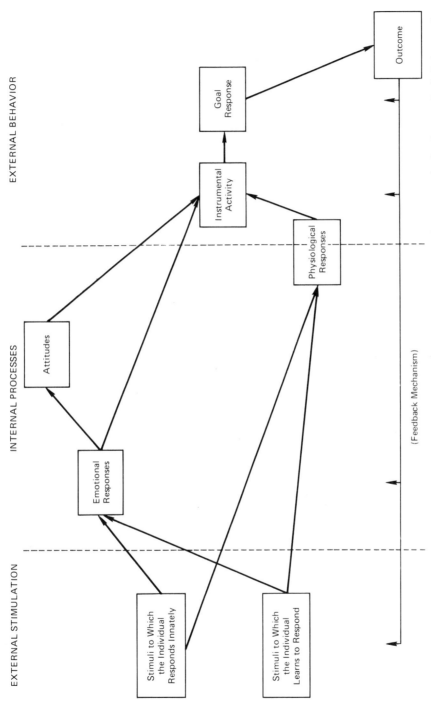

Figure 13-4. Among the internal processes that develop in infancy are positive and negative emotional responses that lead, respectively, to approach and avoidance behavior. In addition, these emotions lead to the development of lasting attitudinal responses. In infancy these "attitudes" are nonverbal, but they form the basis of later, fairly general evaluative responses.

501

negative elements, and they combine to yield a net affective response that varies in direction (positive vs. negative) and in strength.

It should be obvious that there is no way to determine with certainty what a baby feels emotionally. Still, it seems reasonable to assume that an infant feels pleasure in sucking warm milk from a bottle, displeasure in being stuck by a diaper pin, and so forth. More important, the association of such emotions (and mixtures of such emotions) with various external events leads to emotional responses to those formerly neutral events. Thus, mother's smile, a music box, father's voice, the sound of a refrigerator door opening, the sight of a mobile hanging over a crib, the barking of a dog, the smell of baby shampoo, and other stimuli in the environment can come to evoke emotional responses.

The mixed or ambivalent nature of these emotions can be seen; take mother as an example. She is usually connected with a series of very positive emotions (when the infant is fed, rocked, sung to, etc.) and also with a series of very negative emotions (when the infant is left alone, given a bath, taken to a doctor for shots, etc.). The concepts of good mother–bad mother (Sullivan) or madonna–witch (Jung) could very well have their origins in these very early experiences.

Because it is possible to have an infinite variety of emotional experiences in infancy, people can and do learn an infinite range of emotional associations. For example, food can be something totally positive—hunger is quickly satisfied; feeding occurs in the context of love and attention; the milk is neither hot nor cold nor sour; and so forth. Or it can involve strong negative elements—unhappy hunger cries are ignored for a long time before food is supplied; feeding occurs in the context of anxiety and resentment; the milk is an unpleasant temperature or taste, and so forth. Likewise, we can each learn quite different mixtures of emotional responses to father, pets, riding in a car, siblings, music, and everything else in our infant worlds.

As was discussed in some detail with respect to attraction, evaluative responses such as **attitudes** are mediated by emotional responses. Since attitudes involve words and since an infant does not possess language skills, do any attitudes develop in early infancy? It is proposed that very deep, *basic attitudes* are formed during this period. There are no words to express them, but they can be inferred from behavior, as when a baby consistently approaches or avoids a certain thing or makes contented sounds or cries unhappily in response to a given stimulus. For example, one of the authors (DB) knows from family stories that as a very small baby, he must have sorted various aunts, uncles, cousins, and others into positive and negative groups. Many decades later some of these people still remembered being pleased because Donn "liked them" when he was just a babe in arms; those in the other group remembered that infant as much less charming.

One more aspect of emotional-attitudinal responses should be mentioned. In addition to learning specific responses to our immediate surroundings, it seems likely that we acquire some more general, though equally basic and equally unconscious, attitudes. For example, some of us learn that other people are mainly a source of pleasure while some of us learn that other people are often hostile, cruel, indifferent, and rejecting. The basis is thereby formed for lifelong assumptions ranging from "I never met a man I didn't like" to "People are no damn good." Even more generally, the world is perceived as meaningful, predictable, and controllable or as a place filled with random, unpredictable events over which one can never have any control. Some of the basic assumptions made about "human nature" (see Chapter 2) and some of the attitudes expressed on the California F Scale (see Chapter 5) may well represent later verbalized viewpoints based on the evaluative responses acquired in infancy. Because such responses are learned very early, adopted absolutely and without qualifications, and become part of us before they can even be put into words, they tend to be reflected in later life as unshakable convictions that are not open to argument or evidence to the contrary.

Stage 2: Childhood

It should be emphasized that there are no sharp, concrete lines dividing one stage of development from another or even dividing the theoretical constructs of the behavior sequence from one another. Stages overlap and blend into one another, and there undoubtedly are wide variations among individuals as to when they occur. With respect to the constructs, both types of external stimuli can operate at the same time and in complex mixtures; the various internal processes can function all at once; and instrumental activity and goal responses may be mixed, sometimes indistinguishably. Even so, it is useful to describe and to operationalize the various stages and constructs as separate and distinct entities.

Pretending for the sake of clarity that the stages of development occur regularly and in an orderly sequence, it is suggested that **childhood** is the period that begins with language acquisition and ends at puberty. What, then, are the characteristics of childhood?

Language: Evaluating One's Surroundings. The development of language skills and the acquisition of information is a very important aspect of childhood. It should not be assumed, however, that there is an absence of cognitive development in the earliest months (Brazelton, Koslowski, & Main, 1974). Such development is difficult to study because, in the absence of verbal skills, an infant cannot tell us about its thought processes. Even after language is acquired, children are generally unable to recall their earlier experiences. These memory deficits are known as "infantile amnesia." Recent research suggests that infants actually learn a great deal and that what they learn influences their subsequent behavior over long intervals of time. The major problem seems to be an inability to retrieve what has been learned (Rovee-Collier, Sullivan, Enright, Lucas, & Fagen, 1980). The absence of language makes whatever has been learned less accessible to the individual.

There is a quantum leap in development when the child begins to understand and use language. Certainly it is impressive when a dog responds negatively to the packing of suitcases in anticipation of its family going on a trip and leaving him in a kennel. It is even more impressive when chimpanzees begin to communicate their wishes using sign language as described in Chapter 1. All such achievements are overshadowed, however, by the young child who begins to communicate in the verbal symbols of his or her culture (Brown, 1970).

One of the earliest uses of language is to verbalize simple evaluations, that is, consciously to express attitudes. Some of those already existed nonverbally as "basic attitudes" and had been expressed in behavior, but now the child is able to express, often emphatically, his or her feelings. "I love Mommy and Daddy," "I hate Aunt Grace," "I like ice cream" "Carrots taste bad," "Captain Kangaroo is a nice man," "Wicked witch is a bad lady," and on and on. It should be emphasized that such verbalized attitudes can themselves have an influence on instrumental activity. Approach and avoidance responses are strengthened when the person is able to verbalize reactions both internally and to others. Also note that since the outcome of one's goal responses can affect emotional responses, a discrepancy between outcome and previous feelings can lead to change. For example, the child may be induced to try a piece of carrot cake, find that it tastes good, and thus modify his or her evaluation of carrots: "I like carrots *if* they are in cakes."

It has been pointed out that this tendency to evaluate everything in the environment probably was important in human evolution (Clore & Byrne, 1974). Such evaluations led our ancestors to approach that which was safe, familiar, and friendly and to avoid that which was dangerous, strange, and hostile. Those who tended to evaluate whatever they encountered were likely to survive and therefore pass on such tendencies to future generations.

Language: Labeling and Understanding One's Surroundings. Perhaps the most important aspect of language is the fact that it provides a way to label whatever is perceived, to grasp the connections between and among elements, to store this information for future use, to communicate about this material with others *and with oneself*, and to act upon this acquired knowledge (Mischel, 1979; Moran, 1977). The addition of **informational responses** to the system is depicted in Figure 13-5.

The importance of symbolic thought has been recognized by all personality theorists in such concepts as *ego* in Freud's theory. Once the child enters the world of words, the rapid growth of vocabulary is truly

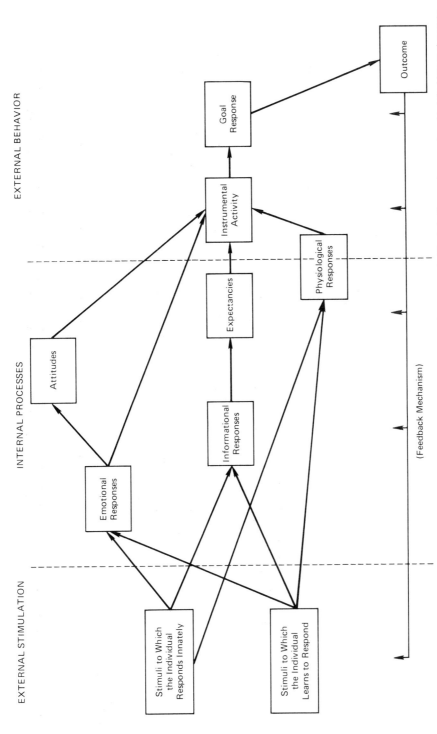

EXTERNAL STIMULATION

INTERNAL PROCESSES

EXTERNAL BEHAVIOR

Figure 13-5. As the child acquires language it becomes possible for him or her to label internal events, to grasp the connections between and among elements, to communicate about this material with self and others, and to act on it. The information can also lead to specific expectancies about the results of engaging in a given activity. Thus, behavior can be self-regulated on the basis of positive and negative expectancies.

505

remarkable. Language opens up the mind, and the child's grasp of his or her immediate surroundings, of other aspects of the world, and of past, present, and future happenings is one of the most significant events in development. A dramatic depiction of the role of language is provided in *The Miracle Worker*. Helen Keller was deaf, dumb, and blind and was thought to be retarded, little better than "a wild, destructive little animal," until at the age of six she was taught letters and words by means of touch (Lash, 1980). Her adult career as an author and lecturer would have seemed impossible to almost anyone who had seen her only as a "wild child" without language. With language, the painful search for information by all of those who preceded us can be summarized and compressed into the personal experience of each one of us. Much of childhood, all of our school years, and for some people, the entire life span consists partly of acquiring and at times correcting a conceptual representation of everything in the universe, including ourselves.

These multiple functions of the informational system involve the kinds of skills discussed earlier with respect to intelligence. That is, IQ consists of the ability to learn, remember, understand, form concepts, and think effectively. Though such activities are partly dependent on inherited abilities, their development is clearly affected by early experience. Thus, studies of environmental enrichment, family influence, and educational experiences consistently show that intellectual stimulation leads to more effective intellectual functioning.

As the child's symbolic representation of the world grows, the information provides a basis on which to anticipate the results of behavior; that is, **expectancies** are formed, as shown in Figure 13-4. For example, a child is told that "the stove is hot." The child has also learned from experience that contact with anything hot is painful (a negative stimulus involving unpleasant emotional responses and a negative evaluation). Thus, the information that a stove is hot leads to the specific expectancy that touching the stove would be very unpleasant, and this expectancy leads to avoidant behavior. Such information and communication make it possible to alter behavior in an adaptive way without the person having to experience negative consequences directly. Once this sort of connection is made, behavior is sometimes guided by verbal instructions to oneself in the form of stated **intentions.** For example, "I won't tease Billy ever again, so I won't get another spanking." Much of childhood is spent learning cause-and-effect relationships and applying that information to one's activities. In Chapter 3, we noted Rotter's emphasis on the importance of expectations in directing behavior.

It is worth mentioning that informational responses actually consist of a mixture of beliefs that are untestable (e.g., belief in invisible ghosts), beliefs that are testable and incorrect (our son in his preschool years dreamed that he was flying over the backyard and briefly believed that he actually had that ability), and beliefs that are testable and correct (our daughter believes that rattlesnakes are dangerous, and they are). With testable beliefs, behavioral outcomes can strengthen or totally alter beliefs and expectancies. Much of the activity of scientists, as discussed in Chapter 1, involves attempts to express beliefs and state expectancies in ways that are testable, arranging procedures to conduct the tests, and using the resulting information as evidence for retaining, altering, or discarding the original belief. It should be added that beliefs, especially in childhood, can be formed and changed on other bases as well. Thus, a child may believe in God simply because "Daddy says so," and a belief may change because someone who is credible strongly expresses a different view—"Johnny says there isn't any such thing as Santa Claus." With respect to testing one's beliefs by comparing expectancies with what actually occurs, we each resemble scientists, just as Kelly proposed (see Chapter 3).

One of the more important belief systems whose formation begins in this period is the set of beliefs that have to do with right and wrong, good and bad (Kohlberg & Gilligan, 1972; Piaget, 1970). Freud's concept of superego suggests that at a very young age the child begins to adopt certain cultural values as defined by the parents. In childhood these values are not organized into any coherent system; rather, they consist of rules learned one by one. They may be very specific ("It's bad to touch myself *down there*") or somewhat general ("Good girls never get mad at their parents"). A very important factor is whether such values are learned simply as a way to avoid punishment and obtain rewards or whether they are internalized as part of the child's own value system. Both Freud and Rogers stressed the importance of the parent–child relationship with respect to the internalization of values. Once a human being has adopted values, goals, and standards, self-reinforcement becomes a powerful factor in behavior (Bandura, 1976). This is another way in which self-regulation can take the place of external rewards, punishments, threats, and promises in directing what the person will do or refrain from doing.

Fantasy: The Power of Imaginative Responses.   The final internal process to be discussed—**imaginative responses**—constitutes one of the strongest and most pervasive systems with respect to its effect on human behavior, as shown in Figure 13-6. One of the more curious aspects of our internal life is the way we weave stories and pictures as if there were a series of brief movies playing almost constantly within our heads. It is proposed that such activity plays a major role in influencing our behavior (Singer, 1973).

For the child, one of the most challenging tasks is sorting out four aspects of the events that begin to occur in the "mind's eye": (1) There are involuntary fantasies that occur during sleep. Unlike Freud's theory of dreams as purely wish fulfillment, current research indicates that the content of our nighttime fantasies is varied and ranges from "replays" of

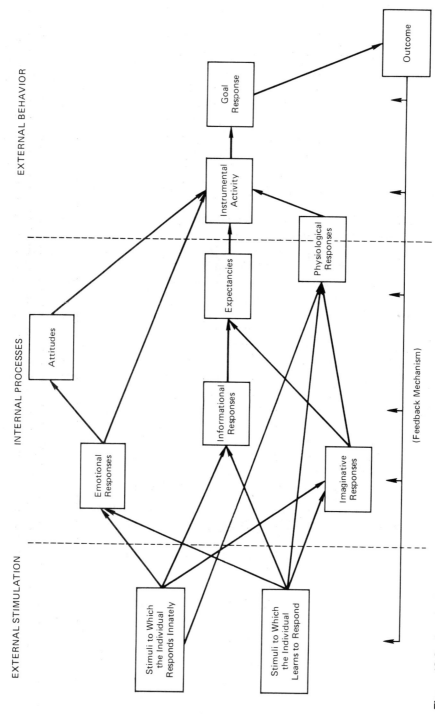

Figure 13-6. Imaginative responses begin to play an important role in childhood as the individual dreams, creates fantasies, and is exposed to the multitude of themes in the songs, stories, myths, and other artistic creations of his or her culture.

EXTERNAL STIMULATION   INTERNAL PROCESSES   EXTERNAL BEHAVIOR

Stimuli to Which the Individual Responds Innately

Stimuli to Which the Individual Learns to Respond

Emotional Responses

Imaginative Responses

Informational Responses

Attitudes

Expectancies

Physiological Responses

Instrumental Activity

Goal Response

Outcome

(Feedback Mechanism)

events in our waking lives (Cohen, 1976) to attempts to find solutions to specific problems (Dement, 1975). (2) While awake, a person experiences sometimes accurate and sometimes distorted memories of past events in his or her life. (3) There is purposeful imaginative play in which roles are assumed and events acted out. (4) Finally, there are anticipatory fantasies about future joys (e.g., going to Disneyland) and terrors (e.g., being attacked by things that go bump in the night). Even for adults with a multitude of cues to guide them, it is sometimes difficult to separate reality from fantasy—"Did I dream that or did it happen?" "Do I really remember that or do I remember what others told me about it?" For children, these various types of imaginative activity tend to blend and at times become indistinguishable. One of the challenges of childhood is to learn to tell the difference between what is real and what is imagined, that is, to become able to function according to Freud's "reality principle" (Bruner, Jolly & Sylva, 1976).

A related aspect of imaginative behavior consists of the fantasies supplied by the culture in the form of stories and songs. In modern society such fantasies are vividly portrayed in books, movies, and television programs. This material provides much more than simple entertainment, both in childhood and in adulthood. First, these external images tend to make up a large part of the content of anticipatory and play fantasies. That is, childhood imaginings are strongly influenced by that which the culture stresses at the time—knights and beautiful maidens, princesses and handsome young men, cowboys and Indians, Donald Duck and his nephews, Batman and Robin, Peter Pan, Cinderella and her fairy godmother, Superman, Wonder Woman, the Cat in the Hat, the Flintstones, the Muppets, and all the rest. Second, these characters and their actions tend to define for the child in a very basic (and often unverbalized) manner *the way things should be.* That is, from the time we can comprehend anything we are all painlessly taught what we should believe about the roles of males and females, the relative values of courage or honesty or achievement or whatever, the definition of justified aggression and vengeance, the role of love, and what a society finds acceptable as racial stereotypes (Morrow, 1978). Third, these fantasies provide each of us with goals and ideals (Cousins, 1977). We learn about people we want to resemble, traits we want to possess, and activities we wish to engage in. The effect of achievement imagery in school readers on subsequent behavior is a well-documented example of this type of influence. Fourth, since the development of photography, many of us have found ourselves playing roles in these "external fantasies." Many children remember what they see themselves do in home movies better than they remember participating in the reality that was photographed.

It might also be noted that an attempt is made to reach children by way of fantasy not only with respect to fictional characters but also with

Figure 13-7. Children's fantasy material can be not only entertaining but a source of beliefs, role models, and motivation that influence future behavior.   (U.P.I.)

respect to much that the culture wishes to pass on to the next generation. For example, historical events (e.g., the ride of Paul Revere) and religious events (e.g., the escape of the Israelites from Egypt) are portrayed in much the same general fashion as the ride of the headless horseman and the escape of Dorothy and her companions from the castle of the evil witch. Advertisers, too, actively attempt to enlist the child's fantasy processes in order to sell food, toys, and other products to their youthful audiences. Watch an hour of Saturday morning television and you will see this in action.

Overt Behavior: Mobility and Manipulative Skills.   Though personality theory is not directly concerned with physical development, some aspects of the behavior acquired during this period are relevant to personality development. That is, not only is overt behavior a result of the processes activated in a behavior sequence; it is also dependent on anatomical functioning and on the perception of the resultant behavior by self and others. One example of a normal aspect of development that can acquire special meaning is the ability to control bowel and bladder functions. Learning to respond to the relevant internal cues and to delay gratification until one reaches a bathroom can be considered simply one of the many perceptual and muscular skills to be learned in childhood. Because of parental anxieties and cultural taboos concerning such functions and their waste products, however, this process can involve the sorts of problems

Freud suggested in describing the psychosexual stages. In addition, anxiety and shame attached to urination and defecation may very well generalize to sexual anatomy and activities.

As a child begins to walk, climb, and use his or her hands to manipulate objects, there are an increasing number of ways in which emotions can be aroused, ideation developed, and fantasies explored. Literally as well as figuratively, one's horizons are expanded. Such behavior increases the amount of pleasure the child can obtain (e.g., satisfying the need to explore and examine, grabbing desired food) and also increases the range of dangers encountered (e.g., falling from a tree, swallowing a poisonous substance). During childhood one is likely to learn to ride a bicycle, swim, fly a kite, skate, turn somersaults, and play a variety of games ranging from table tennis to football. With the ability to move around and to manipulate objects, the child changes from a passive recipient of stimulation to an active seeker of stimulation. Instead of just being acted upon by the environment, the child can now bring about changes in both the physical and the interpersonal world.

Interpersonal skills first become important in childhood, and as Sullivan proposed, each person works out ways to interact with parents, siblings, and peers. In the long run we learn to play certain roles with our teachers, close friends, and strangers. Depending on our role models and on our interpersonal successes and failures, we gradually develop into individuals who are perceived by others as shy, outgoing, kind, cruel, amusing, dull—in other words, we find a niche for ourselves among the observable personality traits and conform to the expectations of others and of ourselves by behaving more or less consistently.

The rewards and punishments connected with all overt activities are of crucial importance, as we have seen in various sections of this book. Do parents expect and encourage early independence and acquisition of skills (e.g., tying shoelaces, crossing streets), or is the child kept dependent as long as possible? Is there rejection not only of certain behavior (e.g., physical aggression) but also of the emotions accompanying it? Are some parts of the body (e.g., the genitals) given inadequate labels and linked with negative emotional responses? Does peer response to the child's behavior encourage or discourage the child's attempts to form interpersonal relationships? Is it all right for a young girl to cry but shameful for a young boy to do so? Is the opposite true of fighting?

In addition to the reactions of others that produce individual differences in behavior, there are also biologically produced differences among individuals in size, strength, coordination, physical attractiveness, and so forth. Especially in the peer culture of childhood, reputations are often based on such external characteristics and behavioral skills. One consequence is that the child begins to define himself or herself as able or clumsy, tough or weak, attractive or ugly, likeable or unpopular. All such reflected assessments are likely to be incorporated into the attitudes, self-descriptions, expectations, and fantasies of the individual.

Childhood, then, is the time during which basic language skills are mastered; many evaluative responses are developed and verbalized; and there is a massive attempt to achieve symbolic understanding of the world and of oneself by means of acquired knowledge and beliefs, the incorporation and creation of multiple fantasies, and the development of many behavioral skills that lead to increased interactions with the physical and interpersonal environment.

Stage 3: Adolescence

Adolescence as a "stage" of development is created mostly by society. In primitive groups adulthood has usually been defined as the time when the person is biologically able to conceive offspring, that is, **puberty.** It should be understood that puberty is not a magic moment at which reproduction suddenly becomes possible but a *period* of growth and change that may last several years. In the United States today puberty begins at about age 11 among girls and age 13 among boys, but with considerable individual variation (in both directions) from these averages. Note also that the ovaries may begin producing ova before the first menstruation and that the testes may begin producing sperm before the first ejaculation.

In most developed societies adulthood is postponed until after a certain amount of schooling or job training has been completed or until some arbitrary age is reached. We will refer to **adulthood** as the period in which a person forms a close interpersonal relationship (most often with a member of the opposite sex) and achieves economic independence. The latter is roughly defined by the completion of schooling, the acquisition of occupational skills, and the establishment of a dwelling place separate from that of the parents. Adolescence, thus, is the period between puberty and adulthood.

Physiological Development. The most obvious feature of adolescence is the series of hormonal changes that lead to the development of sexually mature anatomy and physiological functioning (Tanner, 1970). There are also secondary sexual characteristics, such as growth of body hair, growth of the breasts in females, voice change in males, production of ova and the beginning of the menstrual cycle in females, and the production of sperm and seminal fluid in males. There are changes in the size and responsiveness of the genitals. In both sexes internal and external erotic cues lead to excitement and genital vasocongestion, while extended genital friction can lead to an orgasmic response.

These physical changes all constitute preparation for parenthood and the propagation of the species. They are of psychological importance primarily because of the complex meanings that we have assigned to them. Other physical changes also occur with the final phase of physical growth, and many of these also take on psychological importance. Height and attractiveness become even more crucial than in childhood. Temporary skin problems such as acne can be a source of intense concern. Finally, there are reactions by both self and by others to the size of the breasts in females and of the penis in males. All of these physical attributes (plus some controllable characteristics, such as weight and hair style in both sexes and facial hair in males) can play a major role in affecting the response to the adolescent by both sexes and, hence, his or her self-oriented beliefs and attitudes with respect to attractiveness, self-confidence, and general worth.

Attitudinal Development.   Emotional responses (with their evaluative results) continue to be made. Because the person is in the process of moving from childhood and identification with parents toward adulthood and identification with his or her own nuclear family and social-occupational role, the peer group comes to exercise enormous importance.

For reasons suggested in Chapter 9, people find it extremely important to be similar to their reference group in their judgments of almost everything. Thus, adolescents find it crucial to be with others who share their evaluations of other people, of musical groups, of movies, of clothing styles, and so forth. It is frightening to be too deviant in any respect, and the choice of new friends of either sex must be consistent with the evaluative decisions of one's existing group of friends.

Because physiological needs and emotional reactions are strongly oriented to sexual cues, some of the more important attitudes are those involving sex. Thus, reactions to masturbation, nocturnal orgasms, erotica, premarital sex, contraception, and homosexual desires can become central issues that involve varying degrees of pleasure in one's development as a sexual being as well as conflict, worry, and guilt. As mentioned in Chapter 11, there are great individual differences in emotional and attitudinal responses to sexuality that probably originate in childhood and perhaps even in infancy. Such reactions can be strengthened by adolescent experiences, or they can be altered and even reversed by those experiences. The change that is most commonly described is in the direction of more permissive, more accepting sexual expression. People say that they managed to reevaluate their attitudes and were able to "get rid of old hang-ups" as a result of exposure to new ideas and new experiences during adolescence.

A related, but in many respects more important, task of adolescence is the formation of a close relationship with a member of the opposite sex. As described in Chapter 9, the process of meeting, getting to know, becoming friends with, and loving a member of the opposite sex involves a series of steps in the acquaintance process. Viewed from a distance, adolescence consists in part of a vast and not very efficient sorting task in which the majority of males and females end up in pairs that conform to the prescribed norms of love, marriage, and the formation of new family groups.

Informational Development.   The learning explosion of childhood continues in adolescence as the person acquires more and more knowledge and experience both in the formal school setting and elsewhere. For most, this includes the acquisition of occupational knowledge. In the best of worlds, it also includes broader and deeper knowledge of all aspects of existence such as literature, philosophy, science, economics, and all the other realms of human wisdom and folly.

Perhaps the most common development is the elaboration, consolidation, and justification of existing attitudes with beliefs and selected truths. Most teenagers become able to defend their positions on various issues (religion, politics, morality, etc.) with detailed arguments. A common occurrence is the rejection of previously held beliefs (usually those of parents) in favor of new ones (usually those of peers or a charismatic authority figure). Thus, in generation after generation the teenage years are spent surprising and often shocking the previous generation with a new religious orientation (atheism, Eastern mysticism, or whatever), new political beliefs (radicalism, socialism, or switching from the Republican to the Democratic party or vice versa), and new moral values. For some time this has meant increasing permissiveness, but the reverse has been true at other historical times (Thomas, 1978). Show business figures often serve as focal points for a new and frequently unacceptable style—Frank Sinatra in the 1940s, James Dean, Marlon Brando, and Elvis Presley in the 1950s, the Beatles and Marilyn Monroe in the 1960s, and still others in the 1970s (John Travolta? Bette Midler? the Fonz?) All such change seems to involve a dramatic way of rejecting the values of one's parents, embracing the values of one's current companions and heroes, and in the long run, establishing one's own identity.

Fantasy.   Imaginative responses continue to play an important role in guiding and defining present behavior and holding out a promise of what the future will be like. The story lines of movies, television programs, novels, and plays as well as musical themes continue to affect the imagination. In addition, for many adolescents there is a greater effort than in childhood to create formal fantasies. Many write stories, songs, poems, and books, while others create paintings. For many, there is active participation in the world of music, dance, and the theater.

Even if an adolescent is not actively involved in the creation of overt fantasies that can be communicated to others, almost everyone creates private fantasies. One major area is that of sex and/or love. As we learned in the study of sexual behavior, self-created erotic fantasies tend to accompany masturbation, intercourse, and nonsexual activities. There has been less formal study of love fantasies. We know, however, that purely sexual daydreams often involve an imagined or remembered interaction with a love object. More generally, a scenario in which you find someone with whom you share love, get married and exist from then on in an idyllic love–sex relationship is the image most people have of their own future.

Another major type of fantasy also involves projections of the future. As noted in the study of the achievement motive, a great many people tend to imagine that their lives will be crowned with success—economic success, occupational status, and prestige. Such dreams are fueled not only by private achievement needs but also by the ever-present movies, magazines, TV shows, and advertisements. This external fantasy world seldom includes really unpleasant, ugly, grim poverty and failure (such scenes are reserved for off-Broadway plays and public television). There are, in contrast, fabulous apartments, enormous houses, expensive cars, and decorator bathrooms complete with stereophonic sound. It has been pointed out that one feature of this fantasy world is that no one ever works—the good things in life are simply there, and work is something that you do off-camera or at most in interesting 30-second intervals. It is not surprising that many adolescents look forward to a somewhat vague future in which they live the life of Charlie's Angels, move up to the East Side with the Jeffersons, travel the world like James Bond, or drive their Jaguars to Hollywood premieres accompanied by a movie star or two. Very few of us harbor dreams of a future consisting of a dull job, a drab home, an unhappy spouse, and unappreciative kids.

One aspect of both the love–sex and the success fantasies is that they are usually positive enough to be highly motivating and unrealistic enough so that the stage is potentially set for future disappointment or a nagging sense of failure.

Behavioral Skills.   Learning and change also continue with respect to overt behavior. Some of the new skills are analogous to those of childhood as the adolescent learns to engage in new sports or improve his or her performance in old ones. An adolescent may learn to drive a car or motorcycle or to pilot a boat or airplane. There may be new learning with respect to hobbies, mechanics, construction work, electronics, sewing, or any number of other physical activities ranging from hang gliding to dancing to making love. Many of the behaviors to be learned, whether in school or on the job or at home, are directly relevant to future occupational choices. When teenagers are writing a composition, cooking bacon, appearing in a school play, learning to type, sawing lumber, making change, or whatever, they may be learning and practicing skills that will occupy much of their adult working lives.

Some of the more important behavioral skills are interpersonal ones. As was pointed out in discussing dating anxiety, attraction, and sexual behavior, these skills are seldom formally taught. Instead, most of us must fumble around and learn by trial and error how to deal with members of our own sex and, more important, those of the other sex. The long-term success of books describing how to win friends, deal with business associates, attract dates and mates, and "do it" in bed is evidence of the number of people who do not feel they are skillful enough at such activities.

Adolescence, then, is the time during which physiological development impels the person toward sexual activity and potential parenthood; attitudes become vital sources of contact with peers; emotional-evaluative responses to sex and to potential sexual partners are of central importance; beliefs become elaborated and consolidated and often are in sharp contrast to those of the parents' generation; fantasies of love, sex, and future success serve as guides and powerful motivators, often unrealistic ones; and behaviors ranging from occupational skills to interpersonal skills must be acquired.

ADULTHOOD: THE FUNCTIONING OF THE DEVELOPED PERSONALITY

There is *no* point at which human personality is completely set, never to change again. The rate of change becomes slower throughout the developmental process, however, and the amount of new material added to the system relative to that which is already there becomes smaller for most people each year that they live. Adult human beings, therefore, are relatively stable and consistent with respect to their attitudes, beliefs, fantasies, overt behaviors, and so forth. This is the reason that personality measures are useful in predicting behavior. Behavior is also responsive to the immediate situation, as we have seen, so it is necessary to take stimulus variables into account in making predictions. Having discussed the development of the various aspects of personality, we will now briefly examine the way it operates.

The Dynamic Interactions of the Behavior Sequence

Personality Research and the Behavior Sequence.   The fully functioning behavior sequence is shown in Figure 13-8. All of the elements of the system have been discussed in the description of the developmental process. Keep in mind that each arrow represents a hypothesized antecedent–consequent relationship and that in most situations all of these elements are operating at once. Consider as an example imaginative responses and their effects. A sexual dream can be realistic enough to bring about strong emotional responses (Cohen & Cox, 1975), physiological signs of sexual arousal (Masterson, 1977), and an orgasmic goal response (Katchadourian & Lunde, 1975). Further, imaginative responses suggested by an experimenter have been found to change subjective expectancies about whether the imagined events will occur (Carroll, 1978). Finally, the

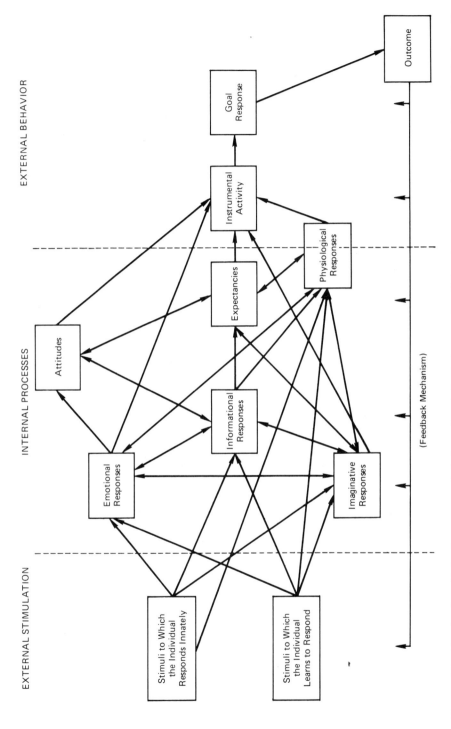

Figure 13-8. The developed behavior sequence, including external stimulation, a series of internal processes, external behavior, the feedback resulting from positive and negative outcomes, and some of the relations among the internal processes.

517

more a person engages in fantasies about a specific activity, the more likely it is that he or she will engage in that activity (Giambra & Martin, 1977). Future research will need to include assessment of each of the indicated constructs, examination of the way they interact to instigate behavior, and alteration of those which are causing problems for the individual and/or society.

The personality research conducted to date has tended to concentrate on only a few elements at any one time. Consider the eight content areas that were covered in previous chapters. Research on authoritarianism has dealt mainly with attitudinal and informational responses. Work on intelligence has been largely confined to informational responses. With manifest anxiety, interest expanded to include emotional, physiological, and informational responses, as well as conditioning and instrumental learning. In the study of achievement need, imaginative responses and expectancies were considered along with attitudinal responses in their combined effect on instrumental activity and goal responses. The study of attraction has centered on emotional and attitudinal responses and the way the person learns to evaluate new stimuli through associational learning. The study of sexual behavior has focused on physiological arousal as well as on imaginative, informational, emotional, and attitudinal responses. The study of morality has concentrated chiefly on stimulus conditions and on informational responses, along with expectancies. The study of aggression has dealt mainly with emotional, physiological, and informational responses. You might find it useful to go back and consider any given experiment or series of experiments and see if you can fit them into this theoretical schema.

Predicting a Specific Behavior.   As an example of how the model might operate if all of the constructs were considered together, let's consider an imaginary study of aggression. Say that a series of male subjects are brought into a laboratory where a stranger administers a mild, moderate, or strong electric shock (stimuli that elicit responses innately) and also makes mildly, moderately, or strongly insulting remarks about them (stimuli eliciting responses after learning has occurred). The subjects then have a chance to use the Buss aggression machine to shock the stranger in a series of trials. We are interested in predicting the button-pressing behavior (i.e., instrumental activity), which the subject is led to believe is a means to hurt the stranger (i.e., goal response). It is quite possible to ignore the internal processes entirely and simply consider the relation between the stimulus manipulations and the responses. It seems probable, for example, that the greatest amount of aggression would occur among subjects receiving the strong shock *and* the strongly insulting remarks, and that less aggression would occur as the instigating stimuli were less strong. Thus, the mild shock and mildly insulting condition should yield the least aggression.

If these assumptions are correct, prediction of aggression in this situation would be greater than chance but still far from perfect. The purpose of considering internal processes would be to attempt to increase predictive accuracy as well as to gain a more comprehensive understanding of the details of the aggressive behavior sequence. Let's consider each of the constructs and how they might contribute to the final response. People undoubtedly differ in *trait anger,* and this aspect of *emotionality* would be a factor that partly determines their responses, along with the degree of situationally determined *state anger.* If we know a person's basic *attitudes about aggression* as well as his or her specific *attitudes about revenge and retaliation,* the predictive process should be enhanced. Next, *informational responses* would involve such things as each subject's labeling of the instigation (e.g., deliberate pain and insult or "The poor guy is too sick to realize what he's doing") and the body of beliefs he or she holds with respect to the morality of retaliation (e.g., an eye for an eye or turn the other cheek) and how others respond to punishment (e.g., as a deterrent to any further aggression or as an invitation to increased hostility). Such beliefs should lead to specific *expectancies* (e.g., aggression will probably decrease because my punishment will teach him a lesson, or I'll probably be hurt even more because he will strike back). Again, prediction should be improved by knowledge of these beliefs and expectancies. *Imagination* could be considered from the point of view of how much exposure each subject has had to aggressive fantasy (in books, movies, and on TV) and how much explicit aggressive imagery is contained in his or her own fantasy productions. Those with the most aggression in their fantasy lives should engage in the most overt aggression. Finally, we need to know the amount of *physiological arousal* that is brought about in each person by the stimulus conditions; presumably amount of arousal is positively related to amount of aggression. It should be noted that if the outcome of the subject's aggression resulted in reward or punishment, subsequent aggressive behavior would be expected to be either more likely or less likely to occur.

It may be seen that such considerations lead us to pay much more attention to what is going on *within* the person in an effort to obtain a more precise prediction of overt behavior. This approach eventually should lead to some very specific statements about each construct's positive or negative contribution to the probability of an overt aggressive response and about the interactions of the various constructs.

Interactions Among Subsystems.   One of the most interesting aspects of the behavior sequence is what happens when there is inconsistency among the internal processes in their influence on the overt response. In our example, the prediction would be simple if *all* of the emotions, beliefs, and so forth operated either to increase the probability of an aggressive response or to decrease that probability.

To illustrate possible inconsistencies, let's consider just two variables—emotions and beliefs—as shown in Figure 13-9. A person feels either pain or pleasure as a result of something a stranger does. In addition, the person's beliefs fall somewhere along a continuum from a strong belief that aggression will deter others from aggressing to a strong belief that aggression only invites aggression from others. There is then a chance to aggress against that person by giving him or her an electric shock. What could we predict about the aggressive responses of individuals A, B, C, and D, whose emotions and beliefs fall at different points along the two dimensions? When beliefs and emotions are consistent, prediction is straightforward. That is, person A feels pain and believes in the deterrent power of aggression—he or she should aggress. Person D experiences pleasure and thinks that aggression invites trouble—he or she clearly has no reason to aggress.

The interesting prediction problems are posed by persons B and C. Person B is caught between his or her emotional response and the belief system. The overt response should be determined by the relative strength of feelings and beliefs. If such strengths could be assessed, the response could presumably be predicted. If the emotions are stronger than the be-

Figure 13-9. Two of the internal processes in the behavior sequence (emotional responses and informational responses) and the way they might vary with respect to consistency in influencing aggressive behavior. Hypothetical individuals A, B, C, and D differ as to where they fall along dimensions of feelings and beliefs that influence aggressive behavior. That is, negative feelings such as pain are consistent with aggressive action, while positive feelings such as pleasure are not. The belief that aggressive acts will deter another person from aggressing is consistent with aggressive action, while the belief that aggression causes further aggression is not.

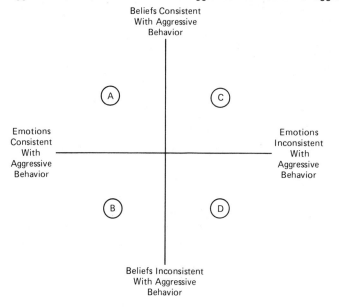

liefs, aggression will occur ("His feelings got the better of him," "She was blinded by emotion"). If the beliefs are stronger than the emotions, aggression will not occur ("He's a person of strong will," "She sets principle above feeling"). Person C is very unlikely to aggress because he or she has no reason to, but if he or she were extreme in beliefs about the positive effects of aggression, C might give the stranger a bit of shock "just on general grounds," "to show him who's boss" and "let him know that C is not someone to take lightly."

You can see that a consideration of just two variables leads to several quite different predictions. When stimulus strength, all six internal processes, and past reinforcement history of the instrumental and goal responses are considered at the same time, it is obvious that future personality research may become much more complex. It is assumed that our eventual predictive statements will rest on a mathematical formulation that takes into account the combined effects of all of the variables.

Possible Neural Correlates of the Proposed Internal Processes. A theoretical system is useful to the extent that it organizes existing knowledge, generates hypotheses that act as guidelines for seeking new knowledge, and most crucial of all, leads to more accurate and precise predictions of a broad range of events. Any theory should be judged only at its own level of complexity. For example, it makes little sense to ask that a theory of economics be judged in terms of its ability to explain the activity of subatomic particles or vice versa. Neither level of theory is more "real" than the other; each can be highly useful in its own realm without making contact with the other, even though the phenomena in question coexist in the same space and time.

With respect to psychological theories, such as those involving learning or personality, the most common question about connections with other areas of research concerns physiology or neuroanatomy. How do the psychological constructs fit in with the "blood and guts" of physiological psychology? Again, it must be stressed that such connections are not necessary to either field. Still, it would be very satisfying to be able to find connecting links between psychological and physiological constructs. Even a few such links would add to the generality of work in both domains. In a *very tentative* way, then, the possible relations between the internal processes described in the behavior sequence and several aspects of neural functioning will be briefly suggested. Figure 13-10 is a schematic diagram of the portions of the central nervous system to be discussed.

The most ancient part of the **central nervous system** is the **neural chassis**, which consists of the **spinal cord,** the **medulla**, the **pons**, and the **midbrain** (Curtis, Jacobson, & Marcus, 1972). The most basic aspects of *physiological arousal* are centered here. The simplest vertebrates, such as fish and amphibians, have developed only this portion of the neural anatomy;

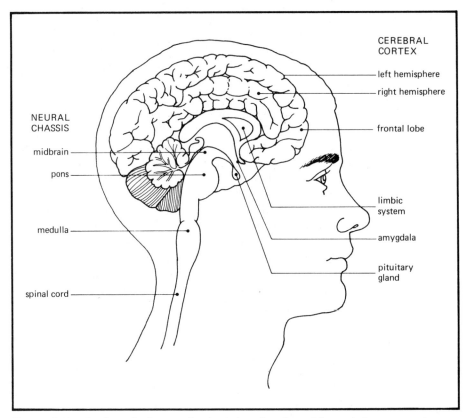

Figure 13-10. A schematic diagram showing selected portions of the central nervous system.

with the neural chassis, they are capable of maintaining bodily functions such as circulation and respiration, reproducing, and fighting or fleeing as acts of self-preservation.

The **limbic system**, which we share with other mammals, is the center of strong, vivid *emotional responses* (Grossman, 1972; MacPhail & Miller, 1968; Robinson, 1973). The **amygdala** is located here, and this body is involved in aggression and fear. In addition, the **pituitary gland** is part of the limbic system, and its domination of the entire **endocrine system** again is tied closely to emotional reactions. Considering what we have learned about the classical conditioning of fear and anxiety as well as the way the conditioning of emotional responses underlies attraction and other *evaluative responses,* it is interesting to note that classical conditioning seems to be a function of the limbic system.

The most complex and most recently developed portion of the brain is the **cerebral cortex.** Human beings and other primates have the largest of these structures relative to our total size, and the most fully developed cerebral cortexes are those of humans, dolphins, and whales. It is here that our cognitive functions occur, and we can receive, recognize, and remember information that we perceive (Masterton & Berkley, 1974). Three areas of the cortex seem most relevant to the behavior sequence: the frontal lobe and the left and right hemispheres.

Expectancies seem to correspond to **frontal lobe** functioning in that this structure is responsible for the anticipation of future events and consequences. Because of frontal lobe functioning, we can look ahead mentally and contemplate what might happen if we behave in a given way. We can compare short- and long-term benefits and dangers, and we can also strive to predict and control future events by means of magic, by constructing legal codes and constitutions, through science, and so forth (Grossman, 1973). The left and right **hemispheres** of the cortex appear to be quite different in functioning, though there is some overlap and some connection between them (Gazzaniga, 1970). The left hemisphere deals with "rational" cognitive skills, such as reading, writing, speaking, and mathematics, in which there is sequential processing of *informational responses* (Gazzaniga, 1967). One could also guess that the rational, verbal component of *attitudinal responses* operates here. The right hemisphere, in contrast, involves pattern recognition, musical ability, art, and various other "intuitive" cognitive skills (Gibson, Filbey, & Gazzaniga, 1970). In other words, *imaginative responses* occur in the right hemisphere. Dreams and other creative acts tend to involve both arousal from the medulla and pons plus the strong emotions of the limbic system, which are woven into a "story" by the right hemisphere in the form of a nightmare, a sexually exciting dream, a myth, a powerful novel, or some other form of imaginative fantasy.

It may be seen, then, that the internal processes of the behavior sequence correspond roughly to specific neural functions that have been identified in physiological research.

Personality Change

Conditions for Change.   Many personality theories have stressed the importance of the earliest years of life in forming the basis for the adult personality. One still sometimes reads statements that each person's basic personality traits are firmly established by the age of 6. A great deal of research indicates, however, that there is no "final" personality and that later experience can undo or modify the effects of early experience (Clarke & Clarke, 1976).

In terms of the behavior sequence, it can be seen that the possibility of change is an integral part of the system. A person frequently encounters new stimulus conditions and hence may behave in a totally new way. For example, new emotional associations may be formed and new attitudes developed. If the person is exposed to new facts or logical arguments, there can be dramatic changes in the information–belief system and, hence, new expectancies and perhaps new emotional responses and attitudes as well. When new fantasies are encountered, the person's expectancies and goals may shift in new directions. Finally, the rewarding or punishing nature of the outcome of goal responses feeds back into the system and frequently results in alteration of one or more of the internal processes. For all of these reasons, personality should probably be thought of as stable only to the extent that conditions remain fairly constant. When external conditions change, internal processes change and, hence, external behavior changes.

Deliberate Change.   Some aspects of personality change occur because of a deliberate attempt by the individual and/or others to alter behavior. People constantly attempt to modify some of their own behaviors that they consider undesirable (e.g., drinking, smoking, overeating, poor work habits) by a variety of means. They try to control external cues (e.g., stay away from bars, decline party invitations), seek new emotional associations (e.g., use a cigarette box that emits a hacking cough when the lid is opened), obtain information (e.g., make a calorie count for each meal), and introduce new fantasies (e.g., think about the praise that will follow success and hard work). Reinforcement can also be manipulated; we know a psychologist who eased his way through graduate school by rewarding himself with an ice cream cone every time he finished a certain amount of required work.

Even more common than such efforts by individuals are institutionalized mechanisms to bring about desired changes. Psychotherapy in its many forms is an attempt to change the personalities of those who seek help. The school system is perhaps the primary way in which society seeks to fit its citizens into a specific mold, regardless of the traits developed in the first six years of life. Schools provide not only information but also a great many overtly expressed values and attitudes (e.g., decisions are best made by majority vote), covertly expressed values and fantasies (e.g., books containing stories that stress achievement need), and attempts at emotional conditioning (e.g., heated rivalries in sports). The least successful of these institutions is the prison system, in which rehabilitation often fails and punishment plus the presence of bad role models only serve to strengthen undesirable traits.

Nondeliberate Change.   Not all personality changes are deliberate. Very often, for example, there are massive changes in external stimulus conditions and reinforcement contingencies that bring about equally massive changes in the people affected. Thus, there are natural disasters and wars that disrupt entire cultures, tear families apart, and create wholly new living conditions for the survivors. People immigrate to a new country and are subjected to new pressures involving most aspects of their lives. Economic changes, both losses and gains, can bring new pressures and conditions that alter what one feels, thinks, and does. A dynamic leader can change the emotional climate of a nation and articulate new goals and philosophies that affect millions of people.

Less obvious are technological changes (such as the invention of the automobile or television) whose side effects can include massive changes in the lives and personalities of those who use them. For example, the automobile was not built with the intention of changing the sexual habits of unmarried adolescents and young adults, but that was one consequence. The purpose of television was not to serve as a fantasy-producing baby sitter for young children, but that was one consequence. Certainly it is impossible to foresee all of the consequences of a given technological change, but it might at least help to identify the existence of such effects after the fact and determine whether we find them acceptable.

Finally, there are the personality changes that occur in everyone as a function of the aging process. While it is not possible to consider this topic in detail here, two aspects are of sufficient importance to note. First, there are physiological changes that occur to some extent in each of us. To the extent that middle or old age is linked with failing eyesight, poor hearing, bad digestion, or assorted body aches and pains, the person's self-perception is also likely to change. Many people believe that sexual interests and abilities wane with age, and if that belief is strong enough, it becomes a self-fulfilling prophecy. In our affluent society many adults tend to eat and drink more while exercising less, so overweight results. All such changes are linked with changes in internal processes, in behaviors, and in the ways others react to the person.

The second type of age-related change is probably more important than the physiological ones. As one moves from adolescence to young adulthood and beyond, there are a succession of situational and role changes that often take one by surprise. The demands of occupation, marriage, parenthood, postparenthood, and retirement can be overwhelming in their effects on feelings, beliefs, and cherished fantasies. Attitudes change; expectancies must be altered; and goals often are not met or are found to be unsatisfying. Also, those who marry almost always think in terms of "forever," and divorce or widowhood may come as a terrible shock and a major challenge to which the person must adjust. A thorough knowledge of personality functioning and change may someday allow us to specify the best way to prepare ourselves for the unavoidable changes that occur throughout the life span.

Personality Adjustment

One of psychology's most difficult tasks is to define what is meant by maladjustment and, at the other extreme, to describe precisely what optimal adjustment might involve. We will first consider **maladjustment**, which is defined here as *any internal or external response that causes psychological distress or unwanted physical pain for the individual engaging in the act and/or for someone else.*

Distress to the Self.   Fear, unhappiness, and depression are emotional responses that deviate from optimal adjustment. It should be noted first that such emotions may be realistic reactions to events in one's environment. Natural and manmade disasters may occur; loved ones may get sick or die; automobile accidents may happen, other people may act unpleasantly; jobs may be lost. In other words, the source of the maladjustment may be external rather than internal. Though most such events are unavoidable, psychological reactions can determine whether the result is personal devastation or a successful attempt to master the situation. That is, a person can give up after a flood destroys his or her home, or it is possible to rebuild the house elsewhere. Loss of a loved one can ruin one's life forever, or the loss can be borne and worked through as new relationships are formed. A person can remain in an unpleasant job or an unhappy marriage, or seek new and more congenial physical and interpersonal surroundings. In general, one can give up and become immersed in sorrow and anxiety, or one can seek to change the external situation or one's own behavior in that situation. When the response is continued emotional upset or a **neurosis** that brings with it a new set of problems, self-distress is the consequence. Bulman and Wortman (1977) report that accident victims who become paralyzed tend to cope badly if they focus on blaming others for the accident. Those who blame themselves cope better, in part because such an approach can lead to an active effort to do something about one's plight.

Another major cause of self-distress is a discrepancy between emotional responses and informational responses. Figure 13-11 shows four possible combinations of informational and emotional variables. There is no problem for the individual when emotion and information are consistent. We engage in many acts ("satisfying pleasures") that we believe to be good, right, proper, moral, healthful, and so forth *and* find pleasant (e.g., eating a delicious nutritious meal, engaging in marital sex, getting a good night's sleep, working on a challenging hobby). Also, most of us easily avoid engaging in acts ("repugnant evils") that we regard as wrong, improper, unhealthful, and so forth *and* would find unpleasant (e.g., torturing a puppy, engaging in sex acts with birds, sleeping on a bed of nails, eating bodily wastes). If there were no other choices than these, life could be a simple matter of seeking satisfying pleasures and avoiding repugnant evils.

The other two sections of Figure 13-11 are the areas where the problems lie. Many things that we must or should do are also unpleasant, so that we are constantly confronted with "duties" (e.g., visiting a dentist for a checkup, going for a job interview, taking a final examination, paying bills).

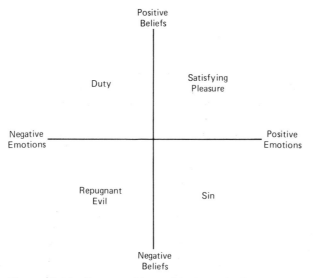

Figure 13-11. Four possible combinations of informational and emotional variables. Self-distress often involves failure to perform *duties* or failure to resist *sins*. We have little trouble engaging in *satisfying pleasures* or avoiding *repugnant evils*.

The choice each time is between immediate pain that has long-term benefits and immediate pleasure that leads to harmful long-term effects. Failure to consider consequences in an explicit way leads many people to realistic distress that was avoidable or to a nagging sense of guilt and self-blame. In the opposite part of the figure lie the pleasures that a person believes to be wrong or harmful; such "sins" might include smoking cigarettes, engaging in what are believed to be immoral sexual acts, eating food that is fattening, or engaging in petty acts of hostility toward a safe target. Failure to resist temptation can again result in realistic distress (e.g., lung cancer or obesity) or guilt and self-blame. The best solution in a given case might be to do one's duty and to resist temptation; an alternative in many instances is to alter an unrealistic or unworkable belief system. The worst solution is to leave the beliefs intact and live a life of regret with respect to duties undone and sins unresisted.

Another major source of self-distress has been touched upon before—expectancies that are either unfulfilled or found unsatisfying. This is a difficult problem for any of us to escape. On the one hand, our expectancies about the future are important and perhaps crucial motivators of current behavior as well as a source of comfort with respect to current problems. Hopes and dreams of what is to come sustain us all. The major fly in the ointment is that many expectations are unrealistic. In part, this means that people can set goals for which the odds are very low (to become world famous, to make a million dollars, to marry an extremely beautiful or handsome spouse, etc.). Such goals are not impossible, since some people actually do become famous, rich, and all the rest. But there should be realistic evaluations and reevaluations of one's chances in the lottery of life. Even when specific goals are more modest and can be met, too often the resulting emotional response is one of disappointment. "Happiness ever after" isn't the usual outcome of marriage, graduation, an increase in income, fame, parenthood, or anything else. We are all some-what conditioned by private and public fantasies to expect that after certain goals are reached, the sky will be bluer and we will dance happily forever to the music of an offstage orchestra. To the extent that our future pro-jections are closer to reality, the resulting disappointments and sense of futility should be lessened. A song asks, "Is that all there is?" We need to realize ahead of time that the answer all too often is yes.

Distress to Others.   There are three major varieties of character-istic behavior that can cause others to feel distress. First, one can behave in ways that are openly cruel, hostile, or aggravating to others. We all know people who have learned a style of interpersonal behavior that is annoying to almost everyone. Some have learned to be insulting, to seek weaknesses and exploit them, to humiliate whoever is present. Though such people tend to be avoided when possible, their presence in one's family, at one's job, or in one's neighborhood can be a source of lasting distress. To the extent that such a person is aware of and concerned about the reactions of others, it is possible for him or her to alter the behavior in a direction that will elicit attraction rather than dislike. Often, however, people find them-selves locked without insight into existing behavioral patterns, and their awareness is limited to the observation that others respond negatively. A familiar complaint to advice columnists is that "people don't like me, but I don't know why." Rather than the panaceas offered by commercials (mouthwash, toothpaste, dandruff shampoo, deodorant, etc.), behavior change is often the only real solution.

A very different type of problem is the person whose behavior involves a belief-emotion inconsistency about which he or she is not as concerned as are friends and relatives. That is, parents, spouse, children, and others may be more upset about a person's unmet duties and unre-sisted sins than the person himself or herself. In general, when a belief system is too weak to overcome emotional responses and someone who cares about the person has a stronger belief system, the result is interper-sonal distress. "Why doesn't she stop drinking?" "Why doesn't he get to work on time?" "Why would she keep on smoking three packs a day?" "Why won't he agree to an operation that may save his life?" A very similar problem arises when belief systems differ. For example, if an adolescent believes that marijuana is a harmless and pleasant way of relaxing while his parents believe that it is a dangerous drug, the adolescent is engaging in behavior he perceives as a satisfying pleasure and his parents perceive as a sin. Various **conduct disorders** fit this description; they range from alcoholism (in which the person may agree that the behavior is harmful) to the **psychopathic personality**, whose emotional responses and belief system differ markedly from those of the majority of people in the culture.

Finally, a person may cause distress to others, even strangers, simply by being deviant from them. As we learned with respect to attraction research, people tend to like those who are similar to themselves and dislike those who are dissimilar. In addition, the dissimilar person is viewed as maladjusted, stupid, and evil (Byrne, 1971). Much of what is labeled as abnormality or deviance in any given culture at a given time consists of ideas or actions that are simply quite different from those of most other members of the culture (Szasz, 1976). Thus, those who are highly dissimilar are threatening and frightening to those who encounter them, and this differentness must be altered or the offending person will be forcibly removed from society. The problem is that the deviance can range from the totally disordered perceptions and thought processes of **psychosis**, brought about by psychological or physiological malfunctioning, to thoughts and acts that just don't happen to conform to what is currently accepted. And it must be noted that it is not always possible to tell which is which.

Optimal Adjustment. Part of the solution to the problem of psychological adjustment was suggested in the preceding discussion. That is, people should be taught to alter their environment or their own behavior in order to escape from realistic stress when it occurs. They should seek to alter either their emotional responses or their belief systems so as to engage in truly necessary dutiful behaviors and avoid truly harmful sinful ones. Their expectancies should be realistic as to attainment and as to what fulfillment might actually constitute.

In more general terms, instrumental activity and goal responses should ideally provide as much immediate and long-term pleasure as possible and as little pain—for both self and others. Beliefs and knowledge should be accurate, and one should be willing to test their predictive accuracy whenever possible. *Accurate labeling* is also critical, so that one responds realistically to the external world and to one's own arousal responses and emotional reactions. People should feel free to play and to explore the world of fantasy, and to seek creative enjoyment in the world of imagination. Realistic and challenging goals—large and small—that are achieved regularly by means of one's own efforts provide a continuing source of satisfaction. Finally, there should always be openness to feedback and willingness to change one's environment, emotional associations, attitudes, beliefs, expectancies, fantasies, and overt behaviors. In a changing world a rigid personality is likely to act as a barrier to optimal adjustment.

Figure 13-12. Optimal adjustment includes enjoying intimacy with others. (Steve Hanson, Stock, Boston)

FUTURE APPLICATIONS OF PERSONALITY RESEARCH

Measuring Personality Traits

Imagine for a moment some future time when all of the major personality dimensions have been identified and measures have been designed to assess individual differences in emotional responsiveness, physiological arousal, attitudes, beliefs, expectancies, fantasies, and overt behavior. The task of providing a *complete* personality description of any one individual would be enormous. The testing alone might well consume days or even weeks. The final product could conceivably take the form of a good-sized book listing the individual's scores and the predictive statements that could be made about him or her. Also, the scores and predictions would be valid only for the present; personality changes over time would require new assessments and a new description. Would it ever be worthwhile to obtain a complete personality description that required such a lavish investment of time, effort, and money?

Though we may only guess about the future, one possibility is that the need for complete personality descriptions will be limited. Only a few very special situations would seem to clearly be appropriate to warrant such an effort. For example, when a person is being selected for a key position in which his or her behavior in a variety of situations has widespread consequences for others, it would seem well worth the investment to be able to predict that behavior as accurately and as completely as possible; candidates for the presidency might qualify. Knowledge of every strength and weakness of such individuals across situations could be of life-and-death importance to all of us. If such personality testing sounds mechanical and impersonal, keep in mind that decisions *must be* and *are being* made about those individuals. The only question is the basis of the decisions, and the relation between the decisions and the consequences. Would you prefer to judge a potential leader on the basis of valid psychological assessment or television commercials and bumper stickers?

Predicting and Controlling
Limited Aspects of Human Behavior

Most predictions that psychologists would reasonably be asked to make in practical situations have to do with specific and limited aspects of behavior. Two sorts of behavioral prediction should be considered. First, there are questions about the behavior of individuals. An example would be, "How well will John Jones do in college?" As the research presented earlier indicates, we know that it would be useful to measure his performance on an intelligence test, to determine his need for achievement, and to assess his anxiety level, specifically including test anxiety. This combination of personality measures would provide a much better than chance prediction of his probable college performance. We do not need to know everything about John Jones, and we do not need to try to describe everything he is likely to do in every situation—we only want to know about his college performance.

Second, there are questions about the responses of people in general. An example would be, "What are the effects of exposing adults to explicit sexual content in books, movies, and magazines?" On the basis of existing research we can answer with respect to probable self-perceived and physiologically indicated levels of sexual arousal, and, taking individual differences into account, we can predict affective responses and behavioral acts. Again, the question has to do with a fairly limited concern and the answer can be quite specific. The more we learn through research, the more accurate the answers to both types of question will be.

There is a further, and potentially more dramatic, use for the knowledge acquired by behavioral science. Neither individuals nor the stimuli they encounter need be thought of in static terms. Change is possible in both. When behavioral science is advanced enough, it should be possible to alter the personality structure of an individual to ensure the most rewarding behavior in a given situation. For example, if we agreed that doing well in college is desirable, we would attempt to devise ways to make John Jones more intelligent, more motivated to achieve, and less anxious. Or we could devise changes in the way college courses are taught so that even students with limited intellectual ability, low achievement need, and high anxiety would be able to learn. In a similar way, if we agreed that sexual activity was beneficial, we could devise ways to make most people feel more emotionally and attitudinally positive about sexual cues and could ensure that erotic materials were models for acceptable sexual behavior and not for sex crimes or aggressive acts.

Whether such manipulations of individuals and external conditions brought about Utopia or Hell would depend on the values of the manipulators in relation to one's own values. Laser beams can be used in performing delicate eye surgery or guiding explosives to their targets. People differ in the relative value they place on these two activities. Thus, one person's Utopia is, in fact, another person's Hell. The best any of us—scientists and nonscientists alike—can do is to attempt to persuade others to share our own (obviously correct) view of the world.

Our long-range hope would be that the people of the future can be creative, bright, happy, democratic, kind, loving, and so on, within the limits of our applied skills and the shared values of our society. Human beings have refused to accept the limits imposed by the physical and biological world. Transportation, communication, comfort, physical health, and conception, for example, are increasingly under our control. We have no reason to believe that personality should or will be left out of humanity's future progress.

SUMMARY

Though most definitions of personality stress a combination of traits, personality research tends to deal with one small segment of the person at a time. Fiction exaggerates the consistency and predictability of human behavior. Some of this novelistic flavor may be seen in the case histories of therapists. Once prediction becomes the goal of personality description, it may be seen that universal generalizations do not provide genuine information about individuals.

Inheritance plays a role in the development of personality with respect to anatomical structure and physiological functioning, factors of appearance and coordination to which there is a social response, and predispositions involving a few behavioral traits. Prenatal influences on personality include the effects of the mother's diet, various drugs consumed during pregnancy, and extreme emotional experiences that may affect the developing fetus.

The *behavior sequence* is a theoretical approach to personality that attempts to tie together the kinds of situational and personality factors discussed throughout this book in a single model of the determinants of human behavior. In this model Stage 1 is infancy (about the first twenty months), during which there is initial reflexive behavior plus simple instrumental activity and goal responses initiated by internal and external stimulation that is physiologically arousing. Associational learning also begins to take place with respect to arousal, emotional responses, and the formation of very general, unverbalized basic attitudes. Stage 2 is childhood (beginning with language acquisition and ending with puberty), which involves the use of language in evaluating one's surroundings; attempts to label and understand the world by way of informational responses and expectancies; the development of imaginative responses; and an array of overt behaviors that provide mobility, the possibility of manipulating aspects of the environment, and the use of interpersonal skills. Stage 3 is adolescence, which extends from puberty to adulthood and includes an initial period of rapid growth and sexual maturation, the development of attitudes that are congruent with those of peers, an increase in knowledge and elaboration of beliefs, an increase in fantasy centered on love–sex relationships and on future success, and an increase in behavioral skills ranging from lovemaking to occupational requirements.

Adulthood involves the formation of a close sexual relationship and the achievement of economic independence. All aspects of the behavior sequence are now formed, and the various processes operate together; future personality research will have to focus on these multiple determinants of behavior. The interactions among the subsystems are of greatest interest when they exert contradictory or inconsistent influences on a given behavior. Possible neural correlates of the internal processes were suggested.

Personality change can occur when stimulus conditions lead to new emotional, informational, or imaginative responses, or when positive and negative outcomes provide feedback to the system that demands change. Such change can be a result of deliberate efforts, such as psychotherapy, or of nondeliberate events, such as aging. Maladjustment involves any internal or external response that causes psychological distress or unwanted physical pain for the person engaging in the act and/or for someone else. Optimal adjustment involves willingness to change the environment or oneself when distress arises, attempts to obtain accurate information, and freedom to enjoy fantasy and creative imagination.

In the future, attempts to describe all of the personality traits of a single individual will probably be confined to very special cases such as the assessment of presidential candidates. Most predictive efforts will be limited to specific questions about a person or about a given stimulus. Personality research should also provide us with knowledge about how to induce individuals to function at a maximal level and how to change the environment to accommodate individuals. Thus, the study of personality can ideally lead to progress that will benefit each of us.

SUGGESTED READINGS

CLARKE, A. M., & CLARKE, A. D. B. (eds.). *Early experience: Myth and evidence.* New York: Free Press, 1976. A collection of chapters in which various investigators examine studies of early experience. There is convincing evidence that traditional ideas about the crucial nature of the first few years of life must be modified in view of the way later experiences are able to "undo" the effects of earlier ones.

CLORE, G. L., & BYRNE, D. A reinforcement–affect model of attraction. In T. L. Huston (ed.), *Foundations of interpersonal attraction.* New York: Academic Press, 1974. Though this chapter deals with a theory of attraction, it presents the model that was later expanded into the behavior sequence. In addition, there is a discussion of the way in which different levels of theory building (from empirical findings to comprehensive theories) are related to one another.

GUBRIUM, J. F. (ed.). *Time, roles, and self in old age.* New York: Human Sciences Press, 1976. A well-coordinated collection of papers dealing with the role changes that occur in later life and their effects on behavior.

HARRÉ, R. (ed.). *Personality.* Totowa, N.J.: Rowman and Littlefield, 1976. A collection of original and reprinted papers dealing with various aspects of a theoretical approach to personality that stresses the way personal traits influence behavior in diverse situations.

KAGAN, J., & COLES, R. (eds.). *Twelve to sixteen: Early adolescence.* New York: Norton, 1972. A collection of original chapters covering a variety of aspects of adolescent development.

MUSSEN, P. H., CONGER, J. J., & KAGAN, J. *Child development and personality.* New York: Harper & Row, 1974. An excellent overview of research on personality development written at a level appropriate to undergraduate college students.

GLOSSARY

Ability trait. In Cattell's theory, the basic source trait that ranges from dull to bright——intelligence.

Achievement need. A learned motive to strive for success and excellence.

Achievement training. The methods used by parents to teach their children to do everything they do as well as possible.

Acquiescent response set. The tendency to agree with a test item regardless of its content.

Actualizing tendency. In Rogers's theory, the inherent motive of the individual to develop all of his or her capacities in ways that serve to maintain or improve the organism.

Adolescence. The stage of development between puberty and adulthood.

Adulthood. The stage of development that begins at different times for different individuals but tends to include the formation of a close interpersonal relationship (most often with a member of the opposite sex) and economic independence (defined by completion of schooling, acquisition of occupational skills, and establishment of a dwelling place separate from that of the parents).

Affiliative behavior. The tendency to seek out other people for companionship and interpersonal contact.

Aggression. Any act designed to harm or injure another person.

Amygdala. A structure within the limbic system.

Anal personality. In Freud's theory, fixation at or regression to the anal stage, which results in either an anal retentive (neat, orderly, compulsive) or an anal expulsive (messy, disorganized, explosive) personality.

Anal stage. In Freud's theory, the second stage of development, in which activities involving the control of bowel functions are of central importance.

Analytical theory. The personality theory of Carl Jung.

Androgyny. A sex role that combines masculinity and femininity.

Anima. In Jung's theory, the archetype of femininity that men possess.

Animus. In Jung's theory, the archetype of masculinity that women possess.

Anti-Semitism. Prejudice directed against Jews.

Anxiety. An unpleasant emotional state characterized by vague fears, physiological arousal, and various bodily symptoms such as rapid heartbeat and perspiration. In Freud's theory, an unpleasant feeling with no specific focus and involving a general sense of helplessness.

Archetype. In Jung's theory, universal symbols contained in the collective unconscious.

Artifact. Anything made by a human being. In research, a finding that is created by the investigator as opposed to something that would occur naturally.

Attitude. Relatively stable evaluative responses that are mediated by emotional responses. Attitudes can be acquired before the person has developed verbal skills; such attitudes constitute deep, basic evaluative orientations. In Cattell's theory, a relatively specific motivational (dynamic) trait that is learned.

Attraction. A person's evaluation of other people along a dimension that includes such attitudes as hate, dislike, indifference, liking, and love.

Authoritarian personality. One extreme of the authoritarianism dimension of personality. It is characterized by conventionalism, submission to a strong leader, aggression toward deviants, a cynical concern with power, a mystical view of the world, distrust of the subjective, a tendency to project, and concern about the sexual activities of others.

Authoritarianism. The personality dimension that ranges from the authoritarian personality to the equalitarian personality.

B-cognition. In Maslow's theory, the kind of nonjudgmental thinking that involves *being*. Examples are thought processes dealing with beauty, goodness, and wholeness.

Behavior modification. Therapeutic techniques designed to alter behavior through procedures based on learning theory.

Behavior potential. In Rotter's theory, the likelihood that a given behavior will occur in a given situation.

Behavior sequence. A theoretical model of personality in which overt behavior is viewed as a function of external stimuli, a series of internal processes (emotions, attitudes, information, expectations, fantasies, and physiological arousal states), and the rewards and punishments that accompany instrumental and goal responses.

Behaviorism. The approach to psychology that assumes that it involves the study of observable behavior rather than hypothetical, unmeasurable mental states.

Binet-Simon Scale. The first successful intelligence test, developed in 1905 by Alfred Binet and Theodore Simon.

Birth trauma. In Freud's theory, the origin of anxiety. The infant is said to feel anxious and helpless at the time of birth because it is forced out of a safe, comfortable womb.

Black Intelligence Test of Cultural Homogeneity. A culture-specific intelligence test designed to reflect the black rather than the white culture.

Blind experimenter. One who is purposely kept unaware of the hypothesis and the expected results so as to avoid conscious or unconscious experimenter effects on the responses of the subjects.

Bootstrap approach. Another name for the internal consistency approach to test construction.

Buss aggression machine. An experimental device used to study aggressive behavior. The subject presses one of ten buttons that supposedly deliver different degrees of electric shock to a confederate.

Bystander calculus. Piliavin and Piliavin's proposal that altruism occurs only when the perceived rewards for helping outweigh the perceived costs.

California F Scale. A test constructed to measure authoritarianism.

Cardinal trait. In Allport's theory, a trait so important that it dominates a person's life.

Case history. A detailed description of the salient aspects of a person's past and present traits, symptoms, and behavior.

Castration anxiety. In Freud's theory, a boy's fear that his father will punish him for sexually desiring his mother by cutting off his penis.

Catharsis effect. The tendency for a given type of behavior (such as aggression) to reduce the probability that one will engage in that behavior later.

Central nervous system. The brain and the spinal cord.

Cerebral cortex. The outer layer of the brain, which contains the frontal lobes and the left and right hemispheres.

Cerobrotonia. In Sheldon's theory, the temperament type involving emotional restraint, desire for privacy, and intellectual interests.

Childhood. The stage of development between language acquisition and puberty.

Classical conditioning. Learning in which a stimulus that elicits a certain response is paired with a neutral one that initially does not elicit that response. After a number of such pairings the neutral stimulus elicits the response.

Client-centered therapy. The therapeutic technique developed by Carl Rogers, in which the emphasis is on perceiving, understanding, and accepting the feelings expressed by the client.

Coefficient of equivalence. An index of reliability that indicates the degree to which two different measures of the same construct are related to one another.

Coefficient of internal consistency. An index of reliability that indicates the degree to which different elements of a test are equivalent to one another.

Coefficient of stability. An index of reliability that indicates the degree to which a measure yields the same score at different times.

Cognitive dissonance. The unpleasant arousal state proposed by Festinger to occur when cognitions are inconsistent.

Cognitive theory. A personality theory that stresses the importance of internal factors that consist of intellectual/rational/conscious processes.

Cognitive therapy. A therapeutic procedure in which efforts are made to alter a person's maladaptive thought processes.

Collective unconscious. In Jung's theory, the inherited influences that reflect the experiences of our ancestors.

Common trait. In Allport's theory, the traits

on which most people in a given culture can be compared.

Complementarity. The proposal that some personality traits should operate in such a way that dissimilarity acts as a positive influence on attraction. For example, a dominant person should get along well with a submissive one.

Complex. In Jung's theory, a collection of related concepts and images in the personal unconscious.

Comprehensive theory. An abstract representation of a phenomenon that brings together a series of generalized laws and indicates how they are related.

Concurrent validity. The correlation between test scores and a current criterion behavior.

Conditioned response. A response elicited by a previously neutral stimulus (the conditioned stimulus) after classical conditioning has taken place.

Conditioned stimulus. In classical conditioning, a previously neutral stimulus that acquires the ability to elicit a response through association with an unconditioned stimulus.

Conduct disorder. A pattern of maladjusted behavior that causes more distress to others than to the person who exhibits the behavior.

Confounded variables. When two or more independent variables are combined in such a way as to make it impossible to determine which is influencing the dependent variable.

Congruent validation. An inadequate verification technique in which new observations that are congruent with a generalization are accepted as evidence of its accuracy. One problem is that incongruent observations are easily ignored.

Conscience. In Freud's theory, the aspect of the superego that guides a person's behavior according to a code of moral standards.

Conscious. In Freud's theory, mental activity of which the person is totally aware.

Construct validity. The total array of relations between a test and other relevant behaviors.

Constructive alternativism. In Kelly's theory, the proposal that there are multiple ways of making sense of the same events.

Content validity. The extent to which a test consists of an adequate sample of a specific body of material.

Control. In an experiment, holding constant the effects of irrelevant variables so that the effects of the independent variable can be observed. In application, the ability to bring about a desired outcome through the manipulation of known variables.

Conventional level (of moral development). A level of moral development at which acts that are approved by others are viewed as "good" while acts that are disapproved of are viewed as "bad."

Conventionalism. Acceptance of conventional moral values simply on the basis of external social pressure.

Coronary-prone behavior. The tendency to be hurried, achievement-oriented, and impatient—characteristics of those with a high risk of developing heart trouble.

Correlational research. Research in which variables are not manipulated. Instead, their correlation or association is observed.

Counterconditioning. A behavior modification technique in which a desired response (such as relaxation) is substituted for an undesirable one (such as anxiety) by means of classical conditioning.

Cross-sectional design. Research in which the variable of age is studied by testing *different individuals* who differ in age.

Cross-validation. In test construction, the use of an item analysis procedure with a second sample of subjects in order to minimize the role of chance in the selection of valid items.

Cue. A weak stimulus that provides information permitting the individual to make a relevant discrimination.

D-cognition. In Maslow's theory, thought processes involving *deficiency* needs. There is a tendency to evaluate, judge, and condemn oneself and others.

Deindividuation. A psychological state characterized by reduced concern with social evaluation, a feeling of anonymity, and a reduction in restraints on forbidden forms of behavior.

Demand characteristics. Any cues in an experiment that suggest the hypothesis to the subjects so that they may behave in such a way as to confirm or disconfirm it rather than in a natural manner.

Dependent variable. In an experiment, the variable whose influence by the independent variable is observed.

Diffusion of responsibility. The fact that when there is more than one witness to an emergency each one's responsibility to act is reduced.

Drive. The state of arousal that occurs when a need has been activated but not satisfied.

Drive reduction. Any activity that results in the lowering of a state of arousal. Drive reduction is reinforcing.

Drive stimulus. An intense stimulus that motivates an organism to act.

Dynamic lattice. In Cattell's theory, a person's interlocking subsidiation chains that constitute his or her motivational structure.

Dynamic trait. In Cattell's theory, a behavioral dimension that involves motivation.

Dynamism. In Sullivan's theory, a recurring behavior pattern or habit.

Ectomorphy. In Sheldon's theory, a body type characterized by a thin, flat-chested, delicate build.

Effectance motive. The drive to be logical, consistent, and accurate in interpreting the world.

Ego. In Freud's theory, the portion of the mind that is reality oriented. It is seen in such activities as reasoning, planning, and learning.

Electra complex. In Freud's theory, the conflict faced by girls during the phallic stage, involving desire for and rejection of the mother, penis envy, and love and admiration of the father.

Emotional response. A positive or negative affective response that is felt as pleasant or unpleasant, is accompanied by characteristic overt responses (e.g., smiling or frowning), and leads to approach or avoidance behavior.

Emotional responsiveness. A characteristic difference among individuals in general level of activation. Anxiety has been defined as one aspect of emotional responsiveness.

Empirical finding. A research result showing that a relation exists between at least two variables.

Empirical law. A functional relation (usually stated in the form of a mathematical equation) between at least two specific variables.

Empirical research. Research that deals with observable variables.

Endocrine system. The series of glands that secrete hormones within the body.

Endomorphy. In Sheldon's theory, a body type characterized by a soft, rounded build.

Entrepreneur. One who organizes and manages one's work on one's own initiative.

Equalitarian personality. One extreme of the authoritarianism dimension of personality. It is characterized by a democratic approach to the role of leader, tolerance for deviant ideas and appearance, lack of interest in power, a scientific view of the world, and concern for the free expression of ideas and feelings.

Equal-interval scale. A scale on which the points are in numerical order of magnitude, but in addition the distance between the points is uniform. A yardstick is an example of an equal interval scale.

Erg. In Cattell's theory, an innate motivational (dynamic) trait.

Erotophile. A person who has positive attitudes about a wide variety of sexual matters.

Erotophobe. A person who has negative attitudes about a wide variety of sexual matters.

Ethnocentrism. The tendency to believe that one's own culture is superior and all others are inferior.

Excitement phase. In the sexual response cycle proposed by Masters and Johnson, the first phase: rapidly mounting arousal.

Expectancy. The anticipation of a positive or negative consequence on the basis of one's information (knowledge and beliefs). In Rotter's theory, a person's estimate that engaging in a specific behavior will result in a particular reinforcement.

Experimental research. Research in which an experimenter manipulates an independent variable in order to determine its effects on a dependent variable.

Experimenter effects. Results that are brought about by something that the experimenter unwittingly does.

External criterion approach. In test construction, the selection of items on the basis of their relation with some existing behavioral difference (correlation) or with some manipulated behavioral difference (experiment).

Externality. In Rotter's theory, the belief that reinforcements are controlled by external factors.

Extinction. The weakening and eventual elimination of a learned response which takes place when it is not reinforced.

Extraversion. In Jung's theory, an inborn tendency to function objectively, with the outside world as the most important consideration.

F Scale. The Fascist Scale, a test constructed to measure authoritarianism.

Face validity. The extent to which a measuring device consists of elements that are logically related to the variable being measured.

Factor analysis. A statistical technique that identifies the homogeneous groupings within a matrix of intercorrelations.

Fear. An unpleasant emotional state characterized by dread of a specific object or event, physiological arousal, and bodily symptoms such as rapid heartbeat and perspiration.

Fear of freedom. In Fromm's theory, the motivating force that causes people to seek the security of totalitarian forms of government.

Fear of success. The tendency to assume that success will have negative consequences.

Fear Survey Schedule (FSS). A checklist of objects and events that is used to identify the kinds of fears a person experiences.

Feeling mode. In Jung's theory, the judgmental mode that involves evaluation of internal and external events.

Field experiment. A field study in which at least one variable is manipulated by an experimenter in order to determine its effects.

Field study. Research conducted in a natural setting rather than in a laboratory.

Frequency count. In measuring behavior, the frequency with which a person engages in a given act.

Frontal lobe. A region of the cerebral cortex.

Frustration-aggression hypothesis. The proposal that a person is motivated to injure whomever or whatever blocks his or her goal-directed behavior.

Functional autonomy. In Allport's theory, the tendency of instrumental behavior (for example, work) to become independent of its origins and to be enjoyed in its own right.

Gender identity. The labeling of a person as male or female.

Generalization. An activity in which a specific, concrete observation is expanded to a more general, abstract proposal.

Generalized law. A functional relation (usually stated in the form of a mathematical equation) between at least two classes of variables.

Genital stage. In Freud's theory, the final stage of development, in which members of the opposite sex are objects of both sexual desire and affection.

Genital vasocongestion. An increase in the blood supply to the genital area that is one component of sexual arousal.

Habit strength. In Hull-Spence theory, the strength of a stimulus-response association that increases whenever that association is followed by reinforcement.

Hemispheres. Part of the cerebral cortex. The left hemisphere deals with various cognitive skills involving sequential processing of information, while the right hemisphere deals with pattern recognition, musical and artistic ability, and the like.

Homophobia. Fear of any stimulus connected with homosexuality.

Hull-Spence theory. The theory of behavior developed by Clark L. Hull and extended by Kenneth W. Spence.

Human nature. The idea that human beings have basic behavioral characteristics that are sometimes disguised by cultural influences.

Humanist. A theoretical position emphasizing the basic goodness of human beings and their potential for growth toward higher and better levels of functioning.

Hypothesis. A prediction deduced from a theory.

I-E Scale. A test that measures Rotter's concept of locus of control. It identifies a subject's beliefs with respect to internality and externality.

Id. In Freud's theory, the totally unconscious portion of the mind, in which there is only striving for immediate satisfaction of needs and wishes.

Ideal self-concept. A person's standards which serve as a goal defining the characteristics he or she would like to have.

Identity crisis. In Erikson's theory, the adolescent crisis that must be resolved as the person tries to figure out who he or she really is.

Idiographic. In Allport's theory, the approach that centers on an individual person rather than on groups and averages. The latter is the nomothetic approach.

Imaginative responses. The thematic images that constitute our verbal and pictorial fantasies. They range from self-created dreams to imaginative creations adapted from the external world.

Independence training. The methods used by parents to teach their children to be independent and able to do things for themselves.

Independent variable. In an experiment, the variable that is manipulated by the experimenter in order to determine its effect on the dependent variable.

Infancy. The stage of development between

birth and language acquisition—about twenty months.

Informational responses. The language symbols that provide labels and connections between and among cognitions. These symbols can be stored for future use and can be communicated both internally and externally.

Instigation. A stimulus (such as a physical attack by another person) that elicits an aggressive response.

Intelligence. The ability to learn, remember, understand, form concepts, and think effectively. In more general terms, the capacity of a person to understand his or her surroundings and the ability to cope with its challenges.

Intelligence quotient (IQ). Originally, a person's mental age divided by his or her chronological age and multiplied by 100. Today, it indicates test performance in relation to the person's age-group.

Intention. A verbal regulator of future behavior involving self-instruction to engage in a given behavior or to refrain from doing so.

Interjudge consistency. An index of reliability that indicates the degree to which different scorers arrive at the same score.

Internal consistency approach. In test construction, the evaluation of items in terms of their relation to the total body of items.

Internality. In Rotter's theory, the belief that reinforcements are controlled by oneself.

Interpersonal Judgment Scale. A measure of interpersonal attraction that yields scores ranging from 2 (extreme dislike) to 14 (extreme liking).

Interpersonal theory. The personality theory of Harry Stack Sullivan.

Introversion. In Jung's theory, an inborn tendency to function subjectively, with oneself as the most important consideration.

Introversion-Extroversion. In Eysenck's theory, one of the three basic dimensions of personality. It indicates a spectrum ranging from careful, thoughtful, passive, quiet individuals to optimistic, active, sociable, outgoing ones.

Intuiting mode. In Jung's theory, the apprehending mode that involves subjective perception of events.

Intuitive approach. In test construction, the creation of items on the basis of armchair logic, theory, or hunch.

Item analysis. In test construction, a proce-

dure in which each item is evaluated in terms of its relation to some criterion.

Jenkins Activity Survey. A test that measures coronary-prone behavior and identifies a subject's standing with respect to Type A and Type B characteristics.

"Just world" hypothesis. Lerner's proposal that most people tend to believe that justice triumphs and that people get the rewards and punishment they deserve.

Laboratory experiment. An experimental investigation conducted in a laboratory setting that provides maximum control over all aspects of the research.

Latency period. In Freud's theory, the period between age six and puberty, when children lose all interest in sexual matters and tend to associate only with same-sex peers.

Libido. In Freud's theory, the energy underlying the life instincts, such as hunger and sex.

Life space. In Lewin's theory, the person plus his or her psychological environment—the factors that determine behavior.

Limbic system. A combination of several brain structures that together play an important role in regulating emotional reactions.

Locus of control. In Rotter's theory, the generalized expectancy that the control of one's reinforcements rests with outside factors (externality) or with oneself (internality).

Longitudinal design. Research in which the variable of age is studied by testing and retesting *the same individuals* at various points in their lives.

Love. An emotional state involving attraction, sexual desire, and concern about the other person.

Love Scale. A test developed by Rubin to measure how much a person loves someone else.

Maladjustment. Any internal or external response that causes psychological distress or unwanted physical pain for the person engaging in the act and/or for someone else.

Manifest Anxiety Scale (MAS). The measure of anxiety developed by Janet Taylor Spence as a way of assessing individual differences in emotional responsiveness.

Measurement error. Inconsistency in a measuring device, such as a test, results in random variations in scores. Thus, part of the score reflects actual differences in the variable being measured and the remainder reflects measurement error.

Medulla. A region of the brain located above the spinal cord.

Mental age. An intelligence test score that has been converted into years and months to indicate the average age of those who perform at a given intellectual level.

Mesomorphy. In Sheldon's theory, a body type characterized by a strong, muscular build.

Meta needs. In Maslow's theory, the higher needs that can be satisfied after the basic biological needs have been satisfied.

Midbrain. A portion of the brain located above the pons.

Minnesota Multiphasic Personality Inventory (MMPI). An objective personality test consisting of scales whose items are answered differently by normals than by individuals with specific psychiatric diagnoses.

Modeling. A behavior modification technique in which the desired behavior is acted out by a live or filmed model.

Modeling effect. The tendency for a person to model or imitate behavior that he or she observes.

Motivation to attain success (M_s). A component of the achievement motive in which the primary goal is success.

Motivation to avoid failure (M_f). A component of the achievement need in which the primary goal is to avoid failure.

n **Ach.** In Murray's terminology, the need for achievement. (See achievement need.)

Need for affiliation (n Aff). The motive to seek interpersonal relations and form friendships.

Need for approval. A personality trait involving the desire to be accepted by others and to be liked.

Need for positive regard. In Rogers's theory, a universal need to be loved and respected.

Need for power. In Adler's theory, a basic human need to be able to control and dominate others.

Need hierarchy. In Maslow's theory, the arrangement of human needs from the most basic physiological necessities to the highest human accomplishment—self-actualization.

Need state. A condition of arousal that occurs when there is a physiological deficit (e.g., lack of food) or surplus (e.g., a full bladder).

Neural chassis. The most ancient part of the central nervous system, consisting of the spinal cord, the medulla, the pons, and the midbrain.

Neurosis. A pattern of maladjusted behavior involving anxieties, worries, fears, bodily concerns, and/or general unhappiness.

Neuroticism. In Eysenck's theory, one of the three basic dimensions of personality. It ranges from stable to unstable behaviors.

Nomothetic. In Allport's theory, his definition of the usual approach of psychological research that deals with groups rather than the preferred approach (idiographic) that concentrates on the individual.

Nonentrepreneur. One who is not free to organize and manage one's own work but is dependent on direction from someone else.

Oedipal complex. In Freud's theory, the conflict between a boy's sexual desire for his mother and his fear of his father's angry jealousy.

Operant. In Skinner's formulation, a response freely exhibited by an organism, not one determined by an external stimulus.

Operant conditioning. A type of learning procedure in which positive reinforcers are presented after a desired response is given, thus increasing the likelihood of that response's occurring again. The procedure can also involve negative reinforcers, which *decrease* the likelihood of a response's occurring. In Skinner's system, a form of learning in which operants are reinforced in order to produce the desired behavior.

Operational definition. A verbal statement that specifies the observable conditions and procedural rules used in defining concepts and variables.

Oral personality. In Freud's theory, fixation at or regression to the oral stage, which results in either a passive, dependent personality (early oral stage) or a verbally aggressive, argumentative personality (late oral stage).

Oral stage. In Freud's theory, the first stage of development in which activities involving the mouth are of central importance.

Oraphilia. A trait involving positive attitudes toward food and the eating process.

Ordinal scale. A scale on which the points are in numerical order of magnitude but the distance between the points is not indicated. For example, when sportswriters or coaches name the top twenty basketball teams, the resulting list of teams is an ordinal scale.

Orgasm phase. In the sexual response cycle proposed by Masters and Johnson, the third phase: an intense rise in excitement followed by a sudden release of sexual tension.

Overcontrolled personality. A person who has learned to be extremely inhibited about expressing aggression, has developed no appropriate aggressive responses, and is likely to respond to a strong provocation with excessive violence.

Ovulation. Release of an egg from an ovary.

Paired-associates learning. A learning task in which subjects are presented with a series of stimulus words and required to learn the response word associated with each one.

Parataxic mode. In Sullivan's theory, the early experiences in which meaning is personally defined and often unrelated to the way others perceive and define the world about them.

Passionate infatuation. An intense and often unrealistic emotional response to another person, interpreted by those involved as "love."

Peak experience. In Maslow's theory, the positive effect of engaging in B-cognition.

Penile plethysmograph. An instrument that measures male sexual arousal by detecting changes in the circumference or volume of the penis.

Penis envy. In Freud's theory, the feeling evoked in a girl during the Oedipal period when she discovers that the clitoris is much smaller than the penis.

Persona. In Jung's theory, the "mask" that we adopt when playing certain roles while interacting with others.

Personal constructs. In Kelly's theory, a person's cognitions that permit him or her to understand, predict, and control the environment.

Personal space. The physical area around each person into which few other people are allowed to enter.

Personal trait. In Allport's theory, the handful of very specific traits that define an individual's personality and make him or her unique.

Personal unconscious. In Jung's theory, the "region of the mind" in which unnoticed, forgotten, or repressed memories are stored.

Personality. The field of psychology that deals with dimensions of individual differences and with situational factors in behavior. With respect to an individual, personality is the sum total of all of the relatively enduring dimensions of individual differences.

Personality theory. A theory developed with the aim of describing and explaining the behavior of individuals.

Personalized system of instruction (PSI). An educational technique in which students set their own pace, hear only a small number of lectures, take tests when they feel that they are prepared, and retake a test if necessary until the material is mastered.

Personification. In Sullivan's theory, one's concept of oneself or of any other person.

Phallic personality. In Freud's theory, the traits that develop when the Oedipal conflicts of the phallic stage are not fully resolved. Males may become homosexuals or promiscuous and unloving heterosexuals. Females may become flirtatious, coldly castrating, or lesbian.

Phallic stage. In Freud's theory, the third stage of development, in which the child has sexual desires toward the mother. Males are in conflict with respect to this desire versus fear of father's retaliation. Females are in conflict with respect to this desire versus rejection of the mother for creating the daughter's "inferior" female genitalia.

Phenomenology. The position stating that each person responds to what he or she perceives rather than to external reality as defined by others.

Pituitary gland. An endocrine gland at the base of the brain whose hormonal secretions play a regulatory role.

Pons. A region of the brain located above the medulla.

Plateau phase. In the sexual response cycle proposed by Masters and Johnson, the second phase: excitement maintained at a high, steady level by continued stimulation.

Pleasure principle. In Freud's theory, the way the id functions in demanding instant gratification.

Popularity. A combination of personality and background factors that elicits positive responses from the people one encounters.

Pornography. Any material whose primary function is to arouse sexual thoughts and cause sexual excitement.

Postconventional level (of moral development). An advanced level of moral development at which the "goodness" or "badness" of various acts is judged by self-chosen moral principles.

Preconscious. In Freud's theory, the stored

memories that a person is able to bring into awareness, though sometimes only after much effort.

Preconventional level (of moral development). A level of moral development at which acts are judged in terms of their outcomes. Those which produce positive outcomes are viewed as "good," while those which produce negative outcomes are viewed as "bad."

Predictive validity. The correlation between test scores and a subsequent criterion behavior.

Press. In Murray's theory, an environmental event that helps or hinders a person's attempt to attain a goal.

Primary need. Motivation based on inborn biological processes.

Proceeding. In Murray's theory, a single behavioral act.

Projective test. A personality test in which the subject responds to somewhat ambiguous stimuli, presumably revealing aspects of his or her unconscious functioning.

Projectivity. The tendency to transfer internal problems to the external world.

Propinquity. Physical nearness. As propinquity between two people increases, the probability of their interacting (and becoming acquainted) increases.

Prosocial behavior. Responses that have no obvious benefits for the responder but are beneficial to the recipient.

Prototaxic mode. In Sullivan's theory, the earliest and most primitive form of experience, in which sensations are perceived without meaning, relation, or sense of time.

Psychoanalysis. The type of psychotherapy developed by Sigmund Freud.

Psychoanalytic theory. The personality theory developed by Sigmund Freud.

Psychosis. Severely maladjusted behavior characterized by distortions in perception, thinking, emotions, and speech.

Psychopathic personality. The type of conduct disorder that involves lack of conscience development, no feelings of anxiety or guilt, and inability to delay gratification.

Psychoticism. In Eysenck's theory, one of the three basic dimensions of personality. It ranges from solitary, insensitive, uncaring behaviors to gregarious, empathetic ones.

Puberty. The point at which a person becomes biologically able to conceive offspring.

Rank order. In measuring behavior, the order in which people differ from most to least is judged by observers. The result is a set of ranks on an ordinal scale.

Rating. In measuring behavior, people can be asked to judge themselves or others along an ordinal scale on which characteristics are differentiated in terms of magnitude or degree.

Reality principle. In Freud's theory, the way the ego functions in dealing with the outside world in a realistic manner.

Refractory period. The period after orgasm during which males are unresponsive to sexual stimulation.

Reinforcement. Any stimulus event that changes the probability of a response occurring.

Reinforcement contingencies. The conditions under which reward or punishment is contingent upon specific responses being made.

Reinforcement value. In Rotter's theory, a person's relative preferences among different reinforcements.

Reinforcement-affect model. The theory stating that evaluation of a stimulus is a positive linear function of the weighted proportion of positive reinforcements associated with that stimulus.

Relaxation training. A procedure in which people are given practice in tensing and then relaxing various muscle groups such as those of the arms, legs, stomach, and face.

Reliability. The consistency with which a measuring instrument assesses a variable.

Repeated exposure. Zajonc's theory that repeated exposure to any stimulus results in a decreased negative response and an increased positive response to it.

Repression-sensitization. A continuum of defense mechanisms ranging from the tendency to deny and avoid threat to the tendency to intellectualize and approach the source of discomfort.

Resolution phase. In the sexual response cycle proposed by Masters and Johnson, the fourth and final phase: a slow decrease in excitement to the level that existed before stimulation.

Role Construct Repertory Test (Rep Test). The measuring device used in Kelly's theory that permits the identification of a person's interpersonal constructs (or roles).

Role playing. A behavior modification technique in which the person practices the desired behavior and receives feedback on his or her performance.

Romeo and Juliet effect. The intensified feeling of love that results when parents interfere in a love affair.

S-R Inventory of General Trait Anxiousness. A scale in which people indicate which of a variety of situations cause them to feel anxious.

Schedules of reinforcement. When reinforcements follow some portion of the responses. For example, a certain *number* of responses must be given before there is a reinforcement or responses must continue for a certain *time period* before being reinforced.

Scientific method. The array of strategies and procedures used by scientists to seek answers to questions.

Secondary need. Motivation that has been learned.

Self. In Sullivan's theory, one's protective image of oneself which reflects the appraisals made by parents and others. See self-concept.

Self theory. A personality theory in which the self-concept plays a central role.

Self-actualization. In Maslow's theory, the highest human need. It includes the need to acquire knowledge, to create, to appreciate beauty, and to achieve.

Self-concept. In Rogers's theory, the collection of attitudes, judgments, and values that a person holds with respect to his or her behavior, ability, appearance, and worth as an individual.

Sensing mode. In Jung's theory, the apprehending mode that involves realistic perception of objective events.

Sentiment. In Cattell's theory, a relatively general motivational (dynamic) trait that is learned.

Serial. In Murray's theory, a succession of related individual acts or proceedings.

Serial learning. A learning task in which the order of a series or list of stimuli must be learned.

Sex guilt. A tendency to punish oneself with anxiety whenever one violates sexual standards in either thought or deed.

Sex role. The degree of socially defined masculinity or femininity that characterizes a person's behavior and description of himself or herself.

Sexism. The tendency to respond to individuals in terms of sexual stereotypes.

Sexual behavior sequence. A theory that deals with sexual responses as a function of external stimulation and several internal processes. Subsequent sexual responses are also influenced by the outcome of a given response.

Sexual conservatism. A restrictive and intolerant attitude toward sexual matters.

Sexual liberalism. A permissive and tolerant attitude toward sexual matters.

Sexual preference. The choice of male or female sexual partners.

Sexual response cycle. Masters and Johnson's description of the physiological responses of sexuality as falling into four phases: excitement, plateau, orgasm, and resolution.

Shadow. In Jung's theory, the unconscious opposite of overt behavioral traits.

Shaping. In operant conditioning, when behavior is gradually molded into some desired form by means of positive reinforcement. Also known as successive approximation.

Sixteen Personality Factor Questionnaire. The test used to measure the basic source traits specified by Cattell's theory.

Social comparison theory. Festinger's theory that people have a need to compare themselves to others.

Social impact theory. Latané's theory that the psychological impact of a group will be a power function of the number of people actually present in the group.

Social learning theory. Rotter's theory of personality that combines learning principles with cognitive processes.

Somatotonia. In Sheldon's theory, the temperament type involving boldness, activity, and aggressiveness.

Somatotype. Sheldon's term for body type, which he classified into the categories of endomorphy, mesomorphy, and ectomorphy.

Source trait. In Cattell's theory, one of the basic traits of personality.

Spinal cord. The portion of the central nervous system that extends from the base of the brain down the back, within the spinal column.

Split-half reliability. A coefficient of internal consistency obtained by correlating two halves of a test (usually the score on all of the odd items with the score on all of the even items).

Stage fright. The anxiety reaction that occurs

when people must speak or perform before a live audience, a microphone, or camera.

Stages of life. In Erikson's theory, the eight periods during which certain crises must be met and resolved.

Stages of ritualization. In Erikson's theory, the six periods during which particular types of fantasies, games, and roles are enacted.

Stanford-Binet Scale. The first successful American intelligence test, developed by Lewis Terman.

State anxiety. Temporary level of anxiety that changes over time in response to stressful situations.

State-Trait Anxiety Inventory. A test designed to measure both state anxiety and trait anxiety.

Stereotypy. The tendency to think in rigid categories with simple, black-and-white explanations of events.

Stimulus-response theory. The kind of personality theory that grew out of attempts to formulate Freudian theory in terms of learning principles. One example is the theory of Dollard and Miller.

Subsidation chain. In Cattell's theory, the series of behaviors that include the expression of an erg, a sentiment, and an attitude.

Successive approximation. In operant conditioning, when behavior is gradually molded into some desired form by means of positive reinforcement. Also known as shaping.

Superego. In Freud's theory, the portion of the mind that contains an image of ideal behavior and the concept of right and wrong.

Surface trait. In Cattell's theory, a specific pattern of behavior that represents one of several alternative ways to express a source trait.

Symbol. In Jung's theory, a word, idea, or image that conveys a relatively unknown thing that cannot be represented more clearly in any other way.

Syntaxic mode. In Sullivan's theory, experiences in which perceptions involve the shared meanings of a given culture.

Systematic observation. Research in which random, unplanned observations of some aspect of the environment are replaced by a planned series of observations of the same phenomenon.

Taylor interaction task. An experimental device used to study aggressive behavior. The subject receives a series of electric shocks from an "opponent" in a competition and then has a chance to shock that opponent.

Temperament. A person's characteristic mood.

Temperament trait. In Cattell's theory, the 15 basic source traits that involve emotions and interpersonal behaviors.

Test anxiety. The anxiety reaction that occurs when a person must take a classroom test, a placement test, a driver's exam, or the like.

Test-retest reliability. The degree to which a measure yields the same score at different times.

Thanatos. A term applied to the energy of the death instincts in Freud's theory.

Thema. In Murray's theory, a combination of a need and a press (an environmental event that frustrates the need or helps to satisfy it).

Thematic Apperception Test (TAT). A projective test developed by Murray that asks subjects to create stories in response to a series of pictures.

Theory. A statement that provides a generalized explanation and description of multiple events.

Thermography. A technique for measuring male and female sexual arousal that detects changes in skin temperature as indicated in photographs.

Thinking mode. In Jung's theory, the judgmental mode that involves the creation of ideas.

Token economy. An application of operant conditioning principles in which certain behaviors (in a mental hospital population, for example) earn tokens which can be exchanged for reinforcements such as food or special privileges.

Traditional family ideology. An autocratic family structure in which the parents stress conventional values, submission, rigid differentiation between the sexes, discipline, and a moralistic rejection of sex and hostility.

Trait. A behavioral dimension along which people differ.

Trait anxiety. A fairly stable level of anxiety that is different for different individuals.

Type A personality. A term applied to coronary-prone individuals who are competitive, hard-driving, aggressive, and pressured.

Type B personality. A term applied to those unlikely to develop heart disease. They are easy-going, relaxed, and unconcerned about time and achievement.

Typology. A theory that classifies people into a limited number of categories or types.

Unconditional positive regard. In Rogers' theory, a totally accepting interpersonal attitude that is the way a parent *should* respond to a child or a therapist to a client.

Unconditioned response. A response that is elicited by an unconditioned stimulus; this stimulus-response sequence occurs naturally without having been learned.

Unconditioned stimulus. A stimulus that elicits a given response naturally.

Unconscious. In Freud's theory, the repressed memories and desires of which a person is totally unaware.

Unsystematic observation. An activity that can occur early in the scientific process in which unplanned and unsystematic observation can lead to new ideas.

Vaginal photoplethysmograph. An instrument that measures female sexual arousal by detecting changes in the amount of blood in the vaginal wall as indicated by the amount of light that passes through.

Validity. The extent to which a measuring instrument is able to predict relevant behavior.

Value. In Allport's theory, the activities that provide a person's life with meaning—his or her philosophy of life.

Viscerotonia. In Sheldon's theory, the temperament type involving sociability, love of comfort, and dependency.

XYY males. Males who have an extra male chromosome and are taller, less intelligent, and more likely to be imprisoned than normal XY males.

REFERENCES

Abramson, P. R., & Mosher, D. L. Development of a measure of negative attitudes toward masturbation. *Journal of Consulting and Clinical Psychology,* 1975, *43,* 485–90.

Acosta, F. X. Etiology and treatment of homosexuality: A review. *Archives of Sexual Behavior,* 1975, *4,* 9–29.

Adams, G. R., & Huston, T. L. Social perception of middle-aged persons varying in physical attractiveness. *Developmental Psychology,* 1975, *11,* 657–58.

Ader, R., & Belfer, M. L. Prenatal maternal anxiety and offspring emotionality in the rat. *Psychological Reports,* 1962, *10,* 711–18.

Adler, F. *Sisters in crime.* New York: McGraw-Hill, 1975.

Adorno, T. W., Frenkel-Brunswick, E., Levinson, D. J., & Sanford, R. N. *The authoritarian personality.* New York: Harper & Row, 1950.

Ahern, S., & Beatty, J. Pupillary responses during information processing vary with scholastic aptitude test scores. *Science,* 1979, *205,* 1289–92.

Albin, R. Adults—Rites of passage. *APA Monitor,* January 1979.

Alker, H. A., & Owen, D. W. Biographical, trait, and behavior-sampling predictions of performance in a stressful life setting. *Journal of Personality and Social Psychology,* 1977, *35,* 717–23.

Allen, B. P., & Potkay, C. R. Variability of self-description on a day-to-day basis: Longitudinal use of the adjective generation technique. *Journal of Personality,* 1973, *41,* 638–52.

Allgeier, A. R. Informational barriers to contracep-

tion. In D. Byrne and W. A. Fisher (eds.), *Adolescents, sex and contraception.* New York: McGraw-Hill, 1981.

Allgeier, E. R., Przybyla, D. P., & Thompson, M. E. Planned sin: The influence of sex guilt on premarital sexual and contraceptive behavior. Unpublished manuscript, Bowling Green State University, 1981.

Allport, G. W. *Becoming: Basic considerations for a psychology of personality.* New Haven: Yale University Press, 1955.

Allport, G. W. *Pattern and growth in personality.* New York: Holt, Rinehart and Winston, 1961.

Allport, G. W. *The person in psychology: Selected essays.* Boston: Beacon Press, 1968.

Allport, G. W., & Odbert, H. S. Trait-names: A psycholexical study. *Psychological Monographs,* 1936, *47* (211).

Allport, G. W., Vernon, P. E., & Lindzey, G. *A study of values.* Boston: Houghton Mifflin, 1960.

Alper, T. G. The relationship between role orientation and achievement motivation in college women. *Journal of Personality,* 1973, *41,* 9–31.

Alper, T. G. Achievement motivation in college women: A now-you-see-it–now-you-don't phenomenon. *American Psychologist,* 1974, *29,* 194–203.

Ames, C., Ames, R., & Felker, D. W. Effects of competitive reward structure and valence of outcome on children's achievement attributions. *Journal of Educational Psychology,* 1977, *69,* 1–8.

Amoroso, D. M., Brown, M., Pruesse, M., Ware, E. E., & Pilkey, D. W. An investigation of behavioral, psychological, and physiological reactions to pornographic stimuli. In *Technical Report of the Commission on Obscenity and Pornography,* vol. 8. Washington, D.C.: U.S. Government Printing Office, 1971.

Anastasi, A. *Psychological testing.* New York: Macmillan, 1976.

Anastasi, A., & d'Angelo, R. Y. A comparison of Negro and white preschool children in language development and Goodenough Draw-a-Man IQ. *Journal of Genetic Psychology,* 1952, *81,* 147–65.

Anastasiow, N. Educational relevance and Jensen's conclusions. *Phi Delta Kappan,* 1969, *51,* 32–35.

Anderson, L. R. Analyses of student demonstrators involved in the overthrow of the Greek military dictatorship. *Journal of Applied Social Psychology,* **1978,** *8,* 215–29.

Andrews, J. D. W. The achievement motive and advancement in two types of organizations. *Journal of Personality and Social Psychology,* 1967, *6,* 163–68.

Arlin, M. Causal priority of social desirability over self-concept: A cross-lagged correlation analysis. *Journal of Personality and Social Psychology,* 1976, *33,* 267–72.

Arling, G. L., & Harlow, H. F. Effects of social deprivation on maternal behavior of rhesus monkeys. *Journal of Comparative and Physiological Psychology,* 1967, *64,* 371–77.

Aronfreed, J. *Conduct and conscience.* New York: Academic Press, 1968.

Arons, S., & Katsh, E. How TV cops flout the law. *Saturday Review,* 1977, *4* (12), 10–14, 16–18.

Asch, S. E. Studies of independence and submission to group pressure: 1. A minority of one against a unanimous majority. *Psychological Monographs,* 1956, *70* (whole no. 416).

Ashton, S. G., & Goldberg, L. R. In response to Jackson's challenge: The comparative validity of personality scales constructed by the external (empirical) strategy and scales developed intuitively by experts, novices, and laymen. *Journal of Research in Personality,* 1973, *7,* 1–20.

Asimov, I. Pure and impure: The interplay of science and technology. *Saturday Review,* 1979, *6* (12), 22–24, 28.

Atkinson, J. W. Motivational determinants of risk-taking behavior. *Psychological Review,* 1957, *64,* 359–72.

Atkinson, J. W. Motivation for achievement. In T. Blass (ed.), *Personality variables in social behavior.* Hillsdale, N.J.: Lawrence Erlbaum, 1977.

Atkinson, J. W., Bongort, K., & Price, L. H. Explorations using computer simulation to comprehend TAT measurement of motivation. *Motivation and Emotion,* 1977, *1,* 1–27.

Atkinson, J. W., Lens, W., & O'Malley, P. M. Motivation and ability: Interactive psychological determinants of intellective performance, educational achievement, and each other. In W. H. Sewell, R. M. Hauser, and D. L. Featherman (eds.), *Schooling and achievement in American society.* New York: Academic Press, 1976.

Atkinson, J. W., & Litwin, G. H. Achievement motive and test anxiety conceived as motive to approach success and motive to avoid failure. *Journal of Abnormal and Social Psychology,* 1960, *60,* 52–63.

Atkinson, J. W., & McClelland, D. C. The projective expression of needs. II. The effect of different intensities of the hunger drive on thematic apperception. *Journal of Experimental Psychology,* 1948, *38,* 643–58.

Auerbach, S. M. Trait–state anxiety and adjustment to surgery. *Journal of Consulting and Clinical Psychology,* 1973, *40,* 264–71.

Auerbach, S. M., Kendall, P. C., Cuttler, H. F., & Levitt, N. R. Anxiety, locus of control, type of preparatory information, and adjustment to dental surgery. *Journal of Consulting and Clinical Psychology,* 1976, *44,* 809–18.

Austin, J. H. The roots of serendipity. *Saturday Review/World,* 1974, *2* (4), 60–64.

Averill, J. R., & Boothroyd, P. On falling in love in conformance with the romantic ideal. *Motivation and Emotion,* 1977, *1,* 235–47.

Azrin, N. H. A strategy for applied research: Learning based but outcome oriented. *American Psychologist,* 1977, *32,* 140–149.

Bachman, J. G., & O'Malley, P. M. Self-esteem in young men: A longitudinal analysis of the impact of educational and occupational attainment. *Journal of Personality and Social Psychology,* 1977, *35,* 365–80.

Balch, P., & Ross, A. W. Predicting success in weight reduction as a function of locus of control: A unidimensional and multidimensional approach. *Journal of Consulting and Clinical Psychology,* 1975, *43,* 119.

Baltes, P. B., & Schaie, K. W. On the plasticity of intelligence in adulthood and old age: Where Horn and Donaldson fail. *American Psychologist,* 1976, *31,* 720–25.

Bandura, A. Social learning theory of aggression. In J. F. Knutsen (ed.), *Control of aggression: Implications from basic research.* Chicago: Aldine, 1971.

Bandura, A. Behavior theory and the models of man. *American Psychologist,* 1974, *29,* 859–69.

Bandura, A. Self-reinforcement: Theoretical and methodological considerations. *Behaviorism,* 1976, *4,* 135–55.

Bandura, A. *Social learning theory.* Englewood Cliffs, N.J.: Prentice-Hall, 1977.

Bandura, A. The self system in reciprocal determinism. *American Psychologist,* 1978, *33,* 344–58.

Bandura, A., Blanchard, E. B., & Ritter, B. Relative efficacy of desensitization and modeling approaches for inducing behavioral, affective, and attitudinal changes. *Journal of Personality and Social Psychology,* 1969, *13,* 173–99.

Bandura, A., & Menlove, F. L. Factors determining

vicarious extinction of avoidance behavior through symbolic modeling. *Journal of Personality and Social Psychology*, 1968, *8*, 99–108.

Bandura, A., Ross, D., & Ross, S. A. Imitation of film-mediated aggressive models. *Journal of Abnormal and Social Psychology*, 1963, *66*, 3–11.

Bandura, A., Underwood, B., & Fromson, M. E. Disinhibition of aggression through diffusion of responsibility and dehumanization of victims. *Journal of Research in Personality*, 1975, *9*, 253–69.

Bandura, A., & Walters, R. H. *Adolescent aggression.* New York: Ronald Press, 1959.

Barclay, A. M. Urinary acid phosphatase in sexually aroused males. *Journal of Experimental Research in Personality*, 1970, *4*, 233–38.

Barclay, A. M. Sexual fantasies in men and women. *Medical Aspects of Human Sexuality*, 1973, *7*, 205–16.

Bard, M., & Zacker, J. How police handle explosive squabbles. *Psychology Today*, 1976, *10* (6), 71, 73–74, 113.

Barefoot, J. C., Hoople, H., & McGlay, D. Avoidance of an act which would violate personal space. *Psychonomic Science*, 1972, *28*, 205–6.

Barker-Benfield, G. J. *The horrors of the half-known life.* New York: Harper & Row, 1976.

Baron, R. A. Reducing the influence of an aggressive model: The restraining effects of discrepant modeling cues. *Journal of Personality and Social Psychology*, 1971, *20*, 240–45.

Baron, R. A. Aggression as a function of ambient temperature and prior anger arousal. *Journal of Personality and Social Psychology*, 1972, *21*, 183–89. (a)

Baron, R. A. Effects of exposure to erotic and nonerotic stimuli on subsequent aggression. Paper presented at the meeting of the Midwestern Psychological Association, Cleveland, May 1972. (b)

Baron, R. A. The aggression-inhibiting influence of heightened sexual arousal. *Journal of Personality and Social Psychology*, 1974, *30*, 318–22. (a)

Baron, R. A. Sexual arousal and physical aggression: The inhibiting influence of "cheesecake" and nudes. *Bulletin of the Psychonomic Society*, 1974, *3*, 337–39. (b)

Baron, R. A. The reduction of human aggression: A field study of the influence of incompatible reactions. *Journal of Applied Social Psychology*, 1976, *6*, 260–74.

Baron, R. A. The aggression-inhibiting influence of sexual humor. *Journal of Personality and Social Psychology*, 1978, *36*, 189–97.

Baron, R. A., & Ball, R. L. The aggression-inhibiting influence of nonhostile humor. *Journal of Experimental Social Psychology*, 1974, *10*, 23–33.

Baron, R. A., & Bell, P. A. Effects of heightened sexual arousal on physical aggression. *Proceedings of the American Psychological Association*, 1973, 171–72.

Baron, R. A., & Bell, P. A. Aggression and heat: The influence of ambient temperature, negative af-

fect, and a cooling drink on physical aggression. *Journal of Personality and Social Psychology*, 1976, *33*, 245–55.

Baron, R. A., & Bell, P. A. Sexual arousal and aggression by males: Effects of type of erotic stimuli and prior provocation. *Journal of Personality and Social Psychology*, 1977, *35*, 79–87.

Baron, R. A., Byrne, D., & Kantowitz, B. H. *Psychology: Understanding behavior.* Philadelphia: Saunders, 1977.

Baron, R. A., & Ransberger, V. M. Ambient temperature and the occurrence of collective violence: The "long, hot summer" revisited. *Journal of Personality and Social Psychology*, 1978, *36*, 351–60.

Bar-Tal, D., & Saxe, L. Perceptions of similarly and dissimilarly attractive couples and individuals. *Journal of Personality and Social Psychology*, 1976, *33*, 772–81.

Bartlett, K. Scientists talk to the animals. *Indianapolis Star*, April 13, 1975, sec. 6, 1, 4.

Bartsch, T. W., & Nesselroade, J. R. Test of the trait-state anxiety distinction using a manipulative, factor-analytic design. *Journal of Personality and Social Psychology*, 1973, *27*, 58–64.

Baruch, G. K. Girls who perceive themselves as competent: Some antecedents and correlates. *Psychology of Women*, 1976, *1*, 38–49.

Baruch, R. The achievement motive in women: Implications for career development. *Journal of Personality and Social Psychology*, 1967, *5*, 260–67.

Batson, C. D. Attribution as a mediator of bias in helping. *Journal of Personality and Social Psychology*, 1975, *32*, 455–66.

Batson, C. D., Cochran, P. J., Biederman, M. F., Blosser, J. L., Ryan, M. J., & Vogt, B. Failure to help when in a hurry: Callousness or conflict? *Personality and Social Psychology Bulletin*, 1978, *4*, 97–101.

Battle, E. S. Motivational determinants of academic competence. *Journal of Personality and Social Psychology*, 1966, *4*, 634–42.

Baugher, D. M., & Gormly, J. Effects of personal competence on the significance of interpersonal agreement and disagreement: Physiological activation and social evaluations. *Journal of Research in Personality*, 1975, *9*, 356–65.

Baughman, E. E. *Black Americans.* New York: Academic Press, 1971.

Baughman, E. E., & Dahlstrom, W. G. *Negro and white children: A psychological study in the rural South.* New York: Academic Press, 1968.

Baumrind, D. An exploratory study of socialization effects on black children: Some black–white comparisons. *Child Development*, 1972, *43*, 261–67.

Beaman, A. L., Barnes, P. J., Klentz, B., & McQuirk, B. Increasing helping rates through information dissemination: Teaching pays. *Personality and Social Psychology Bulletin*, 1978, *4*, 406–11.

Bechtoldt, H. P. Response defined anxiety and MMPI variables. *Iowa Academy of Science*, 1953, *60*, 495–99.

Beck, S. L., & Gavin, D. L. Susceptibility of mice to audiogenic seizures is increased by handling their dams during gestation. *Science,* 1976, *193,* 427-28.

Bell, A. P. *Homosexualities: A study of diversity among men and women.* New York: Simon & Schuster, 1978.

Bell, J. N. Rescuing the battered wife. *Human Behavior,* 1977, *6* (6), 16-23.

Bell, P. A., & Baron, R. A. Aggression and heat: The mediating role of negative affect. *Journal of Applied Social Psychology,* 1976, *6,* 18-30.

Bell, R. R., & Lobsenz, N. M. Married sex: How uninhibited can a woman dare to be? In J. H. Gagnon (ed.), *Human sexuality in today's world.* Boston: Little, Brown, 1977. Pp. 112-18.

Belmont, L., & Marolla, F. A. Birth order, family size, and intelligence. *Science,* 1973, *182,* 1096-1101.

Belmont, L., Stein, Z., & Zybert, P. Child spacing and birth order: Effect on intellectual ability in two-child families. *Science,* 1978, *202,* 995-996.

Bem, D. J., & Allen, A. On predicting some of the people some of the time: The search for cross-situational consistencies in behavior. *Psychological Review,* 1974, *81,* 506-20.

Bem, S. L. Sex-role adaptability: One consequence of psychological androgyny. *Journal of Personality and Social Psychology,* 1975, *31,* 634-43.

Benedict, R., & Weltfish, G. *Races of mankind.* New York: Public Affairs Commission, 1943.

Benson, P. L., Karabenick, S. A., & Lerner, R. M. Pretty pleases: The effects of physical attractiveness, race, and sex on receiving help. *Journal of Experimental Social Psychology,* 1976, *12,* 409-15.

Berg, K. S., & Vidmar, N. Authoritarianism and recall of evidence about criminal behavior. *Journal of Research in Personality,* 1975, *9,* 147-57.

Berkowitz, L. Some aspects of observed aggression. *Journal of Personality and Social Psychology,* 1965, *2,* 359-69.

Berkowitz, L. The frustration-aggression hypothesis revised. In L. Berkowitz (ed.), *Roots of aggression.* New York: Atherton, 1969.

Berkowitz, L. Aggressive humor as a stimulus to aggressive responses. *Journal of Personality and Social Psychology,* 1970, *16,* 710-17. (a)

Berkowitz, L. The contagion of violence. In W. J. Arnold and M. M. Page (eds.), *Nebraska symposium on motivation.* Lincoln: University of Nebraska Press, 1970. (b)

Berkowitz, L. The "weapons effect," demand characteristics, and the myth of the compliant subject. *Journal of Personality and Social Psychology,* 1971, *20,* 332-38.

Berkowitz, L., & Geen, R. G. Film violence and the cue properties of available targets. *Journal of Personality and Social Psychology,* 1966, *3,* 525-30.

Berkowitz, L., & LePage, A. Weapons as aggression-eliciting stimuli. *Journal of Personality and Social Psychology,* 1967, *7,* 202-7.

Berman, R. What's education good for? *New Republic,* 1975, *172* (23), 18-19.

Berscheid, E., & Walster, E. A little bit about love. In T. L. Huston (ed.), *Foundations of interpersonal attraction.* New York: Academic Press, 1974. (a)

Berscheid, E., & Walster, E. Physical attractiveness. In L. Berkowitz (ed.), *Advances in experimental social psychology,* vol. 7. New York: Academic Press, 1974. (b)

Bickman, L., & Rosenbaum, D. P. Crime reporting as a function of bystander encouragement, surveillance, and credibility. *Journal of Personality and Social Psychology,* 1977, *35,* 577-86.

Binet, A. *L'étude experimentale de l'intelligence* (1903). Paris: Alfred Costes, 1922.

Binet, A. *Les idées modernes sur les enfants.* Paris: Ernest Famarion, 1909.

Black, A. H., & Prokasy, W. F. *Classical conditioning II: Current research and theory.* Englewood Cliffs, N.J.: Prentice-Hall, 1972.

Blanchard, F. A., Adelman, L., & Cook, S. W. Effect of group success and failure upon interpersonal attraction in cooperating interracial groups. *Journal of Personality and Social Psychology,* 1975, *31,* 1020-30.

Blass, T. On personality variables, situations, and social behavior. In T. Blass (ed.), *Personality variables in social behavior.* Hillsdale, N.J.: Lawrence Erlbaum, 1977.

Bleda, P. R. Conditioning and discrimination of affect and attraction. *Journal of Personality and Social Psychology,* 1976, *34,* 1106-13.

Bleda, P. R. Effects of smoking on interpersonal attraction. Unpublished ms., Army Research Institute, Arlington, Va., 1978.

Block, J. Personality characteristics associated with fathers' attitudes toward child-rearing. *Child Development,* 1955, *26,* 41-48.

Blumenfeld, W. S. "I am never startled by a fish." *APA Monitor,* 1972, *3* (9, 10), 3, 14.

Bond, M. H., & Dutton, D. G. The effect of interaction anticipation and experience as a victim on aggressive behavior. *Journal of Personality,* 1975, *43,* 515-27.

Bonney, M. E. A study of social status on the second-grade level. *Journal of Genetic Psychology,* 1942, *60,* 271-305.

Bonney, M. E. Relationships between social success, family size, socioeconomic home background, and intelligence among school children in grades III to V. *Sociometry,* 1944, *7,* 26-39.

Bonney, M. E. A study of friendship choices in college in relation to church affiliation, in-church preferences, family size, and length of enrollment in college. *Journal of Social Psychology,* 1949, *29;* 153-66.

Borden, R. J. Witnessed aggression: Influence of an observer's sex and values on aggressive responding. *Journal of Personality and Social Psychology,* 1975, *31,* 567-73.

Boudouris, J. Homicide and the family. *Journal of Marriage and the Family*, 1971, *33*, 667–76.

Bourne, E. Can we describe an individual's personality? Agreement on stereotype versus individual attributes. *Journal of Personality and Social Psychology*, 1977, *35*, 863–872.

Bradburn, N. M. *N* Achievement and father dominance in Turkey. *Journal of Abnormal and Social Psychology*, 1963, *67*, 464–68.

Bradley, R. H., Caldwell, B. M., & Elardo, R. Home environment and cognitive development in the first 2 years: A cross-lagged panel analysis. *Developmental Psychology*, 1979, *15*, 246–250.

Bradway, K. P., Thompson, C. W., & Cravens, R. R. Preschool IQs after twenty-five years. *Journal of Educational Psychology*, 1958, *49*, 278–81.

Bray, R. M., & Noble, A. M. Authoritarianism and decisions of mock juries: Evidence of jury bias and group polarization. *Journal of Personality and Social Psychology*, 1978, *36*, 1424–1430.

Brazelton, T. B., Koslowski, B., & Main, M. The origins of reciprocity: The early mother-infant interaction. In M. Lewis and L. A. Rosenblum (eds.), *The effect of the infant on its caregiver*. New York: Wiley-Interscience, 1974.

Brickman, P., & Bryan, J. H. Equity versus equality as factors in children's moral judgments of thefts, charity, and third-party transfers. *Journal of Personality and Social Psychology*, 1976, *34*, 757–61.

Brickman, P., & D'Amato, B. Exposure effects in a free-choice situation. *Journal of Personality and Social Psychology*, 1975, *32*, 415–20.

Brink, J. H. Effect of interpersonal communication on attraction. *Journal of Personality and Social Psychology*, 1977, *35*, 783–90.

Broad, W. J. Paul Feyerabend: Science and the anarchist. *Science*, 1979, *206*, 534–537.

Brockner, J., & Swap, W. C. Effects of repeated exposure and attitudinal similarity on self-disclosure and interpersonal attraction. *Journal of Personality and Social Psychology*, 1976, *33*, 531–40.

Brody, E. B., & Brody, N. *Intelligence: Nature, determinants, and consequences*. New York: Academic Press, 1976.

Broll, L., Gross, A. E., & Piliavin, I. Effects of offered and requested help on help seeking and reactions to being helped. *Journal of Applied Social Psychology*, 1974, *4*, 244–58.

Broman, S. H., Nichols, P. L., & Kennedy, W. A. *Preschool IQ*. Hillsdale, N.J.: Lawrence Erlbaum, 1975.

Brooks, G. W., & Mueller, E. F. Serum urate concentrations among university professors. *Journal of the American Medical Association*, 1966, *195*, 415–18.

Brown, R. The first sentences of child and chimpanzee. In R. Brown (ed.), *Psycholinguistics*. New York: Free Press, 1970.

Bruce, M. Factors affecting intelligence test performance of whites and Negroes in the rural South. *Archives of Psychology*, 1940 (252).

Bruner, J. S., Jolly, A., & Sylva, K. *Play—its role in development and evolution*. New York: Basic Books. 1976.

Bryan, J. H., & Schwartz, T. Effects of film material upon children's behavior. *Psychological Bulletin*, 1971, *75*, 50–59.

Buckley, N., Siegel, L. S. & Ness, S. Egocentrism, empathy, and altruistic behavior in young children. *Developmental Psychology*, 1979, *15*, 329–30.

Buder, L. Murders at record during 1979 in city. *New York Times*, March 2, 1980.

Bulman, R. J., & Wortman, C. B. Attributions of blame and coping in the "real world": Severe accident victims react to their lot. *Journal of Personality and Social Psychology*, 1977, *35*, 351–363.

Burks, B. C., Jensen, D. W., & Terman, L. M. *The promise of youth: Follow-up studies of a thousand gifted children*. Vol. 3 of L. M. Terman (ed.), *Genetic studies of genius*. Stanford, Calif.: Stanford University Press, 1930.

Burnam, M. A., Pennebaker, J. W., & Glass, D. C. Time consciousness, achievement striving, and the Type A coronary-prone behavior pattern. *Journal of Abnormal Psychology*, 1975, *84*, 76–79.

Burris, R. W. The effect of counseling on achievement motivation. Unpublished doctoral dissertation, Indiana University, 1958.

Burt, C. The inheritance of mental ability. *American Psychologist*, 1958, *13*, 1–15.

Burt, C. The genetic determination of differences in intelligence: A study of monozygotic twins reared together and apart. *British Journal of Psychology*, 1966, *57*, 137–153.

Burt, C., Jones, E., Miller, E., & Moodie, W. *How the mind works*. Englewood Cliffs, N.J.: Prentice-Hall, 1934.

Buss, A. H. *The psychology of aggression*. New York: Wiley, 1961.

Buss, A. H. Physical aggression in relation to different frustrations. *Journal of Abnormal and Social Psychology*, 1963, *67*, 1–7.

Buss, A. H. Instrumentality of aggression, feedback, and frustration as determinants of physical aggression. *Journal of Personality and Social Psychology*, 1966, *3*, 153–62.

Buss, A. H., Booker, A., & Buss, E. Firing a weapon and aggression. *Journal of Personality and Social Psychology*, 1972, *22*, 296–302.

Buss, A. H., Plomin, R., & Willerman, L. The inheritance of temperaments. *Journal of Personality*, 1973, *41*, 513–524.

Butler, M. S., & Haigh, G. V. Changes in the relation between self-concepts and ideal concepts consequent upon client-centered counseling. In C. R. Rogers and R. F. Dymond (eds.), *Psychotherapy and* *personality change.* Chicago: University of Chicago Press, 1954. Pp. 55–75.

Byrne, D. The influence of propinquity and opportunities for interaction on classroom relationships. *Human Relations,* 1961, *14,* 63–69. (a)

Byrne, D. Interpersonal attraction and attitude similarity. *Journal of Abnormal and Social Psychology,* 1961, *62,* 713–15. (b)

Byrne, D. Response to attitude similarity-dissimilarity as a function of affiliation need. *Journal of Personality,* 1962, *30,* 164–77.

Byrne, D. Parental antecedents of authoritarianism. *Journal of Personality and Social Psychology,* 1965, *1,* 369–73.

Byrne, D. *The attraction paradigm.* New York: Academic Press, 1971.

Byrne, D. Social psychology and the study of sexual behavior. *Personality and Social Psychology Bulletin,* 1977, *3,* 3–30.

Byrne, D. Sex without contraception. In D. Byrne and W. A. Fisher (eds.), *Adolescents, sex and contraception.* New York: McGraw-Hill, 1981.

Byrne, D., Allgeier, A. R., Winslow, L., & Buckman, J. The situational facilitation of interpersonal attraction: A three-factor hypothesis. *Journal of Applied Social Psychology,* 1975, *5,* 1–15.

Byrne, D., & Buehler, J. A. A note on the influence of propinquity upon acquaintanceships. *Journal of Abnormal and Social Psychology,* 1955, *51,* 147–48.

Byrne, D., Cherry, F., Lamberth, J., & Mitchell, H. E. Husband–wife similarity in response to erotic stimuli. *Journal of Personality,* 1973, *41,* 385–94.

Byrne, D., & Clore, G. L. Effectance arousal and attraction. *Journal of Personality and Social Psychology Monograph,* 1967, *6* (whole no. 638).

Byrne, D., Clore, G. L., & Worchel, P. The effect of economic similarity–dissimilarity on interpersonal attraction. *Journal of Personality and Social Psychology,* 1966, *4,* 220–24.

Byrne, D., Ervin, C. R., & Lamberth, J. Continuity between the experimental study of attraction and "real life" computer dating. *Journal of Personality and Social Psychology,* 1970, *16,* 157–65.

Byrne, D., Golightly, C., & Capaldi, E. J. Construction and validation of the Food Attitude Scale. *Journal of Consulting Psychology,* 1963, *27,* 215–22.

Byrne, D., Griffitt, W., & Stefaniak, D. Attraction and similarity of personality characteristics. *Journal of Personality and Social Psychology,* 1967, *5,* 82–90.

Byrne, D., & Lamberth, J. The effect of erotic stimuli on sex arousal, evaluative responses, and subsequent behavior. In *Technical report of the Commission on Obscenity and Pornography,* vol. 8. Washington, D.C.: U.S. Government Printing Office, 1971.

Byrne, D., London, O., & Reeves, K. The effects of physical attractiveness, sex, and attitude similarity on

interpersonal attraction. *Journal of Personality,* 1968, *36,* 259–71.

Byrne, D., McDonald, R. D., & Mikawa, J. Approach and avoidance affiliation motives. *Journal of Personality,* 1963, *31,* 21–37.

Byrne, D., & Nelson, D. Attraction as a linear function of proportion of positive reinforcements. *Journal of Personality and Social Psychology,* 1965, *1,* 659–63.

Byrne, D., & Rhamey, R. Magnitude of positive and negative reinforcements as a determinant of attraction. *Journal of Personality and Social Psychology,* 1965, *2,* 884–89.

Calhoun, J. The remediation of interpersonal performance anxiety in the dating situation by behavior modification techniques. Unpublished ms., Purdue University, 1977.

Campagna, A. F., & Harter, S. Moral judgment in sociopathic and normal children. *Journal of Personality and Social Psychology,* 1975, *31,* 199–205.

Campagna, A. G. The function of men's erotic fantasies during masturbation. *Dissertation Abstracts International,* 1976, *36,* 6373-B.

Campbell, C. Portrait of a mass killer. *Psychology Today,* 1976, *9* (12), 110–11, 113, 115–16, 119.

Cantor, N., & Mischel, W. Traits as prototypes: Effects on recognition memory. *Journal of Personality and Social Psychology,* 1977, *35,* 38–48.

Caplow, T., & Forman, R. Neighborhood interaction in a homogeneous community. *American Sociological Review,* 1950, *15,* 357–66.

Carlsmith, J. M., & Anderson, C. A. Ambient temperature and the occurrence of collective violence: A new analysis. *Journal of Personality and Social Psychology,* 1979, *37,* 337–344.

Carlson, E. R., & Coleman, C. E. H. Experiential and motivational determinants of the richness of an induced sexual fantasy. *Journal of Personality,* 1977, *45,* 528–42.

Carlson, R. Where is the person in personality research? *Psychological Bulletin,* 1971, *75,* 203–19.

Carlson, R., & Levy, N. Studies of Jungian typology: 1. Memory, social perception, and social action. *Journal of Personality,* 1973, *41,* 559–76.

Carnegie Commission on Higher Education. *Opportunities for women in higher education.* New York: McGraw-Hill, 1973.

Carroll, J. S. The effect of imagining an event on expectations for the event: An interpretation in terms of the availability heuristic. *Journal of Experimental Social Psychology,* 1978, *14,* 88–96.

Carson, R. C. *Interaction concepts of personality.* Chicago: Aldine, 1969.

Cartwright, D. S. Trait and other sources of variance in the S-R Inventory of Anxiousness. *Journal of Personality and Social Psychology,* 1975, *32,* 408–14.

Carver, C. S., Coleman, A. E., & Glass, D. C. The coronary-prone behavior pattern and the suppression of fatigue on a treadmill test. *Journal of Personality and Social Psychology,* 1976, *33,* 460–466.

Cassell, S. Effects of brief puppet therapy upon the emotional responses of children undergoing cardiac catheterization. *Journal of Consulting Psychology,* 1965, *29,* 1–8.

Cates, J. Psychology's manpower: Report on the 1968 national register of scientific and technical personnel. *American Psychologist,* 1970, *25,* 254–63.

Cattell, R. B. *Comprehensive personality and learning theory.* New York: Springer, 1976.

Cattell, R. B., & Dreger, R. M. (eds.). *Handbook of modern personality theory.* Washington, D.C.: Hemisphere, 1977.

Cattell, R. B., Eber, H. W., & Tatsuoka, M. M. *Handbook for the Sixteen Personality Factors Questionnaire.* Champaign, Ill.: Institute for Personality and Ability Testing, 1970.

Cattell, R. B., Kawash, G. F., & DeYoung, G. E. Validation of objective measures of ergic tension: Response of the sex erg to visual stimulation. *Journal of Experimental Research in Personality,* 1972, *6,* 76–83.

Cattell, R. B., & Kline, P. *The scientific analysis of personality and motivation.* New York: Academic Press, 1976.

Cavior, N., & Boblett, P. J. Physical attractiveness of dating versus married couples. *APA Proceedings,* 1972, *7,* 175–76.

Ceranski, D. S., Teevan, R., & Kalle, R. J. A comparison of three measures of the motive to avoid failure; Hostile press, test anxiety, and resultant achievement motivation. *Motivation and Emotion,* 1979, *3,* 395–404.

Chaiken, S., & Eagly, A. H. Communication modality as a determinant of message persuasiveness and message comprehensibility. Unpublished ms., University of Massachusetts, 1976.

Chapman, A. H. *Harry Stack Sullivan: The man and his work.* New York: G. P. Putnam's Sons, 1976.

Charles, D. C., & Pritchard, S. A. Differential development of intelligence in the college years. *Journal of Genetic Psychology,* 1959, *95,* 41–44.

Cheren, S. If players fight, fans often follow. *New York Times,* January 13, 1980, p. 2 S.

Cherry, F., & Byrne, D. Authoritarianism. In T. Blass (ed.), *Personality variables in social behavior.* Hillsdale, N.J.: Lawrence Erlbaum, 1977. Pp. 109–33.

Cherry, F., & Deaux, K. Fear of success versus fear of gender-inappropriate behavior. *Sex Roles,* 1978, *4,* 97–101.

Cialdini, R. B., Kenrick, D. T., & Hoerig, J. H. Victim derogation in the Lerner paradigm: Just world or just justification? *Journal of Personality and Social Psychology,* 1976, *33,* 719–24.

Clark, M. S., & Mills, J. Interpersonal attraction in exchange and communal relationships. *Journal of Personality and Social Psychology,* 1979, *37,* 12–24.

Clark, R. A., Teevan, R., & Ricciuti, H. N. Hope of success and fear of failure as aspects of need for achievement. *Journal of Abnormal and Social Psychology,* 1956, *53,* 182–86.

Clarke, A. M., & Clarke, A. D. B. (eds.). *Early experience: Myth and evidence.* New York: Free Press, 1976.

Clifford, N. M., & Walster, E. Research note: The effect of physical attractiveness on teacher expectations. *Sociology of Education,* 1973, *46,* 248–58.

Clore, G. L., & Byrne, D. A reinforcement–affect model of attraction. In T. L. Huston (ed.), *Foundations of interpersonal attraction.* New York: Academic Press, 1974.

Clore, G. L., & Gormly, J. B. Knowing, feeling, and liking: A psychophysiological study of attraction. *Journal of Research in Personality,* 1974, *8,* 218–30.

Clore, G. L., & Jeffery, K. M. Emotional role playing, attitude change, and attraction toward a disabled person. *Journal of Personality and Social Psychology,* 1972, *23,* 105–11.

Cohen, D. B. Dreaming: Experimental investigation of representational and adaptive properties. In G. E. Schwartz and D. Shapiro (eds.), *Consciousness and self-regulation,* vol. 2. New York: Plenum, 1976.

Cohen, D. B., & Cox, D. Neuroticism in the sleep laboratory: Implications for representational and adaptive properties of dreaming. *Journal of Abnormal Psychology,* 1975, *84,* 91–108.

Coke, J. S., Batson, C. D., & McDavis, K. Empathic mediation of helping: A two-stage model. *Journal of Personality and Social Psychology,* 1978, *36,* 752–66.

Collins, W. A., & Getz, S. K. Children's social responses following modeled reactions to provocation: Prosocial effects of a television drama. *Journal of Personality,* 1976, *44,* 488–500.

Commission on Obscenity and Pornography. *The report of the Commission on Obscenity and Pornography.* Washington, D.C.: U.S. Government Printing Office, 1970.

Conant, J. B. *On understanding science.* New York: New American Library, 1947.

Conley, J. A., & Smiley, R. Driver licensing tests as a predictor of subsequent violations. *Human Factors,* 1976, *18,* 565–573.

Conrad, H. S., & Jones, H. E. A second study of familial resemblance in intelligence: Environmental and genetic implications of parent–child and sibling correlations in the total sample. *39th Yearbook, National Society for the Study of Education,* 1940, pt. 2, 97–141.

Cousins, N. History and happenstance. *Saturday Review,* 1977, *4* (22), 6.

Cousins, N. The taxpayers' revolt: Act two. *Saturday Review,* Sept. 16, 1978, p. 56.

Cowan, G., & Inskeep, R. Commitments to help among the disabled–disadvantaged. *Personality and Social Psychology Bulletin,* 1978, *4,* 92–96.

Crain, S. A model of sexual role enactment and

motivational attributions in dyadic interactions. Unpublished ms., Duke University, 1978.

Crane, G. W. Trivia "turns off" scholar. *Indianapolis Star,* April 13, 1977, 30.

Cronbach, L. J. Beyond the two disciplines of scientific psychology. *American Psychologist,* 1957, *30,* 116–27. (a)

Cronbach, L. J. Five decades of public controversy over mental testing. *American Psychologist,* 1957, *30,* 1–14. (b)

Cross, K. P. *Beyond the open door.* San Francisco: Jossey-Bass, 1971.

Crouse, B. B., & Mehrabian, A. Affiliation of opposite-sexed strangers. *Journal of Research in Personality,* 1977, *11,* 38–47.

Crutchfield, R. S. Conformity and character. *American Psychologist,* 1955, *10,* 191–98.

Curran, J. P. Examination of various interpersonal attraction principles in the dating dyad. *Journal of Experimental Research in Personality,* 1973, *6,* 347–56. (a)

Curran, J. P. Correlates of physical attractiveness and interpersonal attraction in the dating situation. *Social Behavior and Personality,* 1973, *1,* 153–57. (b)

Curran, J. P. Cross-validation of factors influencing interpersonal attraction in the dating situation. Unpublished ms., Purdue University, 1977. (a)

Curran, J. P. An evaluation of a skills training program and a systematic desensitization program in reducing dating anxiety. Unpublished ms., Purdue University, 1977. (b)

Curran, J. P. Convergence toward a single sexual standard? In D. Byrne and L. A. Byrne (eds.), *Exploring human sexuality.* New York: Harper & Row, 1977. Pp. 194–200. (c)

Curran, J. P., & Lippold, S. The effects of physical attraction and attitude similarity on attraction in dating dyads. *Journal of Personality,* 1975, *43,* 528–39.

Curtis, B. A., Jacobson, S., & Marcus, E. M. *An introduction to the neurosciences.* Philadelphia: Saunders, 1972.

Cvetkovich, G., Grote, B., Bjorseth, A., & Sarkissian, J. On the psychology of adolescents' use of contraceptives. *Journal of Sex Research,* 1975, *11,* 256–70.

Darley, J. M., & Latané, B. Bystander intervention in emergencies: Diffusion of responsibility. *Journal of Personality and Social Psychology,* 1968, *8,* 377–83.

Darwin, C. *On the origin of species by means of natural selection* (1859). New York: Heritage Press, 1963.

Davids, A. The influence of ego-involvement on relations between authoritarianism and intolerance of ambiguity. *Journal of Consulting Psychology,* 1956, *20,* 179–84.

Davidson, F. H. Ability to respect persons compared to ethnic prejudice in childhood. *Journal of Personality and Social Psychology,* 1976, *34,* 1256–67.

Davis, D. J. Birth order and intellectual development: The confluence model in the light of cross-cultural evidence. *Science,* 1977, *196,* 1470–72.

Davis, J., & Lamberth, J. Affective arousal and energization properties of positive and negative stimuli. *Journal of Experimental Psychology,* 1974, *103,* 196–200.

Davis, K. B. *Factors in the sex life of 2,200 women.* New York: Harper & Row, 1929.

Davis, K. E., & Braught, G. N. Exposure to pornography, character, and sexual deviance: A retrospective survey. *Journal of Social Issues,* 1973, *29* (3), 183–96.

Davison, M. L., & Jones, L. E. A similarity-attraction model for predicting sociometric choice from perceived group structure. *Journal of Personality and Social Psychology,* 1976, *33,* 601–12.

Deaux, K. *The behavior of women and men.* Monterey, Calif.: Brooks/Cole, 1976.

DeCasper, A. J., & Fifer, W. P. Of human bonding: Newborns prefer their mothers' voices. *Science,* 1980, *208,* 1174–1176.

deCharms, R., & Moeller, G. H. Values expressed in American children's readers: 1800–1950. *Journal of Abnormal and Social Psychology,* 1962, *64,* 135–42.

Deiker, T. E. A cross-validation of MMPI scales of aggression on male criminal criterion groups. *Journal of Consulting and Clinical Psychology,* 1974, *42,* 196–202.

DeLameter, J. Intrapersonal and interactional barriers to contraception. In D. Byrne and W. A. Fisher (eds.), *Adolescents, sex, and contraception.* New York: McGraw-Hill, 1980.

DeLamater, J., & MacCorquodale, P. *Premarital sexuality: Attitudes, relationships, and behavior.* Madison: University of Wisconsin Press, 1979.

Dembroski, T. M., & MacDougall, J. M. Stress effects on affiliation preferences among subjects possessing the Type A coronary-prone behavior pattern. *Journal of Personality and Social Psychology,* 1978, *36,* 23–33.

Dement, W. C. *Some must watch while some must sleep.* San Francisco: Freeman, 1975.

DeMott, B. Beyond the SATs: A whole-person catalog that works: *Saturday Review/World,* 1974, *1* (17), 68–70.

DePaulo, B. M., & Rosenthal, R. Telling lies. *Journal of Personality and Social Psychology,* 1979, *37,* 1713–22.

Dermer, M., & Pyszczynski, T. A. Effects of erotica upon men's loving and liking responses for women they love. *Journal of Personality and Social Psychology,* 1978, *36,* 1302–9.

Deutsch, M., & Collins, M. E. *Interracial housing.* Minneapolis: University of Minnesota Press, 1951.

DiCaprio, N. S. *Personality theories: Guides to living.* Philadelphia: Saunders, 1974.

Dielman, T. E., Schuerger, J. M., & Cattell, R. B. Prediction of junior high school achievement from IQ and the objective-analytic personality factors U.I. 21, U.I. 23, U.I. 24, and U.I. 25. *Personality: An International Journal,* 1970, *1,* 145–52.

Diener, E. Effects of prior destructive behavior, anonymity, and group presence on deindividuation and aggression. *Journal of Personality and Social Psychology,* 1976, *33,* 497–507.

Diener, E., & DeFour, D. Does television violence enhance program popularity? *Journal of Personality and Social Psychology,* 1978, *36,* 333–41.

Diener, E., Dineen, J., Endresen, K., Beaman, A. L., & Fraser, S. C. Effects of altered responsibility, cognitive set, and modeling on physical aggression and deindividuation. *Journal of Personality and Social Psychology,* 1975, *31,* 328–37.

Diener, E., Fraser, S. C., Beaman, A. L., & Kelem, R. T. Effects of deindividuation variables on stealing among Halloween trick-or-treaters. *Journal of Personality and Social Psychology,* 1976, *33,* 178–83.

Dienstbier, R. A. The role of anxiety and arousal attribution in cheating. *Journal of Experimental Social Psychology,* 1972, *8,* 168–79.

Dion, K. K. The incentive value of physical attractiveness for young children. *Personality and Social Psychology Bulletin,* 1977, *3,* 67–70.

Dion, K. K. Physical attractiveness, sex roles and heterosexual attraction. In M. Cook (ed.), *The bases of human sexual attraction.* London: Academic Press, 1980.

Dion, K. K., & Berscheid, E. Physical attractiveness and peer perception among children. *Sociometry,* 1974, *37,* 1–12.

Dion, K., Berscheid, E., & Walster, E. What is beautiful is good. *Journal of Personality and Social Psychology,* 1972, *24,* 285–90.

Dion, K. K., & Dion, K. L. Self-esteem and romantic love. *Journal of Personality,* 1975, *43,* 39–57.

Dion, K. L., & Dion, K. K. Love, liking, and trust in heterosexual relationships. *Personality and Social Psychology Bulletin,* 1976, *2,* 187–90.

Dixon, N. F. *On the psychology of military incompetence.* New York: Basic Books, 1976.

Dollard, J., Doob, L. W., Miller, N. E., Mowrer, O. H., & Sears, R. R. *Frustration and aggression.* New Haven, Conn.: Yale University Press, 1939.

Dollard, J., & Miller, N. E. *Personality and psychotherapy.* New York: McGraw-Hill, 1950.

Domino, G. Primary process thinking in dream reports as related to creative achievement. *Journal of Consulting and Clinical Psychology,* 1976, *44,* 929–32. (a)

Domino, G. Compensatory aspects of dreams: An empirical test of Jung's theory. *Journal of Personality and Social Psychology,* 1976, *34,* 658–62. (b)

Donnerstein, E., & Donnerstein, M. The effect of attitudinal similarity on interracial aggression. *Journal of Personality,* 1975, *43,* 485–502.

Donnerstein, E., & Donnerstein, M. Research in the control of interracial aggression. In R. Geen and E. O'Neal (eds.), *Perspectives on aggression.* New York: Academic Press, 1976.

Donnerstein, E., Donnerstein, M., & Barrett, G. Where is the facilitation of media violence: The effects of nonexposure and placement of anger arousal. *Journal of Research in Personality,* 1976, *10,* 386–398.

Donnerstein, E., Donnerstein, M., & Evans, R. Erotic stimuli and aggression: Facilitation or inhibition? *Journal of Personality and Social Psychology,* 1975, *32,* 237–44.

Donnerstein, E., Donnerstein, M., Simon, S., & Ditrichs, R. Variables in interracial aggression: Anonymity, expected retaliation, and a riot. *Journal of Personality and Social Psychology,* 1972, *22,* 236–45.

Donnerstein, E., & Hallam, J. Facilitating effects of erotica on aggression against women. *Journal of Personality and Social Psychology,* 1978, *36,* 1270–1277.

Donnerstein, E., & Wilson, D. W. Effects of noise and perceived control on ongoing and subsequent aggressive behavior. *Journal of Personality and Social Psychology,* 1976, *34,* 774–81.

Dorfman, D. D. The Cyril Burt question: New findings. *Science,* 1978, *201,* 1177–1186.

Dovidio, J. F., & Morris, W. N. Effects of stress and commonality of fate on helping behavior. *Journal of Personality and Social Psychology,* 1975, *31,* 145–49.

Dreger, R. M., & Miller, K. S. Comparative psychological studies of Negroes and whites in the United States: 1959-1965. *Psychological Bulletin Monograph Supplement,* 1968, *70,* Pt. 2, 1–58.

Driscoll, R., Davis, K. E., & Lipetz, M. E. Parental interference and romantic love: The Romeo and Juliet effect. *Journal of Personality and Social Psychology,* 1972, *24,* 1–10.

Duck, S. W., & Craig, G. Personality similarity and the development of friendship: A longitudinal study. *British Journal of Social and Clinical Psychology,* 1978, *17,* 237–242.

Dunn, A. F. The dark side of erotic fantasy. *Human Behavior,* 1978, 7 (11), 18–23.

Dunnington, M. J. Behavioral differences of sociometric status groups in a nursery school. *Child Development,* 1957, *28,* 103–11.

Dustin, D. S., & Davis, H. P. Authoritarianism and sanctioning behavior. *Journal of Personality and Social Psychology,* 1967, *6,* 222–24.

Dutton, D. G., & Aron, A. P. Some evidence for heightened sexual attraction under conditions of high anxiety. *Journal of Personality and Social Psychology,* 1974, *30,* 510–17.

Dworkin, R. H. Genetic and environmental influences on person-situation interactions. *Journal of Research in Personality,* 1979, *13,* 279–293.

Dworkin, R. H., Burke, B. W., Maher, B. A., & Gottesman, I. I. A longitudinal study of the genetics of personality. *Journal of Personality and Social Psychology,* 1976, *34,* 510–18.

Dworkin, R. H., & Kihlstrom, J. F. An S-R inventory of dominance for research on the nature of person-situation interactions. *Journal of Personality*, 1978, *46*, 43–56.

Dworkin, R. H., & Widom, C. S. Undergraduate MMPI profiles and the longitudinal prediction of adult social outcome. *Journal of Consulting and Clinical Psychology*, 1977, *45*, 620–625.

Dyck, R. J., & Rule, B. G. Effect on retaliation of causal attributions concerning attack. *Journal of Personality and Social Psychology*, 1978, *36*, 521–529.

Dymond, R. F. Adjustment changes over therapy from self-sorts. In C. R. Rogers and R. F. Dymond (eds.), *Psychotherapy and personality change*. Chicago: University of Chicago Press, 1954. Pp. 76–84.

Dziadosz, T. H., Curran, J. P., & Santogrossi, D. A. Personalized instruction and the attenuation of test anxiety. *Journal of Educational Psychology*, 1980, in press.

Eagly, A. H., & Warren, R. Intelligence, comprehension, and opinion change. *Journal of Personality*, 1976, *44*, 226–42.

Ebbesen, E. B., Duncan, B., & Konečni, V. J. Effects of content of verbal aggression on future verbal aggression: A field experiment. *Journal of Experimental Social Psychology*, 1975, *11*, 192–204.

Ebbeson, E. B., Kjos, G. L., & Konečni, V. J. Spatial ecology: Its effects on the choice of friends and enemies. *Journal of Experimental Social Psychology*, 1976, *12*, 505–18.

Edlin, G. J., & Prout, T. Genetics and IQ. *Science*, 1977, *195*, 6.

Edmiston, S. Murder, New York style: A crime of class. *New York*, 1970, *3* (33), 29–35.

Eisenberg-Berg, N. Development of children's prosocial moral judgment. *Developmental Psychology*, 1979, *15*, 128–37.

Eisenstadt, J. M. Parental loss and genius. *American Psychologist*, 1978, *33*, 211–223.

Elashoff, J., & Snow, R. E. *Pygmalion reconsidered*. Worthington, Ohio: Charles A. Jones, 1971.

Eliasberg, W. G., & Stuart, I. R. Authoritarian personality and the obscenity threshold. *Journal of Social Psychology*, 1961, *55*, 143–51.

Ellis, D. P., Weinir, P., & Miller, L., III. Does the trigger pull the finger? An experimental test of weapons as aggression-eliciting stimuli. *Sociometry*, 1971, *34*, 453–65.

Elms, A. C., & Milgram, S. Personality characteristics associated with obedience and defiance toward authoritative command. *Journal of Experimental Research in Personality*, 1966, *1*, 282–89.

Endler, N. S., & Okada, M. A multi-dimensional measure of trait anxiety: The S-R Inventory of General Trait Anxiousness. *Journal of Consulting and Clinical Psychology*, 1975, *43*, 319–29.

Entin, E. E., & Raynor, J. O. Effects of contingent future orientation and achievement motivation on performance in two kinds of tasks. *Journal of Experimental Research in Personality*, 1973, *6*, 314–20.

Entwisle, D. R. To dispel fantasies about fantasy-based measures of achievement motivation. *Psychological Bulletin*, 1972, *77*, 377–91.

Epstein, R. Authoritarianism, displaced aggression, and social status of the target. *Journal of Personality and Social Psychology*, 1965, *2*, 585–89.

Erikson, E. H. *Childhood and society*. New York: Norton, 1963.

Erikson, E. H. *Toys and reasons: Stages in the ritualization of experience*. New York: Norton, 1977.

Eron, L. D. Relationship of TV viewing habits and aggressive behavior in children. *Journal of Abnormal and Social Psychology*, 1963, *67*, 193–96.

Eron, L. D., Lefkowitz, M. M., Huesmann, L. R., & Walder, L. O. Does television violence cause aggression? *American Psychologist*, 1972, *27*, 253–63.

Estes, W. K. *Learning theory and mental development*. New York: Academic Press, 1970.

Estes, W. K. Learning theory and intelligence. *American Psychologist*, 1974, *29*, 740–49.

Evans, I. M., & Distiller, L. A. Effects of luteinizing hormone-releasing hormone on sexual arousal in normal men. *Archives of Sexual Behavior*, 1979, *8*, 385–95.

Evans, M. C., & Wilson, M. Friendship choices of university women students. *Educational and Psychological Measurement*, 1949, *9*, 307–12.

Evans, P. The Burt affair . . . sleuthing in science. *APA Monitor*, 1976, 7 (12), 1, 4.

Ewen, R. B. *An introduction to theories of personality*. New York: Academic Press, 1980.

Eysenck, H. J. *The structure of human personality*. London: Methuen, 1970.

Eysenck, H. J. *The IQ argument: Race, intelligence, and education*. New York: Library Press, 1971.

Eysenck, H. J. Obscenity—officially speaking. *Penthouse*, 1972, *3* (11), 95–102.

Fantz, R. L. Visual perception from birth as shown by pattern selectivity. *Annals of the New York Academy of Science*, 1965, *118*, 793–814.

Farber, I. E. A framework for the study of personality as a behavioral science. In P. Worchel and D. Byrne (eds.), *Personality change*. New York: Wiley, 1964. Pp. 3–37.

Farquhar, J. Stress and how to cope with it. *The Stanford Magazine*, 1977, *5* (2), 50–55, 71–72, 74–75.

Fechter, L. D., & Annau, Z. Toxicity of mild prenatal carbon monoxide exposure. *Science*, 1977, *197*, 680–82.

Feldman, M. W., & Lewontin, R. C. The heritability hang-up. *Science*, 1975, *190*, 1163–68.

Fenz, W. D., & Dronsejko, K. Effects of real and imagined threat of shock on GSR and heart rate as a function of trait anxiety. *Journal of Experimental Research in Personality*, 1969, *3*, 187–96.

Fenz, W. D., & Epstein, S. Gradients of physiological arousal of experienced and novice parachutists as a function of an approaching jump. *Psychosomatic Medicine,* 1967, *29,* 33–51.

Feshbach, N. D., & Feshbach, S. The relationship between empathy and aggression in two age groups. *Developmental Psychology,* 1969, *1,* 102–7.

Feshbach, S. Dynamics and morality of violence and aggression: Some psychological considerations. *American Psychologist,* 1971, *26,* 281–92.

Feshbach, S. The environment of personality. *American Psychologist,* 1978, *33,* 447–455.

Feshbach, S., & Singer, R. D. *Television and aggression.* San Francisco: Jossey-Bass, 1971.

Festinger, L. A theory of social comparison processes. *Human Relations,* 1954, *7,* 117–40.

Festinger, L. *A theory of cognitive dissonance.* Stanford: Stanford University Press, 1957.

Festinger, L. The motivating effect of cognitive dissonance. In G. Lindzey (ed.), *Assessment of human motives.* New York: Holt, Rinehart, and Winston, 1958.

Festinger, L., Schachter, S., & Back, K. *Social pressures in informal groups: A study of a housing community.* New York: Harper & Row, 1950.

Field, W. F. The effects on thematic apperception of certain experimentally aroused needs. Unpublished doctoral dissertation, University of Maryland, 1951.

Finger, F. W. Changes in sex practices and beliefs of male college students over 30 years. *Journal of Sex Research,* 1975, *11,* 304–17.

Firestone, I. J., Lichtman, C. M., & Colamosca, J. V. Leader effectiveness and leadership conferral as determinants of helping in a medical emergency. *Journal of Personality and Social Psychology,* 1975, *31,* 343–48.

Firkowska, A., Ostrowska, A., Sokolowska, M., Stein, Z., Susses, M., & Wald, I. Cognitive development and social policy. *Science,* 1978, *200,* 1357–1362.

Fish, B., Karabenick, S., & Heath, M. The effects of observation on emotional arousal and affiliation. *Journal of Experimental Social Psychology,* 1978, *14,* 256–65.

Fisher, J. D., & Byrne, D. Too close for comfort: Sex differences in response to invasions of personal space. *Journal of Personality and Social Psychology,* 1975, *32,* 15–21.

Fisher, J. D., Harrison, C. L., & Nadler, A. Exploring the generalizability of donor–recipient similarity effects. *Personality and Social Psychology Bulletin,* 1978, *4,* 627–30.

Fisher, J. D., & Nadler, A. Effect of donor resources on recipient self-esteem and self-help. *Journal of Experimental Social Psychology,* 1976, *12,* 139–50.

Fisher, S., & Greenberg, R. P. *The scientific credibility of Freud's theories and therapy.* New York: Basic Books, 1977.

Fisher, W. A., & Byrne, D. Sex differences in response to erotica? Love versus lust. *Journal of Personality and Social Psychology,* 1978, *36,* 119–25. (a)

Fisher, W. A., & Byrne, D. Individual differences in affective, evaluative, and behavioral responses to an erotic film. *Journal of Applied Social Psychology,* 1978, *8,* 355–65. (b)

Fisher, W. A., Byrne, D., Edmunds, M., Miller, C. T., Kelley, K., & White, L. A. Psychological and situation-specific correlates of contraceptive behavior among university women. *Journal of Sex Research,* 1979, *15,* 38–55.

Fisher, W. A., Byrne, D., & White, L. A. Emotional barriers to contraception. In D. Byrne and W. A. Fisher (eds.), *Adolescents, sex, and contraception.* New York: McGraw-Hill, 1981.

Fisher, W. A., Fisher, J. D., & Byrne, D. Consumer reactions to contraceptive purchasing. *Personality and Social Psychology Bulletin,* 1977, *3,* 293–96.

Flabo, T., & Richman, C. L. Relationships between father's age, birth order, family size, and need achievement. *Bulletin of the Psychonomic Society,* 1979, *13,* 179–182.

Fleming, J. Predictive validity of the motive to avoid success in black women. *Humanitas: Journal of the Institute of Man,* 1977, *13,* 225–244.

Fleming, J. Fear of success, achievement-related motives and behavior in black college women. *Journal of Personality,* 1978, *46,* 694–716.

Flippo, J. R., & Lewinsohn, P. M. Effects of failure on the self-esteem of depressed and nondepressed subjects. *Journal of Consulting and Clinical Psychology,* 1971, *36,* 151.

Folkes, V. S., & Sears, D. O. Does everybody like a liker? Unpublished manuscript, UCLA, 1980.

Frandsen, A. N. The Wechsler-Bellevue intelligence scale and high school achievement. *Journal of Applied Psychology,* 1950, *34,* 406–11.

Frank, A. D. The problem of pornography in cities large and small. *Family Weekly,* January 28, 1979, p. 5.

Frazier, T. M., Davis, G. H., Goldstein, H., & Goldberg, I. D. Cigarette smoking and prematurity: A prospective study. *American Journal of Obstetrics and Gynecology,* 1961, *81,* 988–96.

Freeman, S., Walker, M. R., Borden, R., & Latané, B. Diffusion of responsibility and restaurant tipping: Cheaper by the bunch. *Personality and Social Psychology Bulletin,* 1975, *1,* 584–87.

French, R. L. Sociometric status and individual adjustment among naval recruits. *Journal of Abnormal and Social Psychology,* 1951, *46,* 64–72.

Freud, S. *The interpretation of dreams* (1900). London: Hogarth, 1953.

Freud, S. Jenseits des Lustprinzips. In *Gesammelte Werke,* 1920, vol. 13. London: Imago Publishing, 1940.

Freud, S. Inhibitions, symptoms and anxiety (1926). In J. Strachey (ed.), *The standard edition of the complete* *psychological works,* vol. 20. London: Hogarth and Institute of Psychoanalysis, 1959. Pp. 77-175.

Freud, S. *New introductory lectures on psycho-analysis.* New York: W. W. Norton, 1933.

Freud, S. *An autobiographical study* (1935). London: Hogarth, 1946.

Freund, K., Sedlacek, F., & Knob, K. A simple transducer for mechanical plethysmography of the male genital. *Journal of the Experimental Analysis of Behavior,* 1965, *8,* 169-70.

Friday, N. *My secret garden: Women's sexual fantasies.* New York: Trident Press, 1973.

Frodi, A. Sexual arousal, situational restrictiveness, and aggressive behavior. *Journal of Research in Personality,* 1977, *11,* 48-58.

Fryer, D. Occupational intelligence standards. *School and Society,* 1922, *16,* 273-77.

Gaebelein, J. W., & Mander, A. Consequences for targets of aggression as a function of aggressor and instigator roles: Three experiments. *Personality and Social Psychology Bulletin,* 1978, *4,* 465-468.

Gaertner, S. L., & Dovidio, J. F. The subtlety of white racism, arousal, and helping behavior. *Journal of Personality and Social Psychology,* 1977, *35,* 691-707.

Galbraith, G. G., & Mosher, D. L. Associative sexual responses in relation to sexual arousal, guilt, and external approval contingencies. *Journal of Personality and Social Psychology,* 1968, *10,* 142-47.

Gallagher, J. J. Manifest anxiety changes concomitant with client-centered therapy. *Journal of Consulting Psychology,* 1953, *17,* 443-46.

Gallup, G. G., Jr. Self-recognition in primates: A comparative approach to the bidirectional properties of consciousness. *American Psychologist,* 1977, *32,* 329-338.

"Gallup Youth Survey," *The Indianapolis Star,* October 18, 1978.

Galton, F. *Hereditary genius: An inquiry into its laws and consequences* (1870). New York: Horizon, 1952.

Garcia, L., & Griffitt, W. Authoritarianism–situation interactions in the determination of punitiveness: Engaging authoritarian ideology. Unpublished ms., Kansas State University, 1977.

Garcia, L., & Griffitt, W. Evaluation and recall of evidence: Authoritarianism and the Patty Hearst case. *Journal of Research in Personality,* 1978, *12,* 57-67.

Gardner, R. A., & Gardner, B. T. Teaching sign language to a chimpanzee. *Science,* 1969, *165,* 664-72.

Gardner, R. A., & Gardner, B. T. Early signs of language in child and chimpanzee. *Science,* 1975, *187,* 752-53.

Gass, W. The scientific psychology of Sigmund Freud. *New York Review of Books,* 1975, *22* (7), 24-29.

Gastorf, J. W., Suls, J., & Sanders, G. The Type A coronary-prone behavior pattern and social facilita-tion. *Journal of Personality and Social Psychology,* 1980, *38,* 773-780.

Gastorf, J. W., & Teevan, R. C. Type A coronary-prone behavior pattern and fear of failure. *Motivation and Emotion,* 1980, *4,* 71-76.

Gatchel, R. J. Therapeutic effectiveness of voluntary heart rate control in reducing anxiety. *Journal of Consulting and Clinical Psychology,* 1977, *45,* 689-691.

Gazzaniga, M. S. The split brain in man. *Scientific American,* 1967, *217,* 24-29.

Gazzaniga, M. S. *The bisected brain.* Englewood Cliffs, N.J.: Prentice-Hall, 1970.

Gebhard, P. Sex differences in sexual response. *Archives of Sexual Behavior,* 1973, *2,* 201-3.

Geen, R. G. The meaning of observed violence: Real vs. fictional violence and consequent effects on aggression and emotional arousal. *Journal of Research in Personality,* 1975, *9,* 270-81.

Geen, R. G., & Berkowitz, L. Name-mediated aggressive cue properties. *Journal of Personality,* 1966, *34,* 456-65.

Geen, R. G., & O'Neal, E. C. Activation of cue-elicited aggression by general arousal. *Journal of Personality and Social Psychology,* 1969, *11,* 289-92.

Geen, R. G., & Pigg, R. Acquisition of an aggressive response and its generalization to verbal behavior. *Journal of Personality and Social Psychology,* 1970, *15,* 165-70.

Geen, R. G., Stonner, D., & Shope, G. L. The facilitation of aggression by aggression: Evidence against the catharsis hypothesis. *Journal of Personality and Social Psychology,* 1975, *31,* 721-26.

Geer, J. H. Direct measurement of genital responding. *American Psychologist,* 1975, *30,* 415-18.

Geer, J. H., & Fuhr, R. Cognitive factors in sexual arousal: The role of distraction. *Journal of Consulting and Clinical Psychology,* 1976, *44,* 238-43.

Gelfand, D. M., Hartmann, D. P., Walder, P., & Page, B. Who reports shoplifters? A field-experimental study. *Journal of Personality and Social Psychology,* 1973, *25,* 276-85.

Gengerelli, J. A. Graduate school reminiscences: Hull and Koffka. *American Psychologist,* 1976, *31,* 685-68.

Gentry, W. D. Effects of frustration, attack, and prior aggressive training on overt aggression and vascular processes. *Journal of Personality and Social Psychology,* 1970, *16,* 718-25.

Gerard, H. B., & Miller, N. *Desegregation: A longitudinal study.* New York: Plenum, in press.

Gergen, K. J., Ellsworth, P., Maslach, C., & Seipel, M. Obligation, donor resources, and reactions to aid in three cultures. *Journal of Personality and Social Psychology,* 1975, *31,* 390-400.

Gerrard, M. Sex guilt in abortion patients. *Journal of Consulting and Clinical Psychology,* 1977, *45,* 708.

Gerst, M. S. Symbolic coding processes in observational learning. *Journal of Personality and Social Psychology*, 1971, *19*, 7–17.

Getzels, J. W., & Jackson, P. W. *Creativity and intelligence: Explorations with gifted students.* New York: Wiley, 1962.

Giambra, L. M., & Martin, C. E. Sexual daydreams and quantitative aspects of sexual activity: Some relations for males across adulthood. *Archives of Sexual Behavior*, 1977, *6*, 497–505.

Gibson, J. J., Filbey, R., & Gazzaniga, M. S. Hemispheric differences as reflected by reaction time. *Federation Proceedings, Federation of American Societies for Experimental Biology*, 1970, *29*, 658.

Gide, A. Introduction. In *The essays of Michel de Montaigne.* New York: Heritage Press, 1946.

Gillie, O. Burt's missing ladies. *Science*, 1979, *204*, 1035–1036, 1038–1039.

Girodo, M., & Roehl, J. Cognitive preparation and coping self-talk: Anxiety management during the stress of lying. *Journal of Consulting and Clinical Psychology*, 1978, *46*, 978–989.

Girodo, M., & Wood, D. Talking yourself out of pain. The importance of believing that you can. *Cognitive Therapy and Research*, 1979, *3*, 23–33.

Gjesme, T. Goal distance in time and its effects on the relations between achievement motives and performance. *Journal of Research in Personality*, 1974, *8*, 161–71.

Glass, D. C. Behavioral antecedents of coronary heart disease. Unpublished manuscript, University of Texas, Austin, 1974.

Glass, D. C. Stress, competition, and heart attacks. *Psychology Today*, 1976, *10* (7), 54–55, 57, 134.

Glass, D. C. *Behavior patterns, stress, and coronary disease.* Hillsdale, N.J.: Lawrence Erlbaum Associates, 1977.

Goddard, H. H. *The Kallikak family.* New York: Macmillan, 1912.

Goethals, G. R., Allison, S. J., & Frost, M. Perceptions of the magnitude and diversity of social support. *Journal of Experimental Social Psychology*, 1979, *15*, 570–581.

Goldberg, P. Prejudice toward women: Some personality correlates. *International Journal of Group Tensions*, 1974, *4*, 53–63.

Goldberg, S., Godfrey, L., & Lewis, M. Play behavior in the year-old infant: Early sex differences. Paper presented at the meeting of the Society for Research in Child Development, New York, March 1967.

Goldfarb, W. Effects of psychological deprivation in infancy and subsequent stimulation. *American Journal of Psychiatry*, 1945, *102*, 18–33.

Goldfried, M. R., Linehan, M. M., & Smith, J. L. Reduction of test anxiety through cognitive restructuring. *Journal of Consulting and Clinical Psychology*, 1978, *46*, 32–39.

Goldman, E. K. Need achievement as a motivational basis for the risky shift. *Journal of Personality*, 1975, *43*, 346–56.

Goldstein, E. Effect of same-sex and cross-sex role models on the subsequent academic productivity of scholars. *American Psychologist*, 1979, *34*, 407–410.

Goldstein, J. H., & Arms, R. L. Effects of observing athletic contests on hostility. *Sociometry*, 1971, *34*, 83–90.

Goldstein, J. H., Davis, R. W., & Herman, D. Escalation of aggression: Experimental studies. *Journal of Personality and Social Psychology*, 1975, *31*, 162–70.

Goldstein, M. J., Kant, H. S., & Hartman, J. J. *Pornography and sexual deviance.* Berkeley: University of California Press, 1974.

Goodman, M. Suffer the children of Kent. *New Times*, 1977, *9* (8), 88.

Goodman, N. Ways of worldmaking. New York: Hacket, 1978.

Gordon, H. *Mental and scholastic tests among retarded children.* Education Pamphlet no. 44. London: Board of Education, 1923.

Gorkin, L. The sensuous doctor: Response to sex-role logic problems. Unpublished ms., State University of New York at Stony Brook, 1972.

Gottesman, I. I. Heritability of personality: A demonstration. *Psychological Monographs*, 1963, *77* (9) (whole no. 572).

Gottesman, I. I. Biogenetics of race and class. In M. Deutsch, I. Katz, and A. R. Jensen (eds.), *Social class, race, and psychological development.* New York: Holt, Rinehart and Winston, 1968.

Gouaux, C. Induced affective states and interpersonal attraction. *Journal of Personality and Social Psychology*, 1972, *24*, 53–58.

Gough, H. G., Fioravanti, M., & Lazzari, R. A cross-cultural unisex ideal self scale for the adjective check list. *Journal of Clinical Psychology*, 1979, *35*, 314–319.

Gould, S. J. Morton's ranking of races by cranial capacity. *Science*, 1978, *200*, 503–509.

Granberg, D., & Corrigan, G. Authoritarianism, dogmatism and orientations toward the Vietnam War. *Sociometry*, 1972, *35*, 468–76.

Gray, M. J., & Levin, I. P. Process analysis and scaling of occupational desirability: An example using information integration theory. *Bulletin of the Psychonomic Society*, 1978, *11*, 161–164.

Greenberg, D. S. Biomedical policy: LBJ's query leads to an illuminating conference. *Science*, 1966, *154*, 618–20.

Greene, R. L. Student acceptance of generalized personality interpretations: A reexamination. *Journal of Consulting and Clinical Psychology*, 1977, *45*, 965–966.

Greenwell, J., & Dengerink, H. A. The role of perceived vs. actual attack in human physical aggression. *Journal of Personality and Social Psychology*, 1973, *26*, 66–71.

Greer, G. Seduction is a four-letter word. In E. S. Morrison and V. Borosage (eds.), *Human sexuality: Contemporary perspectives.* Palo Alto, Calif.: Mayfield, 1977.

Greulich, W. W. A comparison of the physical growth and development of American-born and native Japanese children. *American Journal of Physical Anthropology,* 1957, December, 489–516.

Griffith, M., & Walker, C. E. Menstrual cycle phases and personality variables as related to response to erotic stimuli. *Archives of Sexual Behavior,* 1975, *4,* 599–603.

Griffitt, W. Environmental effects on interpersonal affective behavior: Ambient effective temperature and attraction. *Journal of Personality and Social Psychology,* 1970, *15,* 240–44.

Griffitt, W. Response to erotica and the projection of response to erotica in the opposite sex. *Journal of Experimental Research in Personality,* 1973, *6,* 330–38.

Griffitt, W., & Garcia, L. Manipulating authoritarian bias in juror decisions: The impact of verbal conditioning. Unpublished ms., Kansas State University, 1977.

Griffitt, W., & Kaiser, D. L. Affect, sex guilt, gender, and the rewarding–punishing effects of erotic stimuli. *Journal of Personality and Social Psychology,* 1978, *36,* 850–58.

Griffitt, W., & Veitch, R. Preacquaintance attitude similarity and attraction revisited: Ten days in a fallout shelter. *Sociometry,* 1974, *37,* 163–73.

Gross, A. E., Wallston, B. S., & Paliavin, I. M. Beneficiary attractiveness and cost as determinants of responses to routine requests for help. *Sociometry,* 1975, *38,* 131–40.

Grossmann, B., & Wrighter, J. The relationship between selection–rejection and intelligence, social status, and personality amongst sixth-grade children. *Sociometry,* 1948, *11,* 346–55.

Grossman, J. C., & Eisenman, R. Birth order, authoritarianism, and the projection of sex and aggression. *Journal of Psychology,* 1972, *80,* 3–8.

Grossman, S. P. Aggression, avoidance, and reaction to novel environments in female rats with ventromedial hypothalamic lesions. *Journal of Comparative and Physiological Psychology,* 1972, *78,* 274–83.

Grossman, S. P. *A textbook of physiological psychology.* New York: Wiley, 1973.

Grosz, H. J., & Levitt, E. E. The effects of hypnotically induced anxiety on the Manifest Anxiety Scale and the Barron Ego-Strength Scale. *Journal of Abnormal and Social Psychology,* 1959, *59,* 281–83.

Grusec, J. E., Kuczynski, L., Rushton, J. P., & Simutis, Z. M. Modeling, direct instruction, and attributions: Effects on altruism. *Developmental Psychology,* 1978, *14,* 51–57.

Grusec, J. E., Kuczynski, L., Rushton, J. P., & Simutis, Z. M. Learning resistance to temptation through observation. *Developmental Psychology,* 1979, *15,* 233–40.

Grush, J. E. Attitude formation and mere exposure phenomena: A nonartifactual explanation of empirical findings. *Journal of Personality and Social Psychology,* 1976, *33,* 281–90.

Grush, J. E., & McKeogh, K. L. The finest representation that money can buy: Exposure effects in the 1972 congressional primaries. Paper presented at the meeting of the Midwestern Psychological Association, Chicago, May 1975.

Haaf, R. A., & Bell, R. Q. A facial dimension in visual discrimination by human infants. *Child Development,* 1967, *38,* 893–99.

Hahn, E. *Look who's talking!* New York: Crowell, 1978.

Hake, D., & Schmitt, D. R. Paper presented at the meeting of the Association for Behavior Analysis in Dearborn, Michigan, June 1979.

Hall, M. H. A conversation with Abraham H. Maslow. *Psychology Today,* 1968, *2* (2), 35–37, 54–57.

Hamilton, D. L., & Gifford, R. K. Illusory correlation in interpersonal perception: A cognitive basis of stereotypic judgments. *Journal of Experimental Social Psychology,* 1976, *12,* 392–407.

Hamilton, G. V. *A study in marriage.* New York: Alfred and Charles Boni, 1929.

Hampshire, S. The future of knowledge. *The New York Review of Books,* 1977, *24* (5), 14–18.

Handlon, B. J., & Squier, L. H. Attitudes toward special loyalty oaths at the University of California. *American Psychologist,* 1955, *10,* 121–27.

Haney, C., Banks, C., & Zimbardo, P. A study of prisoners and guards in a simulated prison. *Naval Research Reviews,* 1973, *26* (9), 1–17.

Hardy, K. R. Determinants of conformity and attitude change. *Journal of Abnormal and Social Psychology,* 1957, *54,* 289–94.

Hare, R. D. Psychopathy and choice of immediate versus delayed punishment. *Journal of Abnormal Psychology,* 1966, *71,* 25–29.

Harlow, H. F. Lust, latency and love: Simian secrets of successful sex. *Journal of Sex Research,* 1975, *11,* 79–90.

Harlow, H. F., & Harlow, M. H. Learning to love. *American Scientist,* 1966, *54,* 244–72.

Harrell, R. F., Woodyard, E., & Gates, A. I. *The effect of mothers' diet on the intelligence of offspring.* New York: Columbia University, Teachers College, Bureau of Publications, 1955.

Harris, M. B. Mediators between frustration and aggression in a field experiment. *Journal of Experimental Social Psychology,* 1974, *10,* 561–71.

Harris, M. B. Instigators and inhibitors of aggression in a field experiment. Unpublished ms., University of New Mexico, 1977.

Hart, I. Maternal child-rearing practices and authoritarian ideology. *Journal of Abnormal and Social Psychology,* 1957, *55,* 232–37.

Hartshorne, H., & May, M. A. *Studies in the nature of*

character, vol. 1, *Studies in deceit.* New York: Macmillan, 1928.

Hartshorne, H., & May, M. A. *Studies in the nature of character,* vol. 2. New York: Macmillan, 1929.

Harvey, M. D., & Enzle, M. E. Effects of retaliation latency and provocation level on judged blameworthiness for retaliatory aggression. *Personality and Social Psychology Bulletin,* 1978, *4,* 579–582.

Haskell, T. L. Power to the experts. *New York Review of Books,* 1977, *24* (16), 28–33.

Hatch, J. P. Vaginal photoplethysmography: Methodological considerations. *Archives of Sexual Behavior,* 1979, *8,* 357–74.

Hatfield, E., Sprecher, S., & Traupmann, J. Men's and women's reactions to sexually explicit films: A serendipitous finding. *Archives of Sexual Behavior,* 1978, *7,* 583–92.

Hathaway, S. R., Monachesi, E., & Salasin, S. A follow-up study of MMPI high 8, schizoid children. In M. Roff and D. F. Ricks (eds.), *Life history research in psychopathology.* Minneapolis: University of Minnesota Press, 1970.

Hayden, T., & Mischel, W. Maintaining trait consistency in the resolution of behavioral inconsistency: The wolf in sheep's clothing? *Journal of Personality,* 1976, *44,* 109–32.

Hayes, K. J., & Hayes, C. The intellectual development of a home-raised chimpanzee. *Proceedings of the American Philosophical Society,* 1951, *95,* 105–109.

Hearnshaw, L. S. *Cyril Burt, psychologist.* Ithaca, New York: Cornell University Press, 1979.

Heckhausen, H. Achievement motivation and its constructs: A cognitive model. *Motivation and Emotion,* 1977, *1,* 283–329.

Heine, R. W. Foreword. In R. C. Carson, *Interaction concepts of personality.* Chicago: Aldine, 1969.

Heisler, G. Ways to deter law violators: Effects of levels of threat and vicarious punishment on cheating. *Journal of Consulting and Clinical Psychology,* 1974, *42,* 577–82.

Henry, J. The future hustle. *New Republic,* 1978, *178* (5), 16–18, 20.

Henson, C., Rubin, H. B., & Henson, D. E. Women's sexual arousal concurrently assessed by genital measures. *Archives of Sexual Behavior,* 1979, *8,* 459–69.

"Heroes," *New York Review of Books,* 1979, *26* (10), 4, 6.

Herrell, J. M. Sex differences in emotional responses to "erotic literature." *Journal of Consulting and Clinical Psychology,* 1975, *43,* 921.

Herrenkohl, L. R. Prenatal stress reduces fertility and fecundity in female offspring. *Science,* 1979, *206,* 1097–1099.

Herrnstein, R. I.Q. *Atlantic,* 1971, 228 (3), 44–64.

Higgins, R. L., & Marlatt, G. A. Effects of anxiety arousal on the consumption of alcohol by alcoholics and social drinkers. *Journal of Consulting and Clinical Psychology,* 1973, *41,* 426–33.

Hilding, A. C. Obvious question. *Science,* 1975, *187,* 703.

Hiler, E. W. Wechsler-Bellevue intelligence as a predictor of continuation in psychotherapy. *Journal of Clinical Psychology,* 1958, *14,* 192–94.

Hill, C. T., Rubin, Z., & Peplau, L. A. Breakups before marriage: The end of 103 affairs. *Journal of Social Issues,* 1976, *32,* 147–68.

Hodges, L. A., & Byrne, D. Verbal dogmatism as a potentiator of intolerance. *Journal of Personality and Social Psychology,* 1972, *21,* 312–17.

Hodges, W. F., & Spielberger, C. D. The effects of threat of shock on heart rate for subjects who differ in manifest anxiety and fear of shock. *Psychophysiology,* 1966, *2,* 287–94.

Hoffman, L. W. Fear of success in males and females: 1965 and 1971. *Journal of Consulting and Clinical Psychology,* 1974, *42,* 353–58.

Hoffman, L. W. Fear of success in 1965 and 1974: A follow-up study. *Journal of Consulting and Clinical Psychology,* 1977, *45,* 310–21.

Hoffman, M. L. Altruistic behavior and the parent–child relationship. *Journal of Personality and Social Psychology,* 1975, *31,* 937–43.

Hogan, R. Moral Conduct and moral character: A psychological perspective. *Psychological Bulletin,* 1973, *79,* 217–232.

Hogan, R., DeSoto, C., & Solano, C. Traits, tests, and personality research. *American Psychologist,* 1977, *32,* 255–64.

Hokanson, J. E. Psychophysiological evaluation of the catharsis hypothesis. In E. I. Megargee and J. E. Hokanson (eds.), *The dynamics of aggression.* New York: Harper & Row, 1970.

Hokanson, J. E., & Burgess, M. The effects of three types of aggression on vascular processes. *Journal of Abnormal and Social Psychology,* 1962, *64,* 446–49.

Hokanson, J. E., & Shetler, S. The effect of overt aggression on physiological arousal. *Journal of Abnormal and Social Psychology,* 1961, *63,* 446–48.

Holden, C. The criminal mind: A new look at an ancient puzzle. *Science,* 1978, *199,* 511–14.

Hollender, J. Sex differences in sources of social self-esteem. *Journal of Consulting and Clinical Psychology,* 1972, *38,* 343–47.

Holmes, D. S. Conscious self-appraisal of achievement motivation: The self–peer rank method revisited. *Journal of Consulting and Clinical Psychology,* 1971, *36,* 23–26.

Holroyd, K. A. Cognition and desensitization in the group treatment of test anxiety. *Journal of Consulting and Clinical Psychology,* 1976, *44,* 991–1001.

Holt, R. R. Individuality and generalization in the psychology of personality. *Journal of Personality,* 1962, *30,* 377–404.

Holton, G. *Thematic origins of scientific thought: Kepler to Einstein.* Cambridge, Mass.: Harvard University Press, 1973.

Holton, G. On the role of themata in scientific thought. *Science,* 1975, *188,* 328–34.

Honig, A., & Carterette, E. C. Evaluation by women of painters as a function of their sex and achievement and sex of the judges. *Bulletin of the Psychonomic Society,* 1978, *11,* 356–358.

Horn, J. L., & Donaldson, G. On the myth of intellectual decline in adulthood. *American Psychologist,* 1976, *31,* 701–19.

Horn, J. L., & Donaldson, G. Faith is not enough: A response to the Baltes-Schaie claim that intelligence does not wane. *American Psychologist,* 1977, *32,* 369–73.

Horner, M. S. Femininity and successful achievement: A basic inconsistency. In J. M. Bardwick, E. Douvan, M. S. Horner, and D. Gutmann (eds.), *Feminine personality and conflict.* Belmont, Calif.: Brooks/Cole, 1970.

Horner, M. S. The motive to avoid success and changing aspirations of women. In J. M. Bardwick (ed.), *Readings on the psychology of women.* New York: Harper & Row, 1972.

Horton, R. W., & Santogrossi, D. A. The effect of adult commentary on reducing the influence of televised violence. *Personality and Social Psychology Bulletin,* 1978, *4,* 337–40.

House, J. S., & Wolf, S. Effects of urban residence on interpersonal trust and helping behavior. *Journal of Personality and Social Psychology,* 1978, *36,* 1029–43.

Howard, W., & Crana, W. D. Effects of sex, conversation, location, and size of observer group on bystander intervention in a high risk situation. *Sociometry,* 1974, *37,* 491–507.

Hughes, G. American terror. *New York Review of Books,* 1979, *25* (21 and 22), 3–4.

Hull, C. L. *Principles of behavior.* Englewood Cliffs, N.J.: Prentice-Hall, 1943.

Hull, C. L. *A behavior system.* New Haven, Conn.: Yale University Press, 1952.

Humphreys, L. G., Fleishman, A. I., & Lin, P.-C. Causes of racial and socioeconomic differences in cognitive tests. *Journal of Research in Personality,* 1977, *11,* 191–208.

Humphreys, L. G., Lin, P. C., & Fleishman, A. The sex by race interaction in cognitive measures. *Journal of Research in Personality,* 1976, *10,* 42–58.

Hunt, M. *Sexual behavior in the 1970s.* Chicago: Playboy Press, 1974.

Hurd, L. E., Mellinger, M. V., Wolf, L. L., & McNaughton, S. J. Twins: Early mental development. *Science,* 1972, *175,* 914–17.

Hynan, M. T., Harper, S. L., Wood, C., & Kallas, C. Button pushing or aggression? The validity of the shock response in a new paradigm of human aggression. Unpublished manuscript, University of Wisconsin—Milwaukee. 1979.

Insko, C. A., & Wilson, M. Interpersonal attraction as a function of social interaction. *Journal of Personality and Social Psychology,* 1977, *35,* 903–11.

Isen, A. M., Clark, M., & Schwartz, M. F. Duration of the effect of good mood on helping: "Footprints on the sands of time." *Journal of Personality and Social Psychology,* 1976, *34,* 385–93.

Istvan, J., & Griffitt, W. Emotional arousal and sexual attraction. Unpublished ms., Kansas State University, 1978. (a)

Istvan, J., & Griffitt, W. Sexual arousal and evaluations of attractive and unattractive opposite-sex stimulus persons. Paper presented at the meeting of the Midwestern Psychological Association, Chicago, 1978. (b)

"It takes all kinds," *Life,* March 1979, 92–105.

Izzett, R. R. Authoritarianism and attitudes toward the Vietnam War as reflected in behavioral and self-report measures. *Journal of Personality and Social Psychology,* 1971, *17,* 145–48.

Jackson, D. N., Ahmed, S. A., & Heapy, N. A. Is achievement a unitary construct? University of Western Ontario, *Research Bulletin # 273.* 1973.

Jacobs, P. A., Brunton, M., Melville, M. M., Brittain, R. P., & McClemont, W. F. Aggressive behavior, mental subnormality, and the XYY male. *Nature,* 1965, *208,* 1351–52.

Jacobson, L. I. Genetic correlations, squared or unsquared: Can they be accurately computed? *Bulletin of the Psychonomic Society,* 1978, *11,* 123–125.

Jaffe, Y., Malamuth, N., Feingold, J., & Feshbach, S. Sexual arousal and behavioral aggression. *Journal of Personality and Social Psychology,* 1974, *30,* 759–64.

James, W. *The principles of psychology.* New York: Dover, 1950.

Jarvik, L. F., Klodin, V., & Matsuyama, S. S. Human aggression and the extra Y chromosome: Fact or fantasy? *American Psychologist,* 1973, *28,* 674–82.

Jastrow, R. Toward an intelligence beyond man's. *Time,* February 20, 1978, p. 59.

Jenkins, C. D., Zyzanski, S. J., & Rosenman, R. H. *Jenkins Activity Survey.* New York: Psychological Corporation, 1979.

Jenkins, C. D., Zyzanski, S. J., Ryan, T. J., Flessas, A., & Tannenbaum, S. I. Social insecurity and coronary-prone Type A responses as identifiers of severe atherosclerosis. *Journal of Consulting and Clinical Psychology,* 1977, *45,* 1060–1067.

Jensen, A. R. How much can we boost IQ and scholastic achievement? *Harvard Educational Review,* 1969, *39,* 1–123. (a)

Jensen, A. R. Heredity and environment: A controversy over IQ and scholastic achievement. *Berkeley Centennial Fund, University of California,* 1969, *2* (4), 4–6. (b)

Jensen, A. R. *Environment, heredity, and intelligence.* Cambridge, Mass.: *Harvard Educational Review,* 1969. (c)

Jensen, A. R. *Educability and group differences.* New York: Harper & Row, 1973.

Jensen, A. R. Kinship correlations reported by Sir Cyril Burt. *Behavior Genetics,* 1974, *4,* 1–28.

Jensen, A. R. Did Sir Cyril Burt fake his research on heritability of intelligence? Part II. *Phi Delta Kappan,* February, 1977, 471, 492. (a)

Jensen, A. R. Cumulative deficit in IQ of blacks in the rural South. *Developmental Psychology,* 1977, *13,* 184–91. (b)

Jensen, A. R. The current status of the IQ controversy. *Australian Psychologist,* 1978, *13,* 7–27. (a)

Jensen, A. R. Sir Cyril Burt in perspective. *American Psychologist,* 1978, *33,* 499–503. (b)

Jinks, J. L., & Fulker, D. W. Comparison of the biometrical genetical, MAVA, and classical approaches to the analysis of human behavior. *Psychological Bulletin,* 1970, *73,* 311–49.

Johnson, D. F., & Mihal, W. L. Performance of blacks and whites in computerized versus manual testing environments. *American Psychologist,* 1973, *28,* 694–99.

Johnson, D. T. Effects of interview stress on measures of state and trait anxiety. *Journal of Abnormal Psychology,* 1968, *73,* 245–51.

Jolly, A. Lemur social behavior and primate intelligence. *Science,* 1966, *153,* 501–6.

Jones, H. E., & Conrad, H. S. The growth and decline of intelligence. *Genetic Psychology Monographs,* 1933, *13,* 223–298.

Jones, K. L., Shainberg, L. W., & Byer, C. O. *Drugs and alcohol.* New York: Harper & Row, 1973.

Jones, M. B. Religious values and authoritarian tendency. *Journal of Social Psychology,* 1958, *48,* 83–89.

Jones, R. *No substitute for madness.* San Francisco: Zephyros, 1976.

Jovanovic, U. J. The recording of physiological evidence of genital arousal in human males and females. *Archives of Sexual Behavior,* 1971, *1,* 309–20.

Jung, C. G. *Two essays on analytical psychology.* London: Bailliere, Tindall, and Cox, 1928.

Jung, C. G. *The integration of the personality.* New York: Farrar & Rinehart, 1939.

Jung, C. G. *Freud and psychoanalysis.* Vol. 4 of H. Read, M. Fordham, and G. Adler (eds.), *The collected works of C. G. Jung.* New York: Pantheon, 1961.

Jung, C. G. *Memories, dreams, reflections.* New York: Pantheon, 1963.

Jurkovic, G. J., & Prentice N. M. Relation of moral and cognitive development to dimensions of juvenile delinquency. *Journal of Abnormal Psychology,* 1977, *86,* 414–20.

Jurow, G. L. New data on the effect of a "death-qualified" jury on the guilt determination process. *Harvard Law Review,* 1971, *84,* 567–611.

Kagan, J. The magical aura of the IQ. *Saturday Review,* 1971, *54* (49), 92–93.

Kagitcibasi, C. Social norms and authoritarianism: A Turkish-American comparison. *Journal of Personality and Social Psychology,* 1970, *16,* 444–51.

Kahoe, R. D. Personality and achievement correlates of intrinsic and extrinsic religious orientations. *Journal of Personality and Social Psychology,* 1974, *29,* 812–818.

Kamin, L. J. *The science and politics of IQ.* Hillsdale, N.J.: Lawrence Erlbaum, 1974.

Kamin, L. J. Burt's IQ data. *Science,* 1977, *195,* 246–48.

Kane, T. R., Joseph, J. M., & Tedeschi, J. T. Person perception and the Berkowitz paradigm for the study of aggression. *Journal of Personality and Social Psychology,* 1976, *33,* 663–73.

Kangas, J., & Bradway, K. Intelligence at middle age: A thirty-eight-year follow-up. *Developmental Psychology,* 1971, *5,* 333–37.

Kaplan, B. J. Malnutrition and mental deficiency. *Psychological Bulletin,* 1972, *78,* 321–34.

Kaplan, H. B., & Pokorny, A. D. Self-derogation and psychosocial adjustment. *Journal of Nervous and Mental Disease,* 1969, *149,* 421–34.

Kaplan, H. B., & Pokorny, A. D. Self-derogation and childhood broken home. *Journal of Marriage and the Family,* 1971, *33,* 328 37.

Karabenick, S. A. Fear of success, achievement and affiliation dispositions, and the performance of men and women under individual and competitive conditions. *Journal of Personality,* 1977, *45,* 117–49.

Karnilow, A. A comparison of Oedipal and peer sex through the use of hypnotically implanted paramnesias. Unpublished doctoral dissertation, Michigan State University, 1973.

Karylowski, J. Self-esteem, similarity, liking and helping. *Personality and Social Psychology Bulletin,* 1976, *2,* 71–74.

Katchadourian, H. A., & Lunde, D. T. *Fundamentals of human sexuality.* New York: Holt, Rinehart and Winston, 1975.

Kato, T., Jarvik, L. F., Roizin, L., & Maralishvili, E. Chromosome studies in pregnant rhesus macaque given LSD-25. *Diseases of the Nervous System,* 1970, *31,* 245–50.

Katz, I., Cohen, S., & Glass, D. Some determinants of cross-racial helping behavior. *Journal of Personality and Social Psychology,* 1975, *32,* 964–70.

Katzev, R., Edelsack, L., Steinmetz, G., Walker, T., & Wright, R. The effect of reprimanding transgressions on subsequent helping behavior: Two field experiments. *Personality and Social Psychology Bulletin,* 1978, *4,* 326–29.

Kaufman, A. S. Comparison of the performance of matched groups of black children and white children on the Wechsler Preschool and Primary Scale of Intelligence. *Journal of Consulting and Clinical Psychology,* 1973, *41,* 186–91.

Kaufman, I. C., & Rosenblum, L. A.   Depression in infant monkeys separated from their mothers. *Science*, 1967, *155*, 1030-31.

Kazdin, A. E.   The rich rewards of rewards. *Psychology Today*, 1976, *10* (6), 98, 101-102, 105, 114.

Keller, F. S.   "Goodbye teacher..." *Journal of Applied Behavior Analysis*, 1968, *1*, 79-88.

Kelley, K.   Effects of mood and gender differences on passive aggression. Unpublished ms., State University of New York at Albany, 1979. (a)

Kelley, K.   Socialization factors in contraceptive attitudes: Roles of affective responses, parental attitudes, and sexual experience. *Journal of Sex Research*, 1979, *15*, 6-20. (b)

Kelley, K.   Adolescent sexuality: The first lessons. In D. Byrne and W. A. Fisher (eds.), *Adolescents, sex, and contraception*. New York: McGraw-Hill, 1981.

Kelley, K., & Byrne, D.   Strength of instigation as a determinant of the aggression–attraction relationship. *Motivation and Emotion*, 1977, *1*, 29-38.

Kelly, E. L.   Consistency of the adult personality. *American Psychologist*, 1955, *10*, 659-81.

Kelly, G. A.   *The psychology of personal constructs*. New York: Norton, 1955.

Kelsey, F. O.   Drugs and pregnancy. *Mental Retardation*, 1969, 7, 7-10.

Kendall, P. C.   Anxiety: States, traits, — situations? *Journal of Consulting and Clinical Psychology*, 1978, *46*, 280-287.

Kendall, P. C., Finch, A. J., Jr., Auerbach, S. M., Hooke, J. F., & Mikulka, P. J.   The State–Trait Anxiety Inventory: A systematic evaluation. *Journal of Consulting and Clinical Psychology*, 1976, *44*, 406-12.

Kendall, P. C., Williams, L., Pechacek, T. F., Graham, L. E., Shisslak, C., & Herzoff, N.   Cognitive-behavioral and patient education interventions in cardiac catheterization procedures: The Palo Alto medical psychology project. *Journal of Consulting and Clinical Psychology*, 1979, *47*, 49-58.

Kendler, H. H.   Kenneth W. Spence: 1907-1967. *Psychological Review*, 1967, *74*, 335-41.

Kenrick, D. T., & Cialdini, R. B.   Romantic attraction: Misattribution versus reinforcement explanations. *Journal of Personality and Social Psychology*, 1977, *35*, 381-91.

Kenrick, D. T., & Johnson, G. A.   Interpersonal attraction in aversive environments: A problem for the classical conditioning paradigm? *Journal of Personality and Social Psychology*, 1979, *37*, 572-579.

Kenrick, D. T., Reich, J. W., & Cialdini, R. B.   Justification and compensation: Rosier skies for the devalued victim. *Journal of Personality and Social Psychology*, 1976, *34*, 654-57.

Kenrick, D. T., & Stringfield, D. O.   Personality traits and the eye of the beholder: Crossing some traditional philosophical boundaries in the search for consistency in all of the people. Unpublished manuscript, Montana State University, 1980.

Kenrick, D. T., Stringfield, D. O., Wagenhals, W. L., Dahl, R. H., & Ransdell, H. J.   Sex differences, androgyny, and approach responses to erotica: A new variation on the old volunteer problem. *Journal of Personality and Social Psychology*, 1980, *38*, 517-524.

Kerr, N. L., & Kurtz, S. T.   Effects of a victim's suffering and respectability on mock juror judgments: Further evidence on the just world theory. *Representative Research in Social Psychology*, 1977, *8*, 42-56.

Kidd, J. W.   Personality traits as barriers to acceptability in a college men's residence hall. *Journal of Social Psychology*, 1953, *38*, 127-30.

Kilmann, P. R., & Auerbach, S. M.   Effects of marathon group therapy on trait and state anxiety. *Journal of Consulting and Clinical Psychology*, 1974, *42*, 607-12.

Kimble, C. E., Fitz, D., & Onorad, J.   The effectiveness of counteraggression strategies in reducing interpersonal aggression. *Journal of Personality and Social Psychology*, 1977, *35*, 272-78.

"Kind kids are nice to know,"   *Times-Union*, October 21, 1979.

Kinsey, A. C., Pomeroy, W., & Martin, C.   *Sexual behavior in the human male*. Philadelphia: Saunders, 1948.

Kinsey, A. C., Pomeroy, W., Martin, C., & Gebhard, P.   *Sexual behavior in the human female*. Philadelphia: Saunders, 1953.

Kirk, S. A.   *Early education of the mentally retarded*. Urbana: University of Illinois Press, 1958.

Klein, E. B.   Stylistic components of response as related to attitude change. *Journal of Personality*, 1963, *31*, 38-51.

Kleinke, C. L., Meeker, F. B., & LaFong, C.   Effects of gaze, touch, and use of name on evaluation of "engaged" couples. *Journal of Research in Personality*, 1974, 7, 368-73.

Kleinke, C. L., Staneski, R. A., & Weaver, P.   Evaluation of a person who uses another's name in ingratiating and noningratiating situations. *Journal of Experimental Social Psychology*, 1972, *8*, 457-66.

Klineberg, O.   *Negro intelligence and selective migration*. New York: Columbia University Press, 1935.

Klineberg, O.   Negro-white differences in intelligence test performance: A new look at an old problem. *American Psychologist*, 1963, *18*, 198-203.

Klineberg, O.   Black and white in international perspective. *American Psychologist*, 1971, *26*, 119-28.

Knapp, R. H., & Garbutt, J. T.   Time imagery and the achievement motive. *Journal of Personality*, 1958, *26*, 426-34.

Koch, M. B., & Meyer, D. R.   A relationship of mental age to learning-set formation in the pre-school child. *Journal of Comparative and Physiological Psychology*, 1959, *52*, 387-89.

Kogan, N.   Authoritarianism and repression. *Journal of Abnormal and Social Psychology*, 1956, *53*, 34-37.

Kohlberg, L. The development of children's orientations toward a moral order: 1. Sequence in the development of moral thought. *Human Development,* 1963, *6,* 11–33. (a)

Kohlberg, L. Moral development and identification. In H. Stevenson (ed.), *Child psychology.* Chicago: University of Chicago Press, 1963. (b)

Kohlberg, L. A cognitive-developmental analysis of children's sex-role concepts and attitudes. In E. E. Maccoby (ed.), *The development of sex differences.* Stanford, Calif.: Stanford University Press, 1966.

Kohlberg, L., & Gilligan, C. The adolescent as a philosopher: The discovery of the self in a postconventional world. In J. Kagan and R. Coles (eds.), *Twelve to sixteen: Early adolescence.* New York: Norton, 1972.

Kolb, D. A. Achievement motivation training for underachieving high school boys. *Journal of Personality and Social Psychology.*

Komarovsky, M. Cultural contradictions and sex roles: The masculine case. *American Journal of Sociology,* 1973, *78,* 873–84.

Kondracke, M. E. School's out. *New Republic,* March 11, 1978, p. 42.

Konečni, V. J. The mediation of aggressive behavior: Arousal level versus anger and cognitive labeling. *Journal of Personality and Social Psychology,* 1975, *32,* 706–12. (a)

Konečni, V. J. Annoyance, type and duration of postannoyance activity, and aggression: The "cathartic effect." *Journal of Experimental Psychology: General,* 1975, *104,* 76–102. (b)

Konečni, V. J., & Ebbesen, E. B. Disinhibition versus the cathartic effect: Artifact and substance. *Journal of Personality and Social Psychology,* 1976, *34,* 352–65.

Konečni, V. J., Libuser, L., Morton, H., & Ebbesen, E. B. Effects of a violation of personal space on escape and helping responses. *Journal of Experimental Social Psychology,* 1975, *11,* 288–99.

Koocher, G. P. Swimming, competence, and personality change. *Journal of Personality and Social Psychology,* 1971, *18,* 275–78.

Kopkind, A. America's new right. *New Times,* 1977, *9* (7), 20–22, 24, 27–30, 32–33.

Kornberg, A. The irresistible urge to gamble on a quick payoff. *Stanford Observer,* 1977, *11* (6), 5.

Kraemer, H. C., Becker, H. B., Brodie, H. X. H., Doering, C. H., Moos, R. H., & Hamburg, D. A. Orgasmic frequency and plasma testosterone levels in normal human males. *Archives of Sexual Behavior,* 1976, *5,* 125–32.

Krasner, L. The future and the past in the behaviorism-humanism dialogue. *American Psychologist,* 1978, *33,* 799–804.

Kratochwill, T. R., & Brody, G. H. Effects of verbal and self-monitoring feedback on Wechsler Adult Intelligence Scale performance in normal adults. *Journal of Consulting and Clinical Psychology,* 1976, *44,* 879–80.

Krebs, D., & Adinolfi, A. A. Physical attractiveness, social relations, and personality style. *Journal of Personality and Social Psychology,* 1975, *31,* 245–53.

Kuhl, J., & Blankenship, V. Behavioral change in a constant environment: Shift to more difficult tasks with constant probability of success. *Journal of Personality and Social Psychology,* 1979, *37,* 551–563.

Kuhlen, R. G., & Bretsch, H. S. Sociometric status and personal problems of adolescents. *Sociometry,* 1947, *10,* 122–32.

Kukla, A. Performance as a function of resultant achievement motivation (perceived ability) and perceived difficulty. *Journal of Research in Personality,* 1975, *32,* 374–83.

Kukla, A. Preferences among impossibly difficult and trivially easy tasks: A revision of Atkinson's theory of choice. *Journal of Personality and Social Psychology,* 1975, *32,* 338–45.

Kulik, J. A., Kulik, C. L., & Carmichael, K. The Keller plan in science teaching. *Science,* 1974, *183,* 379–83.

Kunen, J. S. Slow down. *New Times,* 1977, *8* (10), 10.

Kutchinsky, B. The effect of pornography: A pilot experiment on perception, behavior, and attitudes. In *Technical report of the Commission on Obscenity and Pornography,* vol. 8. Washington, D.C.: U.S. Government Printing Office, 1971.

Kutchinsky, B. The effect of easy availability of pornography on the incidence of sex crimes: The Danish experience. *Journal of Social Issues,* 1973, *29* (3), 163–81.

Lamb, D. H. Dental treatment as a physical stressor: Changes in state anxiety for persons who differ in trait anxiety. Paper presented at the Midwestern Psychological Association, Cleveland, May 1972.

Lamb, D. H. The effects of two stressors on state anxiety for students who differ in trait anxiety. *Journal of Research in Personality,* 1973, *7,* 116–26.

Lamberth, J., & Kirby, D. A. The lawyers' dilemma: Authoritarianism and jury selection. Paper presented at the meeting of the Midwestern Psychological Association, Chicago, May 1974.

Landers, A. Love or infatuation? Test tells differences. Syndicated column, July 21, 1975.

Landwehr, L. J., & Novotny, R. Juror authoritarianism and trial judge partiality: An experiment in jury decision making. *Journal of Experimental Study of Politics,* 1976, *5.*

Langer, E. J., Janis, I. L., & Wolfer, J. A. Reduction of psychological stress in surgical patients. *Journal of Experimental Social Psychology,* 1975, *11,* 155–65.

Laosa, L. M., Lara-Tapia, L., & Swartz, J. D. Pathognomic verbalizations, anxiety, and hostility in normal Mexican and United States Anglo-American children's fantasies: A longitudinal study.

Journal of Consulting and Clinical Psychology, 1974, *42*, 73–78.

La Porte, T. R., & Metlay, D. Technology observed: Attitudes of a wary public. *Science*, 1975, *188*, 121–27.

Larsen, K. S. Authoritarianism and attitudes toward police. *Psychological Reports*, 1968, *23*, 349–50.

Lash, J. P. *Helen and teacher.* New York: Delacorte, 1980.

Latané, B. Theory of social impact. Paper presented at the meeting of the Psychonomic Society, St. Louis, November 1973.

Latané, B., & Darley, J. M. *The unresponsive bystander: Why doesn't he help?* Englewood Cliffs, N.J.: Prentice-Hall, 1970.

Layzer, D. Heritability analyses of IQ scores: Science or numerology? *Science*, 1974, *183*, 1259–66.

Lee, E. S. Negro intelligence and selective migration: A Philadelphia test of Klineberg's hypothesis. *American Sociological Review*, 1951, *61*, 227–33.

Lemann, T. B., & Solomon, R. L. Group characteristics as revealed in sociometric patterns and personality ratings. *Sociometry*, 1952, *15*, 7–90.

Lerner, M. J. The justice motive: Some hypotheses as to its origins and forms. *Journal of Personality*, 1977, *45*, 1–52.

Lerner, M. J., Miller, D. T., & Holmes, J. G. Deserving versus justice: A contemporary dilemma. In L. Berkowitz and E. Walster (eds.), *Advances in experimental social psychology*, vol. 12. New York: Academic Press, 1975.

Lesser, G. S., Krawitz, R. N., & Packard, R. Experimental arousal of achievement motivation in adolescent girls. *Journal of Abnormal and Social Psychology*, 1963, *66*, 59–66.

Lester, B. M. The consequences of infantile malnutrition. In H. E. Fitzgerald and J. P. McKinney (eds.), *Developmental psychology: Studies in human development.* Homewood, Ill.: Dorsey, 1977.

Leventhal, H., Jacobs, R. L., & Kudirka, N. Z. Authoritarianism, ideology and political candidate choice. *Journal of Abnormal and Social Psychology*, 1964, *69*, 539–49.

Levin, I. P., Ims, J. R., Simpson, J. C., & Kim, K. J. The processing of deviant information in prediction and evaluation. *Memory & Cognition*, 1977, *5*, 679–684.

Levine, C. Role-taking standpoint and adolescent usage of Kohlberg's conventional stages of moral reasoning. *Journal of Personality and Social Psychology*, 1976, *34*, 41–46.

Levine, M. P., & Moore, B. S. Trans-situational effects of lack of control and coronary-prone behavior. Paper presented at the meeting of the American Psychological Association, New York, September 1979.

LeVine, R. *Dreams and deeds: Achievement motivation in Nigeria.* Chicago: University of Chicago Press, 1966.

Levinson, D. J., & Huffman, P. E. Traditional family ideology and its relation to personality. *Journal of Personality*, 1955, *23*, 251–73.

Levitt, E. E. The effect of a "causal" teacher training program on authoritarianism and responsibility in grade school children. *Psychological Reports*, 1955, *1*, 449–58.

Levy, S. Authoritarianism and information processing. *Bulletin of the Psychonomic Society*, 1979, *13*, 240–242.

Lewin, K. *A dynamic theory of personality.* New York: McGraw-Hill, 1935.

Lewin, K. *Field theory in social science: Selected theoretical papers.* D. Cartwright (ed.), New York: Harper, 1951.

Lewis, M. (ed.). *Origins of intelligence: Infancy and early childhood.* New York: Plenum, 1976.

Lewis, M., & McGurk, H. Evaluation of infant intelligence. *Science*, 1972, *178*, 1174–77.

Lewis, R., & St. John, N. Contribution of cross-racial friendship to minority group achievement in desegregated classrooms. *Sociometry*, 1974, *37*, 79–91.

Leyens, J. P., Camino, L., Parke, R. D., & Berkowitz, L. Effects of movie violence on aggression in a field setting as a function of group dominance and cohesion. *Journal of Personality and Social Psychology*, 1975, *32*, 346–60.

Lieber, A. L., & Sherin, C. R. Homicides and the lunar cycle: Toward a theory of lumar influence on human emotional disturbance. *American Journal of Psychiatry*, 1972, *129*, 69–74.

Liebert, R. M., & Baron, R. A. Some immediate effects of televised violence on children's behavior. *Developmental Psychology*, 1972, *6*, 469–75.

Limber, J. Language in child and chimp? *American Psychologist*, 1977, *32*, 280–295.

Lindgren, H. C. Authoritarianism, independence, and child-centered practices in education: A study of attitudes. *Psychological Reports*, 1962, *10*, 747–50.

Lippmann, W. The university. *New Republic*, 1966, *154* (22), 17–20.

Littig, L. W., & Yeracaris, C. A. Achievement motivation and intergenerational occupational mobility. *Journal of Personality and Social Psychology*, 1965, *1*, 386–89.

Lloyd-Still, J. D. *Malnutrition and intellectual development.* Littleton, Maine: Publishing Sciences Group, 1976.

Loehlin, J. C., Lindzey, G., & Spuhler, J. N. *Race differences in intelligence.* San Francisco: Freeman, 1975.

Lombardo, J. P., Steigleder, M., & Feinberg, R. Internality–externality: The perception of negatively valued personality characteristics and interpersonal attraction. *Representative Research in Social Psychology*, 1975, *6*, 89–95.

Loomis, C. P., & Proctor, C. The relationship between choice status and economic status in social systems. *Sociometry*, 1950, *13*, 307-13.

Looney, T. A., & Dove, L. D. Effects of the presence of a home-chamber target on experimental-session attack. *Physiology & Behavior*, 1978, *21*, 283-286.

Lorge, I. Schooling makes a difference. *Teachers College Record*, 1945, *46*, 483-92.

Lott, B. E., & Lott, A. J. The formation of positive attitudes toward group members. *Journal of Abnormal and Social Psychology*, 1960, *61*, 297-300.

Love, R. E., Sloan, L. R., & Schmidt, M. J. Viewing pornography and sex guilt: The priggish, the prudent, and the profligate. *Journal of Consulting and Clinical Psychology*, 1976, *44*, 624-29.

Loye, D., Gorney, R., & Steele, G. Effects of television: An experimental field study. *Journal of Communication*, 1977, *27*, 206-16.

Lumby, M. E. Homophobia: The quest for a valid scale. *Journal of Homosexuality*, 1976, *2*, 39-47.

Lunde, D. T. Our murder boom. *Psychology Today*, 1975, *9* (2), 35-40, 42.

Lundy, J. R. Some personality correlates of contraceptive use among unmarried female college students. *Journal of Psychology*, 1972, *80*, 9-14.

Lynes, R. After hours. Ouch! *Harper's*, 1968, *237* (1420), 23-26.

Maccoby, E. (ed.). *The development of sex differences.* Stanford, Calif.: Stanford University Press, 1966.

Maccoby, E. E., & Jacklin, C. N. *The psychology of sex differences.* Stanford, Calif.: Stanford University Press, 1974.

MacKinnon, D. W. Violation of prohibitions. In H. A. Murray (ed.), *Explorations in personality.* Oxford: Oxford University Press, 1938. Pp. 491-501.

Mackintosh, J. H. Territory formation by laboratory mice. *Animal Behavior*, 1970, *18*, 177-83.

MacPhail, E. M., & Miller, N. E. Cholinergic brain stimulation in cats: Failure to obtain sleep. *Journal of Comparative and Physiological Psychology*, 1968, *65*, 499-503.

Maehr, M. L. Culture and achievement motivation. *American Psychologist*, in press.

Magnusson, D. The individual in the situation: Some studies on individuals' perception of situations. *Studia Psychologica*, 1974, *16*, 124-31.

Magnusson, D., & Ekehammar, B. Anxiety profiles based on both situational and response factors. *Multivariate Behavioral Research*, 1975, *10*, 27-44. (a)

Magnusson, D., & Ekehammar, B. Perceptions of and reactions to stressful situations. *Journal of Personality and Social Psychology*, 1975, *31*, 1147-54. (b)

Mahler, I. Attitudes toward socialized medicine. *Journal of Social Psychology*, 1953, *38*, 273-282.

Maitland, K. A., & Goldman, J. R. Moral judgment as a function of peer group interaction. *Journal of Personality and Social Psychology*, 1974, *30*, 699-704.

Malamuth, N. M., Feshbach, S., & Jaffe, Y. Sexual

arousal and aggression: Recent experiments and theoretical issues. *Journal of Social Issues*, 1977, *33*, 110-33.

Malec, J., Park, T., & Watkins, J. T. Modeling with role playing as a treatment for test anxiety. *Journal of Consulting and Clinical Psychology*, 1976, *44*, 679.

Maller, J. B. Mental ability and its relation to physical health and social economic status. *Psychological Clinic*, 1933, *22*, 101-7.

Manes, A. I., & Melynk, P. Televised models of female achievement. *Journal of Applied Social Psychology*, 1974, *4*, 365-374.

Mann, J., Berkowitz, L., Sidman, J., Starr, S., & West, S. Satiation of the transient stimulating effect of erotic films. *Journal of Personality and Social Psychology*, 1974, *30*, 729-35.

Marks, M. W., & Vestre, N. D. Self-perception and interpersonal behavior changes in marathon and time-extended encounter groups. *Journal of Consulting and Clinical Psychology*, 1974, *42*, 729-33.

Marlatt, G. A. Alcohol, stress, and cognitive control. Paper presented at the International Conference on Dimensions of Stress and Anxiety, Oslo, Norway, June-July 1975.

Marler, P. On animal aggression: The roles of strangeness and familiarity. *American Psychologist*, 1976, *31*, 239-46.

Marquis, P. C. Experimenter-subject interaction as a function of authoritarianism and response set. *Journal of Personality and Social Psychology*, 1973, *25*, 289-96.

Marshall, J. M., & Karabenick, S. A. Validity of an empirically derived projective measure of fear of success. *Journal of Consulting and Clinical Psychology*, 1977, *45*, 564-74.

Marston, A. R. It is time to reconsider the Graduate Record Examination. *American Psychologist*, 1971, *26*, 653-55.

Martin, D., & Lyon, P. *Lesbian/woman.* San Francisco: Glide Publications, 1972.

Martinez-Urrutia, A. Anxiety and pain in surgical patients. *Journal of Consulting and Clinical Psychology*, 1975, *43*, 437-42.

Masling, J. M. How neurotic is the authoritarian? *Journal of Abnormal and Social Psychology*, 1954, *33*, 21-42.

Maslow, A. H. *Motivation and personality.* New York: Harper and Row, 1970.

Masters, W. H., & Johnson, V. E. *Human sexual response.* Boston: Little, Brown, 1966.

Masters, W. H., & Johnson, V. E. *Homosexuality in perspective.* Boston: Little, Brown, 1979.

Masterson, G. *Women's erotic dreams (and what they mean).* New York: Warner Books, 1977.

Masterton, R. B., & Berkley, M. A. Brain functions: Changing ideas on the role of sensory, motor, and association cortex in behavior. In P. H. Mussen and

M. R. Rosenzweig (eds.), *Annual review of psychology*, vol. 25. Palo Alto, Calif.: Annual Reviews, 1974.

Matarazzo, J. D., Guze, S. B., & Matarazzo, R. G. An approach to the validity of the Taylor Anxiety Scale: Scores of medical and psychiatric patients. *Journal of Abnormal and Social Psychology*, 1955, *51*, 276–80.

Matarazzo, J. D., Wiens, A. N., & Shealy, A. E. Correlation of WAIS IQ in 10 pairs of brothers. *Journal of Consulting and Clinical Psychology*, 1978, *46*, 571–572.

Matthews, K. A., & Brunson, B. I. Allocation of attention and the Type A coronary-prone behavior pattern. *Journal of Personality and Social Psychology*, 1979, *37*, 2081–2090.

May, J. L., & Hamilton, P. A. Females' evaluations of males as a function of affect arousing musical stimuli. Paper presented at the meeting of the Midwestern Psychological Association, Chicago, May 1977.

McArthur, L. Z., & Eisen, S. V. Achievements of male and female storybook characters as determinants of achievement behavior by boys and girls. *Journal of Personality and Social Psychology*, 1976, *33*, 467–73.

McBurney, D. H., Levine, J. M., & Cavanaugh, P. H. Psychophysical and social ratings of human body odor. *Personality and Social Psychology Bulletin*, 1977, *3*, 135–38.

McCall, R. B. Childhood IQs as predictors of adult educational occupational status. *Science*, 1977, *197*, 482–83.

McCall, R. B., Hogarty, P. S., & Hurlburt, N. Transitions in infant sensorimotor development and the prediction of childhood IQ. *American Psychologist*, 1972, *27*, 728–48.

McCandless, B. R., Castaneda, A., & Palermo, D. S. Anxiety in children and social status. *Child Development*, 1956, *27*, 385–91.

McClelland, D. C. Some social consequences of achievement motivation. In M. R. Jones (ed.), *Nebraska symposium on motivation*. Lincoln: University of Nebraska Press, 1955.

McClelland, D. C. Methods of measuring human motivation. In J. W. Atkinson (ed.), *Motives in fantasy, action, and society*. Princeton, N.J.: Van Nostrand, 1958.

McClelland, D. C. *The achieving society*. Princeton, N.J.: Van Nostrand, 1961.

McClelland, D. C. *n* Achievement and entrepreneurship: A longitudinal study. *Journal of Personality and Social Psychology*, 1965, *1*, 389–92. (a)

McClelland, D. C. Toward a theory of motive acquisition. *American Psychologist*, 1965, *20*, 321–33. (b)

McClelland, D. C. *Motivational trends in society*. Morristown, N.J.: General Learning Press, 1971.

McClelland, D. C., Atkinson, J. W., Clark, R. A., & Lowell, E. L. *The achievement motive*. Englewood Cliffs, N.J.: Prentice-Hall, 1953.

McClelland, D. C., Clark, R. A., Roby, T. B., & At-kinson, J. W. The effect of the need for achievement on thematic apperception. *Journal of Experimental Psychology*, 1949, *37*, 242–55.

McClelland, D. C., Rindlisbacher, A., & de Charms, R. C. Religious and other sources of parental attitudes toward independence training. In D. C. McClelland (ed.), *Studies in motivation*. Englewood Cliffs, N.J.: Prentice-Hall, 1955.

McClelland, D. C., & Winter, D. G. *Motivating economic achievement*. New York: Free Press, 1969.

McClelland, L. Effects of interviewer–respondent race interactions on household interview measures of motivation and intelligence. *Journal of Personality and Social Psychology*, 1974, *29*, 392–97.

McCordick, S. M., Kaplan, R. M., Finn, M. E., & Smith, S. H. Cognitive behavior modification and modeling for test anxiety. *Journal of Consulting and Clinical Psychology*, 1979, *47*, 419–420.

McElroy, W. D. The global age: Roles of basic and applied research. *Science*, 1977, *196*, 267–70.

McFarland, R. L., Nelson, C. L., & Rossi, A. M. Prediction of participation in group psychotherapy from measures of intelligence and verbal behavior. *Psychological Reports*, 1962, *11*, 291–98.

McGovern, L. P. Dispositional social anxiety and helping behavior under three conditions of threat. *Journal of Personality*, 1976, *44*, 84–97.

McGovern, L. P., Ditzian, J. L., & Taylor, S. P. Sex and perceptions of dependency in a helping situation. *Bulletin of the Psychonomic Society*, 1975, *5*, 336–38. (a)

McGovern, L. P., Ditzian, J. L., & Taylor, S. P. The effect of one positive reinforcement on helping with cost. *Bulletin of the Psychonomic Society*, 1975, *5*, 421–23. (b)

McGowan, J., & Gormly, J. Validation of personality traits: A multicriteria approach. *Journal of Personality and Social Psychology*, 1976, *34*, 791–95.

McGuire, W. J. Vital statistics. *Personality–Social Newsletter*, May 1968, 1–2.

McKay, H., Sinisterra, L., McKay, A., Gomez, H., & Lloreda, P. Improving cognitive ability in chronically deprived children. *Science*, 1978, *200*, 270–278.

McKenna, R. J. Good Samaritanism in rural and urban settings: A nonreactive comparison of helping behavior of clergy and control subjects. *Representative Research in Social Psychology*, 1976, *7*, 58–65.

McKinney, F. Fifty years of psychology. *American Psychologist*, 1976, *31*, 834–842.

McNemar, Q. Lost: Our intelligence? Why? *American Psychologist*, 1964, *19*, 871–82.

McWilliams, N. Personality theory at middle age: Generativity vs. stagnation. *Contemporary Psychology*, 1977, *22*, 25–27.

Meade, R. D. Achievement motivation, achievement, and psychological time. *Journal of Personality and Social Psychology*, 1966, *4*, 577–80.

Megargee, E. I. Undercontrolled and overcontrolled personality types in extreme antisocial aggression. *Psychological Monographs,* 1966, *80* (whole no. 611).

Megargee, E. I. Conscientious objectors' scores on the MMPI *O-H* (Overcontrolled Hostility) Scale. *Proceedings, 77th Annual Convention, APA,* 1969, 507–8.

Megargee, E. I., Cook, P. E., & Mendelsohn, G. A. The development and validation of an MMPI scale of assaultiveness in overcontrolled individuals. *Journal of Abnormal Psychology,* 1967, *72,* 519–28.

Mehrabian, A. Male and female scales of the tendency to achieve. *Educational and Psychological Measurement,* 1968, *28,* 493–502.

Mehrabian, A. The development and validation of measures of affiliative tendency and sensitivity to rejection. *Educational and Psychological Measurement,* 1970, *30,* 417–28.

Melamed, B. G., & Siegel, L. J. Reduction of anxiety in children facing hospitalization and surgery by use of filmed modeling. *Journal of Consulting and Clinical Psychology,* 1975, *43,* 511–21.

Mellstrom, M., Jr., Cicala, G. A., & Zuckerman, M. General versus specific trait anxiety measures in the prediction of fear of snakes, heights, and darkness. *Journal of Consulting and Clinical Psychology,* 1976, *44,* 83–91.

Menachem, A. *Patterns in forcible rape.* Chicago: University of Chicago Press, 1971.

Meredith, H. V. Body size of contemporary groups of one-year-old infants studied in different parts of the world. *Child Development,* 1970, *41,* 551–600.

Merrick, R., & Taylor, S. P. Aggression as a function of vulnerability to attack. *Psychonomic Science,* 1970, *20,* 203–4.

Merton, R. K. Thematic analysis in science: Notes on Holton's concept. *Science,* 1975, *188,* 335–38.

Messenger, J. C. Sexual repression: Its manifestations. In D. Byrne and L. A. Byrne (eds.), *Exploring human sexuality.* New York: Harper & Row, 1977. Pp. 72–77.

Meyer, H. H., Walker, W. B., & Litwin, G. H. Motive patterns and risk preferences associated with entrepreneurship. *Journal of Abnormal and Social Psychology,* 1961, *63,* 570–74.

Meyer, J. P., & Pepper, S. Need compatibility and marital adjustment in young married couples. *Journal of Personality and Social Psychology,* 1977, *35,* 331–342.

Meyer, N. *The seven-per-cent solution.* New York: Dutton, 1974.

Meyer, T. P. The effects of sexually arousing and violent films on aggressive behavior. *Journal of Sex Research,* 1972, *8,* 324–33.

Middlemist, R. D., Knowles, E. S., & Matter, C. F. Personal space invasions in the lavatory: Suggestive evidence for arousal. *Journal of Personality and Social Psychology,* 1976, *33,* 541–46.

Milgram, S. Behavioral study of obedience. *Journal of Abnormal and Social Psychology,* 1963, *67,* 371–78.

Milgram, S. *Obedience to authority.* New York: Harper & Row, 1974.

Miller, C. T., Byrne, D., & Bell, P. A. Facilitating sexual arousal: Anger or dominance? Unpublished ms., Purdue University, 1978.

Miller, J. The call of the wild. *New York Review of Books,* 1976, *23* (14), 10, 12–13.

Miller, N. E. The frustration–aggression hypothesis. *Psychological Review,* 1941, *48,* 337–42.

Miller, N., & Maruyama, G. Ordinal position and peer popularity. *Journal of Personality and Social Psychology,* 1976, *33,* 123–31.

Millham, J. Two components of need for approval score and their relationship to cheating following success and failure. *Journal of Research in Personality,* 1974, *8,* 378–92.

Mills, C. R. Personality patterns of sociometrically selected and sociometrically rejected male college students. *Sociometry,* 1953, *16,* 151–67.

Milton, W., & Waite, B. Presidential preference and traditional family values. *American Psychologist,* 1964, *19,* 844–45.

Minor, C. A., & Neel, R. G. The relationship between achievement motive and occupational preference. *Journal of Counseling Psychology,* 1958, *5,* 39–43.

Mischel, W. Delay of gratification, need for achievement, and acquiescence in another culture. *Journal of Abnormal and Social Psychology,* 1961, *62,* 543–52.

Mischel, W. Theory and research on the antecedents of self-imposed delay of reward. In B. A. Maher (ed.), *Progress in experimental personality research,* vol. 3 New York: Academic Press, 1966. Pp. 85–132.

Mischel, W. *Personality and assessment.* New York: Wiley, 1968.

Mischel, W. Continuity and change in personality. *American Psychologist,* 1969, *24,* 1012–18.

Mischel, W. On the future of personality measurement. *American Psychologist,* 1977, *32,* 246–54.

Mischel, W. On the interface of cognition and personality: Beyond the person-situation debate. *American Psychologist,* 1979, *34,* 740–754.

Mischel, W., & Gilligan, C. Delay of gratification, motivation for the prohibited gratification, and response to temptation. *Journal of Abnormal and Social Psychology,* 1964, *69,* 411–417.

Mischel, W., & Metzner, R. Preference for delayed reward as a function of age, intelligence, and length of delay interval. *Journal of Abnormal and Social Psychology,* 1962, *64,* 425–31.

Mita, T. H., Dermer, M., & Knight, J. Reversed facial images and the mere–exposure hypothesis. *Journal of Personality and Social Psychology,* 1977, *35,* 597–601.

Mitchell, G. D., Arling, G. L., & Moller, G. W. Long-term effects of maternal punishment on the behavior of monkeys. *Psychonomic Science*, 1967, *8*, 209–10.

Mitchell, G. D., Harlow, H. F., Griffin, G. A., & Moller, G. W. Repeated maternal separation in the monkey, *Psychonomic Science*, 1967, *8*, 197–98.

Mitchell, H. E. Authoritarian punitiveness in simulated juror decision-making: The good guys don't always wear white hats. Paper presented at the meeting of the Midwestern Psychological Association, Chicago, May 1973.

Mitchell, H. E., & Byrne, D. The defendant's dilemma: Effects of jurors' attitudes and authoritarianism on judicial decisions. *Journal of Personality and Social Psychology*, 1973, *25*, 123–29.

Monahan, L., Kuhn, D., & Shaver, P. Intrapsychic versus cultural explanations of the "fear of success" motive. *Journal of Personality and Social Psychology*, 1974, *29*, 60–64.

Money, J. Prenatal hormones and postnatal socialization in gender identity differentiation. In J. K. Cole and R. Dienstbier (eds.), *Nebraska symposium on motivation*. Lincoln: University of Nebraska Press, 1974.

Money, J., & Erhardt, A. A. *Man and woman: Boy and girl*. Baltimore: Johns Hopkins Press, 1972.

Montagu, A. *Human heredity*. New York: New American Library, 1959.

Montgomery, R. L., Hinkle, S. W., & Enzie, R. F. Arbitrary norms and social change in high- and low-authoritarian societies. *Journal of Personality and Social Psychology*, 1976, *33*, 698–708.

Moody, K. The research on TV: A disturbing picture. *New York Times*, April 20, 1980, p. EDUC 17.

Moran, L. J. Personal and common components of cognitive dictionaries. *Psychological Reports*, 1977, *40*, 795–806.

Moreault, D., & Follingstad, D. R. Sexual fantasies of females as a function of sex guilt and experimental response cues. *Journal of Consulting and Clinical Psychology*, 1978, *46*, 1385–93.

Moreland, R. L., & Zajonc, R. B. A strong test of exposure effects. *Journal of Experimental Social Psychology*, 1976, *12*, 170–79.

Moreland, R. L., & Zajonc, R. B. Exposure effects may not depend on stimulus recognition. *Journal of Personality and Social Psychology*, 1979, *37*, 1085–1089.

Morgan, C. D., & Murray, H. A. Thematic Apperception Test. In H. A. Murray, *Explorations in personality*. (1938). New York: Science Editions, 1962.

Moriarty, T. Crime, commitment, and the responsive bystander: Two field experiments. *Journal of Personality and Social Psychology*, 1975, *31*, 370–76.

Morris, W. N., Worchel, S., Bois, J. L., Pearson, J. A., Rountree, C. A., Samaha, G. M., Wachtler, J., & Wright, S. L. Collective coping with stress: Group reactions to fear, anxiety, and ambiguity. *Journal of Personality and Social Psychology*, 1976, *33*, 674–79.

Morrow, L. Blacks on TV: A disturbing image. *Time*, 1978, *111* (13), 101–102.

Mosher, D. L. Measurement of guilt in females by self report inventories. *Journal of Consulting and Clinical Psychology*, 1968, *32*, 690–95.

Mosher, D. L. Sex guilt and sex myths in college men and women. *Journal of Sex Research*, 1979, *15*, 224–34.

Mosher, D. L., & Abramson, P. R. Subjective sexual arousal to films of masturbation. *Journal of Consulting and Clinical Psychology*, 1977, *45*, 796–807.

Mosher, D. L., & Cross, H. J. Sex guilt and premarital sexual experiences of college students. *Journal of Consulting and Clinical Psychology*, 1971, *36*, 27–32.

Mueller, C., & Donnerstein, E. The effects of humor-induced arousal upon aggressive behavior. *Journal of Research in Personality*, 1977, *11*, 73–82.

Mueller, E. F., & French, J. R. P., Jr. Uric acid and achievement. *Journal of Personality and Social Psychology*, 1974, *30*, 336–40.

Mulac, A., & Sherman, A. R. Behavioral assessment of speech anxiety. *Quarterly Journal of Speech*, 1974, *60*, 134–43.

Munsinger, H. The adopted child's IQ: A critical review. *Psychological Bulletin*, 1975, *82*, 623–59.

Murray, E. J. Sociotropic-learning approach to psychotherapy. In P. Worchel and D. Byrne (eds.), *Personality change*. New York: Wiley, 1964.

Murray, H. A. *Explorations in personality* (1938). New York: Science Editions, 1962.

Murray, H. A. What should psychologists do about psychoanalysis? *Journal of Abnormal and Social Psychology*, 1940, *34*, 150–75.

Murray, H. A. Preparations for the scaffold of a comprehensive system. In S. Koch (ed.), *Psychology: A study of a science*, vol. 3. New York: McGraw-Hill, 1959. Pp. 7–54.

Murray, J., & Feshbach, S. Let's not throw the baby out with the bathwater: The catharsis hypothesis revisited. *Journal of Personality*, 1978, *46*, 463–473.

Murstein, B. I. *Theory and research in projective techniques*. New York: Wiley, 1963.

Murstein, B. I., & Christy, P. Physical attractiveness and marriage adjustment in middle-aged couples. *Journal of Personality and Social Psychology*, 1976, *34*, 537–42.

Mussen, P. H., Conger, J. J., & Kagan, J. *Child development and personality*. New York: Harper & Row, 1974.

Myers, I. B. *The Myers-Briggs type indicator manual*. Princeton, N.J.: Educational Testing Service, 1962.

Mynatt, C., & Sherman, S. J. Responsibility attribution in groups and individuals: A direct test of the diffusion of responsibilities hypothesis. *Journal of Personality and Social Psychology*, 1975, *32*, 1111–18.

Nadler, E. B. Yielding, authoritarianism, and authoritarian ideology regarding groups. *Journal of Abnormal and Social Psychology*, 1959, *58*, 408–10.

Nahemow, L., & Lawton, M. P. Similarity and propinquity in friendship formation. *Journal of Personality and Social Psychology*, 1975, *32*, 205-13.

Nakazato, H., Inoue, T., & Tanaka, K. Personality similarity and interpersonal attraction—On the dimensions of extraversion and need. *Japanese Journal of Psychology*, 1975, *46*, 109-17.

Nance, J. *The gentle Tasaday.* New York: Harcourt Brace Jovanovich, 1975.

National Committee for Prevention of Child Abuse. *Child abuse hurts everybody.* Chicago, 1978.

Nei, M., & Roychoudhury, A. K. Gene differences between caucasian, Negro, and Japanese populations. *Science*, 1972, *177*, 434-36.

Newcomb, T. M. *The acquaintance process.* New York: Holt, Rinehart and Winston, 1961.

Newcomb, T. M., & Svehla, G. Intra-family relationships in attitudes. *Sociometry*, 1937, *1*, 180-205.

Newman, H. H., Freeman, F. N., & Holzinger, K. J. *Twins: A study of heredity and environment.* Chicago: University of Chicago Press, 1937.

Newtson, D., Engquist, G., & Bois, J. The objective basis of behavior units. *Journal of Personality and Social Psychology*, 1977, *35*, 847-62.

"New Yorkers watch murder in subway," *Lafayette Journal and Courier*, August 8, 1977.

Nezlek, J., & Brehm, J. W. Hostility as a function of the opportunity to counteraggress. *Journal of Personality*, 1975, *43*, 421-33.

Nicholls, J. G. Creativity in the person who will never produce anything original and useful: The concept of creativity as a normally distributed trait. *American Psychologist*, 1972, *27*, 717-27.

Nims, J. P. Imagery, shaping, and orgasm. *Journal of Sex and Marital Therapy.* 1975, *1*, 198-203.

Nisbett, R. E., Caputo, C., Legant, P., & Marecek, J. Behavior as seen by the actor and as seen by the observer. *Journal of Personality and Social Psychology*, 1973, *27*, 154-64.

Nisbett, R. E., & Schachter, S. Cognitive manipulation of pain. *Journal of Experimental Social Psychology*, 1966, *2*, 227-36.

Noonan, J. R., Barry, J. R., & Davis, H. C. Personality determinants in attitudes toward visible disability. *Journal of Personality*, 1970, *38*, 1-15.

Novaco, R. W. Treatment of chronic anger through cognitive and relaxation controls. *Journal of Consulting and Clinical Psychology*, 1976, *44*, 681.

Nydegger, C. N. Timing of fatherhood: Role perception and socialization. *Dissertation Abstracts International*, 1973, *34*, 5355-A.

Nygård, R. *Personality, situation, and persistence: A study with emphasis on achievement motivation.* Oslo, Norway: Universitetsforlaget, 1977.

Nygard, R., & Gjesme, T. Assessment of achievement motives: Comments and suggestions. *Scandinavian Journal of Educational Research*, 1973, *17*, 39-46.

"N.Y. newcomer's nightmare comes true on city street," *Indianapolis Star*, August 27, 1978.

Olweus, D. Aggression and peer acceptance in adolescent boys: Two short-term longitudinal studies of ratings. *Child Development*, 1977, *48*, 1301-1313.

Opton, E., Jr. A psychologist takes a closer look at the recent landmark *Larry P.* opinion. *APA Monitor*, 1979, *10* (12), 1, 4.

Osborne, R. T. Racial differences in mental growth and school achievement: A longitudinal study. *Psychological Reports*, 1960, *7*, 233-39.

Oskamp, S., & Mindick, B. Personality and attitudinal barriers to contraception. In D. Byrne and W. A. Fisher (eds.), *Adolescents, sex, and contraception.* New York: McGraw-Hill, 1980.

Owen, D. R. The 47, XYY male: A review. *Psychological Bulletin*, 1972, *78*, 209-33.

Owens, W. A., Jr. Age and mental abilities: A longitudinal study. *Genetic Psychology Monographs*, 1953, *48*, 3-54.

Pasamanick, B., & Knobloch, H. Early language behavior in Negro children and the testing of intelligence. *Journal of Abnormal and Social Psychology*, 1955, *50*, 401-2.

Passman, R. H., & Mulhern, R. K., Jr. Maternal punitiveness as affected by situational stress: An experimental analogue of child abuse. *Journal of Abnormal Psychology*, 1977, *86*, 565-69.

Patrick, A. W., & Zuckerman, M. An application of the state-trait concept to the need for achievement. *Journal of Research in Personality*, 1977, *11*, 459-465.

Pear, R. Ban is affirmed on homosexuals entering nation. *New York Times*, December 27, 1979, p. A16.

Pedersen, F. A., & Bell, R. Q. Sex differences in preschool children without histories of complications of pregnancy and delivery. *Developmental Psychology*, 1970, *3*, 10-15.

Peplau, L. A. Impact of fear of success and sex-role attitudes on women's competitive achievement. *Journal of Personality and Social Psychology*, 1976, *34*, 561-68. (a)

Peplau, L. A. Fear of success in dating couples. *Sex Roles*, 1976, *2*, 249-58. (b)

Perkins, K. A., & Reyher, J. Repression, psychopathology, and drive representation: An experimental hypnotic investigation of impulse inhibition. *American Journal of Clinical Hypnosis*, 1971, *13*, 249-58.

Perry, D. G., & Perry, L. C. Identification with film characters, covert aggressive verbalization, and reactions to film violence. *Journal of Research in Personality*, 1976, *10*, 399-409.

Pervin, L. A. A free-response description approach to the analysis of person–situation interaction. *Journal of Personality and Social Psychology*, 1976, *34*, 465-74.

Peterson, D. R. *The clinical study of social behavior.* Englewood Cliffs, N.J.: Prentice-Hall, 1968.

Petty, R. E., Harkins, S. G., Williams, K. D., & Latané, B. The effects of group size on cognitive effort and evaluation. *Personality and Social Psychology Bulletin,* 1977, *3,* 579–82.

Petty, R. E., Williams, K. D., Harkins, S. G., & Latané, B. Social inhibition of helping yourself: Bystander response to a cheeseburger. *Personality and Social Psychology Bulletin,* 1977, *3,* 575–78.

Phares, E. J. Locus of control. In H. London and J. E. Exner, Jr. (eds.), *Dimensions of personality.* New York: Wiley, 1978.

Phares, E. J., & Lamiell, J. T. Internal–external control, interpersonal judgments of others in need, and attribution of responsibility. *Journal of Personality,* 1975, *43,* 23–38.

Phillips, D. P. Motor vehicle fatalities increase just after publicized suicide stories. *Science,* 1977, *196,* 1464–65.

Phillips, D. P. Airplane accident fatalities increase just after newspaper stories about murder and suicide. *Science,* 1978, *201,* 748–750.

Piaget, J. *The moral judgment of the child.* Glencoe, Ill.: Free Press, 1948.

Piaget, J. Piaget's theory. In P. H. Mussen (ed.), *Carmichael's manual of child psychology.* New York: Wiley, 1970.

Piccione, A., & Veitch, R. The effect of false arousal feedback on attraction. Unpublished ms., Bowling Green State University, 1978.

Piliavin, J. A., & Piliavin, I. M. Effect of blood on reactions to a victim. *Journal of Personality and Social Psychology,* 1972, *23,* 353–61.

Piliavin, J. A., & Piliavin, I. M. The good Samaritan: Why *does* he help? In L. Wispé (ed.), *Positive forms of social behavior.* Cambridge, Mass.: Harvard University Press, 1976.

Pines, A., & Gal, R. The effect of food on test anxiety. *Journal of Applied Social Psychology,* 1977, *7,* 348–358.

Pines, M. Good Samaritans at age two? *Psychology Today,* June 1979, pp. 66–68, 70, 73–74.

Pisano, R., & Taylor, S. P. Reduction of physical aggression: The effects of four strategies. *Journal of Personality and Social Psychology,* 1971, *19,* 237–42.

Plemons, J. K., Willis, S. L., & Baltes, P. B. Modifiability of fluid intelligence in aging: A training approach. Unpublished ms., Pennsylvania State University, 1976.

Pomerantz, M., & Schultz, C. B. The reliability and validity of two objective measures of achievement motivation for adolescent females. *Educational and Psychological Measurement,* 1975, *35,* 379–86.

Post, A. L., Wittmaier, B. C., & Radin, M. E. Self-disclosure as a function of state and trait anxiety. *Journal of Consulting and Clinical Psychology,* 1978, *46,* 12–19.

Provence, S., & Lipton, R. C. *Infants in institutions.* New York: International Universities Press, 1962.

Puryear, G. R., & Mednick, M. S. Black militancy, affective attachment, and the fear of success in black college women. *Journal of Consulting and Clinical Psychology,* 1974, *42,* 263–66.

Quinn, R. P. Overeducation and jobs: Can the great training robbery be stopped? Paper presented at the meeting of the American Psychological Association, Chicago, August 1975.

Ramirez, M., III. Identification with Mexican family values and authoritarianism in Mexican-Americans. *Journal of Social Psychology,* 1967, *73,* 3–11.

Ray, J. J. Do authoritarians hold authoritarian attitudes? *Human Relations,* 1976, *29,* 307–325.

Raynor, J. O. Relationships between achievement-related motives, future orientations, and academic performance. *Journal of Personality and Social Psychology,* 1970, *15,* 28–33.

Raynor, J. O. Future orientation in the study of achievement motivation. In J. W. Atkinson and J. O. Raynor (eds.), *Motivation and achievement.* Washington, D.C.: Winston, 1974.

Raynor, J. O., & Rubin, I. S. Effects of achievement motivation and future orientation on level of performance. *Journal of Personality and Social Psychology,* 1971, *17,* 36–41.

Reich, C. A. *The greening of America.* New York: Random House, 1970.

Restak, R. The origins of violence. *Saturday Review,* 1974, *6* (10), 16–19.

Rheingold, H. F., Gewirtz, J. L., & Ross, H. W. Social conditioning of vocalizations in the infant. *Journal of Comparative and Physiological Psychology,* 1959, *51,* 68–73.

Richardson, S. K. The correlation of intelligence quotients of siblings of the same chronological age levels. *Journal of Juvenile Research,* 1936, *20,* 186–98.

Rim, Y. Values and attitudes. *Personality: An International Journal,* 1970, *1,* 243–50.

Ringuette, E. L. The stability of individual differences in behavior across experimental conflict situations. *Journal of Research in Personality,* 1976, *10,* 177–82.

Ripple, R. E., & May, F. B. Caution in comparing creativity and I.Q. *Psychological Reports,* 1962, *10,* 229–30.

Roberts, A. H., & Erikson, R. V. Delay of gratification, Porteus Maze Test performance, and behavioral adjustment in a delinquent group. *Journal of Abnormal Psychology,* 1968, *73,* 449–53.

Robinson, D. N. *The enlightened machine.* Encino, Calif.: Dickenson, 1973.

Robinson, P. The measurement of achievement motivation. Unpublished doctoral dissertation, Oxford University, 1961.

Rocha, R. F., & Rogers, R. W. Ares and Babbitt in the classroom: Effects of competition and reward on children's aggression. *Journal of Personality and Social Psychology*, 1976, *33*, 588–93.

Rogers, C. R. *Client-centered therapy.* Boston: Houghton Mifflin, 1951.

Rogers, C. R. Carl R. Rogers. In E. G. Boring and G. Lindzey (eds.), *A history of psychology in autobiography,* vol. 5., Englewood Cliffs, N.J.: Prentice-Hall, 1967, Pp. 341–84. (a)

Rogers, C. R. *The therapeutic relationship and its impact: A study of psychotherapy with schizophrenics.* Madison: University of Wisconsin Press, 1967. (b)

Rokeach, M. *The open and closed mind.* New York: Basic Books, 1960.

Rokeach, M. Authoritarianism scales and response bias: Comment on Peabody's paper. *Psychological Bulletin*, 1967, *67*, 349–55.

Rorschach, H. *Psychodiagnostics.* Berne: Hans Huber, 1921.

Rosen, B. C., & D'Andrade, R. The psychosocial origins of achievement motivation. *Sociometry*, 1959, *22*, 185–218.

Rosen, L. J., & Lee, C. L. Acute and chronic effects of alcohol use on organizational processes in memory. *Journal of Abnormal Psychology*, 1976, *85*, 309–17.

Rosenman, R. H., & Friedman, M. Neurogenic factors in pathogenesis of coronary heart disease. *Medical Clinics of North America*, 1974, *58*, 269–279.

Rosenthal, R., & Jacobson, L. *Pygmalion in the classroom.* New York: Holt, Rinehart and Winston, 1968.

Rosten, L. Marvels overlooked. *Saturday Review/World*, 1974, *1* (24), 54.

Rotter, J. B. *Social learning and clinical psychology.* Englewood Cliffs, N.J.: Prentice-Hall, 1954.

Rotter, J. B., & Hochreich, D. J. *Personality.* Glenview, Ill.: Scott, Foresman, 1975.

Rovee-Collier, C. K., Sullivan, M. W., Enright, M., Lucas, D., & Fagen, J. W. Reactivation of infant memory. *Science*, 1980, *208*, 1159–1161.

Royce, J. R. Toward a viable theory of individual differences. *Journal of Personality and Social Psychology*, 1979, *37*, 1927–1931.

Rubin, R. A., & Balow, B. Measures of infant development and socioeconomic status as predictors of later intelligence and school achievement. *Developmental Psychology*, 1979, *15*, 225–227.

Rubin, Z. *Liking and loving: An invitation to social psychology.* New York: Holt, Rinehart and Winston, 1973.

Rubin, Z. From liking to loving: Patterns of attraction in dating relationships. In T. L. Huston (ed.), *Foundations of interpersonal attraction.* New York: Academic Press, 1974.

Rubin, Z., & Peplau, A. Belief in a just world and reactions to another's lot: A study of participants in the national draft lottery. *Journal of Social Issues*, 1973, *29*, 73–93.

Rudin, S. A. National motives predict psychogenic death rates 25 years later. *Science*, 1968, *160*, 901–3.

Ruff, C. F., Templer, D. I., & Ayers, J. L. The intelligence of rapists. *Archives of Sexual Behavior*, 1976, *5*, 327–29.

Rumbaugh, D. M. (ed.). *Language learning by a chimpanzee: The LANA project.* New York: Academic Press, 1976.

Runyan, W. McK. The life course as a theoretical orientation: Sequences of person-situation interaction. *Journal of Personality*, 1978, *46*, 569–593.

Rushton, J. P. Generosity in children: Immediate and long-term effects of modeling, preaching, and moral judgment. *Journal of Personality and Social Psychology*, 1975, *31*, 459–66.

Rushton, J. P., & Campbell, A. C. Modeling, vicarious reinforcement and extraversion on blood donating in adults: Immediate and long-term effects. *European Journal of Social Psychology*, 1977, *7*, 297–306.

Rushton, J. P., & Endler, N. S. Person by situation interactions in academic achievement. *Journal of Personality*, 1977, *45*, 297–309.

Rushton, J. P., & Teachmen, G. The effects of positive reinforcement, attributions, and punishment on model induced altruism in children. *Personality and Social Psychology Bulletin*, 1978, *4*, 322–25.

Rushton, J. P., & Wiener, J. Altruism and cognitive development in children. *British Journal of Social and Clinical Psychology*, 1975.

Ryan, V. L., Krall, C. A., & Hodges, W. F. Self-concept change in behavior modification. *Journal of Consulting and Clinical Psychology*, 1976, *44*, 638–45.

Rychlak, J. F. Personality theory: Its nature, past, present and—future? *Personality and Social Psychology Bulletin*, 1976, *2*, 213–28.

Ryckman, R. M. *Theories of personality.* New York: Van Nostrand, 1978.

Sackett, G. P. Effects of rearing conditions upon the behavior of rhesus monkeys (*Macaca mulatta*). *Child Development*, 1965, *36*, 855–68.

Sadd, S., Miller, F. D., & Zeitz, B. Sex roles and achievement conflicts. *Personality and Social Psychology Bulletin*, 1979, *5*, 352–355.

Saegert, S. C., Swap, W., & Zajonc, R. B. Exposure, context, and interpersonal attraction. *Journal of Personality and Social Psychology*, 1973, *25*, 234–42.

Sagan, C. *The dragons of Eden: Speculations on the evolution of human intelligence.* New York: Random House, 1977.

Saghir, M. T., & Robins, E. *Male and female homosexuality: A comprehensive investigation.* Baltimore: Williams and Wilkins, 1973.

Sales, S. M. Threat as a factor in authoritarianism: An analysis of archival data. *Journal of Personality and Social Psychology*, 1973, *28*, 44–57.

Salili, F., Maehr, M. L., & Gillmore, G. Achievement and morality: A cross-cultural analysis of causal attribution and evaluation. *Journal of Personality and Social Psychology*, 1976, *33*, 327–37.

Sampson, E. E. Psychology and the American ideal.

Journal of Personality and Social Psychology, 1977, *35,* 767–782.

Samuel, W. Response to Bill of Rights paraphrases as influenced by the hip or straight attire of the opinion solicitor. *Journal of Applied Social Psychology,* 1972, *2,* 47–62.

Samuelson, F., & Yates, J. F. Acquiescence and the F Scale: Old assumptions and new data. *Psychological Bulletin,* 1967, *68,* 91–103.

Sanford, N. The approach of the authoritarian personality. In J. L. McCary (ed.), *Psychology of personality: Six modern approaches.* New York: Logos, 1956. Pp. 253–319.

Sanford, N. Authoritarian personality in contemporary perspective. In J. Knutson (ed.), *Handbook of political psychology.* San Francisco: Jossey-Bass, 1973.

Sappington, A., & Grizzard, R. Self-discrimination responses in black school children. *Journal of Personality and Social Psychology,* 1975, *31,* 224–31.

Sarason, I. G. The Test Anxiety Scale: Concept and research. In C. D. Spielberger and I. G. Sarason (eds.), *Stress and anxiety,* vol. 5. New York: Halsted-Wiley, 1980, in press.

Sarason, I. G. Test anxiety and the self-disclosing coping model. *Journal of Consulting and Clinical Psychology,* 1978, *46,* 102–109.

Sarason, I. G., Smith, R. E., & Diener, E. Personality research: Components of variance attributable to the person and the situation. *Journal of Personality and Social Psychology,* 1980, in press.

Sarason, I. G., & Stoops, R. Test anxiety and the passage of time. *Journal of Consulting and Clinical Psychology,* 1978, *46,* 102–109.

Satz, P., Richard, W., & Daniels, A. The alteration of intellectual performance after lateralized brain-injury in man. *Psychonomic Science,* 1967, *7,* 369–70.

Scarpetti, W. L. Autonomic concomitant of aggressive behavior in repressors and sensitizers: A social learning approach. *Journal of Personality and Social Psychology,* 1974, *30,* 772–781.

Scarr, S., & Weinberg, R. A. IQ test performance of black children adopted by white families. *American Psychologist,* 1976, *31,* 726–39.

Scarr-Salapatek, S. Unknowns in the IQ equation. *Science,* 1971, *174,* 1223–28. (a)

Scarr-Salapatek, S. Race, social class, and IQ. *Science,* 1971, *174,* 1285–95. (b)

Schachter, S. Deviation, rejection, and communication. *Journal of Abnormal and Social Psychology,* 1951, *46,* 190–207.

Schachter, S. *The psychology of affiliation.* Stanford, Calif.: Stanford University Press, 1959.

Schachter, S. The interaction of cognitive and physiological determinants of emotional state. In L. Berkowitz (ed.), *Advances in experimental social psychology.* New York: Academic Press, 1964.

Schafer, R. *A new language for psychoanalysis.* New Haven, Conn.: Yale University Press, 1976.

Schaie, K. W. Translations in gerontology—From lab to life: Intellectual functioning. *American Psychologist,* 1974, *29,* 802–7.

Schaie, K. W., & Parham, I. A. Social responsibility in adulthood: Ontogenetic and sociocultural change. *Journal of Personality and Social Psychology,* 1974, *30,* 483–92.

Schaie, K. W., & Parham, I. A. Stability of adult personality traits: Fact or fable? *Journal of Personality and Social Psychology,* 1976, *34,* 146–58.

Schiff, M., Duyme, M., Dumaret, A., Stewart, J., Tomkiewicz, S., & Feingold, J. Intellectual status of working-class children adopted early into upper-middle-class families. *Science,* 1978, *200,* 1503–1504.

Schill, T., & Chapin, J. Sex guilt and males' preference for reading erotic magazines. *Journal of Consulting and Clinical Psychology,* 1972, *39,* 516.

Schmidt, G. Male–female differences in sexual arousal and behavior during and after exposure to sexually explicit stimuli. *Archives of Sexual Behavior,* 1975, *4,* 353–64.

Schmidt, G., Sigusch, V., & Schäfer, S. Responses to reading erotic stories: Male–female differences. *Archives of Sexual Behavior,* 1973, *2,* 181–99.

Schneider, D. J., & Turkat, D. Self-presentation following success or failure: Defensive self-esteem models. *Journal of Personality,* 1975, *43,* 127–35.

Schrauger, J. S., & Terbovic, M. L. Self-evaluation and assessments of performance by self and others. *Journal of Consulting and Clinical Psychology,* 1976, *44,* 564–72.

Schultz, C. B., & Pomerantz, M. Some problems in the application of achievement motivation to education: The assessment of motive to succeed and probability of success. *Journal of Educational Psychology,* 1974, *66,* 599–608.

Schultz, C. B., & Pomerantz, M. Achievement motivation, locus of control, and academic achievement behavior. *Journal of Personality,* 1976, *44,* 38–51.

Schuster, E., & Elderton, E. M. The inheritance of physical characters. *Biometrika,* 1906, *5,* 460–69.

Schwartz, S. Effects of sex guilt and sexual arousal on the retention of birth control information. *Journal of Consulting and Clinical Psychology,* 1973, *41,* 61–64.

Schwartzman, A. E., Douglas, V. I., & Muir, W. R. Intellectual loss in schizophrenia: Part II. *Canadian Journal of Psychology,* 1962, *16,* 161–68.

Schweder, R. A. How relevant is an individual difference theory of personality? *Journal of Personality,* 1975, *43,* 455–84.

Sears, R. R. Sources of life satisfactions of the Terman gifted men. *American Psychologist,* 1977, *32,* 119–28.

Sears, R. R., Maccoby, E. E., & Levin, H. *Patterns of child rearing.* New York: Harper & Row, 1957.

Seeley, T. T., Abramson, P. R., Perry, L. B., Rothblatt, B. S., & Seeley, D. M. Thermographic measurement of sexual arousal: A methodological note. *Archives of Sexual Behavior*, 1980, *9* (2), 77–85.

Segal, M. W. Alphabet and attraction: An unobtrusive measure of the effect of propinquity in a field setting. *Journal of Personality and Social Psychology*, 1974, *30*, 654–57.

Shaffer, L. S. The Golden Fleece: Anti-intellectualism and social science. *American Psychologist*, 1977, *32*, 814–823.

Shapley, D. California court is forum for latest round in IQ debate. *Science*, 1978, *201*, 1106–1109.

Shattuck, R. *The forbidden experiment: The story of the wild boy of Aveyron.* New York: Farrar, Strauss, & Giroux, 1980.

Shedletsky, R., & Endler, N. S. Anxiety: The state–trait model and the interaction model. *Journal of Personality*, 1974, *42*, 511–27.

Sheldon, W. H., Lewis, N. D. C., & Tenney, A. M. Psychotic patterns and physical constitution: A thirty-year follow-up of thirty-eight-hundred psychiatric patients in New York State. In D. V. Siva Sanker (ed.), *Schizophrenia: Current concepts and research.* New York: PJD Publications, 1969.

Sheldon, W. H., Stevens, S. S., & Tucker, W. B. *The varieties of human physique: An introduction to constitutional psychology.* Darien, Conn.: Hafner, 1970.

Sherman, A. R., Mulac, A., & McCann, M. J. Synergistic effect of self-relaxation and rehearsal feedback in the treatment of subjective and behavioral dimensions of speech anxiety. *Journal of Consulting and Clinical Psychology*, 1974, *42*, 819–27.

Sherwood, J. J. Authoritarianism, moral realism, and President Kennedy's death. *British Journal of Social and Clinical Psychology*, 1966, *5*, 264–69.

Sherwood, J. J., & Nataupsky, M. Predicting the conclusion of Negro-white intelligence research from biographical characteristics of the investigator. *Journal of Personality and Social Psychology*, 1968, *8*, 53–58.

Shipley, R. H., Butt, J. H., Horwitz, B., & Farbry, J. E. Preparation for a stressful medical procedure: Effect of amount of stimulus preexposure and coping style. *Journal of Consulting and Clinical Psychology*, 1978, *46*, 499–507.

Shipley, T. E., & Veroff, J. A projective measure of need for affiliation. *Journal of Experimental Psychology*, 1952, *43*, 349–56.

Shope, G. L., Hedrick, T. E., & Green, R. G. Physical/verbal aggression: Sex differences in style. *Journal of Personality*, 1978, *46*, 23–42.

"Shoplifting loss $7 billion a year—$200 a person." *The Indianapolis Star*, March 4, 1979.

Shortell, J. R., & Biller, H. B. Aggression in children as a function of sex of subject and sex of opponent. *Development Psychology*, 1970, *3*, 143–44.

Shotland, R. L., & Huston, T. L. Emergencies: What are they and do they influence bystanders to intervene? *Journal of Personality and Social Psychology*, 1979, *37*, 1822–34.

Shotland, R. L., & Straw, M. K. Bystander response to an assault: When a man attacks a woman. *Journal of Personality and Social Psychology*, 1976, *34*, 990–99.

Shuey, A. M. *The testing of Negro intelligence.* Lynchburg, Va.: J. P. Bell, 1958.

Shuey, A. M. *The testing of Negro intelligence* (2nd ed.). New York: Social Science Press, 1966.

Shuntich, R. J. Some effects of attitudinal similarity and exposure on attraction and aggression. *Journal of Research in Personality*, 1976, *10*, 155–65.

Shuntich, R. J., & Taylor, S. P. The effects of alcohol on human physical aggression. *Journal of Experimental Research in Personality*, 1972, *6*, 34–38.

Sigall, H., & Landy, D. Radiating beauty: Effects of having a physically attractive partner on person perception. *Journal of Personality and Social Psychology*, 1973, *28*, 218–24.

Silverman, L. H. Psychoanalytic theory: "The reports of my death are greatly exaggerated." *American Psychologist*, 1976, *31*, 621–37.

Simonton, D. K. Biographical determinants of achieved eminence: A multivariate approach to the Cox data. *Journal of Personality and Social Psychology*, 1976, *33*, 218–26.

Simpson, M. Authoritarianism and education: A comparative approach. *Sociometry*, 1972, *35*, 223–34.

Singer, D. L. Aggression arousal, hostile humor, and catharsis. *Journal of Personality and Social Psychology Monograph Supplement*, 1968, *8*, 1–14.

Singer, J. L. *The child's world of make-believe: Experimental studies of imaginative play.* New York: Academic Press, 1973.

Singh, R. Reinforcement and attraction: Specifying the effects of affective states. *Journal of Research in Personality*, 1974, *8*, 294–305.

Sintchak, G. H., & Geer, J. H. A vaginal plethysmograph system. *Psychophysiology*, 1976, *12*, 113–15.

Sirota, A. D., Schwartz, G. E., & Shapiro, D. Voluntary control of human heart rate: Effect on reaction to aversive stimulation. *Journal of Abnormal Psychology*, 1974, *83*, 261–67.

Sirota, A. D., Schwartz, G. E., & Shapiro, D. Voluntary control of human heart rate: Effect on reaction to aversive stimulation: A replication and extension. *Journal of Abnormal Psychology*, 1976, *85*, 473–77.

Skinner, B. F. *Walden two.* New York: Macmillan, 1948. (a)

Skinner, B. F. "Superstition" in the pigeon. *Journal of Experimental Psychology*, 1948, *38*, 168–172. (b)

Skinner, B. F. *Beyond freedom and dignity.* New York: Knopf, 1971.

Skinner, B. F. *Science and human behavior.* New York: Macmillan, 1953.

Skinner, B. F. *About behaviorism.* New York: Knopf, 1974.

Skodak, M., & Skeels, H. M. A final follow-up of one hundred adopted children. *Journal of Genetic Psychology*, 1949, *75*, 85–125.

Slutsky, J. M., & Allen, G. J. Influence of contextual cues on the efficacy of desensitization and a credible placebo in alleviating public speaking anxiety. *Journal of Consulting and Clinical Psychology*, 1978, *46*, 119–125.

Smith, A. J. Similarity of values and its relation to acceptance and the projection of similarity. *Journal of Psychology*, 1957, *43*, 251–60.

Smith, C. P. (ed.). *Achievement-related motives in children*. New York: Russell Sage, 1969.

Smith, R. E., Ascough, J. C., Ettinger, R. F., & Nelson, D. A. Humor, anxiety, and task performance. *Journal of Personality and Social Psychology*, 1971, *19*, 243–46.

Smith, R. E., Keating, J. P., Hester, R. K., & Mitchell, H. E. Role and justice considerations in the attribution of responsibility to a rape victim. *Journal of Research in Personality*, 1976, *10*, 346–57.

Smith, R. E., Meadow, B. L., & Sisk, T. K. Attitude similarity, interpersonal attraction, and evaluative social perception. *Psychonomic Science*, 1970, *18*, 226–27.

Smith, R. E., Wheeler, G., & Diener, E. Faith without works: Jesus people, resistance to temptation, and altruism. *Journal of Applied Social Psychology*, 1975, *5*, 320–30.

Snow, B. Level of aspiration in coronary prone and noncoronary prone adults. *Personality and Social Psychology Bulletin*, 1978, *4*, 416–419.

Snyder, C. R. Why horoscopes are true: The effects of specificity on acceptance of astrological interpretations. *Journal of Clinical Psychology*, 1974, *30*, 577–80.

Snyder, C. R., & Larson, G. R. A further look at student acceptance of general personality interpretations. *Journal of Consulting and Clinical Psychology*, 1972, *38*, 384–88.

Snyder, C. R., Shenkel, R. J., & Lowery, C. R. Acceptance of personality interpretations: The "Barnum effect" and beyond. *Journal of Consulting and Clinical Psychology*, 1977, *45*, 104–14.

Snyder, M., & Swann, W. B., Jr. Behavioral confirmation in social interaction: From social perception to social reality. *Journal of Experimental Social Psychology*, 1978, *14*, 148–162.

Solomon, B. Emotional stress under air raids. *American Journal of Psychiatry*, 1942, *7*, 142–49.

Solomon, H., & Solomon, L. Z. Effects of anonymity on helping in emergency situations. Paper presented at the meeting of the Eastern Psychological Association, Washington, D.C., March 1978.

Solomon, L. Z., Solomon, H., & Stone, R. Helping as a function of number of bystanders and ambiguity of emergency. *Personality and Social Psychology Bulletin*, 1978, *4*, 318–21.

Sommerschield, H., & Reyher, J. Posthypnotic conflict, repression, and psychopathology. *Journal of Abnormal Psychology*, 1973, *82*, 278–90.

Sorrentino, R. M., & Short, J.-A. C. The case of the mysterious moderates: Why motives sometimes fail to predict behavior. *Journal of Personality and Social Psychology*, 1977, *35*, 478–484.

Spence, J. A., & Spence, K. W. The motivational components of manifest anxiety: Drive and drive stimuli. In C. D. Spielberger (ed.), *Anxiety and behavior*. New York: Academic Press, 1966.

Spence, J. T. The TAT and attitudes toward achievement in women: A new look at the motive to avoid success and a new method of measurement. *Journal of Consulting and Clinical Psychology*, 1974, *42*, 427–37.

Spence, K. W. Learning and performance in eyelid conditioning as a function of the intensity of the UCS. *Journal of Experimental Psychology*, 1953, *45*, 57–63.

Spence, K. W. A theory of emotionally based drive (D) and its relation to performance in simple learning situations. *American Psychologist*, 1958, *13*, 131–41.

Spence, K. W. The empirical basis and theoretical structure of psychology. In K. W. Spence, *Behavior theory and learning*. Englewood Cliffs, N.J.: Prentice-Hall, 1960. Pp. 71–88.

Spence, K. W. Anxiety (drive) level and performance in eyelid conditioning. *Psychological Bulletin*, 1964, *61*, 129–39.

Spence, K. W., Farber, I. E., & McFann, H. H. The relation of anxiety (drive) level to performance in competitional and noncompetitional paired-associates learning. *Journal of Experimental Psychology*, 1956, *52*, 296–305.

Spence, K. W., & Taylor, J. A. Anxiety and strength of the UCS as determiners of the amount of eyelid conditioning. *Journal of Experimental Psychology*, 1951, *42*, 183–88.

Spence, K. W., & Townsend, S. A comparative study of groups of high and low intelligence in learning a maze. *Journal of General Psychology*, 1930, *3*, 113–30.

Spielberger, C. D. The effects of anxiety on complex learning and academic achievement. In C. D. Spielberger (ed.), *Anxiety and behavior*. New York: Academic Press, 1966.

Spielberger, C. D. Anxiety as an emotional state. In C. D. Spielberger (ed.), *Anxiety: Current trends in theory and research*, vol. 1. New York: Academic Press, 1972.

Spielberger, C. D., Auerbach, S. M., Wadsworth, A. P., Dunn, T. M., & Taulbee, E. S. Emotional reactions to surgery. *Journal of Consulting and Clinical Psychology*, 1973, *40*, 33–38.

Spielberger, C. D., Gorsuch, R. L., & Lushene, R. E. *Manual for the State-Trait Anxiety Inventory*. Palo Alto, Calif.: Consulting Psychologists Press, 1970.

Spielberger, C. D., & Katzenmeyer, W. G. Manifest anxiety, intelligence, and college grades. *Journal of Consulting Psychology*, 1959, *23*, 278.

Spielberger, C. D., & Smith, L. H. Anxiety (drive), stress, and serial-position effects in serial-verbal learning. *Journal of Experimental Psychology*, 1966, *72*, 589–95.

Spranger, E. *Types of men* (trans. P. J. W. Pigors). Halle: Max Niemeyer Verlag, 1928.

Stagner, R. Traits are relevant: Theoretical analysis and empirical evidence. In N. S. Endler and D. Magnusson (eds.), *Interactional psychology and personality*. Washington, D.C.: Hemisphere, 1976.

Stallings, F. H. A study of the immediate effects of integration on scholastic achievement in the Louisville public schools. *Journal of Negro Education*, 1959, *28*, 439–44.

Stang, D. J. Effects of "mere exposure" on learning and affect. *Journal of Personality and Social Psychology*, 1975, *31*, 7–12.

Stang, D. J., & Crandall, R. Familiarity and liking. In T. M. Steinfatt (ed.), *Readings in human communication*. Indianapolis: Bobbs-Merrill, 1977.

Staub, E. *Positive social behavior and morality*, vol. 2, *Socialization and development*. New York: Academic Press, 1978.

Steigleder, M. K., Weiss, R. F., Balling, S. S., Wenninger, V. L., & Lombardo, J. P. Drive-like motivational properties of competitive behavior. *Journal of Personality and Social Psychology*, 1980, *38*, 93–104.

Steigleder, M. K., Weiss, R. F., Cramer, R. E., & Feinberg, R. A. Motivating and reinforcing functions of competitive behavior. *Journal of Personality and Social Psychology*, 1978, *36*, 1291–1301.

Steinmetz, S. K. The use of force for resolving family conflict: The training ground for abuse. *The Family Coordinator*, 1977, *26*, 19–26.

Stephenson, W. *The study of behavior. Q-technique and its methodology*. Chicago: University of Chicago Press, 1953.

Sternberg, R. J. The nature of mental abilities. *American Psychologist*, 1979, *34*, 214–230.

Stewart, F. A. A sociometric study of influence in Southtown. *Sociometry*, 1947, *10*, 11–31.

Stewart, N. A.G.C.T. scores of army personnel grouped by occupation. *Occupations*, 1947, *26*, 5–41.

Story, M. D. A longitudinal study of the effects of a university human sexuality course on sexual attitudes. *Journal of Sex Research*, 1979, *15*, 184–204.

Strickland, B. R. *Locus of control and health related behaviors*. Paper presented at the XV Interamerican Congress of Psychology, Bogota, Colombia, December 1974.

Stumphauzer, J. S. Increased delay of gratification in young prison inmates through imitation of high-delay peer models. *Journal of Personality and Social Psychology*, 1972, *21*, 10–17.

Sue, D. Erotic fantasies of college students during intercourse. *Journal of Sex Research*, 1979, *15*, 299–305.

Suinn, R. M. How to break the vicious cycle of stress. *Psychology Today*, 1976, *10* (7), 59–60.

Sullivan, H. S. *Conceptions of modern psychiatry*. Washington, D.C.: William Alanson White Psychiatric Foundation, 1947.

Sullivan, H. S. Tensions interpersonal and international: A psychiatrist's view. In H. Cantril (ed.), *Tensions that cause war*. Urbana: University of Illinois Press, 1950. Pp. 79–138.

Sulloway, F. J. *Freud, biologist of the mind: Beyond the psychoanalytic legend*. New York: Basic Books, 1980.

Suls, J., & Kalle, R. J. Children's moral judgments as a function of intention, damage, and an actor's physical harm. *Developmental Psychology*, 1979, *15*, 93–94.

Swanson, E. O. The relation of vocabulary test-retest gains to amount of college attendance after a 24-year period. *American Psychologist*, 1952, *7*, 368.

Swap, W. C. Interpersonal attraction and repeated exposure to rewarders and punishers. *Personality and Social Psychology Bulletin*, 1977, *3*, 248–251.

Swart, C., & Berkowitz, L. Effects of a stimulus associated with a victim's pain on later aggression. *Journal of Personality and Social Psychology*, 1976, *33*, 623–31.

Swertlow, F. S. Barbara Walters and ABC: Which is she—journalist or Cher? *TV Guide*, 1977, *25* (7), 15–16, 18.

Szasz, T. *Schizophrenia: The sacred symbol of psychiatry*. New York: Basic Books, 1976.

Takooshian, H., Haber, S., & Lucido, D. J. Who wouldn't help a lost child? You, maybe. *Psychology Today*, February 1977, pp. 66–68.

Tanner, J. M. Physical growth. In P. H. Mussen (ed.), *Carmichael's manual of child psychology*, vol. 1, New York: Wiley, 1970.

Taylor, J. A. The relationship of anxiety to the conditioned eyelid response. *Journal of Experimental Psychology*, 1951, *41*, 81–92.

Taylor, J. A. A personality scale of manifest anxiety. *Journal of Abnormal and Social Psychology*, 1953, *48*, 285–90.

Taylor, J. A. Drive theory and manifest anxiety. *Psychological Bulletin*, 1956, *53*, 303–20.

Taylor, S. P., & Epstein, S. Aggression as a function of the interaction of the sex of the aggressor and the sex of the victim. *Journal of Personality*, 1967, *35*, 474–86.

Taylor, S. P., & Gammon, C. B. Effects of type and dose of alcohol on human physical aggression. *Journal of Personality and Social Psychology*, 1975, *32*, 169–75.

Taylor, S. P., Gammon, C. B., & Capasso, D. R. Aggression as a function of the interaction of alcohol and threat. *Journal of Personality and Social Psychology*, 1976, *34*, 938–41.

Taylor, S. P., & Pisano, R. Physical aggression as a function of frustration and physical attack. *Journal of Social Psychology*, 1971, *84*, 261–67.

Taylor, S. P., Vardaris, R. M., Rawtich, A. B., Gammon, C. B., Cranston, J. W., & Lubetkin, A. I. The effects of alcohol and delta-9-tetrahydrocannabinol on human physical aggression. *Aggressive Behavior*, 1976, *2*, 153–61.

Teevan, R. C., & McGhee, P. E. Childhood development of fear of failure motivation. *Journal of Personality and Social Psychology,* 1972, *21,* 345–48.

Teichman, Y. Predisposition for anxiety and affiliation. *Journal of Personality and Social Psychology,* 1974, *29,* 405–10.

Telfer, M. A., Baker, D., Clark, G. R., & Richardson, C. E. Incidence of gross chromosomal errors among tall criminal American males. *Science,* 1968, *159,* 1249–50.

Temerlin, M. K. *Lucy: Growing up human, a chimpanzee daughter in a psychotherapist's family.* Palo Alto, Calif.: Science and Behavior Books, 1975.

Terman, L. M. *The measurement of intelligence.* Boston: Houghton Mifflin, 1916.

Terman, L. M. (ed.), et al. *Mental and physical traits of a thousand gifted children,* vol. 1. Stanford, Calif.: Stanford University Press, 1925.

Terman, L. M. Trials to psychology. In C. Murchison (ed.), *A history of psychology in autobiography,* vol. 2. Worchester, Mass.: Clark University Press, 1932.

Terman, L. M., & Buttenwieser, P. Personality factors in marital compatibility: I. *Journal of Social Psychology,* 1935, *6,* 143–71. (a)

Terman, L. M., & Buttenwieser, P. Personality factors in marital compatibility: II. *Journal of Social Psychology,* 1935, *6,* 267–89. (b)

Terman, L. M., & Merrill, M. A. *Measuring intelligence.* Boston: Houghton Mifflin, 1937.

Terman, L. M., & Merrill, M. A. *Stanford-Binet intelligence scale.* Boston: Houghton Mifflin, 1960.

Terman, L. M., & Oden, M. H. *The gifted child grows up.* In L. M. Terman (ed.), *Genetic studies of genius,* vol. 4. Stanford, Calif.: Stanford University Press, 1947.

Terman, L. M., & Oden, M. H. *The gifted group at mid-life: Thirty-five years' follow-up of the superior child.* In L. M. Terman (ed.), *Genetic studies of genius,* vol. 5. Stanford, Calif.: Stanford University Press, 1959.

Terrace, H. S. How Nim Chimpsky changed my mind. *Psychology Today,* 1979, *13* (6), 67–68, 71–72, 75–76.

Terrace, H. S., Petitto, L. A., Sanders, R. J., & Bever, T. G. Can an ape create a sentence? *Science,* 1979, *206,* 891–902.

Tesser, A., & Paulhus, D. L. Toward a causal model of love. *Journal of Personality and Social Psychology,* 1976, *34,* 1095–1105.

Thelen, M. H., Dollinger, S. J., & Roberts, M. C. On being imitated: Its effects on attraction and reciprocal imitation. *Journal of Personality and Social Psychology,* 1975, *31,* 467–72.

Thomas, K. The rise of the fork. *New York Review of Books,* 1978, *25* (3), 28–31.

Thomas, M. H., Horton, R. W., Lippincott, E. C., & Drabman, R. S. Desensitization to portrayals of real-life aggression as a function of exposure to television violence. *Journal of Personality and Social Psychology,* 1977, *35,* 450–58.

Thompson, R. J., Jr., & Kolstoe, R. H. Physical aggression as a function of strength of frustration and instrumentality of aggression. *Journal of Research in Personality,* 1974, *7,* 314–23.

Thorndike, E. L., & Woodyard, E. Differences within and between communities in the intelligence of children. *Journal of Educational Psychology,* 1942, *33,* 641–56.

Thorpe, J. G. An investigation into some correlates of sociometric status within school classes. *Sociometry,* 1955, *18,* 49–61.

Thurman, C., Baron, A., & Klein, R. *Journal of College Student Personnel,* 1979, *20,* 546–550.

Tidd, K. L., & Lockard, J. S. Monetary significance of the affiliative smile: A case for reciprocal altruism. *Bulletin of the Psychonomic Society,* 1978, *11,* 344–46.

Tims, A. R., Jr., Swart, C., & Kidd, R. F. Factors affecting pre-decisional communication behavior after helping requests. *Human Communication Research,* 1976, *2,* 271–80.

Townes, C. H. Quantum electronics, and surprise in development of technology: The problem of research planning. *Science,* 1968, *159,* 699–703.

Trehub, S. E., & Rabinovitch, M. S. Auditory-linguistic sensitivity in early infancy. *Developmental Psychology,* 1972, *6,* 74–77.

Trent, R. D. The relationship of anxiety to popularity and rejection among institutionalized delinquent boys. *Child Development,* 1957, *28,* 379–84.

Tresemer, D. W. *Fear of success.* New York: Plenum, 1977.

Tribich, D., & Messer, S. Psychoanalytic character type and status of authority as determiners of suggestibility. *Journal of Consulting and Clinical Psychology,* 1974, *42,* 842–48.

Trippett, F. Science: No longer a sacred cow. *Time,* March 7, 1977, 72–73.

Tryon, R. C. Genetic differences in maze-learning ability in rats. *Thirty-ninth Yearbook of National Social Studies Education,* 1940, Pt. 1. Pp. 111–19.

Tryon, R. C. Psychology in flux: The academic-professional bipolarity. *American Psychologist,* 1963, *18,* 134–43.

Tucker, I. F. *Adjustment, models and mechanisms.* New York: Academic Press, 1970.

Tudor, T. G., & Holmes, D. S. Differential recall of successes and failures: Its relationship to defensiveness, achievement motivation, and anxiety. *Journal of Research in Personality,* 1973, *7,* 208–24.

Turner, C. B., & Fiske, D. W. Item quality and appropriateness of response processes. *Educational and Psychological Measurement,* 1968, *28,* 297–315.

Turner, C. W., & Layton, J. F. Verbal imagery and connotation as memory-induced mediators of aggressive behavior. *Journal of Personality and Social Psychology,* 1976, *33,* 755–63.

Turner, C. W., Layton, J. F., & Simons, L. S. Naturalistic studies of aggressive behavior: Aggressive stimuli, victim visibility, and horn honking. *Journal of Personality and Social Psychology*, 1975, *31*, 1098–1107.

Turner, J. H. Entrepreneurial environments and the emergence of achievement motivation in adolescent males. *Sociometry*, 1970, *33*, 147–65.

Turner, R. H., & Vanderlippe, R. H. Self-ideal congruence as an index of adjustment. *Journal of Abnormal and Social Psychology*, 1958, *57*, 202–6.

Tyler, L. E. *The psychology of human differences.* Englewood Cliffs, N.J.: Prentice-Hall, 1956.

Udry, J. R. *The social context of marriage.* New York: Harper & Row, 1971.

Ulrich, R. E. Pain as a cause of aggression. *American Zoologist*, 1966, *6*, 643–62.

Uranowitz, S. W. Helping and self-attributions: A field experiment. *Journal of Personality and Social Psychology*, 1975, *31*, 852–54.

Vance, F. L., & MacPhail, S. L. APA membership trends and fields of specialization of psychologists earning doctoral degrees between 1959 and 1962. *American Psychologist*, 1964, *19*, 654–58.

Vanderbeck, D. J. A construct validity study of the *O-H* (Overcontrolled Hostility) Scale of the MMPI, utilizing a social learning approach to the catharsis effect. Unpublished doctoral dissertation, Florida State University, 1972.

Varela, J. A. Social technology. *American Psychologist*, 1977, *32*, 914–923.

Vassiliou, V., Georgas, J. G., & Vassiliou, G. Variations in manifest anxiety due to sex, age, and education. *Journal of Personality and Social Psychology*, 1967, *6*, 194–97.

Veitch, R., & Griffitt, W. Good news, bad news: Affective and interpersonal effects. *Journal of Applied Social Psychology*, 1976, *6*, 69–75.

Vernon, P. E. *Intelligence and cultural environment.* London: Methuen, 1969.

Vernon, P. E. Genes, "G" and Jensen. *Contemporary Psychology*, 1970, *15*, 161–63.

Videback, R. Self-conception and the reactions of others. *Sociometry*, 1960, *23*, 351–59.

von Hoffman, N. Down the down staircase. *Penthouse*, 1977, *9* (2), 51–52.

Vore, D. A., & Ottinger, D. R. Maternal food restriction: Effects on offspring development, learning, and a program of therapy. *Developmental Psychology*, 1970, *3*, 337–42.

Wade, N. IQ and heredity: Suspicion of fraud beclouds classic experiment. *Science*, 1976, *194*, 916–19.

Wade, N. Scandal in the heavens: Renowned astronomer accused of fraud. *Science*, 1977, *198*, 707–709.

Wagner, R. V. Complementary needs, role expectations, interpersonal attraction, and the stability of working relationships. *Journal of Personality and Social Psychology*, 1975, *32*, 116–24.

Waldrop, M. F., Bell, R. Q., McLaughlin, B., & Hal-

verson, C. F., Jr. Newborn minor physical anomalies predict short attention span, peer aggression, and impulsivity at age 3. *Science*, 1978, *199*, 563–65.

Walker, L. E. *The battered woman.* New York: Harper & Row, 1979.

Walker, L. J., & Richards, B. S. Stimulating transitions in moral reasoning as a function of stage of cognitive development. *Developmental Psychology*, 1979, *15*, 95–103.

Walker, R. N. Body build and behavior in young children. Body build and nursery school teachers' ratings. *Monographs in Social Research on Child Development*, 1962, *27*, Serial No. 84.

Wallace, D. H., & Wehmer, G. Evaluation of visual erotica by sexual liberals and conservatives. *Journal of Sex Research*, 1972, *8*, 147–53.

Wallach, M. A., & Leggett, M. I. Testing the hypothesis that a person will be consistent: Stylistic consistency versus situational specificity in size of children's drawings. *Journal of Personality*, 1972, *40*, 309–30.

Waller, J. H. Achievement and social mobility: Relationships among IQ scores, education, and occupation in two generations. *Social Biology*, 1971, *18*, 252–259.

Walsh, N. A., Meister, L. A., & Kleinke, C. L. Interpersonal attraction and visual behavior as a function of perceived arousal and evaluation by an opposite sex person. *Journal of Social Psychology*, 1977, *103*, 65–74.

Walster, E., & Piliavin, J. A. Equity and the innocent bystander. *Journal of Social Issues*, 1972, *28*, 165–89.

Walster, E., & Walster, G. W. *Equity: Theory and research.* Boston: Allyn & Bacon, 1978.

Warren, N. Malnutrition and mental development. *Psychological Bulletin*, 1973, *80*, 324–25.

Wechsler, D. *The measurement of adult intelligence* (3rd ed.). Baltimore: Williams and Wilkins, 1944.

Wechsler, D. Intelligence defined and undefined: A relativistic appraisal. *American Psychologist*, 1975, *30*, 135–39.

Wegner, D. M., & Schaefer, D. The concentration of responsibility: An objective self-awareness analysis of group size effects in helping situations. *Journal of Personality and Social Psychology*, 1978, *36*, 147–55.

Weidner, G., Istvan, G., & Griffitt, W. Beauty in the eyes of the horny beholders. Paper presented at the meeting of the Midwestern Psychological Association, Chicago, 1979.

Weidner, G., & Matthews, K. A. Reported physical symptoms elicited by unpredictable events and the Type A coronary-prone behavior pattern. *Journal of Personality and Social Psychology*, 1978, *36*, 1213–1220.

Weiner, B. New conceptions in the study of achievement motivation. In B. A. Maher (ed.), *Progress in experimental personality research*, vol. 5. New York: Academic Press, 1970.

Weinstein, M. S. Achievement motivation and risk preference. *Journal of Personality and Social Psychology,* 1969, *13,* 153–72.

Weiss, R. F., Boyer, J. L., Lombardo, J. P., & Stich, M. H. Altruistic drive and altruistic reinforcement. *Journal of Personality and Social Psychology,* 1973, *25,* 390–400.

Weissbrod, C. Noncontingent warmth induction, cognitive style, and children's imitative donation and rescue effort behaviors. *Journal of Personality and Social Psychology,* 1976, *34,* 274–81.

Weitzman, L., Eifler, D., Hokada, E., & Ross, C. Sex-role socialization in picture books for preschool children. *American Journal of Sociology,* 1972, *77,* 1125–50.

Wellman, B. L., & Pegram, E. L. Binet IQ changes of orphanage pre-school children. *Journal of Genetic Psychology,* 1944, *65,* 239–63.

Wessberg, H. W., Mariotto, M. J., Conger, A. J., Farrell, A. D., & Conger, J. C. Ecological validity of role plays for assessing heterosocial anxiety and skill of male college students. *Journal of Consulting and Clinical Psychology,* 1979, *47,* 525–535.

West, S. G., & Brown, T. J. Physical attractiveness, the severity of the emergency and helping: A field experiment and interpersonal simulation. *Journal of Experimental Social Psychology,* 1975, *11,* 531–38.

Wheeler, L., & Nezlek, J. Sex differences in social participation. *Journal of Personality and Social Psychology,* 1977, *35,* 742–54.

"When to confess," *Times,* September 3, 1973, pp. 69–70.

Whimbey, A. You can learn to raise your IQ scores. *Psychology Today,* 1976, *9* (8), 27–29, 84–85.

White, L. A. Erotica and aggression: The influence of sexual arousal, positive affect, and negative affect on aggressive behavior. *Journal of Personality and Social Psychology,* 1979, *37,* 591–601.

White, L. A., Fisher, W. A., Byrne, D., & Kingma, R. Development and validation of a measure of affective orientation to erotic stimuli: The Sexual Opinion Survey. Paper presented at the meeting of the Midwestern Psychological Association, Chicago, May 1977.

Whiting, J. W. M., & Child, I. L. *Child training and personality: A cross-cultural study.* New Haven, Conn.: Yale University Press, 1953.

Whyte, W. W., Jr. *The organization man.* New York: Simon & Schuster, 1956.

Wiggins, J. S. A psychological taxonomy of trait-descriptive terms. The interpersonal domain. *Journal of Personality and Social Psychology,* 1978, *37,* 395–412.

Wilkie, F., & Eisdorfer, C. Intelligence and blood pressure in the aged. *Science,* 1971, *172,* 959–62.

Willerman, L., Naylor, A. F., & Myrianthopoulos, N. C. Intellectual development of children from interracial matings. *Science,* 1970, *170,* 1329–31.

Williams, A. F. Social drinking, anxiety, and depression. *Journal of Personality and Social Psychology,* 1966, *3,* 689–93.

Williams, R. L. The BITCH-100: A culture-specific test. Paper presented at the meeting of the American Psychological Association, Honolulu, September 1972.

Williams, R. L. Scientific racism and IQ—silent mugging of the black community. *Psychology Today,* May, 1974.

Williams, R. M. Why children should draw. *Saturday Review,* 1977, *4* (23), 10–16.

Willingham, W. W. Predicting success in graduate education. *Science,* 1974, *183,* 273–78.

Wilson, E. O. *On human nature.* Cambridge, Mass.: Harvard University Press, 1978.

Wilson, J. P. Motivation, modeling, and altruism: A person situation analysis. *Journal of Personality and Social Psychology,* 1976, *34,* 1078–86.

Wilson, L., & Rogers, R. W. The fire this time: Effects of race of target, insult, and potential retaliation on black aggression. *Journal of Personality and Social Psychology,* 1975, *32,* 857–64.

Wilson, W., & Nakajo, H. Preference for photographs as a function of frequency of presentation. *Psychonomic Science,* 1965, *3,* 577–78.

Wilson, W. C., & Abelson, H. I. Experience with and attitudes toward explicit sexual materials. *Journal of Social Issues,* 1973, *29* (3), 19–39.

Winchel, R., Fenner, D., & Shaver, P. Impact of coeducation on "fear of success" imagery expressed by male and female high school seniors. *Journal of Educational Psychology,* 1974.

Winder, C. L., & Rau, L. Parental attitudes associated with social deviance in preadolescent boys. *Journal of Abnormal and Social Psychology,* 1962, *64,* 418–24.

Winick, M., Meyer, K. K., & Harris, R. C. Malnutrition and environmental enrichment by early adoption. *Science,* 1975, *190,* 1173–75.

Winslow, C. N. A study of the extent of agreement between friends' opinions and their ability to estimate the opinions of each other. *Journal of Social Psychology,* 1937, *8,* 433–42.

Winter, D. G., Stewart, A. J., & McClelland, D. C. Husband's motives and wife's career level. *Journal of Personality and Social Psychology,* 1977, *35,* 159–66.

Winterbottom, M. R. The relation of need for achievement to learning experiences in independence and mastery. In J. W. Atkinson (ed.), *Motives in fantasy, action, and society.* Princeton, N.J.: Van Nostrand, 1958.

Wissler, C. *The correlation of mental and physical tests.* New York: Columbia University Press, 1901.

Witkin, H. A., Mednick, S. A., Schulsinger, F., Bakkestrom, E., Christiansen, K. O., Goodenough, D. R., Hirschhorn, K., Lundsteen, C., Owen, D. R., Philip,

J., Rubin, D. B., & Stocking, M.   Criminality in XYY and XXY men. *Science*, 1976, *193*, 547-55.

Wolf, T. H.   *Alfred Binet*. Chicago: University of Chicago Press, 1973.

Wolpe, J., & Lang, P. J.   A fear survey schedule for use in behaviour therapy. *Behaviour Research and Therapy*, 1964, *2*, 27-30.

Worbois, G. M.   Changes in Stanford-Binet IQ for rural consolidated and rural one-room school children. *Journal of Experimental Education*, 1942, *11*, 210-14.

Worchel, S.   The effect of three types of arbitrary thwarting on the instigation to aggression. *Journal of Personality*, 1974, *42*, 300-18.

Worchel, S., Arnold, S. E., & Harrison, W.   Aggression and power restoration: The effects of identifiability and timing on aggressive behavior. *Journal of Experimental Social Psychology*, 1978, *14*, 43-52.

Worchel, S., Hardy, T. W., & Hurley, R.   The effects of commercial interruption of violent and nonviolent films on viewers' subsequent aggression. *Journal of Experimental Social Psychology*, 1976, *12*, 220-32.

Worell, J., & Worell, L.   Support and opposition to the women's liberation movement: Some personality and parental correlates. *Journal of Research in Personality*, 1977, *11*, 10-20.

Wright, F. H.   A controlled follow-up study of small prematures born from 1952 through 1956. *American Journal of Diseases of Children*, 1972, *124*, 506-521.

Wright, L.   Intellectual sequelae of Rocky Mountain spotted fever. *Journal of Abnormal Psychology*, 1972, *80*, 315-16.

Wrightsman, L.   Effects of waiting with others on changes in level of felt anxiety. *Journal of Abnormal and Social Psychology*, 1960, *61*, 216-22.

Wrightsman, L. S., Jr., Radloff, R. W., Horton, D. L., & Mecherikoff, M.   Authoritarian attitudes and presidential voting preferences. *Psychological Reports*, 1961, *8*, 43-46.

Wyant, K. W., Lippert, J. A., Wyant, F. W., & Moring, D. G.   The duration and generalization of attraction. *Journal of Research in Personality*, 1977, *11*, 347-55.

Yarmey, A. D., & Bull, M. P., III.   Where were you when President Kennedy was assassinated? *Bulletin of the Psychonomic Society*, 1978,*11*, 133-35.

Yarrow, L. J.   Separation from parents during early childhood. In M. L. Hoffman and L. W. Hoffman (eds.), *Review of child development research*, vol. 1. New York: Russell Sage, 1964.

Yates, B. T., & Mischel, W.   Young children's preferred attentional strategies for delaying gratification. *Journal of Personality and Social Psychology*, 1979, *37*, 286-300.

Yerkes, R. M.   Psychological examining in the U.S. Army. *Memoirs: National Academy of Science*, 1921, *15*, 1-890.

Zajonc, R. B.   Attitudinal effects of mere exposure. *Journal of Personality and Social Psychology Monograph Supplement*, 1968, *9*, 1-27.

Zajonc, R. B.   Family configuration and intelligence. *Science*, 1976, *192*, 227-36.

Zander, A., & Forward, J.   Position in group, achievement motivation, and group aspirations. *Journal of Personality and Social Psychology*, 1968, *8*, 282-88.

Zanna, M., Sheras, P. L., Cooper, J., & Shaw, C.   Pygmalion and Galatea: The interactive effect of teacher and student expectancies. *Journal of Experimental Social Psychology*, 1975, *11*, 279-87.

Zeichner, A., & Pihl, R. O.   Effects of alcohol and behavior contingencies on human aggression. *Journal of Abnormal Psychology*, 1979, *88*, 153-160.

Zemore, R.   Systematic desensitization as a method of teaching a general anxiety-reducing skill. *Journal of Consulting and Clinical Psychology*, 1975, *43*, 157-61.

Zigler, E., & Trickett, P. K.   IQ, social competence, and evaluation of early childhood intervention programs. *American Psychologist*, 1978, *33*, 789-798.

Zillman, D.   Excitation transfer in communication-mediated aggressive behavior. *Journal of Experimental Social Psychology*, 1971, *7*, 419-34.

Zillmann, D.   *Hostility and aggression*. Hillsdale, N.J.: Lawrence Erlbaum, 1978.

Zillmann, D., Bryant, J., & Carveth, R. A.   The effect of erotica featuring sadomasochism and bestiality on motivated intermale aggression. *Personality and Social Psychology Bulletin*, 1980, in press.

Zillmann, D., Johnson, R. C., & Day, K. D.   Provoked and unprovoked aggressiveness in athletes. *Journal of Research in Personality*, 1974, *8*, 139-52.

Zillmann, D., Katcher, A. H., & Milarksy, B.   Excitation transfer from physical exercise to subsequent aggressive behavior. *Journal of Experimental Social Psychology*, 1972, *8*, 247-59.

Zillman, D., & Sapolsky, B. S.   What mediates the effect of mild erotic on annoyance and hostile behavior in males? *Journal of Personality and Social Psychology*, 1977, *35*, 587-96.

Zimbardo, P.   The psychological power and pathology of imprisonment. A statement prepared for the U.S. House of Representatives Committee on the Judiciary. (Subcommittee no. 3, Robert Kastenmeyer, chairman; hearings on prison reform.) Unpublished paper, Stanford University, 1971.

Zimbardo, P. G.   On the ethics of intervention in human psychological research: With special reference to the Stanford prison experiment. *Cognition*, 1974, *2*, 243-56.

Ziv, A., & Israeli, R.   Effects of bombardment on the manifest anxiety level of children living in kibbutzim. *Journal of Consulting and Clinical Psychology*, 1973, *40*, 287-91.

"Zoo's wolves maul toddler," *Lafayette Journal and Courier*, January 5, 1976.

Zuckerman, M.   Development of a situation-specific trait-state test for the prediction and measurement of affective responses. *Journal of Consulting and Clinical Psychology,* 1977, *45,* 513–523.

Zuckerman, M., & Gerbasi, K. C. Belief in a just world and trust. *Journal of Research in Personality,* 1977, *11,* 306–17.

Zuckerman, M., & Reis, H. T. Comparison of three models for predicting altruistic behavior. *Journal of Personality and Social Psychology,* 1978, *36,* 498–510.

Zuckerman, M., Tuchup, R., & Finner, S. Sexual attitudes and experience: Attitude and personality correlates and changes produced by a course in sexuality. *Journal of Consulting and Clinical Psychology,* 1976, *44,* 7–19.

AUTHOR INDEX

Mihal, W. L., 222
Mikawa, J., 338
Mikulka, P. J., 262
Milavsky, B., 391
Milgram, S., 192, 193
Mill, J. S., 202, 446
Miller, C. T., 383, 436, 437
Miller, D. T., 143
Miller, E., 206
Miller, F. D., 310
Miller, J., 41
Miller, K. S., 223, 227
Miller, L., 111, 401
Miller, N., 227, 330
Miller, N. E., 93, 97, 113, 246, 379, 380, 522
Millham, J., 472
Mills, C. R., 330
Mills, J., 461
Milton, W., 167
Mindick, B., 437
Mischel, W., 99, 114, 136, 138, 140, 233, 298, 473, 504
Mita, T. H., 333
Mitchell, G. D., 269, 387
Mitchell, H., 345
Mitchell, H. E., 185, 186, 189, 453
Moeller, G. H., 316
Moller, G. W., 269, 387
Monachesi, E., 132
Monahan, L., 311
Money, J., 423, 438, 442, 495
Montagu, A., 411, 495
Montgomery, R. L., 178
Moodie, W., 206
Moody, K., 393
Moos, R. H., 428
Moran, L. J., 504
Moreault, D., 421
Moreland, R. L., 333
Morgan, C. D., 130
Moriarty, T., 479
Moring, D. G., 353
Morris, W. N., 340, 459
Morrow, L., 509
Morton, H., 26
Mosher, D. L., 420, 421, 424, 426, 436
Mowrer, O. H., 379
Moyer, K. E., 411
Mueller, C., 408
Mueller, E. F., 303
Muir, W. R., 236
Mulac, A., 266, 268
Mulhern, R. K., Jr., 377
Munsinger, H., 210
Murray, E. J., 231
Murray, H. A., 82–86, 113, 130, 283
Murray, J., 407
Murstein, B. I., 286, 341
Mussen, P. H., 482, 496, 534
Myers, I. B., 61
Mynatt, C., 467
Myrianthopoulos, N., 227, 228

Nadler, A., 466
Nadler, E. B., 179
Nahemow, L., 332
Nakajo, H., 334
Nance, J., 378
Nataupsky, M., 221

Naylor, A. F., 228
Nei, M., 221
Nelson, D., 344
Nelson, D. A., 260
Ness, S., 457
Nesselroade, J. R., 262
Newcomb, T. M., 343
Newman, H. H., 207, 209
Newtson, D., 496
Nezlek, J., 360, 361, 407
Nicholls, J. G., 232
Nichols, P. L., 215
Nims, J. P., 431
Nisbett, R. E., 44, 476
Noble, A. M., 185
Noonan, J. R., 364
Novaco, R. W., 409, 411
Novotny, R., 185
Nydegger, C. N., 292
Nygard, R., 287, 294

Oden, M. H., 237
Okada, M., 265
Oliver, C., 32
Olweus, D., 385
O'Malley, P. M., 229, 295
O'Neal, E. C., 411
Onorad, J., 408
Opton, E., Jr., 224
Osborne, R. T., 227
Oskamp, S., 437
Ostrowska, A., 215
Ottinger, D. R., 217
Owen, D. R., 379
Owen, D. W., 492
Owens, W. A., Jr., 234

Packard, R., 305
Page, B., 480
Palermo, D. S., 330
Parham, I. A., 139, 450
Park, T., 272
Parke, R. D., 397
Parker, D., 359
Pasamanick, B., 227
Passman, R. H., 377
Patrick, A. W., 286
Paulhus, D. L., 355
Pear, R., 438
Pearson, J. A., 340
Pechacek, T. F., 273
Pedersen, F. A., 384
Pegram, E. L., 213
Peplau, L. A., 311, 360
Pepper, S., 351
Pepys, Samuel, 15
Perkins, K. A., 55
Perry, D. G., 397
Perry, L. B., 429
Perry, L. C., 397
Pervin, L. A., 139, 140
Peterson, D. R., 142
Petitto, L. A., 16
Petty, R. E., 467
Phares, E. J., 98
Phillips, D. P., 399
Piaget, J., 446–51, 481, 507
Piccione, A., 353
Pigg, R., 389
Pihl, R. O., 404

Piliavin, I. M., 458, 459, 460, 466
Piliavin, J. A., 458, 459
Pilkey, D. W., 434
Pines, A., 275
Pines, M., 451
Pisano, R., 382, 408
Plemons, J. K., 235
Plomin, R., 72
Pomerantz, M., 287, 294, 297
Pomeroy, W. B., 17, 422, 424
Post, A. L., 259
Prentice, N. M., 474
Price, L. H., 286
Pritchard, S. A., 214
Proctor, C., 330
Prokasy, W. F., 498
Prout, T., 225
Provence, S., 498
Pruesse, M., 434
Przybyla, D., 420, 437
Puryear, G. R., 310
Pyszczynski, T. A., 435

Rabinovitch, M. S., 500
Radin, M. E., 259
Radloff, R. W., 167
Ramirez, M., 111, 169
Ransberger, V. M., 403
Ransdell, H. J., 422
Rau, L., 330
Rawtich, A. B., 406
Ray, J. J., 166
Raynor, J. O., 294, 295, 324
Reeves, K., 340
Reich, C. A., 293
Reis, H. T., 463
Resnick, L. B., 241
Restak, R., 377
Reyher, J., 55
Rhamey, R., 352
Rheingold, H. F., 500
Ricciuti, H. N., 297
Richard, W., 236
Richards, B. S., 450
Richardson, C. E., 379
Richman, C. L., 292
Rim, Y., 178
Rindlisbacher, A., 315
Ringuette, E. L., 139
Ripple, R. E., 232
Ritter, B., 273
Roberts, A. H., 474
Roberts, M. C., 351
Robins, E., 439
Robinson, D. N., 522
Roby, T. B., 284, 285
Rocha, R. F., 381
Roehl, J., 273
Rogers, C. R., 104–10, 114, 492, 507
Rogers, R. W., 381, 401
Roizin, L., 495
Rokeach, M., 176
Rorschach, H., 130
Rosen, B. C., 290
Rosen, L. J., 236
Rosenbaum, D. P., 479
Rosenblum, L. A., 269
Rosenman, R. H., 91
Rosenthal, R., 472
Ross, C., 305

SUBJECT INDEX

F Scale (*See* California F Scale)
Factor theory, 88–92
Family: cultural differences in, 169–70; discipline in, 170–71; ideology, traditional, 168–69; violence in, 376–78
Fantasy: in adolescence, 514–15; in childhood, 507–10; sexual, 429–33
Fascist classroom, creating, 174–75
Fascist Scale (*see* California F Scale)
Fathers: and achievement need, 288–89, 291–92; loss of, and achievement, 319
Fear (*see also* Anxiety): and affiliation, 339–40; interpersonal, 270–71; and sexuality, 416–17
Fear Survey Schedule (FSS), 251
"Feebleminded," identifying, 202
Fiction, personality description in, 489
Frequency count, 121
Friendship, 341–53: and love, 358–61
Frustration-aggression hypothesis, 370–81
Functional distance, 332

Gays (*see* Homosexual behavior)
Gender identity, 438
General-arousal hypothesis, 391
Generalization, 23–24
Genetics: of behavior, 494; and intelligence, 207–11; and IQ, 224–26
Genital vasocongestion, 428
Giftedness, 236–38
Grades, 229–31: and IQ, 294; and success, 294–95
Gratification: delayed, 298–99, 472–74; immediate, 446; Freud's concept of, 448; and moral behavior, 446; and sexuality, 416–17, 420–22

Habit strength, 248
Heat, effects of, 403–4
Help, effects of receiving, 466
High need achiever, development of, 288–92
Homophobia, 438
Homosexual behavior: causes of, 438–39; and social-psychological adjustment, 439–40; stereotypes, 437–38
Hormones, 427–28: and adolescence, 512
Hostility, 182–84
Hull-Spence theory, 245–48
Human nature, 41
Human needs, 84–85
Humanistic theories, 100–109
Humor: and anxiety, 260–61; hostile, 399

Id, 49, 74, 85, 446
I-E Scale, 98
Imaginative responses, 507–10
Incentive, 296
Independence training, 289–90
Infancy (stage 1), 496–503
Infants, emotional responses of, 500–503
Infatuation, passionate, 354–57
Informational development in adolescence, 514
Informational responses, 504
Instigation, 381–84

Instruction, personalized system of (PSI), 268
Intelligence: defined, 201; differences in, 206–14; and environment, 211–14; and expectations, 238–39; and grades, 229–31; measuring, 202–6; and occupation, 215; and race, 220–29; and socioeconomic factors, 215–20
Intelligence quotient (IQ), 206: and aging, 233–36; and "experiments of nature," 208–10; and grades, 294; and psychotherapy, 231–32; racial differences in, 220–29
Intelligence testing, 201–6
Intent, perceived, 382–83
Intentions, 506
Interference, 478–81
Internal consistency approach to test construction, 125–26
Internalization, 474–75
Interpersonal interactions, positive, 361–66
Interpersonal Judgment Scale, 344
Interpersonal skills, acquiring, 511
Interpersonal theory, 63–69
Intuitive approach to test construction, 125
Item content, 124

Judgment, moral (*see* Moral judgment)
Just World hypothesis, 453
Just World Scale, 452–54

Language: and evaluation, 503–4; as labeling device, 504–7
Learning: associational, 498; paired-associates, 254–55; serial, 253–54
Learning theory, 92–99
Lesbianism (*see* Homosexual behavior)
Libido, 51
Limbic system, 522
Longitudinal research, 234–35
Lore, 353–61 (*see also* Attraction)
Love Scale, 358
Lying, 472

Maladjustment, 257–58, 525
Manifest Anxiety Scale (MAS), 247–51
Manipulative skills, 510–12
Marijuana, and aggression, 404, 406
Measurement error, 121
Mental age, 206
Minnesota Multiphasic Personality Inventory (MMPI), 132, 133
Mobility, 510–12
Modeling effect, 394
Moral behavior: big-city vs. rural life and, 480–81; Hogan's model, 447; and interference, 478–81; Kohlberg's model, 446; Piaget's model, 446; situational factors in, 454–64; television and, 457; and temptation, 471–78
Moral judgment: changing, 450; levels of, 446, 447; studies of, 448–51
Mother, early separation from, 369
Motivation to attain success (M_s), 294
Motivation to avoid failure (M_f), 294
Motivational taxonomy, 82–88
Motive, 296

Movies, and mood, 347–48
Murder, 375–76
Music, and feelings, 348–49

n Ach, 283–91 (*see also* Achievement need)
n Aff, 338, 340
Nations: achievement need in, 314–22; predicting economic growth of, 316–19
Need state, 496
Neurosis, 526

Observation, 22–23
Occupation, and intelligence, 215
Operant conditioning, 94–97
Opinion change, 232
Opinions, open-minded expression of, 362–63
Orgasm phase, 428

Paired-associates learning, 254–55
Parent-child interactions, 109, 475, 507
Parents (*see also* Fathers): learning aggressive behavior from, 386–88; and sex education, 425–26
Penile plethysmograph, 429
Personal constructs, 111–13
Personality: authoritarian (*see* Authoritarian personality); characteristics of, 60–63; comprehensive theory of, 496; criminal, 378–79; as a field of psychology, 31–34; overcontrolled, 388–89; psychopathic, 529; science of, 7–9; three systems of, 49–51
Personality adjustment, 525–29
Personality change, 523–25
Personality description, 489–92
Personality development: biological aspects of, 492–95; psychological aspects of, 495–516
Personality measurement, 129–31: integrating trait and situational approaches, 144–47; situational approach, 140–44
Personality research, 488–89: and the behavior sequence, 516–18; future applications, 530–32
Personality test, constructing, 127–28
Personality theory, 41: success of, 74–76; types of, 45–74
Personalized system of instruction (PSI), 268
Physiological development, in adolescence, 512–13
Plateau phase, 428
Pleasure principle, 50, 446
Political aggression, 372–73
Politico-Economic Conservatism Scale, 178
Popularity, 330–31
Pornography, 433
effects of, 434–35
Postconventional level of moral judgment, 447
Power, 160
Preconventional level of moral judgment, 446
Prediction, 11–16: and personality de-

591